ENVIRONMENTAL POLLUTION

MONITORING AND CONTROL

ENVIRONMENTAL POLLUTION

MONITORING AND CONTROL

SECOND EDITION

S M KHOPKAR

MSc., PhD
Professor Emeritus
Department of Chemistry
Indian Institute of Technology, Bombay
Mumbai

Publishing Globally

NEW AGE INTERNATIONAL (P) LIMITED, PUBLISHERS
LONDON • NEW DELHI • NAIROPI
Bangalore • Chennai • Cochin • Guwahati • Hyderabad • Kolkata • Lucknow • Mumbai
Visit us at www.newagepublishers.com

Published by New Age International (P) Ltd., Publishers
First Edition: 2004
Second Edition: 2015
Reprint: 2018

GLOBAL OFFICES

- **New Delhi** **NEW AGE INTERNATIONAL (P) LIMITED, PUBLISHERS**
 7/30 A, Daryaganj, New Delhi-110002, (INDIA)
 Tel.: (011) 23253771, 23253472, **Telefax:** 23267437, 43551305
 E-mail: contactus@newagepublishers.com • Visit us at www.newagepublishers.com
- **London** **NEW AGE INTERNATIONAL (UK) LTD.**
 27 Old Gloucester Street, London, WC1N 3AX, UK
 E-mail: info@newacademicscience.co.uk • Visit us at www.newacademicscience.co.uk
- **Nairobi** **NEW AGE GOLDEN (EAST AFRICA) LTD.**
 Ground Floor, Westlands Arcade, Chiromo Road (Next to Naivas Supermarket)
 Westlands, Nairobi, KENYA, **Tel.:** 00-254-713848772, 00-254-725700286
 E-mail: kenya@newagepublishers.com

BRANCHES

- **Bangalore** 37/10, 8th Cross (Near Hanuman Temple), Azad Nagar, Chamarajpet, Bangalore- 560 018
 Tel.: (080) 26756823, **Telefax:** 26756820, **E-mail: bangalore@newagepublishers.com**
- **Chennai** 26, Damodaran Street, T. Nagar, Chennai-600 017, **Tel.:** (044) 24353401
 Telefax: 24351463, **E-mail: chennai@newagepublishers.com**
- **Cochin** CC-39/1016, Carrier Station Road, Ernakulam South, Cochin-682 016
 Tel.: (0484) 2377303, **Telefax:** 4051304, **E-mail: cochin@newagepublishers.com**
- **Guwahati** Hemsen Complex, Mohd. Shah Road, Paltan Bazar, Near Starline Hotel
 Guwahati-781 008, **Tel.:** (0361) 2513881, **Telefax:** 2543669
 E-mail: guwahati@newagepublishers.com
- **Hyderabad** 105, 1st Floor, Madhiray Kaveri Tower, 3-2-19, Azam Jahi Road, Near Kumar Theater
 Nimboliadda Kachiguda, Hyderabad-500 027, **Tel.:** (040) 24652456, **Telefax:** 24652457
 E-mail: hyderabad@newagepublishers.com
- **Kolkata** RDB Chambers (Formerly Lotus Cinema) 106A, 1st Floor, S N Banerjee Road
 Kolkata-700 014, **Tel.:** (033) 22273773, **Telefax:** 22275247
 E-mail: kolkata@newagepublishers.com
- **Lucknow** 16-A, Jopling Road, Lucknow-226 001, **Tel.:** (0522) 2209578, 4045297, **Telefax:** 2204098
 E-mail: lucknow@newagepublishers.com
- **Mumbai** 142C, Victor House, Ground Floor, N.M. Joshi Marg, Lower Parel, Mumbai-400 013
 Tel.: (022) 24927869, **Telefax:** 24915415, **E-mail: mumbai@newagepublishers.com**
- **New Delhi** 22, Golden House, Daryaganj, New Delhi-110 002, **Tel.:** (011) 23262368, 23262370
 Telefax: 43551305, **E-mail: sales@newagepublishers.com**

ISBN: 978-81-224-3804-8

C-17-08-10685

Printed in India at Ajit Printing Press, Delhi.
Typeset at Pegitek Graphics, Delhi.

PUBLISHING GLOBALLY
NEW AGE INTERNATIONAL (P) LIMITED, PUBLISHERS
7/30 A, Daryaganj, New Delhi - 110002
Visit us at **www.newagepublishers.com**
(CIN: U74899DL1966PTC004618)

Dedicated
to
my beloved wife
Dr. Sucheta

Preface to the Second Edition

Since the last decade when the first edition of this book was published, several transformations have taken place in the field of the environmental science and engineering. The newer areas have emerged and the priority of monitoring and control have radically changed. These areas include statistical analysis, recycling of waste water, utilisation of the solar energy and demographic changes in the field of population. Such changes promoted me to add additional chapters as well as the new data and novel information in the various chapters of this revised and enlarged edition.

For instances on account of famine resulting due to inadequate precipitation (rain) an acute shortage is felt all over Maharashtra. In the places like Marathwada even a pale of drinking water is not available. This situation led to rethinking as to why we cannot recycle and reuse the waste water but not sewage. Leave aside potable water but for other requirements like washing one can easily use recycled water. The application of the technique of Reverse Osmosis and the electrodialysis proved to be ideal for conversion of sea water to pure water. Further rain water harvesting is the long-term solution to pressure water supplies. Similarly, in the field of energy on account of acute shortage of coal many thermal power plants have closed in various states in India. The other alternative is nuclear or the solar energy. Unfortunately, inspite of having greater knowhow in nuclear energy with our scientists the establishment of nuclear plants in Tamil Nadu, Maharashtra are strongly resisted by people on account of recent tragedy in Japan at Fukoshima due to tsunami. The last alternative to harness energy is solar energy in tropicalised country like India. Number of solar energy plants are being put up in metropolitan cities like Mumbai to have solar energy for street lightening. Guest houses and few educational institutes have solar heaters. The solar panels are perfectly working as new source of energy. The third problem is of population. Inspite of having census in 1991, 2001, 2011 many unknown facts have come out on migration of population. This necessitated to search for correlation of environment and population. The field of statistical analysis played significant role in the process of enumeration. Similarly apart from physical and chemical methods the versatile, biomonitoring methodology has evolved recently in monitoring and control of environmental pollution with significant advantages.

Therefore, in order to keep abreast with new development and dissemination of valuable knowledge as many as six new chapters have been added to the text-book dealing with the above aspects. In addition a lot of new data has sprung up into existence for air, water, effluent and noise pollution. Therefore, all chapters are supplemented with novel data in form of tables, figures and new write up in the text. All these new additions have resulted in addition of few pages in the original book but with better utility. I am very confident that readers would find new data to be more interesting and useful. I expect the book would be received with the same inquisitiveness and joy of gaining new knowledge in the environmental science as was done with earlier editions to the students in under-graduate and postgraduate level in the universities and institutions.

I take this opportunity to thank *Mr. Saumya Gupta*, Managing Director of New Age International (P) Ltd. Publishers and his able team of efficient editorial assistants for excellent production of this book. I take this opportunity to thank my son Samir and his family Madhavi and Rohan; so also my daughter Dr. Supriya and Ketan, Ruchir for their cheerful words and encouragement throughout the writing of this book.

Finally, I shall be failing in my duties if I do not thank my wife Dr. Sucheta for bestowing patience perseverance and for creating conductive atmosphere in home while writing of this mighty task of the compilation of the monograph. The constructive suggestions are always welcome from my valued readers.

S.M. KHOPKAR

Professor Emeritus, Chemistry
Indian Institute of Technology,
Mumbai–400076

Preface to the First Edition

There is an excessive awareness in society for environmental pollution. However the degree of such pollution is not known primarily due to the lack of knowledge on monitoring methodology. Some workers who painstakingly collect data on the nature and extent of pollution, do not know how to process this valuable information not only for the control of pollution but also for future planning and forecasting in designing novel methods for control. With these objectives in mind this book is specially designed to explain what is pollution, what are the methods of the monitoring, how best one can control the pollution, since many laboratory methods are useless for monitoring. One can use infact the precious data on the pollution for future forecasting, planning and designing efficient control measures.

Therefore first three chapters dwell on general introduction to pollution, choice of methods of analysis and overview of modern methods of monitoring and analysis. Environmental toxicology constitutes an integral component of health and is therefore considered in depth. The next two chapters on air pollution not only cover characterisation, monitoring but also meteorology of air pollution for dispersion and analysis. Subsequent two chapters on water pollution cover not only characterisation and analysis but also treatment of water for all purposes. Industrial effluents and sewage are the areas wherein now a days biological methods of treatment are used in large scale which is therefore considered. Agricultural pollution mainly due to misuse of pesticide is then considered.

In last few decades solid waste, hazardous waste and the biomedical waste have attained sizeable problem of characterisation, treatment, transport and disposal. A through account of these vitally important parameters is included. A discussion on environmental pollution shall not be complete without the consideration of noise pollution, thermal pollution, radiation hazards specially disposal of radioactive waste which is alarming proposition all over the world.

Lastly environmental impact assessment (EIA) has achieved greater significance in environmental planning during setting of new plants. Similarly to keep environment clean, one must design environmental models from existing database to formulate novel methods for mitigation of pollution. Hence a brief account is presented in last two chapters of this presentation.

Every attempt is made to include data on Indian condition to suit our environmental understanding. At end of each chapter upto date references to recent books in the field are included. I am quite confident that this book will prove to be quite useful for the graduate and postgraduate programmes in environmental science and engineering specially majoring in monitoring and control technology. It may prove useful to serious research workers, practising chemist and confirmed environmentalists.

I take this opportunity to thank my son Samir and his wife Madhavi; as well as my daughter Dr. Supriya and her husband Ketan for encouraging me from time to time during writing of this book. Further I would like to thank my wife Dr. Sucheta for creating favourable atmosphere for writing and showing patience and perservance during execution of the mighty task of writing this book.

S.M. Khopkar

Professor Emeritus
Indian Institute of Technology
Powai Mumbai 400076

Contents

1 Introduction

1.1 INTRODUCTION

Environmental science is the science which deals with the complex interactions occuring amongst the terrestrial, atmospheric, aquatic, living and anthropogenic environment. It includes all the disciplines of physical, chemical and biological sciences. We make statement that it is study of earth, air, water, living organisms and the man with his impact on activity. It is natural history called 'ecology'. The environment in which we live gets affected by the activities of the man. Environmental science encompasses atmosphere, hydrosphere, geosphere and biosphere. 'Atmosphere' is air surrounding the earth. While 'hydrosphere' pertains to earth's water. 75% of earth is water and we are concerned with activities of man with surface or ground water. 'Geosphere' is composed of solid earth and soil. One which is in contact with atmosphere and hydrosphere is termed as 'Lithosphere' (about 50–100 km of thickness). The 'biosphere' is region in which the earth is stationed. Biosphere is also place of residence for biotic or living organism.

1.2 ENVIRONMENTAL CHEMISTRY

It covers various areas of interactions of pesticides, freon, volatile organometallic compounds. It is the investigation related to the sources, reactions, transport or migration and ultimate fate of chemical species in either hydrosphere, lithosphere, atmosphere or living organism. The study of environment has commenced in 1978 by scientists who were not trained as environmentalist but were experts in allied fields. Many scientists were deeply concerned with environmental problems. The present day chemist must know the consequence of chemicals which they are producing in the environment. It is not always possible to solve immediately the complex problems of an environment. The extent of pollution caused and the components responsible for such effects are in the perview of environmental chemical analysis.

Environmental chemistry is in fact truly interdisciplinary in nature within it has many branches of natural sciences. It encompasses intricate relationship with inorganic, organic, physical and biochemistry. It is also related to biology, toxicology and public health engineering. It summarise the study of sources, reactions, transport and fate of chemical entities in air, water, soil, environments as well as their effects on human health and the natural environment. Science is not merely concerned with the aspects of pollution but also related to behaviour of natural chemicals in nature. It is concerned with developing clear understanding of chemist.

1.3 ENVIRONMENTAL CHEMICAL ANALYSIS

In order to keep the environment clean it is necessary to measure the damage caused by pollution. Without understanding the extent of damage caused, it may not be possible for us to control it. Such work involves devising suitable control measures. Now these suitable control measures can be meticulously planned, provided if we know what should be the level of pollution is? Hence, in order to understand the level of pollution, we should undertake the analysis or measurement of pollution. This analysis or measurement is termed as environmental pollution analysis, which throws light on exact degree of pollution. It will guide us to recover valuable products from waste and help us to take appropriate control measures to minimise pollution. With this objective in mind we should try to learn environmental pollution analysis. In order to undertake the analysis, we must know the type of pollution.

Environmental chemistry has major challenges to determine nature and quantity of specific pollutant in environment. This is known by chemical analysis which is first step in the investigations related to the environments. The significant level of pollutant may contain less than trace level of pollutant. In water pollution, one ppm of metal like beryllium is considered objectionable. The present day environmental chemical analysis demands very low limit of detection. Environmental chemistry is however not analytical chemistry, as latter involves intricate knowledge of measurement. The accuracy sought in former is not so critical as it is in analytical chemistry. Analytical chemistry is a fundamental vital part of our endeavour to understand the nature, reactions and transport of the chemical species in the environment.

Environmental chemical analysis involves air, water, land wastewater or sewage, pollutants are present at lower level. In order to ascertain their concentration environmental chemical analysis demands sophisticated instruments like gas chromatography, ion chromatograph or inductivity coupled plasma atomic emission spectroscopy. It needs also potentiometer and conductometer to ascertain the quality of environment at tracer concentration.

What is the need for monitoring environmental pollution or analyse the data which is collected? One cannot think of control measures unless one knows what is the extent of pollution? A lot of noise is made about pollution, a great awareness can be created in society in large cities on pollution, but we cannot effectively control pollution in the absence of authentic data about air pollution, water pollution, industrial effluents, sewage management, land and pesticides pollution or abatement of noise pollution. Such measures can be effective only if we have reliable data on levels of pollution. Such reliable data can be generated by monitoring the environmental at site. The knowledge of levels of pollution will enable us to use and adopt effective, reliable and economic measures for control. To control pollution, which is growing in alarming proportion, the most effective way is to analyse environmental pollution and then adopt a strategy for its control. Therefore, it is envisaged to consider ways and means to analyse environmental pollution.

1.4 IMPACT OF MAN ON ENVIRONMENT

Environment is composed of atmosphere, earth, water and space. If it remains clean, it is enjoyable. The interaction of the atmosphere, lithosphere, hydrosphere and biosphere continues for years together. Unfortunately, on account of the various activities of man, the composition and complex nature of environment gets changed. Such activities include industrialization, construction and transportation. These activities, although essential for human development and welfare, lead to generation and release of objectionable materials into the environment. It makes our life miserable and uncomfortable.

The natural environment is clean, but due to multifarious activities of man it gets polluted resulting in what is called as *environmental pollution*. Our main aim is to keep our environment clean. One way of achieving it is by curbing all of our activities. However, in order to keep pace with the rapid industrialization world over, we cannot afford to arrest industrial activity. What we can do is to select such industrial processes, which would cause minimum or zero pollution. It is necessary to undertake pollution control measures, to keep the environment clean.

Our environment is simple as well as complex. It is simple so long as it remains clean. It gets complex when industrial activities grow. To comprehend this complex nature of environment, we need knowledge of all disciplines of chemical, physical and biological sciences. To device control measures, we need knowledge of engineering and technology. Environmental science and engineering is truly interdisciplinary in nature. To understand atmosphere we need knowledge of physics and meteorology, for knowing hydrosphere and air we need knowledge of chemistry, the complex behaviour of living organism can be really explained with a knowledge of the life sciences, the interaction in lithosphere can be best understood from principles of earth sciences, while the entire control mechanism can be devised only with intricate knowledge of engineering and technology. In the process of monitoring we collect enormous data, which can be interpreted and understood only if we are conversant with statistical analysis and computer programming. We first look into the problem of population.

It is worthwhile to watch world population as well as the Life expectancy of persons as shown in Table 1.1. The latest figure as well as the one projected population after half century (*i.e.,* 2050) are worth, comparing. As expected the highest population is in China 1300 millions while India would cross China in next century with highest population of the country as 1620 millions. Fortunately small countries like Brazil, Nigeria and even Japan have controlled growth of population. One axiom is more is the population one encounters more of the environmental pollution. For developed countries like UK, USA, Europe have good life expectancy of 70-80 years while developing countries like India, Russia, have poor figure for Life expectancy ranging from 30-70 years. A close look at

Table 1.1 shows that the life expectancy of women is better than that of man (of 75 and 80 resp. in USA) in the year 2005.

Table 1.1 World Population and Life expectancy (present and future)

S. No.	*Country*	*Population 2005 (million)*	*Population 2050 (million)*	*Life duration in 1900 Male (Ys)*	*Life duration in 1900 Female (Ys)*	*Life duration in 2005 Men (Ys)*	*Life duration in 2005 Women (Ys)*
1.	Brazil	184	260	–	–	–	–
2.	Congo	–	183	–	–	–	–
3.	China	1304	1437	–	–	–	–
4.	Ethopia	–	170	–	–	–	–
5.	Bangladesh	144	231	–	–	–	–
6.	Indonesia	222	308	–	–	–	–
7.	India	1104	1628	23	23	61	63
8.	Pakistan	162	295	–	–	–	–
9.	USA	297	420	46	48	75	80
10.	Japan	128	–	42	44	78	85
11.	Russia	143	–	31	3	59	72
12.	Nigeria	132	258	–	–	–	–

Table 1.2 Open spaces in Mumbai

Place	*Area sqm total*	*Population dcm/sq. mt*	*Open space needed for 100 persons (sqm)*	
			Actual	*Required*
Chembur	19.31	11.525	466	3035
Borivili	77.56	7.244	216	3035
Malad	19.13	19.54	197	3035
Andheri	23.50	22.251	632	3035

Table 1.3 Outburst of population in world (in millions) in last 50 years

Country	*Name of city*	*1950*	*1990*	*2000*
India	Kolkata	4.5	11.8	15.9
	Mumbai	2.9	11.1	15.4
	New Delhi	1.4	8.6	12.8
America	New York	12.3	15.7	16.1
	Los Angeles	4.1	10.5	10.9
England	London	10.3	10.6	10.8
Japan	Tokyo	6.7	20.5	21.3
	Osaka	3.8	10.5	11.2
China	Beijing	6.6	9.7	11.5
	Shanghain	10.3	12.6	14.7
Pakistan	Karachi	2.6	9.1	11.6
Bangladesh	Dhaka	0.4	6.4	11.3

A concerted effort is to be made to keep our environment clean. It will lead to betterment of our lives. At this stage it is worthwhile to examine what causes the deterioration of an environment? With greater urbanisation natural environment is spoiled. *e.g.*, Table 1.2 indicates extent of available open space in Mumbai for man to live. Table 1.3 shows how there is outburst of population within last 50 years all over the world. Table 1.3 gives also life expectancy. It is interesting to specially note rise for India and China. There is outburst of population which (Table 1.3) would cause scarcity of water, food and other essential things in life. One shudders to think what will be actual consequence of population in year 2050. Table 1.3 shows that there is a rise in population in every country.

1.5 INTERACTION WITH VARIOUS SPHERES OF ENVIRONMENT

Water occurs in all spheres of an environment such as land, air and biosphere and geosphere. These are essential part of living system. Atmosphere in reality acts protective blanket on earth. It is source of vital gases like O_2, N_2, CO_2 needed for respiration, fixation and photosynthesis. The UV light is prevented to enter sphere of earth from atmosphere. Geosphere or earth is the place for human being to live in. We consider Lithosphere is outer layer of earth. Soil is formed by disintegration or weathering action on rocks. The anthrosphere is real sphere of interaction. Science pertains to discovery, explanation and theoretical development of natural phenomena of energy, matter space and time. While on basis of fundamental knowledge of science and engineering it provide plans and means to accomplish definite objectives. The science and engineering together leads to technology plans for growth. Technology is used by interweaving ecology with environment. Simultaneously it used with advancement of technology for the benefit of mankind. One must observe environmental impact. It is essential to consider the environmental protection.

1.6 ECOLOGY AND ENVIRONMENT

Ecology is the science which concerns with relationship between living organism with their physical environment. We consider it from the angle of organisms and how these organisms adjust to environment. A ecosystem consists of mutually interacting organisms and their environment in which matter is interchanged. The environment in which a particular organism reside is called 'habitat'. Environment is then divided into four categories as terrestrial environment, fresh water environment, marine environment and symbiotic environment. Alternatively in simple words it is classified in terms of pollution.

Environmental pollution is classified into various groups. The pollution of air is termed as the *atmospheric pollution*, the pollution of hydrosphere or water is termed as *water pollution*, while pollution due to disposal of waste water is termed as *industrial effluent's pollution*. Similarly, indiscriminate dispersal of domestic sewage or sullage is called *domestic effluent* or *sewage pollution*. In addition to these major sources of pollution we have pollution of lithosphere called *soil pollution*. Pesticide residue contributes towards soil pollution. Urban areas are blessed with the menace of noise, which at times becomes intolerable. This is called *noise pollution.* Some kind of pollution leads to generation of smell or odour; and as such its measurement becomes important.

Ecosystem accounts for population or population explosion which leads to depletion of resources. Ecosystem ecology and population ecology are two important areas of consideration. The functional ecology explains how things work. At this stage we must consider biosphere. Biosphere is part of an environment consisting of living organism. This is made of hydrosphere and geosphere. Environment influences biosphere. This is based upon plant synthesis fixing solar energy in form of photochemical reactions. The degradation in the presence (aerobic) or absence of (anaerobic) oxygen leads to reduction of biomass with liberation of CO_2 gas. Biosphere and anthrosphere are closely related. Human being depends upon biosphere. The anthrosphere is that part of the environment made or modified by human being and used for their various activities.

1.7 CLASSIFICATION OF ENVIRONMENTAL POLLUTION

Pollution is defined as an unfavourable alteration of the environment from the effects of changes in energy patterns, radiation level; chemical or physical constitution or the abundances of organism. Pollutants are generated by natural sources as well as by human activity. Some are natural others are largely related to human being. Pollutant even if it is natural, has some adverse effect on human health. Even traces of pollutant can create deleterious consequences. Some pollutants are biologically concentrated so their concentration on human vary. Environmental pollutants can affect men, animals, plants or materials causing injury to health or reduction of growth of plants or corrode metals. The effect may be local or global. Pollutants interact with each another, to produce synergistic effects. The combination of pollutants produces severe effect. Such effects may extend much further as they are transported through air or water. Some pollutants have the cumulative effect which persists for longer period. At present there is greater awareness of deadly pollutants like carcinogenic compounds. Some pollutants have restricted effect.

Much of the pressure on the environment from pollutants is due to population as shown in Table 1.1. Large population needs large food, a reservoir with disposal of large waste. This is only part of big picture. A rising standard led to more transportion, per capita energy consumption, and substantial industrial growth. New technologies produce more energy but also generate more pollution. Consequently, there is greater pressure on energy and other natural resources used. Thus, there is "limit to the growth".

For the purpose of investigation environmental pollution has been classified into different groups. Pollution dealing with atmospheric changes is called *air pollution* which is most important. One which contaminate water, irrespective of it being used for drinking or industrial purposes is called *water pollution.* Now pollution caused by water after use is called *waste water* or *effluent* which causes pollution. The domestic effluent or sewage has harmful effect if not properly treated. Apart from air, water effluent and sewage we have pollution due to solid waste, hazardous waste or biomedical waste which is rising in alarming proportion. We have specific pollution due to noise, pesticides, food, metals and thermal pollution which must be also considered. We shall take brief account of every class of pollution with suitable examples.

1.8 AIR POLLUTION

Atmosphere plays a significant role in global processes supporting life on earth. It serves as an efficient heat reservoir. Troposphere is a zone very close to earth. It is an important zone for living world. Stratosphere is next zone to the troposphere. Ozone is an important component of this stratosphere. Mesosphere and thermosphere are next zones to stratosphere which contain highly reactive gas species as O_2^+, NO^+ and O^+. They protect earth by absorption at short wave radiation. The unpolluted atmosphere is composed of 78.1% N_2, 21%O_2, 0.9% Ar and 0.03% CO_2. The water vapour accounts for 1.3% in air. The photochemical reactions result in atmospheric changes as O_2 absorbs UV radiation to produce O_3 in stratosphere, CO_2 level is 360 ppm and is rising by 1 ppm per year. Excess of CO_2 in air causes "Greenhouse effect" *i.e.,* warming up of troposphere. Excess of CO_2 will prevent blood from transporting O_2 to body tissues. Two oxides of nitrogen *viz.* NO and NO_2 are injurious to health. They are written as NO-NO_x. They enter in photochemical reaction to produce NO_2. Very small particulates are called *condensation nuclei,* which promotes precipitation or rain formation. The colloidal particles in air are called '*aerosols*'. Atmosphere is protective blanket which nurtures the earth and protects it from the hostile environment of outer sphere which comprises of stratosphere, mesosphere and thermosphere. It provides CO_2 for plants and O_2 for man for respiration. The stratospheric chemistry of the ozone layer; ground level chemistry leading to the formation of acid rains, and the Greenhouse effect leading to the global warming are three giant trouble shooters of environment. These phenomena are discussed in greater details in next chapter on Air Pollution. With this introductory or preliminary section let us consider how air pollution has grown? What is status of air pollution in Indian cities? How is dust pollution, or benzopyrene cause menance and noise pollution problem for the mankind?

Amongst the various types of pollution, air pollution is of significance as it causes immediate health problems. The obvinoxous gases that lead to pollution are oxides of carbon, nitrogen and sulphur (Table 1.4). Particulate matter also causes air pollution.

It is interesting to study Tables 1.4 and 1.5 which give the status of air pollution in city of Mumbai and another in city of Kolkata. The important pollutants considered are SPM, SO_2, NO-NO_x in both the Tables. It is noted that in Mumbai SPM and SO_2 are highest in mill area of Lalbaug while NO-NO_x is high in Khar and in Parel which is another predominant labour area. The picture in Kolkata is slightly different. The Maniktala area near Sealeda station has high level of SPM while the Tollygunj industrial area has high concentration of SO_2. Interestingly Dalhousie square in central Kolkata has prepondrance of cars, trucks and other vehicles has highest level of NO-NO_x. This was picture between 1992 to 1996 now it must be more alarming.

Table 1.4 Air quality in Mumbai (1996) (μg/m^3)

S.No.	Location	Town	SPM	SO_2	NO-NO_x
1.	North East	Chembur	341	65	51
2.	Central	Lalbaug	454	128	–
3.	North West	Khar	349	11	77
4.	Central	Babula Tank	318	56	56
5.	Central	Parel	326	47	70
6.	Central	Dadar	–	60	–
7.	North East	Sewree	–	60	–
8.	North East	Ghatkopar	407	75	–
9.	North East	Sakinaka	–	49	–

Table 1.5 Air quality in city of Kolkata (1992) (μg/m^3)

Location	Area	SPM		SO_2		NO-NO_2	
		Mean (annual)	Max (monthly)	Mean (annual)	Max (monthly)	Mean (annual)	Max (monthly)
South	Bhowanipur	290	550	20	50	15	30
Central	Dalhousie Sq.	390	700	25	75	20	45
Central	Manikatala	400	750	40	130	20	30
North	Howrah Stn.	400	700	50	125	20	30
South east	Tollygunj	500	1000	40	200	15	35

Looking at the alarming picture of air pollution in the city of Mumbai and Kolkata, it is necessary and worthwhile to consider status of air pollution in other important cities in India like New Delhi, Chennai, Nagpur, Hyderabad, Ahmedabad, Kanpur and Jaipur with special reference to same pollutants *viz* SPM, SO_2 and NO-NO_x.The findings are quite interesting. The city of Kanpur with main ganges river flowing and lot of agricultural land has high level of SPM (590 mg/m^3) while Chennai has substantial !evel of NO-NO_x. Ahmedabad a city of textile-fabric has substanial level of SO_2 (0.040 ppm) (Table 1.6).

Table 1.6 Air pollution level in major cities in India (μg/m^3)

S. No.	Town	SPM	NO-NO_x	SO_2
1.	New Delhi	530	85	220
2.	Chennai	60	139	140
3.	Nagpur	300	150	500
4.	Hyderabad	130	40	300
5.	Ahemadabad	342	50	400
6.	Kanpur	590	5	300
7.	Jaipur	440	30	200
8.	Mumbai	250	50	500

One thing is certain no city in India is free from air pollution. Further, these are typical levels at particular point of time and may vary during year, or even during day also on account of the consequences of the meteorological parameters, which would be considered in a greater depth in subsequent chapters. Table 1.6 gives particle (SPM) size of dusts from different sources.

Thus, suspended particulate matter is worst among pollutants. There are no-efficient devices to remove dust. However success of such separation largely depends upon particle size (Table 1.7) and source or origin of particulate mater (SPM) in Indian cities (Table 1.8).

Table 1.7 Relative size of suspended particulate matter (SPM) in different products

Source	*Size in (mm)*	*Source*	*Size (mm)*
Fog	50	Pigment	4.0
Flourmill	20	Sulphuric acid mist	0.8-4.0
Grain	15	Tobacco smoke	0.25
Talcum	10	Ammonia smoke	0.1
Coal mines	10	Smelling zinc oxide	0.05

Table 1.8 Particulate matter in major Indian cities (1978) (μ_g/m^3)

City	*Urban area*	*Sub-urban area*	*Residential area*
Mumbai	123	150	221
Kolkata	352	324	246
Delhi	361	256	391
US Standard (EPA)	75	75	75

The level of suspended particulate matter in big cities of India is shown in Table 1.8. The emission due to auto-exhaust causes serious pollution of air due to formation of oxides of nitrogen and benzopyrene. Table 1.9 indicates the level of BaP *i.e.*, Benzopyrene in various towns of the world, and Table 1.10 shows, level pollution at various places in Mumbai. It is generated by incomplete combustion of petrol. It is a serious air pollutant as it has carcinogenic properties causing lung cancer.

Table 1.9 Benzopyrene level in different nations of world

Country	*Town*	*Level mg/m³*
Germany	Hamburg	17-1863
Hungary	Budapest	32-1060
Iran	Tehran	0.61-63
Japan	Osaka	11.1
Poland	Warsaw	29-133
Spain	Madrid	0 9.4
Sweden	Stockholm	15-27
USA	Urban average	0.5-18.6

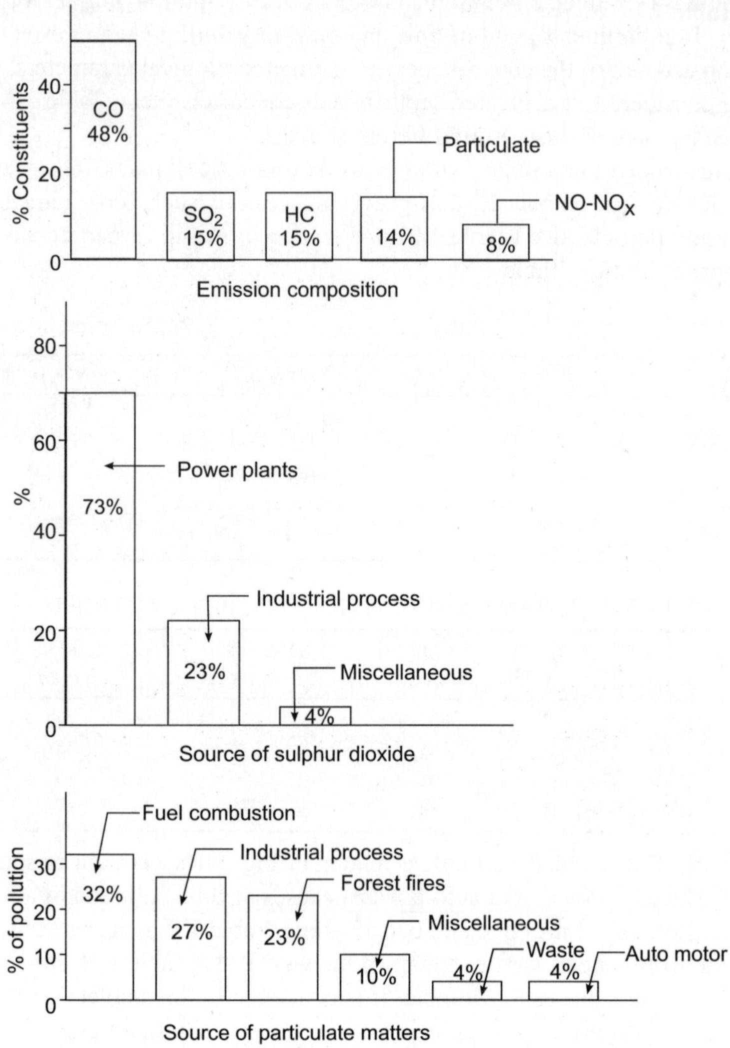

Fig. 1.1 Primary air pollutants

Table 1.10 Benzopyrene levels in Mumbai in various localities

City of Mumbai	*Range of concentration mg/m³*	*Source of emission*
Lalbaug	165.0 to 861.0	Gas plant where coal is burnt.
Dadar	7.1 to 16.2	When gas plant is shut-down.
Sion	15.0 to 36.0	Automobile exhaust omissions
Koliwada	17.4 to 225.1	Kiln for firing pottery
Trombay	2.0 to 13.0	Petrochemical complex
Bhandup	0.8 to 2.0	Residential area
Colaba	3.1 to 3.9	Residential area

Table 1.11 Source of overall atmospheric pollution in various years (%) in different locations of world

Source	*1973*	*1978*	*1983*	*1986*	*1990*	*2000*
Domestic	34.2	43.5	47.12	53.58	55.00	60.0
Commercial	4.92	6.15	6.34	6.95	7.00	7.5
Industrial	43.8	51.2	56.4	64.4	70.0	70.0
Power generation	12.2	12.2	48.94	46.95	40.0	50.0
Transportation	39.8	64.6	10.63	13.14	15.6	20.0
Others	40.0	64.6	10.64	13.15	15.0	70.0

The combustion of sulphur containing coal generates sulphur dioxide (Table 1.12). Though wood causes zero pollution, but its calorific value is

Table 1.12 Amount of sulphur in fuels emitting SO_2

Substance	*%S*	*Calorific value*
Wood	0	18
Peat	1	18
Lignite	1.3	23.2
Bituminous	1.6	25.5
Semibituminous	1.2	36.0
Anthracite	1.0	34.0
Coke	<1.0	29.0
Crude oil	0.5-3.0	—
Fuel oil	2-4	43.5
Coaltar fuel	0.5	37.8
Town gas	0	18.6
Natural gas	Trace	34.0
Producer gas	0	4.5

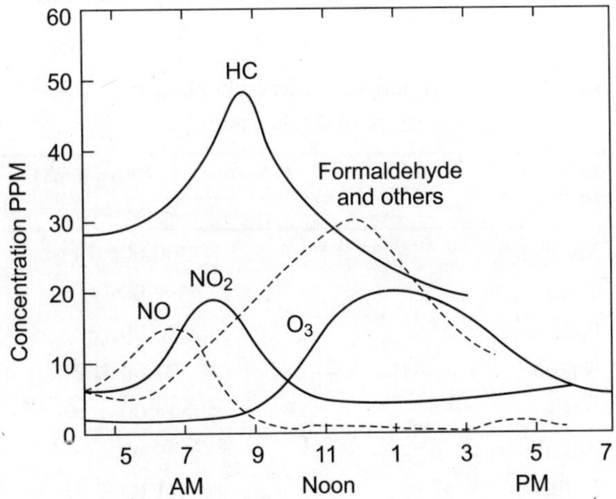

Fig. 1.2 Different pollutants in photochemical smog

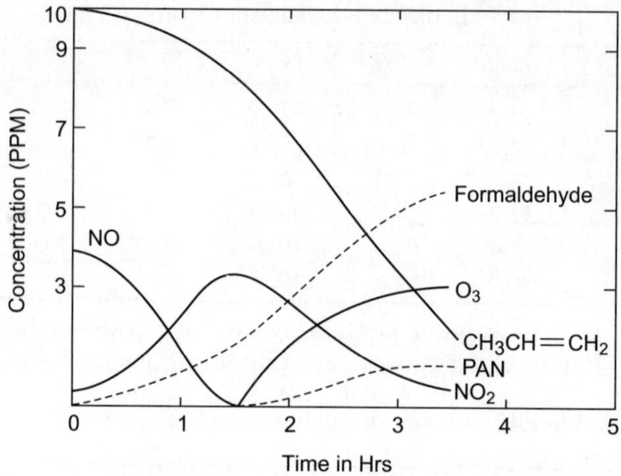

Fig. 1.3 PAN and other pollutants in smog

poor,while oil produces pollution due to SO_2 but it has high calorific value. Transportation is a major source of pollution causing the highest pollution in big cities in India. Table 1.13 lists the population of two-wheelers (bikes) in various cities of Maharashtra, while Table 1.14 lists overall production of two-wheelers in India, which are responsible for vehicle emissions. The growth rate shows that as the activity of production increases, vehicle pollution also rises. The photochemical smog which is generally produced by combination of smoke and fog contributes several pollutants to air (Figs. 1.2 and 1.3) *e.g.*, CO, CO_2, NO-NO_x, SO_2, hydrocarbon (HC). The thermal power plants are responsible for cause extensive air pollution.A typical thermal power plant in the capital of India throws daily 80 tons of flyash and several tons of SO_2 in the atmosphere. Delhi and Kanpur have the highest dust fallout, Mumbai emits highest SO_2 emissions while Kolkata dispersed highest level of NO-NO_x.

Table 1.13 Population of two-wheelers in various districts of Maharashtra

Districts	*Number in (thousands) (Ten years ago)*
Mumbai	200.00
Thane	7.00
Pune	150.00
Nagpur	77.00
Nasik	14.00
Aurangabad	29.00
Kolhapur	21.00

Table 1.14 Manufacture of two-wheelers in India (in thousands)

Year	*Two-wheeler over 150 CC*	*Scooters*	*Mopeds*
1970–75	43,000	58.40	11.70
1975–80	70,000	101.70	36.20
1980–85	11,600	210.00	105.00
1985–90	175,000	400.00	425.00

We have various sources, such as domestic viz. burning of coal and coke, industrial emissions, commercial activities, thermal power generation unit and last but not the least is transportation. Table 1.11 lists various sources of atmospheric pollution (Fig. 1.1). Table 1.12 indicates as to how much air pollution is caused by ignition of the fuel. Kolkata contributes its share by emitting large proportion of NO-NO_x in the air. Table 1.15 gives composition of photochemical smog.

Table 1.15 Typical concentration of trace constituents in photochemical smog

Constituent of smog	*Concentration, ppm*
NO-NO_X	20
NH_3	2
H_2	50
H_2O	2×10^6
CO	4×10^3
CO_2	4×10^4
O_3	50
CH_4	250
Higher paraffins	25
C_2H_4	25
Higher olefins	25
C_2H_2	90
C_6H_6	10
Aldehydes	60
SO_2	20

The average composition of photochemical smog is shown in the Table 1.15. It largely contains oxides of nitrogen, hydrocarbon and other gaseous pollutants.

1.9 WATER POLLUTION

The total amount of water on surface of earth is 3.5×10^{20} gallons of which 97% is found in sea while fresh water is merely 37 million km^3. Of this 0.8% occurs in polar ice water which percolates in ground is called 'ground water' and it emerges on surface of earth as river or lake water. Due to hydrological cycle on water, earth is in constant circulation by evaporation, precipitation, percolation and run off. There is natural balance between evaporation and precipitation (*i.e.*, raining). The ground water (*i.e.*, aquifers) is mainly used for drinking. 'Limnology' is the study of fresh water. The knowledge on chemistry of natural water has developed enormously with development of chemical sciences. In ancient times whole civilization had disappeared due to water scarcity by climatic variations. In olden days the water-born diseases like cholera and typhoid killed several people. The increase in population has resulted in large amount of the consumption of water. The microorganisms are indicators of the quality of water. The study of water is called '*hydrology*'. The main supply of water from earth is called 'hydrological cycle'. Hydrosphere and lithosphere (earth) interaction is of great significance. The human consumption relates to fresh water and ground water. There is however uneven distribution of water. Water has excellent characteristics such as good solvent properties, high dielectric constant, and surface tension; transparent appearance, maximum density at 4°C, high heat of evaporation with higher latent heat of fusion of ice and higher heat capacity. Surface water occurs in river streams and lakes while esturine water originates from ocean in which stream flow. In such water the marine organisms thrive very well.

Unfortunately this fresh water does not remain pure but gets polluted by several agencies. Sewage and oxygen demanding waste is main culprit. In addition infecting agents, plant nutrients, exotic organic chemicals, inorganic materials and compounds sediments and heat totally spoil the quality of water.

The important sources of water pollution are domestic waste, industrial waste, agricultural and shipping waste. Several legislations starting from 1899 till date have been passed in various states (including Maharashtra) in India since ages to preserve the quality of water, because the water quality is of major concern for everyone. The discharge of pollutants in navigable water is also prohibited. The process of contamination or degradation consumes oxygen and its total level in water is lowered. The waste level is assessed from knowledge of biological oxygen demand (BOD). The Coliforma bacteria or *E.coli* spread water-born diseases. Plant nutrients like phosphorus and nitrogen lead to growth of undesirable organism like algae leading to eutriphication.

Therefore, water pollution has been studied in great details. The indiscriminate disposal of water after use in the form of waste water causes water pollution. The tragic incident of Minnamata in Japan is well known. A paper factory using mercury compounds carelessly dumped its waste effluents into the sea, which formed $(CH_3)_2Hg$ and $(CH_3CH_2)_2$ Hg, it in turn was consumed by the sea-fish. The Japanese people who consumed such sea-fish indicated symptoms of mercury poisoning like gingivitis, vomiting, fever, diarrhoea, paralysis of extremities.

Therefore, quality of drinking water has been factor in ascertaining human welfare. Feccal pollution marrs water quality. Water-born toxic chemicals are great threat to the quality of water. Several kinds of substances cause water pollution *e.g.*, trace elements (Hg, Cd, Pb), organometallic compounds, radioisotopes, inorganic pollutants, asbestos, algal nutrients, organic pollutants, pesticides, petroleum waste, sewage, pathogens, detergents, sediments and few of the carcinogenic compounds. Heavy metals like Cd, Hg, Pb and few of the metolloids like arsenic, organic tin spoil the quality of water. Thus, water supplies get

Table 1.16 Potable water standard in India (mg/ml)

S. No.	Property	Level Minimum	Level Maximum	S. No.	Property	Level Minimum	Level Maximum
1.	Turbidity	5.0 (NTU)	25.0 (NTU)	9.	Cl^-	200	600
2.	Colour	5.0	50.0	10.	SO_4^{2-}	200	400
3.	pH	7.0 – 8.5	6.5 – 9.2	11.	F^-	1.0	1.5
4.	Hardness	100	500	12.	NO_3^-	4.5	45.0
5.	Mg	30	150	13.	Zn	5.0	15.0
6.	Fe	0.1	1.0	14.	Oils	0.01	0.30
7.	Mn	0.05	0.50	15.	Detergents	0.20	1.0
8.	Cu	0.05	1.0	–		–	–

Table 1.17 Quantum of world's water supply

Location	Kind	Volume (km^3) 1×10^4	% of Total Supply
Surface	Fresh	12.0	0.009
	Saline	10.0	0.008
	Stream	0.12	0.001
Subsurface	Soil	6.5	0.005
	Ground water	400	0.3
Other source	Ice-cap glaciers	2900	2.1
	Atmosphere	1.3	0.001
	Ocean	1315.00	97.3

contaminated by phosphate, soaps and detergents and anaerobic degradation of organic matter. Table 1.16 and Table 1.18 gives idea about standard of drinking water in India. While Table 1.17 gives source of water supply.

Table 1.18 Standards for Potable water (by WHO)(mg/ml)

Parameter	Average	WHO Maximum	WHO Minimum	Indian (average) Standard
Turbidity	5	25	2.5	5.0 NTU
pH	7.0–8.5	6.5–9.2	7.0–8.5	6.5
Total solids	500	1500	500	–
Hardness	100	200	100	100
Calcium	75	200	75	–
Magnesium	30-50	150	30	30
Iron	0.1-0.3	1.0	0.1	0.1
Chloride	200	600	200	200
Sulphate	200	400	200	200
Fluoride	1.0	1.5	1.0	1.0
Nitrate	45	45	4.5	4.5
Lead	0.05	0.05	0.10	–

Table 1.19 shows that bigger is the river greater is pollution. We have Ganga water authority plan to clean up such large rivers. All rivers are contaminated by industrial effluents.

The water which emerges out after use from industries is called as the *industrial effluent*. Such effluents have no definite composition, as anything which is not required is carelessly dumped into its stream. Such unwanted disposable material is contributed by chemical firms, food and beverage industry, textile and apparel industries, electronics and electrical material industries, or thermal power plants. The quality of such water is characterised by the study of its various physical, chemical and biological properties. The disposal of arsenic compounds by paper industry, or toxic chemicals by fertilizer plant had caused serious problem in western India. In many places in India, town *e.g.* in Maharashtra Ahemednagar municipal authorities have not hesitated to let up sewage into streams or brooks or rivers, assuming that dilution would solve the pollution problem. The biological matter and bacteria such as *coliform, Sterpococcii, feccal coliform, crenthronix,* are not eliminated by mere dilution. Such water needs chemical treatment, like disinfection, which would also kill pathogenic bacteria.

Table 1.19 Quality of river water in various states of India

State	*Name of river*	*Polluting industry*	*Pollutants released*
Central Maharashtra	Ulhas	Rayon	Zinc
Uttar Pradesh	Ganges	Jute, Sugar	Organic pollutants
Punjab	Sone	Paper pulp	Arsenic, sulphite
Madhya Pradesh	Narmada	Paper	Arsenic, black liquor, bagasee
Uttarakhand	Yamuna	Insecticides	Organic mercury compounds
Kerala	Chaliyar	Rayon	Zinc, Cadmium
Karnataka	Kaveri	Rayon, Sugar	Bagasee, metal pollutants
Andhra	Godawari	Paper, small scale industries	Metal pollutant, organics
Gujarath	Mahi	Dyestuff	Dyes, intermediate
Western Maharashtra	Mullamutha	Antibiotic	Organics, antibiotics
Assam	Brahmaputra	Paper pulp	Black liquor
Goa	Juhari	Fertilizers	Alkali metals, ammonia
Eastern Maharashtra	Patalganga	Organic chemicals	Pesticides organics

1.10 INDUSTRIAL WASTE WATER

Waste water contains chemicals, waste from paper, petroleum, food, transport, textile, electronic and ancillary industries. The pollution by industrial waste water amounts to several times greater than one caused by domestic waste water. In past it has increased at greater proportion with alarming rate. The waste from heavy industrial community is much polluted (Table 1.20). The waste water from food industry undergoes putrification with very high BOD. Beet sugar refining industry waste has also high BOD thus food processing involves danger of growing infectious disease (Table 1.20). While textile waste has high BOD, it is alkaline. The impurities in fiber give waste. Cattle processing waste has low BOD. Paper and pulp mills waste contains air pollutents. Effluent is a mixture of chemicals used in processing. Table 1.21 gives characteristics quality of typical effluent. The water is deep brown in colour and interferes with aquatic photosynthesis. A wide variety of pollutants are encountered in waste from the chemical industry with pH 6.0. It contains pesticides like DDT, 2,4D. Oil drilling waste includes mud, brine hydrocarbons petroleum waste and coal mines. The waste contains minerals and suspended solids, the waste from polymer industry has high BOD bad taste and odour it renders water unpotable. Metal industries waste is acidic and contains cyanogen, phenols, limestone; other industries have variety of water pollutants *e.g.* leather or tannery waste, it is alkaline full of dichromate solution used for hide cleaning operation. The quality of inland effluent is described in Table 1.20 while biological standard of waste water in terms of its quality is depicted in Table 1.22.

Table 1.20 Quality of different industrial effluents

Industry	*Quantum of solids (billion m^3)*	*BOD (10^2 kg of O_2)*	*Suspended solids (10^6 kg) (SSM)*
Chemical	4.0	4400	86
Paper	7.2	2670	136
Petroleum	4.9	230	208
Food	2.6	1950	3000
Transport	0.9	54	—
Polymer	0.6	18	23
Textile	0.5	400	0
Electronics	0.3	31	9
Sewage	20	3300	4000

Table 1.21 Characteristics of typical industrial effluent

S. No.	*Parameter(s)*	*Level (ppm)*	*S. No.*	*Parameter(s)*	*Level (ppm)*
1.	pH	5.5–9.0	10.	Cd^{2+}	2.0
2.	Suspended solids	100	11.	Cr^{3+}	0.1
3.	Temperature	40°C	12.	Cu^{2+}	3.0
4.	NH_3	50	13.	Ni^{2+}	3.0
5.	BOD_5 (mg/L)	30	14.	Se^{4+}	0.05
6.	COD (mg/L)	250	15.	Zn^{2+}	5.0
7.	As^{3+}	0.2	16.	PO_4^{3-}	5
8.	Hg^{2+}	0.01	17.	F^-	10
9.	Pb^{2+}	0.1	18.	Oil, Grease	10

Table 1.22 Biological standard of waste water

Class	*Application*	*Quality (MPN or ppm)*
A	Domestic water	*E.coli* 50/100 ml
B	Recreation water	*E.coli* 100/100 ml
C	Fishing	DO—3 ppm, CO_2—40 ppm
D	Industrial water	No odour or SPM, poor DO

This table indicates waste water which not only contains the offensive chemicals but also bacteria like *E.coli*. It is worth comparing their standard with that of water used for drinking, in swimming pools and fishing purposes.

1.11 POLLUTION DUE TO SEWAGE

Very few cities in India have sewage treatment plants. Even major metropolitan cities in India do not have plants to treat all sewage and sludge. The most of our villages are fitted with antiquited treatment plants or septic tanks. The growth of slums in bigger metropolitan cities is posing alarming problems of sewage disposal. In fact the greatest problem which existed for Ganga water Authorities during their preliminary operation. They faced the indiscriminately disposal of sewage. The untreated domestic sewage causes serious health problems. In China inspite of very large population, effluents are clean, because they have efficient sewage disposal network. The release of untreated sewage in sea causes serious problem with marine life, *e.g.*, a huge amount of sardines in Mumbai sea shore were killed a decade ago due to release of sewage from a nearby plant without proper treatment. The oil pollution deteriorates the aquatic marine environment, as several grades of oil are nondegradable.

Table 1.23 Quality of sewage in cities

Source of pollution	*Component(s)*	*Environment impact*
Human fecces, organic products	Oxygen demand	Oxygen consumption rises
Industrial effluents	Organics	Fish Flora killed
Human waste, toilets	Viruses	Causes epidemic diseases
Domestic effluents	Detergents	Asthetic affected
Liquid soap industry	Phosphates	Algae bloom, eutrification
Food industry	Grease, waxes	Aquatic life affected
Human waste, water softener	Salts, solids	Bad for living organism
Chemical industry	Heavy metals	Toxic metals bad for health
Detergents, industry waste	Complexing agents	Transport, ion solublisation

Table 1.23 shows characteristic of typical sewage. Many impurities can be removed by primary or secondary treatment. Sewage lead to formation of the sludge. The quantum of sewage produced is enormous, hence a very careful control is essential. The carboceous organic matter, oxidisable by the microorganism to CO_2 and H_2O are major constituents of sewage. Their presence is actually calculated from knowledge of BOD_5 of sewage for five days. Septic conditions are present when DO is very low as much ≤ 3 mg/L while the fresh water has DO of 9.2 mg/L. The S, N, P, C get oxidised to SO_4, P_4, NH_3, NO_3, PO_4, CO_2 in bad sewage water. The degradation leads to depletion of oxygen level affecting living organism giving bad taste, odour, and the colour. The sludge or sediments are commonly present in sewage. They reduce sunlight penetrating in waste water. The disposal of sewage is also complex formidable task. Water closets increase load of sewage. Sewage cannot be directly disposed in ocean as it needs pretreatment. This concept led to

building of sewage treatment plants. Nowadays, 95% of sewage is treated and the septic tanks or cesspools are discarded as they are considered unhygenic modes of disposal. The water-borne diseases were thereby eliminated. Thus, the treatment of sewers was major factor of good sanitation. Sewage, treatment consists of primary, secondary and tertiary treatment which would be covered in great details in chapter on sewage treatment and disposal. The primary treatment is simple ensuring mechanical removal of solid and sludge secondary treatments are biological analogus to natural degradation process. The removal of phosphorus or nitrogen is effected by tertiary treatment, as phosphorus lead to eutriphication of water-ways and algal boom. Indian railways are facing perinal problem of the disposal of waste in train compartment and on rail tracks.

1.12 SOLID WASTE, HAZARDOUS WASTE AND BIOMEDICAL WASTE

So far few studies were made with solid wastes. With greater industrialisation, the production of colourful, boxes and packings for food, beverages, edible oil. We have an alarming problem of solid waste disposal. It is further aggravated due to nondegradable nature of plastic and polymeric materials. A survey was made in the city of Mumbai in particular month for accumulation of solid waste. It is composed of garbage, paper, glass, plastic, etc. It was found that it had animal waste (1500 tons) which constitutes the largest share followed by mineral waste (1100 tons), agricultural waste (550 tons), household waste (250 tons) per year. In comparison, paper (30 tons) and plastic waste (4 tons) was small. The methods for disposal of such solid waste are equally tedious. They include—physical compositing, incineration and land filling. All these methods available for their disposal are expensive. Table 1.24 gives percentage of solid waste in different towns in India as well as in typical cities of America, England, Japan and Switzerland. Such waste has all components of nature. The highest garbage in India was encountered in Pune; while paper and glass was disposed heavily in American cities; rags found extensive usage in Japanese solid waste, while Mumbai headed the list having maximum of plastic waste which is banned nowadays because it is nondegradable.

Table 1.24 Composition of solid waste (tons/month)

Location	*Place*	*Garbage*	*Paper*	*Glass*	*Rags*	*Plastic*
World	America	5.0	54.4	9.1	2.6	1.7
	England	13.0	50.0	6.0	3.0	–
	Switzerland	14.5	33.5	8.5	3.0	2.0
	Japan	36.9	24.8	3.3	7.1	2.2
India	Nagpur	31.4	0.2	0.07	0.3	0.2
	Pune	67.6	8.7	0.6	1.6	0.7
	Kanpur	35.8	4.5	1.0	5.7	0.8
	Kolkata	45.1	3.2	0.4	3.6	0.6
	Mumbai	52.3	12.0	0.5	4.3	2.7

The science and technology of solid waste has expanded tenfold in last decade. We have solid waste, hazardous waste and biomedical waste of which solid waste was well-known to a man. Systematic investigations on their effect on human health were made and various sources of solid waste were identified. Good amount of work was carried out on their characterisation and versatile methods were developed for their treatment such as physical, chemical and biological modes. Recycling was best mode which also includes land fillings. However, the study of the hazardous waste is of recent origin. Many substance constitute hazardous waste. They were identified and their chemical and physical properties were examined. These include flammable toxin, reactivity, and corrosive components. The sources of such waste was clearly identified and difficult methods for their quantitive analysis were evolved. Several treatment procedures were recommended. Many Governments like one in Maharashtra passed a legislation for transportion of hazardous waste. In addition to incineration, the methods of treatment include concentration, detoxification etc. Land filling was rarely used for disposal. The discovery of biomedical waste is of very recent origin. This is true for metropolitan towns where super speciality hospitals are located. Unfortunately very few hospitals have systematic treatment or disposal plants. Most of the hospitals throw such waste with cities domestic solid waste for further processing. It is serious as it may lead to outbreak of serious diseases. It is absolutely imperative to segregate hospital waste containing blood, pathogenic organism, sharps, bandages, tissues, etc. Transportion has to be done only after preliminary sterilisation at hospital premises. The principal treatment methods encompass disinfection, steam sterilisation followed by suitable disposal mode like incineration, thermal gas sterilisation or chemical treatment. One has to minimise waste generation and guard against occupational hazards and diseases.

1.13 OTHER KINDS OF POLLUTION

We have so far considered the important modes of pollution namely air pollution, water pollution. This was followed by pollution due to waste water as well as sewage and sludge contamination. Finally, we have considered solid waste problems from hazardous and biomedical waste.

However, apart from above major mode of pollution there are other modes of pollution which do not fall under any of the above categories but are of prime importance. They include:

(*a*) Noise pollution
(*b*) Pesticide pollution
(*c*) Food pollution including environmental carcinogens
(*d*) Metal pollution
(*e*) Thermal pollution
(*f*) Pollution due to radiation.

Although some of them like pesticides are covered under related fields such as agricultural or soil pollution, or metal pollution with toxicology, noise pollution or thermal pollution is special class of air pollution. An attempt is made in this concluding section of this chapter to have a glimpse of specific pollutants. Apparently they appear to be less harmful but when one considers the problems created by these pollutants one feels it is obligatory to consider them. The study of the environmental impact assessment (EIA) is considered in final chapter of book. We need details of other related areas like population, production and the consumption, energy and the environment, radiation, economics and legislation. Since the main objective of this monograph is to provide significance of environmental pollution monitoring and control and to focus subsequently on analysis inclusive of characterisation and determination and control, which are briefly covered here from angle of monitoring as well as control.

(a) Noise Pollution

Noise is another source of pollution. Noise is measured in decibels *i.e.,* dB. Table 1.25 list levels of noise in general while Table 1.26 gives noise in industrial town

Table 1.25 Levels of noise pollution in daily life

Source	*Noise level (dB)*
Garden	20
Bedroom	25
Library	30
Living room	40
Conversation	60
Business office	67–70
Average street traffic	80–85
Heavy truck traffic	90
Pneumatic chipper	100
Pop music	110
Jet take off at airport (at 100 m distance)	125
Jet engine (at 25 m distance)	130
Threshold of pain	140

Table 1.26 Noise level in two industrial towns in South (Nos. 1–8) and East (Nos. 9–16) of India

Visakhapatnam (S. India)			*Rourkela (E. India)*		
S. No.	*Location*	*Noise level (dB)*	*S. No.*	*Location*	*Noise level (dB)*
1.	Aseelemetta	81	9.	Near Court	85.5
2.	Gopalpatnam	82	10.	Mangal Bhavan	86.1
3.	Gyanapuram	78	11.	Daily market	83.2
4.	Gurudwara Junction	77	12.	Near Nala Road	76.3
5.	Dondaparthi	76	13.	Old Bus Stand	80.5
6.	Old Kotha Road	73	14.	Madhusudan Market	84.8
7.	Ram Nagar	72	15.	New Bus Stand	84.5
8.	Siddartha Nagar	76	16.	Near UCO Bank	76.6

and Table 1.27 presents noise level in Mumbai in various places. This is domestic noise. A person can tolerate on an average 45 to 60 dB without much discomfort, however, beyond this limit. It causes mental fatigue, irritation and other health hazards.

Table 1.27 Noise level during diwali festivals in Mumbai

S.No.	*Locality*	*Noise level (dB)* *In festival*	*Normal times*
1.	Prabhadevi	101	70
2.	Pedder Road	108	75
3.	Opera House	98	70
4.	Tejpal Ground	90	68
5.	Goregaon (West)	88	55
6.	Colaba	57	60

Noise is unwanted sound. It is measured in terms of the intensity level. There are two nearly identical log scales expressed in decibel (dB). For measuring high sound levels of any type will be leading to hearing loss. The effects of noise is related to total sound energy received by ear. It produces psychological and physiological effects in man. The physiological effects leads to constriction or narrowing of blood vessels. The Transport produces highest noise. However, noise can be controlled by restricting sound production at the source by barriers or ear protectors. It is also possible to dampen the level of noise by synthetic maternal used for manufacture of wall partitions. It is done around I.I.T. in Bombay.

(b) Pesticide Pollution

Pesticide residue is the vital source of pollution of land and soil. A list of pesticides in use is quite lengthy and is given in subsequent chapter. The most important ones like DDT, malathion, para-malithion, aldrine, dialdrin, cause a serious problems of land pollution. Their characterisation and determination is complex. These pesticides have deleterious effect on health. Several of them are carcinogenic and cause long-term harmful effects upon health and hence they need analysis. Hence it is worthwhile to consider some of them very briefly.

They are basically special chemicals to remove insects and weeds in the crop. They lack persistance in environment hence are repeatedly used. In 1948, Miiller was awarded Noble Prize for the discovery of DDT used in pest-control. In 1962 ecological problems of DDT were confirmed and restrictions on consumption were clamped. The pesticides pyrethrum is not harmful to human. They are categorised as herbicide (*e.g.*, carbamate), insecticide (organic phosphates), fungicides (dithiocarbamate). On the basis of chemical structure they are classified as the chlorinated hydrocarbons, organophosphates, carbamates, phenoxyactic acids, 2, 4D, 2, 4, 5T belonging to chlorinated hydrocarbons. The environmental characteristics shows their slow degradation with long half-life, (~ 15½ yrs) *e.g.*, DDT degrades to DDE in several years. The organophosphorus pesticides include malthione, parathion. They have high mammalian toxicity. They are chemically reactive and hydrolyse at high pH. Their retention in soil is short lived (max. 40 days). They are partially soluble in water and have no biaccumulation capacity due to low lipophilicity. The carbamates are class of compounds which include propoxur (*i.e.,* Baygon in market). They are polar compounds, water soluble (~ 2 gms/L) and have limited persistance in environment. Some are deadly toxic and biodegradable to hydrolysis and oxidation products. Pyrethrins and pyrethroides is another class used in flowers. The phonoxyacetic acid herbicides have auxin structure. They are harmonic weed killers and are polar soluble in water, less toxic with low persistance in the environment. In 1962, Rachel Carson published a book entitled "Silent spring" on pesticides. Some pests are resistant to pesticides. Wildlife is also affected by them. Chlorinated pesticides like DDT have killed birds. Organophosphorus pesticides proved fatal for human beings. Crop-rotation reduces their toxicity. In 1972, US–EPA prevented indiscriminate use of pesticides *e.g.*, DDT aldrin, dieldrin and mercury compounds. They were finally banned in developed countries.

Table 1.28 Lifecycle of some pesticide

Pesticide	*Life (years)*	*Pesticide*	*Life (years)*
DDT	10	2-4 5T	1/2
BHC	11	Moinuron	3
Heptachlor	6	Atrazinc	1
Aldrin	9	Simarzine	I½
Chlorodine	12	Diuron	I¼
Toxaphone	6	Parathion	¼

Table 1.29 Colour code for identification

Level of Toxicity	*Sign*	*Colour code*	*Lethal Dose*
Deadly	Poison	Red (Bright)	Few drops
Highly	Poison	Yellow (Bright)	30 ml dose
Moderate	Danger	Blue	309–500 ml
Average	Caution	Green	> 500 ml

Table 1.30 Annual production of pesticides in India

Pesticide	*Production (tons)*	*Pesticide*	*Production (tons)*
BHC	3000	Phorate	600
Carbanyl	5000	Methyl parathion	1500
DDT	5000	$CuSO_4$	3000
Endosulphon	1200	Sulphur compounds	1500
Lindane	1000	2-4 D	1200
Malathion	1400	$AlPO_4$	1000

Table 1.30 lists annual production of pesticides in India in terms of tons per year indicating highest production rate of 5000 ton/yr for DDT. The Table 1.28 indicates lifecycle of pesticide in soil (*i.e.,* retention time) the highest retention is

for DDT (10 years) with low level in parathion (3 months). Pesticides are sold under different names *e.g.*, insecticides for killing invertebrates, nematicides for roundworm, rodenticides for rodents, aricides for repel birds, piscicides for fish, herbicides for plants, fungicides for killing fungie and algicide for destroying algae. Arsenic Oxide was used to kill weeds but it is nondegradable.

The analysis of pesticides at microgram concentration needs mass spectrometer. For the analysis of several organic pollutants the colour code is internationally used to export toxic or hazardous materials such color code is indicated in Table 1.29.

(c) Food Pollution and Environmental Carcinogens

Mostly food products get contaminated with the excessive applications of pesticides or similar organic compounds notably fatty acids parafins, sodium benzoate (food preservative), amino acids (for emulsification), preservative or nutrient additive. Table 1.31 list important food additives and their function and applications in order to emphasize that it is not only the pesticides which foul agricultural products but also excessive use of food additives spoil the crop and render it unfit for eating. It is worth studying food additives as is shown in Table 1.32.

Since early years attention was paid on the adulteration of food supplies. However, these days the major concern is on avoidance of food poisoning from either chemical agent or their derivatives. The safety of food additives is extensively practised in western world. Such additives are either artificial or synthetic which are extensively used for variety of purposes (Table 1.31). Several additives had to be banned during Second World War when it was having questionable origin so were totally unsafe for human consumption. In fact, FDA has passed stringent laws to prosecute manufactures of the dangerous products by giving impressive advertisement on TV and in media.

Table 1.31 Food additives and their function and applications

Additive	*Role*	*Applications in*
Carbon dioxide	Soft drink	Aeration gas liberation
Chlorine	Bleaching colour	Wheat flour
Acetic acid	Rendering acidic	Jelly, jams, drinks
Calcium phosphate	Anticoking agent	Commercial salt
Amino acids	Nutrient additive	Bread ceral
Sodium benzoate	Preservation	Jam, bread, pickles
Saccharine	Artificial sweetner	Diabetic Patient's food
Fatty acids	Emuslifier, disperser	Chocolates, Icecream
Parafins	Coating, glazing agent	Chocolates, sweets

Apart from food, several of the organic compounds encountered in environment cause cancer. Their chemistry is complex and as such it is really difficult to ascertain the mechanism of interaction. 3-4 Benzopyrene (BaP) is one such deadly compound, which causes cancer of lung. BaP is found in auto exhaust emissions, is in incompletely burned tobacco and cigarette. Various levels of BaP exist in different towns in the world. In winter, the central Mumbai region shows a high level of BaP as 400 μg/m^3 due to location of coal gas manufacturing unit in the Lalbaug area of Mumbai. South Mumbai had 3.5 mg/m^3 while north Mumbai had 1.4 μg/m^3. The eastern suburbs of Mumbai had varying limit of 15-36 μg/m^3 due to location of several brick and kiln factories. A consumption of 1000 cigarettes emits 2-122 μg/m^3 BaP, which is sufficient to kill a large human population. A survey of the workers in England working in gas plant, gas retorts with coal or producer gas, crane operators, printers, chimney sweepers, asphalt workers, street cleaners showed that they were largely affected by cancer of lung, etc. A large number of organic compounds like benzidine, β-napthylamine, 4-aminodiphenyl, 4-dimethyl-aminobenzene, 4-nitrodiphenyl are confirmed as carcinogenic compounds which are injurious to human health.

If we examine carefully Table 1.32 the food additives we observe that they are used for sweetening. Flavour production, dispersing and bleaching agent, color for-mation and those generating gases like CO_2 for the purpose of fermentation of wine.

Table 1.32 Food additives and their applications

S.No.	*Additives*	*Illustration*	*Applications*
1.	Sweetening agents	Saccharine	In Diabetic food and special formulation
2.	Preservatives	Sorbic/Benzoic acid	Pickles, Jams, bread and chicken preparation
3.	Flavoring agents	Essential oils	Soft Drinks, Chewing gum; sweets and confectionary
4.	Nutrients	Lysine, Vitamins	Bread, Cereal, Rice, Dal
5.	Dispersing agents	Fatty acids	Choclate, Toffees, ice-cream with gelatin
6.	Glazing/coating agents	Wax, Paraffin	Chocolates, Toffees
7.	Bleaching agents	Chlorine, Sulphur dioxide	Wheat, flour, food items
8.	No Lumping agents	Calcium Phosphate, Starch	Common Salt, Table salt
9.	Coloring agents	Turmeric, Saffron	Sweets, Drinks, Food items like Jalebees
10.	Gas producing agents	Carbon dioxide gas	Soda water, Lemon drink, aerated drinks

Amongst the sweetening agents Saccharine is used in diet or food for diabetic patients, while benzoic acid is used as preservative for pickles. The soft drinks, chewing gum involve use of flavouring agents like vanilla. Most of the vitamins are added as supplement for diet to balance food intake. The coloring agents are extensively used in preparation of sweets like *Jalebi* or *Barfi*. All kind of soft and cold drinks promote generation of gases like carbon dioxide. In spite of strict regulations by Food and drug (FDA) authorities. We observe large scale consumption of prohibited compound like Metanil Yellow in the preparation of sweets. On extensive scale in cities Milk is tampered with the addition of dirty water and carry out generation of butter from edible oils. One cannot enjoy happy and peaceful life unless all these activities are eliminated.

(d) Metal Pollutants

We have more than 104 elements in the periodic classification, of which 80 are metals but, of these only 17 are toxic. Some of these are commonly utilized metals, while other are less frequently used and are termed as rare metals. The important toxic metals are: Be, Os, Pt, Hg, T1, V, Te, Co, U, Se, Cd, Pb, As, Sb, Cr, Ni, Zn, Mn. Their toxicity varies with threshold limiting value (TLV) between 2 $\mu g/m^3$ to 5000 $\mu g/m^3$. It is the maximum tolerable limit for a human being. The different metals have different degrees of toxicity. Mercury causes tremor, renal disorder; lead causes plumbism, gastric and colic problems, cadmium is a cumulative poison, causes anaemia and hepatic disorder; vanadium causes wheezing dyspnea, arsenic causes skin cancer and dermatitis; osmium causes halo around eyes and bronchitis, while tellurium consumption gives garlic odour to breath and sweat. Some of these metals are carcinogenic. They lead to cause cancer of lung, nose, liver pleura, thyroid. Source of these metal pollutants are varying, some of these pollutants are encountered in water and air, effluents, solid waste and sewage. We need reliable method for their characterisation and quantitative determination. They are emitted out from various sources, *e.g.*, waste water from electroplating industry (Cr, Ni), air emission from fluorescent lamps (Cd, Be), paint pigment waste (Pb, Cr), auto-exhaust emissions (Pb, Te).

Those elements with high atomic weight are called *heavymetals*. Out of several metals environmentally mercury, lead, arsenic and cadmium are most toxic. They cause the pollution of air, water or soil. All of them are non-degradable. Of all the four metals mercury is highly toxic. They have high affinity for >SH group from enzymes. The antitode is BAL (British Antilewstic) which has a structure similar to (Fig. 1.4) EDTA is antitode for actual poisoning due to these metals. Toxicity is related with kind of 'species' present in environment *e.g.*, Methyl mercury is toxic but not mercury chloride or calomel. In Castner Kellner cell for the manufacture of soda one uses the mercury amalgam with sodium metal. Hg $(CH_3)_2$ is most toxic as it is soluble in fats. Fish is main source of mercury pollution. Minnamata tragedy in Japan was caused by methyl mercury in (1950). Cerebral palsy symptoms were shown by infants. Through food chain it is ingested in body as $(C_6H_5Hg^+)$ phenyl mercury acetate are highly toxic.

Like mercury, cadmium is cumulative poison which resides in body for as long as ten years and then start showing toxic effects in old age. It is used as stabiliser in electric cell or PVC manufacture with alkaline batteries. The accident occurs due to cadmium contamination from smelting in mining operations. It would cause degenerative bone disease. It accumulates in liver and kidney and causes disease called 'Itai-itai' detected in Japan. The main source of cadmium poisoning is zinc smelting mills and mining operation.

Arsenic is environmentally important metal. Zn is toxic as it is used in pesticides. It has tendency to form ionic bonds. It is present in Pb $(AsO_4)_2$ or Cu_3 $(AsO_4)_2$ which are pesticides. Drinking water is main source for contamination. It is carcinogenic compound leading to lung, liver and bladder cancer. The smoking synergistically enhances rate of reaction in body. It causes gasterointestinal damage As(III) is more toxic than As(V) while compounds as H_3AsO_4 is water soluble and toxic compounds. Insect food is present as $(CH_3)_4As^+$ or CH_2COOH (As) compound ~ 2.5 ppb is tolerated in the drinking water. Next environmentally important metal is lead. Table 1.33 gives source of heavy metal pollutants while Table 1.34 gives pH for extraction of metals with ADPC before AAS analysis.

Table 1.33 Source of heavy metal pollutants (μg/g)

Metal	*Earth*	*Soil*	*Plants*	*Sewage*	*Sludge*
Cd	0.2	0.06	0.2	0.62	5.9
Co	40	8	0.05	–	–
Cr	200	100	0.2	0.31	7.71
Fe	70	20	4	8.75	71.79
Hg	50,000	38.000	140	320	–
Mn	0.5	0.03	0.015	–	–
Mo	1000	850	15	5.03	15.81
Ni	2.5	2	1	–	–
Pb	16	40	1	6.5	67.0
Zn	80	50	8	2.20	8.84

Table 1.34 Optimum pH range for extraction with ADPC in MIBK*

Element	*pH (range)*	*Element*	*pH (range)*
Ag	~ 3.5	Cu	0.1–8.0
Cd	10–6.0	Fe	2.0–5.0
Co	2.0–10.0	Mn	~ 2.0–4.0
Cr	3.0–9.0	Ni	z-4.0
Zn	2.0–6.0	Pb	0.1–6.0

* This is followed by atomic absorption spectroscopic method.

Arsenic is widely dispersed in environment. Lead is extensively used in the industry such as leadshots for gunshots in alloys like solder. Bivalent lead is stable. Old water pipes were made out of lead and as such it was consumed in drinking water, lead phosphate forms protective coating and does not dissolve in the potable water, so phosphate is added to water if lead is present in water $Pb_3(AsO_4)_2$ pesticide was having deliterous effect on health.

It is used in pigments as oxide or chromate which on scaling off can contaminate food or container. Lead sulphide and carbonate dissolves in water by reaction of anion with water. The storage accumulator if not properly handled emits lead in atmosphere. Tetramethyl lead (ICA) was used as antiknock $Pb(CH_3COO)_4$ in petrol to prevent soot deposition in gears.

Table 1.35 World standard of heavy metals in potable water

Heavy metal	*EPA (ppb)*	*WHO (ppb)*	*Canada (ppb)*	*India (ppb)*
As	2	10	25	10
Cd	5	5	5	5
Pb	20	50	10	40
Hg	2	1	1	1

Ethylene bromide or chloride is added in petrol to convert lead to its halides which in turn degrades to oxide. Methylation of lead occurs in atmosphere. Methyl cyclopentademyl manganese tricarbonyl (MMT) is added as catalytic convertor in petrol to reduce lead contents in exhaust gas in place of other antiknocking agents. MMT turns to Mn_3O_4. Lead present formation of haemoglobin by interfering with enzyme involved. It affects liver, kidney and heart. Children readily get affected by toxic lead. Amount more than > 30 μg/100 blood affects person lead readily affects brain tissues in children. Other toxic elements are Be, Zr, Se, Ni, Sn, Sb, Zn, Cr, Ag.

(e) Thermal Pollution and Radiation Hazards

The boilers produce large amount of waste heat which can create problems and cause adverse environmental effects. These are referred as thermal pollution. Inspite of second law of thermodynamics heat is not converted to mechanical or electrical energy but is simply wasted. The loss may be to the extent of one-third of total heat energy. Thermal plant consume 40% while nuclear power plants use 35% of energy. Most heat is released in water by way of cooling. Such heat decreases the viscosity of water leading to phenomena of sedimentation, and decrease in dissolved oxygen of the water (DO). This in turn threatens the existance of flora, fauna and living organism in water. Heat also enhance reaction rate, high temperature. Some times it leads to better growth rate of organisms or even shorten

Table 1.36 Social life in metropolitan towns in India (%)

Cities	*New Delhi*	*Mumbai*	*Chennai*	*Kolkata*
Transport	62.0	70.0	58.0	60.0
Power	44.0	76.0	52.0	58.0
Water	56.0	76.0	52.0	56.0
Law order	48.0	62.0	54.0	42.0
Education	68.0	70.0	70.0	44.0
Hospital	64.0	58.0	60.0	54.0
Housing	56.0	40.0	54.0	52.0
Open Spaces	58.0	16.0	40.0	42.0
Shopping	70.0	70.0	66.0	58.0
Hoteling	70.0	72.0	66.0	58.0
Leisure	62.0	70.0	60.0	60.0
Heritage	72.0	60.0	58.0	64.0

lifespan of some species with loss in biomass. Sudden rise in temperature introduces behavioural changes in living matter. Ecologist have therefore studied aquatic ecosystems. Waste heat can be released in form of evaporation of water or heat can be directly transferred to atmosphere by heat exchangers in dry cooling towers. The buildings can be heated in cold climate. Radiation hazards have same adverse effects on environment pollution. The social life in India with reference to day-to-day activities is shown in Table 1.36.

The perusal as given in Table 1.36 shows the quality of social life in four metropolitan cities in India such as New Delhi, Mumbai Chennai and Kolkata.

The existence of transport, power, water supply and law and order is best in Mumbai. While housing, open spaces, heritage, shopping is good in city of New Delhi. However Chennai can claim as best town from the view point of education and hospitals. Kolkata has nothing remarkable things to claim. This city has chronic problem of water and power limited open spaces, education complexes. While in Mumbai the situation of open spaces is vowefully worst (16%) followed by giant problem of housing due to unplanned growth of slums. There is recurring problem of Power, law and order in New Delhi. In case of Chennai it has similar problem of open spaces like Mumbai, as well as shortage of potable water. From all view point of comfort we note that Mumbai is best city with transport, power, water, education, Hotels and restaurants, and recreation theaters and commercial malls in the city.

1.14 CONCLUSION

Environmental pollution has grown by leaps and bounds needing immediate attention from mankind. To understand this problem one needs basic knowledge of environmental chemistry and specially of environmental chemical analysis. The impact of man on the environment and interaction with various spheres of environment originated pollution. The ecology and environment are closely related. The environmental pollution has been classified into five main groups as air pollution, water pollution, industrial waste water, sewage pollution and solid waste. In last decade pollution has reached a level in alarming proportion all over the world. The transportation is the main culprit leading to rise of photochemical smog. The water pollution was known to man since ages with reference to the quality of drinking water. Most of rivers are highly polluted. Waste water generated after use of water in industry causes serious problem of the pollution. It depends upon the source of the effluent. Pollution due to sewage is rampant in India. This is accompanied by pollution due to solid hazardous and biomedical waste which is receiving prompt attention in last few years. Apart from these major sources we have noise pollution; pesticide pollution; food pollution; pollution due to metal pollutants and thermal pollution and radiation hazards. With the indiscriminate use of nuclear energy death due to radiation hazards may increase. Mostly all the countries have excellent legislation to prevent pollution. Unfortunately the implementation mechanism is far from satisfactory. The developing countries have successed to some extent in managing environmental pollution but the underdeveloped third world countries the position is far from satisfactory.

Thus the environmental pollution is the most burning problem, requiring immediate attention by the society. A survey of basic needs of man in India revealed that people wanted consideration of issues such as vandalism, odour, bus fare, parks, employment, noise, medical care, schools, roads, garden and home in that order (Table 1.36). However, they gave top priority to the stoppage of degradation of their environment in preference to other important issues. In England there was greater awareness since 1952. With the enforcement of clean air act (1968), air was cleaned, while in the USA, Environmental Protection Agency (US EPA) was established. In India since 1962 Maharashtra was the first state to enact Water Pollution Act, followed by draft proposal for Air Pollution Control in 1980. Fortunately our Government is aware of these problems. It has passed comprehensive environmental protection bill in 1986 to include legislation on abatement of noise pollution. Maharashtra was first to introduce a bill for transportation of hazardous chemicals (1988). In spite of this we have tragedy of spilling of chemicals on highways. State boards for abatement and control of air and water pollution is there in every state. However, these control measures shall not be effective, unless environmental education is imparted from primary school to college and university level. We have the Department of Environment and Forest of the Central Government under the Ministry of Environment. The agencies to control environmental pollution which will be effective only if we properly monitor pollution. No doubt future is certainly bright for India, provided we are alert on monitoring and control of environmental pollution.

ADDITIONAL READING

1. R.A. Horne, *'Chemistry of Environment'*, Wiley Interscience (1978).
2. A.S. Boughey, *'Man and Environment'*, 2nd Edition, MacMillian Publishing Co. Inc., New York (1975).
3. E.T. Chanlett, *'Environmental Protection'*, 2nd Ed., McGraw Hill Kogakusha Ltd. (1979).
4. I.L. Marr and M.S. Cresser, *'Environmental Chemical Analysis'*, International Textbook Co., New York (1983).
5. C.N. Sawyer and P.L. McCarty, *'Chemistry for Environmental Engineers'*, 3rd Ed. McGraw Hill Book Co., (1978).
6. A.K. Sen, *'Environmental Management and Planning'*, Wiley Eastern Ltd. (1988).
7. B. Patel, *'Proceeding of the Seminar on Management of Environment'*, Wiley Eastern (1980).
8. *Water Treatment Handbook,* 5th Ed., Degremont (1979).
9. A. K. De, *'Environmental Chemistry'*, 5th Ed., New Age Intl. (p) Ltd., (2003).
10. R. Nash, *'Environment and Americans—a problem of priorities'*, Holt Rinhart and Winston (1972).
11. H.B. Elkins and L.D. Pagnotto, *'Industrial health hazards in Treatise of Analytical Chemistry'*, Ed. I.M. Kolthoff, P.J., Elving, Part III, Volume 4 Section B, Wiley Interscience (1980).

12. J.W. Moore and E.A. Moore, *'Environmental Chemistry'*, Academic Press, New York (1976).
13. K.J. Irgolic and A.E. Martell, *'Environmental Inorganic Chemistry'*, VCH Publishers Inc. USA (1985).
14. L. Hodges, *'Environmental Pollution'*, Second Edition. Holt Rinhart and Winston New York (1977).
15. C. Baird, *'Environmental Chemistry'*—W.H. Freeman and CO New York (1995).
16. D.W. Connet, *'Basic Concept of Environmental Chemistry'*. Lewis Publishers Bocca Raton (1997).
17. S.E. Manahan, *'Environmental Chemistry'*, 7th Edition. Lewis Publishers (2000).
18. G.N. Ewing, *'Environmental Analysis'*, Academic Press (1977).
19. K. Shah, *'Basics of Solid and Hazardous Waste Management Technology'*—Prentice Hall USA (2000).
20. S.M. Khopkar, *'Environmental Pollution Analysis'*, Second Ed., New Age International (P) Ltd., (2012).

2 Environmental Analysis

2.1 INTRODUCTION

Environmental analysis provides a source of valuable knowledge and information. The analysis is concerned with quantitative analysis. During such analysis a suitable reference or standard is required for the purpose of the comparison. The chemical analysis of environmental samples helps us to understand the biological pathways or cycles specially those involving harmful materials. In order to understand the seriousness of harmful materials as pollutants, it is sometimes necessary to know sociological and economical aspects to know hazardous nature of the material in addition to levels of pollutants.

2.2 ENVIRONMENTAL IMPACT ASSESSMENT (EIA)

Environmental impact assessment gives information on likely status of pollution. The action of man on environment leads to disturbances, assimilation or transformation leading to the degradation of an environment and quality of life. Thus, EIA is a procedure which tries to explain, define, assess the effect of proposed project so that better informed decision can be made. EIA considers (*a*) the impact of the environment by proposed work (*b*) recognises unavoidable adverse effects (*c*) provides an alternative to action (*d*) recognises and provides monitoring scheme and finally (*e*) suggests devices to mitigate or decrease the environmental impact. The decision makers initially need EIA report before taking decision to set up plant or industry. It helps to control environmental pollution. EIA uses mathematical models for predictions of degradation of environment in future. Environmental chemistry helps us to design monitoring programme. It also stipulates threshold limiting value of toxic substances and defining emission standards. EIA is objective and not exact science but predicts the future.

2.3 CRITERIA OF SELECTING A METHOD OF ANALYSIS

A success of an analytical method depends largely upon analyst in selecting right choice of method in the project. For such purpose literature should be consulted (*e.g.*, Analytical or environmental abstracts). The criteria of selection of the method depends upon the accuracy and precision sought, the sensitivity and selectivity of method, possible interferences. Speed and cost of analysis, skill are finally decide the working. We have to ask question as to what kind of accuracy or precision is aimed in experiment? One can get good precision but not necessary with good accuracy. One must test reproducibility of the method and should not much depend too much on repeatability of work. The sensitivity defines the smallest concentration of material which can be easily analysed. The selectivity is measure of exclusiveness of method for particular element or the component during analysis *e.g.*, Dimethylglyoxime is selective for the analysis of nickel. Interference marr the good method of analysis during measurements and are therefore removed before determination. The speed of analysis should not be very long. The analysis must be completed as quickly as possible *e.g.*, biological examination of the water. The time for analysis of individual component as well as analysis of all constituents as a whole should be reasonably small to the extent possible. The overall cost of analysis is very important in country like ours. Like cost, operator's skill is also important specially when interlaboratory comparison is made. One should preferably select a familiar technique. The scale of operation is very critical. The sensitivity and availability of sample influences the scale of operation when sensitivity represent smallest fraction of sample to be analysed.

2.4 ERRORS IN ANALYSIS

The steps in analysis are mainly sampling, dissolution, separation and quantitative determination. These steps can go wrong if some error creeps in any one of the above four steps. Even a laboratory environment can also introduce an error in the analysis. For example, glove box must be clean and free from any contamination specially in environmental analysis, we badly need a clean room. The type of containers used for analysis must be also clean. The adsorption of ions on the surface of glass container is not favourable. The adsorption loss is more at lower concentration and the magnitude of loss depends upon the solvent used. The pH of solution also influences such error. Glass with low thermal coefficients is preferable. Fused silica is best material for container. The cleaning of glass wax is also critical. The relative performance of container material is not always easy to assess. For instance borosilicate glass is best material for the manufacture of container. The voltalisation leads to loss of material to be analysed. The organometallic compounds are lost due to voltalisation. The reagents used must be reasonably pure and of 'Anal R' grade. All volatile liquids should be purified by process of distillation. In market the grades of reagents with the varying degree of purity are available. Thus, purity of compound is somewhat of complex significance. A pure chemical will be having exact theoretical composition. They are good to prepare 'standard' in instrumental analysis. Water is universal solvent. It can be best purified by distillation. The high purity water is obtained by double distillation in glass-quartz apparatus. One can also use millipore reagent grade water. The preparation of such water is rather expensive.

2.5 STATISTICAL ANALYSIS

Such analysis can be carried out provided we have large set of results of analysis. We commonly use the term standard deviation *e.g.* If a_1 a_2 a_3 a_4 ... a_n are values then mean is $\left[\frac{a_1 + a_2 + a_3 + a_4 \ldots. a_n}{n}\right]$ for each value then would be some deviation from mean value (either positive or negative) *e.g.*, if a is mean then $(a_1 - a)$ $(a_2 - a)$ $(a_3 - a)$ are differences as δ_1, δ_2 δ_3 ... δ_n. The square root of sum of all these differences divided by $(n - 1)$ gives standard deviation $s.d. = \sqrt{\frac{\Sigma\delta^2}{n-1}}$ = Standard deviation of single measurement if n = total number of determinations.

The errors in calculations are random and they may result gross errors. Random errors are one where the deviation of any one result is positive or negative. Error is matter of chance. We have "systemic" errors. These are one which always remain constant in all determinations. The caliberation of instrument can eliminate such systemic error. The gross errors are expected to occur only to other analyst by accidently dropping sample. Q-test is used to ascertain the reliability of results. The precision of analytical result is measure of repeatability of analysis. While accuracy of analysis is a measure of its correctness. There are limits of detection and determination. All instrumental analysis need calibration graph. The choice of scale for both x and y axes are important for the optimum readability of link with slope close to 45°. The 'regression' analysis is a statistical tool useful for handling raw data used to construct calibration curve. The best way is to make five measurements and calculate the constant '*k*' and '*b*' for the line in equation $A = Kc + b$ and evaluate concentration '*c*' from measured physical property such as absorbance. The regression analysis or the least square method is used for calculating best straight line of each set of data.

Finally, the comparison of results of analysis is also important. We calculate student '*t*' test as follows:

$t = \frac{9A - 9B}{g} \cdot \sqrt{\frac{n}{2}}$. This value is compared in Table of '*n*' values against values for degree of 90, 95, 99% confidence limit. The greater details of this subject is provided in Chapter 4 on statistical analysis.

2.6 SAMPLING

The sampling of water and air are critical but it is most important to get reliable results of analysis. The sample should not be heterogenous. The sample should be taken at different points and different depths in soil or water. Air samples must be collected on scattered area taking into account the meteorological parameters specially in case of air pollution analysis. The sampling should be done on the continuous basis all round the year. The container should be such that it should not contribute to pollution level of air or water. The storage and preservation of the sample is equally important so the samples like food, plants, tissue change their composition in air. So they should be stored in cold storage to preserve their components.

Let us first consider special features of air sampling. All samples must be collected from troposphere which is 11 km from earth above. The grab sampling is common method for air. It has limitations of leakage in transportation and contamination and availability of limited volume for analysis. Nowadays continuous monitoring sampling units are available. The sampling should be preferably be done in open atmosphere. The sampling of auto exhaust emission should be done at exhaust stock and exhaust pipe in car.

In water sampling morphological information, is very useful. Morphotetry is the study of morphological features of the basin of body of water. The type, location, historical background, of sample must be studied. The area, length between two sampling points, the depth for collection of sample must be predetermined. For large bodies sampling stations should be set up. Water may be collected in glass or polythene container. 'Van Dorn Water Sampler' is also useful. Other types are "Ruttner sampler" or "Dussart flask sampler". Thermos flask can be used for sampling. Temperature, pH, free CO, and alkalinity, dissolved oxygen, sulphide should be immediately recorded. The sample during transportation and storage must be kept in freezer. If a large number of samples are collected then a baseline can be easily established for the purpose of comparison. Gas cylinder often contains smell of organic or analogous substances which should be kept aside for some time and then the sample may be collected and proceed for the quantitative analysis.

2.7 DISSOLUTION OF THE SAMPLE

This is also called as the opening of the sample. Such decompositions either involves oxidation or reduction or none of these two reactions. If solvation energy exceeds the crystal lattice energy, solid dissolves. The water is best solvent. The dichloromethane, chloroform, toluene and hexane are best solvents for the organic materials. For inorganic materials, acids may be used for the dissolution. Hydrochloric, nitric or perchloric acids, are also used depending upon the need. Teflon container is must if hydrofluoric acid is used. The process of fusion is also used for minerals with potassium bisulphate, borax, alkali hydroxide, alkali nitrate or carbonate are best for fusion in platinum crucibles or silver container. The heating of sample should not exceed ten mts. The cooled solid mass should be dissolved in dilute acids. He, O_2, H_2, are used for dissolution, during process of combustion. In hydrogen, the organic compound experiences pyrolysis. Vacuum is used for determination of dissolved gases in metals by gas chromatography. The sampling of soil is simple. The surface soil samples are collected.

2.8 ELIMINATION OF INTERFERENCES

A detailed account of various separation methods is included in next chapter. The separation in many instances is must before any instrumental analysis is carried out to eliminate interferences during step of determination. Such kind of the separation by phase change, or partition between two liquid phases are used. In two phase separation system, the phases are separated and retained separately for further treatments. A phase change can facilitate separation *e.g.*, a transformation from solid to liquid is done by melting while liquid to gas conversion is done by volatilization but change from solid to gas is done by sublimation. The process is reversible *e.g.* gas can be condensated to solid or liquid and liquid can solidify to solids as shown in Fig. 2.1.

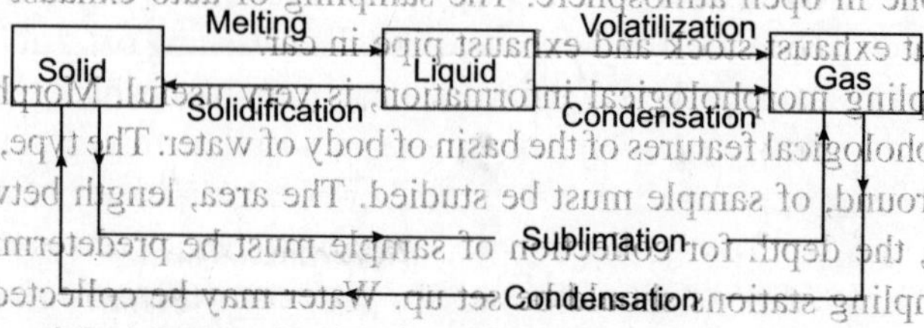

Fig. 2.1

Many separations are based upon partition between two phases where both phases are liquids or one is solid and other is liquid. The component of interest is partitioned between two phases *e.g.*, separation of solid by filter paper or separation of two liquids immiscible with each other by solvent extraction in separatory funnel. This permits quantitative separation. The separation is based upon the difference in magnitude of partition coefficient. The details of such technique are given under liquid-liquid extraction in the next chapter. Apart there are several practicle separation techniques. A birds' eye view is taken for them in this chapter and details are discussed in next chapter. Such techniques include diffusion, condensation, stripping, volatilization extraction, adsorption, desorption, ion exchange and precipitation. We consider the following few techniques:

(*a*) *Diffusion*: It makes use of three phases of which two are similar one and third phase is isolated *e.g.*, gas diffusion through membrane. This permits the transfer dissolved gas from one solution to other. The difference in diffusion rate can be also exploited to device separation, but here temperature control is critical.

(*b*) *Condensation*: It means trapping less volatile impurities in stream of gas. Liquid nitrogen cannot be used as coolant, but liquid oxygen can be used as coolant, CO_2 in propon-2-ol or ice water can be also used for the process of condensation thereby accomplishing good separation.

(*c*) *Stripping*: The dissolved volatilies are separated by bubbling N_2 gas and its subsequent scrubbing to recover volatile matter. One can strip organic solvent from aqueous phase in solvent extraction.

(*d*) *Volatilization*: Volatilization of gas or vapour is used to separate nonvolatile components. Head space analysis separates volatile part from solution. This can be confirmed by nothing loss in weight of the sample.

(*e*) *Distillation*: This is best method if two liquids boil at different temperatures of *e.g.*, ethanol from sugar solution. The essential oils from food can be thus separated.

(f) *Solvent Extraction*: The solute is transferred from one liquid to another liquid by shaking the two phases. Two phases are immiscible. The method is good for trace analysis specially for metals and few organic compounds. The selection of extractant and control of pH or acidity during extraction is most critical.

(g) *Adsorption-desorption*: It is basis of adsorption chromatography. Gas phase absorption of inert gases on activated coal is the classic example of this technique. The process of desorption occurs at high temperature. The washing solid absorbent also releases adsorbed matter. The contact time, particle size, packing pattern, total load are all vital factors.

(h) *Ion exchange*: Ion exchange is special class for separation of ionic species from non-ionic or one ionic species from another ionic species provided their exchange potentials are different. By regeneration one can reuse ionexchange resin. By process of elution, material is taken up by ion exchange resin *e.g.* mixtures of anions can be effectively separated. Liquid anion exchangers can be used for separation of anionic metal complexes which are negatively charged.

(i) *Precipitation*: Precipitation is classical method for separation of insoluble ionic solids from solution. It is used in gravimetric analysis. We exploit the difference in solubility of two species for the purpose separation. To remove trace species coprecipitation can be also carried out.

(j) *Dissolution*: Dissolution is good if we have mixture of a salt and sand to analyse as the latter can be filtered and thus separated. There are few problems associated with separation methods. Before ascertaining optimum conditions of separation, large number of parameters have to be studied to know their influence on process of separation. In most of the instrumental methods of determination, separation is a prerequisite to get reproducible results. Amongst instrumental techniques only atomic absorption spectroscopy does not need elimination of interferences before quantitative analysis.

2.9 THE QUANTITATIVE ANALYSIS

Most commonly used methods cover classical or spectral or electroanalytical methods. These methods are discussed in great details in next chapter. One cannot differentiate between classical and instrumental methods as a complete analytical procedure consist of both methods. Depending upon amount of the constituent one can decide which instrumental method one should follow to get reliable results. The digital read out on instruments are better than analogue form as they are cheap, readable, linear and time saving and of course simple to operate. The instruments consist of signal which varies with references to some physical property like absorbance, diffusion current, emission etc.

2.10 COMPLETION OF ANALYSIS

One has to guard source of errors in any analytical determination. Minimum handling of the sample is beneficial. Fewer steps in analysis are preferred to avoid the errors. Nanogram (10^{-9}) samples can be perfectly analysed if one reduces number of steps of operations and selects right kind of the instrumental method for the purpose of analysis. Errors can creep in form at stage of sampling, weighing, decomposition, separation or determination. There may be contamination by operator, container, solvent, reagent etc. Loss may be observed due to loss of air in container. Other factors which contribute to error are inhomogeneous sample, not caliberated glassware or measuring instruments lead to pitfall in analysis. The best thing is to consider all sources of error and interferences to check method from this angle before commencing analysis. It must be born in the mind that monitoring of the pollutant is most crucial as the methods for the control depends upon their level of pollutant present in environment. Further the toxic manifestations of pollutant is also dependent on level.

2.11 ENVIRONMENTAL LEGISLATION

Table 2.1 shows as to how legislations were passed in course of time.

Table 2.1 Environmental legislation (laws) in USA and India

S.No.	*Name of act and year*	*Special features*
Acts in USA		
1.	Air quality (1967)	In various part of states level was monitored and based upon these results standards were stipulated.
2.	Clean air act (1970)	United states environmental pollution association was formed. The primary and secondary standards (for air) were established. Hazardous pollutants were identified.
3.	Clean air act (1977)	Pollution by auto exhaust emission was controlled. Computer programming is used to prepare a model.
4.	Clean air act (1990)	Lowest achievable emission rate was established.
5.	Clean air act (1997)	Amendated act to cover Green house gases including ozone were formulated.
Act in India		
1.	Water pollution (1960)	Only in Maharashtra act came into existence with setting of Pollution Control boards and standards established.
2.	Water pollution (1974)	In all States of India Pollution Control boards were established with sufficient powers to look at industries.
3.	Air Pollution (1965)	For first time air pollution control norms were stipulated.
4.	Environmental protection bill (1986)	A comprehensive act covering both air and water pollution was devised.
5.	Noise regulation (2000)	New act was passed, standards were prescribed. Noise during festivals was regulated.
6.	Comprehensive Environment Protection	All aspects of pollution in air, water, effluent, noise, odour were regulated.

A perusal of Table 2.1 demonstrates as to how awareness of the pollution was created and how effective legislations were passed in assemblies and parliament. Finally our own standards were established.

It is worth considering regulation (Table 2.1) on pollution control in America as well as in India. It shows how awareness was created in society both in developed and developing countries.

2.12 CONCLUSION

Before proceeding for the environmental analysis one must understand the scope and methodologies to be adopted. This parameter attains special significance while preparing a report on environmental impact analysis. There are various criteria for selecting method of analysis. These include accuracy, speed, cost and level of analysis. In all such analytical procedures the source of errors in analysis must be identified and carefully guarded to ensure reproducible results. While considering errors, one must be quite conversant with statistical parameters like standard deviation or regression analysis. Most vital step especially in air pollution analysis is technique of sampling. It involves several steps. But before that dissolution of the sample is very important which can be done in mineral acids or fused alkalies. Most of the instrumental methods do not tolerate interferences. Such interferences have to be before hand eliminated. There are variety of methods for such separation but distillation, solvent extraction and ion exchange are the most popular methods. For quantitative analysis one can use classical methods if level is high or best use instrumental techniques involving spectrophotometry, electroanalytical methods like polarography. The radio analytical techniques like activation analyses are rarely used. One must not forget that the entire operation will not be complete unless one carries out complete analysis to account for all the constituents in air, water, soil or solid waste sample.

ADDITIONAL READING

1. S.M. Khopkar, *'Basic Concepts of Analytical Chemistry'*, Third Edition, New Age International Publisher (2010).
2. S.M. Khopkar, *'Analytical Chemistry Problems and Solutions'*, Second Edition, New Age International Publisher (2012).
3. I.L. Marr, M.S. Cressor, *'Environmental Chemical Analysis'*, International Textbook Company Chapman and Hill (1983).
4. K. Eckschlager, *'Errors, Measurements and Results in Chemical Analysis'*, Van Nostrand Reinhold., London (1973).
5. H.A. Lattenen, W.L. Harris, *'Chemical Analysis'*, Second Edition, McGraw Hill and Co. New York (1975).
6. R. Bock, I.L. Marr, *'Decomposition Methods in Analytical Chemistry'*, International Textbook Co. (1979).
7. J.A. Dean, *'Chemical Separation Methods'*, Van Nostrand Reinhold and Co. (1969).
8. E.W. Berg, *'Physical and Chemical Methods of Separation'*, McGraw Hill and Co. (1963).

9. A.K. De, S.M Khopkar, R.A. Chalmers, '*Solvent Extraction of Metals*', Van Nostrand Reinhold and Co. (1970).
10. S.M. Khopkar, '*Analytical Chemistry of Macrocyclic and Supramolecular Compounds*', Second Edition, Springer Verlag (2008).
11. E.W. Ewing, '*Environmental Analysis*', Academic Press (1977).
12. R.L. Grob, '*Chromatographic Analysis of Environment*', Marcell Dekker (1983).
13. E.B. Sandell, '*Colorimetric Determination of Traces of Metals*', Interscience Publishing (1964).
14. S.M. Khopkar, '*Environmental Pollution Analysis*', Second Edn., New Age International Publisher Ltd. (2012).

3 Modern Methods of Analysis

3.1 INTRODUCTION

The control measures for the abatement of pollution cannot be properly devised unless we are aware of the extent or level of pollution. Such level can be ascertained by precise measurement, and analysis of the environmental pollution. There are numerous methods for the measurement of pollution. They consist of classical methods of analysis like gravimetric or volumetric methods.These methods are generally applicable at milligram concentrations. Several of the pollutants are present in environment at microgram levels, *e.g.*, dust and particulate matter, while few metal pollutants like beryllium are having their threshold limiting value as 2 μg/m^3. As such spectral methods or electroanalytical methods are best suited in analysis. Many times the pollutants are found in association with one another. Under these circumstances determination becomes more complicated. One has to resort to various separation techniques, like chromatography for the isolation of these pollutants. In this chapter, an endeavour is made to present a brief review of various methods utilised for the analysis of the various pollutants. It is not envisaged here to describe what the said method is? It is presumed that the reader is quite conversant with the basis of these methods. Only, an attempt will be made to highlight applications of these methods in environmental pollution analysis. For knowing basic concepts of the methods, the reader is referred to the book—'*Basic Concepts of Analytical Chemistry*' Third Edition (2010).

In the techniques of environmental chemical analysis, it is very much essential to know quality and quantity of the pollutants. This is specially of crucial importance if the pollutant is present at lower concentration in form of the species to be characterised. Several of these techniques are common to analysis of soil, water, air and biological samples. During such analysis one may encounter various errors which may be termed as "random" or "bias" errors (deviation from true value). The values closer to true values are called 'accurate' values. The process of identification and control of such errors is called as 'quality control'. Since many pollutants are present at microgram levels we should know methods of analysis. The lowest concentration of analyse which can be measured determines sensitivity of method. We encounter instrumental detection limit or lower level of detection. Former limit is three times standard deviation value while latter is an amount which will give measurable signal. Sometimes method for the detection limit or practical quantitative limit is also used in the quantitative environmental analysis.

3.2 SEPARATION METHODS

In environmental pollution analysis, the separation methods have their unique position in the scheme of analysis of pollutants. This is because one rarely encounters a pure or uncontaminated sample of air or water. The great strides have been made in the instrumental methods of analysis as far as speed, level and cost is considered. Most of methods suffer from serious drawback of the interferences. With the exception of atomic absorption spectroscopy, all other instrumental methods demand removal of interfering species before the quantitative chemical analysis. Such instrumental techniques include molecular absorption spectroscopy (UV visible, IR), light scattering Raman spectroscopy methods turbidimetry nephelometry, atomic emission methods (like FES ICP-AES) and molecular emission spectroscopy (Fluoroscence/Phosphorescence) methods. Similarly, electroanalytical or radioanalytical techniques also demand clean uncontaminated sample. To overcome these limitations several separation methods are invented. They include separation involving precipitation, froth-flotation but they are not good at low concentration of pollutants. There are methods based upon phase separation like solvent extraction and chromatography. These chromatographic methods are based upon the principles of differential migration of species on column due to either adsorption (column chromatography) or partition (such as paper, TLC, gas liquid, extraction chromatography). Some methods depend upon the difference in migration due to the difference in the molecular geometry of species like (Gel permeation/ion-exclusion) or differential migration of ions under the influence of electrical potential (*e.g.*, Electrochromatography). However, from the environmental point of view, gas chromatography, HPLC, ion chromatography and many of these instrumental techniques coupled upon with mass spectrometry or plasma spectroscopecy have shown miracles in the analysis. The conventional chromatographic methods are also equally effective.

3.3 CHROMATOGRAPHIC METHODS

We have effective methods, let us consider at this stage relevant methods of the separation.

(a) Adsorption Chromatography

This method largely consists of columnar methods and gas-solid chromatography. These methods are based up on the phenomenon of adsorption. Unfortunately, both techniques have limited applications in environmental separations. The forces involved in the process of adsorption include dipole induced dipole interaction or van der Waals interaction or London forces between solute particles and the stationary support like silica, alumina or diatomaceous earth packed in column. The gas solid chromatography is extensively used in radiochemical separation of radio nucleotides like iodine, krypton and xenon in gaseous state. These columnar methods have relatively less utility in analysis. The other less common techniques are exclusion and electrochromatography which are mainly based upon difference the in geometry of particles or rate of migration of ions under the influence of electric potential.

(b) Exclusion Chromatography

It is based upon the segregation of solute on basis of difference in molecular geometry or size of species. This technique is based upon the separation of molecules depending upon difference in their size. Gel filtration is an example of this technique. This technique has limited use in environmental analysis, excepting for the separation of biological products. Gel filtration is best used in biotechnology applications. We have also technique based upon migration under influence of potential as 3.3(*c*).

(c) Electrochromatography

Electrophoresis is not truly chromatographic method as it involves only one phase while electrochromatography involves two phases. Electrochromatography has limited applications in environmental pollution analysis. It is used for the separation of metals from effluents to a limited extent. Such separation occurs due to differential migration under the influence of difference in electrical potential.

3.4 PARTITION CHROMATOGRAPHY

Partition chromatography is most widely used method of separation in environmental pollution analysis.

This technique is based upon the exploitation of difference in partition coefficients for solute thereby promoting differential migrations. The important methods under this class are paper chromatography, thin layer chromatography, gas-liquid chromatography. Liquid-liquid partition chromatography (LLPC) and reversed phase partition chromatography (RPPC). All these methods have extensive applications. Paper chromatography (both ascending and descending and circular) are used for the separation of inorganic as well as organic species, *e.g.*, separation of Hg, As, Pb with ethylacetate, butanol mixture as stationary phase with hydrochloric acid as mobile phases. The thin layer chromatography is used for characterisation and separation of pesticide residues. The gas liquid chromatography has extensive applications in separation of organic pollutant analysis. GC-MS *i.e.*, hyphenated gas chromatography mass spectrometry is very useful for the separation of volatile and thermally stable organic pollutants, specially from air. All hydrocarbons, polymers, from air can be characterised by GC with appropriate detectors like TCD, FID and ECD. Of these flame ionisation detector finds extensive applications in the environmental pollution analysis. Mass spectrometers have various kinds of analysers like single channel, double channel, time of flight and quadrupole analysers. Of these, the last one is best suited for analysis.

3.5 GAS CHROMATOGRAPHIC SEPARATIONS

This is most efficient tool. Since 1950 gas chromatography has played an important role in separation of interfering contaminants. It can be used for the qualitative and quantitative analyses as it is rapid sensitive as well as selective for the purpose of separations. When a mixture of volatile component is passed through column along with carrier gas like helium, nitrogen, each volatile component is partitioned between carrier gas and solid or liquid with high boiling point coated on stationary support (*e.g.*, chromsorb). The amount of time needed by the volatile component to travel down the column is directly proportional to the degree at which each component is retained by the stationary phase on the column. Such phase consists of high boiling solvents consequently different component due to difference in their partition coefficient are retained on column. Those with less affinity for column due to less partition coefficient would emerge out first from the column followed by those which have high affinity due to high partition coefficient emerge latter. This will lead to differential migration fronts resulting in separation of various components in different fractions of the effluent from the column. Now if appropriate detector is available it can measure the time at which component emerges from column and hence amount of component to be measured. A graph of retention time versus detector response is used to evaluate the exact concentration of each component in the mixture. Ar, He, Ne, N_2 are used as one of the carrier gas. The sample in form of liquid or vapour is injected into the column. The stationary support is one which has large surface area. The capillary column with long tubes are becoming very popular TCD *i.e.* thermal conductivity detector is commonly employed. ECD *i.e.,* electron capture detector is used for separation of halogenated hydrocarbons and phosphorus compounds. FID *i.e.*, flame ionisation detector is very sensitive for organic compounds. Mass spectrometer can be used as the detector in hyphenated techniques *e.g.,* for GC-MS, Compound must be thermally stable and volatile for separation. The aqueous samples are not used but the extracted solvent is injected in the column. In packed column, stationary phase is coated on stationary support. Temperature at inlet and outlet must be carefully controlled to get reproducible results. Methylene chloride, chloroform and halogenated hydrocarbons linger in column and must be first removed. The loss of column coating is called 'column bleed' which occurs at high temperature. The ghost peaks occur due to contamination but they can be removed by injecting more diluent in column. ECD is best for detection of halogens, peroxides, quinones and nitro groups. FID is widely used as it has high sensitivity for oxygen-carbon compounds, it ignores impurities in carrier gas, it has large linear dynamic response (LDR), is reliable and has low detection dead volume, is inert towards inert gas and is non combustile materials which is considered assest in analysis.

3.6 GAS CHROMATOGRAPH—MASS SPECTROMETRY

This hyphenated technique of mass spectrometer is particularly useful for characterisation of specific organic pollutants. While gas chromatography works for isolation/separation of species. It works on principle of generation of ions by electric discharge, followed by separation based upon charge/mass (e/m) ratio. An output is recorded as mass spectra. The compound must be preferably pure. They must have ability to detect wide variety of compounds. From fragmentation pattern one can elucidate structure. The quadrupole mass spectrometer is most useful in environmental analysis with 70 eV beam of 0 to 200 eV. Then depending upon (e/m) ratio differential segregation occurs. One kind of e/m particle travel in quadrupole analyser (based upon difference in their mol.wt.). Mass scan be obtained from their fragmentation pattern. The pattern is matched with one of known compound with baseline to identify the other components. A compound is source which is quickly detected. Some mass ions present due to air components that leak in the system, *e.g.*, N^{14}, N^{18}, O^{16}, O^{32} or C^{14}, Ar^{40}, He^{4}. The compounds which are isolated by gas chromatography are PCB derivatives, phenol, polynuclear, aromatic hydrocarbons, toxaphonic, trihalogen, methane. While GC-MS technique is used for the characterisation and determination of volatile compounds and extractants, such as dibromomethane, dibromochloropropane, herbicides, pesticides, volatile halocarbons.

3.7 HIGH PERFORMANCE LIQUID CHROMATOGRAPHY

This is a kind of technique which is applicable to any kind of chromatographic separation. As such it is not separate class of chromatography method but a separate technique useful for all chromatographic methods. For nonvolatile liquids which are thermally unstable this technique is beneficial. One gets high resolution when very high pressure is used. Refractive index and UV detector are employed. Like GC-MS one can use LC-MS for better identification and determination. HPLC is technique where in, liquid mobile phase containing hot gas transfers sample through the column containing liquid stationary phase. The components are held up on column phase by affinity expressed as physical property like adsorption, partition, ion exchange, size selectivity or electrical potential difference. Mostly the UV detector is used or photo-diode is also used which measures absorbance of sample, detector has problem of interferences like masking of absorbance region of HPLC mobile phase and its additives specially at wavelength of 200-300 nm thereby causing interferences. Postcolumn reaction is inline sample derivatisation. The less sensitive compounds can be analysed with postcolumn reaction. However, with fluoroscence detector interferences are minimised. This is used with postcolumn reaction. It is extremely sensitive. HPLC is used for analysis of chlorophyll, 6–9 polynuclear aromatic hydrocarbons and similar organic constituents causing environmental pollution.

The success of gas chromatography method is attributed to the use of most efficient detectors to quantify the sample after separation. The principal amongst many detector are ECD, FID, TCD which stands for electron capture detector, flame ionisation detector and thermal conductivity detectors respectively. The mass spectrometric detector (MSD) was discovered latter. However the most commonly used detector was TCD *i.e.* thermal conductivity detector. It has reasonable limit of detection viz 10^{-8} m *i.e.* almost nano level analysis but the range of FID detector was quite large viz 10^{-11} the highest limit of the range of detection *i.e.* Linear dynamic range (LDR) is maximum for the electron capture detector. All these detectors facilitate separation of several organic compounds containing nitrogen, phosphorus and sulphur. The basic requirement is simple the compound must be thermally stable and is reasonably volatile. If one is interested in analysis of organo metallic compounds the best detector used is TCD and to some extent flame ionisation detector (FID).

Another important variable in Gas Chromatography is kind of stationary support used upon which high boiling liquid is impregnated as the stationary phase specially in Gas-Liquid Chromatography (GLC). Variety of materials are used as the stationary support which include chromsorb, silica, kieselghur and diatomaceous earth. The first one is synthetic sorbant. The activated charcoal is also extensively used in Gas-Solid chromatography (GSC). The separation in such system is accomplished with adsorption of component on appropriate sorbant which participates in holding solute molecule due to London forces, dipole induced dipole interaction or weak vander Waals forces. They are holding the solute on stationary supper in the column. On account of the difference in adsorbility various kind of compounds are separated. Trevor and Ramsay and his group accomplished the separation of inert gases by Gas solid Chromatography.

It should be noted that activated charcoal/coal is best material used in gas solid chromatography. It facilitates measurement of several parameters such as bulk density, porosity, surface activity, weight loss. In fact the separation of individual components is of greatest relevance in Environmental analysis. Table 3.2 demonstrates the utility of charcoal as the stationery support.

Table 3.1 Type of detectors used in gas chromatography

S. No.	*Name of Detector*	*Abbre-viation*	*Limited detection (M)*	*Linear dynamic range (LDR)*	*Applications*	*Remarks*
1.	Electron capture (ECD)	ECD	10^{-13}	10^{2}	Halo, nitro-oxygenated compounds	Varying response
2.	Flame ionisation (FID)	FID	10^{-11}	10^{6}	Organic compounds	Most common in use
3.	Flame photometry	FID	10^{-11}	10^{3}	Phosphorus Sulphur compounds	Variable response
4.	Mass Spectrometry	MSD	10^{-11}	10^{2}	All organic volatile compounds	Used for separation and determination
5.	Thermal conductivity (TCD)	TCD	10^{-8}	10^{4}	Thermally Stable compounds	Widely used technique

Table 3.2 Charcoal as the adsorbant in adsorption chromatography

S.No.	Characteristics facilitating separation	Magnitude
1.	Bulk density measurement	0.24 g/cm
2.	Chemical contents of elements present; Al, K Na, Ca, Mg, Fe	0.5–1.5%
3.	Loss of mass after contact with water	8%
4.	Porosity in one day contact with stability	0.055 BTU
5.	Surface area of the sorbant	280 g/cm^2
6.	Specific activity of the particles	1.20
7.	Contact pH for aqueous solution	5.7

3.8 ION EXCHANGE CHROMATOGRAPHY

The cation as well as anion exchange chromatography are very useful in environmental analysis. The well-known process of deionisation of water is based upon the principle of ion-exchange methods. Apart from this, any kind of separation of anions can be done by anion exchange methods. All cationic impurities can be isolated by cation exchange chromatography. Liquid anion exchangers are based on similar principles of anion exchange chromatography. In addition to separation of inorganic compounds, the organic compounds like protein, carbohydrates, aminoacids can be best separated by ion exchange chromatography.

This technique is useful and flexible mode at atmospheric or at high pressure. Both inorganic as well as organic ions can be separated. They are in H^+ form for cation resin and Cl^- form for anion exchange resin. In water analysis, ion-exchangers are used to remove interfering ions, determine total ion concentration, and concentration of trace quantities of cations. The batch method of ion exchange is useful for sample volume less than 100 ml, while columnar method is used for any volume of the sample. In batch method, sample is shaken with resin in beaker without column while the columnar method provides continuous contact between resin and sample, it facilitates the rapid exchange reaction. As solution passes through the column containing resin, ions are separated depending upon their exchange potential. It depends upon ionic size, and charge of ionic species. The greatest advantage of ion exchange method is one can use the same resin again and again after suitable regeneration process. The mineral acid regenerates cation exchange resin in column. The resin should be kept under liquid/water. The efficiency of separation on column depends upon flow rate employed during separation. As 0.1–1 ml/mt is considered best flow rate. After columnar separation the component is analysed with colorimeter using a suitable chromogenic ligand for a cation. Turbidity should be scruplously avoided during photometric measurement. The chromogenic ligands used are dithizone for Cd, Pb, Hg, Ag, Zn. The other method for analysis include atomic absorption spectroscopy, flame emission spectroscopy, plasma spectroscopy (ICP-AES), Potentiometry, (ion selective electrode) ISE. One can use polarography, or anodic stripping voltammetry. (These method are discussed in some details in subsequent sections of this chapter). GC-MS is also useful for quantitative analysis. "Ion chromatography"—is the best method. This technique is mainly used for separation of boron, removal of cation, or sulphate, isolation of surfactants, to get ammonia free water; and preparation of deionised water. Several anions also can be separated. In early years resins were imported, but now indigenous resins synthesised in India are cheaply available, and they are comparable with the imported resins in quality.

3.9 ION CHROMATOGRAPHY

The ion chromatography has come to the forefront only recently. It has helped us for characterisation, identification and determination of anions from the samples of water. It is being used for the speciation of metal pollutants. The chemical speciation is having greater ramification, as the nature of species in the environment will throw light on the toxicity of such metals on human beings. The nature of Hg, Cr or Fe in water was ascertained by ion chromatography. The sodium salts are used for the elution of ions taken up by ion-exchange column. This eluant is subsequently passed on anion exchange column (supressor), which in turn generates corresponding acid to give rise in conductivity. Such change in conductivity is related to quantum of anions present in the solution.

The most significant contribution of the ion chromatography is the possibility of analysis of any kind of anions which otherwise was a arduous task. The supressor column in the system helps for the detection of anions. Apart from common anions, oxyanions like arsenite, borate, and complex anions like carbonate chlorate, chloride and cyanide, hypochlorite, hypophosphite, nitrate, nitrite, phosphate, pyrophosphate, selenate, selenite, sulphite, sulphate, sulphide, trimetaphosphate and tripoly phosphate can be quantitatively analysed by ion chromatography. All cations can be also analysed by it. Ion chromatography can easily distinguish between chemically similar ions such as (Br^-, Cl^-, F^-) (SO_3^{2-}, SO_4^{2-}) or (NO_3^-, NO_2^-). In this technique the water sample is injected in stream of (carbonate-bicarbonate) eluent and passed through column. The anions are separated on the basis of their relative affinity for the resin. The separated anions are passed through cation exchanger. In the suppressor column the separated anions are converted to highly conductive acids form. The alkali carbonate-bicarbonate eluent is then converted to H_2CO_3 acid. The anions are then successively analysed by measurement of their electrical conductivity. By measuring peak area one can calculate % in plot of conductivity versus volume of eluent. Low molecular weight organic acids interfere in high concentration of fluoride and chloride. The sample dilution eliminates interferences otherwise the impurities give spurious peaks. The small sample must be used, some interference are eliminated by preconcentration, gradient elution or reinjection and recycling of the sample.

The lowest detection limit is 0.1 mg/L or μg/ml. For routine analysis of fluoride with chromogenic ligands like SPADNS, zirconiumalizarine sulphonate is used. The photometer should be preferably used. A use of guard column identical to separation column to protect separation column is used to avoid fouling of resin by the organic compounds. The suppressor column contains strongly acidic cation exchange resin. The fiber supressor or membrane suppressor is also used to convert anions to their acid form. It is essential to construct calibration plot before actual analysis with standard solution of anions. The resins from column is regenerated and reused.

Table 3.3 Precision of analysis by anions chromatography (mg/L)

Anion(s)	*Taken*	*Found*	*Precision*
Cl^-	0.76	0.86	0.18
NO_2^{2-}	0.45	0.49	0.09
Br^-	0.25	0.25	0.04
PO_4^{3-}	0.18	0.16	0.06
NO_3^-	0.50	0.56	0.16
SO_4^{2-}	0.51	0.57	0.07

The several anions from water samples can be analysed by ion chromatography. They include, bromide, cyanide, nitrate. The method can resolve a mixture of seven anions like F^-, Cl^- NO_2^-, Br^-, NO_3^- and SO_4^{2-} in less than twenty minutes period. So also F^- NO_2^-, HPO_4^-, Br^-, NO_3^-, SO_4^{2-} were resolved in eight minutes with Na_2CO_3–$NaHCO_3$ as eluents. The most remarkable application of ion chromatography is the 'environmental speciation' as toxicity of polluting material depends upon knowledge of what form cation or anions are present in sample. Metals in the different oxidation states were separated by ion chromatography with photometric detector with 4 (pyridylazo resorcinol (PAR) as chromogenic ligand.

3.10 SOLVENT EXTRACTION METHOD

This is the most versatile method for separation. It does not need very sophisticated instruments, excepting a good separatory funnel. The separations are largely based upon exploiting the difference in distribution coefficient of solute in two immiscisible solvents. Various kinds of solvating solvents as ethers, ketones, aldehydes and alcohols have been used for the purpose. In many instances the macrocyclic polyethers like crown ethers and high molecular weight amines, *i.e.*, liquid anion exchangers are used for separation of metal complexes. When the distribution ratio is exceedingly small, one has to resort to extraction chromatographic technique, where in hydrophobic extractant is coated on stationary support and interesting separations are carried out with mineral acids, as the mobile phase. The success of such a method depends upon the availability of large number of theoretical plates in the chromatography column. The chelating extracts such as β-diketone, oxine, oximes cupferron, dithizone, naphthol and azonaphthol, xanthates, sodium diethyldithiocarbamates and dithols are used. These extractants not only permit separation at microgram concentration, but also facilitates simultaneous extraction and spectrophotometric determination in one single stage.

The chemistry of alkali metals and alkaline earths was neglected. Only with the discovery of macrocyclic polyethers *i.e.* crown ethers, it was possible to separate and analyse any element belonging to s-block elements.

Solvent extraction has served as the complimentary tool. For instance although the analysis of metallic ions by atomic absorption spectroscopy is rapid in order to have better sensitivity, the metals are better extracted in hexanone (MIBK) or with suitable complexing agent. Similarly, 8-hydroxyquinoline complexes of metals in chloroform are directly injected into atomiser to provide greater selectivity.

Even in gas chromatography, the sample of organic compound is first extracted in suitable solvent before it is injected into the port so as to give better elution peak with good sensitivity. This shows instrumental methods are not adequate and need help of solvent extraction for separation.

Several developments have taken place in chemistry of transition elements extraction with crown ethers, cryptants and supramolecular compounds like calix(n)arine. The crown ethers act like host with metal ion as guest. When cavity of crown ether is similar to the cationic size of metal it is extracted as host guest complex, permitting separation from other cations. The interesting contributions were made with calix(n)arine. It has cone shaped conformation. It permits separation of metals of same group of classification. Metals with varying size from same group of the periodic classification can be extracted by calixarine. In stripping operations the metal ions came out of cavity according their size. The solid-phase extraction (SPE) is new area emerging in the environmental analysis. SPE contains extracting solid in column. The activated carbon is used for many years however, synthetic materials like long chain hydrocarbons (C_1-C_{18}) bound to solids have been used for the purpose A polymer of DVB with styrene can remove pesticides from water. Ethyl acetate is used to eluate pesticide residue from the column and analysed by gas chromatography. Another example of use of SPE is analysis of sulphide. Its reaction with NN'—dimethyl-p phenylene-diamine sulphate and ferric chloride give methylene blue. The solution is forced through sep-Pak C_{18} solid phase extractor to remove methylene blue which is attached to SPE. Methanol hydrochloric acid mixture is used to stripp out methylene blue. It is determined spectrophotometrically at 660 nm. Solid phase microextractor is specialised device used for analysis of haloethers. A other device use disk made of substance which bind with SPE and remove where water is filtered through it *e.g.,* solid phase extraction disk can remove radion nuecleotides from water *e.g.,* Sr^{90} or Cs^{137}.

3.10.1 Extraction Chromatography

Reversed phase extraction chromatography is in between SPE and solvent extraction. The hydrophobolic extractants is coated on stationary support as stationary phase which extracts several metal ions and are subsequently eluted with hydrophillic mineral acid in order of their affinity for column.

It can be seen that not all the methods available in analytical chemistry are always useful in the environmental pollution analysis. At the same time one cannot depend upon sophisticated instrumental methods, as on several occasions simple classical methods have furnished valuable data on the extent of pollution. What is more important is the level of analysis and background of analyte sample? One cannot all the time use instrumental methods specially in fields, as one needs a method suitable for the continuous measurements or monitoring. It is essential to have radically different approach while selecting a method for monitoring. In a developing country like India, another factor is the cost-benefit analysis. The method should be sensitive and economical. Such criteria must be taken into account while selecting a method for the air and water pollution monitoring on long-term basis.

3.11 CLASSICAL METHODS OF ANALYSIS

The gravimetric and volumetric analysis are two important classical methods. Such methods are largely used for the analysis at milligram level. The acidity or alkalinity of water is ascertained by volumetry. First part involves titration with base (pH 4.5) with methyl orange as indicator then titration to pH 8.3 with phenolthalein gives total acidity. While alkalinity of water is determined by titration with acid at pH 8.3 (or pH 4.5) at low pH we get total alkalinity. Similarly, hardness of water can be measured by complexometric titration with EDTA. The famous Winkler's method for analysis of dissolved oxygen also involves redox titration.

The gravimetric methods are used when the pollutant is present in the environment at milligram levels, *e.g.*, the lead candle method is used for analysis of SO_2 from air. It is based upon this principle, where a candle of PbO_2 on exposure to SO_2 forms $PbSO_4$, which is weighed to find out SO_2 in the air. The method involves simple weighing of PbO_2 and $PbSO_4$ before and after exposure respectively, to find the amount of SO_2 present. The other example is the determination of suspended particulate (SPM) matter from air. We resort to weighing of particulates deposit on millipore filter paper. The residue is collected by sampling procedure involving high volume sampler. In analysis of water pollution we rarely use gravimetric methods.

The volumetric or titrimetric methods are classified into four groups involving acid-base titrations, redox reactions, precipitation methods and complexometric technique. These methods are used for monitoring of air as well as water pollution, *e.g.*, the acid-base titration with conductance measurement is used for the analysis of SO_2 from air or boron from sample of soil. The simple acid-base titration is also used for ascertaining the acidity or alkalinity of sample of water. The application of the redox titration is well-known. The Winkler's method for the determination of dissolved oxygen (DO) from water is based upon redox reaction of manganese salt. It is reacted in the presence of potassium iodide when the liberated iodine is titrated with standard thiosulphates solution. Many of the organic pollutants from air can be determined by redox titrations. In all these cases, analysis is restricted to milligram level. The precipitation titration has wide ranging applications in water analysis, *e.g.* the determination of the dissolved chloride from sample of water can be accomplished by Volhard's method or Mohr's method. The complexometric titrations has maximum utility in pollution analysis. For instance, the hardness of water can be ascertained by titration of calcium or magnesium with EDTA (disodium salt), with suitable metallochromic indicator like Patterson Reed indicator. Similarly, level of iron or manganese from polluted sample of water can be ascertained by complexometric titrations. In comparison to water analysis, the complexometry technique has limited applications in analysis of air pollution. In spite of great advancement of instrumentation and with development of DO (dissolved oxygen) analysers, the Winkler's method with redox titration is still considered the best and the most reliable for analysis of DO, and for BOD (Biological oxygen demand). The chemical oxygen demand (COD) for water can be ascertained only by the redox titration involving $K_2Cr_2O_7$, H_2SO_4, KI and $Na_2S_2O_3$. The main reactions in Winkler's methods are:

$$Mn^{2+} + 2OH^- + \tfrac{1}{2}O_2 \rightarrow MnO_2 + H_2O$$

$$MnO_2 + 2I^- + 4H^+ \rightarrow Mn^{2+} + I_2 + 2H_2O$$

$$2S_2O_3^{2-} + I_2 \rightarrow S_4O_6^{2-} + 2I^-$$

A back calculation from the amount of $S_2O_2^3$ gives original amount of dissolved oxygen. BOD is obtained from DO by adding a microbial seed to the sample and maintaining it for 5-days to get value in mg/L. More details are available in subsequent chapters. However, for quantitative analysis at microgram level one uses instrumental methods. There are several methods for quantitative analysis of pollutants. These methods are applicable when the pollutant is present at milligram (10^{-3} g) to femtogram concentration (10^{-15}g). Table 3.2 lists such methods. The classical gravimetric and volumetric methods can analyse a pollutant upto 10^{-4} g concentration, while analytical absorption or emission spectroscopic method facilitate analyse pollutants to the level of nanogram (*i.e.*, 10^{-9} g) concentration. Other methods involving light scattering or molecular luminescence spectroscopy operates upto microgram levels. The radioanalytical or electroanalytical methods can work in the range 10^{-7} to 10^{-9} concentration. While method of capillary electrophores permits at ato level (10^{-18}) of analysis.

3.12 THE CLASSIFICATION OF SPECTROSCOPY METHODS

This is indicated in Table 3.4. It includes absorption, emission, fluoroscence, light scattering methods including Raman and nephelometry. Of these technique few are used for structure elucidation.

Amongst the various spectral methods of analysis the quantitative method like absorption spectroscopy find extensive applications in the environmental analysis. In comparison the other spectral methods are less commonly used. The main reason for popularity of atomic absorption spectroscopy is the easy availability of instruments. It is readly availability for plethora of organic analysis. There is chromogenic ligands and it provides reasonable limits of detection. (Table 3.4) Amongst spectral methods those methods which are used for the elucidation of structure include NMR, ESR, (ORD-CD) *i.e.*, optical rotatory dispersion and circular dichromism. AAS is one of the most common method used in absorption spectroscopy. For the characterisation of organic compounds one can take resort to infrared (IR) or ultraviolet (UV) and selected fluoroscence spectral methods of analysis. The technique of nephelometry is mainly used to measure suspended particulate matter (SPN) from the atmosphere. NMR, ESR, Raman, XRD are frequently used for the elucidation of the chemical structure of the pollutant. Atomic and molecular fluoroscences and phosphorescence methods are of recent origin, while Mossbaüer and γ-ray spectrometry are specialised methods for the characterisation of pollutant containing metals like Iron (III), cobalt (II) or radio active isotope of the sample. The popularity of the method of analysis not only depends upon sensitivity or accuracy but also on easy availability of instruments. Since indigenous Photometers or spectrometers including AAS are locally available these methods have become popular.

Table 3.4 Classification of spectral methods of analysis

S.No.	*Absorption spectroscopy*	*Emission spectroscopy*	*Fluoroscence spectroscopy*	*Raman spectroscopy*	*Scattering radiation*
1.	Atomic absorption	Atomic Emission	Atomic Fluoroscene	Resonance	Nephelometry
2.	UV visible spectroscopy	Flame emission	Molecular Luminances	Raman spectra conventional	Turbidimetry
3.	IR spectro-scopy	Electron spectro	Chemi-Luminance		
4.	NMR	γ-ray spectroscopy	Phospho-metry		
5.	ESR		X-ray Fluori-metry		
6.	Mössbaüer spectroscopy	–	Fluorimetry		

Table 3.5 Level of quantitative analysis by various methods

Method	*Conc. level*	*Symbol*	*Range*
Gravimetry	mg	mili	10^{-1} – 10^{3-}
Volumetry	mg	mili	10^{-1} – 10^{3-}
UV/visible/infrared spectroscopy	μg	micro	10^{-3} – 10^{6-}
Emission spectroscopy	ηg	nano	10^{-6} – 10^{9-}
Atomic absorption spectroscopy	ηg	nano	10^{-6} – 10^{9-}
Molecular luminescence	ηg	nano	10^{-3} – 10^{9-}
Light scattering	μg	micro	10^{-3} – 10^{6-}
Radioanalytical	ηg	nano	10^{-6} – 10^{9-}
Electroanalytical	μg	micro	10^{-3} – 10^{6-}

3.13 MOLECULAR ABSORPTION SPECTROPHOTOSCOPIC METHODS

In methods such as molecular absorption spectroscopy involves the atomic or molecular absorption. These methods include UV, visible IR spectrophotometric methods. They were also called as the 'colorimetric methods of analysis'. One measures either % transmittance or absorption of monochromatic light passing through the sample in comparion with one passing through reagent blank. So A = abC wherein A = absorbance, a = absorptivity, b = optical path, C = cocentration. This is called as **Bear's Law**. A plot of A against C gives a straight line graph passing through origin. The coloured species is extracted into the organic solvent to give more intense colour in extractive photometry. Several methods are used for the spectrophotometric analysis of sample with suitable chromogenic ligands as shown in the brackets as *e.g.* NH_3 (Nesslers reagent), Boron (curcumin), chlorine (o-toludine), fluoride (zirconium fluoride and alizarine) nitrite (NEDA), phosphate (molybdenum blue), selenium (diaminobenzidine), sulphide (methylene blue) and nitrate (brucine).

(a) Ultraviolet and Visible Spectrophotometric Methods

This is the most popular technique, with maximum utility in the pollution analysis. The principal reason for such popularity is the easy availability of colorimeters or spectrophotometers. The principle of visual colorimetry also forms the basis of Ring Oven technique. Table 3.6 indicates how UV spectroscopy can be used for the characterisation of organic functional group/chromophores. The task is complicated, when one has to characterise organic compound as the pollutant which is contaminated.

Table 3.6 Ultraviolet absorption of pollutant with chromophores

Chromophore	*Absorption peak (nm)*	*Molar absorptivity* ε	*Electronic transition*
Alkene	177	1.3×10^4	$\pi \to \pi^*$
Carbonyl	186	1.0×10^{-3}	$n \to \pi^*$
Amide	214	0.6×10^1	$n \to \pi^*$
Azo	339	0.5×10^1	$n \to \pi^*$
Nitro	280	2.2×10^1	$n \to \pi^*$
Olefin	184	1.0×10^4	delocalise π^*
Ketone	280	2.7×10	$n \to \pi^*$
Methanol	184	1.5×10	$n \to \sigma^*$
Methyl chloride	173	2×10^2	$n \to \sigma^*$
Benzene	204	7.9×10^3	$n \to \sigma^*$
Toluene	207	7.9×10^3	$\pi \to \pi^*$
Phenol	211	6.2×10^3	$\pi \to \pi^*$
Aniline	230	8.6×10^3	$\pi \to \pi^*$
Naphthalene	286	9.3×10^3	$\pi \to \pi^*$
Styrene	244	1.2×10^4	$\pi \to \pi^*$

* These represent antibonding orbitals.

A peak at 280 nm indicates presence of Keto group; or a peak at 186 nm indicates presence of carbonyl group; the peaks at 240 to 280 nm indicates the presence of aromatic compounds like napthalene or styrene, respectively. The visible spectrophotometry has made the greatest revolution. In air pollution analysis, SO_2

is determined with p-roseaniline (PRA) method or NO–NO_2 from air is determined by Saltzman method using; napthylethyl diamine (NEDA)H_2S is analysed spectrophotometrically with molybdenum-blue method; in water pollution analysis metal pollutants like iron (1–10 phenanthroline), Cr (sym diphenylcarbazide), Mn (formaldioxime); nickel (Dimethylglyoxime); zinc (dithizone) methods are well-known, where a chromogenic ligand is reacted with metal pollutant to form coloured complex. So long as the system adhers to Beer's law one can easily use this technique for analysis of majority of the metal pollutants in air and water (Fig. 3.1).

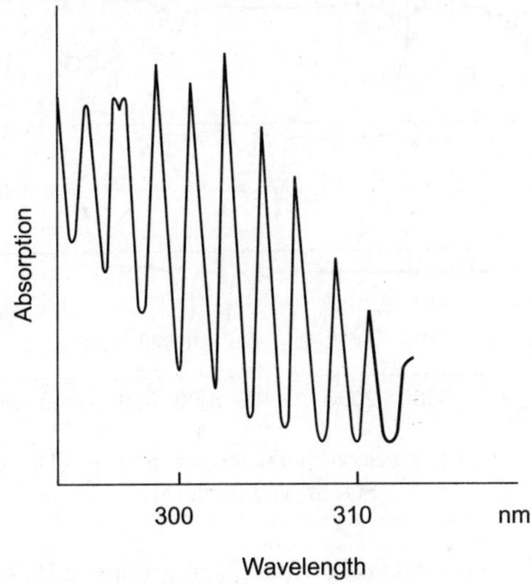

Fig. 3.1 UV spectra of sulphur dioxide

(b) Infrared Spectroscopic Methods

While characterising the organic pollutant from air or water, only one technique may not furnish reliable information. It may be necessary to use more than two or more methods, to definitely ascertain the presence of certain pollutants. Infrared

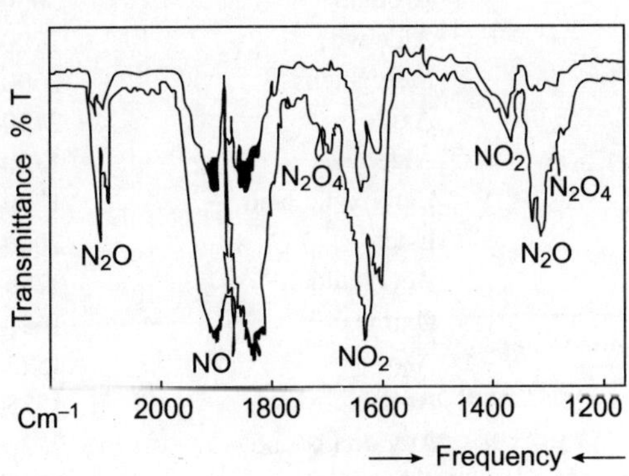

Fig. 3.2 IR spectra of NO–NO_x

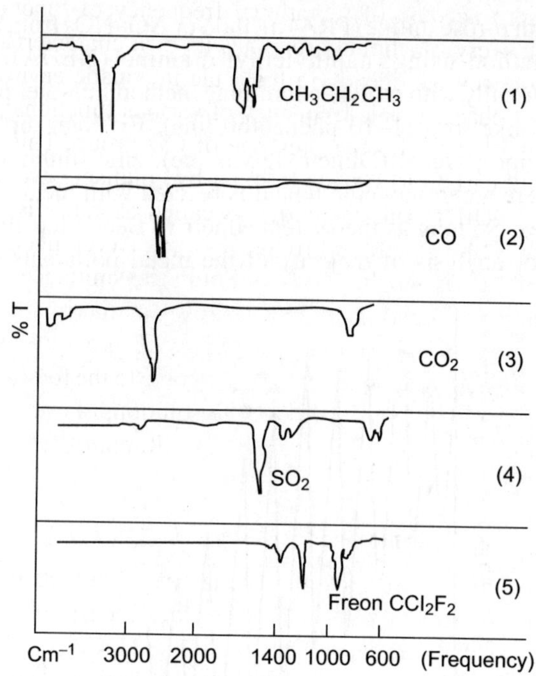

Fig. 3.3 IR spectra of few gaseous pollutants *viz.* propane (1), CO (2), CO_2 (3), SO_2 (4) and freon (5)

Table 3.7 Characterisation of functional groups in IR spectroscopy

Group	*Environment*	*Frequency (cm^{-1})*
OH	Alcohol	3580–3650
	Acid	2500–2700
NH	Amine	3500
	Amide	3140–3320
CH	Alkyne	3300
	Aromatic	3030
	Aldehyde	2700–2900
SH	Mercaptans	2500–2700
—N_3	Azide	2120–2160
> CO	Aldehyde	1720–1740
	Carboxylic acid	1700–1725
	Ester	2000–2300
	Acyl halide	1795–1850
NOH	Oxime	1640–1690
—N = N—N	Azo	1575–1630
N—N	Amine	1575–1650
—$(CH_2)n$	Any compound	722
CN	Alkyl nitrile	2240–2260
CNS	Isocyanate	2240–2275

spectra originates on account of vibrational frequency of functional group in a molecule. As such every functional group has its own characteristic frequency. A typical group frequency can identify a molecule in aquatic environment or in air. Table 3.7 lists such characteristic frequency of various functional groups. A peak at 1720 to 1740 cm^{-1} indicates the presence of CO group. This had formed the basis for analysis of carbon monoxide from air by nondispersive infrared spectroscopic technique (NDIR). This technique is called as **non-dispersive**, because we carry out measurements at fixed frequency or wave number, *e.g.* 1800 cm^{-1}. The presence of azo group would show maximum transmittance at 2120 cm^{-1}, the effluent sample from dyestuff industry shows a maxima transmittance at 3500 cm^{-1} for amines. It is 1575 cm^{-1} for azo group present in sample of water (Figs. 3.2 and 3.3). The Raman spectroscopy has come to the forefront only recently. It is more useful for the analysis of aqueous solutions. Further, it is useful for remote sensing and detection of air pollutants. Raman spectroscopy involves measurement of scattered radiation.

(c) Light Scattering Techniques

Amongst these techniques we have turbidimetry and nephelometry and Raman spectroscopy. The turbidimetry technique involves measurement of absorbance of turbid solutions *e.g.* like one containing $PbCrO_4$ or $HgCrO_4$, while nephelometry involves measurement of the intensity of scattered radiation by suspended particles *e.g.* ($BaSO_4$). The classical method involving measurement of turbidity of water was carried out by Jackson's candle meter however it is not reliable. The unit involved is JU. This method may involve personal error during such measurements. Instead a nephelometry with NTU units is a more reliable method. The best method for the analysis of SO_4^{2-} from water is by measurement of $BaSO_4$ by nephelometry. The choice of the method depends upon the nature and the particle size. For very fine particle size nephelometry is best method.

The Raman scattering is useful for measurement of aqueous solution. In this technique one can ascertain functional groups of pollutant. The infrared spectroscopy is useless for analysis of aqueous solution but Raman spectroscopy permits analysis of aqueous solution due to Rayleigh scattering. With change of frequency of stroke and antistroke line we get typical spectra. The frequency of incident and reflected light is not same.

3.14 ATOMIC ABSORPTION SPECTROSCOPY METHOD

The atomic absorption spectroscopy is most predominant method specially suitable for determination of metal pollutants in environment. This method is dependent upon the absorption of radiation by a cloud of atoms of analytical metal. The atomisation can be carried out either by flame or by the graphite furnace. This is most popular technique in the environmental analysis because one can analyse many metals simultaneously at microgram concentration in the presence of each another. The significant advantage is unlike in other instrumental methods of analysis it is not necessary to eliminate the interference of other ions before analysis.

This technique has made a great revolution in quantitative chemical analysis. The another reason for popularity of this method is the possibility of analysing large number of samples simultaneously. It is useful for multi-element analysis. It is applicable at micro and nanogram concentration of the metal pollutants. The notion that there is no need of a chemist if AAS is available in laboratory is false as it is totally ill conceived. Certain critical analysis of metals like As, Sb, Sn, Se, Te, Bi need hydride generator and one must know what kind of thermal stability the hydrides have. Table 3.9 lists prospective metal pollutants which can be determined by AAS. In spite of the discovery of cold vapour AAS technique for mercury, most of the state pollution control laboratories prefer Bindscheiderr's green method by spectrophotometry. A look at sensitivity (Table 3.8) indicates certain metals like mercury and uranium have poor sensitivity for AAS method.

Amongst the instruments, flame atomic absorption spectrophotometry is most popular. The method can be broadly divided into six subgroups depending upon the kind of metal and its concentration present in the sample.

1. Determination of Sb, Bi, Cd, Ca, Cs, Cr, Co, Cu, Au, Ir, Fe, Li, Mg, Mn, Ni, Pt, K, Rh, Ru, Ag, Na, Sr, Ti, Sn, Zn. (direct aspiration into air acetylene flame).
2. Determination of low concentration of Cd, Cr, Co, Cu, Fe, Pb, Mn, Ni, Ag, chelation by with ammonium pyrrolidine dithiocarbamate (APDC) extraction in MIBK is hexanone followed by aspiration into air acetylene flame.
3. Determination with nitrous oxide acetylene flame for Al, Be, Mo, Os, Si, Th, Ti, V (due to high temp. of atomisation).
4. Determination at low level of metal after extraction with oxine in MIBK for Al, Be.
5. Determination with argon-hydrogen or nitrogen-hydrogen flame As, Se (Hydride method).
6. Determination by cold vapour atomic absorption technique Hg (because it's volatile and sublimes in flame).

This AAS method resembles emission spectroscopy or flame photometry. However, in AAS amount of light absorbed by atomised elements is measured. A hollow cathode lamp of particular elements is used as each metal has its own characteristic absorption wavelength. The intensity of energy of the characteristic absorption wavelength varies. Absorption is directly proportional to the concentration of element in the sample. The chemical interference may be due to incomplete dissociation of metal during atomisation or inadequate temperature provided for dissociation.

Phosphate interferences is eliminated by addition of lanthanumol salts while the interference of silica is eliminated by addition of calcium. MIBK and APDC extraction is necessary for real samples. One must know sensitivity, detection limit and optimum range of concentration (LDR) for analysis. Sensitivity is defined as metal concentration that produces absorption of 1% (*i.e.*, 0.0044 absorbance) while detection limit (LDR) is defined as the concentration which possess absorption equivalent to twice the magnitude of the background fluctuations. Hollow cathode or electrodeless discharge tube is used. The multielement hollow cathodes gives lower sensitivity. In hydride generator method for As or Se electrodless discharge lamp (EDL) is preferred but it takes little more time for warming.

Table 3.8 Atomic absorption spectrometric analysis

Element	*Flame*	*λ (nm)*	*Sensitivity (μg/cm)²*	*LDR (Linear dyamic range)*
Ag	AA	328	0.01	0.1–4
Al	NA	309	0.10	5–100
As	NH	194	0.002	0.002–0.02
Au	AA	243	0.01	0.5–2.0
Ba	NA	554	0.03	1–20
B	NA	235	0.005	0.05–2
Bi	AA	223	0.06	1–50
Ca	AA	423	0.003	0.2–20
Cd	AA	229	0.002	0.05–2
Co	AA	241	0.03	0.5–10
Cr	AA	358	0.02	0.2–10
Cs	AA	852	0.02	0.5–15
Cu	AA	325	0.01	0.2–10
Fe	AA	248	0.02	0.3–10
Hg	AH	254	0.20	10–300
Mg	AA	285	0.005	0.02–3
Mn	AA	280	0.01	0.1–10
Mo	AA	313	0.1	1–20
Ni	AA	232	0.02	0.3–10
Os	NA	291	0.08	–
Pb	AA	283	0.05	1–20
Pt	AA	266	0.1	5–75
Rh	AA	344	0.3	–
Ru	AA	350	0.5	–
Sb	AH	218	0.07	1–40
Se	AH	196	0.002	0.002–0.02
Si	NA	252	0.3	5–150
Sn	AA	225	0.8	10–200
Sr	AA	461	0.03	0.3–5
Ti	NA	365	0.3	5–100
V	AA	318	0.2	2–100
Zn	AA	214	0.005	0.05–2

AA - air acetylene, AH - air hydrogen, NA - nitrous oxide-acetylene, NH-Hydride generation.

Apart from flame AAS, electrothermal AAS is equally popular and is efficient method. It uses heated graphite atomiser which facilitates determination with better sensitivity as well as better linear dynamic range (LDR) of analyt. No sample preconcentration is necessary. One can use small samples (1-100 μ*l*). It avoids interference from suspended solids and permits use of wide variety of the solvents and also facilitates atomisation at high temperature. Although time needed is more it has greater matrix effect. The current is successively raised to permit, evaporation, charging and atomisation in that sequence. The chemical interference is seen. The absolute sensitivity for all the elements is 10^{-10} to 10^{-12} g. A shortest possible atomisation time is preferred to remove error. The major advantage of graphite furnace model is that it gives detection limit upto 1000 times lower than those offered by flamed model. Finally a special cold vapour technique is used for analysis of mercury. The method involves at room temperature reduction of mercury to the elemental state in vacuum by stanous chloride solution, followed by sweeping of mercury into an absorption cell with air (10^{-9}) *i.e.,* nanograms of mercury could be analysed at 254 nm (Table 3.8).

Table 3.9 Atomic absorption spectroscopic analysis of important polluting elements

S. No.	*Name*	*Symbol*	*First wavelength (nm)*	*Second wavelength (nm)*	*Detection Limit ng/m³*	*Optimum concentration ng/m³*	*Range of analysis ng/m³*
1.	Lithium	Li	323	670	2.0	0.7	3–30
2.	Beryllium	Be	235	–	2.0	0.3	4–40
3.	Chromium	Cr	358	425/521	12–60	6–20	120–300
4.	Iron	Fe	249	372/392	10–200	20–30	40–600
5.	Cobalt	Co	241	391	20–1000	–	30–100
6.	Nickel	Ni	232	341/362	10–50	1–10	20–200
7.	Osmium	Os	291	426	70–1000	18	100–300
8.	Silver	Ag	328	338	20–100	5–20	30–500
9.	Zinc	Zn	214	376	0.5–300	0.1	1–15
10.	Mercury	Hg	253	–	100	20	200–400
11.	Tin	Sn	286	–	11.0	3.6	20–200
12.	Lead	Pb	217	283.0	20–30	5	40–200
13.	Arsenic	As	194	–	0.24	3	40–400
14.	Bismuth	Bi	223	228	20-300	3–100	5–800
15.	Selenium	Se	196	204	25–300	5	40–200

Although Table 3.8 indicates the list of elements which can be analysed by AAS, it shows the toxic metal pollutant which can be analysed by AAS. The principle reason for the popularity of AAS methods in the environmental monitoring stems from two observations namely these methods can be carried out without removal of interference before measurement. Another reason is multielement analysis facilitate analysis of 3–4 metals in one step and finally the level of analysis. Though the Table 3.9 shows first and second wavelength one which is used for quantitive analysis is termed as 'resonance wavelength.' This table not only shows detection limit but also optimum concentration as well as range of analysis with special reference to metal pollutants in the environmental samples.

3.15 ATOMIC EMISSION SPECTROSCOPY

The conventional flame photometry or flame atomic emission as well as plasma spectroscopy technique belong, to this category. The spectral lines emitted are measured for their intensity at very high temperature. Lower detection limits are possible as emission increases directly with temperature. Many metalloids like As, B, Se can be analysed by plasma spectroscopy. We can simultaneously analyse as many as thirty two metals in one single operation in atomic emission spectroscopy. It is a quite useful technique specially it is powerful for multi-element analysis.

Of these methods, flame photometry is relatively cheap and dependable. Table 3.10 lists metal pollutants which can be analysed by flame photometry. The greatest advantage of this technique, is that, it is relatively a cheap with appropriate filters available in the market. All determinations can be carried out in visible region of the spectra. A greater accuracy can be sought by standard addition and the internal standard method. Only metals like Rb or Cs can be determined at near IR region, for which appropriate light filters are not easily available at present.

Table 3.10 Flame emission spectroscopic analysis of toxic metal pollutants

Element	*Wavelength* (λ) *nm*	*Sensitivity* $\mu g/ml$	*Source of pollution*
Li	670	0.017	Glass, photocells
Na	589	0.003	Water, soap, alkali
K	766	0.009	Soap, photocells, pharmacy
Ca	422	0.013	Milk, plants, water, vegetation
Sr	460	0.041	fission reaction, soil, leaf
Ba	554	0.20	Vegetables, glass, X-ray

(a) Inductively Coupled Plasma Spectroscopy (ICP-AES)

The ICP-AES technique is of recent origin. Although it is quite expensive, it is very rapid and reliable. It is useful for the multi-element determination of large number of samples containing metal pollutants. The accuracy obtained is quite satisfactory. An argon torch is used for the purpose of excitation with radio-frequency generation. It is also used as the hyphenated technique by coupling with HPLC or mass spectrometer.

It has several advantages over conventional atomic emission or flame emission spectral methods *viz.*:

(*a*) It permits analysis of as many as twenty five elements in one single operation within short period of time.

(*b*) The temperature for atomisation ranges from 8000 to 10000°K. It ensures complete atomisation of sample.

(*c*) In conventional flame photometry only 15% of sample reaches into flame while 85% sample is discharged in drain. But in ICP-AES due to comflaging effect of flame 100% sample goes into ICP torch.

(*d*) The level of analysis is very low as little as 0.1 ηg/ml of metal can be analysed by ICP–AES.
(*e*) Plasma is generated by radiofrequency generator at 4 to 50 MHz and 2 to 5 kW attaining maximum temperature of 10,000°K. The lower detection limit is related to high emission intensity.
(*f*) Metalloids like As, B, Se can be analysed by the plasma spectroscopy as chemical reactions are totally minimised inside plasma of argon.
(*g*) Plasma atomisation combined with mass spectrometry forms hyphenated techniques which is most powerful means for the multi-element analysis. It has low detection limit.

Table 3.11 Plasma spectroscopic analysis

Element	*λ max (nm)*	*Lower Limit (μg/L)*	*Upper Limit (mg/L)*
Al	308	40	100
Sb	207	30	100
As	193	30	100
Ba	455	2	50
Be	313	0.3	10
B	250	5	50
Cd	226	4	50
Ca	318	10	100
Cr	268	7	50
Co	229	7	50
Cu	325	6	100
Fe	260	7	100
Pb	220	40	100
Mg	274	30	100
Mn	250	2	50
Mo	202	5	100
Ni	232	15	50
Se	196	75	100
SiO_2	212	20	100
Ag	328	7	50
Sr	407	0.5	50
Ti	191	40	100
V	292	8	50
Zn	212	2	100

We encounter during analysis spectral and nonspecific interference in ICP-AES analysis. In such case alternate wavelength is selected to avoid overlaps (see Table 3.9). A background correction is also applied. The sample neutralization and transport process cause physical interference. A change in viscosity or surface tension of sample causes physical interference. High dissolved solids cause drift in the instrument if present at tip of nebuliser. Chemical interference is caused by formation of molecular compound, ionisation and thermochemical effects associated with sample vaporisation and atomisation in the plasma but all these can be easily eliminated.

Thus, the examination of Table 3.11 shows that the most sensitive detection is possible for boron, cadmium, copper, manganese, strontium and zinc below 5 μg/ml of metal by ICP-AES. While the method is insensitive for elements like aluminum, antimony, arsenic, lead, magnesium, selenium and thallium with detection limit of more than 40 μg/L which is high.

3.16 MOLECULAR LUMINESCENCE METHOD

These methods are termed as chemiluminescence techniques. They have made a spectacular progress in the analysis of gaseous pollutants like SO_2, H_2S or NO-NOx from atmosphere. These are most reliable methods. The analysis of Be (morin, *i.e.*, pentahydroxy-flavanol), Th (Alizarin), Al (quinalzarine) by fluorescence technique is very well-known. The analysis of organic compounds, *e.g.* riboflavin, thiamine hydrochloride, quinine from waste water emanating from pharmaceutical industry, is best carried out by fluorescence spectroscopy. In comparison, the phosphorescence spectroscopy is not popular in environmental analytical chemistry. With the rise in pollution in sugar industry, this technique may pickup. A relatively cheap set of fluorimeters or phosphorimeters shall make this technique more popular in future years.

The fluoroscence is an example of delayed emission. The electrons through excitation by Raman or xenon lamp gets excited. They are promoted to higher energy level. However, these excited electrons cannot remain all the time in the higher orbital. Therefore, they release energy in form of emission and return back to ground state. If time required between excitation and emission is 10^{-9} to 10^{-12} the phenomena is called 'fluoroscence' however if time needed is 10^{-3} to 10^{2} with longer delay the effect it is called as the 'phosphorescence.' The former is used for characterisation of air pollutant *e.g.*

$$SO_2 + h\gamma \rightarrow S^*O_2;\ S^*O_2 \rightarrow SO_2 + \text{(Fluoroscence energy)}$$

$$NO_2 + h\gamma \rightarrow N^*O_2;\ N^*O_2 \rightarrow NO_2 + \text{(Fluoroscence energy)}$$

(Star indicates excited state of the molecules)

Thus, SO_2 or NO_2 are excited to give S^*O_2, N^*O_2 which in turn release energy to get back to ground state as SO_2 or NO_2 which have lower energy. Large number of pollutants which are present in waste water can be analysed quantitatively by fluorimetry. A group of organic complexing ligands are available which on complexation with metal show characteristic fluoroscence *e.g.* Al, Zr, Th, Be, Sb, Pb, Mn. The corresponding fluorinating ligands are alizarine, quinalizarine 8-hydroxyquinoline; morin, rhodamine, eosin and erythrosine, respectively. However, substances promoting decrease in fluoroscence intensity (*i.e.* Quenching) must be absent. Several organic compounds like aniline, analide promote quenching. Secondly, wavelength for absorption and emission should not be same (If it is same called as **resonance fluoroscence**). Finally, as for instrumentation light source

Table 3.12 Electroanalytical techniques

S.No.	*Name of method*	*Technique used*	*What is measured*	*What is controlled*	*Remarks*
1.	Potentiometry	Potentiometry	Potential	Current	Popular method good quantity analysis
2.	Potential controlled	Voltammetry-polarography Cyclic voltammetry Rotating disc polarography method Chronoamperiometry Electrolysis	Diffusion current Diffusion current Diffusion current potential Control potential	Fixed resistance	Maximum used in coordination chemistry
3.	Controlled current	Chronopotentiometry Coulometric Titration	Diffusion current	Current	Good at microlevel
4.	Conductometry	High frequency method Normal conductometry	Conductance Conductance	Potential fixed	Fast and reliable method
5.	Polarography	Square wave DC, AC method	Diffusion current	Fixed resistance	Most popular method
6.	Coulometry	measured quantum of electricity used	Substance generated	Fixed current or fixed voltage	Used on the preparator scale

should be always kept at right angles to detector like photocell or photomultiplier tubes in fluoroscence measurements.

3.17 ELECTROANALYTICAL TECHNIQUES

These techniques comprises of four major methods *viz.* potentiometry, conductometry, coulometry and polarography. Various electroanalytical methods are summarised in Table 3.12.

Inspite of simplicity and low cost, electroanalytical methods have not become popular like Spectroscopic techniques in Environmental monitoring. In fact a method like Polarography not only facilitates quantitive analysis but also provides a method for identification or characterisation of metal pollutant (in the aquatic environment from the knowledge of the half wave potential ($E_{1/2}$) one can identify the unknown element. The technique depends on the supporting electrolyte used in the analysis. All these methods largely use Ohm's law and Faradays laws of electrolysis. All measurements either pertain to measurement of current, or potentional or resistance. In potentiometry we measure voltage in polarography we measure 'diffusion current' while in the technique of conductometry we measure reciprocal of resistance called as the conductances. Table 3.12 gives vivid account of electroanalytical methods. It also points out what is measured and what is controlled. Final column brings out special feature of the said method. It is hoped that in the course of time in future these methods may become very popular.

3.17 (a) Potentiometric Methods

Potentiometric methods involve measurement of the potential. The indirect application of this technique in pollution analysis is the measurement of pH of solution. The technique of chronopotentiometry is used for the analysis of the metal pollutants. The potentiometric method is used for indirect determination of amount the metal pollutant. The technique of conductometry is used to ascertain quality of water. Apart from measuring purity of water, conductometric technique is used for the continuous measurement of SO_2 from air. The coulometry technique is based upon the Faraday's law of electrolysis. The electrical generation of bromine is compared with generation of bromine from KBr with SO_2 by reduction. This led to monitoring of SO_2 by coulometry. The anodic stripping voltametry (ASV) is an instance of the specialised category of the coulometric method. In recent years, ASV has become very popular. This method involves two cells for reduction,

Table 3.13 Limits of analysis of polarographic methods

	Limit	*Sensitivity*
AC polarography	10^{-4}–10^{-5}	5×10^{-7}
Classical polarography	10^{-5}–10^{-6}	1×10^{-5}
Sq. wave polarography	10^{-6}–10^{-7}	5×10^{-8}
Pulse polarography	10^{-7}–10^{-8}	1×10^{-8}
Anodic stripping voltametry	10^{-7}–10^{-9}	1×10^{-9}

while ion selective electrode (ISE) is an instance of potentiometric technique. With the easy availability of specific ion electrodes, the analysis of anions from water is a matter of minutes. Even with advancement of solid state – enzyme electrode as well as electrodes fitted with liquid ion-exchangers, crown, ethers, the analysis of cationic species is reducted to single measurement.

Amongst electroanalytical techniques, polarography or voltammetry has the greatest advantage over other methods. Table 3.14 summarises important metal pollutants with their half-wave potentials ($E_{1/2}$), which can be analysed by polarography. The distinct advantage of such a technique is the possibility of identification of metal pollutant from the effluent sample. $E_{1/2}$ is the characteristic potential of a metal under a set of specific supporting electrolyte, which helps one to identify a metal. The polarography has distinct advantage for analysing even for the organic pollutants, *e.g.* the pesticide residues can be best analysed by this technique with a suitable electrolyte like lithium hydroxide.

Table 3.14 Polarographic characterisation of toxic metals

Metal pollutant	*Half-wave potential ($E_{1/2}$) in KCl*
Cd	– 0.76 V
Co	– 1.46 V
Cu	– 0.47 V
Fe	– 1.12 V
Pb	– 0.76 V
Zn	– 1.50 V

Thus, several techniques for water analysis use electrochemical sensor *e.g.* potentiometry, voltammetry or amperiometry. The potentiometry uses Nerst equation as

$$E = E^{\circ} + \frac{2.3\,RT}{nF} \log\left[\frac{\text{oxid}}{\text{red}}\right],$$

If E^0 = standard electrode potential

R = universal gas constant

T = temperature in absolute scale °K

Since $\left[\frac{2.303\,RT}{F}\right] = 0.0591$ at room temperature

F = Faraday's constant

n = no electrons transferred.

We use reference electrode filled with saturated calomel (SCE) with its standard potential $E^{\circ}_{SCE} = 0.246$ V for saturated solution of KCl. For bivaloni metal we write Nerst Equation ($n = 2$, $T = 273 + 25$°K).

$$E = E_m^0 + \frac{0.592}{2} \log [M^{2+}]$$

The technique of measurement of anion concentration by the ion selective electrode is of recent origin. Glass electrode is also useful as ion selective electrode for hydrogen. Similarly, the fluoride electrode is most common in environmental analysis. The electric output is in the form of a potential signal which is directly proportional to log of concentration of ion.

Polarography or voltammetry is used for characterisation as well as determination of metal pollutant we use Ilkovic equation as

$$i_d = 607\, nD^{1/2}\, m^{2/3}\, t_d^{1/6}\, C$$

where i_d = diffusion current
c = concentrate ion
m = rate of flow of liquid
n = number of electrons transferred
t_d = time between two successive drops
D = Fick's diffusion coefficients

The technique of differential pulse polarography is also very useful for water analysis where potential is applied in small pulses and current is read at end of voltage pulse and is compared to current before generation of pulse. While the anodic stripping voltammetry involves deposition of metals on electrode surface over a period for time followed by stripping it rapid with sweep. A differential pulse anodic stripping voltammetry is used to analyse Cu, Pb, Cd, Zn from the tap water.

The half-wave potential ($E_{1/2}$) is very useful for identification of metals in polarography. The value of $E_{1/2}$ depends upon the supporting electrolyte. Different metals will have different values of $E_{1/2}$ with a particular supporting electrolyte. However, the same metal may have different $E_{1/2}$ values in different supporting electrolytes. In voltammetry since diffusion currents is directly proportional to the concentration *i.e.*, $id \propto C$ with other factor constant one can easily find out current if $id/id_x = C/C_x$ if C_x is an of unknown with id_x as diffusion current C = known current and id_x known diffusion current.

3.18 RADIOANALYTICAL METHODS

Amongst nuclear methods of the analysis, neutron activation analysis and isotope dilution methods are most useful. However, the greatest limitations of these methods is the nonavailability of radioactive isotopes. The neutron source with high flux is available only with atomic research centres, with restricted access. In more advanced countries like Canada and France, such facility is readily available through private enterprises to any common research worker.

In neutron activation analysis, a sample to be analysed is irradiated with slow neutron source to form unstable isotope, with mass number greater by one unit. Such unstable isotope undergoes transmutation (n, γ) reaction to revert to its original isotope, with emission of γ-radiation. These emitted gamma (γ)-radiation are proportional to the amount of metal irradiated. By comparing known weight and the activity, it is possible for us to ascertain weight of the unknown by measuring its activity on irradiation. Many metal pollutants like Fe, Mn, Cu, Sb, Bi, Cd, Zn, V can be easily determined at nanogram concentrations by neutron activation analysis technique (NAA).

e.g. $$U_{92}^{238} + n_0^1 \rightarrow U_{92}^{239} + \gamma$$

In this equation we note that unstable isotope of U_{92}^{238} is U_{92}^{239}

$$U_{92}^{239} \rightarrow U_{92}^{238} + \gamma$$

(The amount of γ-radiation generated is proportional to concentration)

In the activation analysis the reduced equation is used

$\frac{A_1}{A_2} = \frac{C_x}{C_2}$ if A_1, A_2, C_2 is known, unknown can C_x.

One must have reasonably stable isotope for irradiation and one must possess facility for γ-counting in the laboratory.

The second largely used technique is the method of isotope dilution (IDM). This method involves the dilution of active isotope with active material. Consequently, the reduction in activity is measured and from this indirectly the concentration of material is evaluated. $W_1(A/A_1 - 1) = W$ (unknown species)

It would take quite some time to popularise these methods, unless a cheap source of neutron for irradiation and easy availability of γ-ray counters are available.

So also adequate protection measures are secondary. Therefore safety of worker is of primary importantce. The use of personal dosimeter is mandatory in the laboratory. Pocket ionisation dosimeter, thermoluminescence dosimeter or thumble chamber is available. Thin window Griegor Müller counter is best for measuring the activity. Second important problem is disposal of radioactive waste. This involve the dilution and dispersion or secondly the concentration and confinement. I, ky, Xe are radioactive gases to be controlled in hood. However, other waste like PCB, dioxide and asbestos are more dangerous. The γ and β counting is less expensive and less hazardous. Cs, I, Sr, H_1^3, U are measured radiometrically.

3.19 RING OVEN TECHNIQUE

Ring oven technique is most suitable method for carrying out analysis of metal pollutants in water or air. What is done is circular filter paper is taken, at the centre of which sample containing metal pollutants is applied. By capillary action different ions migrate at different rates toward edge of circular paper. This rate is related to capillary migration or may be due to difference of partition coefficient if solvent system is used. The paper is taken dried on ringoven (special kind of dryer) and various chromogenic reagent(s) are sprayed. We note different concentric rings of different metals of varying color intensity. These rings are then punched out and compared with standard rings of same metal with same chromogenic ligand. By visual comparison it is possible to compare intensity of analyte sample with ring with a known concentration. In order to get approximate concentration of metal in unknown sample. By some regular practise it is quite easy to tally analyte sample with standard sample, *e.g.* if we have mixture of Ag, Pb, Hg and if the mixture is applied to centre of circular filter paper in presence of HCl and ethylacetate mixture the migration of ions occurs at different speed, faster being lead slowest being silver. Now if we spray circular paper with K_2CrO_4 we get inside ring of silver then we have pale green ring for mercury and outer ring of lead being turmeric yellow. These rings can be punched and compared with standard rings made similarly with know concentration.

This technique is largely recommended by SCOPE for the analysis of metal pollutants. This is a relatively cheap method, easy to operate and dependable and useful for semiquantitative analysis. It is best suited for outdoor work, field analysis and *in situ* analysis. By comparison of rings with standard rings obtained by interaction of chromophroic group with the metal pollutant, it is quite possible to qualitatively analyse and get semiquantitative information of the metal being analysed. Table 3.15 shows results of analysis of metal pollutants from air by ring oven method.

Table 3.15 Ring oven technique

Metal ion present ($\mu g/m^3$)	*Ring oven ($\mu g/m^3$)*	*Spectral method ($\mu g/m^3$)*
Pb	340	360
–	220	230
V	78	73
–	62	68
Se	26	27
–	24	28
Cd	13.5	14
–	16	19

3.20 CONCLUSION

From the foregoing discussion, we come to the conclusion that methods for environmental analysis are not similar to methods of chemical analysis due to interferences and their small concentration. The separation methods are most important to eliminate the interferences before undertaking instrumental analysis. Such separation methods are largely composed of adsorption, exclusion, electro- or partition chromatography, or more sophisticated techniques such as gas, GC, or GC-MS, HPLC, ion-exchange or ion chromatography. The last method has several applications for analysis of anion or in the study of environmental speciation. Solvent extraction is no doubt the simplest and rapid method of separation. If metal pollutant is present in milligram level one can use gravimetry but for analysis of dissolved oxygen, acidity/alkalinity of water or hardness volumetric method like complexometry are still most popular. However, molecular absorption spectroscopy involving UV, visible, IR or light scattering methods are most common for analysis of organic as well as inorganic pollutants. Atomic absorption spectroscopy is much sought after as many metals can be easily analysed in the presence of one other. The plasma spectroscope is slowly replacing AAS when large samples are present at nanogram concentration. The fluoroscence and phosphorescence methods are less frequently resorted but electroanalytical techniques involving either potentiometry (for ISE) or voltammetry (Polarography) are most useful as the latter can identify the metal pollutant from effluent. In comparison radio chemical methods involving activation analysis or isotopic dilution method are less popular however ring oven technique as recommended by SCOPE, is best for field analysis. In conclusion we can state that choice of method of analysis depends largely on the level, the interferences, speed, number of sample handled what kind of accuracy or precision is required.

ADDITIONAL READING

1. L. Erdey, *'Gravimetric Analysis'*, Pergamon Press (1963).
2. A.I. Vogel, *'Textbook of Quantitative Inorganic Analysis'*, 4th Edn. Longman & Green (1980).
3. F.J. Welcher, *'Analytical Uses of Ethylenediamine Tetracetic Acid'*, Van Nostrand (1958).
4. C. Schwarzenbach and H. Flaschka, *'Complexometric Titrations'*, Metheuen and Co. Ltd. London (1969).
5. A.K. De, S.M. Khopkar and R.A. Chalmers, *'Solvent Extraction of Metals'*, Van Nostrand Reinhold (1970).
6. O. Samulson, *'Ion Exchange Separations in Analytical Chemistry'*, John Wiley, 2nd Edn. (1963).
7. E. Lederer and M. Lederer, *'Chromatrography—Theory and Practice'*, 2nd Edn. Van Nostrand (1957).
8. J.M. Bobbitt, *'Thin Layer Chromatography'*, Reinhold, New York (1963).
9. J.A. Dean, *'Chemical Separation Methods'*, Van Nostrand Reinhold, London (1970).
10. D.W. Grant, *'Gas-Liquid Chromatography'*, Van Nostrand Reinhold (1971).
11. M.G. Mellon, *'Analytical Absorption Spectroscopy'*, Wiley, New York (1950).
12. D.M. Hercules, *'Fluorescence and Phosphorescence Analysis'*, Wiley Interscience, New York (1966).
13. R.M. Silverstein, G.C. Bassler and T.C. Morrill, *'Spectroscopic Identification of Organic Compounds'*, 6th Edn. Wiley, New York (1990).
14. I. Fleming and D.H. Williams, *'Spectroscopic Methods in Organic Chemistry'*, McGraw Hill, New York, 3rd Edn. (1980).
15. J.A. Dean, *'Flame Photometry'*, McGraw Hill, New York (1960).
16. G.F. Krikbright, *'Atomic Absorption Spectroscopy and Related Methods'*, Marcell Dekker (1977).
17. H.J. Arnikar, *'Essentials of Nuclear Chemistry'*, Wiley Eastern, 2nd Edn. (1990).
18. L. Meites, *'Polarography Technique'*, Interscience, New York (1952).
19. S.M. Khopkar, *'Basic Concepts of Analytical Chemistry'*, Third Edn. New Age International (2008).
20. R.C. Kapoor & G.A. Agarwal, *'Polarography'*, Wiley Eastern (1991).
21. S. Manahan, *'Environmental Chemistry'*, 7th Edn. Lewis Publishers, New York (2000).
22. APHA, *'Standard Method for Examination of Water and Waste Water'*, American Public Health Association 20th Edn. (2000).
23. C. Baird, *'Environmental Chemistry'*, W.H. Freeman and Co. (1995).
24. S.M. Khopkar, *'Enviromental Pollution Analysis'*, New Age International (P) Publisher, Second Edn. (2010).

4 Statistical Methods in Environment

4.1 INTRODUCTION

Analytical chemistry is science of measurements. This is because all quantitative analytical methods invariably involve the use of instrumental methods of analysis. While environmental monitoring is a part of analytical methods involving collection of data in the environment from air, water, wastewater, land, agricultural pesticides, noise, odour. There is growing tendency amongst young research workers to painstakingly collect enormous numbers of environmental data; such as pH, DO, BOD, COD, TDS. The worst part is such valuable data remains embedded in the literature as it is not used for further processing. The data should be no doubt reliable. One can easily proceed further to use this data for the construction of environmental models which in turn can be used for future forecasting. Apart from this environmental impact (EIA) assessment constitutes an important aspect of environmental monitoring provided if the data is reliable, reproducible and representative one. In order to ascertain these criteria one has to entirely depend upon statistical methods of analysis. It is perfectly logical that the information on the some aspect to know how good are your reading, how good is its reliability and to what extent it can be reproduced. In view of this demand an endeavour is made in this chapter to consider the various parameters involving statistical information. The various points to be considered include evaluation of terms such as means, median, deviation, standard deviation, range and the important confidence limits of the environmental monitoring. We can also further test the validity of such measurements involving the tests such as Q-test for rejection of results. Student '*t*' test and F-test. The important criteria for the rejection of the results from the enormous environmental data collected during systematic, investigation is important.

4.2 VARIOUS TYPES OF DEVIATIONS

When we handle a numerical data, we should know whether it involves any error(s). Such kind of error is expressed in terms of % (percentage) or ppt (*i.e.* percent per thousand). Therefore, we calculate absolute and relative difference. We get an absolute error from expression: % Error = $\left(\frac{E}{T}\times 100\right)$ if T – true value. Also we calculate it in terms of thousand as $\left(\frac{E}{T}\times 1000\right)$= parts per thousand (*i.e.* ppt). It roughly gives preliminary idea about quality of data.

It is usual practise to calculate the mean value as well as the average deviation of the mean *e.g.* In set of five readings such as : 0.1010, 0.1020, 0.1005, 0.1030, 0.1015. For these five readings the "mean value" is 0.1016. We can proceed ahead with the calculation of average deviation of the mean from the different means of 0.1016 = δ as follows:

$\Sigma\delta = (0.0006 + 0.0004 + 0.0009 + 0.0014 + 0.0001)$. Total divided by (5) = n is the number of reading. It works out tube: 0.0034/5 = 0.00068 = d = δ

The average deviation of mean is statistically expressed as follows:

$$D = \frac{d}{\sqrt{n}} = \frac{0.00068}{\sqrt{5}} = \frac{0.00068}{2.236} = 3.041\times 10^{-4} \text{ or } 0.0003041$$

In this 'n' is number of reading d = δ is average of difference while δ is actual difference from the mean.

However it is general practise to express such deviation in the form of "standard deviation (S) and "standard deviation of the mean". We use same above five readings and use their differences for calculation as:

$\Sigma\delta^2 = (0.006)^2 + (0.0004)^2 + (0.0009)^2 + (0.0014)^2 + (0.0001)^2 = 33 \times 10^{-7}$

Standard deviation (s) = $\sqrt{\frac{\Sigma\delta^2}{n-1}}$ if δ = is difference from each value n = nos. of reading so

$SD = \sqrt{\frac{33\times 10^{-7}}{4}} = 0.0009$. This is called as the standard deviation(s) while standard deviation of the mean is $S = \frac{S}{\sqrt{n}} = \frac{0.0009}{\sqrt{5}-1} = \frac{0.0009}{\sqrt{4}} = 0.00004025$ so standard deviation is 9×10^{-4} and standard deviation of the mean is (S) = 4.025×10^{-5}. The relative standard deviation i.e. called also as coefficient of variation it is $RSD = \frac{\text{Standard deviation}}{\text{nos. of readings}}\times 100 = \frac{S\times 100}{n} = \frac{0.0009\times 100}{5} = 0.8858\%$ .This is commonly used to know approximate reliability. So far we have considered significance of mean (m), average deviation (d) average deviation of mean (D), standard deviation (S) and standard deviation of the mean (S) in ascertaining reliability of the procured readings.

4.3 CRITERIA FOR REJECTION OF RESULTS AS WELL AS WHAT IS MEDIAN VALUE AND RANGE?

When we consider set of values, we can easily calculate the mean, average deviation of mean or standard deviation of the mean. However, some times we encounter a value which shows very large deviation. Such value appears to be out off the track. Therefore, we are tempted to reject this odd value. In our previous example we had the highest value (0.1030) while (0.1005) is lowest value. The difference between two values is called as range *i.e.* (0.1030 – 1.005) = 0.00250. This value is called as "range". It gives rough estimate of the quality of value we have got from experimental set of work. Assuming the particular value in set of readings is having difference from mean is (0.1016 ~ 0.1316) = 0.300. Since this difference is more than average deviation of 0.00003041 (it is several times bigger) this reading must therefore be rejected. The difference should not be more than (2 ½ or 4) times the average deviation of mean. Now as regards the median value, in above example which have five readings. In this set we have two values *viz.* 0.1005, 0.1010 are below and another two values are 0.1025, 0.1030 above values the middle value is 0.05. It is called as median value. For odd number of readings it is easy to ascertain median value, but for even number of readings we have to take average of two adjacent values *e.g.* In 10, 11, 12, 13 and 15. The median value is 12. It indicates half the results (2) are above the median value and another half value of the results are below median value of (12).

If we have four readings *viz.* 10, 11, 12, 14 four values then the median value is calculated from average of middle two values as (11 + 12)/2 = 23/2 = 11.5 is actual median value of results. Now let us undertake another example of rejection of value from Q-value. If the difference (δ) $\geq 4d$ above average deviation, we reject then such value while some worker allow difference of only (δ) $\geq 2.5d$ we accept such values also *e.g.* If the value is 22.62 with deviation (d) as 0.022 and if average deviation is (δ) = 0.193 we compare it with 'd' actual difference encountered as actual difference = (4 × 0.022) = 0.088 is less than (δ) average deviation of difference *i.e.* 0.088 < 0.193. We therefore accept the value as difference is very small and can be considered as the negligible number during statistical analysis.

4.4 SIGNIFICANCE OF TEST, STUDENT 'T' TEST AND 'F' TEST

(*a*) The Q test is another way of ascertaining the reliability of the result and the criteria for acceptance or rejection of the particular value is given as follows:

Range $Q_n = \dfrac{(M_n - M_{n-1})}{(M_n - M_1)}$, where in M, is first reading. M_n = last reading (M_n – 1) last but one reading.

M_2 = Second reading, n = total number of readings. In an example with values as 6.593, 6.942, 7.146, 7.098 and 7.256. We have in all (5 = n) values

M_1 = 6.593, M_2 = 6.942, ($M_5 - M_1$) = (7.256 – 6.593) range is 0.668. We have Q_1 value

$$Q_1 = \frac{(M_2 - M_1)}{(M_5 - M_1)} = \frac{(6.942 - 6.593)}{(7.256 - 6.593)} = 0.527$$ and 0.64 (it is average deviation *i.e.* δ). So we conclude that the value obtained may be accepted during statistical analysis. It is accepted if M_2 = 6.942, M_1 = 6.593, ($M_5 - M_1$) = 0.668 is accepted

value $Q_2 = \dfrac{(M_5 - M_4)}{(M_5 - M_1)} = \dfrac{(7.256 - 7.098)}{(7.256 - 6.593)}$ = 0.17 < 0.64 (If δ = 0.64) is accepted as (M_5 = 7.256, M_4 = 7.098 then ($M_5 - M_1$) = 0.668. So value Q_1, Q_2 are both accepted.

(*b*) Student '*t*' test: We first evaluate a standard deviation to find out the value of '*t*' is obtained from table in annexure (Table A) dealing with various levels of probability. The limit for dependence is given by equation as $\left(\text{mean} + \frac{ts}{\sqrt{n}}\right)$ *e.g.* mean (m) = 9.46, standard deviation (S) = 0.17% and n = 6 the value of '*t*' shall be 2.02 for six values. So we have $9.46 + \frac{2.02 \times 0.17}{\sqrt{6}} =$ is acceptable if m = 9.46, t = 2.02, s = 0.17, n = 6.0.

It is possible to use either Q-test or '*t*'-test to ascertain the reliability. However, we need to use table '*t*' for knowing the different levels of probability. It is all such tables are provided in form of annexures (Table-A).

4.5 REGRESSION ANALYSIS AND ANOVA

Both are very important in environmental analysis. The regression analysis is defined as statistical devise with which we can find out the unknown value with one variable from the other known values of the another variable; presuming '*x*' (ebsisa) is variable and is independent and not subjected to error, while '*Y*' (ordinate) is dependent. The regression lines are different assuming $Y = f(x)$ *i.e.* $Y = (mx + c)$ C is intercept on Y-axis m = numerical constant. It will be clear from following numerical problem.

Example 1: The analysis of Lead from soil and plant showed following results:

Table 4.1 Lead analysis (mg)

S. No.	Conc. of lead (x) in soil	Conc. of lead (y) in plants	$(x)^2$	x^2	xy	$(x \times y)$
1.	20	30	$(20)^2$	400	600	20 × 30
2.	30	45	$(30)^2$	900	1350	30 × 45
3.	40	50	$(40)^2$	160	2000	40 × 50
4.	45	60	$(45)^2$	2025	2700	45 × 60
5.	50	70	$(70)^2$	2500	3500	50 × 70
6.	55	70	$(70)^2$	3025	3850	55 × 70
7.	60	75	$(75)^2$	3600	4500	60 × 75
8.	65	80	$(80)^2$	4225	5200	63 × 80
9.	70	85	$(85)^2$	4900	5950	70 × 85
10.	75	85	$(85)^2$	5025	6375	73 × 85
11.	Mean = $(\bar{x})$ = 51	Mean = $(\bar{y})$ = 65	Σx^2	x^2	xy	$x \times y$
12.	Σx = 370	Σy = 630		Σx^2 = 28,800	Σxy = 3,31,500	

Here we calculate

$\Sigma x = 570$, $\Sigma y = 650$, $\Sigma x^2 = 28{,}800$ $\Sigma y^2 = 45{,}300$, Mean = $\bar{x} = 51$, Mean = $\bar{y} = 65$,

Σxy = 3,31,500. From this problem we evaluate the value of m and c in equation $y = (xm + c)$, c = intercept, $m = \dfrac{(n\Sigma xy - \Sigma x\Sigma y)}{(n\Sigma x^2) - (\Sigma xy^2)}$; $c = (\bar{y} - m\bar{x})$. We substitute value of Σxy, Σx, Σy. If n = 10 number of readings.

$$m = \frac{10(36023 - 33150)}{10(28800) - (510)^2} = \frac{(360250 - 331500)}{(288000 - 260100)} = \frac{28750}{27900}, \; m = 1.03$$

Now, $c = (\bar{y} - \bar{x}m)$ if $\bar{x} = 51$, $\bar{y} = 65$ mean. If bar above x and y represent mean $C = (\bar{y} - \bar{x}m) = 65 - (1.03 \times 51) = 12449$, if $y = (xm + c) = 1.30 + 12{,}449$.

This shows regression in between x and y as it varies between two limits.

ANOVA: Let us consider significance of analysis of variance (ANOVA). It is used to identify sources of variability from one or more source. This method is useful in interpretation of data from industry. Anova is used either for comparison of one set or comparison of several sets of readings. It is either simple analysis or its multiple analysis. It is the method for testing two or more data in treatments to determine the variation. Hence is called as analysis of variable (ANOV).

Example 2: Analysis of variance (ANOVA) we get data as shown in Table 4.2.

Table 4.2 Analysis of variance

Replicate (x)	F_1	F_2	F_3	F_4......F_n	*Total*
R_1					
R_2					
R_3					
R_4					
R_5					
Total					

The correction factor (c) $= \Sigma x^2/n$,

Total sum of square $= \Sigma x^2 = (x_1^2 + x_2^2 + x_3^2 \ldots) - c$

The sum of squares due to factors of F values.

$$\Sigma F^2 = \left[\frac{(\Sigma F_1)^2 + (\Sigma F_1)^2 + (\Sigma F_3)^2 \ldots (\Sigma F_n)^2}{n} - C\right]$$

If n = nos. of replicates. The least significant difference (LSD) is obtained as

$$\text{Standard error of difference} = \sqrt{\frac{2(Mss \text{ of error})}{n}} \quad \text{if } LSD = (t \times SE)$$

If t = table value at 5% level is known.

Example 3: Three students (x, y, z) performed analysis (four times) what is value of ANOVA?

	I	*II*	*III*	*IV*	*(T)*
X	10	8	6	4	28
Y	12	10	6	5	33
Z	8	12	8	10	38

Answer:

	(T)	(T^2)
X	$(10 + 8 + 6 + 4) = 28,$	$(28)^2 = 787$
Y	$(12 + 10 + 6 + 5) = 33$	$(33)^2 = 1089$
Z	$(8 + 12 + 8 + 10) = 38$	$(38)^2 = 1444$

893 = It is the sum of square of all four readings for x, y, z studied

$\sum x, y, z$ = Grand total $(T) = (28 + 33 + 38) = 99$

$$\text{Correction factor} = \frac{C^2}{n} = \frac{(99)^2}{12} = \frac{9801}{12}$$

$$\text{Total } S - S = (RSS - CF) = (893 - 816.7) = 76.3$$

$$\text{Nos. of treatments} = \frac{(T_1)^2}{n} + \frac{(T_2)^2}{n} + \frac{(T_3)^2}{n}$$

$$= \left(\frac{28}{4}\right)^2 + \left(\frac{33}{4}\right)^2 + \left(\frac{38}{4}\right)^2 - 816.7 = 12.50$$

We summarize ANOVA table as shown in Table 4.3

Table 4.3 Summary of ANOVA values

S.No.	*Source of variation*	*SS*	*d.f.*	*MSS*	*Variance ratio*
1.	Nos. of treatment	12.5	$3 - 1 = 2$	$Y_1 = 12.5/2 = 6.25$	$F = v_1/v_2$ 6.25/7.08
2.	Error	63.75	$12 - 3 = 9$	$Y_2 = 63.75/9 = 7.08$	= 0.882
	Total	76.25		The difference are insignificant	

4.6 CONFIDENCE LIMIT

As stated before if 'n' is small than, S or s it will not be reliable and it shall be uncertain. If here S = standard deviation and s = standard deviation of the mean. From S *i.e.* standard deviation (S) the lower and upper limits of confidence limits are obtained by dividing $(n - 1)S^2$ by two numbers taken from Table of Chi square (Annexure B) *i.e.* $n = 7$, $(n - 1) = 6$, then we have.

$$\text{Lower confidence limit} = 0.47s^2 = \frac{(n-1)s^2}{\text{ch. sq.-value at 90\% confidence limit at 90°}}$$

while for upper limit it is confidence limit

$$= 3.67s^2 = \frac{(n-1)s^2}{\text{ch. sq.-value at 95\% confidence limit}}$$

Based upon these confidence limit values we calculate, the values between 5% and 95% limits, we calculate lower and upper confidence limit. Assuming nos. of reading (n) are 10, standard deviation (S) = 0.308, we have

$$\text{Lower limit} = \frac{(n-1)s^2}{18.307} = 0.0518$$

$$\text{Upper limit} = \frac{(n-1)s^2}{3.940} = 0.2407$$

In this problem for '*n*' value the Chi square value for 90% and 95% confidence limit is available from Chi square Table (Appendix B).

Provide if from Table 18.307; 3.940 values are taken for 90% and 95% confidence limit respectively.

Confidence interval: It is more informative to state an interval within which the values of parameter is expected to lie *e.g.* A; (1 – α) confidence interval for the population mean can be considered by equation $\left(\bar{y} - s_y t_{a/2}\right) < \eta < \left(\bar{y} + s_y t_{w/2}\right)$ where in $t_{1/2}$ and s have $v = n - 1$ degree of the (by a lower and upper limit) freedom. The confidence interval is bounded between two limits *viz.* lower and upper. If a series of random sets of '*n*' observation is sampled from normal distribution with 'η' mean fixed (also α) then (1 – α) confidence interval ($\bar{y} \pm s$), $t_{\alpha/2}$ is considered. There is a (1 – α) probability that the true value falls within this confidence interval. The use of confidence interval is equivalent to making two sided test of the null hypothesis, *e.g.* 90% and 95% is confidence interval for 'η' which the mean value is known.

Finally graphic presentation is portrayed as (1) Line graphs, (2) Scattered graph (3) bar graphs (4) histograms, (5) Frequency polygens (6) Frequency curves and (7) π-graphs are important.

In the following pages we shall now consider solved problems.

SOLVED PROBLEMS

Example 4: In analysis of dissolved oxygen from water the following results were obtained as 9.990, 9.982, 9.983, 9.980, 9.973. Calculate the mean, average deviation standard deviation of mean and median value.

Answer: The mean is 9.980 = (9.990 + 9.982 + 9.983 + 9.980 + 9.973 = 9.990)

The median is 9.982, average deviation $n = 5$ five readings mean is

$$D = \frac{d}{\sqrt{n}} = 3.16 \times 10^{-6} = 6.3 \times 10^{-3}$$

Thus standard deviation = 6.3×10^{-3}, relative standard deviation is

$$\frac{\left(6.3 \times 10^{-3}\right) \times 100}{9.982} = 0.0631 \text{ i.e. } 6.31 \times 10^{-2}$$

Example 5: The analysis of oxygen from polluted atmosphere showed following results:

56, 55.95, 56.04, 56.08, 56.23 can the last value be rejected?

Answer: The average value of $(\bar{x})$ is

$$= \frac{56+55.95+56.04+56.08+56.23}{5} = \delta = \frac{280.3}{5} = 56.06$$

The difference between mean $m = 5$ (55.98) and the last value (M_{n-1}) (56.23) is 0.28. The last (M_n) and last but one (M_{n-1}) value the difference is (56.23 – 56.08) = 0.15. Q-value for five determination is 0.64. The difference between the last value M_n and average value is $\overline{M}$ (56.23 – 55.95) = 0.28. We get value of Q as $Q_{exp} = 0.15/0.28 = 0.54$ $Q_3 = 0.64 > 0.054$. Last reading is acceptable.

Example 6: The total dissolved solids (TDS) in a sample of spring water is

22.81, 26.62, 22.73, 22.75, 22.78, 22.79, 22.83, 22.84, 22.87, 22.92, 22.94.

Calculate (*i*) mean and average deviation of mean (*ii*) Standard deviation and standard deviation of mean (*iii*) Median value and the range (*iv*) relative difference in high and low value (*v*) Upper and lower confidence limit?

Answer: (*i*) The mean value is average of eleven values $\bar{v} = 22.813$

(*ii*) $d = \frac{\Sigma d^2}{n} = \frac{0.242}{11} = 0.022$ it is average deviation of mean. We also know

(*iii*) Standard deviation $= \sqrt{\frac{\Sigma S^2}{n-1}} = 0.308$. The S.D. of mean is $\frac{0.308}{\sqrt{n-1}} = 0.028$.

The coefficient of variation $\left(\frac{S}{m} \times 100\right) = 1.22\%$ *i.e.* relative standard deviation

(*iv*) Median value is middle of high (22.94) and low (22.62), value is 22.83 while the range is (22.94 – 22.62) = 0.32. The relative difference is 14 ppt. The confidence limit at lower and upper values are from Table-C (Annexure).

Upper level $= \frac{(n-1)s^2}{3.904} = \frac{10 \times (0.308)^2}{3.309} = 0.24$. If 3.904 is lower confidence value from Table

Lower level $= \frac{(n-1)s^2}{18.307} = \frac{10 \times (308)^2}{18.307} = 0.0518$. If 18.307 is upper confidence value from Table.

The values *viz.* 3.904 and 18.307 are obtained from Table of Chi square (Appendix B) with $n = 10$ degrees of freedom.

Example 7: The analysis of autoexhaust emission for lead released from exhaust pipe is:

1.12, 1.15, 1.11, 1.16, 1.12 μg. Calculate the arithematic mean, mean deviation, probable analytical error, confidence limit, standard deviation of mean and standard deviation noted from these readings.

Answer: The mean of five reading

$$(\bar{x}).s = \left[\frac{1.12+1.15+1.11+1.16+1.12}{5}\right] = 1.13$$

The deviation of mean is $\Sigma S^2 = \Sigma(1 - 0.1)^2 + (0.002)^2 + (00.02)^2 + (0.03)^2 + (-0.01)^2 = 0.018\%$ while the deviation of mean = (0.0001 + 0.0004 – 0.0004 + 0.0009) is

$\Sigma\delta^2 = 0.019$ the standard deviation (s) $= \sqrt{\dfrac{\Sigma\delta^2}{n-1}} = \sqrt{\dfrac{0.0019}{4}} = \pm 0.022$

The probable analytical error is $\Sigma = \dfrac{\pm t_s^{\sigma}}{\sqrt{n}} = \dfrac{2.78 \times 0.022}{\sqrt{5}} = \pm 0.027\%$

Finally the confidence limit is = 1.13 ± 0.027%, upper (99%) confidence limit

$= \dfrac{4.60 \times 0.022}{\sqrt{5}} = \pm\, 0.045\%.$

So actual value is = 1.13 ± 0.045

Example 8: Calculate the average deviation, standard deviation, rejection of results 90% confidence limit and t-distribution from the analysis of calcium from hard water?

The readings are: 112.25, 112.36, 112.21, 112.30, 112.36, 112.32 mg (n = 6), state also whether that mean value 112.30 differ too much from accepted figure of 112.40?

Answer: We evaluate standard deviation $\sqrt{\dfrac{\Sigma S^2}{n-1}} = 0.060.$ The quantity (↓)

$t = (112.30 - 112.40)\sqrt{\dfrac{6}{0.006}} = 4.1$ from table of confidence limit (Appendix C).

$v = 5$, $t = 4.032\%$ at confidence limit and 4.773 at 99.5 confidence limit. There is huge error so reject it.

Example 9: Calculate 50% and 95% confidence limit for following results of analysis of (NO – NOx) from the polluted atmosphere when readings are as: $R_1 = 1.80$, $R_2 = 1.58$, $R_3 = 1.64$?

Answer: $\text{Mean}(\bar{x}) = \dfrac{(1.80+1.58+1.64)}{n=3} = 1.673$, standard deviation ($SD$) is

$S = \sqrt{\dfrac{\Sigma\delta^2}{n-1}} = 0.10.$ From tables in appendix for 50% confidence limit the value is $t = \pm\, 0.067$ and for 95% confidence limit it is ± 1.96

So 5% confidence limit $= \left[1.67 \pm \dfrac{0.67 + 0.10}{\sqrt{3}}\right] = 1.67 \pm 0.04$ as $\left[x + \dfrac{t+s}{n-1}\right]$ *i.e.* we use the formula as

$$\text{mean} = \frac{t\text{-value} + \text{stand. deviation}}{\sqrt{n_{os}}\ \text{of reading or freedom}} = \text{mean} \pm \frac{t_{\text{value}}}{\sqrt{n}}$$

Now we shall consider the important statistical parameters in pictorial form or graphic representation and what is the significance of lea^t square method?

4.7 GRAPHIC REPRESENTATION AND PROBABILITY OF DISTRIBUTIONS

The sample is a group of 'n' observations which are available. Population is large set of samples. The random variable is the soul of observations while observation is the origin of random sample. The error has discrepancies in replicate observation from one experiment to another experiment. We examine it in mathematical terms.

A first stage is to plot a data either as dot diagrams where one uses plots *viz.* histograms (Fig. 4.1) or data density plot. The ordinance of the histograms may be actual count in interval or be relative frequency ($f_1 = n_1/n_2$). If n = total nos. of values. Let us consider probability of distribution curve when 'n' is large, frequency distribution becomes smooth to give population frequency distribution curve. It is represented by probability density function (Fig. 4.2).

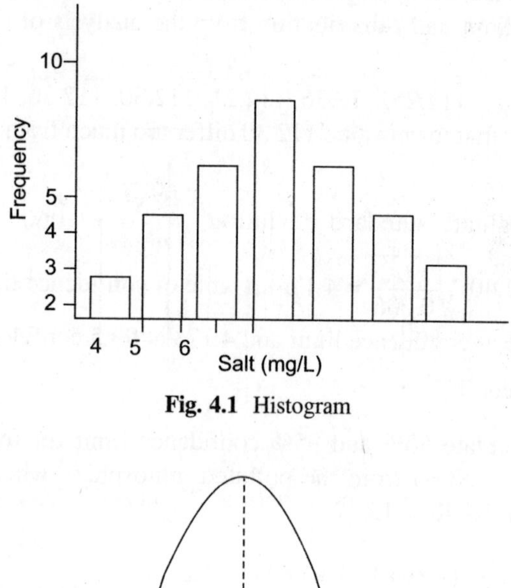

Fig. 4.1 Histogram

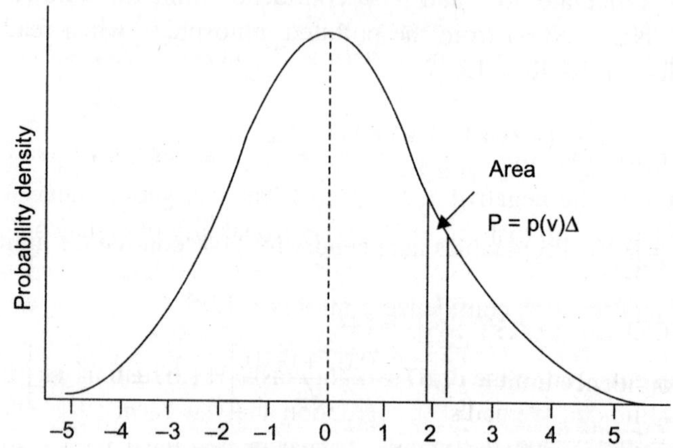

Fig. 4.2 Probability density function graph

The ordinate $p(y)$ of the distribution is not probability itself. It is given by the area under probability density function (Fig. 4.2). It shows normal uniform distribution curve called as "Gaussian distribution curve".

4.8 ACCURACY, REPRODUCIBILITY

The accuracy is a function of both bias and precision. A bias measures systematic errors. The accurate results have good precision, with zero bias. Such bias can be identified by checking experimental data. The bias cannot be evaluated in absence of knowledge of true value. Precision results have small random errors. Reproducibility or repeatability are same terms however, they carry many times with different meaning. Normality means that the error from measurement (e) is assumed to originate from normal probability distribution. We get symmetrical bell shaped distribution curve as shown in Fig. 4.2. (Gaussian curve)

Let us finally examine normal distribution, bell shaped curve (Fig. 4.3). It is called 'Gaussian distribution curve', $n = 8$ nos. of readings, $\sigma^2 = 1$ is a variance, mean = η

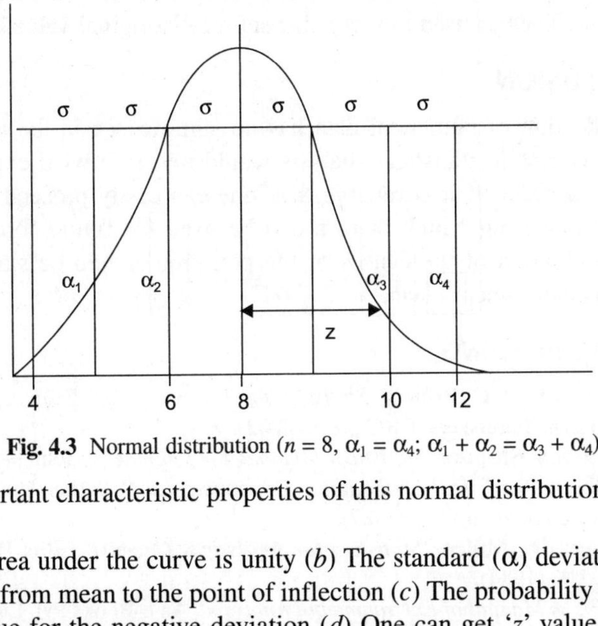

Fig. 4.3 Normal distribution ($n = 8$, $\alpha_1 = \alpha_4$; $\alpha_1 + \alpha_2 = \alpha_3 + \alpha_4$)

The important characteristic properties of this normal distribution curve are as follows:

(*a*) The area under the curve is unity (*b*) The standard (α) deviation measures the distance from mean to the point of inflection (*c*) The probability is $(\alpha_1 + \alpha_2) = (\alpha_3 + \alpha_4)$ true for the negative deviation (*d*) One can get 'z' value which is $z = (y - \eta)/\sigma_2$ if z = has no distribution (*e*) The probability of a standardized normal deviation is 5.82%.

4.9 METHOD OF LEAST SQUARES

The fitting an equation to the data is mighty task. The equation may be empirical or mechanical model. We had seen regression analysis earlier. It is also called the curve fitting or parameter estimation. Linear or nonlinear model uses data *e.g.* Mode $y = \beta x^2$ is for nonlinear plot. We give equation for least square method as

$$S = \sum_{i=1}^{n} (C_1)^2 = \sum_{i=1}^{n} (y_1 - \eta_1)^2$$

If the minimum sum of all square is called the residual sum of squares (S_R). The mode is to ascertain the parameter which is called as the "method of least square". It is useful for both nonlinear as well as linear models. The method of least squares is used in analyzing a data from actual experiments. So also data from unplanned happenings. The residual error ($\sigma = y - \eta$) be random. In statistical analysis geometric mean is the antilog of the arithmetic mean of the logs and values of available. Similarly if standard deviation (S) is divided by the mean and multiply by 100 we get $\left(\frac{S}{m} \times 100\right)$ is called as the "coefficient of variance "(CV) or relative standard deviation is percentage. A sample is a sub-set of population and consists of a group of 'n' observations taken from analysis. Thus statistics are random variables and are characterized by (a) probability distribution that has a mean and variance values. The variance is square of the standard deviation. It is σ^2 or S^2. The ANOVA is used to recognize source or original valuation.

4.10 CONCLUSION

The mere collection of numerical data has no significance in the abatement of pollution. A systematic statistical analysis would reveal to what extent our data acquisition is in order. If it is reliable then one can easily proceed to construct mathematical modeling which in turn can be used for future forecasting. An intensive investigation of the causes of the pollution should be simultaneously made to keep environment clean.

ADDITIONAL READING

1. P.M. Berthouex, L.C. Brown, *'Statistics for Environmental Engineering'*, Second Edition, Lewis Publishers, CRC press (2002).
2. G.J. Hahn, S.S. Shapiro, *'Statistical Methods for Engineers'*, John Wiley (1967).
3. R.O. Gilbert, *'Statistical Methods for Environmental Pollution Monitoring'*, Van Nostrand Reinhold and Co. (1987).
4. J.C. Miller, J.N. Miller, *'Statistics for Analytical Chemist'*, Ellis Harwood Ltd., Chinster, UK (1984).
5. N.C. Aery, *'A Manual of Environmental Analysis'*, An e-Books Pvt. Ltd., New Delhi (2010).
6. S.M. Khopkar, *'Analytical Chemistry, Problems and Solution'*, Second Edition, New Age International Publishers (P) Ltd., New Delhi (2013).
7. G.E.P. Box, W.G. Hunter, J.S. Hunter, *'Statistics for Experimentors; An Introduction to Design Data Analysis and Model Building'*, Wiley Interscience, New York (1978).
8. W.W. Peigorsch, A.J. Bailor, *'Statistics for Environmental Biology and Toxicology'*, Chapman and Hall, New York (1997).

5 Environmental Toxicology

5.1 INTRODUCTION

The environmental toxicology and health are two inseparable areas, as human ecology constitutes an important sector of health. Environmental toxicology is a subject that concerns with source of toxic substances, manner in which they reach to the man, and most important is their biological effects on human health. The inhalation is principal route for ingestion of toxic pollutants in human body. Water vapour and dust are important carriers of toxic materials to man. Through food chain substantial amount of toxic substances are deposited in human body *e.g.* caesium^{137} or strontium^{90} which are deposited on grass which is consumed by cows, then through their milk man also gets contaminated. Water is another important pathways for toxicants for human. This is consumed by fish, which in turn it is consumed by man who gets contaminated by pollutants.

5.2 PRINCIPLES OF TOXICOLOGY AND STANDARDS

The effect of toxic substances on man varies with dose, and its chemical properties. Animal experiments give indications of part of organ which is affected. Toxic effect may be short-term exposure or long-term effects *e.g.* Inhalation of beryllium dust causes pulmonary edema but patient can be cured if kept away from further exposure. While some materials on prolonged exposure cause cumulative effects which are in turn injurious to health. Synergism is an effect when person is exposed simultaneously to two toxic compounds which in turn gives stronger ill effects on man rather than what each compound singularly would have given. There are several synergistic compounds. It is worthwhile to know what are standards for such substances? The standards are called **threshold limiting values** (TLV). It is defined as the permissible limit for exposure of toxic pollutant during 40 hrs (8 × 5) per week. Toxic effects can occur but their effects are not immediately known. Carbon monoxide poisoning is detected immediately. Vinyl chloride on prolonged exposure causes cancer. The zero risk for toxicant is not possible on several occasions. The material which is very toxic for human being not may be for the animals *e.g.* vinyl chloride causes liver cancer for man but not influencing animal. Further, it depends upon individual health as some persons have better immunity to toxic effects in comparison with the another individual. The exposure

Table 5.1 Health effects of toxic organic pollutants from atmosphere

S. No.	Name of the toxic pollutant	Chemical formula	Per annum Production (1b/year)	Source of contamination	Adverse effects
1.	Nitro benzene	$C_6H_5NO_2$	8.5×10^8	Aniline compounds, Dyes	Carcinogenic (animal)
2.	Styrene	–	7.5×10^9	Paint industry Plastic factory	Carcinogenic (animal)
3.	1.4 dioxane	–	–	Pigment industry, solvent	Carcinogenic (Human)
4.	Toluene	$C_6H_5(CH_3)$	11.9×10^9	Auto exhaust emissions, solvent	Lungs, liver affected
5.	Benzene	C_6H_6	12.7×10^9	Auto exhaust emissions, solvent	Carcinogenic (Human)
6.	Xylene	$C_6H_4(CH_3)_2$	11.1×10^9	Accepted solvent, no adverse effect	No toxicity effects
7.	Chlorobenzene	C_6H_5Cl	3.6×10^8	Solvent, contaminant	Carcinogenic (animal)
8.	Carbon tetrachloride	CCl_4	7.5×10^8	Fluoro carbon factory Refrigeration Plant	Carcinogenic Human and animal
9.	Chloroform	$CHCl_3$	3.3×10^8	Fluoro carbon production good solvent	Carcinogenic
10.	Vinyl Chloride	–	7.5×10^9	PVC manufacturing unit	Carcinogenic

to industrial workers cannot be compared with ordinary person. In former, it is restricted only to 40 hrs a week while in latter case such exposure may be for longer duration. A dose response curve gives a 'sigmoid' curve indicating that initially toxic effect is less with lapse of time, as time passes the toxic manifestations are increasing. US citizen can tolerate one rad per year radioactivity while Indian citizen can tolerate 5 rad/year of radioactivity. There are no apparent signs of leukemia. The rate at which the dose is delivered has an important bearing on the influence on human being.

It is worthwhile at this stage to consider toxic organic compounds in day to day use. Table 5.1 List such compounds along with their source and their toxicological manifestations. It is surprising to note common organic solvents such as Benzene, Chloroform, carbon tetrachloride which are consumed day to day life are extremely toxic and carcinogenic in nature. Their production per annum exceeds 12.7×10^9 to 7.5×10^8 lbs/year. The other less injurious organic compound is nitrobenzene with bitter almonds odor, it is very toxic. In plastic and pigment industry, styrene, divinyl benzene, vinyl chloride are used on large scale unfortunately they are all carcinogenic compounds. A commonly used solvent viz 1-4 dioxane, or THF are dangerous material. For all practical purposes now a days in chemical research laboratory benzene a tolume are replaced by xylene as the solvent in research investigations specially in the field of solvent extraction separation.

Table 5.2 Leading causes of disease in world

S.No.	*Name of disease*	*Rank in 2020 (%) (Future)*	*Rank in 1990 (%) (Past)*
1.	Heart disease	1	5
2.	Depression	2	4
3.	Accident on Road	3	9
4.	Stroke Paralysis	4	6
5.	Lungs Problem	5	11
6.	Pneumonia	6	1
7.	Tuberculosis	7	7
8.	Battle field death	8	–
9.	Diarrhea	9	2
10.	Aids; HIV	10	–
11.	Fight Quarel	12	–
12.	Hereditary Problems	13	10
13.	Suicide tendency	14	–
14.	Respiratory Problems	15	–
15.	Childhood Problems	11	3
16.	Malaria, Dengue	–	12

If we consider the rate of mortality, Japan stands first for long life with longitivity of male is 70 years, for the women 75 years. In comparison this rate in India is 65-68 years. In the south eastern asiatic nations including Africa the rate is poor viz 45-48 years. The death toll largely includes children. Their are various kinds of ailments starting from cardiac problem to malaria and dengue all over world. These diseases in spite of government control are not wanning, fortunately those diseases like polio, paralysis, pulmonary diseases are wanning. The situation is more satisfactory in well developed countries. India stands in between with no success to irradicate, malaria. The third and fourth column in Table 5.2 provides rank of killer diseases—Heart, lungs, brain, sickness are not easily curable. The ranking in 1990 is not same as in year 2010 due to meticulous careful planning all over world by health departments and hospitals.

In most of the cases we see decline of disease *e.g.* S. No. 6, 10, 12 and 15 show decline (Table 5.2).

Table 5.3 Metal pollutants released (tonnes in thousand) by atmospheric pollution

Metal	*Human contribution*	*Natural release*	*Total release in tonnes*	*Ratio of Human/natural release*
Pb	2006	6	2006	333
Sb	38	1	39	38
Zn	840	36	876	23
Cd	6	0.3	6.3	20
Cu	260	19	279	14
Se	14	3	17	4.7
As	78	21	99	4
Ni	98	28	126	4
V	210	65	275	3
Cr	94	58	152	2

Table 5.4 Source of toxic pollutants in environment

Source industry	*Toxic pollutant released*	*Average level (ppm)*
Sulphuric acid	SO_2	10–30
Steel	Suspended particulate matter (SPM)	10–1000
	CO	40–400
Chemicals	NO–NO_x	10–200
	$HCrO_4$	18 mg/m^3
	Al_2O_3	30 mg/m^3
	NH_3	2–50
	SO_2	1–40
Pesticides and solvents	DDT, parathion	18 mg/m^3
	Ethanol	800
	Benzene	150
	Phosgene	1
	Fe_2O_3	60 mg/m^3
Heavy engineering goods	Al_2O_3, SiO_2, C, Fe dust	—
Rayon	CS_2	40

Most of the pollutants encountered in air, water or waste water are toxic. Hence, it is worthwhile to consider them in different groups like toxic metal pollutants, toxic gases and the toxic organic pollutants. The source of pollution, toxicological manifestations, methods of analysis and measures to control their ill-effects to man are also considered.

5.3 TYPES OF TOXIC POLLUTANTS

All the compounds used in industry are not toxic or injurious to health, but few of them cause serious health hazards. Majority of toxic materials exist in gaseous or vapour form, while a few exist in the form of fluids or solids. Amongst gaseous pollutants, one can easily name: AsH_3, SbH_3, H_2S, CO or freon ($CCl_2 F_2$) as toxic. They are absorbed through skin and eyes by the process of inhalation and they are ingested in the body. Several organic solvents, specially those having boiling point less than 120 to 150°C are by and large toxic in nature. They affect skin and cause problems on inhalation. Dust, fumes and suspended particulate matter are hazardous, as they get ingested into the lungs. Similarly, minerals containing Pb, Mn, Be, silica, asbestos cause serious lung diseases. They produce cancer of lung, and impaired respiratory function. Pesticides and polymers are very harmful to health. Pesticide residue causes intoxication. Since plastic and polymers are nondegradable, their disposal poses a serious problem. These products on decomposition or combustion are very dangerous to the health. Many polymers are skin irritants, called primary irritants or sensitizers. The latter do not cause any irritation on first contact to skin, but later cause dermatitis. Dyes, soaps, oils, resins, explosive plasticizers, cosmetics, coal (Table 5.5) derivatives are irritants by nature. Acids, alkalies, salts and organic solvents belong to this category of primary irritants. The physiological manifestations of toxic pollutants is quite interesting.

Table 5.5 Summary of Toxicity of metal pollutants

S.No.	*Elements*	*Highly toxicity*	*Intermediate toxicity*	*Low toxicity*
1.	Transition elements (d-block)	Hg(II) Cu(II) Cd(II) Au(III)	Ag(I) Pt(IV), Mn(II) Fe(III) Ni(II) Co(II)	–
2.	Main group elements (p-block)	Zn(II), Sn(IV) As(III) Pb(II)	Ba(II) Al(III)	–
3.	Inner transition elements (f-block)	None All radioactive elements	Ce(IV), La(III)	known Lanthanides
4.	Alkali metals (S-block)	None	Sr, Cs, Be	Li, Na, K, Rb, Mg, Ca, Ba

We have already seen in Table 5.3 toxic metals released in the environment. We can group them according to extent of toxicity. The release of toxic elements in air is expressed in tons/m^3. It shows that the highest release is for Lead (2006 ton/m^3) while selenium, antimony are released in very small concentration. Other toxic elements are let off in air are zinc, copper, vanadium and chromium in some form or other. A perusal of Table 5.4 indicates that few metals are highly toxic. Those include zinc, tin, Mercury, Cadmium, Arsenic and Lead while alkali and alkaline earth elements like calcium, barium, potassium and sodium are not harmful. It is yet to be ascertained as to how many inner transition metals like Lanthanides are toxic, although it is confirmed that other inner transition elements like actinide is (*5f*) metals series are confirmed as harmful to health on account of release of radio activity.

5.4 COMMON TOXIC MANIFESTATIONS

The brain, heart, lungs, kidney and liver are vital organs of our body. These vital organs get affected by toxic pollutants. Any problem with heart is termed as cardiac disfunction. Disorder of lung is termed as pulmonary, while problems that of kidney is renal disorder and one with liver are called hepatic disorder. The central nervous system, operated mainly by brain also gets affected by sensitisers. There are problems associated with blood vascular system, digestive system and skin ailments. Let us first consider their effects on health.

(a) Asphyxiation

The absence of oxygen used for breathing causes breathing problem and lead to fatality. Several gases react chemically and produce asphyxiation, *e.g.,* CO, HCN, $COCl_2$ leading to death of inhaler.

(b) Irritation

The corrosive acids and caustic alkalies produce irritation of eyes, skin and respiratory passage. Those causing harm to lower respiratory passage are more harmful, such as NO_2, PH_3, CdO, BeO. Aldehydes, alcohols or ketones are all injurious to the lung.

(c) Pneumoconiosis

This is a problem related to lung. It is caused due to exposure to dust or other pollutants. The compounds like quartz, asbestos, beryllium cause pneumoconiosis.

(d) Narcosis

Many organic solvents are narcotic in nature, *e.g.,* halogenated hydrocarbons, esters, ketones, ethers. Even benzene and carbontetrachloride cause intoxication. Fortunately, such effects are not of permanent nature, as many effects are irreversible causing no problem to the health.

(e) Systemic Intoxication

It causes irreversible damage with slow recovery of vital organs, nervous system or haemoropoletic system. Haemotoxic effects are caused by benzene and can even lead to leukemia. Anemia is caused by lead-poisoning. Carbon monoxide converts haemoglobin in blood to methaehemoglobin, which in turn leads to instanteneous death due to asphyxiation for inhaler. Aromatic and nitro-organic compounds are bad for the health (Table 5.6).

Table 5.6 Health hazards encountered in various chemical factories or processes

Health hazards	*Chemical factory or process*	*Incidence (%)*
Pneumoconiosis	Coal and zinc	34
Toxicity due to CS_2, Zn	Rayon industry	27
Toxicity due to Mn and V	Ferromanganese, steel industry	73
	processing and refining of products	16
Ulceration of wounds	Dichromate exposure to health	20
Insecticide poisoning	DDT affects lung	30
	Parathion	21
Byssinosis (chest disease)	Cotton fibre dust deposited in lung	8
Chronic bronchitis	Textile and jute mill process	10
Lead toxicity	Printing press	25
	accumulator or car batteries	11
Dyes interaction	Dyestuff, carcinogenic compounds like benzidine, β–naphthylamine	7

(f) Hepatic and Renal Disorder

The problems of liver and kidney belongs to this category. Compounds of Hg, Se, U, As, TNT, halogenated hydrocarbons cause damage to liver and kidney. The primary function of the liver is to form blood, while kidney is an efficient filtration unit to remove toxins from the body. Neurotoxic effects are indirect fallout of renal or hepatic disorder. Person may suffer from tremor, paralysis, mental fatigue due to exposure to CH_3Br, CS_2, Mn or Hg compounds. The bile fluid if mixed with blood causes jaundice, excess drinking of wine causes cirrhosis of liver, urinary infection cystitis and nephritis.

(g) Dermatitis

This is an occupational disease, primarily caused by contact of skin with corrosive chemicals. Dermatological examination reveals cause of such problems. In order to get reliable information our sampling process must be dependable and accurate.

5.5 THE BIOLOGICAL SAMPLING

Several problems of body are accurately diagnosed by proper sampling process. Air, blood and urine are used for such purposes. Some poisons like cadmium compounds remain in body for as long as 10 years. We call them cumulative toxins, while a few others are excreted instantaneously, like compounds of vanadium. Very useful and specific information is obtained from biological sampling of toxic material.

(a) Breath Sampling

Volatile and unreactive substances can be measured in breath sample. Chlorinated hydrocarbons, carbon monoxide and radioactive gases can be easily identified in breath samples.

(b) Urine Analysis

An environmental scientist can detect 90% of toxic materials in urine, *e.g.* Pb, Hg, As, Sb, Cd, Se, Te, U and fluorides are easily detected in urine. Few are detected at late stage. Organic substances are usually excreted such as DDT resides in the body for a longer time. A large presence of say proteinuria or coproporphyrine in urine indicates indirect presence of Cd or Pb in the body.

(c) Blood Analysis

Few substances are easily detected in blood, *e.g.*, Pb, Mn, heavy metals are easily identified in the body by blood test. The chemiluminescence effect on blood can be measured. The organophosphorus pesticides like Tik-20 can be detected due to the formation of carboxy hemoglobin in blood. CH_3Br is also instantaneously detected in blood.

Table 5.7 Source and level of Toxic metals in Pollutants (%)

S. No.	*Source*	*Fe*	*Ni*	*Mn*	*Cu*	*Cd*	*V*	*Pb*	*Zn*	*Highest level of metal*
1.	Road dust	2.5–6	3.7–6.5	0.067	0.08	Nil	2.0–4.0	0.18	0.70	Ni
2.	Street dust	–	–	0.14	0.039	–	0.030	0.24	0.10	Pb
3.	Soil dust	2.0	0.002	0.06	0.039	–	0.030	0.06	0.10	Zn
4.	Auto emission	0.09	0.8	1.2×10^{-3}	7.2×10^{-3}	5×10^{-5}	–	1.0	0.02	Pb
5.	Furnace oil	0.90	0.008	0.15	0.20	0.10	–	9.7	12.0	Zn
6.	Incinerator	0.33	0.079	0.027	0.17	0.016	–	6.9	11.0	Zn
7.	Farm soil	2.0	2×10^{3}	6×10^{-2}	2×10^{-2}	–	4×10^{-3}	6×10^{-2}	1×10^{-2}	Fe
8.	High ways	2.75	0.004	0.035	0.008	2×10^{-4}	–	0.1	0.045	Fe

It is very interesting to examine the Tables 5.6 and 5.7 the first Table shows extent of damage caused by pollutant release from specific industry. In our day to day life we encounter metal pollutant from road dust, auto exhaust emission, incinerators. The high incidence of problems of lungs is encountered from steel plants (73%), zinc factory (34%), and printing industry (25%). Further the specific metal pollutants like Lead, Cadmium, Zinc, Manganese in terms of % from various sources are given in Table 5.7. Road dust contains too much of iron compounds while furnace oil releases substantial amount of Zinc and Lead. In all we summarise that the roads streets, soil, highways are all potential source of environmental pollution.

(d) Nail and Hair Analysis

Certain compounds like As, V, Sb are easily detected in hair and nails even after long years. The cystine contents of nail gets affected by their presence. Several cases of murder, bride burning suicide were detected by analysis of nail and hair. Even from ashes in the grave after lapse of several months toxic metals are detected.

(e) Tissue Analysis

This is a sure test of detecting malignant growth. The autopsy is carried out for dead tissue, while biopsy is carried out for living tissue. It gives important information or clue on lesion in the tissue. Now, there is growing trend to examine DNA in body.

5.6 THRESHOLD LIMITING VALUE (TLV)

This is an unique measure of toxicity. It refers to airborne concentrations of substances and indicates condition under which a worker is continuously exposed day after day without adverse effects, however, there is a wide variation in the individual susceptibility due to varying immunity. It is interesting to note that on an average, a person of Indian origin can tolerate more dose of a toxin due to intrinsic immunity in comparison with a person from abroad. Thus,TLV represents time weighed average concentration for 7 to 8 hours work per day, or 40 hours per week. It provides a guideline to control the of health hazards. It permits an exposure above the prescribed limit, if there is compensation by equivalent exposure below the limit during working day or working week. TLVs are based on best available information from human or animal studies of exposures. TLVs are not always used for knowing relative index of hazards, evaluation of air pollution nuisances, estimation of toxic potential or proof of disease. Most important factor is that, the working conditions differ from country to country. *e.g.,* those in the United States of America cannot be compared with those living in India.

5.7 TOXIC METAL POLLUTANTS AND THEIR ANALYSIS

There are only eighteen toxic metal pollutants. In periodic classification of elements, we have many (hundred fourteen) elements, of these approximately eighty are metals; fortunately, out of these eighty metals only eighteen metals are toxic. The important source for these metal pollutants is indicated in Table 5.12, while the general toxic effects on health of very important metal pollutants are listed in Table 5.13, the general toxic manifestations caused by metals are listed in Table 5.14 the threshold limiting values of important metals are listed in Table 5.15, the TLV of several other elements, which are also considered to be toxic. The source, toxic effects, important analytical methods for analysis of these toxic metal pollutants are discussed. Group I–beryllium, Group II–zinc, cadmium, mercury, Group III–thallium, Group IV–lead, Group V–vanadium, arsenic, antimony, Group VI–chromium, uranium, selenium, tellurium, Group VII–

manganese, Group VIII–cobalt, nickel, osmium and platinum are all toxic. Table 5.12 indicates classification of metals on basis of their toxicity.

Table 5.8 Sources of metal pollutant from industry

S. No.	*Metal*	*Source*	*S. No.*	*Metal*	*Source*
1.	Be	Fluorescent lamps	10.	Se	Glass, photocells
2.	Os	Catalyst, staining agent	11.	Cd	Cladding alloy, alkali cells
3.	Pt	Catalyst, alloy, thermocouple	12.	Pb	Auto-exhaust emission
4.	Hg	Chloroalkali and pesticides	13.	As	Paper pulp pesticides
5.	Tl	Rodenticides; pesticides	14.	Sb	Alloys, pharmaceuticals preparations
6.	V	Furnace oil, metal mills	15.	Cr	Plating, paints, alloys, ether
7.	Te	Auto-exhaust emission	16.	Ni	Alkaline cell, alloys, catalyst process
8.	Co	Ink pigment, magnets	17.	Zn	Galvanisation process, alloys
9.	U	Nuclear reactors	18.	Mn	Mines, minerals

Table 5.9 Toxic effects of some metal pollutants

Metal	*Effects on human health*
Hg	Tremor, gingivitis, renal disorder, asphyxiation
Pb	Plumbism, gastric problems, colic, anaemia and irritation of lungs, pneumocomosis
Cd	Shortness of breath, anaemia, liver trouble and necrosis, hepatic and renal disorders
V	Catarrah, cough, wheezing, dyspnea and dermatitis, sore throat
As	Cancer of skin and nasal septum, jaundice
Cr	Dermatitis, ulcer, cancer
Os	Halo around eyes, bronchitis
Te	Garlic smell to sweat and breath

Table 5.10 Toxicological effects of compounds

Toxic effects	*Compounds*
Asphyxiation	CO, HCN
Irritation	CdO, BeO, NO_2
Pneumoconiosis	Be
Narcosis	$CHCl_3$, CCl_4
Systemic intoxication	Organic compounds
Hepatic and renal disorders	As, AsH_3
Haemotoxic	Pb, organolead compounds
Neurotoxic	Hg, Mn
Dermatitis	Alkalies, phenols
Carcinogenicity	Cr(VI). $Ni(CO)_4$, Pt, As,

Table 5.11 Threshold limits of toxic metal (μg/m³)

Transition Elements (d-block)				Main Group Elements (p-block)			
Metal	*TLV*	*Metal*	*TLV*	*Metal*	*TLV*	*Metal*	*TLV*
V	100	Os	2	Be	2	As	500
Cr	500	Pt	2				
Mo	5000	Cu	1000	In	100	Sb	500
Mn	5000	Zn	500				
Co	100	Cd	200	TI	100	Sn	2000
Ni	1000	Hg	10	Pb	200	Se/Te	200

Table 5.12 Classification on basis of toxicity of metals

Low Toxic (TLV < 5.0 μg/m³)	*Medium Toxicity (TLV < 200 μg/m³)*	*High Toxicity (TLV < 2000 μg/m³)*	*Nontoxics elements (TLV > 5000 μg/m³)*
Sb	Cd	Al	Ca
Sr	Cu	Mo	Na
Th	Hg	Zr	K
Ti	Pb	W	Rb
Cs	V	Zn	Li

The individual elements from the view-point of their source, toxicity, method of analysis and control are prescribed in the following sections.

(a) Toxic Metal Pollutants and Analysis

(*a*) Vanadium is a highly toxic metal. The emissions from furnace oil boilers, milling operations in steel industry, catalyst discharge in waste water, heat exchangers fired with residual oil causes pollution.

The vanadium is an important component of steel and alloys. The toxic symptoms include low synthesis of amino acids, lipids, uneven haemoglobin distribution in the body. It causes cardiovascular disease. The irritation of gastrointestinal track and respiratory system gets affected. It causes problem such as bronchitis, dysepnea, rhinorrhoea, coughs wheezing, infection of pharynx. Those workers who clean oilfired boilers suffer from poisoning and respiratory disease. Excess dose of vanadium can turn the colour of tounge to green. During summer its concentration is high as the emission from furnace oil release are dispersed very quickly in the atmosphere.

Most inexpensive technique for the analysis of the vanadium is ring oven technique (limit 0.01 μg). It can be colorimetrically analysed by oxidation with H_2O_2 or as complex with at 8–hydroxyquinoline. The method of polarography is also beneficial for its analysis from the atmosphere. Neutron activation analysis is also suitable for such analysis. The TLV for oxide is 0.1–0.5 mg/m³. Only vanadium carbide can be tolerated in large dose of 4 mg/m³. In Russia accepted TLV is 0.002 mg/m³ while in Germany its accepted limit for Vanadium is 0.001 mg/m³.

For collection from atmosphere cyclone and electrostatic precipitator (ESP) is ideal. For large particle size high volume sampler are most suitable. In the air it is present in form of pentaoxide. Most of colorimetric methods involve its analysis in the pentavalent form by extractive photometry. The method involving photometry of magenta black colour permits analysis in the range of 1 to 50 $\mu g/m^3$. In AAS it is analysed at 318 mm with graphite furnace at level of 0.033 mg/m^3, but flame AAS gives in comparison poor results.

(b) Chromium

Chromium (III) is not toxic as hexavalent chromium. Main source of chromium is paint industry, alloy stainless steel; glass industry, electroplating bath and tanneries waste, where $K_2Cr_2O_7$ is used for hide cleaning and leather treatment. Such waste is alkaline. It causes dermatitis, ulceration and perforation of nasal septum, chromic mist leads to chest trouble, hexavalent chromium compounds cause lung cancer, to workers working in paints, pigment and tannery industries. A concentration of 3.8 μg/litre is detected in urine. It is determined spectrophotometrically with symm-diphenylcarbazide. It is determined also by polarography. In AAS air acetylene flame is used to analyse it at 357 nm with a sensitivity of 0.55 μg/ml.

The inhalation of atmosphere containing chromium dust can lead to respiratory cancer. The chromate of zinc, lead and barium are harmful to the health. Corrosin inhibiters are made of chromium compounds. The leather tanning containers, cooling towers anodising bath have on an average of 40 to 180 mg/L of chromium. The pigments like chrome green, yellow and orange are hazardous. High volume sampler can be used to collect dust containing chromium from air. It can be collected on membrane filter. In high dosage idometric titration can be used. By ring oven method as low as 0.15 mg of chromium can be analysed. The AAS cannot distinguish between Cr(VI) and Cr(III) species. Therefore, Cr(VI) is extracted with ammonium pyrroldine (APDC) dithiocarbamate in MIBK. 1, 5 diphenyl carbohydrazine (DPCH) is a good extractant. The complex however has limited stability. From water it can be analysed by fluoroscence, spark source mass spectrometry, and by X-ray fluoroscence.

The threshold limiting value of chromates is 0.1 mg/m^3 but for soluble chromate it is higher *viz* 0.5 mg/m^3. For potable water tolerance level is 0.05 ppm. Electrostatic precipitator is widely used method for collection of chromium from air. The scrubbers can be used with advantage for collection of chromium mist. For collection of chromium from water ion-exchange, solvent extraction and reverse osmosis techniques are very effective. SO_2 is used to reduce Cr(VI) to Cr(III). The cation exchanger separates Cr(III) from effluents. The precipitation can be also resorted to isolate $Cr(OH)_3$ from water. Tributylphosphate can be used for solvent extraction separation of chromium.

The control measures include utilisation of the solid waste for land filling, the ocean disposal and incencration. Ocean dumping method has created a major concern and is being slowly discarded all over the world.

Table 5.13 Level of chromium in food (μg/kg)

Food	*Level*	*Food*	*Level*
Flour	20	Cereals	0.50
Bran	50	Pulses	0.79
Meat	10–60	Leafy vegetable	5.25
Fish	10–30	Spices	2.61
Vegetables	140	Common salt	2.0
Milk	10	Milk powder	0.32
Cheese	10–130	Red meat	0.24
Sugar	20	Nonleafly vegetables	5.47
Egg	200	Aquatic plants	6.11

Table 5.14 Daily intake of chromium in food in different countries (*μg/day*)

Country	*Intake of chromium*	*Country*	*Intake Chromium*
Canada	189–282	England	80–100
Europe	11–195	N. America	5–115
Japan	202–110	S. America	25–224
New Zealand	39–190	Russia	88–126

From Tables 5.13 and 5.14 it is seen that in foodstuff is present in form of fish and meat. The amount of chromium is (10–60 μg/kg), the egg yoke contains 200 μg/kg. The leafy vegetable have high contents of chromium (5.47 μg/g). A comparison with countries all over world (Table 5.14) for the consumption of chromium range shows that Europe has least contamination in food (11–20 μg/day) while Japanese people consumes very high contents of chromium (200–180 μg/day) in food in form of fish.

(c) Molybdenum

It is a transition element most commonly used in oxyanionic form for the detection of phosphorus. It is essential element in enzymes like xanthine oxidase, oxidising them gets to uric acid. Very small amount of molybdenum is encountered in diet. It has low order of toxicity. It can accumulate in kidney, liver and bones as much as 1 μg/g. Although gastrointestinal track readily absorbs molybdenum from food, fortunately it is readily excreated in the form of urine. The excess intake leads to diarrhea, anemia, for their poisoning copper compounds are best antitodes for it. It causes "heart disease". The dust of molybdenum can give pulmonary disorder. If it is orally taken in dosage of 15 mg/day it causes joint disorders and gout. In human body it leads to the formation of uric acid from Xanthine oxidase enzyme.

The best method for detection is to form complex with alkali thiocyanate which can be extracted in methylethylketone and measured colorimetrically. It also forms extractable complex with toluene 3-4 dithol which can be photometrically analysed. As low as 1 mg/ml of molybdenum can be analysed. It is either complexed with 8-hydroxyquinoline or N-pyrrolidithiocarbemic acid in neutron activation analysis. Neutron activations analysis is best method which gives 0.1/mg/ml of Mo but the method is not reproducible. From sea-water it is isolated on cation exchange resin and analysed by flameless AAS. It has TLV of 5 mg/m^3 for soluble and 10 mg/m^3 for insoluble compounds. In potable water it should not exceed the limit of 0.05 mg/L.

(d) Uranium

Amongst radioactive elements, it is highly toxic. The main source is atomic reactors. It causes histological damage to kidney and is slowly absorbed in the body. U^{235}_{92} amongst all isotopes causes radiation hazards. A concentration of 0.03 to 0.3 µg/litre is detected in urine. It is analysed by α-counting. In spectro-photometric analysis, dibenzoylmethane, 8-hydroxyquinoline and 2-thenoyl-trifluoroacetone (TTA) are used as extracting agents to give coloured complex for photometric determination. It can also be determined by polarography. Due to poor sensitivity (*viz.* 113 µg/ml), AAS is not a good method, even if one uses a flame of nitrous oxide-acetylene or graphite furnace measurement at 358 nm still the sensitivity is very poor.

(e) Manganese

The main source of manganese is milling factory, alloy industry, mines and minerals depots, smelting operations, and glass industry. It affects the central nervous system, causes gait and speech disturbance, tremors, mask-like face and uncontrollable laughter and lung troubles. The symptoms are visible after 2 to 3 months of exposure. Blood test is most dependable. MnO_2 causes pharyngitis, pneumonia. It is carried in bile through gastrointestinal tract to affect lungs.

Although it is best micronutrient for soil, it is systemic respiratory poison lung liver, blood and nervous system is affected by manganese. It can cause cardiac problems and even cancer. The school going children in Japan with school within radius of 8 km of factory were affected by its dust to show problems with their upper respiratory track, when the level was 160 to 260 µg/m^3 in city of Kanazawa. The hallucination, apathy and emotional instability is also caused in period of 15 years. Ferromaganese plants emit out large oxides in air. The dry cell manufacturing unit discharges it in effluents. The methyl cyclopentadienyl manganese carbonyl is used as the catalyst in petrol as antiknocking agent instead of $(C_2H_5)_4Pb$ in gasoline. Foggy whether promotes the level of manganese in atmosphere. Manganese is oxidised to MnO_4^- and it is measured colorimetrically as its complex with formaldioxime at 470 nm. The AAS and NAA are more sensitive methods where the level of analysis is 0.1 ppb. At 279 nm it is analysed by AAS with sensitivity of 0.21 µg/m^3. The threshold limiting value of manganese is 5 µg/m^3. The potable water should not contain more than 0.05 µg/L of manganese. Electrostatic precipitor and Venturi scrubbers are recommended for its collection from atmosphere. From water it is removed by pH adjustment or by use of cation exchange process; or by percipitation method in the suitable form. Since iron is chemically similar; it also gets removed along with the manganese. At high pH, there is risk of scale deposition on the container to give tinting. The sensitivity for photometry is 0.1 μg/g while for neutron activation analysis sensitivity is 0.001 μg/g and for AAS it is 0.01–0.21 mg/m^3 while flame photometry permits analysis of as low as 0.1 μg of manganese. The level in food is given in Table 5.15. It is high in walnut and low in butter.

Table 5.15 Manganese in foodstuff (mg/kg)

Food	Level	Food	Level	Food	Level
Barley	9.9	Rice	9.6	Fish	0.5
Corn	3.8	Wheat	13.7	Eggs	0.3
Butter	0.1 (lowest)	Tomato	0.6	Apple	0.3
Milk	0.5	Spices	1.8	Walnut	19.7 (highest)

(f) Cobalt

The main source of cobalt is magnet making factory, while nickel originates from hydrogenation of oil industry and paint factories. $Co(CO)_8$ is most toxic and causes lung problem such as pulmonary edema, while nickel causes dermatitis, pneumonia, lung and nose cancer due to nickel carbonyl or giddiness, headache, nausea, vomiting. Cobalt is determined spectrophotometrically with nitroso R-salt or with cupral extraction in chloroform or with α-nitroso β-napthol. It is not accurately measured by AAS, as the sensitivity is not satisfactory. It is determined at 240 nm.

Since nickel is extensively used in our households utensils in the form of stainless steel alloys we must consider its toxic effects. The harmful effects have been noted. A dose of 0.1 mg/ml is harmful in industry due to exposure to nickel carbonyl.

(g) Nickel

The toxicity of cobalt and nickel is identical. Nickel dust produces cancer of lungs and sinus. It causes respiratory disorder and dermatitis. It is carcinogenic but it is not fully confirmed by physicians. In 1967 in Germany, inhalation of its nickel carbonyl caused death of two persons. It had caused severe respiratory problems. The oral dose of diethyldithiocarbamate is an effective antitode for nickel poisoning. It causes eczema and itching. There is hypersensitivity in lymphocytes and leucocytes. The emission from stacks and from metallurgical operation of nickel is very hazardous to health. The upper respiratory track is severely affected. The crude oil contains nickel (~ 10 ppm). Water from silver refinery contains substantial amount of nickel. In waste water it is present as soluble salt. Nickel contents in plating industry is very high as shown in Table 5.16.

The best method for the detection and determination of nickel is with dimethylglyoxime to give pink complex which is easily extractable in to chloroform or carbon tetrachloride. Infrared technique directly analyses its carbonyl compounds with optical cells with longer optical path. The atomic emission spectrography was also used for trace analysis.

Table 5.16 Nickel concentration in plating industry (μg/g)

Industry	*Table ware*	*Metal finish*	*Machine fabrication*	*Plating plants*	*Average acid waste*	*Average alkaline waste*
Range	10–130	12–60	5–35	2–200	10–48	0.4–21

Ring oven technique is practical method for the analysis of nickel. The TLV for nickel is 0.001 ppm in air and in water it is 1 μg/m^3 but 0.1 μg/m^3 is optimum for atmosphere. The bag collection is best method for collection of nickel sampling from air. From water it is collected as its hydroxide. By the process of ion-exchange it can be removed from water. The reverse osmosis is used with advantage for the purpose of its isolation economically.

(h) Osmium and Platinum

The source of osmium is staining agent, organic synthesis osmium tetraoxide introduces–C–C–linkage; while platinum is used in thermocouples and as catalyst. Tetraoxide is volatile (m.p. <45 °C; b.p > 100°C), it causes irritation of eyes, halo around eyes and heaviness of eyelids and impairment of vision. It causes headache and bronchitis, pulmonary edema, while plantinum causes respiratory diseases, nasal irritation, asthma, dermatitis and eczema and photophobia. Osmium is determined spectrophotometrically with thiourea, while platinum is determined photometrically with p-dimethylaminobenzoyl rhodanine as chromogenic ligand. For AAS sensitivity is not good. It is below a concentration of 1.2 μg/ml. They are analysed at 295 and 495 nm for osmium and platinum respectively.

(i) Copper

Copper is used extensively in household utensils hence it is worth considering. It has good thermal and electrical conductivity. It is one of the metals which is used highest in alloys like brass, in manufacturing bronze, german silver and type metal. The gases from Beessemer convertor contain good amount of copper. The excess dose of copper causes fatal hemolytic anemia and hepatic necrosis. About 0.01 to 1.7 ppm of copper in water has deleterious effect on health. It is more toxic in ionic form. It causes fatty metamorphosis of liver, necrosis of kidney. It is used as base metal for silver. Jewellery effluents contains large amount of copper. It is determined by emission spectroscopy. NAA, AAS, ICP–AES and polarography are the best methods for analysis of copper.

However in reality, there are large number of methods for the analysis. If it is present in large amounts gravimetry with salicyldioxime is the best method. In relatively low concentration, volumetric iodimetric method is most suitable. For colorimetric analysis of copper we have several chromogenic ligands as α-benzonoxime (*i.e.,* cupron), anthranalic acid, semicarbazide, PAN. The atomic absorption spectroscopy is good at lower concentrations. The permissible level is 1 ppm for potable water and for soil it is 0.2 ppm. In waste water it should not be more than 0.5 ppm. The prescribed TLV is 1 mg/m^3 but it is practicable to have

0.2 mg/m^3. ESP is used for collection of copper dust from air. The bag house effects can be also used in copper refineries. The venturi scrubbers can be used for collection of small particle size of copper. The other methods are evaporatory recovery, the direct electrolytic refining of pure copper from industrial effluents. In destructive treatment it is treated with lime when hydroxide solubility increases at high pH perhaps due to the phenomena of the complexation. In the Table 5.17 good amount of copper is present in foodstuffs.

Table 5.17 Copper contents in food (μg/g)

Food	*Level*	*Food*	*Level*
Rice	2.60	Animal food	12.26
Maize	1.75	Wheat flour	9.26
Wheat	3.47	Maize flour	3.68
Gram	6.96	Gram flour	8.00
Gram dal	7.22		

This shows that wheat flour, animal feed and gram or gram flour contains large amount of copper. It is difficult to digest these products by human being when taken food.

Table 5.18 Copper level of waste water (mg/L) from industry

Industry/process	*Level*	*Process/Industry*	*Level*
Plating waste	20–120	Alkaline waste	0–1.0
Brass dip	4.4–8.5	Large plates	0–100
Copper mill	19–74	Silver plating	3–900
Metal process	204–370	Acid silver plating	30–590
Tube mill	74	Alkaline silver plating	3.2–19
Wire mill	988	Pickel path	40–23
Rolling mill	34	Machine bath	28–7.8
Appliance	0.5–11.0	Tube mill	5.2–4.1

From Table 5.18 it will be seen that highest copper level in waste water is from metal process, wire mills, silver plating baths has considerable amount (1000 mg/L) of copper while the acid pickle bath has also objectionable amount of copper. The alkaline waste relatively contains small amount of copper.

(j) Zinc

The main source of zinc is galvanisation industry and alloy industry. It causes chills, nausea, vomiting and metal fume fever, but patient recovers in 48 hours as a person can acquire some immunity on long exposure. Zinc chloride produces skin diseases. The oxide is bad for the lung. Good amount of zinc is lost from disposal of effluents from metal processing, plating, silica coatings and rayon industries. ESP impingers are used to collect zinc dust. The chromogenic ligands like zincon 1–(2 thiazolylazo) 2 napthol PAN, o-meocaptothenalaniline is used for the colorimetric analysis. From water it is analysed by AAS at 214 nm or fluorimetrically but photometry with dithizone is the best method. The TLV for zinc in water is 5 mg/L. The effluent should not contain more than 10 ppm of zinc. From air zinc dust can be collected by ESP, or by the venturi scrubbers or bag house filters. In rayon effluents the zinc can be recovered by ion-exchange. It is best method with minimum cost.

Table 5.19 Level of zinc in foodstuffs (mg/kg)

Food	*Zn*	*Food*	*Zn*
Beef	20–60	Milk	3.6
Milk (Processed)	4.0	Spinach	10
Fish	15	Onion	3.5
Wheat	18	Tomato	1.6
Vegetables	2	Potato	3.6
Rice	10	Cabbage	3.3
Maize	14	Peas	3.2
Gram	41	Rice	7.4
Animal food	35	Chicken meat	30.0
Wheat flour	16.8	White meat	10.0
Maize flour	17	Red meat	20.0
Bread	30	Pork and fish	25.0

The Table 5.19 shows that beef, chicken meat, gram, bread, fish contain considerable amount of zinc, while tomatoes has low contents of zinc.

Table 5.20 Level of zinc in air and water in different states of India(mg/l)

State	*Air*	*Water*	*State*	*Air*	*Water*
Andhra Pradesh	1.42	0.018	Kerala	0.081	0.073
Bihar	0.721	0.078	Punjab	1.471	0.177
Gujarat	0.310	0.056	Orissa	0.675	0.055
Himachal Pradesh	0.238	0.058	Rajasthan	0.217	0.056
Haryana	0.530	0.019	Utter Pradesh	0.388	0.091
Karnataka	0.75	–	West Bengal	0.821	0.076

Since Arsenic, Mercury, Lead and Cadmium are present in the major concentration in food, water, air, they are discussed separately in Chapter 6.

From the above Tables 5.19 and 5.20 we draw the inferences—that atmosphere in Punjab and Andhra Pradesh has significant amount of zinc while water in Punjab, U.P. and Bihar have remarkable level of zinc.

(k) Beryllium

The main source of pollution due to beryllium is emissions from fluoroescent lamp industry. It causes dermatitis and pneumoconiosis and poses respiratory disorder. Fine particles are more hazardous. It can cause lung problem for a person exposed even in radius of 1 to 2 km of the factory. It is determined by spectrophotometry with eriochrome cynine R.

It is determined fluorimetrically with morine (*i.e.*, pentahydroxy flavanol) or 8–hydroxyquinoline. It can be also determined by atomic absorption spectroscopy at 235 nm with nitrousoxide-acetylene flame with sensitivity of 0.016 μg/m^3. As small as 0.005 μg/m^3 is detected in air or tissue. Other effective chromogenic reagents for spectrophotometry of beryllium are p-nitrophenylazoresorcinol and chromoazurol–S.

Within the metals, the most toxic element is beryllium. The disease 'Beryllosis' is common in the workers working in flurosecent tube industry. The compounds produces conjunctivities and cancer but the latter effect is as yet no confirmed. It is sampled by high volume sampler from atmosphere. The TLV for metal is 25 μg/m^3. This limit was brought down to 2 μg/m^3 on animal experiments. WHO has prescribed limit of 0.002 μg/m^3 *i.e.*, 2 mg/m^3. Large number of control measures for its abatement are recommended however, the best method is to reduce its industrial applications and find out some substitute for use in industry.

(l) Indium

Indium is mainly used in alloys like solder (25%) in dental preparations semiconductors. (10%) transistors (25%) bearing (20%) lamps (10%) and research (10%). It is moderately toxic, causes intoxication and.degeneration of tissue and adverse effect on liver, heart, kidneys. The acidic food-stuff is favouring the absorption of indium in the body. The prolonged exposure causes tooth decay, pain in joints and bones, nervous and gastrointestinal disorders, heart pain and the general debility. Radioactive indium induces cancer. It gives vascular shade if injected in body within ten minutes. It is not toxic when used in semiconductors and lubricants.

It imparts blue colour to flame at 450 nm and is analysed by flame photometry. Alizarine and quinalazarine impart characteristic colour to complex which is colorimetically analysed but aluminium interferes. It is masked by fluoride. The common ions like zinc, iron, cobalt, nickel are masked by complexation with alkali cyanide 0.01 to 1 mg/ml of indium is analysed by this method. Gravimetrically, it can be analysed as trioxide after ignition of trihydroxide to oxide. It is complexed with 8-hydroxyquinoline and directly weighed in gravimetric method as its oxinate complex.

The TLV for indium is 100 μg/m^3. In the sample of water it is removed by precipitation as it forms insoluble hydroxide.

(m) Thallium

The main source of pollution is pesticide and cosmetic industry. It is largely used as the depilatory agent. It causes chronic poisoning. It is extracted in amylacetate and is determined spectrophotometrically with methyl violet as chromogenic ligand. It is also analysed polarographically. AAS is not very useful for thallium analysis because the sensitivity and working range are poor for this metals.

(n) Antimony

The main source is safety match industry, drug and alloy industry. It causes violent and continuous vomiting, profuse diarrhea, muscle weakness and damage to kidney and liver. The fatty degeneration of spleen and liver is accelerated by its compounds. The sulphide is main component used in safety match. It causes loss of appetite. It affects the heart, it causes myocardial infraction; the metal is more dangerous than its compounds. It is used in fireworks. Stibine dissolves readily in gastro-intestinal track, and causes damage of liver. It is determined spectrophotometrically at 565 mm, with rhodamine B as the chromogenic ligand. A concentration of 0.2 mg/ml of antimony can be detected. It is determined by AAS at 218 nm in air-acetylene flame, with limits of 10 to 40 μg/ml with hydride generator.

The potassium antimonyl tartarate is used in drug as emetic and the treatment of tropical diseases. Gallin is another chromogenic ligand which is used for the analysis. Malachite and brilliant green are also popular reagents for analysis. The TLV is 0.005 ppm (mg/L) in air and 0.05 ppm in water. Few compounds are hazards. Seafood contains good amount of antimony. It is controlled by precipitation as its sulphide.

(o) Tin

It is not very toxic. It is extensively used in food and canning industries. It is used in packing and plating of sheet to prevent corrosion although it is anodic to metal which is to be coated. Inorganic tin is harmful. Dust containing tin can get ingested in the lungs. Organic tin is also toxic in relation to the inorganic tin. Tributyl tin compound is highly caustic in nature. It affects skin of lower abdomen, thigh and groin of exposed workers. It causes mild headache, nausea and visual disturbances. In 1967, in Kuwait people were poisoned by drinking juice stored in tin container (~ 400 ppm was consumed per person). Diethyltindiodine is used in medium but it proved to be very harmful. Symptoms are vomiting, headache, vertigo, abdominal pain and retention of urine. It leads to cardiac or the respiratory failure. Milk stored in container coated with tin can disolve 40 ppm of tin in about six months.The atomic emission spectroscopy is best method for its detection. With hydrogen peroxide in sulphuric acid it forms yellow coloured complex which is photometrically measured. The TLV for tin is 2 mg/m^3 for inorganic tin and 0.1 mg/m^3 for the organic tin. The oxide is tolerated in high dosage of 10 mg/M^3. In water it is removed by precipitation as the hydroxide. Such oxides can be disposed by land filling. It is the most effective method of control of excess of tin or its compounds.

(p) Selenium and Tellurium

The source for both is glass and photocell industry, while source for tellurium is auto-exhaust emission, as Hexaethyltellurium [$(C_2H_5)_6$ Te] is used to combat the ill-effect of residual lead from antiknocking action. Selenium compounds are irritating and toxic. The oxide causes bronchitis, dyspnea, rales, wheezing, headache, sleeplessness, nervous and cardiac disorders, loss of appetite, H_2Se

(less than 3 ppm) causes damage to liver and spleen; $SeOCl_2$, SeO_2, H_2Se are all harmful. Tellurium is more toxic, it causes fatal intoxication, epigastric distress, metallic taste, and bad odour to breath and sweat (infact it is a good symptom to know its toxicity). The blue sol is reduced by $SnCl_2$ and is measured directly by nephelometer. It is also extracted in n-amylalcohol and analysed by spectrophotometer. AAS need air-hydrogen flame for selenium or air-acetylene flame for tellurium. They are measured at 196 and 214 nm respectively, with sensitivity of 0.47 and 0.26 μg/ml, respectively.

The soluble selenium compounds are very toxic. They cause gastrointestinal disturbances. Sneezing, garlic taste to mouth and nose bleeding called **catarrh** occurs on breathing. Dermatitis is caused by oxide, while H_2 Se causes oilfactory fatigue. Finger nails get affected and in women it causes irregular menses. From glass manufacturing unit some selenium volatilises in air and fouls atmosphere. In xeroxing or photocopying, prolonged exposure in close room is very dangerous to the health. The exhaust from reverberatory furnace contain selenium compounds. Liquid impingers can be used for collection. On account of the presence of organic matter non-destructive methods of analysis is preferred *viz.*, neutron activatism analysis. Diamines are used for photometric analysis. Thiourea, diphenyl hydrazine, 2-3 diaminonapthalene and pyrrol or 3-3′ diaminobenzaline are used in photometric analysis. In range of 0.1 to 0.5 mg Se, diaminobenzidine method is ideal. The standard TLV for selenium is 0.2 mg/m^3 for metal and 0.05 mg/m^3 for compounds like H_2Se or SeF_6. Since many compounds are warm compounds cooling before sampling is necessary ESP method is not suitable. From water it is removed by precipitation or by ion-exchange method.

5.8 TOXIC GAS AND NONMETAL POLLUTANTS

Amongst nonmetals, we have boron, carbon, nitrogen, phosphorus, oxygen, sulphur and halogen compounds, which are toxic in nature and invariably cause atmospheric pollution. They are listed in Table 5.21.

Table 5.21 TLV of gaseous pollutants in atmosphere

S. No.	*Pollutants*	*Formula*	*ppm*	*Concentration (1×10^5) mg/m^3*
1.	Carbon monoxide	CO	50	0.55
2.	Phosgene	$COCl_2$	0.1	0.004
3.	Ammonia	NH_3	50	0.0003
4.	Nitrogen dioxide	NO_2	5	0.09
5.	Phosphine	PH_3	0.3	0.004
6.	Ozone	O_3	0.1	0.002
7.	Sulphur dioxide	SO_2	5	0.13
8.	Fluorine	F	0.1	0.00
9.	Chlorine	Cl	1	–
10.	Bromine	Br	0.1	0.007
11.	Hydrogen sulphide	H_2S	10	0.15

5.9 ORGANOMETALLIC COMPOUNDS

Those of the organometallic compounds involving arsenic, mercury and lead are environmentally important. Several organometallic compounds are used as catalyst, semiconductors, but are not toxic. They have mild organic behaviour if ingested in body. Amongst them $Pb(C_2H_5)_4$ is colourless oily liquid which is used as the antiknock in gasoline. They affect lipids and enter through skin in body, and thus affect central nervous system causing fatigue, weakness, restlessness, atoxia, psyonosis and convulsions. It proved fatal even with two days of exposure. In the organotin compounds tributyl tin is used as the bactericide. It causes skin rash. It affect mitochondria function by readily combining with sulphur. Metal carbonyls like $Ni(CO)_4$ are hazardous, $Co(CO)_4$ is also bad $Fe(CO)_5$ is injurious. They are all volatile. Diethyl zinc $Zn(C_2H_5)_2$ on combustion produces oxide which on exposure cause zinc metal fume fever and chills.

5.10 TOXIC INORGANIC COMPOUNDS

The compounds of the heavy metals are toxic. The information on the toxicological chemistry of various toxic substances is listed in documents entitled toxicological profiles published by Americax health authorities. A CD rom of these compounds is also available. Apart from metals in inorganic chemicals several of the compounds of the nonmetallic elements are toxic and hazardous to the health. The principal nonmetal are, oxygen, carbon, nitrogen, sulphur and halogens. Inorganic compounds of silicon like SiO_2 are also hazardous. They cause silicosis. Silanes are not considered to be toxic. Silicon halides and hydrohalides have bad odour and cause irritation to the eyes and lung. Asbestos is a fibrous silicate mineral $[Mg_3(Si_2O_5)(OH)_4]$ which is very good heat insulating material but its inhalation causes pneumonia, mesothelioma tumor in chest cavity near lungs and cancer of the lung. Therefore, its use must be restricted. Toxic compounds are discussed in subsequent sections.

(a) Inorganic boron Compounds

Boric acid is a dressing material. It is less toxic in comparison with various hydrides like di and tri borane. Of this diboron is a respiratory irritant and a nerve poison. It is estimated by nonaqueous conductiometric titration with manitol, or by spectrophotometry with crimson red as chromogenic ligand.

(b) Inorganic Carbon Compounds

Amongst these CO, CO_2 are environmental pollutants comparatively CO is more harmful. It is colourless, odourless and tasteless gas detected in tube as $I_2O_5 + CO \rightarrow CO_2 + I_2$ (violet vapour). Other methods of detection are $HgO + CO \rightarrow Hg$ (luster) $+ CO_2$, $PdCl_2 + CO \rightarrow COCl_2 + Pd$ (luster). It readily reacts with haemoglobin of blood to form methaemoglobin, which causes coagulation of blood, then asphyxiation and death. CO is formed by incomplete combustion. It causes headache, dizziness, nausea, impaired brain function, weakness and death. In blood it is tested with pyrotannic acid. Carbon dioxide is not a pollutant in the real sense but its excess amounts in air causes rapid breathing and headache.

The CO is generated due to incomplete combustion of fuels and from burning of petrol. Power plants generates monoxide. Cigarette smoke contains 4% carbon monoxide. It is readily absorbed in lungs to react with the haemoglobin in blood to generate obvinoxous methaemoglobin. The carboxy haemoglobin is very stable product. The high level in the ambient air is extremely injurious to health. The biological effects were investigated 20% saturation causes poisoning. The psychomotor function is impaired. It leads to cardiovascular problems.

(c) Inorganic Nitrogen

NH_3, NH_2-NH_2, NO-NO*x* and MCN are the main pollutants compounds of nitrogen. Ammonia causes irritation of nose, throat and eyes. A concentration greater than 50 ppm is not tolerable. Hydrazine (NH_2-NH_2) which is used as the rocket propellant causes damage to the liver and kidney. It causes skin trouble. It is determined spectrophotometrically with p-dimethylaminobenzaldehyde. NO-NO_x contains oxides in form of several gases like NO, NO_2, N_2O_3, N_2O_4 and N_2O_5, of which NO-NO_2 are more toxic. They irritate the eyes, cause problems with lower respiratory passage, vertigo, vomiting, asphyxiation, inhibit enzyme activity in the body. The metal cyanide (MCN) are deadly poisonous (limit 100 ppm is fatal).

The oxides of nitrogen are more toxic than other nitrogen nonoxy compounds. NO, NO_2 have adverse effects on health. The source is IC-engines and photochemical smog with rise of ozone level. The oxides of nitrogen mainly causes respiratory problems specially of lower respiratory passage. NO_2 is toxic to animals also. The symptoms are similar to the ozone exposure. The pulmonary edema and similar symptoms are encountered after breathing.

(d) Phosphorus Compounds

White phosphorus causes anaemia, gastrointestinal dysfunction, bone brittleness and eye damage "Phossy Jaws' is a disease caused by excessive exposure which deteriorates jaw bone and it is fractured. Toxicologically, important compounds in this group are PH_3, P_4O_6, P_4O_{10} and metal phosphides. They are used as rodenticides and pesticides. Organophosphorus compounds are toxic. They cause necrosis and phossy jaw for workers, specially working in the match industry with exposure to white or red phosphorus. PH_3 is toxic gas causes diarrhoea, nausea, tightness of chest and epigastric pain. It is used for fumigation of wheat and corn. It is colourless gas, undergoes auto ignition at 100°C. It is potent hazard in the laboratory. Pulmonary tract irritation and depression of central nervous system is noted on exposure to PH_3. P_4O_{10} is corrosive irritant to skin, eyes and mucous membrane PX_3 and PX_5 the halides of phosphorus are strong irritants to eyes. Phosphorus oxihalide ($POCl_3$) is strong irritant to eye, skin and mucous membrane. Fortunately, they are not extensively used in the industry.

(e) Inorganic Compound belonging to Oxygen Groups

The ozone is generated by photochemical reaction in the stratosphere. Other products of the reaction are peroxyacyl nitrate. The high level of oxidant is indication of gross pollution in the atmosphere. They show mutogenic effects and affect tissues. Eye, nose and throat get irritated. However, upto level of 500 $\mu g/m^3$, no adverse effect is noted. Lungs gets affected (400 – 1400 $\mu g/m^3$) by ozone. The athletic performance in sports gets affected with exposure to these pollutants. (> 200 $\mu g/m^3$). Its exposure leads to pulmonary macrophages reduction. It is not clear whether ozone is tolerated at same level by human beings. It definitely causes pulmonary edema, cause lipid peroxidation in high dosage. High pressure oxygen or pure oxygen is harmful, but not diluted oxygen, with inert gas or nitrogen, as it exists in the environment. Ozone formed by silent electric discharge in air, is toxic, oxygen by interaction with UV radiation or during welding of high voltage electric discharge produces ozone.

(f) Inorganic Sulphur Compounds

Amongst sulphur compounds, sulphur dioxide and hydrogen sulphide are harmful. More than 10 ppm of oxide causes health hazards while H_2S is an odourous gas which can paralyse respiratory tract, cause conjuctivitis and eye irritation. A dose more than 500 to 1000 ppm is fatal for animals; 10 to 20 ppm of it causes eye trouble called *keratitis*. Mild dose of it causes headache, dizziness, and malfunctioning of central nervous system.

The other toxic compounds of sulphur are S_2F_2, SF_4, SF_6, S_2Cl_2, SCl_4, SO_3, SO_2Cl_2, COS and CS_2. Halo compounds of sulphur are as toxic as their acids. Thioxyhalides are corrosive, toxic and irritating liquids. Amongst oxides like SO_2 which is more toxic. The source is combustion of coal containing 1 to 5% of sulphur. The residual oil from petroleum product contains 1 to 6% of sulphur. SO_2 in stack is inversely proportional to square of the height of chimney, and SO_2 occurs at greater distance from the point of release. It emits out from stack of height of 100 to 200 feet. The release occurs at height of 1000 to 1500 feet. SO_2 has bad effect on health. The lungs gets congested. At the best 5 ppm can be tolerated by healthy human beings. It affects upper respiratory track or bronchial passage. Dust contaminated with SO_2 has ill effects on lower respiratory passage *i.e.,* bronchoconstriction. In 1952, in London fog, the senior citizen is suffered heavily due to high level of SO_2 in air. This led to enactment of clean air act in England. About 3500 to 4000 person died due to gas poisoning of lungs. Sunlight dilutes its level in air. Amongst the atmospheric pollutants the pollutant which is more commonly monitored is SO_2 due to availability of simple methods of analysis. During heat waves level of SO_2 in air increases considerably high. The bad smokers suffer from cancer, emphysema and bronchitis. CO_2 and SO_2 affect cardiorespiratory system. The space heating produces SO_2 as well as NO_2. To control SO_2 from air, desulphurised fuel should be only used. The use of tall stacks can dilute pollutant in upper atmosphere. To control SO_2 pollution one can use Venturi scrubbers to dissolve SO_2 in fine stream of water to form sulphurous and sulphuric acid which in turn can be treated before final disposal. If one can recover sulphur in the form of H_2SO_4, $(NH_4)_2SO_4$, $CaSO_4$ it will be economics for reuse. The desulphurisation of coal or oil is quite expensive proposition. At that value even diesel oil which is so freely used for heavy vehicle movement must be first desulpherised in order to maintain the atmosphere clean and free of sulphur.

(g) Inorganic Halogen Compounds

Most of them have toxic effects on health. The famous experiment of Moseley's during synthesis of fluorine caused irrepairable damage of tissues. The incurable wounds are natorious. Calcium gluconate injection is the best antidote. Chlorine gas causes burning of eyes, cough, substernal pain and respiratory distress. In tube railway in England, several persons fainted due to leakage of chlorine in duct. A concentration of ClO_2 is less than 0.1 ppm which is not harmful, a greater dosage causes bubling in chest *i.e.,* Rales. Bromine is corrosive but less toxic. Iodine in true sense is not toxic. Phosgene ($COCl_2$) a gas used in biological warfare, causes pulmonary edema. Methylene chloride formed by burning of kerosene is bad for health. Many compounds containing halogens are toxic.

Fluorine containing compounds are most dangerous within the various halogens. They cause fluorosis. The fluorides occur in water, soil, and dust. The fluoride ion is physiologically very active. Aluminum plants emit out fluoride in atmosphere. Fluoride readily gets absorbed and accumulated in body, specially of children. The intake in man increases with age of the person. Persons with lung and kidney problems is readily affected by fluoride poisoning. There is increase in the erythrocytes in blood. It gets accumulated in nails, hair and urine. However, small dose of fluoride helps dental health, but high dose increases collagen formation. Aorlic calification is decreased in residents of fluoride factory. A town named Manduser in Madhya Pradesh has high level of fluoride in water.

Amongst acids of halogens HF and HCl are bad for health. On contact with HF on skin causes ulcer and lesions. They are incurable and lead to gangrene. The gaseous hydrogen chloride is less toxic. In stomach very dilute solution of acid is present. The inhalation of acid vapour causes spasms of larynx and lead to put accumulation fluid inside the lung. It has greater affinity for water and in this process it gets diluted and rendered harmless to tender skin. Within interhalogen compounds ClF, BrCl and BrF_3 readily reacts with water to give corresponding acids. They are corrosive invariably dehydrate tissue, skin, mouth, throat, the mucous membrane is affected by them. Within haloxides OF_2, Cl_2O, ClO_2, Cl_2O_2 and Br_2O are harmful and reactive. ClO_2 when reacted with water produces trihalogens which are injurious to health. Amongst haloxy acids HOCl is most reactive it readily reacts with eyes, tissues, skin to produce acid and free O_2.

5.11 TOXIC ORGANIC COMPOUNDS AND PESTICIDES

Several organic compounds are toxic. Second hazardous substances like DDT and pesticides; polychlorinated biphenyls (PCB). The organic chemicals industry in spite of its phenomenal growth is associated with problem of occupational health. PCB and DDT are halogenated hydrocarbons and carbon tetrachloride is another injurious product, causing liver injury. Freon (CCl_3 F Freon-11) and CCl_2F_2 (Freon 12) a refrigerant is responsible for causing depletion of ozone in air and ozone hole in the atmosphere. They lead to transmission of harmful ultraviolet radiation to the earth. Apart from DDT, aldrin, dieldrin, endrin, heptachlor and chlorodane are all injurious pesticides. The worst finding was in 1950 it was discovered that they cause cancer to mammals. From 1939 to 1950 farmers used it indiscriminately as effective and powerful pesticides but since 1960 a red alert was given by WHO all over world about its toxicity. This was first announced in book entitled "silent spring". The DDT contents of human tissue varied from 5 to 8 ppm. The polychlorinated biphenyl *i.e.,* PCB is injurious chemical. This is used to provide noninflammable insulation to electrical instruments. It is sold as "Halowax". The chlorinated napthalenes are highly toxic. PCB is used as the dielectric spacer in sealed equipments or as plasticizers in paints industry. In Japan, PCB contaminated rice gave signal to give skin complaints called "Yasho disease," PCB has hundreds of isomers. In 1972, in America, EPA banned use of PCB in certain preparations having human consumption.

Most of the organic compounds have adverse effect on central nervous system. It is difficult to consider their toxicity in terms of individual compound. It is better to consider them in groups, on the basis of (*a*) compounds containing carbon and hydrogen, (*b*) compounds containing carbon, hydrogen, oxygen, (*c*) compounds containing carbon, hydrogen, nitrogen and finally, (*d*) compounds containing carbon, hydrogen, sulphur and phosphorus.

(a) Hydrocarbons and their Derivatives

Table 5.22 lists all hydrocarbons. They have narcotic effect on human system. Butadiene, isoprene affects bone marrow. Benzene causes respiratory disorder and narcosis. It causes blood dyscrasia and blood anaemia. It is usually determined spectrophotometrically at 244, 249, 255 or 261 nm, as its dinitro derivative. Toluene (C_6H_5—CH_3) in comparison to benzene is less toxic. It causes lymphocytosis. It has bad effect, if the dose exceeds 200 ppm. It causes drowsiness, mild headache, impaired coordination. Fortunately, it cannot penetrate through the skin. It is excreted through urine as hippuric acid. It's dinitroderivative is determined spectrophotometrically at 530 nm. Amongst aromatic hydrocarbons xylene (C_6H_4 $(CH_3)_2$) has least toxicity. A high dose produces liver and kidney damage and hyperplasia of bone marrow. It is a narcotic. Ethylbenzene $(C_2H_5)C_6H_5$ is a substitute for antiknock for aviation fuel. It causes irritation of eyes and skin. Terpentine is a mixture of hydrocarbons, a universal solvent which can cause lung irritation and paralysis of central nervous system. Terpentine a common solvent must be carefully handled.

Chloroform ($CHCl_3$) was a classical anaesthetic agent in surgery, but is not used nowadays as it affects heart and causes cardiac sensitization. Carbon tetrachloride (CCl_4) is harmful, as it has depressing action on central nervous system, it causes gastrointestinal disturbance and causes liver, kidney and lungs problems. It leads to loss of appetite, vomiting. Tetrachloroethylene is a substituent for CCl_4 for the purpose of dry cleaning. Freon (CCl_2F_2) is a gas which is used extensively for filling compressor in refrigerators. It affects the lung. Methyl (CH_3Cl) chloride is a substitute refrigerant, which also causes symptoms of drunkenness and inebriation; pulmonary congestion, cardiac failure.

The gases like methane, ethane, propane, butane are considered as the asphyxiants. The liquid hydrocarbons lead to dermatitis. Hexane and cyclohexane cause polyneuropathy *i.e.*, muscle weakness. Ethylene is phototoxic propylene is also neutrotoxic compound. Acetylene is narcotic gives headache. In body benzene gets converted to phenol leading to bone marrow damage. Benzene lowers the white cells in blood and prevents clotting of blood. Napthalene exposure leads to anaemia and lowering of red cells in blood or failure of kidney. Other polyaromatic hydrocarbons are also risky. Threshold limiting values of hydrocarbons are listed in Table 5.22.

Table 5.22 Toxic level of hydrocarbons

Hydrocarbon	*ppm*	*1 × 10*^{5}µg/m^3
Benzene	25	0.8
Butadiene	1000	2.2
Cumene	50	2.45
Cyclopentadiene	75	2.0
Styrene	100	4.2
Toluene	200	7.5
Xylene	100	4.35
Hexane	500	18.0
Heptane	500	20.0
Octane	500	23.5
Cyclohexane	300	10.5

(b) Compounds Containing Carbon, Hydrogen and Oxygen

The commonly used compounds are listed in Table 5.22. Methanol (CH_3OH) causes blindness, diminution of vision, and enlargement of liver. The country wine mainly contains methanol. It is analysed spectrophotometrically with chromotropic acid. Ethanol causes inebriation and temporary drowsiness and affects liver. n-Butanol irritates eyes and causes corneal inflammation. Acetone (CH_3COCH_3) is narcotic in nature and it causes irritation of mucous membrane. MEK, MBK, MIBK are less toxic, with minor problems like throat irritation, nausea, headache. Mesityl-oxide (4-methyl-3-pentane-2-one) is an efficient extractant for metal separations, but it is toxic if present in concentration more than 12 ppm. It irritates eyes, lung, and throat. A concentration of 25 ppm causes discomfort to lungs and kidneys, the dioxane and tetrahydrofuran (THF) are not truly toxic.

The unsaturated hydrocarbon like ethylene and propylene are also toxic and are mutogenic and carcinogenic to animals. They cause cynosis, pulmonary edema, kidney failure. 1, 2, 3, 4 butadiene is also confirmed as the carcinogenic compound.

The methanol toxicity causes deterioration of optical nerve and affects the retinal ganglion cells of eyes causing blindness. Ethanol (0.5%) causes cirrhosis of lever. Ethylene glycol *i.e.,* (CH_2OH-CH_2-OH) is used as the coolant in car. It causes edemia and affects kidney. Nitrophenols are harmful as they are protoplasmic poison and on inhalation within thirty minutes proves fatal. The spleen, pancreas and kidney are affected by it—cresol, napthol, napthophenol and pentachloro phenol are also toxic in nature > C=O *i.e.,* carbonyl group containing compounds such as aldehydes and ketones *e.g.,* formaldehyde, acetaldehyde, acetone, MEK and acrolein. Formaldehyde is toxic (Formulin 35-70%). It causes persensivity. It is lung carcinogen due to formation of formic acid. Acetaldehyde is less toxic than acrolein. Latter has choking odour. The ketones are less toxic with pleasant smell, but high dosage promotes skin irritation. MEK causes neuropathic disorders. The acids *viz* formic or acetic acids are corrosive and affects esophageal tissue. The ethers like methylether or ethylether have low toxicity. They are used as the mild anaesthetic agents to paralyse central nervous system in medicine. The acid anhydride like acetic anhydride is systematic poison. It is corrosive and affects upper respiratory track. Many esters like methylacetate, vinylacetate, di(ethylhexyl)phathalan and allylacetate are volatile but when passed through pulmonary system cause major problems. They hydrolyse in water. Many esters are asphyxiant and narcotic in action. Allylacetate is not toxic. DEHP is used as plasticizer in polymer which is common contaminant in water. It is used in medicine

Table 5.23 Threshold limit values of some organic solvents

Compound	*Concentration*	
	ppm	*1 × 10⁵* $\mu g/m^3$
Acetic acid	10	0.25
Amyl acetate	100	5.25
Cresol	5	0.22
Dioxane	100	3.6
Formaldehyde	5	0.08
Formic acid	5	0.9
Phenol	5	0.19
Tetrahydrofuran	200	5.9
Terpentine	100	5.6
Butyl alcohol	100	3.0
Iso amylalcohol	100	3.6
Ethyl acetate	400	14.0
Butyl acetate	150	7.1
Diethylether	400	12.0
Mesityl oxide	25	1.0

to fill bags with medicine in interavenous injection. Excess dose of DEHP causes blood haemophilias effect and kidney failure.

(c) Organonitro Compounds

This constitutes a large group of compounds comprising of trimethylamine, ethylenediamine, pyridine, aniline, 2-napthylamine, acrylonitrile, benzidine and nitrobenzene (Table 5.24). Lower amines are rapidly taken up by body. They cause necrosis of liver and kidneys. Lung problems and oedema. Ethylenediamine damages eye tissues. The carbocylic aromatic amines like aniline, α-napthylamine, benzidine are all carcinogenic. They convert Fe(II) to Fe(III) *i.e.* methaemoglobinemia in haemoglobin of blood leading to cynosis. Benzidine causes haemolysis bone marrow depression kidney and liver damage. Pyridine has offensive odour but is luckily less toxic. It causes mental depression. Nitrites contain $\rangle C{=}N$ group *e.g.*, acetonitrile is reactive and readily absorbed through skin. Nitrocompounds *e.g.*, nitromethane and nitrobenzene both are liquids which cause anorexia, nausea vomiting renal failure. Nitrosamines are highly dangerous. They contain —N=O. They cause cancer, liver damage and kidney trouble dimethyl nitrosoamine is hazardous. Isocyanate specially methyl isocyanate (MIC) had caused disaster in Bhopal in 1984 killing thousands of persons. It causes shortness of breath and lung damage, nausea and body pain.

(d) Organophosphorus Compounds

They have varying degree of toxicity. Organophosphate esters *e.g.*, trimethyl phosphate, paraoxon, tetraethyl pyrophosphate, triocrylphosphate damage nerves, degradation of neutrons, vomiting and diarrhoea leading to partial paralysis. Tetraethyl pyrophosphate is deadly toxic for man. The organophosphorus compounds containing sulphur such as the phosphorothionate and phosphorodithionate ester used as the insectiside are very dangerous. They arrest nonezymatic hydrolysis due to > P=O group with P=S group. The pesticide malathion or parathion are important members of this class of compounds. Sarin a powerful military poisonous gas, is the systemic poison of central nervous system (0.01 mg/kg is fatal dose).

(e) Organosulphur Compounds

Most harmful compound is CS_2. It causes hysteria, mental fatigue, reacts with amino acids and show problems in the body to form chelates of heavy metals. Organosulphur compounds are relatively less toxic in spite of offensive smell. Alkylthiols (*e.g.* CH_3—SH) cause nausea and headache, cold hands, feet and cynosis. They are percursors to cytochrome oxidase poison (CH_3—HSO_4) or the dimethyl sulphate is skin irritants and is carcinogenic. It causes conjunctivitis and swelling of respiratory membrane. It affects kidney, liver, lungs and cause cloudiness of cornea in eyes if exposured for long time. The sulphur mustards are compounds used in millitary *e.g.*, bi (2-chloro-ethyl) sulphide is mutogenic and causes blisters on body. It readily penentrate in skin and causes damage.

(f) Organohalide Compounds

CCl_4 is toxic solvent, it causes depression of the central nervous system. In 1970, food and drug authorities banned its use in America. It affect liver, kidney, and gastrointestinal tract.

Table 5.24 Threshold limiting value of organonitro, organosulpho and organophosphosphates.

Compound	*Concentration*	
	ppm	*1× 10^5 μg/m³*
Acetonitrile	40	0.7
Acrolein	0.1	0.002
Aniline	5	0.19
Hydrazine	1	0.013
Methylamine	10	0.12
Toluidine	5	0.22
Trinitrotoluene	–	0.015
Dinitrobenzene	–	0.01

The CCl_4 mechanism of toxicity involves electron transfer reaction in radical species. Lipid per oxidation in liver causes problems. The alkylhalides like vinyl chloride and tetrachloroethane are extensively used and indiscrimantely disposed in the environment. Nervous system, hepatic and renal problems are caused by them. They are carcinogenic also. The cis isomer is less toxic however trans form causes gastrointestinal problems, tremors, cramps and nausea. It causes liver cancer. Arylhalides cause respiratory disorders, cynosis. p-dichlorobenzene is used as freshner and mothballs but is confirmed carcinogenic compound. They cause rhinitis, nausea, jaundice, liver cirrhosis, weightloss, anorexia. It is used in electrical equipment as hydraulic fluids but it is readily dispersed in an environment causing harm. PCB belongs to this class of compounds. Most of the organo halide pesticides like 2.4 T, 2 4.5 T, TCDD have been discussed under pesticides on Chapter. DDT is important member of this group.

5.12 ENVIRONMENTAL CARCINOGENS

Cancer is a disease which can attack almost all tissues of the body. These cells proliferate without any control. Carcinoma commence in epithelial tissues, sarcoma develops in liver, leukemia is cancer of blood, but lung, intestine and breast cancer are most prevalent. Some chemicals cause cancer but cancer can be prevented if detected early. The effects caused by environmental factors are known at very late stage. Tobacco and panmasala chewing and smoking causes cancer of lung, mouth, bladder, kidney, liver, stomach. Heavy drinkers of alcohol also suffer from cancer of pharynx and mouth. Tannic acid is a harmful chemical. Nitrosoamines obtained from smoked food are toxic. Benzopyrene is generated by incomplete combustion of coal or coke. It causes scrotal cancer. Air pollution can produce lung cancer. POM *i.e.*, polycylic organic matter is carcinogenic. The over exposure to the

X-rays promotes cancer of lungs, bone, benzidine β napthylamine all are carcinogenic compounds. Asbestos exposure causes cancer. The excessive use of fertilisers, food preservatives, drying agents are very injurious in food chain. There is no safe dose of chemicals beyond which it causes cancer. A human diet contains a great variety of mutogens and carcinogens. Mutagen damages DNA and starts degeneration of cell. Some drugs are also dangerous *e.g.,* one preventing abortion *viz,* diethylbestrol causes vaginal cancer in girls. The list of thirtysix chemicals associated with cancer induction in human are known. The significant chemicals which are in day to day used are listed in Table 5.23. The carcinogenic compounds are alfatoxin; asbestos; benzene, benzidine, beryllium compounds, chloromethyl ether; cadmium compounds, carbon tetrachloride, chromium compounds, dimethyl sulphate, ethylenoxide, irondextran, mustard gas, isopropyl alcohol, β-napthylamine, nickel compounds, phenacetis, polychlorinated biphenols, vinyl chloride. They also cause cancer. Arsenic compounds are dangerous. The chemotherapeutic agents work by killing cancer cells (few normal cells are sometimes killed also) by radiation. It causes nausea, vomiting and hairloss.

Some attempts were made to observe few points for the prevention of cancer. They are to use nutritionally balanced food; eat variety of food, avoid fat and alcohol; with no smoking; intake of vitamins, take fibrous food; do not eat salty food or drink hot liquids, avoid charred food or one with fungal infection. Avoid exposure to strong sunlight, take good exercise and keep body clean.

(a) Tetratogenesis (Mutagenesis in Compounds)

The tetratogens are chemical species that cause birth defects arising out of damage to embryonic cells. The mutations also cause birth defects. They cause enzyme inhibiton by xenobiotics, interfere with energy supply. While mutagenesis alter DNA to produce inheritable traits. It is natural process and is harmful. It causes birth defects change in nitrogenous basis of DNA decides nature of RNA, inhibiting enzyme formation *e.g.* HNO_2 is mutigenic in nature. Alkylation of DNA causes mutogenesis. Dimethylnitrosoamine, 3, 5 dimethyl-phenyl triazine, 1, 2 dimethyl hydrazine are mutogenic compounds. Carcinogenic compounds are one like nitrosoamines and polycyclic aromatic hydrocarbons (PAH) biological agents like hepadna or retroviruses or ionising radiation or selective breeding. The synthetic and naturally occurring chemicals also cause cancer. Xenobiotic produce chemical carcinogenes. Chimney sweepers, dye manufacturers, tobacco processor are affected by severe cancer.

Cancer has two stages *viz* initial stage and promotional stage. First stage starts with reaction of DNA by epigentic carcinogen. The latter are promoters and show increase in number of tumor cells. The compounds like benzopyrene, vinyl chloride require bioactivation while ethylenediamine dimethylsulphate do not require bioactivation. For few immune system acts a body's natural defense system to protect it from xenobiotic chemicals. Hypersensitivity is caused due to excessive action of immune system. PAH are confirmed exoestrongens compounds like Be, Cr, Ni, formaldehyde are xenobiotic promoting carcinogenicity.

(b) Polycyclic Aromatic Hydrocarbons (PAHs)

In 1930, in London the Chimney sweepers showed cancer of scortum due to the presence of PAH in soot deposits of chimney. PAH contains two or more fused six membered carbon atom aromatic rings *e.g.*, napthalene, benzopyrene. They have low water solubility. They are produced by combustion. PAH has number of benzene rings. Corone (VIII) is PAH with large molecular weight. PAH are also composed of five membered ring compounds like acenapthalene.

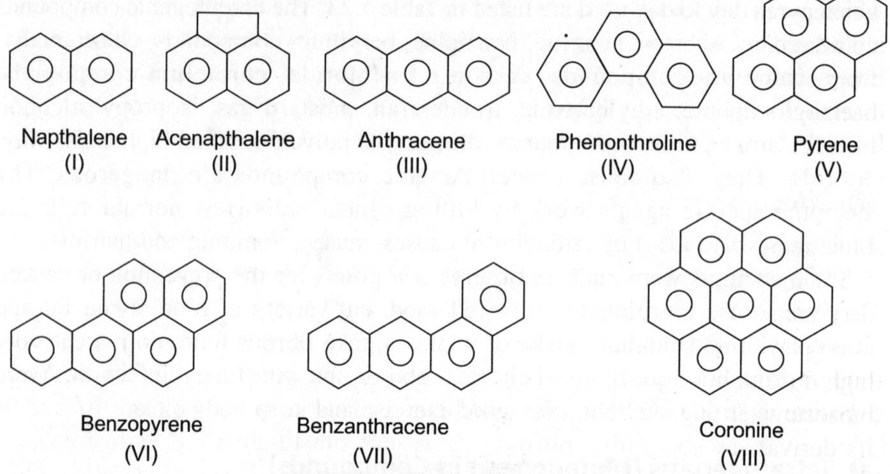

Fig. 5.1 Heterocyclic compounds

Most of them are solid with increase in m.p°C with mol. weight. They have low vapour pressure. They are formed in environment which is oxygen deficient. At high temperature less alkyl substituted PAHs or formed.

(c) Source of PAHs in Environment

Forest fires, volcanoes are main sources. The other is anthropogenic source like power plant, and autoexhaust emission.

Table 5.25 Source of Benzo(a) pyrene ($\mu g/m^3$)

Source	*Thermal power plant*	*Town incinerator*	*Open air combustion*	*Autoexhaust emission*	*Tobacco combustion*
Level	30-930	17-2700	2800-173,000	25-700	0.8-2.0

From Table 5.25 it will be seen that Tobacco consumption is very injurious to health.

(d) Occurrence in Environment

The carcinogen PAHs are present in environment (Table 5.26) in large concentration. They have six membered aromatic rings. They have strong UV-visible absorption spectra. Chemical photolytic or metabolic process degrades them in air. In water the chlorination degrades them. In presence of oxygen sample in sunlights they degrade with low half-life (less than 1 hr). The persistance of PAH is proportional to its size. In clear water, their presence is less but in sediments it is abundant (*e.g.*, BaP in water is 0.034 while in sediments 200 to 300 μg half-life).

(e) Toxicity of PAHs

All of these compounds are prone to produce cancer. Benzoanthracene and benzopyrene are deadly carcinogenic in nature. Xenobiotic lipophilic compounds converted by enzyme to polar water soluble products like mixed function oxidase from cytochrome P_{450}-group. PAHs get converted to dihydrosol epoxides to bind haemoglobin and DNA. The reaction proceeds very slowly and over long period of time. Solar radiation increases the toxicity of PAH compounds.

(f) Effects on PAH on Health

Mutogenic and carcinogenic effects are predominant in PAHs. Benzopyrene (Table 5.27) induce chromosome aberrations or cause epidermal hyperplasia and neoplasia. PAHs occurs in soil, air and biota. PAH are lipophilic. PAHs persist in atmosphere for longtime. Graphite is the ultimate product of PAH. Lobsters contains high dose of PAH. BaP is produced by incomplete combustion of fossil fuel. It bioaccumates in food chain. Diesel engine exhaust is potent source of PAH and its derivatives containing nitro group as the substituents *e.g.*, nitropyrene or dinitropyrene are highly toxic and are mutogenic and produce cancer (Fig. 5.2).

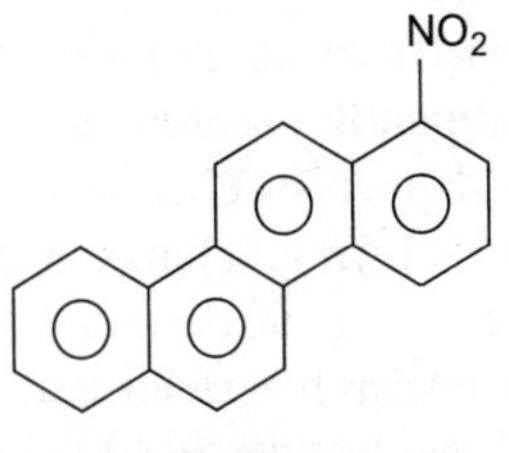

1-nitropyrene (IX)

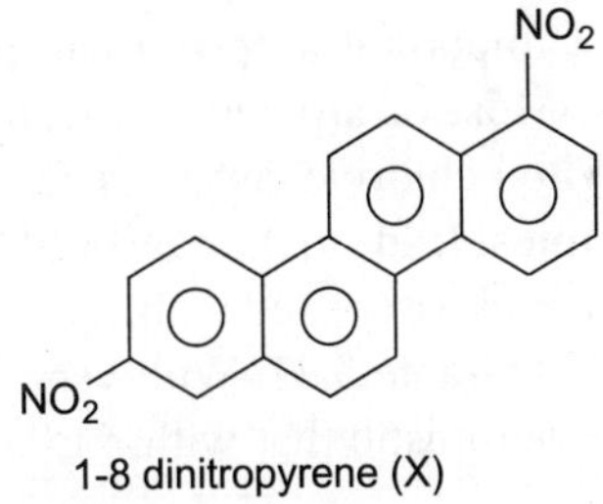

1-8 dinitropyrene (X)

Fig. 5.2 Sub. pyrene

These compounds are formed in car engine by action with NO-NO*x*.

Table 5.26 Toxic products from environment of PAH

Source of	*PAH*	*Perylene*	*Flouran-thene*	*BaP*	*Pyrene cirthraone*	*Benzo anthrane*	*Benz Coronone*
Cigarette (μg/m³) smoking	11	99	22	66	35	100	–
Combustion (mg/kg)	0.1-138	4-400	0.2-64	–	–	2-160	0.1-40
Structure in Fig 5.1		(vi)	(v)		(vii)	(viii)	

Table 5.32 indicates the level of BaP all over world in the important cities, with their source or origin.

5.13 CANCER

So far we have considered the effects of (BaP) benzopyrene and various forms of PAH as cancer generating compounds. It is essential to know the source of BaP from various fuels (Table 5.27). It shows that the rate of consumption by human being and industries is remarkable while Table 5.28 point out cancer promoting activity of Tobacco consumption, nitrogenous food consumption wrong intake of medicine and most important being synthetic food additives added in diet in our day to day consumption. Table 5.29 shows the extent of curing of cancer by radiotherapy and chemotherapy as well as surgery. Both treatment are very useful for the cure of cancer patients. The total death of patient from disease of cancer is alarming. Various medical hospitals in India and abroad are spending huge sums of money, in research with good deal of scientific manpower to find out definite drug which can permanently cure cancer of various organs. Table 5.30 shows which organs of body are commonly affected by cancer. It includes bladder, ovary, uterus, prostate glands, testes and pharynx with varying degree of cancer. The cobalt therapy and exposure in high energy accelerator for the purpose of treatment shows positive results. The deep X-rays are beneficial for cure of cancer of testies and scrotum, while cobalt therapy is useful for the cure of the cancer of the retinoblastoma or cervix and uterus. The exposure to high energy accelerator shows positive improvement. Patient suffer from the cancer of uterus (cervix) and prostate gland.

The most important a person can practise is to no exposure to carcinogenic compounds. Most of aromatic as well as aliphatic unsaturated compounds (*e.g.* benzidine, vinyl chloride, asbestos are very dangerous chemicals as the exposure to these chemical leads to the cancer of bladder, liver and lungs. A detailed account of these problems associated with deadly disease with no definite cure are discussed in Table 5.27 to Table 5.31. With very brisk research activities all over the world, one must be optimistic that within two to three decades in future of this century,

Table 5.27 Benzopyrene

S. No.	*Fuel*	*User's area*	*Bap (ηg/Btu) (Reported rate)*	*Consumption by human being*	*Consumption (energy)*	*Total Emission (annual) (kg) output*
1.	Coal	Utilities	58 μr/10^6 Btu	2.6×10^9	7.34×10^{13}	4.5
2.	Wood	Residential	6 ηg/3	1×10^6	2.7×10^{13}	6.37
3.	Oil	Resident	0.1 mg/kg	4.1×10^9	1.6×10^{14}	0.40
4.	Natural gas	Resident	20 μg/10^6 Btu	7.4×10^9	4.0×10^{14}	0.10
5.	Auto fuel	Streets	73 μg/gal.	8.5×10^9	3.8×10^{14}	228
6.	Diesel of truck	Road ways	321 μg/gal.	8.2×10^8	3.7×10^{13}	85.0

cancer will be declared as curable disease. The same fate is for the brain disease called dementia or Alzhiemer which has no cure so far although thousands of people in India are suffering from this fatal disease and all new drugs are under clinical trials in U.S.A.

We have seen in general more important organic compounds which are toxic in nature in earlier sections. The Table 5.23 list the level of concentration both in ppm and micrograms per cubic meter of common organic solvents frequently used in chemical laboratories. This Table shows Formic acid, Formaldehyde, Phenol and mesityloxide have very low tolerance limit. Tables 5.24, 5.25, 5.26 show threshold limiting, values of organic compounds which are commonly used in day to day activities of human being. The Tables 5.25–5.29 show the important aspect of organic compounds leading to rise of cancer. In auto exhaust emission the objectionable product is Benzopyrene (see Figs. 5.1 and 5.2). The largest source of benzopyrene in atmosphere is due to incomplete combustion of fuels like coal, natural gas, diesel oil (Table 5.25). This table also shows their consumption and their annual emission in air. Wood is real culprit to release BaP in air on combustion. The auto fuels like petrol and diesel oil show largest consumption and pollution. The users are from residential areas. The compressed natural gas, (CNG) is least harmful with 0.10 kg as annual consumption and most preferred instead of petrol in all public vehicles like autos, taxis and city buses on average.

Table 5.28 Cancer promoting materials and occupation

S. No.	*Substance occupation*	*Exposure estimated*	*Tolerable limit*	*Kind of cancer*
1.	Tobacco (Gutkha, Cigar, Pan masala)	30	25-40	Cancer of mouth
2.	Alcohol (country wine)	3	2–4	Lung, brain cancer
3.	Food (Nitrogen compounds)	35	10–70	Liver and Pancreas Cancer
4.	Sex (excessive indulgence)	7	1–10	Cervic, breast cancer
5.	Occupation (Foundry Smithry)	4	2–8	Chest
6.	Petrol (auto exhaust)	2	1-5	Lungs
7.	Indust. Exposure (BaP expose)	1	1–2	Lungs
8.	Wrong medicine (carcinogenic)	1	0.5–3	Stomach, Intestine, Kidney
9.	Infection (via HIV)	10	1	Fallopian tubes, uterus
10.	Surrounding Environment	3	3	Lungs
11.	Synthetic food additives	1	1	Intestine, stomach

The Table 5.28 list materials/occupation responsible for causing cancer. The tolerance limit for food additives is low. Although Tobacco bags the place of high tolerance level it leads to problem of cancer of Lungs and mouth. The consumption of gutakha, pan masala, Jarda are all extremely dangerous to health with quite low tolerance limit with the highest (30%) exposure to human being. The list is long for cancer promoting activities. Most prevalent is breast cancer, Liver, Lungs and intestine. Unfortunately no single remedy is so far discovered to mitigate the problem of cancer. Several international agencies all over world are trying to have cure in developed countries. They are pouring dollars to unfold the mystery of decaded disease of cancer.

Table 5.29 Cancer cure by radiation therapy and surgery (%)

S. No.	*Site of cancer*	*X-ray deep treatment*	*Cobalt therapy*	*Accelerator and radin*	*Radiation (%)*	*Surgery (%)*	*Radiation and surgery (%)*
1.	Bladder	0–5	25–30	40–50	38	24	38
2.	Breast	–	–	–	16	34	54
3.	Cervix uterus	35-45	50–55	60–65	95	5	0
4.	Digestive track	–	–	–	3	50	5
5.	Larynx	–	–	–	68	10	22
6.	Pharynx	20–25%	30–35%	45–50%	90	0	10
7.	Oral cavity	–	–	–	80	5	15
8.	Lung	–	–	–	85	5	10
9.	Skin	–	–	–	70	20	10

The location of site or place of cancer is of equal importance specially from the survival point of view. Table 5.29 indicates such sites. Many of these problems are circumvented by radiation therapy and surgery. In women about 35-45% toll is taken by cervic cancer but it is curable by radiation (90%). The survival rate is highest for breast cancer if diagnosed in initial stages while problem of Pharynx are all fatal as shown in Table 5.29. The extensive research for long duration is essential to unfold the mystery, the causes and mode of prevention of cancer.

Table 5.30 Rate of survival of patients in cancer treatment (%)

S. No.	*Organ affected*	*Deep X-ray (%) (Survival)*	*Cobalt therapy (Survival)*	*High engine accelerators (Survival)*
1.	Bladder	0–5%	25–30%	40–50%
2.	Ovary/Fallopian tubes	15–20%	35–40%	50–60%
3.	Cervix/uterus	35–45%	50–55%	60–65%
4.	Prostate	5–15%	40–45%	50–60%
5.	Testis/Scrotum	65–70%	75–80%	85–95%
6.	Retinoblastoma	30–40%	40–55%	80–90%
7.	Pharynx/nose	20–25%	30–35%	45–50%

We had seen in Table 5.30 rate of survival. However it all depends upon the history of health of each and every patient is having. Table 5.30 list some survival rates provided by treatment of deep X-ray, cobalt therapy or use of high energy accelerator. The last mode is best for survival of patient suffering from retino-blastoma. Deep X-ray helps to cure uterus cancer. Cobalt therapy can cure cancer of testis. However this is just observation. Unfortunately inspite of having extensive research no remedy has been so far found to avoid fatality in human being.

Before closing this long story of environmental carcinogens, it is better to identify sources or chemicals from which a person should preferably remain away and avoid excessive exposure. Liver, lungs, breast, brain are vital organs which get affected by killer disease. The β-napthylamine (from dye industry) vinyl, chloride (polymer industry) Aflatoxin (latex factory) in general are all unsafe chemicals therefore attention should be paid to minimise their use in day to day life. One can avoid over exposure to certain industries like dyestuff, food, leather,

Table 5.31 Cancer producing chemicals

S.No.	*Reagent/Surrounding*	*Affected site*	*S.No.*	*Surrounding/Reagent*	*Affected site*
1.	Benzidine	Bladder	11.	Isopropyl alcohol	Nasal
2.	Cyclophosphamide	Bladder	12.	Leather materials	Nasal
3.	2-napthylamine	Bladder	13.	Phenacein	Kidney
4.	Late age wedding/ pregnancy	Breast	14.	Melphalan	Marrow (Bone)
5.	Hamartoma – contraceptive	Liver	15.	Buslphan, benzene	Marrow (Bone)
6.	Vinyl Chloride	Liver	16.	Cadmium compounds	Prostate
7.	Virus – Hepatitis-B	Hepatoma	17.	Arsenic	Skin
8.	Aflatoxin	Liver	18.	UV-radiation	Skin
9.	Asbestos	Lung	19.	Betal, Tobacco, Lime	Mouth
10.	Chromium/ Phenoxy acid	Lung	20.	Mustard gas	Larynx, Lung

plastic and polymer factories, tobacco and cigarette manufacturing units as they are all potential source of carcinogenic compounds. Even in refrigerator industry chlorofluoro carbon (CCl_2F_2) is used in compressor. It is also carcinogenic however in the course of time better substituents have been discovered. In India on an average 30 lakhs persons suffer from cancer per year of these 14 lakhs are only women who suffer from cancer of uterus or breast. Unfortunately, the survival rate is extremely poor.

Table 5.32 Benzopyrene in various cities

Country	*City*	*Level* (μg × $10^{-2}/m^3$)	*Source*
America	Chicago	0.4–3.9	Aeroplanes
	Deteroit	1.10–5.4	and automobile emissions
	New York	0.5–4.0	–
	Philadelphia	0.6–5.9	–
	Los Angles	0.16–10	Too many cars
Switzerland	Zurich	4.1–7.7	Cars and sea
Japan	Kyushu	5–10	Sunlight
England	London	5–10	Sunlight
Iran	Teheran	6–6.3	Automobile emission
Norway	Oslo	6–2.6	Automobile emission
India	Mumbai	2–6.0	Dyestuff industries

5.14 TOXIC MINERALS AND DUST

Table 5.33 indicates dispersion of metal dust, grit and particulate matter in the atmosphere with varying size.

Thus, minerals and solid mixtures of organic matter can also cause toxicity. Their inhalation causes mechanical loading of lung and fibrosis of lung cells. Of the materials tested silica and asbestos are highly objectionable. SiO_2 causes silicosis, shortness of breath, decreased chest expansion and ultimately tuberculosis of lung. The toxic level is 2.5 million particles per cubic foot. While asbestos causes fibrosis of lung, silica can cause lung cancer. It absorbs protein from human body. Talcum, soapstone, mica, limestone, dolomite, coal, alumina are also injurious to health. Amongst organic dust, we have cotton dust or jute dust, which causes disease called byssinosis on exposer by the mill workers. This was prevalent in mill area of Mumbai and Ahmedabad. All dust particulate is best analysed by nephelometry, *i.e.*, light scattering methods and expressed in NTU units (Table 5.34).

Table 5.33 Metal concentration in common flyash with varying size

Metal pollutant	*Level and size*	
	25-12.5 μm	*1.5 μm or less*
Al (III)	54,300	59,300
Cd(II)	5	100
Cr(III)	130	300
Fe(III)	59,000	32,000
Mn(II)	240	500
Ni(II)	200	300
Pb(II)	200	500

Table 5.34 Grit and dust in different localities

Type of site/area	*Grit and dust fall out (mg/m^2d)*
Industrial	139
Fashioned housing	116
Low density housing	82
Commercial town	112
Town centre	90
Outskirts of a village	70
Countryside, open highways	38

5.15 CONCLUSION

It is interesting to study environmental toxicology, which imparts knowledge of harmful nature of the pollutants. Several industries release toxic materials in air or water. Toxicity is related to disfunctioning of lungs, liver, kidney and heart. The biological sampling of breath, urine, blood, nail, hair and tissue give positive information. The toxicity is measured in terms of threshold limiting value (TLV). Several metals are toxic *e.g.,* As, Sr, Sn, Ti, Cs are highly toxic while Cd, Cu, Hg, Pb and V have got intermediate toxicity while Al, Mo, Zr, W, Zn have low toxicity and Ca, Na, K, Rb and Li have virtually no toxic manifestations. While considering these metals their source, toxic effects, methods of analysis and finally control should be considered. Of several metals only 18 are worthy of consideration due to their toxic effects. In all cases food items containing these metals are important. Several organic compounds are deadly toxic, so also inorganic compounds such as non metals like boron, carbon, nitrogen, sulphur and phosphorus. Halosubstituted inorganic compounds are harmful. Amongst toxic organic compounds aromatic hydrocarbons, polyhydric alcohols, organonitro, organophosphorus organosulphur, and organohalides are worth examining as most of them are highly toxic, and are environmental carcinogens. Many of which are identified as cancer producing compounds. Many have tetrogenic and mutogenic effects on the health. Most of polyclic aromatic hydrocarbons are dangerous. Several compounds and their sources have been identified. Those causing cancer have been recognised. The kind of treatment to cure cancer by cobalt radio therapy or chemotherapy have been investigated. The status of autoexhaust emission containing benzpyrene (BaP) have been established and measures are suggested to control their effects with antiknocking agents. The minerals and dust in high dosage are also injurious. One has to be very careful while dealing with these compounds if one wants to avoid further deleterious consequences on the health.

ADDITIONAL READING

1. C. Baird, *'Environmental Chemistry'*, W.H. Freinon and Co. (1998).
2. J.D. McKinney, *'Environmental Health Chemistry'*, Ann Arbor Publication (1990).
3. M. Sitting, *'Toxic Metals Pollution Control and Workers Protection'*, Noyes Data Co. (1976).
4. M. Richardson Edn, *'Environmental Toxicology Assessment'*, Taylor and Pranas Publishers (1995).
5. J.W. Patterson, R. Passiono, *'Metal Speciation, Separation and Recovery'*, Vol. II. Lewis Publisher (1989).
6. S.E. Manahan, *'Environmental Chemistry'*, Seventh Edition, Lewis Publishers (1999).
7. C.H. Walker, S.P. Hopkin, R.M. Sibly, D.B. Peakall, *'Principles of Ecotoxicology'*, Taylor and Francis (1992), New Delhi.
8. N. Rajvaidya and D.K. Markande, *'Advances in Environmental Science'*, Vol. 4, APH Publishers (1998), New Delhi.
9. F.A. Patty, *'Industrial Hygiene and Toxicology'*, Vol. 1 and 2, Interscience, New York (1963).
10. E.A. Brown, *'Toxicity of Metals'*, Butterworth Pub. (1968).
11. K. Anderson and R. Scott, *'Fundamentals of Industrial Toxicology'*, Ann Arbor (1981).
12. H.G. Seiler and H. Sigel, *'Handbook on Toxicity of Inorganic Compounds'*, Marcel Dekker, New York (1988).

13. N.I. Sax, *'Dangerous Properties of Industrial Materials'*, Reinhold Publishing Corporation, New York, 6th Ed. (1984).
14. M. Sitting, *'Handbook of Toxic and Hazardous Chemicals'*, Park Ridge, Noyes (1981).
15. M. Eisenbud, *'Environmental Toxicology and Health'*, MacMillan Press London (1979).
16. E.E. Hinnawi and M.H. Hashmi, *'The State of the Environment'*, Butterworth Publication (1987).
17. C.R.K. Murthy and P. Viswanathan, *'Toxic Metals in Indian Environment'*, Tata McGraw Hill and Co. (1991).
18. WHO, *'Health Hazards of the Human Environment'*, WHO Pub. (1972).
19. S.M. Khopkar, *'Environmental Pollution Analysis'*, Second Edition, New Age International (P) Publisher (2011).

6 Environmental Chemistry of Common Toxic Metals

6.1 LEAD, CADMIUM, ARSENIC AND MERCURY AND ENVIRONMENTAL HAZARDS

The problem of cycling of these four toxic pollutants is very complex; specially in industry. Therefore, it is worthwhile to consider the impact of these metal pollutants in environment with special reference to Indian environment. Good amount of cadmium, lead, arsenic and mercury is released in air. It is of great significance to consider their presence in our environment. The survey in north India for presence of arsenic in vegetable indicated that 2–30 μg/100 gm of arsenic is present in most of the vegetables such as cabbage, peas, onions, radish, spinach and bananas (raw). Arsenic contents in farm manure specially those containing superphosphate indicated 187.8 mg/100 of arsenic while cow-dung (11.2), poultry (13.3–23.7) have substantial amount of arsenic on an average mean level of arsenic in water is 3–15 μg/100 gm. The boring wells showed as high as 54.5 μg/100 g of arsenic in water. A survey in Mumbai for these three elements (*viz.* Hg, Cd, As) in food is shown in Table 6.1.

Table 6.1 Toxic metals in food (Mean Concentration (ηg/gm) and range as in 1978)

Sample	*Arsenic (II)* (ηg/g)	*Cadmium (II)* (ηg/g)	*Mercury (II)* (ηg/g)
Potable water	–	–	1.9 (0.72–8.6)
Milk	–	–	(7.2–27.1)
Fruits	–	–	1.9(1–2.8)
Fish	56.0 (20.5–141.5)	40.1 (4.6–282.6)	40.1 (4.6–282.6)
Vegetables	3.1 (1–8.2)	43.8 (16.5–98.1)	6.5 (0.75–30.3)
Cereals	25.7 (1–88.2)	37.9 (15.2–79.8)	7.0 (0.75–31.1)

6.2 METALS IN ENVIRONMENT

The range and mean concentrations of these elements is given in Table 6.1. The coal contains arsenic in good proportion (~1–10 mg/kg). The fly ash in capital of

Table 6.2 Amount of cadmium in food

Item	*Food*	*Wheat*	*Rice*	*Corn*	*Soyabean*	*Peanuts*	*Onions*	*Carrot*	*Tomatoes*	*Spinach*	*Lettuce*
Metal	Cd (mg/kg)	0.048	0.013	0.014	0.064	0.090	0.100	0.250	0.270	0.830	0.620

Table 6.3 Amount of lead in food

Item	*Food*	*Peanut*	*Onion*	*Carrot*	*Tomato*	*Fruits*	*Milk*	*Cabbage*	*Potato*	*Apple*	*Plum*	*Butter*	*Eggs*	*Cheese*	*Bean*
Metal	Pb (mg/kg)	0.22	0.22	0.04	0.79	0.14	0.05	0.10	0.26	0.11	0.04	0.09	0.12	0.22	0.30

Table 6.4 Amount of mercury in food

Item	*Food*	*Cereals*	*Vegetables*	*Fruits*	*Milk*	*Fish*	*Blood*	*Hair*
Metal	Hg (mg/kg)	7.0	6.5	40.1	1.2	40.1	26.6	8.5

India at Indraprastha power plant is as high as 0.091%. It varies in the range of 0.091–1.328 ppm. Cadmium is present in Rice (0.079 ppm), maize (6.061 ppm), wheat (0.089), gram (0.074), gramdal (0.033) and wheat flour (0.2). In fertilizers cadmium contents is high. The crops grown on waste water shows level in maize (0.85, 1.98), Spinach (0.50, 3.29), cauliflower (0.48, 2.24) is cadmium and lead respectively.

The fly ash contains significant amount of cadmium. The sea coast of Chennai showed 0.001–0.047 mg/kg of cadmium. The animal feed had 0.9–1.8 ppm of Cd. A study in Gujarat in city of Ahmedabad showed lead contents as high as 0.35-1.7 $\mu g/m^3$ with 0.013 μg/gm in portable water. The lead contents in vegetables cultivated on waste water showed as 14–24 μg/gm. The decocation of tea in Punjab showed 0.002–0.012 ppm of lead. Animal feed has 9.66–5.94 ppm of lead. Typical tap water from Uttar Pradesh contains 0.004–0.008 ppm of lead. While fly ash from Indraprastha Industrial Estate has 110–260 gm/gm of lead. The autoexhaust emission is main source of Lead. The atmosphere in Mumbai is also greatly polluted by Lead. It varies from μg/gm: in Bus (57), Truck (160), Jeep (32), Car (256), Taxis (22), Bike (88), Tempo (6). Finally, let us consider mercury the worst contributor in air. The estuarine environment in Chennai has 0.0015–0.0045 ppm of Mercury. It is 0.1–0.33 present in sediment in ppm. The sea water has 0.0003 ppm mercury. In Bangalore (0.94), Calcutta (negligible), Trombay (0.16–1.29), Chembur have (21.5) $\eta g/m^3$ of mercury. The mercury balls are used to preserve crops which contains 0.1–0.4 mg of mercury specially in wheat and Rice.

The food on frying lowers down the contents of mercury due to loss on account of sublimation. About 40% level is reduced to lower limit for mercury. Thane creek in Mumbai showed 0.5 ppm with average of 78 ηg/liter of mercury. The soil in coal belts of Vidarbha contains too much of lead and mercury. The fly ash in Delhi had 4–14 μg/gm of mercury. About 170–190 tonnes is produced in India while rest of the mercury is imported specially for use in chloro alkali industries.

6.3 TOXIC METALS AND HUMAN HEALTH

Except arsenic other three elements are nonmetalloids. The occupational investigations showed adverse effects on human health. The bad effect of lead in America or ill effect of mercury in Japan have been thoroughly investigated. In 1981, the arsenic poisoning was noticed by WHO in Japan. The health effect has greater significance because of all four metals have created big problem with death of people in various states such as W. Bengal, Madhya Pradesh, Maharashtra and Gujarat. In Japan and America showed confirmed cases of pollution due to mercury.

The identification of species in what form is present as mercury or arsenic is most essential *e.g.* It is present as $(CH_3)_3Hg$, $(C_2H_5)_2Hg$ and Arsenicbetane and Arsenoetholine. The ingestion vai food is common route of entry. The cadmium goes into lung during smoking. Arsenic accumulates in nail, hair and skin while methylmercury is toxic to brain. We are considering individual metals from view point of their toxicity.

Table 6.5 Route of entry of toxic metal in human health

S. No.	Route of entry in body	Arsenic	Cadmium	Lead	Mercury
1.	Process of excretion	Urine	Urine	Urine	Foetus
2.	Half life (biological isotope)	10–30 hrs	>10 yrs	20 yrs	70 days
3.	Major route entry	Ingestion	Inhalation	Inhalation	Ingestion
4.	Accumulation	Keratinous tissue	Kidney, liver	Bone, kidney, liver	Brain, liver, kidney
5.	Extent of absorption %	80%	5%	10%	90%

(a) Effect of Lead

The central nervous and renal system severely gets affected by exposure to lead. In renal system, mitochondrial damage is caused while there is intranuclear inclusion in bodies with neuropathy. In nervous system it causes cognitive problems which is specially high in children. The encephalopathy also arises. In haematological system ALA-D (δ ammolevulinic acid) is generated. The haemo synthesis and anemia is encountered in its presence of Iron in protoporphyrine lead inhibits the transmitochondrial transfer of Iron (III). ALA-D causes neutrotoxic manifestation. As told earlier children get severely affected. Low lead level leads to neuropsychologic deficient with low IQ valve. The main source is (ICA) as ignition control addictive or antiknocking agent which is added to Petrol in order to prevent formation and deposition of soot in cylinders of automobile engine.

(b) Effects of Mercury

The tragedy of minamata is well known. In 1950, the methyl and ethyl mercury from chloroalkali industry were consumed by fish which in turn entered in food chain. It was swallowed by human being in city of Minamata in Japan thereby showing symptoms of gingvits; swelling of lower limbs; affecting eyesight. There is paraesthesia of Lungs body extremities. Several cases *viz.* 160 death and 3300 of suspected poisoning was noted with alkyl mercury. It is used as the fungicide for wheat. It was interesting to know that the bread prepared from it showed damaging influence on health (*e.g.* Iraqi epidemic). About 6000 persons were poisoned with 500 death in hospitals. In Pakistan (100), Guatemala (45), Ghana (150) several clinical cases clearly identified as of mercury poisoning.

(c) Effect of Cadmium

The kidney is readily affected by it. Proteins get excreted in urine causing Proteniuria. Glomerular dysfunction is another problem. In Japan at place called Nigita it caused disease called "Itai-Itai". There was loss of amino acids. The nonferrous metal mines in Japan discharged cadmium solutions in effluents. Rice readily absorbs cadmium causing renal problems, women severely gets affected by cadmium poisoning. It leads to the renal dysfunction. It causes nephritis in human beings. It was noticed in Europe in Belgium. Nephrosis is also caused due to ingestion of cadmium by men and women. Therefore, intensive investigation were carried out in Japan and Europe on cadmium.

(d) Effect of Arsenic

Inorganic arsenic is dangerous for human beings. It affects skin, lung, liver, central nervous system, reproductive organs and causes blood poisoning. In skin, it causes skin tumors, lungs get cancer; liver is affected leading to Cirrhosis or Jaundice. It also causes hearing loss and disturbed erythropoiesis. Palm and feet gets affected. They give rise to the skin tumors. The peripheral vascular disturbances are also caused, leading to gangrene or black foot disease. Unfortunately, so far the lung cancer is incurable. The milk processed by sodium phosphate is contaminated with arsenic. It causes hearing loss, Japan had recorded it in milk. The drinking water in W. Bengal in the area of Damodar Valley is seriously infected by arsenic compounds. The large scale exposure leads to chronic effects. Such cases were discovered also in Japan, Argentina, Taiwan, USA and Canada. Copper and melters and pesticide plants influenced the phenomena of arsenic poisoning. Fowler's solution is sodium arsenic which is used to cure Leukaemia but it caused serious side effects. In Czechoslovakia, what was detected was 1000 μg/gm of arsenic from Lignite coal. It resulted the loss of the hearing in children in Table 6.6 shows chronic effects of metal pollutants.

Table 6.6 Chronic exposure and threshold values of toxic metals

S. No.	*Metal*	*Effect on health*	*Threshold limit value (TLV)*	*Reported actual threshold limit*	*Significant effects*
1.	Arsenic (III)	Skin cancer	200 μg/L	2 μg/L	Prolonged exposure causes problem (~ 70 yrs) exposure
2.	Cadmium (II)	β_2 m cancer	150 μg/day	20–70 μ/d	50 yrs exposure affects fat person
3.	Mercury (II)	Early	20 μg/gm · symptoms	2 μg/gm	Fish consumption affects pregnant women
4.	Lead (II)	ALA-D-EEP	11 μg	10–20 μg	Children affected, 10% prevalence

6.4 SPECIATION OF METAL POLLUTANTS

Time scaling of cycles with the chemical speciation if of critical significance. The oxidation state is most vital. The studies in oxygenated water indicated reliable results. The stability constant, general trends, complexation, redox speciation, adsorption and residence time of all these four toxic metals are considered in following sections.

How the speciation is important will be illustrated by simple example. Thus, mercury which is present in the form of $(CH_3)_3$ Hg or $(C_2H_5)_3Hg$ are toxic but $HgCl_2$, $HgNO_3$ is not toxic. Similarly, chromium (III) is very toxic but not chromium (VI) compounds. This illustrates how the oxidation state of the toxic metal influences toxicity. Similarly in the case of mercury to know what kind of anion is attached to mercury is great value *e.g.* NO_3^-, Cl^- if attached to mercury is not toxic but if we attach (CH_3^-), $(C_2H_5^-)$ or (C_6H_5) groups to mercury it is rendered highly toxic. These examples clearly show that the importance of speciation in the environmental studies is most important. For instance, in oxygenated water all the four elements are in bivalent state; with exception of arsenic which is mostly present in +5 oxidation state, leading to stabilization of (H_3AsO_4) arsenic acid. Therefore, evaluation of stability constant is most essential. The preliminary studies showed that cadmium and mercury which form chlorocomplexes are hazardous. Apart from chlorocomplexes the hydroxy and carbonate species in oxygenated water are also harmful. Arsenic gets converted to H as O_4^{2-} species. Mercury also forms bromocomplexes. Cadmium forms mixed ligand complexes. The s-block metals like Na, K, Ca, Mg form stable phosphato complex while arsenic is most in form of negatively charged complex in aqueous environment. The amount of free metal ion shows that the strength of complexing cation is in order as: Cd < Pb < Hg in sea water. In chloride solution order for complexation is: Pb < Cd < Hg while in hydroxyl media the order is: Cd < Pb < Hg. The salinity determines the kind of speciation for toxic metal pollutant.

In the organic media complex formation (*e.g.* Hg complex) is noted specially in the presence of fulvic and humic acids. They influence the speciation pattern. In this complexation investigations in sea water the order is Cd < Pb < Hg. The range of methyl mercury species present is (CH_3Hg^+), $(CH_3Hg\ OH)$, $(CH_3Hg\ Cl)$, (CH_3l_2Hg), (CH_3HgS) and $(CH_3Hg)_2S$. The methyl mercury species can not be formed in anoxic environment in living system (CH_3Hg^+) is stable complex and can remain as such for long time. In natural water, monomethyl and dimethyl arsenic compounds facilitates great contribution to the speciation of arsenic in natural water. Let us now consider some special features of these toxic metal pollutants.

6.5 ARSENIC IN ENVIRONMENT

The metal enters in body through ingestion and inhalation. The metal is of public scrutiny on toxicity. It has local health effects in environment, it is widely distributed. Both inorganic as well as the organic mercury was studied. Methylated arsenic was also well studied. It originates from anthropogenic source as copper smelting and coal refining or combustion process. The volcanic activity at low temperature of voltization is noticed. The sources of arsenic is logical methylation. It was predicted quite early. In aerosol the speciation was not investigated. The database for aquatic environment is well documented. The soil source is worth studying for arsenic. The certain variety of fish species are potential source of arsenic (III) poisoning. The surface and groundwater studies are equally important for tracing mercury. The health effects are quite well known. Tobacco has the synergic effect on it causing serious health problems in smokers.

Table 6.7 LD_{50} of arsenic compounds (mg/kg)

S. No.	*Name of compound*	*LD_{50} (mg/kg)*	*S. No.*	*Name of compound*	*LD_{50} (mg/kg)*
1.	Arsenic oxide	34.5	5.	Monomethyl arsenic	1800
2.	Sodium arsenite	4.5	6.	Dimethyl arsenic	1200
3.	Sodium arsenate	14.8	7.	Trimethyl arsenic	10.6
4.	trimethyl arsenic	8000	8.	Tridimethylamino arscenate	88.0

The Table 6.7 indicates LD_{50} level of compounds of the arsenic. Trimethylarsenic has highest tolerance value (8000) while Tridimethylammino arsenate has lowest tolerance limit of 8 mg/kg. While sodium arsenite is very toxic.

Table 6.8 Arsenic level in marine organism (μg/g)

Kind	*Organism*	*Fish*	*Shell fish*	*Brown algae*	*Sea urchin*	*Sea squirrel*	*Brown algae*	*Sea cucumber*
Inorganic	(Level) (μg/g)	0.28	0.01	36.5	0.22	0.05	0.6	0.1
Organic	(Level) (μg/g)	15.34	15.9	15.2	7.0	24.3	6.5	11.3

A close look of Table 6.8 indicates that inorganic arsenic is less toxic in comparison to organic arsenic. The sea squirrel shows highest arsenic level (~ 24.3) organic form while sea cucumber has low tolerance of 0.1 μg/g.

Table 6.9 Arsenic in water and urine (mg/L)

Sample No	*1*	*2*	*3*	*4*	*5*
In water (mg/L)	0.04	0.05–0.14	0.15–0.25	0.26–0.30	0.4–0.8
In urine (mg/L)	0.03	0.059	0.127	0.152	0.228

If we look at Table 6.9 it shows good amount of arsenic in water and urine. Few samples have 0.4–0.8 arsenic. Water excretes excreta maximum 0.228 mg/L in the urine. It is negligible in some samples.

Table 6.10 Variation of arsenic according to depth of well in north east India

Depth of well (meter)	*2–16 m*	*70–150 m*	*150–250 m*	*250–300 m*	*300–500 m*
Arsenic (mg/L) level	0.007 (low)	0.0095	0.157	0.217	0.251 (high)
Wells	11	7	12	37	5
Average value ratio (depth/level)	2/0.007	70/0.0095	150/12	250/37	300/5.0

The Table 6.10 indicates that deeper is well more is level of arsenic located. As 300–400 m deep well has as much as 0.251 mg/L of arsenic, while shallow well with depth of 2–16 meter has only 0.007 mg/L of arsenic compounds.

Table 6.11 Arsenic in human morbidity with age of person (mg/L)

Arsenic in water (mg/L)	*0.21*	*0.23*	*0.34*	*0.39*	*0.56*	*0.75*
Rate of morbidity (%)	0.3	1.5	6.5	13.7	31.4	46.4
Age of man (years)	~10	~20	~30	~40	~50	~60
Incidence (%)	14.3	30.1	73.2	83.1	71.7	46.4

Table 6.11 shows as age increases rate of morbidity also rises with high percentage at 0.39 mg/L to 83.1% while lowest morbidity at 0.21 level is 14.3%.

6.6 LEAD IN ENVIRONMENT

Anthropogenic lead is spread everywhere. The leaded petrol which was used as ignition control additive was the principle source of lead. It is very toxic for children. Food chain is also affected by lead. In the form of ingestion it accumulates with residence time which is very high.

The examination of Table 6.12 shows that the highest production of lead is in America, but America has also maximum consumption (%). The lowest production is in China and Korea where corresponding consumption is 4.5% and 5.0% respectively. It indicates that the use of lead outstrips the production in France, Japan, USA, China and Korea.

Table 6.12 World production and consumption of lead

S. No.	*Country*	*% production*	*% consumption*	*S. No.*	*Country*	*% production*	*% consumption*
1.	America	15	22 (+7)	6.	France	4.4	4.8 (+0.4)
2.	Australia	11	10 (+1)	7.	Germany	7.3	6.1 (+1.2)
3.	Canada	10	4.5 (–5.5)	8.	Japan	5.4	6.0 (+1.6)
4.	China	4	4.5 (+0.5)	9.	Korea	3.0	5.0 (+2.0)
5.	England	5.9	5.5 (–0.4)	10.	Russia	17.0	14.0 (–3.0)

Table 6.13 Lead contents of waste water from few typical industries

S. No.	*Source water*	*Level (mg/ml)*	*S. No.*	*Source of water*	*Level (mg/ml)*
1.	Litharage battery	5–48	4.	Steel works	0.1–0.50
2.	Electroplating	2–140	5.	Sewage in drain	0.5–1.5
3.	Dye stuff	3.0	6.	ICA-industry (Automobile fuel)	127–135

It should be noted from Table 6.13 that the maximum amount of lead is encountered in waste water from lithrage battery and automobile industry (S.No. 1

and 6). This is because ICA *i.e.*lead tetraethyl is used ($Pb(C_2H_5)_4$) as antiknock agent in petrol. Similarly, lithrage battery has electrodes made out of lead.

Both inorganic/organic lead in human system has varying toxic effects. For instance organic lead causes loss of sleep, vertigo and nausia while inorganic lead leads to diarrhea, vomiting. The study of lead speciation shows that in bi and tetravalent state it is present both in inorganic and organic form. Organometallic lead originates from voltalization of gasoline. The additives (~5%) are released in uncombustible form. Air pollution and Lead emission are closely linked specially at high temperature. Lead in Land goes to food chain due to grazing of grass by animals. The microorganism accumulates lead in their bodies. Anthropogenic source is more harmful than the natural source of lead. It is found in volcanogenic dust, windblown dust, forest fire and sediments from ocean. The gasoline and combustion products of petrol contain highest amount of lead. In future the demand for lead would grow fast. Therefore, a better and planed monitoring is needed with special reference to the bioavailability. Lead pigments as $PbSO_4$ were commonly utilised. It is used in alloy like solder and water pipes due to its flexibility. The monitoring in health of children is very cumbersome. The erythrocyte, protoporphyrin fluoroscerice or blood lead levels are measured in biosphere. Lead from paints and pigments industry is easily replaced by TiO_2 or $BaSO_4$ as the substitute for toxic lead in Titanex paints.

6.7 CADMIUM IN ENVIRONMENT

It is rare metal pollutant, occurring in nature in ores. There is change in global cycling of the metal. Many times it is associated with mercury. Just like Minamata tragedy in Japan in 1940, it had caused serious problem in place called Nigata a small town in Japan where it caused a disease called 'itai-itai'. Inspite of that it is used for several purposes as metal coating, nuclear reactor, alkaline, fuel cells and low feasible alloys. Rubber tyre plastic on combustion release the vapours of cadmium (0.5 μg/m^3). Vegetables like spinach, lettuce, soyabean plants can tolerate as high as 3.4 μg/kg of the cadmium compounds. Table 6.2 indicates level of cadmium encountered in various samples of food. It severely affects kidney and causes renal problems, lungs and respiratory disorder. In 1951 in Europe senior citizens were affected by adverse effect of cadmium. The countrywise distribution in different years is shown in Table 6.14. The presence of cadmium in different countries show in all nations, it is definitely detected in air and water but not traced in places like USA. Similarly, in north sea, it is encountered only in aquatic environment.

The volcanic eruptions are major source of emission of cadmium in air. The oceans spray, forest fire, release considerable amount of cadmium. The metal mines are reliable source; where it is found in association with zinc. Mexico provides highest level of cadmium. Nickel-cadmium alkaline batteries manufacturing units release good amount of cadmium in the aquatic environment. In Europe, it is consumed at highest level. It is present in negligible level in potable water (< 20 μg). The cigarette smoke is dispersed as aerosals *e.g.* 20 cigarettes contain 25–30 μg of cadmium. It is analysed by Atomic absorption spectroscopy (AAS) at 229 nm in air-acetylene flame. The limit of detection is 0.5–2 μg/mL with sensitivity of 0.0004 μg/mL.

Table 6.14 Distribution of cadmium in various countries

S. No.	*Year of study*	*Country*	*Source (Natural)*	*Environmental saturation in*			*Remarks*
				Air	*Water*	*Soil*	
1.	1978	Denmark	–	×	×	×	Natural origin
2.	1981	Switzerland	–	×	×	×	In all places
3.	1979	W. Europe	×	×	×	×	Natural, all places
4.	1978	Sweden	–	×	×	–	Not in soil
5.	1979	America	–	×	×	×	Not natural origin
6.	1982	North sea	×	–	×	–	Only in aquatic environment
7.	1970	World wide	×	×	–	–	Only in air

x = presence detected; – = no information.

6.8 MERCURY IN ENVIRONMENT

In environmental perhaps this is the only metal pollutant which has been extensively studied due to Minamata (Japan) tragedy. The chloroalkali industries in Castner-Kellener cell use one of the electrode in the form of mercury. The production of sodium hydroxide with mercury diaphram in Dowson or Castner Kellener process occurs. When it leaks in aquatic environment, it combines with organics in water to form $(CH_3)_3Hg$ or $(CH_3CH_2)_2Hg$. This in turn is consumed by specially those bony fish. These varieties of fish with greater thorns is finds way in food chain consumption. The adverse effects of mercury poisoning like gait, hearing loss, visual disturbance, atoxia, pathological and primitive reflux are known. Such effects are indicated in Table 6.15.

Table 6.15 Toxic effects of mercury

Toxic manifestations	*% persons affected*	*Toxic manifestations*	*% person affected*
Atoxia	94	Salivation	24
Gait	82	Speech disturbance	88
Hearing loss	85	Swallowing problem	94
Muscle weakness	27	Tendon effects	34
Mental imbalance	71	Visual disturbance	100
Pathological	12		–
Primitive reflex	0		–

It will show that the maximum damage of health is done of eyes, then hearing loss, gait, speech disturbance and severe problem for swallowing of food. The salvation and pathological refluxes are negligible. An examination of fish and nonfish eaters, in blood and urine show in fish eaters contains 26.6, 20 and 8.5 ηg/mL respectively, while in non-fish eater problem is not acute. One encounters it corresponding level around in blood, urine and hair as much as 14.1, 11–0 and 2–0 ηg/mL respectively.

The impact of mercury poisoning on human health is shown in Table 6.16.

Table 6.16 Impact of mercury toxicity on health (%)

Toxic indications	*% Exposure*	*Level*	*Toxic indications*	*% Exposure*	*Level*
Blood pressure	~50	Medium	Shyness	5–25	Low
Cough and cold	~20	Medium	Tremors	5–25	Medium
Diarrhea	1–10	Low	Weight loss	10–70	High
Insomia	5–50	Medium	Eyes-ear infection	90–100	Very high
Loss of apetite	10–70	High	Throat problems	20–70	High

The Table 6.16 shows maximum damage is caused to eyes, ears and throat. While digestive system is marginally affected. The neurological effects leads to tremors, insomia, shyness and hypertension in affected population of people. It is most interesting to look at the level of exposure as low, high or medium.

The main pathway to man is by ingestion via aquatic organism *e.g.* Fish methyl mercury is most toxic compound. Their vapours are also very toxic. The food chain transfer is major source for consumption of mercury. It undergoes biomagnification the chronic effects are unknown. The knowledge of speciation is most vital for understanding its ill effects on health. Hg° has zero solubility in water. Both major physical as well as in chemical speciation would furnish real picture of its toxicity. In sediments the process of methylation is favoured. It not only depends upon metabolic activity of bacteria but also on pH, redox potential, organic substrate reaction and the temperature. The anaerobic condition is most favourable to promote this process. By and large the level of move than 0.5–1 μg/gm is injurious to the human health. Low pH is favourable for bacterial methylation. Methylation is maximum in soil or sediments. Hg–Se combination reduces toxicity of mercury for certain organism in ratio of 1:1:: Hg:Se. There is demethylation of mercury which in turn reduce its toxicity.

In conclusion while discussing toxic metal pollutants as well as polluting compounds present in India is concerned we have to seriously contemplate about these four elements. There are serious instances of arsenic poisoning in West Bengal specially in Damodar river area. Similarly, the problem of mercury nusiance is widely distributed in the marine environment of Arabian sea in coastal zone of Bombay, Trivendrum and Chennai. The next pollutant relevant to India is lead. On account of its extensive application as anti-knocking agent (in form $(CH_3)_2Pb$ or $(CH_3CH_2)Pb$) we record automobile pollution in large cities like Kolkata, Mumbai, Delhi, Chennai, Hyderabad and Benglaru. Finally, the role of cadmium is significant in metal operation in areas of Bihar and Rajasthan. It is always associated with zinc therefore, Hindustan Zinc Industry in Rajasthan have significant adverse effect of health of population. Other toxic metals have not been studied so intensively as compared to the four metal pollutants.

6.9 MONITORING AND CONTROL MEASURES

In fact extensive research work has been carried out in monitoring of these four metals. Most of it is discussed in earlier chapters on toxic metal pollutant. We briefly summarize it as:–

(a) Mercury: It is best determined by cold vapour atomic absorption spectroscopy. Brillian Green and several triphenyl basic dyes are used in absorption spectroscopy. In electroanalytical methods as polorography is best method. Neutron activation is also fine.

(b) Lead: The best method for its analysis is polarography with dimethy-sulphoxide as the supporting electrolyte. It can be also analysed by AAS or ICP-AES. The spectral method consists of the extraction photometry with dithozone. EDTA is used in volumetry analysis.

(c) Cadmium: It is best analyzed by extractive photometry using dithizone in chloroform. AAS or ICP-AES is another method. Finally, one can also use polarography technique for quantitative analysis of cadmium at low level.

(d) Arsenic: The best method is arsenophosphomolydic complexation for measurement in spectrometry. In AAS we have to use hydride generates to analyze it. Electroanalytical method is rarely utilized in analysis.

As regards method for control, we must follow few norms. For mercury cathode, Kastner Keller cell should not be used as Dowson process is preferable. For the preservation of food seed $(C_6H_5)_2Hg$ should not be used. The mercury while desposing in stream should not get mixed with organic pollutants to form organo-mercury compounds.

As regards lead main source of pollution is auto exhaust emission in form of ICA which is used as the anti-knocking agent to prevent soot formation in gear box. All lead compounds should not be used in pigments as $PbCr_2O_7/PbCrO_4$ as additive with TiO_2 in Titanex whitner. The pipe fittings in the sanitary ware should not use flexible lead pipes. They can be replaced by flexible plastic tubes.

The cadmium is mostly used as the protective coating in reactors. It is advisable to replace it with tin if the surface is anodic. In the alkaline cadmium batteries one should avoid using cadmium electrodes.

Finally, for prevention of arsenic from getting contaminated with potable water it should be separated *e.g.* Salverson which is extensively used in dysentry contains substantial amount of arsenic. Similar in cosmetics it is used in form of 'surma' for cooling eyes but it is deadly toxic.

6.10 CONCLUSION

Inspite of availability of modern methods for the monitoring of more toxic metals, environmentalist must look forward to have more selective more specific and the methods with the excellent sensitivity. This is possible provided research for better method or new reagents is continued.

ADDITIONAL READING

1. T.C. Hutchinson & K.M. Meema, *Lead, Mercury, Cadmium and Arsenic in the Environment SCOPE-31*, John Wiley and Sons, New York. (1987).
2. M. Sitting, *Toxic metals Pollution Control and Workers Protection*, Noyes Data Co. (1976).
3. F.A. Patty, *Industrial hygiene and Toxicology*, Interscience Vols. 1 and 2, New York (1963).
4. E.G. Hinnawi and M.H. Hashmi, *State of Environment Butterworth* (1987).
5. J.O. Nriagu, *Arsenic in Environment*, John Wiley and Co. (1994).
6. R. Hartung, B.D. Dimon, Ed. *Environmental Mercury Contamination*, Annarbor Science Publication (1974).
7. R.M. Harrison, D.P.H. Laxen, *Lead Pollution, Causes and Control*, Chapman and Hall London (1981).
8. C.R.K. Murthy and P. Vishwanathan, *Toxic Metals in Indian Environment*, Tata McGraw Hill and Co. (1991).
9. E. A. Brown, *Toxicity of Metals*, Butterwidth Pub. (1968).
10. C.H. Walker, S.P. Hopkin, R.M. Sibly, D.B. Peckcall, *Principles of Ecotoxicology*, Taylor and Francis (1992).
11. S.M. Khopkar, *Environmental Pollution Analysis,* Second Edition, New Age International Publishers (2012).
12. S.M. Khopkar, *Basic Concepts of Analytical Chemistry*, Third Edition, New Age International (P) Publishers Ltd. (2008).
13. I.L. Marr, M.S. Cresser, *Chemical Analysis*, International Textbook Co., New York, Blacki and Sons Ltd. (1983).
14. J.N. Moore, *Inorganic Contamination of Surface Water*, Research and Monitoring Springer, Verlag (1990).
15. N.F. Voznaya, *Chemistry of Water and Microbiology*, Mir Publishers, Moscow (1981).

7 Air Pollution Analysis

7.1 INTRODUCTION

Taj Mahal is one of the nine wonders of the world. Unfortunately on account of activity of the man in the surrounding environment, the monument is threatened with ill-effects of pollution. The survey conducted by National Environmental Engineering Research Institute (NEERI) Nagpur revealed that 500 $\mu g/m^3$ of (SPM) suspended particulate matter and 50 $\mu g/m^3$ of sulphur dioxide in the atmosphere is present around the monument. One really wonders in such picturesque environment of Taj Mahal, how SO_2 is present? In the super gagnatic plain there is good amount of suspended particulate matter. The white marble is slowly tarnished to yellow colouration with dark spots by pollutants. NEERI had made thorough investigations of atmosphere of city of Agra and confirmed that the atmosphere around Taj is seriously polluted by industrial activity of small scale industries. The industries such as ferrous alloy plants (3–373 kg/h) chemicals and rubber processing (34 kg/h) refractory and lime processing works (18 kg/h) belch-out not only SPM (as shown by figures in brackets) while SO_2 is ranging from (20–600 kg/h). The CO was also present in large proportion (30–705 kg/h). There are highest number of units of ferrous casting, which should be immediately shifted or changed. The Mathura refinery which is in neighbourhood is also contributing its own share by fouling the atmosphere around Taj Mahal (Table 7.1).

Since 1930, the awareness of air pollution was created all over the world. The world conference on air pollution was held at Stockholm in 1978. The International conference was held in Sweden to assess global destruction. Since then Indian government had taken serious note of pollution thereby leading to establishment of pollution control boards in every state as well as Central Pollution Control Board (CPCB) at New Delhi. In 1992, Earth Summit was held in Rio–de–Janeiro in Brazil under auspicious of United Nation which discussed the present magnitude of the pollution all over the world. The problem of chlorofluorocarbon (CFC) causing depletions of ozone layer was discussed. The Montreal protocol in 1987 in Canada solemnly declared that by 2000 AD all countries should halt production of CFC. Chlorofluorocarbon in different forms as is CCl_3F, CCl_2F_2 and CCl_2FCClF_2 (*i.e.*, Trade name as CFC–11, 12, 13 respectively or Freon).

By 1986, 43% CFC was generated in Europe alone 30% in USA and only 0.03% in India. CFC was useful not only in refrigerators and airconditioning but also in manufacture of plastics, fire extinguishers and aerosol propellants. In India attempts are made to phase out CFC in order to protect ozone layer. Instead of CFC, nowadays HCFC is recommended as an alternative substitute for it. The air pollution in Indian cities as recorded in 1978 is shown in Table 7.2 while pollutants in the atmosphere are listed in Table 7.1.

Table 7.1 Atmospheric pollutants

S. No.	Name of pollutant	Formula	Important characteristics	Impact of pollutant on nature/health
1.	Sulphur dioxide	SO_2	Colourless, Soluble gas has choking fumes	Vegetation damaged bad for human health
2.	Sulphur trioxide	SO_3	Water soluble gas	Very corrosive in nature
3.	Hydrogen sulphide	H_2S	Rotten egg smell, no odour at high concentration	Very much poisonous
4.	Nitrous oxide	N_2O	Colourless, carrier gas	Nongeneration in burning inactive
5.	Nitric oxide	NO	Colourless gas	Obtained at high temp. and pressure
6.	Nitrogen dioxide	NO_2	Brown gas	Part of photochemical smog
7.	Carbon monoxide	CO	No odour or color	generated by incomplete combustion
8.	Carbon dioxide	CO_2	No colour or odour	Antropogenic, part of very poisonous greenhouse gas
9.	Ozone	O_3	Reactive, interaction	Photochemical smog component bad for vegetation
10.	Hydrocarbons	HO	Several derivatives with varying property	Exist from car, injurious, industrial operations
11.	Methane	CH_4	Combustible, it has no odour	Greenhouse gas
12.	Chlorofluorocarbon	CFC	good thermal properties unreactive	dissociate ozone

Thus, it is seen that Indian cities are relatively free from pollution. In 1986, Comprehensive Environmental Protection bill was passed by the Parliament with clamping of vigorous standards. They were designated as ISI standard of 5182 (Part I–XX). We are expected to adhere to it (Table 7.1).

With so much of awareness and health problems, one cannot remain silent but must act to control air pollution. The historical development of pollution all over the world is interesting. One must know what is air pollution, and its ill-effects on health of man, plants, animals, objects and planets? We should be aware of what are the important sources of air pollution and what are stationary and mobile sources. The meteorological parameters like wind velocity, wind direction, wind roses are the deciding parameters influencing the dispersion of air pollutant. The sampling and monitoring of ambient air quality as well as stack emission needs great attendation. The methods for analysis of suspended particulate matter (SPM),

SO_2, NO–NO_x, CO, CO_2, hydrocarbons should be reviewed. The transportation is major culprit of air pollution, hence it should be considered with their characteristics specially along with that of autoexhaust emission involving four stroke petrol engines and diesel engines as the mobile source of the pollution.

7.2 HISTORY

In early years, the public health engineers have paid great attention to water pollution problems, however, relatively study of air pollution was somehow neglected. Several tragedies and catastrophic events all over the world persuaded environmentalist to consider atmospheric pollution which is very harmful to human health.

The water pollution act was formulated in Bombay in 1962. The Clean Air Act came into existence only in 1986. The developed countries like UK, USA and Canada passed Clean Air Act as early as in 1952.

Apart from SO_2, NO–NO_x, CO, CO_2 which cause pollution of the atmosphere another important component of the atmosphere is suspended particulate matter (SPM) which is great source of trouble, and it is generated from dry earth by man's activity. In high dose, it is also injurious to health. The small size particulates are very harmful as they are retained in lungs. The air pollutant dumping place is called 'sink'. Chlorofluorocarbon (CFC) used in refrigerator is accumulated in troposphere of earth destroying natural protective layer of ozone. This depletion causes penetration of ultraviolet radiation from sun which causes harm. The 'receptor' is badly affected by polluted air, where a person, plant or animal are all receptors. Transport is the mechanism of movement of pollutants from the source to the receptor. Wind drives pollutant to receptor. The migration of gaseous pollutant proceeds by process of diffusion.

In 1930, in Belgium, there was a very bad fog in a Menuce valley due to temperature inversion. In 1948, in Donara in America had haze and mist causing death of several persons by respiratory diseases. In 1952, worst tragedy occurred in England. The people experienced dense fog due to inversion of pollution leading to the death of as much as 4000 persons due to lung troubles. In 1956 and 1962 similar kind of smog was noticed in America called as the *Los Angles smog*. The word originated from bad photochemical smog which was observed in 1945 in Los Angles in California. It contained harmful products like PAN (*i.e.,* peroxyacetyl nitrite) which is generated due to autoexhaust emission by interaction of aldehydes and aromatic compounds leading to thick fog formation. In 1970, apart from America and England, Japan experienced thick fog over city of Tokyo. It took toll of 6000 people who were taken ill due to eye irritation, bad throat and respiratory problems. The worst tragedy in Bhopal in India took a toll of more than 2500 innocent lives. Several hundreds of persons were permanently disabled, due to leakage of MIC (methyl iso cyanate) from tank in pesticide manufacturing unit on December 3, 1984 when it was cold wintry night. The disaster took place in dead of night, due to accumulation of air pollutants. Though it was obligatory for company to take prevention before disaster occurred and killed several hundreds of innocent persons in India was not done.

In order to understand what is air pollution we must first consider nature of unpolluted atmosphere.

A look at Table 7.1 shows that, it is worthwhile to identity the atmospheric gaseous pollutants. They include oxides of sulphur and nitrogen, Hydrocarbons ozone. As shown in Table 7.1 one can note that the most toxic gases are CO, O_3, NO–NO_X, and few organic compounds. In fact some gases like CO, CO_2, SO_2, NO-NO_2 form the integral component of greenhouse gases while few are constituents of photochemical smog, while gas like CF_2Cl_2 (*i.e.* Chlorofluorocarbon) is used in refrigeration but it is dangerous as it is capable of effecting depletion and destroying of ozone layer from the atmosphere. This is turn and permits infrared radiation to enter to earth. Most of the oxides of nitrogen have deliterious effect on health. They are normally encountered during rainy season in thunder bolt and lightening of atmosphere.

Table 7.2 Sulphur dioxide (μg/m^3) in air in Mumbai

Location in city of Mumbai	*2012*	*2011*	*2010*	*2009*	*2008*	*Remarks*
Worli	14	8	9	13	14	Rising
Khar	10	7	9	12	11	Steady
Andheri	11	8	12	13	11	Steady
Bhandup	12	10	14	18	14	Decrease
Borivali	9	7	7	8	8	Steady
Meera Road	16	10	16	16	18	Lowering

Table 7.3 NO-NO_x in air: Oxides of nitrogen (μg/m^3) in Mumbai

Location	*2012*	*2011*	*2010*	*2009*	*2008*	*Remarks*
Worli	44	32	41	67	31	Increasing
Khar	57	44	47	84	47	Increasing
Andheri	56	40	53	86	47	Rising
Bhandup	40	34	29	7	34	Steady
Borivali	20	14	22	31	19	Steady
Meera Road	60	50	65	69	54	Steady

Table 7.4 Suspended particulate matter μg/m^3) in atmosphere in Mumbai

Location	*2012*	*2011*	*2010*	*2009*	*2008*	*Remarks*
Worli	205	197	201	183	185	Rise
Khar	299	221	250	252	258	Rise
Andheri	238	203	227	263	281	Decrease
Bhandup	273	198	200	206	268	Rise
Borivali	158	125	113	129	32	Rise
Meera Road	760	642	603	389	439	Rise

Table 7.5 Atmosphere pollutants in air

S.No.	*Name of gas*	*Formula*	*% by Volume*	*% by weight*	*Toxic effects*
1.	Nitrogen	N_2	78.03	8.7×10^8	Inert, no effect
2.	Oxygen	O_2	20.99	2.7×10^8	Life supporter
3.	Argon	Ar	0.94	1.47×10^7	Asphyxiating gas
4.	Carbon dioxide	CO_2	0.033	5.5×10^5	Short of breathing
5.	Neon	Ne	0.0015	–	Causes asphyxiation
6.	Oxygen	O_2	20.00	2.6×10^5	Fast bread thing and pulse

Table 7.6 Common organic pollutants encountered in atmosphere

Comp/Formlu	*Spgr /den*	*m.p./b.p°C*	*Solu-bility (water)*	*Comp/Formula*	*Spgr /den*	*m.p./b.p°C*	*Solu-bility (water)*
Acetic acid	1.05	16.7	–	Hydrogen Sulphide	1.18	–59.6	437
Acetone	0.79	56.5	12	Iodine	4.93	184.4	0.016
Acrolein	0.84	52.2	40	Methane	0.55	–161.4	0.35
Acrylic nitrite	0.81	78.9	–	Methanol	0.79	64.7	–
Amyl acetate	0.87	142	0.25	Methylethyl ketone	0.80	79.6	37
Benzene	0.87	80.1	0.07	Neon	0.67	–245.9	2.6
Benzoyl chloride	1.212	197.2	–	n-Pentane	0.63	36.3	–
Bromine	3.2	58.78	3.13	Phenol	1.07	181.4	8.2
1, 3 Butadiene	0.62	–4.41	–				
Butane	0.60	–0.6	15	Propanol	0.854	96.6	–
n-Butyl acetate	0.88	125.1	0.7	Syrene	0.90	145.5	–
n-Butyl celluslove	0.88	171.2	–	Toluene	0.866	+10.8	–
				Tin chloride	1.32	74.1	–
Butyl ether	0.79	142.2	20.05				
Carbon dioxide	1.56	–78.2	179.7	Turpentine	0.86	155	–
Carbon disulphide	1.26	46.3	0.2	Vinyl chloride	0.90	–12	–
Carbon monoxide	195	–192°	0.004	Xylene	144	–	0.88
Carbon tetrachloride	1.59	76.8	0.097	Ammonia in-organic pollutants	0.817	–33.4	89.9
Chlorine	1.56	–34.6	1.46	Arsine	2.69	–55.0	20
Chlorobenzene	1107	132.1	–	Barium per oxide	4.95	–0.8	–
Chloroform	1.48	61.2	0.82	Epoxy oxide	1.48	150	–
Cresol (o.m.p.)	1.03–1.05	196–202	1.8–2.5	Nitric oxide	1.03	–151	7.34
Cynogen	0.86	–20.5	4.50	Nitrogen dioxide	1.05	21.3	–
Dichloride ether	1.22	178.5	1.07	Nitrous oxide	1.53	–90.7	130.9
Diethy amine	0.68	7.4	–	Nitroglycerin	1.60	160	0.18
Ethane	0.54	–88.6	4.7	Ozone	1.65	–112	0.49
Ethyl acetate	0.90	77.1	8.5	Sulphur dioxide	2.26	–10	22.8
Ethyl alcohol	0.78	98.4	–	Sulphuric acid	1.83	340	00
Ethyl ether	0.78	34.6	7.5	Phosphine	1.14	–85	2.6

It is interesting to examine Table 7.5 dealing with the atmosphere pollutants which are injurious to the human health. The highest amount of gas is nitrogen (~78%) is atmosphere but is not harmful.

Then we have high percentage of oxygen (~21%). The rest of the gases like carbon dioxide, inert gases are present in negligible proportion. Hydrogen, nitrous oxide, methane (Table 7.1) are present in very small concentration (~4.0–7.5 × 10^2 by volume).

The toxic gases causes all kinds of ill effects on the health. There are several kinds of organic compounds specially hydrocarbons as show in (Table 7.6) which are present in air. Their solubility along with m.p./ b.p. are provided in Table 7.6. They are washed with rain and descend on the earth to show that toxic effects *e.g.* Acetone, cynogen, hydrogen sulphides, ammonia, nitrous oxide. Thus Table 7.6 we have pollutants, reasonably soluble in aqueous medium while carbon monoxide, nitroglycerin, ozone have insignificant presence in air. Their solubility in water renders them less injurious to human health.

7.3 COMPOSITION OF ATMOSPHERE

Table 7.7 Composition of pure atmosphere

Constituents	*ppm (dry)*	µg/m³ *(dry basis)*	µg/m³ *(wet basis)*	%
N_2	780,000	8.95×10^8	8.67×10^8	78
O_2	209,400	2.74×10^8	2.65×10^8	20
Ar	9300	1.52×10^7	1.47×10^7	0.9
CO_2	315	5.67×10^5	5.49×10^5	0.03
He	5.2	8.50×10^2	8.25×10^2	0.05
CH_4	1.2	7.87×10^2	7.63×10^2	0.01
N_2O	0.5	9.00×10^2	8.73×10^2	0.005
H_2	0.08	4.29×10^2	4.00×10^2	0.0008

As seen in Table 7.7, atmosphere is composed of nitrogen and oxygen as major components. Carbon dioxide is present in significant proportion in atmosphere. While oxides of nitrogen, hydrocarbon, hydrogen are minor components. If the composition of this atmosphere is changed on account of the activity of man in environment leading to generation of high levels of CO, CO_2, SO_2, NO–NO_x hydrocarbons it indicates air is polluted. The exhaust emission increases level of CO, NO–NO_x and hydrocarbons in atmosphere. By combustion of coal containing sulphur, enormous amount of SO_2 is liberated which affects the health. Most of the pollutants generated in air are having ill-effects on health.

In order to understand complexity of existance of the air pollutants, it is most essential to consider their abundance in the atmosphere, their tolerance limit and location of different spheres of the earth where they exist.

We consider the abundance of elements in solar atmosphere, important components are metals as well as nonmetals. It would be seen that (Table 7.8) carbon, nitrogen, oxygen, hydrogen are present in various concentrations, *e.g.*, carbon is present in the range of 10,000 × 10^4 atoms in the solar atmosphere, while nitrogen is 21,000 × 10^4, oxygen 2.8 × 10^{10} and hydrogen as 5.1 × 10^{12} atoms. On sun we have more of hydrogen and helium (1 × 10^{12}). Out of 114 elements in the periodic classification, approximately 80 are metals and around 24 are nonmetals. Out of these 24 nonmetals, only 10 are of real concern from the viewpoint of atmospheric pollution. Table 7.7 shows composition of the atmosphere. On an average there is 78% nitrogen, 21% oxygen and 1% of other gases. The major constituents among these other gases are CO_2 and water vapour. Now by anthropogenic activity if this composition changes and if there is undue generation of toxic gases like SO_2, H_2S, CO, CO_2, NO–NO_x, O_3, suspended particulate matter or hydrocarbons or organic compounds, then the atmosphere is said to be polluted. These gases are all injurious to health. Table 7.9 describes the highest tolerance limit of industrial gases. The gases like phosgene ($COCl_2$), chlorine and methylisocyanate are tolerated in very small concentrations. Table 7.9 gives the threshold limiting values of polluting gases in the atmosphere. This table shows that only CO_2 is anthropogenic and not in the real sense a pollutant and it is tolerated in higher ratios, while SO_2(5), NO_x(5), CO(5O), NO(25), Cl_2(1) and O_3(0.1) are tolerated in very small concentration.

Table 7.8 Abundance of few elements in the solar atmosphere

Element	*Atomic number*	*Atomic mass*	*Abundance (× 10^6) atoms*
H	1	1.00	0.05 × 10^8
C	6	12.01	100
N	7	14.00	210
O	8	16.00	0.028 × 10^6
Mg	12	24.31	170
S	16	32.06	43
Ca	20	40.08	8.7
V	23	50.94	0.059
Cr	24	52.00	2.0
Mn	25	54.93	1.5
Fe	26	55.84	270
Co	27	58.93	0.55
Ni	28	58.71	4.7
Cu	29	63.54	0.87
Zn	30	65.37	0.31

In order to understand dispersion of pollutant in the earth's atmosphere it is necessary to understand how the atmosphere is composed of? There are different spheres as are troposphere, stratosphere, mesosphere and thermosphere (Table 7.9).

Thus, if we consider the altitude in km, the area upto 8 to 10 km is called **troposphere**; 1 0 to 50 km is called as **stratosphere**; 50 to 150 km is termed as **mesophere** and 150 to 400 km is called as **thermosphere**. The lowest temperature in troposphere is about –60°C; in stratosphere –88°C; in mesophere –100°C and in thermosphere it continues to rise. The highest temperature in troposphere is 20°C, stratosphere 80°C, mesosphere 100°C and thermosphere greater than 500°C. An aircraft flies up to a height of 20 km and experiences a minimum temperature of –60°C. The highest peak of the Himalayas, *viz*. Gaurishankar or Mt. everest is at a height of 6 to 8 km, with the approximate minimum temperature of –40°C. In the upper atmosphere, there is atomic oxygen and nitrogen, while the middle air contains diffusion of oxygen and nitrogen and it is called as **homopause** or **diffusion layer**, while the ground bottom layer contains a mixture of oxygen and nitrogen. One significant feature of temperature change is, as we go beyond 10 km, temperature decreases continuously, then a further ascend upto 50 km shows a continuous temperature rise, upto 90 km temperature again it falls and beyond 90 km till more than 800 km, temperature continuously rises. This drop in temperature and pressure with height in troposphere causes inversion and change in velocity and direction of wind. The pressure drop is from 100 to 10 kpa or to 0.0001 kpa (Fig. 7.1).

Table 7.9 Tolerance limit of industrial gases

S.No.	*Gaseous pollutant*	*Threshold limit ppm (TLV)*
1.	NH_3	2.5
2.	Cl_2	1.0
3.	CO	5.0
4.	SO_2	5.0
5.	$COCl_2$ (Phosgene)	0.1
6.	HCN	10
7.	H_2S	10
8.	CH_3CN (MIC)	0.02
9.	CO_2	5000
10.	NO	25
11.	NO_2	5
12.	O_3	0.1

Table 7.10 Toxic effects of gases and vapours on man

Effects	*Pollutants*	*Action*
Asphyxiants	N_2, CH_4, CO, CO_2	Causes oxygen deficiency
Irritants	H_2SO_4, HCI, NH_3	Nasal problems
	SO_2, Br_2, Cl_2	Irritates lower lung
	NO–NO_x	Bronchitis, asthma
Anaesthetics	Petrol	Depresent
	CH_3 CH_2 OH	anaesthetic effects
	C_2 H_5 OC_2 H_5	
	C_6 H_6	action on blood
	CH_3 OH, CS_2	Nervous system affected

Within these spheres the activities of man by and large are confined to the troposphere which has a variable temperature of –50°C to +40°C. The phenomena of inversion would be considered in next chapter on air pollution and meteorology. It is noteworthy to examine Table 7.10 which shows the source from where pollutants emerge and their toxic effects.

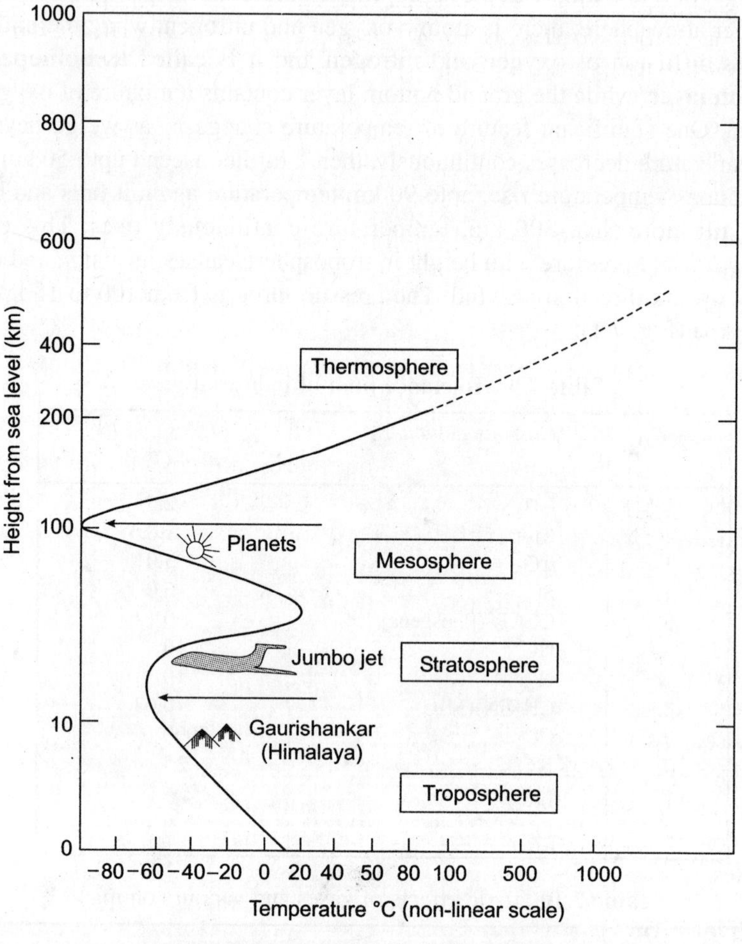

Fig. 7.1 Temperature zones of atmosphere

7.4 EFFECTS OF AIR POLLUTION

The air pollutants causes adverse effects on human health. Apart from human beings vegetation and plants also get severely affected on exposure to polluted atmosphere. Various kinds of materials get tarnished or spoiled by air pollutants. The whole atmosphere is made up of several planets and stars. Consequently, the atmospheric components also get seriously affected by air pollution. It is worthwhile to consider such effects on various constituents of the earth. Some known toxic effects on human being are summarised in Tables 7.12 and 7.13.

Table 7.11 Source of pollutants

S.No.	Source of pollution	Name of element present	Toxic effect on
1.	Soil dust	Al, Si, Ti, Sc, Mn.	Silicolysis, Lung problem
2.	Marine environment	Na–Cl.	High blood pressure
3.	Lime stone industry	Ca	Cardiac problems
4.	Steel industry	Mn, Fe, Cr	Blood anemia
5.	Auto exhaust emission	Pb, Br	Lever affected Cirrhosis
6.	Combustion-refuse	Zn, K, Pb, Sb	Metal flume fever
7.	Combustion-oil	V, S. As	Lung throat affects
8.	Combustion coal	Al, SO_2, S.	Dementia, alzarmine
9.	Diesel oil exhaust	C	Throat infection
10.	Nonferrous metal factory	Cu, Zn, As, Sb.	Fever, anemia, Vomiting

It will be observed from Table 7.13 that there is significant effect of gaseous pollutants like SO_2, Cl_2, NO–NO_x, O_3 act on materials like metals, paints, pigments, leather, paper, textiles, dyes, rubber, glass and ceramics. Table 7.13 describes the physiological action of toxic gases on human beings. This also includes toxic vapours. The principal toxic effects caused are asphyxiation, irritation, and anaesthetic manifestations. This action includes irritation of nose, lungs, and central nervous system.

It is worthwhile to investigating how these pollutants are released in the atmosphere. A perusal of Table 7.11 shows that the main source is dust and suspended particulate matter (SPM). This source also includes emissions from cement, steel, oil and alloy industry. Thus in addition to toxic gases we have the presence of inorganic components like metal pollutants such as lead, manganese, arsenic, cadmium which are very toxic in nature. The combustion of diesel or analogous oil also produces toxic metals like vanadium, arsenic, antimony. The autoexhaust emission is worst source of atmosphere pollution. The main element is released in air is lead which is component of ignition control additive or (ICA). It is added in oil to prevent deposition of soot in the car engines. As a rule $Pb(C_2H_5)_4$ is added as antiknock to fuel which in turn dissociated to elemental lead and it in turns combine with soot, *i.e.* carbon which is removed from gear boxes of the vehicles.

(a) Effects on Health

The air pollution have deleterious effect not only on human health but also on vegetation and animals, materials and structure of atmosphere, soil and water bodies. The carbon, sulphur and fluoride cycle in nature on large scale affects man. SO_2 is released in troposphere. Fertilisers release fluoride which gets accumulated in vegetation and harms our teeth and bones. The total body burn means how much of material accumulates in body in blood, tissue, teeth, bone and urine. The body can discharge these pollutants *e.g.*, lead can get ingested in body and cause problems with brain. While CO interacts with blood generating carboxy haemoglobin and arrest flow of blood. The human respiratory system is most sensitive towards atmospheric pollutants.

The nasal, trachea bronchial or pulmonary portion of respiratory system gets affected by air pollutants (Fig. 7.2). The pollutants invariably affect the chest causing pulmonary edema specially with SPM and toxic gaseous pollutants. SPM gets mostly deposited in trachea and bronchial region. Sneezing removes obstruction in the passage (*i.e.,* mucociliary escalator) SO_2 is absorbed in major portion of the respiratory system. Air pollution affects respiratory, circulatory and olfactory system. Clinical epidermiological and toxicology, studies reveal adverse effects of air pollution. Most reliable information is obtained from clinical investigation. Such of the adverse effect are listed in Tables 7.10 and 7.11. The presence of other pollutants in air also shown (Table 7.12) for physiological effects.

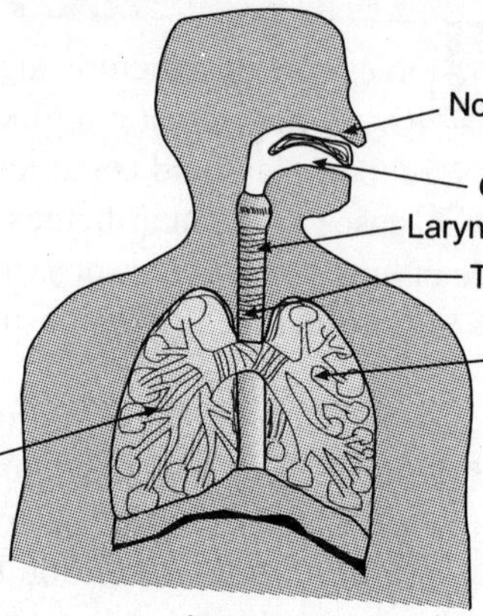

Fig. 7.2 Human breathing pattern

Table 7.12 Physiological effects on health

Pollutant	*Effects on human health*
CO	Circulatory system affected, cardiovascular disease noted.
NO_2	Respiratory pathogens increase, causes eye irritation.
O_3	Coughing, chest problem.
Pb	Neuromotor and neurocongitivits disease, brain is affected.
PAN	Eye irritation, burning, sneezing, cough and cold.
SO_2	Respiratory disorder, chronic problem, chest disease.

(b) Effect on Vegetation and Animals

The low concentration of pollutant in air does not affect plants even on long exposure, but they have biochemical changes with some physiological response and symptoms of deterioration and death of epidermal cells. The 'stomataes' are affected (Fig. 7.3). Fumigation—an old agricultural practice leads to destruction of plants. Fruit yield is decreased. O_3, SO_2, NO–NO_x, PAN are deadly harmful to plants. The earth has 1.9 J × 10^{10} mm coverage of the forest *i.e.,* 1/5 of total available land. At low dose forest acts as sink for pollutant but same forest also acts as source of CO_2, NH_3 and NO–NOx. They are formed by the biological denitrification process.

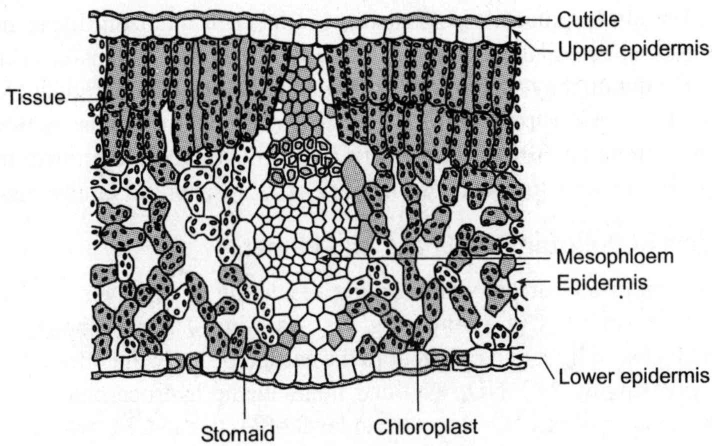

Fig. 7.3 Structure of leaf

The intake of PAN, O_3 develops immunity in plants for pest infection. The acid rain or acid deposition pertains to transfer of the acidic components from atmosphere (*e.g.*, SO_2, NO_2, HNO_3, SPM) to the earth. This leads to acidification of lakes leading to adverse effects on flora and fauna, fish and animals. Arsenic, lead and mercury are deadly harmful pollutants to the animals. Plants suffer from the effect of pulmonary oedema. Intake of heavy metals is more serious for animals Arsenic lead and mercury intake has caused diarrhoea, anaemia, discouloration of hair of the animals. Fluoride from phosphate fertiliser is also bad. It causes fluorosis.

(c) Effect of Pollutants on Material

Table 7.13 Effect on materials

Maternal	*Effects on materials*	*Pollutants for exposure*
Metals	Loss of lustre	SO_2, NO–NOx
Pigment	Bleaching action	SO_2, Cl_2,
Paints	Discolouration	SO_2, H_2S, SPM
Leather	Bad gloss with no shine	SO_2, CO_2
Paper	Increase brittleness	SO_2, CO_2, H_2S
Textile	Decrease in durability	SO_2, CO_2
Dyes	Bleaching action	NO_2, Cl_2, H_2S
Rubber	Cracks, fatigue	O_3, CO_2, CO
Ceramic and glass	Rough surface	Acid vapours

In Table 7.12, we notice that the most significant effect is seen on metals by the loss of characteristic metallic lustre. They are corroded if they are wet. Aluminum has no effect by SO_2. Galvanised plates show also depletion of zinc layer on exposure to pollution. Copper and silver form protective coating and prevents corrosion on exposure to pollution. The exposure of building to SO_2, CO_2, shows the destruction of surface of wall. The dyes and fabric get affected with pollutants like SO_2. The SPM, spoils fabric and textile products. While ozone bleaches design on cloth. SO_2 affects glass, paper and leather on prolonged exposure. H_2S reacts with lead paint with the formation of sulphide giving black colouration. O_3 attacks the rubber leading to its cracking. The smog causes haze and mist in the air and scattering of radiation. SPM largely reduces visibility due to scattering of particles. The particles of size 1 μm reduces visibility of atmosphere to almost zero.

(d) Effects of Pollutants in Space and Planets

The long-term effects are global warming, depletion of O_3 layer in atmosphere and greenhouse effect. CO_2 promotes global warming. The greenhouse gases are those which absorb light and radiate it to the earth (specially the infrared radiation of long wavelength). NO–NO_x, CO and nonmethane hydrocarbon cause global warming. Another ill-effect is decrease in level of O_3 due to CFC from air causing "Ozone hole." The UV–radiation converts O_2 to O_3 through the formation of atomic oxygen in normal atmosphere.

The UV radiation can be absorbed by O_3 to undergo dissociation. As such O_3 prevents UV radiation to reach on surface of earth. But chlorofluorocarbon from cyrogenic sources destroys O_3 layer. The CFC undergoes degradation on exposure to sunlight.

Table 7.14 Greenhouse effect

S.No.	*Greenhouse gas*	*Formula*	*ppm in 1800*	*ppm in 1900*		*% Level of rise/fall*	*Duration in years*
1.	Carbon monoxide	CO	40	60	ppb	0.20	Long time
2.	Carbon dioxide	CO_2	280	353	ppm	0.5	150 ys
3.	Methane	CH_4	0.8	1.7	ppm	1.0	10 ys
4.	Dinitrogen oxide	N_2O_4	288	310	ppb	0.20	150 ys
5.	Nitrogen dioxide	NO_2	40	250	ppb	0.30	Many days
6.	Hydrocarbon	HC	500	900	ppt	–	Many days
7.	Chlorofluoro compound (C-11)	C-11	0	280	ppt	4	65
8.	Chlorofluoro compound (C-12)	C-12	0	484	ppt	4	130

Table 7.14 shows rise and fall of greenhouse gases. They mainly compose of CO, CO_2, CH_4, HC, N_2O_4, and Chlorofluoro compounds sold in industry under trade mark C-11 and C-12.

It is worthwhile at this stage to consider (Table 7.14) the figures for the 19th and 20th century and to record fall or rise of their level in the atmosphere. The levels of CO, CO_2, HC, oxides of nitrogen all are rising alarmingly in air at the level of ppm or ppb or ppt levels. Such gases remain stationary in atmosphere unless wind direction and wind velocity changes in order to remove them from atmosphere. Further one cannot always rely on metrological factors for their elimination. The city planners must take stringent measure against industries which are not treating released air or the effluent before which latter is let off in open atmosphere or sewers. The cost of the treatment of pollutant in effluent or air is much less than the pollutant treatment taken after the released in town or big metropolitan cities like Mumbai, Kolkata, Chennai, Bengalore and New Delhi.

Apart from CFC other greenhouse gases can also cause damage to protective layer of O_3 in the universe and render the earth usually warm.

7.5 GLOBAL EFFECTS OF POLLUTION

(a) Greenhouse Effect and Acid Rain

In 1959, the level of CO_2 in air was about 316 ppm, but it rose to 320 ppm in 1962, further it went upto 324 in 1969 and was more than 350 in 1990 now it may be more than 400 ppm. The level of CO_2 is successively rising in the atmosphere. Such increase in CO_2 warms up the surface of the earth. The increase in atmospheric turbidity like smog or pollution reduces the intensity of falling sunrays on earth and decreases the temperature of the lower atmosphere. However, due to balancing effect of these two factors, man has succeeded in changing climate of the earth. Trees are important source for assimilating large amounts of CO_2 in day time and producing CO_2, in night time to biosphere and also atmosphere. The combustion of the fossil fuels, industrial, domestic and transportation activities, has increased the percentage of CO_2. By 2100, we may have 495 ppm of CO_2 in the air, which is objectionable concentration, it promotes grim warming to earth. This anthropogenic production of CO_2 consumes it through photosynthesis and replenishes supply of O_2 in the atmosphere in day time. Fortunately, any increase in the greenhouse effect due to manmade emission of CO_2 is far out weighs by more long-range events. Even if temperature of earth increases day by day, H_2O vapour in air also

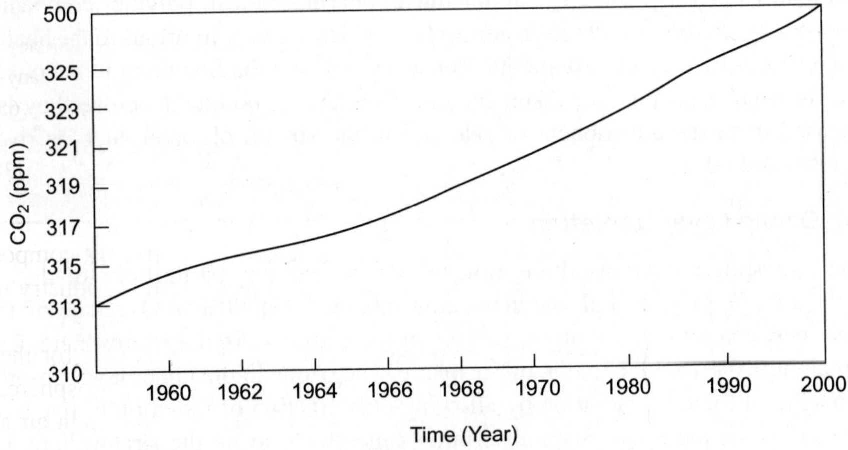

Fig. 7.4 Variation in CO_2 level in air as extrapolated to 2000

rises and in turn increases absorption of gases. Thus, greenhouse effect does the job of balancing the constant level of CO_2 in air. This in turn leads to the philosophy of grow more trees on the earth. This is because in day time CO_2 absorbs any amount of the excess of CO_2 generated by industries in atmosphere but at the same time also releases O_2 to air on account of photosynthesis to refresh the quality of air. However, in night-time they release CO_2 and inhale oxygen.

Consequently, due to this cycle of inhalation and exhalation of CO_2 the atmosphere maintains optimum level of CO_2 in air. It does not allow to exceed minimum level of CO_2 in atmosphere preventing thereby warming of earth and atmosphere. This kind of effect is termed as "Greenhouse effect". It is conducive for human beings. In fact, we are surviving on earth due to this effect. In soil, it is worthwhile to note industrial pollutants (Table 7.15).

Table 7.15 Industrial pollutants

S.No.	*The industry*	*Emitted pollutant*
1.	Metal finish	Alcohol, Celluslove acetate, phthalates
2.	Motor car painting	Phenols, Toluene, Xylene Ketones
3.	Paper and pulp	Latex, high, boiling organic compounds
4.	Rubber processing	Latex, vinyl chloride, mercaptans
5.	Chemical processing	Any kind of voltile component
6.	Pharma products	Toluene, hydrocarbons, isopropanol
7.	Beverage production	Several form of hydrocarbons
8.	Confectionary factory	Ethyl alcohol; flavouring agent source
9.	Printing press	Alcohols, glycerols, ink
10.	Soil treatment	Benzene, toluene, xylene, ethylene

Apart from conventional gases reasonable amount of organic products are released in the atmosphere by various chemical industries Table 7.15 shows paper, rubber, pharmaceutical, food beverages industries letting off lots of harmful pollutants in air. One has to carefully characterise them by gas-liquid chromatography. By and large all chemical, pharmaceutical, polymer companies release obvinoxous pollutants in atmosphere which are very injurious to the health. Therefore in EIA *i.e.* environmental impact assessment the first thing to be looked into is what measures are taken for the abetment of pollutant before they are released in to the atmosphere or released in the stream of water such as river, brooks, and lakes.

(b) Ozone Layer Depletion

The atmosphere contains three molecules of ozone per 10 millions of the air molecules. O_3 plays a vital role in the atmosphere. About 90% of O_3 resides in the layer between 8 to 20 km above surface of the earth *i.e.*, in the stratosphere. The remaining 10% ozone is in the meso sphere. The ozone in the upper layer absorbs damaging ultraviolet radiation by allowing only fraction of radiation to reach on the surface of the earth. Such absorption generates heat on the stratosphere. O_3 controls temperature of the atmosphere. In absence of protective layer of ozone all the ultraviolet radiation from sun descend on the surface of the earth. Ozone from atmosphere is generated as per the following reactions. In laboratory it is called Sieman's reaction with silent electric discharge.

$$O_2 + \text{UV radiation} = O + O; O_2 + O \rightarrow O_3(g)$$

It is measured in Dobson units. The concentration of the ozone is 10^{12} molecules/ cm^2 at 20 km rising upto 10^{14} mg/cm^3 at 45 km. It is interesting to know how depletion of this ozone layer occurs? It was experimentally verified by NASA in America that such layer over Antarctica is depleted (60%) causing antarctic ozone hole (AOH). Several chemicals are also responsible for causing the ozone hole in the atmospheres. Such chemicals are largely made out of chlorine, fluorine, bromine with carbon and hydrogen. One of them is fluorocarbons or chlorofluorocarbons (CFC) which are responsible for depletion of ozone layer in the atmosphere.

In addition to CFC; *i.e.,* methyl chloroform is also very dangerous. These compounds are used in refrigerators, airconditioners, foam blowing, cleaning electrical contacts, and as solvents. Ozone is destroyed in atmosphere in following transformation:

$$2O_3 + 2Cl_2 = 2ClO + 2O_2$$

$$2ClO + 2O \rightarrow 2Cl + 2O_2 \rightarrow Cl_2 + 2O_2(g)$$

i.e., O_3 gets easily converted to oxygen and liberates free chlorine. This chlorine atom can decompose 100,000 ozone molecules in the air.

The depletion of O_3 layer leads to skin cancer, eye irritation and problems with immune system. By obstructing phytoplankton, on ocean surface, food chain is affected. The Montreal Protocol was passed in 1987 to completely reduce use of CFC and conserve ozone layer. Thus, the halocarbons, CCl_4, methylchloroform, hydrobromofluorocarbons, methylbromide and bromochloromethane are banned for use by Montreal treaty. Instead of using CFC ozone friendly products were developed like HFC 134a, HCFC 22, HCRF, HN_3 HFC 152a for the refrigeration and use them in compressors, foam sector, and fire fighting devices. CCl_4 is to be replaced by per chloroethylene as the solvent. India is signatory to Montreal Protocol (1987) so attempts are made to phase out CFC or analogus products. The protocol was modified in July 2000 for developing countries. The developed countries like England, Denmark, Austria, Canada and China have made little progress in abatment of CFC and maintaining protective layer of ozone in stratosphere and troposphere stating that it is thus not possible to avoid use of CFC.

(c) Acid Rain

Acid rain is ascribed to the rainfall which is more acidic (pH $<$ 4.0) than natural rain. It has pH range between 4.0 to 5.0 against normal rain fall with pH between 6.5 to 8.5. The acid rain is an outcome of the air pollution which is caused by different chemical industries. The existance of acid rain must be born in mind while preparing environmental impact assessment (EIA) during the setting new industries.

Several European countries, Canada and America suffered from problem of acid rain. In India some years ago such rain was detected in Mumbai and Kolkata. Acid rain is very harmful. It not only spoils potable source of the water but also destroys buildings, monuments, and shining surfaces and structures. By lowering the pH, aquatic life in lakes is killed. It prevents fish from laying eggs. Algae in water is destroyed by acid rain. In jungles vegetables plants trees the leaves are all affected by acid rain. Even land becomes barren due to loss of micronutrients in the soil. The microbiological activity of land is ruined and it is rendered barren.

The important factors causing acid rains are the presence of SO_2, NO–NO_x, hydrocarbons in rain water. SO_2 is generated in large amount due to combustion of coal containing sulphur and various metallurgical operations while NO–NO_x is generated by photochemical smog and autoexhaust emissions. The oxides of nitrogen form atomic oxygen and nitrogen dioxide and finally nitric acids:

$$NO_2 + h\nu \rightleftharpoons NO_2 \uparrow$$

$$NO_2 \rightleftharpoons NO + O \text{ (atomic);}$$

$$O + O_2 + M \rightleftharpoons O_3 + M,$$

$$O_3 + NO \rightleftharpoons NO_2 + O_2 \uparrow$$

Then $$2NO_2 + O_2 \rightarrow N_2O_5 + O$$

$$N_2O_5 + H_2O \rightarrow 2HNO_3 \text{ (Acid rains)}$$

In case of emission by sulphur dioxide reactions are as follows:

$$SO_2 + h\nu \rightleftharpoons SO_2 \uparrow$$

$$SO_2 + O_2 \rightleftharpoons SO_4^-;$$

$$SO_4^- + O_2 \rightarrow SO_3^- + O_3;$$

$$SO_3 + H_2O = H_2SO_4 \text{ (acid)}$$

Thus, sulphuric acid is produced.

The Earth Sumit in 1992 held at Rio De Janero Brazil seriously considered problem of the acid rain in the developed countries and marked out strategy for the control of the acid rain in the atmosphere. All problems on greenhouse effect, depletion of ozone layer and acid rain were discussed in the conference in great details to dispel these universal problems and render the earth clean.

Table 7.16 Effect of gases pollutant on health

S.No.	*Pollutant*	*Maximum level (mg/m^3)*	*Damage caused to the health*
1.	Oxides of Nitrogen (NO–NO_x)	20	Harmful for health causes anemia
2.	Ammonia (NH_3)	15	Harmful in high concentration
3.	Sulphur dioxide (SO_2)	500	Throat infection and lung
4.	Vinyl Chloride	5	Neurogenic poison
5.	Benzene (C_6H_6)	5	Carcinogenic effects
6.	1-2 dichloroethane ($C_2H_3Cl_2$)	5	Less toxic
7.	Hydrogen Chloride (HCl)	30	Creates lungs problem
8.	Particulate (SPM)	20	Bysnosis, lung affected

Table 7.16 indicates the maximum level of the atmospheric gases which are tolerated. Beyond these levels they are likely to cause health problems *e.g.* 5 $\mu g/m^3$ is level of organic vapours composed of benzene dichloroethane, vinyl chloride. Even suspended particulate matter as well as NO–NO_x should not exceed the limit of 20 $\mu g/m^3$. On the whole the investigation have been carried out by various agencies effect of pollutants (gas) on water or wastewater contamination. However, the close investigation on air pollution is lacking. It is no doubt problem of big cities but there are in existence equally big measures for their control in the atmosphere (Table 7.17).

Table 7.17 Gaseous pollutants

S. No.	*Gas*	*Character*	*Remarks*	*S. No.*	*Gas*	*Character*	*Remarks*
1.	CH_4	Odourless, burn	Greenhouse gas	7.	NO_2	Brown gas	Present in smog
2.	CFC	Reduce O_3 layer	Thermal properties	8.	N_2O	Colourless gas	Inert
3.	HC	Many virtues	Autoemission releases this	9.	SO_2	Pale yellow choking smell	Bad for vegetable
4.	CO	No colour odour	Components combustion	10.	SO_3	Soluble in water	Very corrosive
5.	CO_2	No odour or colour	Greenhouse gas	11.	H_2S	Rotten eggs odour	Poisonous
6.	NO	No colour	High temp. combustion production	12.	O_3	Reactive gas	Photo-chemical smog

The gaseous pollutant levels in air is high. Table 7.17 list important chemical characteristics of these pollutants. CO, CO_2, CH_4 are all greenhouse gases while NO–NO_x, O_3 are important components of photochemical smog while many organic vapours are part of autoexhaust emissions. The oxides of sulphur originate from combustion of nondesulpharised coal and coke, at this stage.

(d) Photochemical Smog

Many cities like Los Angles, Mexico and Zurich suffered severely from photochemical smog. In 1952, in London the photochemical smog laced with SO_2 called as sulphurous smog reduced the visibility to distance to 3–miles. The oxides of nitrogen and hydrocarbons promote fog formation. Automotive emission enhances this formation process. In America automotive emission standard are fixed with following figures. Total hydrocarbons (0.41 gm/mile, CO (3.4 g/mile), NO_2(0.4 gms/mile). In the course of reactions hydrocarbons in air get oxidised to CO_2. The reactions are $CH_4 + O \rightarrow CH_3^* + OH^*$. This further forms peroxyl radical $H_3C^* + O_2 + M \rightarrow H_3COO + M$ (methyl pyroxyl radical). The other reacts as $CH_4 + OH^* \rightarrow CH_3^* + H_2O$ and $H_3COO^* + NO \rightarrow H_3C^* + NO_2$. Then action is H_3COO^* +

NO_2, M $\rightarrow$ $CH_3COO\ NO_2$ + M, $H_2O + h\nu \rightarrow$ Photochemical organic compounds undergo photochemical reaction to give free radical.

(*i*) *Mechanism of smog formation:* The atmospheric oxidants like O_3, H_2O_2, $ROOR^1$, ROOH or PAN are formed as per reactions given below: If R = aryl or alkyl.

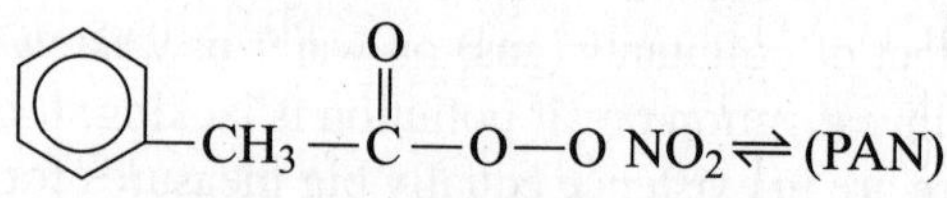

Fig. 7.5 Peroxy nitrite reaction

It gets converted to PAN. It is powerful eye irritant. The overall mechanism of the formation of photochemical smog is very complex. Figure 7.6 shows increasing level of NO_2 and decrease level NO level in air. The reactions lead to the formation of OH^- radicle. The overall reaction proceeds in four ways:

(*i*) initial photochemial reaction giving atomic oxygen

$NO_2 + h\nu \rightarrow NO + O$ (atomic)

$O_2 + O + M \rightarrow O_3 + M$; $O_3 + NO \rightarrow NO_2 + O_2$ (M = methyl)

$RH + O \rightarrow R^+$ + other product, $O_3 + RH \rightarrow R^* + OH$ products

$NO + ROO^- \rightarrow {}^*NO_2$ + Product, $NO_2 + R^* \rightarrow$ Product + PAN

(*ii*) reaction of oxygen species to generate ozone

(*iii*) generation of organic free radical to form RH

(*iv*) Chain propagation branching and termination.

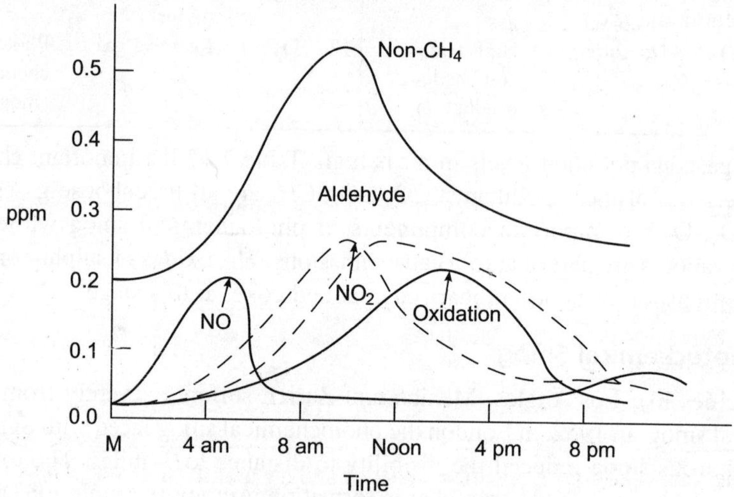

Fig. 7.6 Photochemical smog

Important Reactions in smog formation are:

$OH^- + NO_2^- \rightarrow HNO_2 \rightarrow OH^- + NO^-$; $2OH^- \rightarrow H_2O_2$

$2HOO^- \rightarrow H_2O_2 + O_2$

$NO_2^- + O_3 \rightarrow NO_3^- + O_2$, $NO_3^- + RH \rightarrow HNO_3 + R^-$

$NO_2^- + NO_3^- \rightarrow N_2O_5$; $N_2O_5 + H_2O \rightarrow 2HNO_3$

NO_3^- is the important species of atmosphere which is more prevalent in night. In day, it degrades as $NO_3 + h\nu \rightarrow NO + O_2$ or $NO_2 + O$. In reaction NO_3^- is slow radical than OH^- in air. The reactivity of hydrocarbons in smog formation is important specially with OH^- ion. The inorganic products from smog are SO_4^{-2} and NO_3^- leading to the acid precipitation, decrease in visibility and adverse effects on health. N_2O_5 forms HNO_3 in fog. This with NH_3 gives NH_4NO_3 having adverse effects upon plants and animals.

(*ii*) *Effects of Smog:* It affects health, damages material and is toxic to plants and affect stability of the atmosphere. O_3 (0.15 ppm) causes coughing. By the process of the polymerisation aerosol particles give smog forming reaction. Plants get affected due to oxidants like O_3, PAN and NO–NO_x of these PAN is most toxic to plants. Photochemical smog is an example of O_3 in wrong ground level. The overall reactions can be called *giant chemical reactions*. The net level being 100 to 120 ppb in air. The volatile organic compounds accelerate the process of fog formation. NO' is primary pollutant while O_3 and HNO_3 are generated later as secondary pollutants. At high temperature nitrogen converts to NO nitric oxide and sub-sequently to NO_2.

(*iii*) *Removal of Photochemical Smog*: One must eliminate NO_2 and HC from air to reduce fog. O_3 level in grouped strata should be reduced. The generation of NO or NO_2 in combustion emission must be decreased by using the catalytic convertor. Rhodium convertor is best to convert $NO_2 \rightarrow N_2$ and $CO \rightarrow CO_2$. They also reduce the formation of hydrocarbons. The addition of NH_3 converts NO^- to elemental nitrogen.

(*iv*) *Ecological Effects of Photochemical Smog:* NO^- is not soluble in water but long exposure converts it to HNO_3. Wet deposition of pollutants transfers them to earth surface in form of rain snow or fog formation in the period of ten years. It is worthwhile to examine emission standard abroad to prevent fog.

Table 7.18 Emission standards in various countries in world. ($\mu g/m^3 \times 10$)

	Hydrocarbons		*CO*		*NO_2*	
State	*1980*	*1990*	*1980*	*1990*	*1980*	*1990*
New York	0.41	0.05	7.0	3.4	2.0	1.0
California	0.39	0.25	9.0	3.4		1.0–0.4
Ontario	–	0.25	–	3.4	–	1.0
Mexico	4.8	0.40	53	3.4	–	1.0

The Table 7.19 gives primary and secondary standard of pollutants.

7.6 SOURCES OF POLLUTION

The most important sources of air pollution are transportation, fuel combustion. The stationary source is industrial process, solid waste disposal and other miscellaneous sources. It is noteworthy to see in Fig. 7.7 that maximum CO is emitted by transportation, while maximum SO_2 is liberated due to fuel combustion from stationary sources. The auto exhaust emission generates 10^{-8} million tonnes

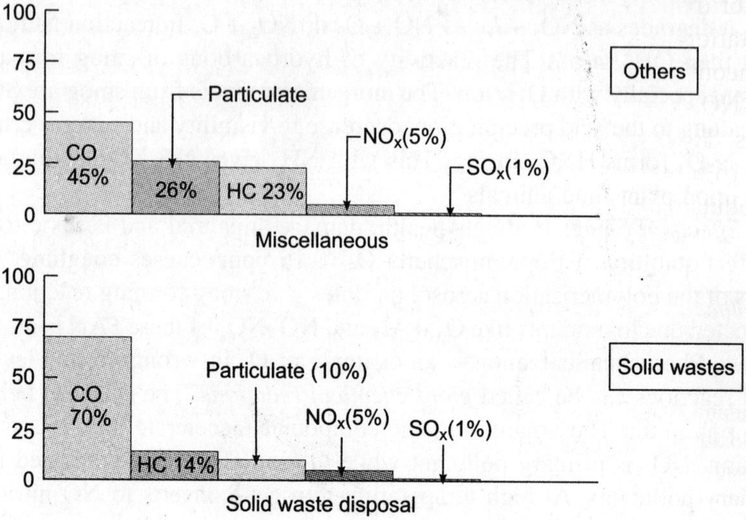

Fig. 7.7 Sources of pollution

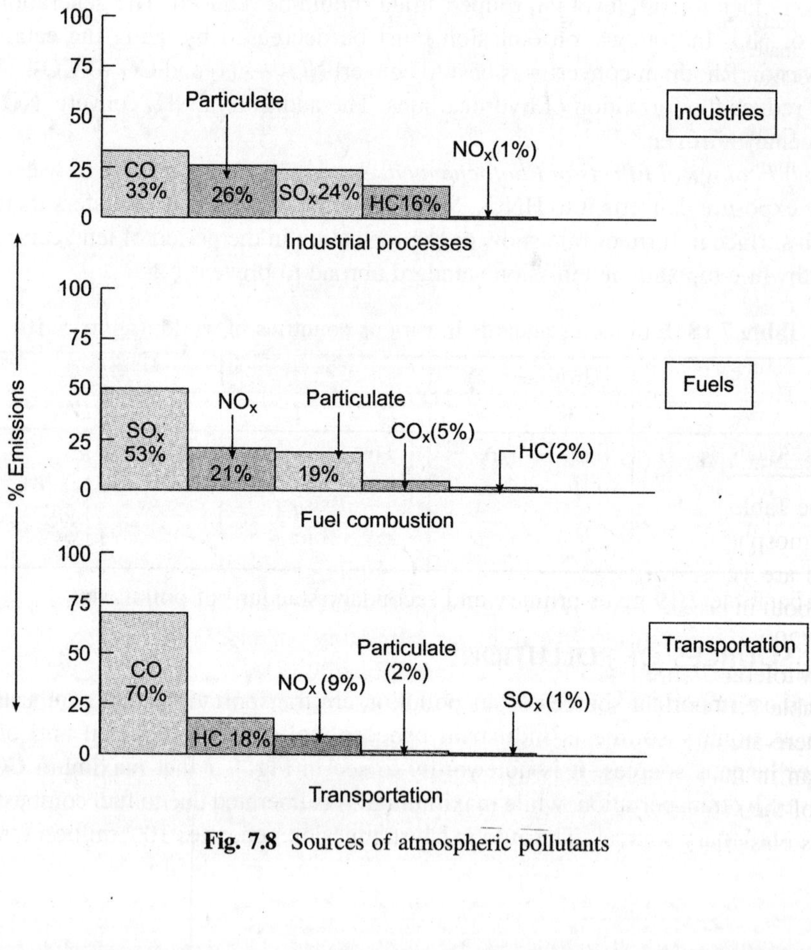

Fig. 7.8 Sources of atmospheric pollutants

per year of oxides of nitrogen. Highest amount of hydrocarbon are liberated by transportation industry while suspended particulare matter is generated by miscellaneous sources and also by fuel combustion. Amongst these pollutants SO_2 and NO–NO_x are major culprits. Figure 7.7 outlines the major sources of SO_2 emissions. The coal combustion generates 41% pollutants, while petrol burning liberates 16%, smelting give 5%, refinery product give 7% and other sources give 5% of pollutants. Thus, the major source of pollution is coal burning.

Table 7.19 Air quality standards

S.No.	*Pollutant*	*Chemical formula*	*Standards* Primary $\mu g/m^3$	*Standards* Secondary $\mu g/m^3$	*Source of contamination in air*
1.	Sulphur dioxide	SO_2	60–80	80–260	Combustion of coal containing sulphur
2.	Oxides of nitrogen	NO–NO_x	60–90	80–100	Vegetation affected gives photochemical smog
3.	Suspended particulate	SPM	130–200	150–300	Collects due to lack of moisture in air
4.	Respirator particulate matter	RPM	60	120	Very fine particles affects lung
5.	Ozone	O_3	157	210	From stratosphere it descends on earth
6.	Carbon monoxide	CO	2	5–10	Incomplete combustion of fuel
7.	Hydrocarbon	HC	160	160	Release from chemical industries
8.	Lead	Pb	0.75–1.5	1.0–1.5	Auto exhaust emissions
9.	Poly aromatic Hydrocarbon	PAH	0–10	0–0.10	Plastic and Polymer industries
10.	Carboxylic acid (oliphane)	–COOH	40–1300	PPb < 0.1ηg	Food and drug industries
11.	Nonmethane	Non CH_4	500–1200	–	decaying matter, vegetable decay
12.	Formaldehyde	HCHO	20–80	0.1–1.0	Produced from atmosphere lightening
13.	Ammonia	NH_3	0.1–10	0.1–80	Release from effluent

The Table 7.19 list the level of primary as well as of the secondary standards in the atmospheric gases. It is related to National ambient air quality standards. Such levels are very low for organic pollutants while greenhouse gases have higher limit both in primary as well as in secondary standards. SPM has high permissible limit (200 $\mu g/m^3$) however for RPM *i.e.* respiratory polluting matter has (60 $\mu g/m^3$) as low tolerance limit. Very small concentration of CO, NH_3 are tolerated as shown in (Table 7.19).

There are numerous sources of air pollutants which are generated by activity of man in the environment. The natural process also generates pollutants. One way of the source of air pollution is classified as the natural pollutant and second one is classified as man-made pollutants. Table 7.20 list man-made pollution.

From the data in Table 7.20, we can infer that transportation is worst polluting source emitting 92% CO, 65% hydrocarbons and 42% of NO–NOx. While chemical industries as well as thermal power plants release substantial amount of SO_2 due to the combustion of coal containing sulphur (32–48%). The hydrocarbons also emerge from traffic (~ 65%).

Table 7.20 Source of man-made pollution

Source	*CO* %	*SO_2* %	*HC* %	*NO–NOx* %
Transportation	92	4	65	42
Industries	4	32	26	21
Power plants	–	48	–	32
Space heating	3	12	3	5
Combustion	1	4	6	0

7.7 NATURAL SOURCES

An erupting volcano emits particulate matter, along with SO_2, H_2S and CH_4. The accidental fires in forest give rise to large amount smoke, unburned hydrocarbons, CO, CO_2, NO–NO_x and ash. The ocean emits aerosols in atmosphere. The pollen emitted from plant causes air pollution. The anthropogenic source includes industry, utilities and personal sources. The industries which are most important source of air pollution are power plant, refuse, incinerators, cement, glass, minerals, metals, chemical fertilisers, plastics, pesticides, petrochemicals paper, agricultural products and food. Those manufacturing new products from raw materials are bound to create pollution. Industrial sources are sometimes designated as stationary source of pollution. The domestic activity also produces large amount of air pollution. The heating of houses or waste handling machines produce air pollution. Personal sources cause definite pollution by process involving automobile, cooking, open refuse burning house heating, recreation and incinerators.

(a) Combustion as the Source

The combustion produces CO_2 and water vapour. It releases lethal air pollutants like CO, CO_2, SO_2, NO–NOx, smoke, fly ash, polynuclear hydrocarbons. Since the process is dependant on free radical chain reaction, time, temperature and turbulence must be considered for combustion generating sources. Fuels containing volatile materials do produce pollution. The solid fuel is worst. At high temperature combustion produces more of oxides of nitrogen, CO and hydrocarbons. Auto exhaust emissions givcs mostly NO–NO_x, CO.

(b) Stationary Sources

These sources are numerous in number. They are complex. Their emission can be controlled by modifying processes or recovery of used products. The important industries, causing pollution of air are the liquid soap factory which gives odour, while sulphuric acid factory produces in atmosphere mist or haze; plastic industry produces nondegradable organic waste (PVC) and emits obvinoxous odour. Paints industry emits gases like acrolein in air. Acid manufacturing units liberate SO_2, SO_3 and aerosols. The phosphatic fertiliser industry gives particulate matter and gaseous fluoride. Major inorganic chemical plants produce lime dust, ammonia, chlorine and oxides of nitrogen. Petrochemical industry emits hydrocarbons and reduces gaseous emissions, CO, SPM and odour. The metal industries emit SO_2, dust, smoke, and fumes in form of aerosol plume. The nonferrous metal industry; generates enormous amount of SO_2. Fluoride is also thrown in air from aluminium plant. Glass industries generate SPM. Paper and pulp industry gives out SO_2, SPM and offensive odour detectable even from distance of 100 km. The plastic paint, nonferrous metals industries are worst while food, cement, steel and ceramic industry are less hazardous as they release lesser air pollutants.

7.8 MOBILE SOURCES

The moving objects like car, scooters, motorcycles, trucks and trailers are all producing pollution. They liberate CO, CO_2, SO_2, NO–NO_x, particulate and hydrocarbons. The worst is car running on petrol. To account for this kind of pollution emission inventory must be made. High octane gasoline and its incomplete combustion causes severe air pollution.

Particulates contain carcinogenic products like benzopyrene ($61 \eta g/m^3$) and lead particulates. Any diesel exhaust also gives strong odour due to aldehydes, SO_2 and NO–NO_x which promote generation of odour. It is shown in the Table 7.23.

In Table 7.21 comparative account of combustible products emitted by various power plant incinerators is given.

Table 7.21 Comparison of combustion products (g/kg)

Pollutant	*Power plants*	*Incinerator*
CO	Nil	50.0
SO_2	20	1.5
NO–NO_x	0.43	2.0
Aldehyde/ketones	0.01	3.0
Suspended particulates	75	11.0
Hydrocarbons	0.43	7.3

The source of air pollutant is dust storm, forest fires volcanoes, sea spray and plant pollen as natural source. The domestic industrial and traffic pollution is equally hazardous. They are classified on the basis of sources such as point source, line source and volume or area source. The *original* pollutant is named as primary pollutant while one generated by *interaction* of primary pollutant with component of air are called as *secondary pollutants*, which are present in gaseous state. In order to understand intricasies of pollution due to the autoexhaust emission we should examine critically both Tables 7.22 and 7.23.

7.9 AUTOEXHAUST EMISSION—CHARACTERISATION AND ANALYSIS

In India, we have two types of automobiles one which works on petrol while other one working on diesel. Compressed Natural Gas (CNG) is of recent origin and is more popular in spite of having high cost of petrol and extent of pollution it causes. In petrol powered engines we have two types of engines *viz.*, two stroke engines and four stroke engines. The two stroke engines are fitted in autorickshaw, scooter, motorcycle while four stroke engines are fitted in cars, taxis, van, etc. Table 7.22 shows emission from these both kinds of vehicles.

Table 7.22 Autoexhaust emissions (g/L)

Pollutants	*Scooter Two stroke engine*		*Car Four stroke Engine*	
	Petrol (g/L)	*Diesel (g/L)*	*Petrol gm/kg*	*Diesel vehicle gm/kg*
CO	291.0	6.0	165	50
Hydrocarbons	52.4	18.0	33	30.0
NO–NO_x	11.3	22.2	16.5	16.5
SO_2	0.9	4.0	0.8	7.5
Aldehydes	0.4	1.0	0.8	1.6
Particulate matter (SPM)	1.1	11.0	0.05	30.0

Table 7.23 Emissions while running engine

State of operation	*NO_x%*	*HC%*	*CO%*
Idling engine	1.0	1.0	1.0
Accelerating stage	100	0.4	0.6
Cruising stage	66	0.3	0.6
Deaccelerating stage	1.0	11.4	0.6

The emission by car, two and four wheelers are worth examining (see Table 7.23). The quality of gas present in exhaust according to working condition of the engine are shown *e.g.*, level of HC, goes on increasing in deaccelerating process (11.4%) while levels of NO–NO_x (100) rise during process of accelerating of engine.

The amount of exhaust gases released during various stages of operation of two or four wheelers are worth examining. The Table 7.23 shows no pollution when machine in idling, but while cruising operation pollution is highest. So also accelerating period is unsafe as good amount of NO–NO_x CO, and hydrocarbon are released in air. Therefore, it is absolutely essential to dampen them and undertake periodical cleaning of carburator of the automobile.

This shows autoexhaust emission from petrol fuelled engine gives large amount of CO (165), Hydrocarbon (33) and NO–NO_x (16.5) and SO_2 (0.8), SPM (0.05) organics (0.8) all in g/kg. While the diesel engine gives NO–NO_x, (16.5) suspended particulate (30), SO_2 (7.5) and aldehydes (1.6) and hydrocarbon (30) all in g/kg. The emission standards prescribed by EPA in America from time to time for automobile are given in Table 7.24.

The pollution from car can be controlled by improving design of engine, use of the better fuel, good town planning, and driving practices and better road keeping and traffic management.

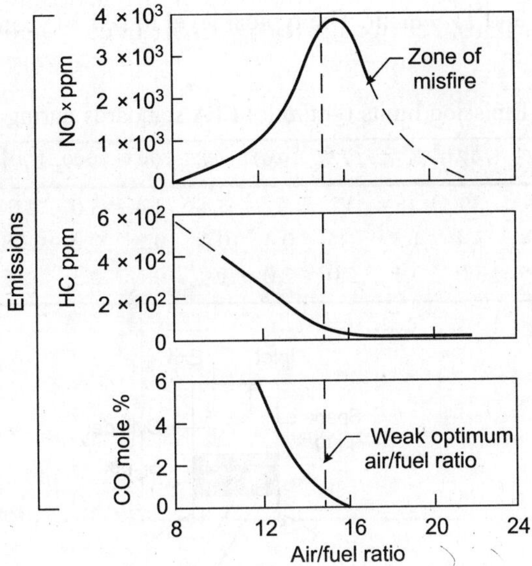

Fig. 7.9 Influence of fuel–air ratio on autoexhaust emission

In order to understand the working of car which is solely responsible for generating pollutants the working of typical car engine is considered and how it produces pollutants is examined.

7.10 WORKING OF ENGINE

The working of a four stroke engine is considered with spark ignition (SI) (Fig. 7.10). The position (I) represents intake stroke with inlet open and exit closed, when air and hydrocarbons are sucked in. Now (II) shows compression stroke with inlet and exit both closed when the piston moves up with compressing air–fuel in the ratio of 7 : 12. Then the spark ignition occurs in position (III), it represents power or work stroke when both inlet and exit are closed and combustion occurs. At this time temperature rises and expanding combustion products pushes up the piston with exit open. Finally, in position (IV), exhaust stroke exit is open, inlet is closed and exhaust gases go out. The carburetor is located near the inlet control the mixture of air and fuel (15 : 1), which is sprayed by intake stroke. Ideal fuel is iso-octane (C_8H_{17}, *i.e.*, 2,2,4 trimethyl pentane).

(*a*) The combustion occurs as per the following reaction:

(*i*) $C_8H_{17} + 12.5\ O_2 + (N_2) \rightarrow 8CO_2 + 9H_2O + (N_2)$.

(*ii*) $C_8H_{18} \rightarrow C_{17}H_{15} + CH_3^+$ (cracking of hydrocarbons)
(*iii*) $CH_3^+ + C_8H_{18} \rightarrow CH_4 + C_8H_{17}$
(*iv*) $C_8H_{17} \rightarrow CH_3 + C_7H_{14}$

A peroxide radical is formed along with peroxide chain. The final products in exhaust gases are H_2, O_2, formaldehyde, higher ketones, CO, CO_2 and water vapour. This may lead to octane dilemma. A Clean Air Act (1970) stipulated definite ratios of HC, CO, NO_2 and TPS in air. The typical level in last 30 years are as presented in Table 7.24.

Table 7.24 Emission limits (gm/mile) EPA standards during last 30 years

Pollutants	*1972*	*1974*	*1976*	*1979*	*1980*	*1992*	*1995*	*1999*	*2001*	*Remarks*
CO	39	39	15	15	7	3.4	3.4	3.0	2.0	Decreasing
Hydrocarbon	3.4	3.4	1.5	1.5	0.4	0.4	0.2	0.2	0.20	Decreasing
NO–NO_x	3.5	3.0	3.1	2.0	2.0	1.0	0.4	0.3	0.25	Slow decrease

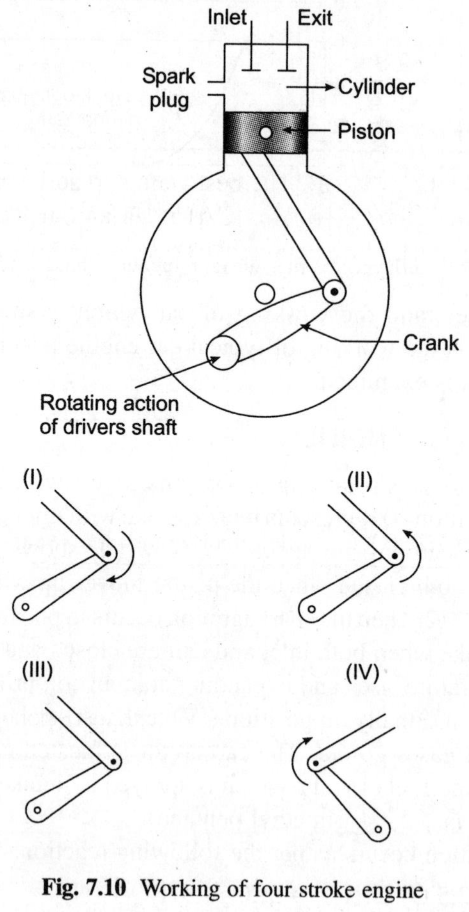

Fig. 7.10 Working of four stroke engine

In order to control the problem of pollution due to exhaust several chemical additives are added to petrol. We call it as unleaded petrol. Some advanced countries in west do not permit use of unleaded petrol for consumption of cars, autos and bikes. The use of unleaded petrol is compulsory. The Table 7.25 indicates composition of unleaded gasoline. Their solubility in common organic solvents is considered. Toluene, Xylene, Pentane can absorb high % w/w of obvinoxous gases which are released by vehicles (Table 7.25).

Table 7.25 Composition of unleaded petrol

S. No.	*Constituents*	*Formula*	*% by w/w*	*Exposure range (PPM) (maximum)*
1.	Toluene	$C_6H_5(CH_3)$	10–12	25
2.	Xylene	$C_6H_4(CH_3)_2$	8–10	100
3.	Pentane	C_5H_{12}	9–11	100–200
4.	Heptane	C_7H_{16}	6–8	50–500
5.	Hexane	C_6H_{12}	6–8	600–1000
6.	Butane	$CH_3CH_2CH_3$	4–6	300
7.	Benzene	C_6H_6	0–3	1–5
8.	Cyclohexane	C_6H_{12}	0–1	100–125
9.	Trimethy benzene	$(CH_3)_3C_3H_6$	0–3	25
10.	Ethyl benzene	$C_2H_5–C_5H_6$	0–2	400–500

An ideal fuel to air ratio is 1 : 13. The best way is to add a catalyst to reduce emission of toxic gases. Pb $(C_2H_5)_4$ or (ICA) is an antiknocking agent which prevents deposition of soot. The hydrocarbons which are emitted by petroleum combustion are oleifins, parafins, aromatics, with carbon chain ranging from C_1 to C_{35} while the residue has carbon chain ranging from C_{35} to C_{90}. The gasoline supply to engine can be enhanced by cracking, polymerisation, alkylation, or reforming high knocking agents to reduce knocking products. The common and most efficient catalyst used for such purposes is AK 33 X. It is methylcyclopentadienyl manganese–carbonyl which reduces deposition of soot inside the engine. The octane dilemena is shown in Table 7.26.

Table 7.26 Octane dilemma (%) in last 80 years

S.No.	*Pollutant*	*1905*	*1970*	*1976*	*1980*	*1990*	*Trend*
1.	HC	11	2.2	0.5	0.25	0.06	decrease
2.	CO	80	23	11	4.7	2.1	decrease much
3.	NO–NO_x (NO_2)	4	–	0.9	0.4	0.2	decrease marginal
4.	SPM	0.3	–	0.1	0.03	0.01	good decrease

7.11 CHARACTERISTICS OF EMISSION

A pollutant is defined as one which causes human response, like physiological, economical or asthetic. The pollutants are classified on the basis of their physical state. If a pollutant is dispersed in air, it is called *gaseous pollutants*, but a highly polymerised aggregate of liquids or solid substances lumped together are called *aerosols*. They contain solids and liquids. There are inherent difficulties of collection. The atmosphere with its load of pollutants constitute highly inhomogeneous and dynamic mixture, not in equilibrium or a steady state. The coexistence is possible due to dilution. An efficient mode of collection of pollutants is essential. If the concentration of pollutant in air is low, then large air samples are required to be collected to facilitate concentration of sufficient material for analytical purposes. All the interfering substances are assumed to be present before actual analysis. A simple syringe or hypodermic syringe with needle may cause severe fluctuations or variations in the composition to ascertain it with any degree of accuracy. The methods of sampling of aerosols and gases pollutants are of crucial importance. Due to inhomogeneous nature of aerosols, sampling becomes more complex.

In autoexhaust emissions along with CO_2, CO is also emitted, it is the worst gas that is emitted. Three wheelers, cars, generate enormous amounts of CO in the air. If one maintains air/fuel ratio of 15:1, there is higher generation of NO_x (4000 ppm) with hydrocarbon (HC) of about 100 ppm and CO of about 2 ppm. The ideal carburettor setting is done at a ratio of 13:16. The composition of autoexhaust varies from model to model and for same model with the particular year of car production. Only from 1963 abroad strict regulation for control of automobile emission were clamped due to photochemical smog formation. As told earlier control of air fuel ratio (15:1 best) can reduce emission due to NO–NO_x and hydrocarbons in the atmosphere.

(a) Emission from Petrol Engine

The crankcase emission is most definite source of trouble. Better ventilation through control valve can prevent large emissions specially CO. This is called '*Positive Crankcase Ventilation*' (PCV). The evaporative emission from tank and carburettor is another source. The control of air to fuel ratio, ignition timing, compression ratio, engine speed, deposits and condition can reduce emissions. The control of exhaust emission for unburned hydrocarbon and CO is done by fuel modification with use of LPG, or CNG or minimization of emission from combustion chamber, with better design of engine or further oxidation of pollutant outside combustion chamber by process of catalysis. The catalytic converter is effective for emission control. NO–NO_x emission is lowered by recirculation of exhaust gas with incoming fuel air charge, to lower temperature or one can use also catalytic convertor.

(b) Emission from Diesel Engine

People have myth that diesel engine does not produce pollution and is very safe. On the contrary, it emits more of NO–NOx, SO_2, and particulate. See Table 7.21. These are compression engines. The cycle of fuel flow can be controlled by controlling the diesel powered engine with fuel modification one can prevent over fueling. To this present date USA–EPA stipulation of particulate is 0.37 gm/km and NO–NO_x at 0.93 gm/km. Secondly diesel is becoming as expensive as petrol.

(c) Autoexhaust Emission Analysis

Engine operated device called dynamometer is used for sampling of gases. All well-known methods *viz.*, NDIR for CO, chemiluminescences for NO–NO_x PRA colorimetry for SO_2, and for hydrocarbons by the gas chromatography facilitates characterization of aldehydes, and light scattering techniques measures the level of particulate matter. Heritage smoke meter is used to measure smoke from exhaust pipe. The permissible limit of smoke in America is 70HSO fair is injected near exhaust value, which is at high temperature it promotes oxidation of unoxidised matter like hydrocarbons. While crankcase ventilation can control also emission of nitrogen oxides, oxides of carbon, hydrocarbons, unsaturated organic compounds and aromatic products like 3.4 benzopyrene. In addition several metal pollutants like lead, cadmium, vanadium, selenium are also encountered which in turn can be easily analysed by atomic absorption spectroscopy or plasma spectroscopy.

7.12 AMBIENT AIR QUALITY MEASUREMENT

The analysis of air pollution can be carried out in two ways (*a*) one involving laboratory analysis (*b*) while second involving monitoring on the site. The ambient air quality can be ascertained by conventional laboratory analysis however, the stack monitoring cannot be carried out in the laboratory. One has to go to field to collect the samples and if possible to analyse the pollution at the source. It is necessary to resort to continuous monitoring of large number of samples. The methods of analysis on micro scale may not be valid for continuous measurement of the air sample. We need information on meteorological parameters. Therefore, we shall discuss the laboratory scale analysis of air pollutants while continuous measurement or monitoring of large number of samples in field shall be considered in next chapter.

In order to get reliable results of analysis, one needs reliable sample for analysis. Further during the collection of sample, wind direction, wind velocity and temperature may change. Therefore, it is essential to have good method of sampling. We ask when was the sampling technique used for sampling of the aerosols? The method is not same as sampling of gaseous pollutants as later is much as simpler because one gets homogeneous sample. The aerosols are mixture of liquids and solids pollutants from the atmosphere. The methods of sampling of aerosols as well as those for the sampling of the gaseous pollutants are summarised in following sections of this chapter (Figs. 7.11 to 7.13).

(a) Sampling of Air

The atmosphere contains particulate matter and gases as the main pollutants. In order to get reliable information we must have representative samples before the actual analysis. One must collect adequate samples at proper intervals. The sampling process should not change the chemical or physical properties of the pollutants. A sampling unit consists of inlet manifold, air mover, collection medium

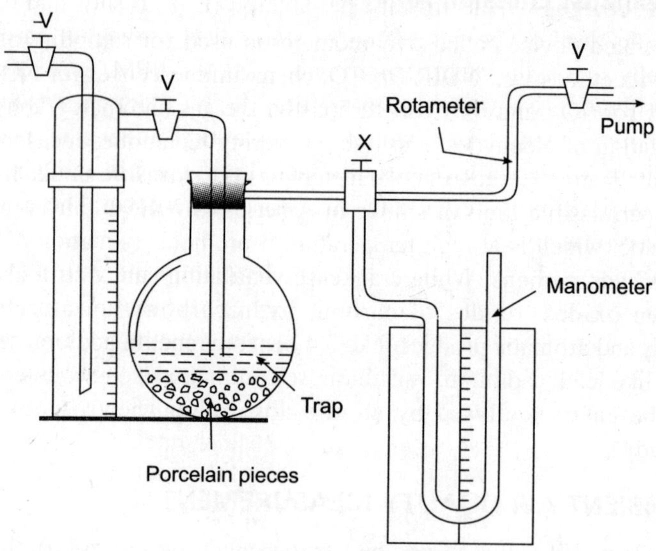

Fig. 7.11 Sampling unit

and finally rotameter for flow measurement (see. Fig. 7.11). The material of construction for them is inert substances like glass or teflon or stainless steel. Pumps act like air remover. There are several ways of sampling aerosols. In inertial method during flow of gas and aerosols the direction of flow is suddenly changed with the result that the aerosols get deposited on the impinger while gas passes away. While the gravitational sampling involves induction of centrifugal field in order to collect heavy particles in sedimentation chamber, but in gradient sampling, a difference in physical properties of aerosols such as electrical mobility

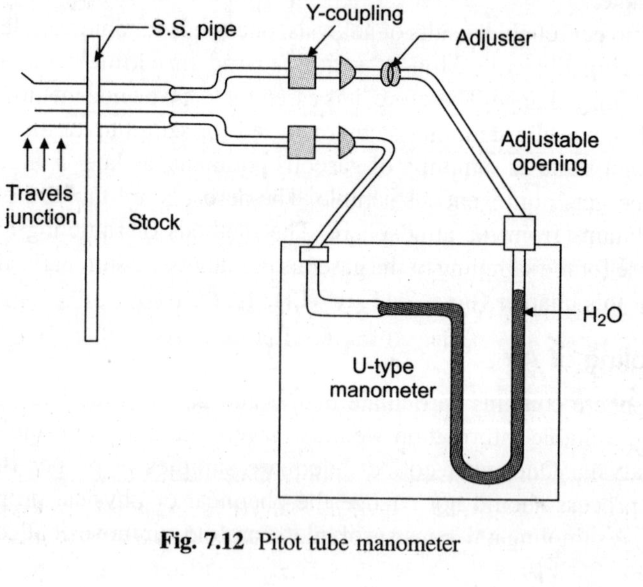

Fig. 7.12 Pitot tube manometer

or difference in charge as in electrostatic precipitator (ESP) is shown in Figs. 7.12 and 7.13. On account of the generation of static electricity light particles are attracted thereby separating them from heavier particles (SPM). Only precaution is that ozone should not be generated by friction and by silent electric discharge. The thermophoresis method is based on the separation under the influence of thermal gradient; while diffusoforesis is technique wherein the aerosols are separated by exploiting difference in diffusion phenomena. These diffusion technique is very effective.

The sieving and filtration technique is less frequently utilised. The aerosols contain liquid or solid particulate matter of varying size and dimensions. After considering the basic principles involved in different methods of sampling, we consider each technique, in some detailes. The sampling of gaseous pollutant is relatively simple however sampling of (solid/liquid particles collectively called) *aerosols* is some what complex. Let us first consider methods for sampling of aerosols followed by methods for sampling of the gaseous pollutants.

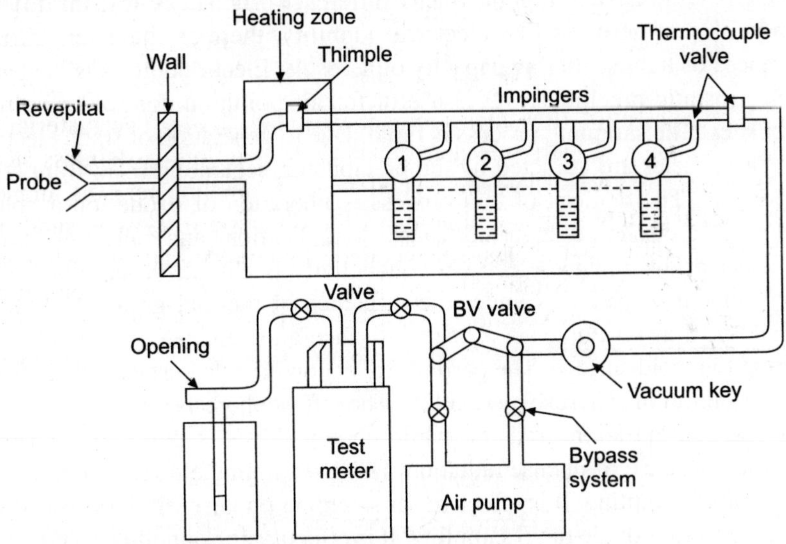

Fig. 7.13 Particulate sampler

(b) Sampling Methods for Aerosols

In all there are six methods for sampling of aerosols. They are inertial, gravitational, gradients, diffusional, sieving and filtration. Let us consider them in details.

(c) Inertial Sampling

A large group of techniques for separation of particles from gases may be termed as *inertial*. The inertia of a particle is greater than that of a gas molecule. If the direction of a gas stream is changed suddenly, due to collision the larger particulate are deposited on the obstructing surface. With impingers (*i.e.*, obstructing objects), some sort of action occurs under liquid surface, as the liquid washes off the surface to provide more chance for air collection. The only limitation is, during bouncing action such particles are shattered and decomposed and not useful for subsequent analysis, hence it should be avoided.

(d) Gravitational Sampling

In this technique particles are induced to leave air particles when they travel by induced gravity of centrifugal force. This principle is employed in sedimentation chamber. The centrifugal collector are used for the purpose of sampling. The larger particles settle down quickly. There is no reaction after collection therefore it is clean process.

(e) Gradient Sampling

The gravitational methods involve motion of particle under the influence of gravity. In gradient sampling, advantage is taken of the difference in some physical characteristics to effect sampling. Such a difference originates due to the difference in properties of aerosols like electrical mobility, thermal character, diffusion, differences of light scattering capacity of aerosols. Electrophoresis is the basis of the electrostatic precipitator. It is useful for air pollution control and airborne particulates. The sampling process is rapid. Due to generation of static electricity, the light particles are attracted by the precipitator, separating them from heavier components. The demerit of this process is liberation of ozone, on account of silent electric discharge. It further causes complications and collecting substrate pose a big problem,when electrical conductivity is absent. 'Thermophoresis' is the movement of particles under the influence of thermal gradient. A thermal precipitator draws sample on a heated surface and separates it out from those adhering to a cold surface. The particle collection on cold surface is beneficial in high concentration of aerosol particulate. The diffusophoresis is motion of particles in vapour concentration gradient, while photophoresis is migration of aerosols under the influence of intense radiation. However, both the forces are too slow to provide rapid sampling. It is effective for sampling photosensitive aerosols which are too small to provide rapid sampling. It is effective for sampling photosensitive pollutants.

(f) Diffusion Method

This technique is very effective for particles of small size. This is a statistical process, where in collecting surface and small particles are brought together by the phenomenon of random Brownian motion of the suspended particles in the process of collision.

(g) Sieving of Samples

The largest airborne sample particulates may be collected by sieving with the help of fine mesh. This method is useful for filtering out insects from aerosols.

(h) Filtration of Samples

This is the most widely used single technique of removing particles from air. The membrane filters are used, which have small pore size. For dust and particulate matter, this is the most efficient sampling technique. Let us consider sampling of gaseous pollutant now.

7.13 SAMPLING OF GASEOUS POLLUTANTS

In comparison with sampling of aerosols which are heterogeneous, sampling of gaseous pollutants is relatively simpler, because they are homogeneous. Unfortunately, both for aerosols as well as gaseous pollutants the task is difficult, because of sudden variation in wind velocity, wind direction, changes in sample composition and temperature for such considerations. For several meteorological parameters are accountable. Let us consider important methods for sampling of gaseous pollutants. The sampling methods for gases are classified as one involving storage or a grab sampling, condensation, adsorption and absorption.

(a) Grab Sampling

A portion of ambient air is closed in a container and stored. Just isolation without concentration is possible by this technique. Storage sampling is another name for this method. The storage at atmospheric pressure is made in rigid containers. Glass or stainless steel is used as container material. In a few instances, mylar—a special kind of material is used, as it is elastic and non-odourant. The nature of container selected will be decided on the basis of quality and kind of the pollutant which is being collected.

(b) Condensation

The low temperature condensation called cryosampling is an excellent method for air sampling at low temperature. The species condenses and gets concentrated. The cooling agent used consists of liquid hydrogen or even liquid oxygen. This sampling technique provides an additional advantage of concentration.

(c) Adsorption

The gas is adsorbed on solid material at reduced temperature and then evacuated or flushed out with an inert gas like N_2 or Ar at elevated temperature. The material used for adsorption consist of porous substance like silica, alumina, Kieselguhr, diatomaceous earth or activated carbon. Large amount of gas can be easily sampled by this technique. Only limitation of this method is that, polar substance cannot be easily desorbed after adsorption from solid substrate. The process of adsorption is a surface phenomenon, which is used for purification of air for experimental purposes, like sampling by dilution.

(d) Absorption

This is the most popular method for sampling of gaseous pollutants. The reactive pollutants are absorbed in aqueous solution, *e.g.*, SO_2 is absorbed in water or

H_2O_2; ozone is absorbed in a solution of potassium iodide; the absorption of NO_2 is effected in NaOH, as its absorption in water is very slow; CO is absorbed in a solution of ammonical cuprous chloride; O_2 is absorbed in the solution of alkaline pyrogallol; CO_2 is absorbed in the solution of alcoholic KOH. In fact, this forms the basis of Orsat gas analyser. By the process of absorption, a component of gas phase is transferred into a bulk of solid or liquid phase. The transfer process involves a chemical interaction and fixing of a particular species in the liquid phase. The ventilation, spraying, bubbling ensures intimate contact between gas and liquid or solid absorption; such sampling can also be classified as active and passive absorption sampling. The use of ion exchange resin in packed bed column can also be used as the excellent sampling medium. However, it is essential to maintain the sample in an extremely dry state so as to get successful, reliable and reproducible results of the final analysis.

(e) Analysis of Aerosols

We would consider separately analysis of aerosols and gaseous pollutants. The purpose of such analysis is to ascertain the composition of the entire sample in terms of its various constituents. This will enable one to obtain information of individual particles. The method employed is bulk method, where total content of atmosphere is expressed in terms of $\mu g/m^3$ (or ppm) for large samples, which are collected by electrostatic precipitator or by filtration. The sample is then dissolved and analysed for its contents of metal pollutant by AAS, ICP–AES, or spectrophotometry. The gravimetric or volumetric methods are useless for such purposes. The ring oven technique is ideal for such operation in the fields. This single particle method is composed of three parts, *viz.*, morphological examination, micrurgy test and microspot investigation. In morphological examination, an attempt is made to recognise a chemical species by mere observation or sight. In micrurgy test, the sample identification or characterisation is done under light microscope with the use of precise micromanipulator. Finally, in microspot investigation, a specific reagent is used for the identification of a material, *e.g.*, nickel with dimethyl-glyoxime. The identification of radioactive material is done by radioactography. There are numerous organic ligands which are specific for the detection of the aerosols. The analysis of aerosols is done by ambient air quality monitoring. So we shall first consider ambient air quality measurement in the laboratory.

Table 7.27 Cost for pollution control of SO_2

S. No.	*Abetment Process*	*Cost \$ (Dollar)*	*Level of reductions Decrease in SO_2 level*	*Approx. cost ₹ (Rs.)*
1.	Injection in the sorbent	50–100	30–70%	2500–5000
2.	Desulphurisation of dry SO_2 gas	80–170	70–90%	4000–8500
3.	Desulphorisation of wet SO_2 gas	80–170	90–100%	4000–8500

It is necessary to estimate the cost of gases, pollutant in the developing country like India which is very high. The process of desulpharisation or unleading of petroleum is very prohibitive. Such cost exceeds from ₹ 2000–10,000 which in turn is prohibitive. For developed countries like USA, UK, Europe this problem is not dominant but for South East Asian countries as UAR, North African do not have much problem of availability of fuel. Since the economy is dependent on other resources, they are able to sale gas fuel at much cheaper price (Table 7.27).

7.14 ANALYSIS OF THE GASEOUS POLLUTANTS

Ambient air pollution or ambient air measurement is essential here to distinguish between air outdoors causing pollution by transport and diffusion of wind (*i.e.*, ambient air pollution) from the contamination of air indoor by the same substance. The pollution within the factory premises is called as *Indoor Pollution*. The day-time pollution is more intense than one in night time obviously due to closure of factories in night. Pollutants which are directly emitted from source are called *Primary Pollutants* and are not always harmful. The pollutants generated in air due to interaction of pollutants with the components of atmosphere lead to release of *Secondary Pollutants e.g.*, smog haze are secondary pollutants. The size fraction below a diameter of 10 μm (PM_{10}) is selected as standard for airborne particulate matter *i.e.*, SPM. The method for the characterisation and determination of atmospheric polluting gases are more or less individual and specific. The use of different sampling methods for gas depends upon the availability and diversity of analytical technique used for the determination. The non-selective methods include condensation of samples and analysis by mass spectrometry. Most reactive gases cannot be analysed by gas chromatography (GLC), as pollutants are lost during collection. Non-selective methods are useful for less reactive, pollutants and closely related homologous series of hydrocarbons and aldehydes. GLC involves the use of FID (flame ionisation detector) or ECD (*i.e.*, electron capture detector). In the specific analyser, polar traces of gases are absorbed in solution. No method of analysis is perfect and every method is subject of controversy. Such of the methods which have been selected have minimum interference. In years to come, it is hoped that newer methods will be invented or old methods will be modified for better selectivity during analysis.

Table 7.28 Level of tolerance of pollutants

S.No.	*Type of gaseous pollutant*	*Formula*	*Level of tolerance (mg/m³)*
1.	Benzene	C_6H_6	5 (0.1 ppb in factory)
2.	Ammonia	NH_3	15
3.	1-2 dichloroethane	$CCl_2–CH_3$	5 (1 ppb in factory)
4.	Hydrogen chloride	HCl	10
5.	Susp. particulate matter	SPM	20
6.	Oxides of nitrogen	$NO–NO_x$	300
7.	Sulphur dioxide	SO_2	500
8.	Vinyl chloride	...	5 (0.4 ppb in factory)

From the air several organic compounds can be tolerated at different levels. A close look at Table 7.28 shows that HCl gas, benzene, ammonia are tolerated at very low concentration of < 5 mg/m^3 from the atmosphere. Very few compounds are tolerated at higher concentration such as oxides of nitrogen, sulphurdioxide.

An endeavour is made to consider laboratory methods for the analysis of SO_2, H_2S, NO–NO_x, CO, CO_2, O_3 ammonia, organic vapours. Such methods consist of mainly spectrophotometric methods. The volumetric technique, conductometric analysis, infrared method, fluorescence measurement technique are also described.

7.15 SULPHUR DIOXIDE ANALYSIS

Three properties of SO_2 are used for its quantitative analysis. The details of analysis is as follows:

(a) Acid Titration

The important properties of SO_2 are acidity, reducing character and precipitation which is used in gravimetry. There are also spectrophotometric methods. SO_2 is collected over H_2O_2 or H_2O and corresponding change in acidity is measured by titration or by measuring a change in conductivity, but the latter method is more reliable. Only drawback of this method is that, HF, HCI if present in atmosphere interfere with positive error but NO_2 does not interfere due to low solubility in water. NH_3 if present interferes with negative error.

(b) Reduction Method

The second method involves the use of reducing property of SO_2. It is allowed to react with excess of KI and the liberated iodine is titrated against standard solution of $Na_2S_2O_3$. SO_2 is collected over NaOH and redox titration is carried out. The reduction method suffers from positive interference from other redox pollutants such as H_2S. Organic matter also interferes in such a determination, O_3 also interferes but NO_2 does not interfere in the redox titration for reasons stated above as it has limited solubility in water.

(c) Lead Candle Method

In the lead candle method PbO_2 is exposed to atmosphere of SO_2 to undergo the reaction as: $PbO_2 + SO_2 \rightarrow PbSO_4$. The change in weight of candle gives an idea about SO_2 in the air. The only limitation of this method is that dust and particulate matter can get deposited on lead peroxide to give erroneous results.

However, the best method for laboratory analysis of sulphur dioxide is spectrophotometric method. Such methods are summarised in Table 7.29.

(d) Spectrophotometric Determination of Sulphur Dioxide

Three methods are most common (Table 7.29). The first method is used for direct analysis of SO_2 with absorbing solution H_2O_2 and barium chloroanilate to give a red coloured complex with absorption maxima at 530 nm. This method is good

Table 7.29 Spectrophotometric determination of sulphur dioxide

1. SO_2 in H_2O_2, barium chloroanilate → Red complex (λ_{max} = 530 nm)		
2. $FeCl_3$, NH_4Cl, HCl, 1,10—phenanthroline → coloured complex (λ_{max} = 510 nm) PRA is most popular method		
3. Absorbing solution	:	NaCl, $HgCl_2$
Reagent	:	PRA (para roseaniline leucobase and formaldehyde
λ_{max} = 560 nm;		$\varepsilon = 3.0 \times 10^4$
Colour development in 20 minutes		
Working range	:	1–10 µg/ml
Interferences are negligible.	:	Nil

for flue gases, but it lacks sensitivity required for ambient air analysis. The second method is based on absorption of SO_2 into a mixture of ferric chloride, ammonium chloride, hydrochloric acid and *o*-phenanthroline solutions. A coloured complex so formed is spectrophotometrically measured at 510 nm. The development of the colour is rapid, but the fading of colour is also equally fast. H_2S shows strong interference. The third but ideal method is one known as PRA method. In this sodium chloride and mercury chlorides are reacted with p-rosaniline (leucobase) in formaldehyde to give intense red-violet colour of p-rosaniline methylsulphonic acid, showing strong absorbance at 560 nm. The mechanism of reaction is described in Fig. 7.14. At pH > 1.6, colour is measured at 548 nm, which at pH < 1.2 is measured at 575 nm. The sensitivity of the method is in the range of 1 to 10 ppm and the colour is stable for long time. The method is simple and reproducible.

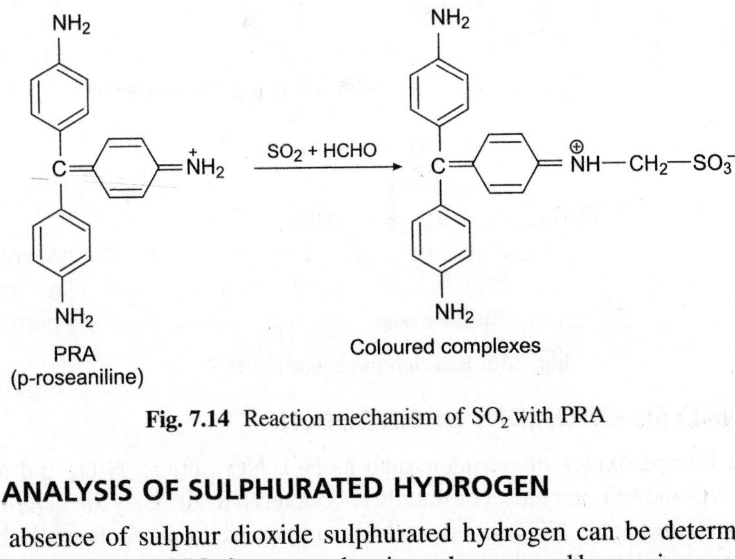

Fig. 7.14 Reaction mechanism of SO_2 with PRA

7.16 ANALYSIS OF SULPHURATED HYDROGEN

In the absence of sulphur dioxide sulphurated hydrogen can be determined by reduction technique. If SO_2 is present then it can be removed by passing gas mixture on glass fibre filter impregnated with K_2CO_3. H_2S forms coloured precipitate with second group metals of qualitative analysis. Pb acetate turns black. In iodometric titration H_2S solution reacts with KI and liberated iodine is titrated with standard solution of thiosulphate. So redox titration is applicable if level of H_2S is hıgh.

(i) Spectrophotometric Determination of Sulphurated Hydrogen

There is only one reliable method called *ethylene blue method* (Table 7.30) for the colorimetric analysis of H_2S. The absorbing solution, contains $CdSO_4$ and NaOH. The dye called as the *ethylene blue* so formed by interaction of $FeCl_3$ and N–N′–diethylphenylene diamine is measured at 670 nm. Beer's law limit is 1 to 10 μg/m with molar absorptivity $\varepsilon = 3.5 \times 10^4$. The reaction mechanism is depicted in Fig. 7.15. Gases like SO_2, O_3, NH_3 do not interfere, but sulphites, thiosulphates show strong interference, which can be eliminated by action with $FeCl_3$. The method is more sensitive if such complex is extracted in chloroform. Cd, Pb or As are most useful for formation of coloured sulphides in spectrophotometric determination.

Table 7.30 Spectrophotometric determination of hydrogen sulphide (Ethylene blue method)

Absorbing solution	:	$CdSO_4$, NaOH, $FeCl_3$
Chromogenic reagent	:	N–N′ diethyl p-phenylene diamine
Colour formed	:	Ethylene Blue
Wavelength for measurement	:	670 nm $\varepsilon = 3.5 \times 10^4$
Working Range 1 to 10 μg/ml		
Extractive spectrophotometry in $CHCl_3$ has better sensitivity		

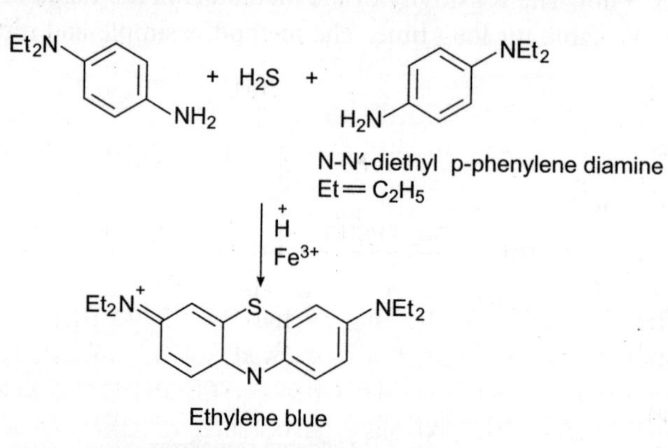

Fig. 7.15 Reaction mechanism of H_2S

7.17 ANALYSIS OF OXIDES OF NITROGEN

There are several oxides of nitrogen such as NO, NO_2, N_2O_3, N_2O_4 and N_2O_5. However, NO and NO_2 are most commonly encountered in air. They are determined by gas chromatography. NO converts to NO_2 to give rise to photochemical smog. The most useful method is "Saltzman method", performed by using a spectrophotometer for quantitative analysis of NO and NO_2.

(i) Spectrophotometric Determination of NO–NO$_x$ if x = 1, 2, 3, 4, 5

There are several methods for analysis as shown in Table 7.31. In phenol-disulphonic acid method, reaction of nitrogen oxide in H_2O_2 and H_2SO_4 is used to develop colour complex measurable at 400 nm. The reactions during transformations are as:

$$2NO + H_2O_2 \rightarrow 2HNO_3$$
$$2NO + 3H_2O_2 \rightarrow 2HNO_3 + 2H_2O$$
$$HNO_3 + HO\ C_6H_3\ (SO_3H)_2 \rightarrow HOC_6\ H_2(NO_2)\ (SO_3H)_2 + H_2O$$

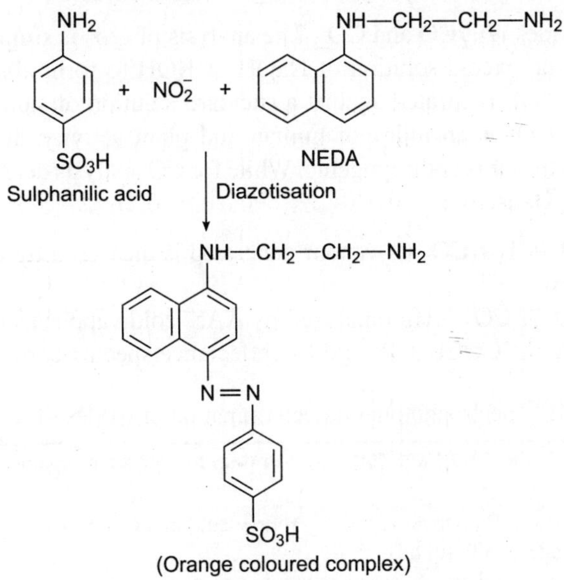

Fig. 7.16 Reaction mechanism of NO–NO$_x$

The method is not valid beyond 25 ppm for NO–NOx. Organic nitrogen shows strong interference. In xylenol orange method, nitrite ion reacts with $KMnO_4$ and propylene glycol with 2 to 4 xylenol to give a yellow coloured complex with absorption maxima at 435 nm. The limit of analysis is 2 to 5 μg/ml. All operations are performed in single step. In the third method, sodium arsenite is absorbed on H_2O_2, in the presence of sulphamide; when H_2SO_4 and N–(naphthyl) ethylene diamine hydrochloride (NEDA) forms a red coloured complex which is measured at 550 nm. SO_2 does not interfere. The limitation is $NaAsO_3$ is toxic in nature. In triethnolamine method, the sample is absorbed in an aqueous solution of triethanolamine in butanol. The colour is developed by diazotization reaction using NEDA (N–naphthylethylene diamine chloride) to give orange coloured complex with maximum absorbance at 550 nm. The range of analysis is 0.005 to 0.5 ppm. In modified method, absorbing solution of NaOH is used instead of hydrogen peroxide. It is treated with H_2O_2, sulphanilamide, H_3PO_4, NEDA to form a coloured complex with the limit of analysis as 0.04 to 1.5 ppm. However, Saltzman's method is the best and more widely accepted for the analysis of NO–NO$_x$. The important reactions involved in such analyses are depicted (Fig. 7.16) . A mixture of NaOH, triethanolamine, sulphanilic acid, glacial acetic acid and NEDA is used. The colour is developed instantaneously due to process of dye formation. It is measured at 550 nm. The molar absorptivity is 4×10^4 with sensitivity of 0.01–1.5 μg/ml^1/cm^2. The principal interferences is due to O_3 and high concentration of SO_2 in the sample. The important reaction is summarised in (Table 7.31).

7.18 ANALYSIS OF OXIDES OF CARBON

(a) Analysis of Carbon Dioxide by Volumetric Method

There are two oxides *viz.*, CO and CO_2. The analysis of CO_2 is simple, where it is bubbled through an excess solution of NaOH or KOH to form alkali carbonate. Then unreacted alkali is titrated against a standard solution of suitable acid. The measurement of CO_2 is an index of human and plant activity, as a significant portion of CO_2 in the air is anthropogenic. While for CO analysis detection methods involves use of I_2O_5 as:

$I_2O_5 + CO \rightarrow I_2 + CO_2$ (I_2 vapour generated is measured by visual colorimetry)

$HgO + CO \rightarrow CO_2 + Hg$ (analysed by AAS–cold vapour technique).

$PdCl_2 + CO \rightarrow COCl_2 + Pd$ (Pd by reflectance spectroscopy is measured).

Table 7.31 Spectrophotometric determination of oxides of nitrogen

1. Phenoldisulphonic Acid (λ = 400 nm) useful up to 25 μg but organic nitrogen interferes
2. Xylenol, $KMnO_4$, Propylene glycol → Yellow coloured complex λ_{max} 435 nm (Working range 2–500 μg/ml)
3. $NaAsO_3$ (H_2O_2, sulphamide, H_3PO_4, NEDA) λ = 550 nm
4. Triethanolamine, n–butanol λ_{max} 550 nm
5. Saltzmann Method
   Absorbing solution: Triethynolamine in NaOH
   Reagents: NEDA, Sulphanilic acid and Acetic acid
   λ_{max}: 550 nm, ε = 4.0 5 104
   Colour development: 15 minutes (stability : 24 hours)
   Working range: 0.01 – 1.5 mg/ml

(b) Spectrometric Method for Analysis of Carbon Monoxide

Since CO is odourless, colourless, and tasteless gas, the indicator tubes are very useful in mines and deep sea operations. The indirect methods for analysis of CO are already summarised in Table 7.32. In indirect method CO reduces yellow silicomolybdate to form molybdenum blue. The colour changes from yellow-green to green and then to a permanent blue obtained. Silica impregnated to with ammonium molybdate in H_2SO_4 is reacted with CO to give blue solution with absorption maxima at 660 nm. The method is sensitive. Only organic compounds, like H_2S, moisture reduce molybdenum and give errors in results. This method is comparable with nondispersive infrared spectroscopy technique. The method of nondispersive infrared measurement (NDIR) is best well suited for continuous measurement of carbon monoxide from autoexhaust air emissions.

Table 7.32 Spectrophotometric determination of carbon monoxide

(I) Mercuric Oxide—Reflectance spectroscopy measurements ($HgCl_2$, CO) of Hg, H_2O, Olefins, interfere

(II) Palladium Chloride—Reflectance spectroscopy measurement ($PdCl_2$, CO) metallic Pd is measured.

(III) SiO_2, $(NH_4)_2 MoO_4$, CO → Molybdenum blue colour is measured by absorption spectrophotometrically.

λ_{max} = 660 (absorption maxima)
Absorbing solution : Silica gel impregnated with ammonium molybdate
Colour development: Instantaneous
Working range: 1–10 μg/ml
Interference: Organic, H_2S and Moisture

7.19 THE ANALYSIS OF OZONE FROM THE ATMOSPHERE

We have already considered depletion of ozone layer in atmosphere. Now let us consider analysis of ozone. The volumetric method involving redox titration is the most popular method of analysis. The reaction involved is $O_3 + 2KI + H_2O \rightarrow O_2 + 2KOH + I_2$ (at > 0.5 ppm of O_3); however in this reaction, interfering substance must be absent. Excess of 2% KI is buffered at pH 7. Final iodine concentration is measured volumetrically. Ozone can also be determined spectrophotometrically at 352 nm. The alkaline solution of KI is used. The solution is added to a mixture of phosphoric and sulphuric acid. The method is useful for field analysis of O_3. Such redox titrations can be carried out as linear titration like amperometry or colorimetrically. A fluorimetric method involves interaction of O_3 with dye fluorescent acridine to give fluorescence, but the reliable techniques are spectral methods as it is simple and selective. The number of spectrophotometric methods are described in Table 7.33.

(a) Spectrophotometric Determination of Ozone

Various methods for such analyses are summarised in Table 7.33. The phenolphthalein method is based on the development of pink colouration with reduced form of dye. It is oxidised by H_2O_2 with $CuSO_4$ as catalyst to give a pink colour with the maximum absorbance at 530 nm. SO_2 interferes in this method. The reaction of O_3 with 1–2–di–4(–pyridyl)—ethylene in acetic acid (glacial) gives a yellow coloured complex measurable at 442 nm. The aldehyde forms coloured complex with 3–mcthyl–2–bcnzothiazolone hydrazine hydrochloride The intense yellow coloured complex is measured at 442 nm. In N–tetramethyldiaminodiphenyl methane in dilute acetic acid gives a violet colour, measurable at 565 nm. When NO–NO_x are present, green colour turns to yellow (λ_{max} – 565 nm). In diphenylamine sulphonate method, perchloric acid sodium diphenylamine gives turquise–red colour (λ_{max} = 593 nm). While in 4–4′ dimethoxystilbene method, blue colour (λ_{max} = 610 nm) is obtained where-in NO_2, SO_2 do not interfere. The reaction of phosphate buffered KI solution is used at λ = 352 nm. The interference of SO_2, NO_2 and peroxyacetyl nitrite H_2S is eliminated by using suitable sequistering agent.

Table 7.33 Spectrophotometric determination of ozone from air

1. Phenolphthalein, H_2O_2, $CuSO_4 \rightarrow$ pink coloured complex (λ_{max} : 530 nm)
2. 1, 2–di (4–pyridyl) Ethylene $\rightarrow$ (λ_{max} : 442 nm) Yellow coloured complex
3. N–tetramethyldiaminophenyl methane $\rightarrow$ Blue–violet colour complex (λ_{max} : 565 nm)
4. Diphenylamine sulphonate
   Sodium diphenylamine, $HClO_4 \rightarrow \lambda_{max}$ = 593 nm
   Turquise red–violet coloured complex
5. 4–4′ dimethyl Stilbene $\rightarrow$ Blue (λ_{max} : 610 nm)
6. Iodide Method
   Absorbing solution: Phosphate buffer KI solution
   Reaction: $O_3 + 3KI + H_2O \rightarrow KI_3 + 2KOH + O_2$ λ_{max} : 353 nm
   Interference: SO_2, NO_2, peroxyacetyle nitrate and H_2S

7.20 ANALYSIS OF AMMONIA FROM ATMOSPHERE

The method for determination of ammonia involves the absorption of gas into dilute H_2SO_4. Various methods for analysis are summarised in Table 7.34. In indophenol method, $(NH_4)_2SO_4$, phenol, sodium–nitroprusside and NaOCl are reacted to give a blue coloured complex, measurable spectrophotometrically at

Table 7.34 Spectrophotometric determination of ammonia

1. Indophenol—$(NH_4)_2$ SO_4, Phenol, Sodium nitroprusside NaOCI
   blue λ_{max} = 630 nm
   but formaldehyde interfere
2. $(NH_4)_2$ SO_4, HOCI, $Br_2 \rightarrow NO_2^-$ formed diazotization orange (λ_{max} = 550 nm)
3. NH_3 in quartz cell at λ = 204 nm and e = 2–6 × 10_3
4. 1, 4–Dioxane, Benzene sulphimido–p–benzoquinone $\rightarrow \lambda_{max}$ 480 nm
5. Nessler's method
   Absorbing solution: H_2SO_4
   Reagents $HgCI_2$, KI in NaOH
   λ_{max}: 450 nm
   Working range 10–100 μg/ml
   Interference: ammonium salts, aliphatic amines, and sulphurated hydrogen

630 nm but formaldehyde interferes. Sensitivity is 0.025 to 1 ppm. The nitrite method is based upon the reaction of $(NH_4)_2$ SO_4 with HOCI and Br_2 gas to give coloured complex (λ_{max} = 550 nm). The direct determination of NH_3 in air can be achieved at 204 nm in a 100 mm quartz cell where $\varepsilon = 2.7 \times 103$ with sensitivity of 7 ppm. A direct one–step method for analysis of ammonia involves its absorption in dioxone solution containing o–(benzene sulphonamido) p–benzoquinone. It gives a coloured complex (λ_{max} = 480 nm) (Table 7.34).

The Nessler's method is the ideal method. The brown colour so developed is measured at 450 nm. The important reaction is $2Hg^{2-}_4 + NH_3 + 3OH^- \rightarrow NH_2$ Hg_2IO (brown) + $7I^-$ + $2H_2O$. It is a sensitive method; however it shows interference of aliphatic amines and H_2S. The method is simple with minimum interferences.

7.21 ORGANIC AIR POLLUTANTS

Organic pollutants have strong effect on atmosphere. They have direct and secondary effects on air. Major hydrocarbons are alkanes, alkenes, alkynes and aryl compounds. They originate from petroleum products. Many of them lead to the smog formation. By interaction with OH^-, alkyl radicals are formed. The alkyenes like ethylene, propylene, styrene are released into air from IC–engines and petroleum products. Acetylene originates from welding operation. O_3 and NO_3^- also reacts with them. Aryl hydrocarbons specially polyaromatic hydrocarbons are main sources of the pyrene benzene, ethyl benzene. Plasticiser is another source of pollution in plastic industry. Biphenyl occurs in smoke of diesel engine carbonyl compounds like aldehyde and ketones which are also encountered in air. *e.g.*, HCHO (Formaldehyde) is generated by interaction of hydrocarbon and OH^- radical. CH_3CHO is produced from the preparation of plastics or by microorganisms, where >C=O is chromophore. They give rise to peroxyacetyl nitrate. Acrolan also occurs in air. Acetone produces PAN. Sometimes aliphatic alcohols, phenols, ethers and carboxylic acids are encountered in air *e.g.*, CH_3OH, C_2H_5—OH are starting materials for synthesis. Ethyleneglycol is anti-freezing agent. Phenols are mostly present in water and they rarely occur in air. This is the starting material for bakelite preparation. Similarly, ethers rarely occurs in air. They are unreactive. The oxides ethylene and propylenoxide are common in air. In the organohalides, chloromethane, dichloromethane, dichlorodifluoromethane and trichloroethane. They are present in marine environment. Last two compounds are used as the refrigerants. Vinyl chloride is injurious to health, it causes liver cancer. They have high vapour pressure Trihalomethane is in water and occur in air. Chlorofluorocarbons (CFCs) are many $CC_{13}F$, $CC_{12}F_2$, $C_2C_{13}F_3$, $C_2C_{12}F_4$ and C_2ClFs called as CFC–11, 12, 13. Halon are compounds like $CBrCF_2$, ClCBr F_3 are used as fire extinguisher.

They are specially used in aircrafts, but they rapidly destroy O_3 from atmosphere. They are $CBrCF_2$, $CBrF_3$ and $C_2Br_2F_4$ (called as Halon 211, 1301, 2402 respectively. Perfluorocarbons (CF_5 C_2H_6) are used as etching agents. They are destroyed by photolysis at 130 mm. Half-life is long. They cause greenhouse warming. CH_3SH is produced by microorganism Thiophene, methanethiol are common. In organonitro compounds amines, like CH_3NH_2, CH_2CHCN, aniline pyridine and nitrobenzene are most common as anthropogenic source. The aryl amines like benzidine β–naphthylamine are dangerously harmful being carcinogenic. However, the nitrosoamines are well-known atmospheric pollutant. They attach alkyl $\begin{matrix} R \\ R' \end{matrix}\!\!>\!N—N=O$ group to DNA giving cancer producing DNA in modified form. All these compounds are found in tropospherereazone very close to the earth. The next is stratosphere which contains atmospheric O_3. Source of OH^- radicle is photolysis of HNO_2, H_2O_2 or reaction of HO_2 with NO and $O_2 \rightarrow O_3$ converted O_3.

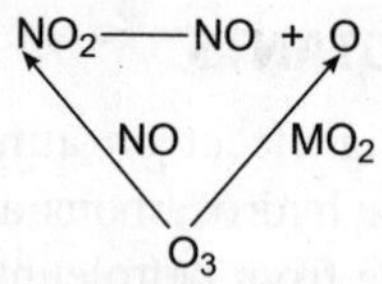

Fig. 7.17 Leigntion cycle

By this Leigntion cycle O_3 is continuously created and also consumed. NO^-_3 in air is formed from oxides of nitrogen. The troposphere contains CFC while stratosphere contains O_3.

(a) Reactions of Organic Compounds in the Atmosphere

The main reactions are with OH^- radicals. Such reaction is as highest during day-time with rise of methane (CH_4) water and methyl radical. It forms CH_3—CHO, HCHO, C_2H_6, and CO_2 while O_3 reacts with hydrocarbons to give rise to aldehyde, ketones and carboxylic acid. Transbutene and Limonene are generated. O_3 is electrophillic *i.e.,* those which have love for electrons, NO^-_3 radicals also reacts similar to OH^- radical. There is phototransformation where molecules absorb photons from atmosphere. The sources of organics is the main emission from industries or transportation or the generations of the gases by interaction of microorganisms with atmospheric gases. The important reactions involve ether interaction with OH^- radicle or NO^-_3 radicle or O_3 from air which undergo photochemical reaction.

(b) Analysis of Organics

The gas chromatography is used for volatile compounds in few instances GC–MS is also used for quantitative analysis. The spectrophotometry in UV or visible region is also used. The important compounds are volatile organics, methane, volatile aromatic organics, volatile hydrocarbons, trihalomethane (in water only) phenols PCB, PAH. The initial BOD analysis gives idea of total biodegradable organic present in air. Total organics is ascertained by CHN analysis. Wet oxidation method is rarely used. Adsorption pyrolysis and titrimetry is adopted for degradable products. Adsorption chromatography is used for phenols which are analysed by colorimetry or gas liquid chromatography. The chloroform extraction is employed for analysis of phenols and pyrene. It is followed by spectrophotometry. Organics and volatile acids are estimated by adsorption chromatography followed by titration with NaOH. There are numerous methods for the analysis of trihalomethanes.

Lighter organics are determined by adsorption chromatography (GSC), CH_4 is determined at ppb level by GLC. 3–4 benzopyrene–a carcinogenic and polycylic compounds is determined by GLC and fluorimetrically. HCHO is a component of photochemical smog and is determined with spectrophotometrically with chromotropic acid in H_2SO_4. Olefins and acroleins are analysed by gas chromatography. It is not possible to get definite information by GLC, but hyphenated GC–MS offers reliable information in characterisation of organic pollutants.

For rapid analysis of gaseous pollutants in environment, the best method is spectrophotometry. These methods are simple, inexpensive, with availability of innumerable organic ligands.

The high performance liquid chromatography is used for the analysis of nonvolatile organics. Several compounds are analysed by GC–MS. The volatile compounds are analysed by pure and trap packed column of GC–MS *e.g.*, acrylonitrile CH_4 is analysed by titration of generated CO_2 to HCO_3 acid. Volatile hydrocarbons are analysed by GC. PCB and PAHs followed by extraction. The organics are mostly isolated by GC and then analysed by MS or absorption spectroscopy with suitable chromogenic ligand.

7.22 CONCLUSION

Air pollution is attaining an alarming level with the growth of industries. Even heritage objects are not spared from the devasting consequences of air pollution. Several episodes took place all over the world, which led to formulation of air pollution control legislation in most of the European and American nations. When normal composition of the atmosphere is fouled or altered with addition of pollutants the air pollution occurs. The effects of air pollution on men, animals and vegetation are alarming. However, global consequences leading to greenhouse effect, depletion of ozone layer, acid rains or photochemical smog formation is of serious concern. There are various sources of air pollution like stationary and mobile sources. Combustion is big sources of pollution. Autoexhaust emissions is worst source amongst mobile sources. To ascertain their magnitude it is necessary to conduct ambient air quality monitoring. It involves aerosols and gaseous pollutant. Their sampling methods are dependable for getting reproducible results. There are efficient methods for laboratory analysis of sulphur dioxide sulphurated hydrogen, oxides of nitrogen, oxides of carbon, ozone and ammonia. Such methods, are largely include simple volumetric or spectrophotometric methods of analysis. Enormous amounts of organic compounds are encountered in the atmosphere. Some of these are even carcinogenic. Their methods of analysis is composed of gas chromatography or GC–MS with FID and ECD detectors. The spectral methods of analysis are resorted. In conclusion, unless the quantitative analysis of air pollutants in atmosphere is carried out carefully one cannot predict the extent of damage caused to the nature.

ADDITIONAL READING

1. Mayuri Gandhi and S.M. Khopkar, *Ind. J. Env. Prot.* **9**, 343 (1989).
2. *Environmental Pollutants: Selected Analytical Methods* SCOPE **6** (1975), Butterworths, London.
3. A.C. Stem, *Air Pollution*, Vol. 3, 3rd Ed. (1976), Academic Press, New York.
4. A. Attri, T.P. Igiebki and B. Jaselskis, *Anal. Chem.*, **42**, 1282 (1970).
5. P.W. West and G.C. Gaeke, *Anal. Chem.*, **28**, 1816 (1956).
6. M.B. Jacobs, M.M. Braverman and S. Hochheiser, *Anal. Chem.*, **29**, 1349 (1957).
7. S.M. Khopkar, *Res. Ind.*, **29**, 86 (1984).
8. B.E. Saltzmann, *Anal. Chem.*, **26**, 1949 (1954).
9. APHA, *Methods for Air Sampling and Analysis,* American Public Health Association, p. 337 (1992).
10. H. Yagoda and F.H. Goldmann, *J. Ind. Hyg. Toxicol.*, **25**, 440 (1943).
11. A.A. Christie, R.G. Lidzey and D.W.F. Radford, *Analyst,* **95,** 519 (1970).
12. D.A. Levaggi, W. Sin and M. Feldstein, *J. Air Pollut. Const. Ass.*, **23**, 30 (1973).
13. EPA 'United States Environmental Protection Agency', *Fed. Regist.* **36**, 8200 (1971).
14. R.C. Robbings, K. M. Borg and E. Robinson, *J. Air Pollut. Control. Ass.*, **18**, 106 (1968).
15. A.J. Haagensmit and M.F. Brunnelle, *Int. J. Air Pollut.,* **1** 31 (1958).
16. T.R. Hanser and D.W. Bradley, *Anal. Chem.*, **38**, 1529 (1966).
17. C. Arnold and C. Mentzel, *Ber. Dent. Chem. Ges.*, **35**, 1324 (1902).
18. H.H. Bravo and R.J. Robinson, *Anal. Chem.*, **33,** 1115 (1961).
19. H.H. Bravo and J.P. Lodge, *Anal. Chem.*, **36,** 671 (1964).
20. D.H. Byers and B.E. Saltzmann, *Am. Ind. Hyg.* **19,** 252 (1958).
21. HS Intersociety Committee, *Health Lab. Sci.*, **10,** 115 (1973).
22. V.W. Truesdale, *Analyst,* **96,** 584 (1971).
23. F.A. Gunther, J.H. Borkley, M.J. Kolbenzene, R.C. Blinn, *Anal. Chem.,* **28,** 1985 (1956).
24. D.N. Karmer and J.M. Sech, *Anal. Chem.*, **44,** 395 (1972).
25. M. Buck and H. Stratmann, *Z. Anal. Chem.*, **213,** 241 (1965).
26. S.K. Santic and S. Tyagi, *Employment News Weekly,* **26** (2002).
27. S.E. Manahan, *Environmental Chemistry,* 7th Ed. Lewis Publishers NY (1999).
28. D.W. Connell, *Basic Concepts of Environmental Chemistry*, Lewis Publishers Boca Raton (1997).
29. C. Baird, *Environmental Chemistry*, W.H. Freeman and Co. (1995).
30. APHA *Standard Methods of Examination of Water and Waste Water,* 20th Ed. (2000).
31. H. Loggen, *Environmental Pollution*—2nd Ed. Holt Reinhort Wintson (1978).
32. S.M. Khopkar, *Environmental Pollution Analysis,* Second Edition, New Age International Publishers (2012).

8 Air Pollution and Meteorology

8.1 INTRODUCTION

The sampling of air pollutant is most important as the characteristics of sample changes within few seconds from place to place. The presence of wind, the change into velocity of wind or even an abrupt change in direction of wind or flow rate alters composition of atmosphere. The temperature of atmosphere at the time of measurement is also important. A change in temperature causes change in convection currents in atmosphere. This in turn changes the pattern of wind. It results in the formation of photochemical smog due to dispersion in air. A close study of the terrain is most important. If there is mountain, or valley in path of wind the direction due to dispersion of air pollutants is altered. Thus, before sampling or measurement of the pollutants, it is essential to study the behaviour of the various meteorological parameters. The meteorology is science of the atmosphere. From the knowledge of various parameters of the meteorology, one can predict pattern of dispersion of the pollutants in the atmosphere. In order to understand air pollution survilence and monitoring, we need to study the 'wind roses'. These are graphical representation of the direction or velocity of wind against time. These wind roses give precise

Table 8.1 Environment around planets in universe

S. No.	*Name of the planet*	*Distance from sun (10^9 m)*	*Radius at equator (10^9 m)*	*Temp° kelvin K°*	*Pressure bars*	*Gases encountered*
1.	Pluto	5900	1.5	50	1×10^{-5}	Unknown
2.	Neptune	4497	25.2	56	1×10^{2}	H_2, He
3.	Uranus	2870	26.2	58	1×10^{2}	H_2, He
4.	Saturn	1427	60.3	97	1×10^{2}	H_2, He
5.	Jupiter	778	71.4	129	1×10^{2}	H_2, He
6.	Mars	228	3.4	218	$7 \times 10^{3-}$	CO_2, N_2, Ar
7.	Earth	150	1.7	288	1.0	N_2, O_2, Ar
8.	Moon	150	6.4	244	2×10^{-4}	Ne, Ar, He
9.	Venus	108	6.0	730	90	CO_2, N_2
10.	Mercury	57.9	2.4	440	2×10^{-15}	He, H

information of location of pollution, one must understand the impact of the various meteorological parameters on the dispersion of air pollution. It includes consideration of wind, wind velocity, wind direction, effect of temperature, phenomena of inversion. After detailed studies of these parameters it is worthwhile to undertake the air pollution monitoring or measurement on continuous basis. This provides reliable information of the pollutants. These studies are taken into account in first part of this chapter. It is interesting to examine the environment around the plants. A further investigation on northern hemisphere environment is most interesting.

We examine Table 8.1, in recent years thorough investigations are being carried out in space. On account of the brisk activities in space sputniks are located. Everyone is keen to know what kind of life exist on the other planets in the universe? A successful landing on the moon has revealed marvells and mysteries of universe. A next stage of investigation is to set land on the Mars. A comparative study of earth and mars indicates that there is good possibility of existence of life on the mars as atmosphere is to earth. But it is close to sun (~ 228×10^9 metres) while the planet farthest from the sun is pluto (~ 5900×10^9 metres). There is varying degree of temperature from 50° K at pluto to 288° K on the earth. The moon temperature is close to that of earth *viz.* 274° K. Venus however has high temperature of 730° K. The pressure varies from planet to planet, it is very low at planet called mercury (~ 2×10^{-15} bars) and it is very high at venus. Very little information is available in details on the status of environment on these planets. Now let us examine the conditions on the northern hemisphere of the earth (Table 8.2).

Table 8.2 Condition on north hemisphere with pollution at different pressures

S. No.	*Property*	*Low pressure*		*High pressure*	
		Nonpermanent	*Thermal*	*Nonpermanent*	*Thermal*
1.	Storm generation	Possible	Rarely	No	No
2.	Cloud cover	Cloudy	No clouds	No clouds, sunny	No clouds
3.	Air pollution	Decreases	Decreases	Increases	Increases
4.	Wind speed	Fast	Changing	Weak	Changing
5.	Wind direction	Counter clockwise	Counter clock	Clockwise moving	Clockwise
6.	Pressure	Strong	Changing	Weak	Changing
7.	Pressure gradient	Strong	Changing	Weak	Changing
8.	Range of latitude	45–65° N	24–45° N	24–45° N	45–65° N

The study of atmosphere on the northern hemisphere of the earth is interesting. However, more interesting observations are possible on our own planet namely earth. The study of the environment in northern hemisphere is most challenging both at low and high pressure. There are no clouds in the north pole. At high pressure air pollution increases as seen in Table 8.2. The wind speed is rapid at low pressure. It is however difficult to standardize atmosphere condition even on the earth. The main reason being enormous variation in meteorological parameters such as wind velocity. The wind direction influences the temperature and pressure in the atmosphere.

8.2 METEOROLOGICAL PARAMETERS

We consider first different meteorological parameters which influence dispersion of pollutant. Such factors decide the mode of measurement of pollutants.

(a) Winds

Winds are caused by pressure difference, leading to the difference in temperature in the atmosphere. It occurs on large area and lead to significant climatic changes. The intervening valley, trees, buildings, change their direction as well as speed. Wind plays a significant role in distribution of pollutants in the atmosphere. In view of this the consideration of changes in its velocity or direction and impact of the temperature on the course of its flow must be considered.

(b) Wind Velocity

The change in velocity with altitude depends upon, the kind of terrain through which it is flowing. The time or location where wind is blowing is equally important.The buildings, trees, large size water bodies affect its velocity. The specific direction of transportation of pollutants is determined by wind direction at the source. The air pollution at point source is more severe and sensitive as it is concentrated in location. If wind is flowing over the source, it causes the dispersion of the concentration of the pollutants. The direction of the plume, transport from slack is important for transporting pollutant. With variation in height of stack, there is a change in wind direction. At ground level, wind circulates clockwise. The horizontal thermal structure, affects the direction to shift it to counter clockwise direction with rise in height of chimney. The presence of the cold and warm air also affects wind direction. Wind velocity rises with height. Wind velocity dilutes the released pollutants at point of emission. Such dilution occurs in the direction of plume transporting from the stack. Wind speed is used to determine plume direction and dispersion at top of stack. It affects travel time of pollutant from source to receptive object like man. It is irregular motion of wind. The erratic flow of wind moves in random motion and sets eddy current (Fig. 8.1). Superheated air ascends to top. The slow flow of atmospheric wind leads to formation of thermal turbulence. Such turbulences are quite large. The mixing of pollutant in turbulence by dispersion is called "eddy diffusion". The dispersion ability can be measured. Wind forces have a centrifugal path in circulation. The direction of wind is related to temperature gradient. The wind velocity increases with height of stack due to decrease in surface friction in upper atmosphere (Fig. 8.2). The wind velocity is measured as $u/u_o = (Z/Zo)^{\mu}$. In this equation u = wind speed at height 'Z' and u_0 is wind speed at height 'Zo' and μ is parameter of fit = 1/7 for 2 to 10 meter height. This is called as 'Power law' of wind velocity. The change in velocity of wind with height depends upon the type of terrain and time of flow. Its nature, density,

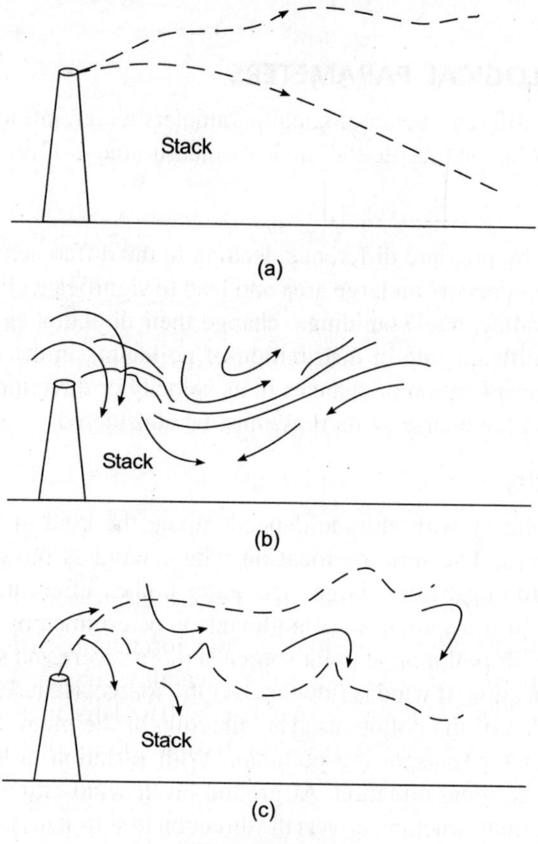

Fig. 8.1 Eddy formation

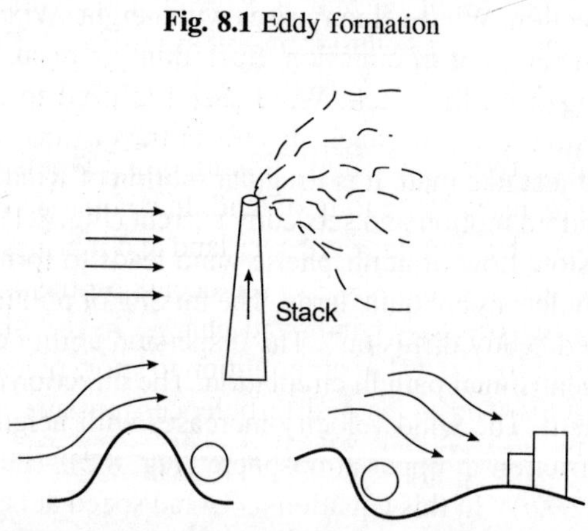

Fig. 8.2 Location of stack position and wind direction

size, presence of building affects gradient. Flow of wind is smooth on smoother surface but on rough terrain it produces mechanical turbulence (Fig. 8.3).

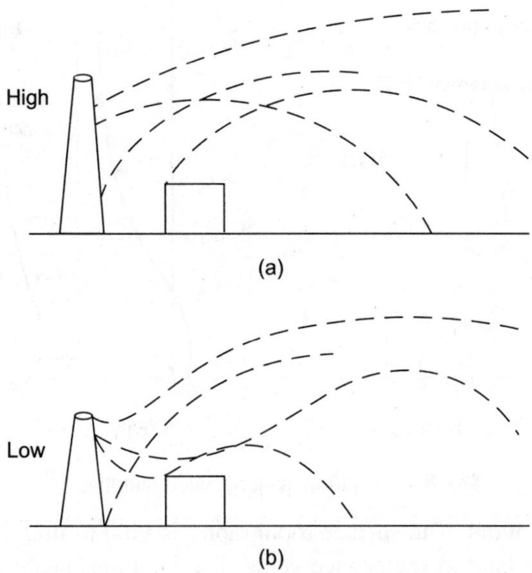

Fig. 8.3 Plume behaviour over building and turbulence

The thermal turbulence gives rise to large eddy formation, leading to the change in the motion of plume. The 'α' is called as "stability constant". It has value of 0.11 for large lapse rate; 0.14 for small lapse rate, 0.20 for large inversion and 0.33 for very large inversions. The cyclones and anticyclones are also worth considering.

(c) What are Cyclones and Anticylones?

There is large scale circulation of wind. The cyclones do cause at ground level counter clockwise circulation of air and at more height of stack, it causes the clockwise circulation of air. Air pollution problem is severe at the high altitude because the large mass or parcel of air moves by circulation. It has different temperature regions to regions toward which it is moving. The junction with local air is called 'front'. Sea-breeze and valleys are important points in topography of winds. Sea-breezes are caused by heating of land. In comparison heating of water is slow. By the process of heating, air rises over land and it brings heavier air from water to land. A reverse *i.e.,* land-breeze to sea occurs on the cooling cycle. The valley causes channeling of cross-winds and change in the direction of wind. Therefore, it is important for analyst of air pollution to know preciously the dimension of transport phenomena; winds and turbulence, pressure and temperature. The humidity must be also known. Winds are also measured horizontally for direction (Fig. 8.4) around a building.

(d) Wind Direction

The wind direction is very critical. The effect of ocean, and mountain valley on the direction of wind is of significance. The obstacles like building lead to change

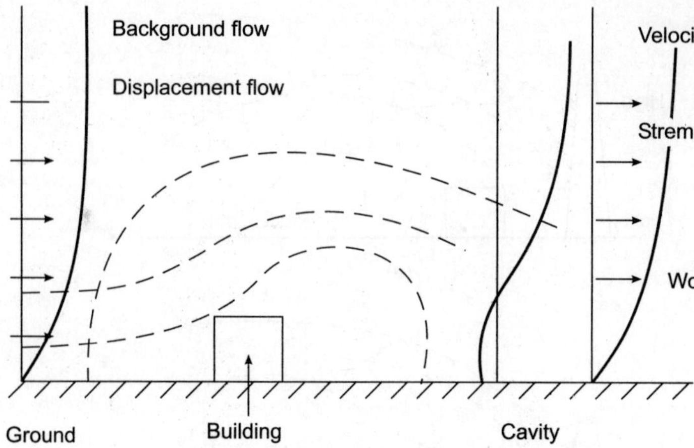

Fig. 8.4 Windflow pattern round building

in the direction of wind. The surface topography is vital to understand the effect of sea-breeze from land to sea or vice versa. The land gets heated quickly in day but it gets cooled also quickly in night. The hot air over heated land moves to sea in day time and it reverses its direction of flow to land from sea in night-time leading pleasant breeze on land in night. As regards effect of the mountain or valley on winds, in day time, the base of mountains is heated. The wind goes up and flow over valley and mountain slopes. However in night land is cooled leading to change in air density, so cold dense air flows from sea to mountain to occupy the valley. If polluting source is located in valley, the pollutants are trapped in the valley during day time when it is warm, pollutant disperse from mountain to move upto valley. If wind returns to valley in night it leads to shift of wind towards lower end of valley. This circulation of wind gives rise to accumulation of pollutant to dangerous level. The location of non-uniform heights of buildings relative to stack height affects behaviour of plume and formation of mechanical turbulence (Figs. 8.3 and 8.4). If the location of stack is behind the building or hill (1) it leads

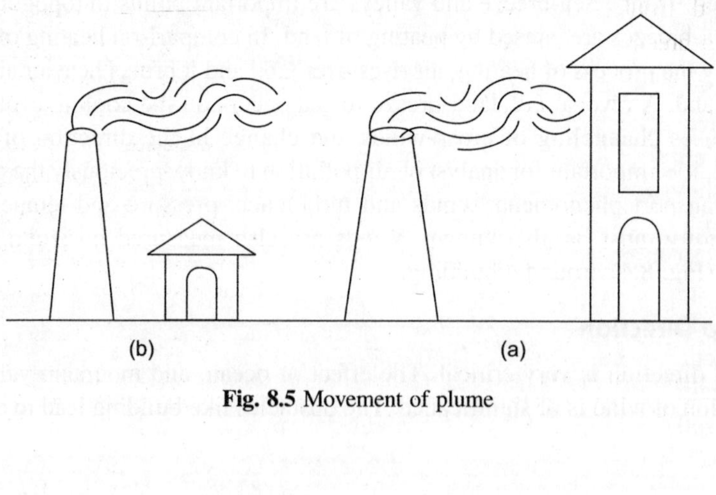

Fig. 8.5 Movement of plume

to rising plume above stack level and the pollutant are carried away from the stack provided if gas and ambient velocities are identical. However, the flow depends upon the height of stack. If the stack height is more than building, then plume goes away from building but with rise in turbulence more dispersion occurs. If the height of stack is less than building, pollutants flow to base of the building (see Fig. 8.5 parts *a* and *b* respectively). Therefore, it is most essential to have stack height of more than 2.5 times height of adjacent building.

(e) Measurement of Meteorological Variables

Meteorology is the science, which deals with the atmosphere and its variations. These meteorological studies are useful in understanding emission rates, stack design, plant site and selection and forecasting of air pollution area. It is most essential to measure variables or meteorological parameters during monitoring of air. The factors are pressure, temperature, relative humidity, wind speed and intensity of solar radiation. The pressure is measured by mercury barometer or with aneroid barometer. At sea level pressure is 760 mm, aneroid barometer is less accurate than mercury barometer. Thermometer is used to measure temperature but at a time the thermocouple is also used as it is based on current flow in circuit. The humidity is measured by sling psychrometer or wet and dry thermometer. In latter the one end of thermometer is covered with wet cloth while other end is kept dry. Temperature and humidity are measured simultaneously. Wind speed is measured by an instrument called 'anemometers (cup type)'. The rate of rotation of shaft to which cups are attached is recorded electrically. In gusty winds it is possible that the wrong readings may be recorded. So wind variations are combined to give both speed and direction of wind on same chart. The intensity of sunlight is measured by sunshine recorder. The instrument for measuring intensity of sunlight is called "pyrheliometer". The bright surface and black surface are connected and difference between two sides is measured on thermocouple with good sensitivity.

(f) Wind Roses

Wind data at particular spot is expressed in terms of "Wind roses". Wind roses represents velocity of the wind against time indicating at what fraction of time a given velocity of wind prevails. This is graphical representation of wind data giving percent frequency of wind velocity, and its direction at given spot. Since wind motion is circular, it is easier to interpret and imagine the frequency of the wind-flow by showing wind roses or wind frequencies in each direction. It is done on interval of 3 or 5 hourly basis (Fig. 8.6).

In Fig. 8.6 highest frequencies are from south to west and lowest frequencies are from southeast to east. The wind roses show stability frequencies in each direction. The roses are drawn by plotting either the average concentration for each direction or the frequency of concentrations above some particular concentration against time. In wind roses spike indicates direction of blowing wind, the width of spikes indicate the velocity and length of spike which is proportional to the percent time at given velocity and the direction. The eight spike wind roses are plotted. Unfortunately it cannot record wind at low speeds. Since winds carry air pollution, it can dilute wind roses. Wind roses can be constructed on hourly basis for total period of month. Wind variability or its gustiness is important to measure the turbulence. Wind roses is graphical representation of wind data giving percentage frequency of wind speed and wind direction for a particular location. It can be drawn for day, month or even year. For such purpose the knowledge of velocity of wind, wind direction and period or time of blowing is essential. The

$$\text{percent frequency of wind} = \frac{\text{Period of wind in blowing } (h \times 100)}{\text{Unit period say 24 hrs}}$$

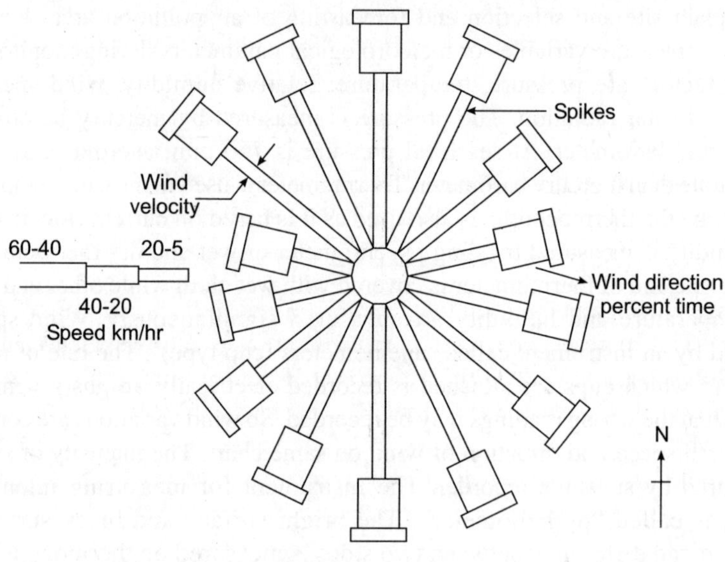

Fig. 8.6 Wind roses

(g) Effect of Temperature

The potential temperature gives an idea about atmospheric stability. It is expressed by an equation as

$$\theta = T\,(1000/p)^{0.288}$$

if θ = potential temperature for stability and T = absolute temperature, p = pressure (in milli bar, mb). At this temperature, packet of dry air would have stability if it is brought to dry state adiabatically to a pressure of 1000 milli bars. If potential temperature decreases with height, the atmosphere is stable. The earth surface absorbs solar radiation and it radiates to the atmosphere with the result that air near earth surface becomes warm and drifts away by expansion. It is less dense and has less pressure. The warm air when it comes in contact with cold air, it gives room and push forward from high pressure to low pressure at more height (see Fig. 8.7). The temperature at the equator is high while at poles it is low and cold.

Now if warming parcel of air remains warm, it rises upward at point of displacement. The atmosphere is rendered 'unstable'. However, if rising packet of air is cool and dense, air packet moves downward to render atmosphere 'stable'. At high pressure system at northern hemisphere vertical motion of air is downwards and horizontal motion is clockwise. At low pressure air vertically moves upward and horizontal motion is anti-clockwise. The decrease in temperature with altitude is called as "lapse rate" such lapse rate is also called "ambient lapse rate."

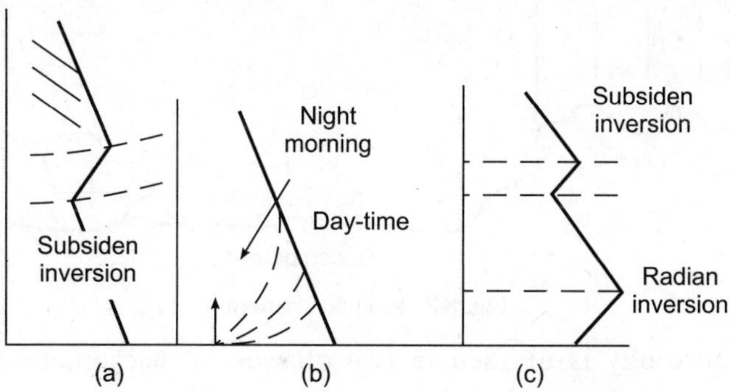

Fig. 8.7 Inversion and pattern of wind-flow

If change in temperature is without heat loss or transfer it is called as 'adiabatic lapse rate'. This represents decrease in temperature with altitude due to adiabatic cooling. In ideal gas, it is 1°C per 100 metre. If the environmental lapse rate is more than dry adiabatic lapse rate (DALR) it is termed as "super adiabatic lapse rate" one which is lower than DALR it is called "subadiabatic" lapse rate. If lapse rate is zero it is called *isothermal i.e.,* no change in temperature with height.

(h) Inversions

If the temperature of earth's surface is cooler than temperature at high altitude, then the temperature increases with altitude *i.e.,* negative lapse rate or inversion. Such rise in temperature with altitude is called 'Inversion'. Natural inversion is possible due to first cooling of earth than air, it is intense. The shallow inversion is due to thermal mixing in morning, which is mechanical. The inversions at the surface are caused at night by cooling air near the earth. The 'subsidence' inversion is explained by following diagrams (Figs. 8.7 and 8.8).

This is due to sinking packet of air in high pressure area (anti-cyclones) at reasonable height. Such sinking package leads to rise in temperature. The humidity decreases in this process. The top part of sinking packet is warmer. Inversions are of considerable importance to air pollution to understand the effect stabilization of atmosphere leading to vertical spreading of pollutants and arresting vertical motion. In day time air near earth warms up and receive heat by radiation till evening. But after sunset loss of heat on earth takes place leading to cooling of earth. Since there is inversion due to radiation it is called as "radiation inversion". This is followed by subsidence inversion as shown in (Fig. 8.7*a*).

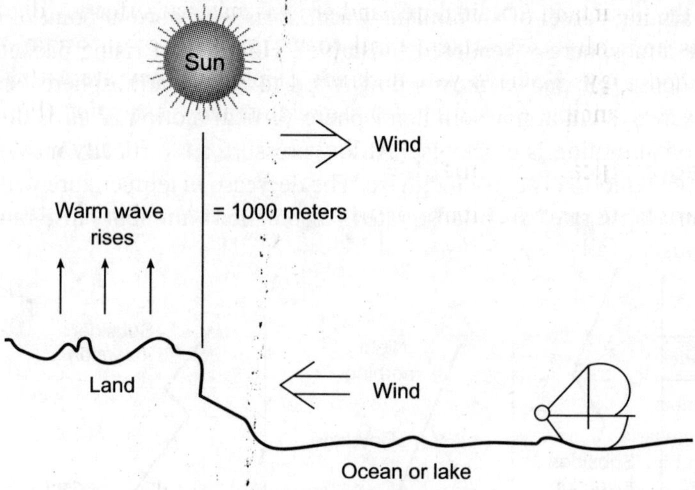

Fig. 8.8 Inversion pattern

The meteorology is divided in two classes as macrometeorology and micrometeorology. The macrometeorology pertains to large mass of air movement due to change in temperature, pressure and rotation of earth leading to the dispersion. The humidity and clouds also affect movements of air mass. The

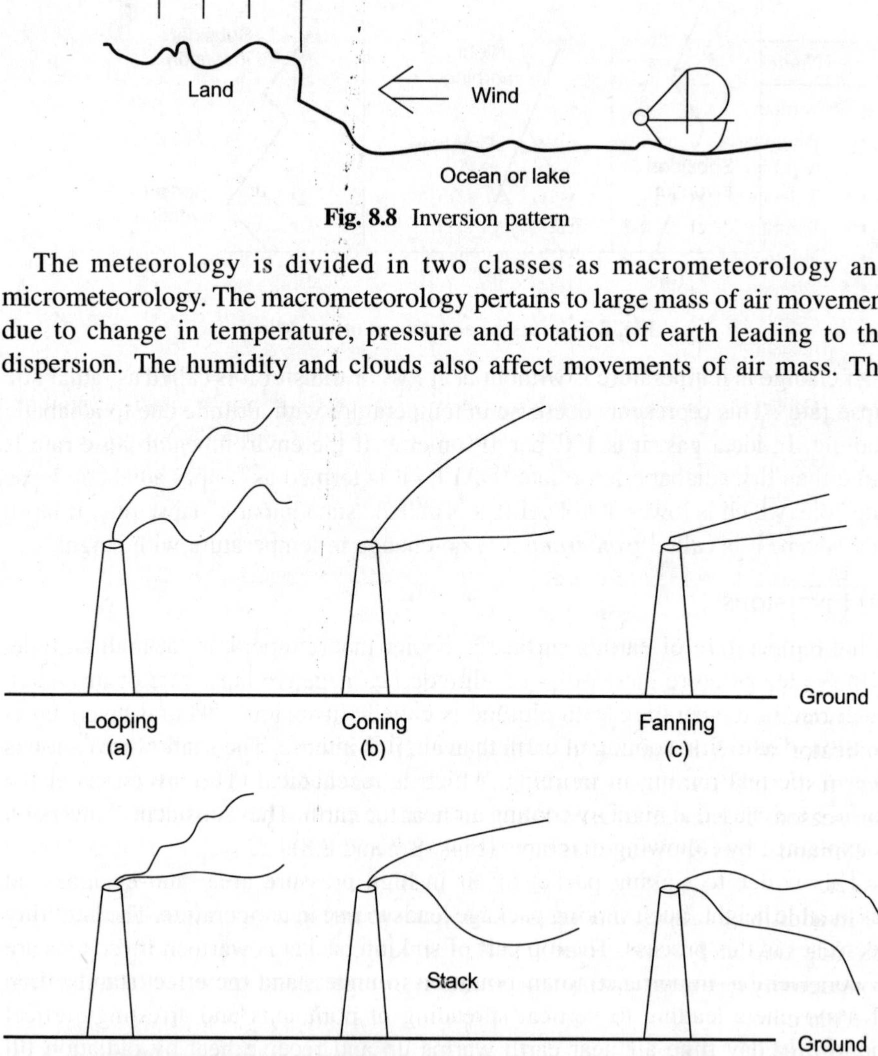

Fig. 8.9 Kind of plumes

micrometeorology pertains to study of air circulation and temperature in its valleys, slopes of the mountain, building, tree and ground material, affecting dispersion of pollutants specially from stack wind roses, give lot of information in the micromethodology. We have various kinds of plums. They are as (*a*) looping, (*b*) coning, (*c*) fanning, (*d*) lofting, (*e*) fumigation and (*f*) trapping (Fig. 8.9).

(i) Meteorological Instruments

In comparison to air pollution monitoring instruments, these instruments are indigeneously available in any part of India (see Table 8.3).

Table 8.3 Meteorological instruments

Name of instrument	*Property measured*	*Kind of technique*
• Temperature recorder	Temperature	Temperature sensor by diode
• Anemometer and wind meter	Wind velocity and wind direction	Velocity threshold
• Tide and wave meter	Wave and tide	Hydrostatic pressure
• Salinity meter	Salinity of system	Conductivity cell
• Telemeter	Measurement of depth	Hydrostatic sensing probe
• Temperature logger	Temperature recorder	Probe with thermistors
• Water speed measurement	Water flow meter	Signal conditioners and loggers
• Water level meter	Water level	Resistance variation
• Capacitance bridge	Height and level of water indicator	Capacitance sensors measurement of difference
• Telemetry design	Data transmitter	UHF radiolink used
• Rain gauge	Rainfalls	Rain gauge measurement
• Humidity indicator	Humidity measurement	Measurement with thermistor probes

Among these instruments temperature recorder is most useful. One can also use temperature logger. The most useful instrument is anemometer. It is a device which measures wind velocity as well as wind direction. By making use of anemometer one can easily construct beautiful wind roses. We also need humidity indicator which is measured by wet and dry bulb thermometer. One also uses thermistor probe for measurement. The rain gauge is used to record the rainfall in the season. Telemeter is used to measure the depth mostly in water. Water level meter and water speed meters are useful to record level as well as rate of flow of water.

In addition to these there are special kinds of meteorological instruments. They include tide and wave meter (used near sea coast), salinity meter (based on conductivity measurement), and capacitance bridge. However, these are not always used in comparison to main meteorological instruments.

By making use of above instruments we can measure wind velocity, wind direction, temperature gradient, temperature, inversions, rain level, leading to construction of wind roses and deciding mode of control of air pollution.

8.3 MONITORING AND ANALYSIS

There is definite difference between these two terms *viz.* monitoring and analysis. The first term relates to continuous long-term measurement of pollution on site, or in outdoor environment while latter term pertains to the laboratory scale analysis of pollutants collected from site involving measurements in laboratory.

We have considered laboratory methods of air pollution analysis. When the pollutant is emitted ceaselessly and specially when it is necessary to measure it at site such as in a field, or in any other outdoor location, several of the laboratory methods fail to furnish reliable information. At a time it is difficult to collect the sample and bring it to the laboratory for further analysis. There is a good possibility that we have to take several measurements on regular basis at constant and regular intervals, for which we need rapid methods which can analyse air pollutants on a continuous basis. Few of the laboratory methods are also used for the outdoor locations. It is always possible to use basic principles underlying laboratory methods for testing of pollutants so as to devise a novel method for continuous measurement. Such continuous measurement is termed as 'monitoring'.

Monitoring is confined to two aspects. One what is called as ambient air quality management while latter is termed as "stack emission" monitoring or analysis. The ambient air quality monitoring is confined to a specific place or location while stack monitoring is restricted to the larger area adjacent to stack. This is because of the dispersion of pollutants is rapid by wind, temperature changes as considered under various meteorological parameters.

The status of monitoring instrument in India is considered from the view point of their working principles and availability followed by the detailed discussion of ambient air quality monitoring of specific gases. The monitoring in stack emission from atmosphere is also covered.

The various control measures resorted for abatement of the pollution are based on this knowledge. The control measures are considered at the end of this chapter.

(a) Air Pollution Monitoring Instruments

The monitoring instrument is composed of three components, *viz.*, air remover, transducer and recorder. The air remover consists of a flow meter and a pressure gauge. It measures rate of flow of air passing and the pressure under which gas pollutants exist. Transducer in fact is the heart of the instrument, which measures intensity as in physical property, while the recorder notes change in physical property of gaseous pollutant, *e.g.*, flow colorimeters or spectrophotometers are used to measure the concentration of the pollutant. The instrument should be checked for response time, specificity, sensitivity, noise level, maintenance and downtime and overall accuracy. Very few instruments are available for aerosol analysis in this country, but some progress has been made for fabrication at academic institutions.

The common air pollution monitoring instruments for measurement are summarised in 8.3. The limits of analysis are specific, the techniques of measurement are given in the last column of Table 8.3. There are a good deal of instruments for measurement of SO_2, CO, CO_2, NO–NO_x and H_2S. They are based upon measurement of various physical properties *e.g.,* for SO_2 monitor use of either conductance measurement or coulometric technique is made. On the contrary, for H_2S we have only one method involving flow colorimetry. The other pollutants like oxygen, ozone, smoke and dust, organic pollutants as well as metal pollutants, are monitored on a continuing basis. In such techniques, apart from conventional methods one uses measurements of light scattering phenomena (for smoke), fluorescence quenching (organic pollutant), emission and absorption spectroscopy (metal pollutants) for quantitative analysis (Table 8.4).

Table 8.4 Air pollution monitoring instruments and their range

Instrument	*Pollutant measured*	*Range (ppm)*
• IR gas analyser	CO, CH_4 and HC	10–1000
• NDIR analyser	CO, CO_2	10–1000
• Car exhaust meter	Auto exhaust analysis	No limit
• CO-monitor	Catalytic oxidation	0–50
• SO_2 monitor	Conductivity	0–100
• SO_2 monitor	Coulometric titration	0–40
• O_3 monitor	Chemiluminescence	0–0.1
• NO-NOx-monitor	Chemiluminescence	0– 0.5
• H_2S analyser	Colorimetry	0–40

(b) Status of Monitoring Instruments in India

At this stage, it is worthwhile to take stock of the situation of the available monitoring instruments in India. In the last two decades, our country had made spectacular progress in enactment of pollution control measures and we have succeeded in controlling pollution upto a reasonable limit in the urban areas as well as in few metropolitan cities.

In India, on the front of development of monitoring instruments, little progress has been made. While prescribing standards for pollutants there was awareness of our limitations, but while prescribing methods of analysis, one never thought of whether a particular instrument is easily and cheaply available in India. Table 8.4 lists status of minimum monitoring instruments used in India. It will be interesting to note that out of these basic instruments six are not fabricated in India, while 50% of listed instruments need refinement; and of this only 25% instruments are in the process of development. Table 8.4 gives such approximate idea of important instruments. This remark is based upon reports prepared by the special committee of DST on environmental monitoring instruments of the Government of India. One encouraging feature is that although simple instruments like pH meter, and spectrophotometer was imported 50 years ago, but now they are easily available in India. Similarly, since past decade sophisticated instruments like AAS,

Table 8.5 Air monitoring instruments and technique of analysis

Instruments	*Pollutant measured*	*Technique of analysis*
• Conductometric analyser	SO_2	Conductometric measurement
• Continuous SO_2 monitor	SO_2	Coulometric measurement
• Gas liquid chromatography	CO, NO, organics hydrocarbons	Gas chromatography with different detectors
• Nitric oxide monitor	NO–NOx	Fluorescence technique
• O_3 analyser	O_3 in atmosphere	Emission spectrography
• Ozone monitor	O_3	Chemiluminiscence technique
• Infrared gas analyser	CO, CH_4 and other hydrocarbons	Infrared absorption NDIR technique
• Fluorescence spectroscopy	Organic pollutants	Fluorescence or phosphorescence methods
• Smoke meter	Smoke, smog	Light scattering technique
• Atomic absorption spectroscopy	Trace metals analysis	Atomic Absorption Spectroscopy
• Emission spectrography at tracer levels	Metal pollutants	Emission spectroscopy ICP-AES

GLC, C, H, N analysers and all meteorological instruments are indigenously fabricated. They are readily available in India. The day will not be too far when NMR, GSMS, NDIR will be also designed and fabricated in India. The reason is simple, we have infrastructure, facilities and know how available. With little effort and proper utilisation of expertise and manpower, we will be self-supporting on this count of design and development of these instruments. We must fabricate only such monitoring devises which suit Indian conditions and environment. Table 8.5 lists monitoring instruments so far developed by various scientific and academic institutions in India.

Table 8.6 Some minimum air monitoring set-up

Instrument	*Parameter measured*
• High volume sampler	Dust load
• Microscope	Particulate size
• SO_2 analyser	Conductance
• NO–NO_x meter	Absorbance
• O_3 analyser	Absorbance
• O_3 analyser	Chemiluminescence
• CO	Infrared absorption (NDIR) CO, CO_2
• Hydrocarbon	FID–ionisation GC

Table 8.7 Monitoring instruments developed in India till (2003)

Instrument developed in India
• Smoke meter
• Recording stack smoke density meter
• Stack monitoring kit
• High volume sampler
• Size selective gravimetric dust sampler
• Portable multigas sampler
• CO monitor as NDIR
• SO_2 monitor
• H_2S monitor
• O_3 monitor
• $NO–NO_x$ monitor
• NDIR-CH_4 monitor
• Fluorescent SO_2 monitor
• Electro deposited lead dioxide plate
• Wind speed recorder
• Wind direction recorder
• Temperature sensor
• Sunshine recorder
• Anemometer
• Telemetry instrument

(c) Principles of Monitoring Methods

If it is necessary to measure air pollution on a regular basis, then one must identify some physical property of the pollutants for such measurements. The component of instrument which measures such physical parameters is called as 'Transducer'. A specific property, characteristic of a particular pollutant such as light transmittance or absorbance, electrical conductivity; change in potential, generation of current by passage of electricity, nucleation of fog formation or radioactivity is measured. Such properties are summarised in Table 8.8.

Although many air pollution monitoring instruments have been designed and developed in research institutions, very few have been put up in market. This is because the prototype models are designed and left at this stage by the research workers and no attempts are made to commercially produce them on large scale *e.g.*, H_2S, SO_2. Noise meter have been known since long in India but no one wants to take onerous responsibility of fabricating them at reasonable price for users.

Table 8.8 Physical principles involved in various monitoring methods

Physical principle	*Illustrations*
• Molecular absorbance (UV/visible/IR)	SO_2, NO_2, H_2S, CO
• Atomic absorption (AAS)	SO_2, Hg, Pd
• Atomic emission (ICP–AES)	SO_2 metal pollutant
• Molecular luminescence (Fluoroscence)	SO_2, NO_2, H_2S
• Light scattering (Nephelometry and Turbidimetry)	Particulates SPM,
• Magnetic resonance/Electron spin resonance (NMR/ESR)	Organics
• Polarograph amperometery (diffusion current)	Pesticide, metals
• Conductance, high frequency light (conductivity)	SO_2
• Potential–pH measurement, ionselective electrodes	NO–NO_x, metals
• Coulometry—anodic stripping voltametry (ASV)	SO_2, anions
• Radioanalytical (NAA/IDM) methods	Radioactive pollutants
• Gas chromatrography (GC)	Organics volatile complexes thermally stable

(d) Environmental Monitoring Programmes and Survilence

Monitoring programmes can be classified into various groups. The priority is given in the order, ambient environmental monitoring; source monitoring; inplant monitoring and personal monitoring. The ambient environment monitoring covers the monitoring of ambient air. The source or stack monitoring is carried out by enforcement agencies to confirm to the standards led down by controlling authorities. Last two groups, *viz.*, inplant and personal monitoring is carried out to accomplish the proper enforcement of control strategies. The fixed station ambient monitoring is done by mobile monitoring van. The stationary or stack monitoring is carried out in many process industries at the place of origin. At source the concentration of pollutant is quite high.

Now we would consider broadly two class of monitoring namely ambient monitoring and stack monitoring. There are several methods which are common between laboratory scale analysis and field monitoring. However, many times one has to sacrifice accuracy if one has to monitor large number of samples field in open air. The methods of sampling of the gaseous pollutant are more or less similar to those discussed earlier.

The ambient air quality monitoring for SO_2, H_2S, NO–NO_x, CO, CO_2 hydrocarbon and trace elements in the atmosphere is considered.

(e) Sampling of Gaseous Pollutant

The technique for sampling of gaseous pollutants involves either grab sampling, condensation, adsorption or absorption. In grab sampling, at random interval gas sample is collected for analysis. While in condensation method *i.e.,* cryosampling gas is cooled, and the species are condensed and concentrated. While in adsorption technique gas is adsorbed on surface of solid adsorbent at reduced temperature.

Silica, alumna, kieselguhr diatomeceous are used as adsorbents. From the polar substances after adsorption it is difficult to remove pollutant from solids even on heating. The most commonly used technique is absorption in suitable solvent *e.g.*, oxygen is absorbed in alkaline pyrogallol, CO is absorbed in ammonical cuprous chloride, SO_2 is absorbed in hydrogen peroxide and ozone in potassium iodide to liberate free iodine; CO_2 is absorbed in alcoholic potash in cascade impinger sampler (Fig. 8.10). The sample must be dry. The ion exchange resins are also used. Tenax–XAD and activated carbon are used for absorption of gases. The static sampling is done in the absence of pump *e.g.*, lead dioxide for collecting SO_2 from air. The method is simple, rapid, easy, reliable and inexpensive. It works on diffusion or permeation principle. The important step after sampling of aerosol (including particulate matter) or gaseous pollutant is to monitor. The analyses of suspended particulate matter SPM. SO_2, NO-NO_x, CO, CO_2, NH_3, H_2S, O_3, hydrocarbons and lead from the polluted atmosphere is then carried out.

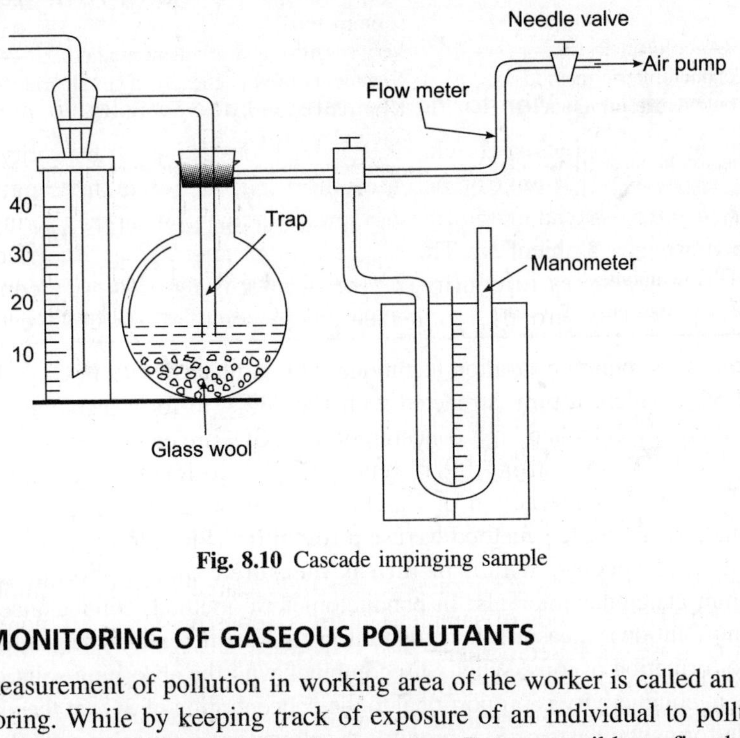

Fig. 8.10 Cascade impinging sample

8.4 MONITORING OF GASEOUS POLLUTANTS

The measurement of pollution in working area of the worker is called an inplant monitoring. While by keeping track of exposure of an individual to pollution it leads to what is called as *personal monitoring*. It was possible to fix, threshold limiting value of toxic pollutant from the knowledge of personal monitoring. Whatever strategy is used for air pollution analysis it is extended for air pollution monitoring. Broadly the air pollutants can be classified due to presence of particulate matter, sulphur compounds, hydrocarbons (HC); nitrogen compounds, halogens, carbon compounds, inorganic compounds and organic compounds in the atmosphere. The monitoring of air quality parameters is done according to importance of pollutants like suspended particulate matter, SO_2, hydrocarbons, carbon dioxide, carbon monoxide, oxides of nitrogen and ozone.

(a) Monitoring of Sulphur Dioxide

The various methods used for the monitoring of SO_2 are summarised in Table 8.9. The important methods are based upon measurement of either colour or electrical conductance, or use of electrochemical transducer. The technique of the chemiluminescence, NDIR spectroscopy, or gas chromatography is also used.

Table 8.9 Monitoring methods for SO_2

Method	*Remarks*
• $Ba(ClO_4)_2$ titration	Valid till 500 ppm but many metals interfere
• Flow colorimetry	Barium chloroanilate used as the chromogenic ligand but NO–NO_x interference in spectrophotometry
• PRA–colorimetry	Very sensitive and excellent method.
• Conductometric method	Commonly used is cheap and simple to operate.
• Coulometric titrations	KBr reduction by SO_2 with the use of three electrodes assembly.
• Electrochemical transducer	Semipermeable membrane is used in ion selective electrode
• Pulses fluorescence spectroscopy	Very sensitive at ppm level in UV region.
• NDIR technique	*In situ* monitoring very accurate and reliable
• GLC (flame photodetector)	Specific for SO_2 is fast and selective method.

In barium perchlorate titration technique, SO_2 is reacted with H_2O_2 or H_2O to form H_2SO_4, which in turn is reacted with $Ba(ClO_4)_2$ to form insoluble $BaSO_4$. This method is valid when high concentrations of SO_2 are encountered, but many metals like lead show strong interference. Flow colorimetry is the best technique. This involves interaction of Ba-chloroanilate with SO_2 to give coloured compound, while in PRA method we use p-rosaniline (PRA) to react with SO_2 to give coloured species, which in turn is measured spectrophotometrically at 540 mm at regular intervals. In conductometeric method, conductance of an absorbing solution is measured at regular intervals. The increase in the conductance is due to formation of ions. When SO_2 combines with the absorbing solution, the increase in conductivity is proportional to the concentration of SO_2 in the air. This principle forms the basis of SO_2 monitor developed indigenously in IITB (Table 8.10). The liquid used for selective absorption is monoethanol and triethanolamine, H_2O_2 and formaldehyde is used to eliminate interference of other gaseous pollutants like CO, H_2S, NO–NO_x and NH_3. The SO_2 monitor permits analysis in the range of 0.1 to 80 ppm (Fig. 8.11). The levels of SO_2 in atmosphere is 4 to 40 ppm. Other working details are also provided in Table 8.10. In coulometric technique, in alkali halide solution like KBr, a constant halogen-to-halide ratio is maintained by electric current. It measures the current required to regenerate the halogen depleted by SO_2. Such current is proportional to the quantity of SO_2 which is converted from halogen to halide. The only limitation of this technique is the periodic replacement of the reagent and the need of constant cleaning of electrodes.

Fig. 8.11 SO_2 analyser

A cell containing acidic potassium bromide with four electrodes is taken, SO_2 is passed when free Br_2 is liberated, which causes imbalance in circuit. The signal is amplified and current is passed to generate enough free bromide coulometrically to restore null balance in the circuit. The generating current which is indirectly proportional to SO_2 present is continuously measured. In electrochemical transducer, a sealed coulometric devise is used. SO_2 selectively diffuses through a semipermeable membrane and as a dissolved gas passes through thin-film electrode. Current generated by oxidation of SO_2 is a measure of its concentration. The selectivity is determined by the choice of the membrane electrolyte and electrode materials of construction. The most efficient and common technique is pulsed fluorescence spectroscopy. A pulsed ultraviolet source excites the SO_2 molecules, which emit a characteristic fluoroscence with intensity proportional to the quantity of SO_2 gas present. This is also called as *chemiluminescence* technique. It work as follows:

$$SO_2 + h\nu \rightarrow \overset{*}{SO_2};\ \overset{*}{SO_2} \rightarrow SO_2 + \text{Fluorescence}$$

Such fluorescence is detected by a photomultiplier tube and after suitable signal processing feeded to the meter and recorder. The only limitation of this method is humidity, which quenchs fluorescence intensity. In nondispersive IR method, a broad spectral absorption is measured and sensitized for a particular gas by a detector. Limitations are H_2O, CO, aromatic compounds show strong interferences, in the same region of SO_2 absorption. Measurement with filters can be used to eliminate interference. In gas chromatography, flame ionisation detector technique is useful for specific measurement of SO_2, but not for H_2S. There is a urgent need to develop these instruments in India or further to develop more selective method for analysis. The prominent methods of monitoring of SO_2 are summarised in Table 8.9.

The principal methods include acid-basic or redox titration, gravimetry and photometry. In titration technique, SO_2 is bubbled through hydrogen peroxide and change in acidity is measured by titration with alkali hydroxide. At this stage one can also measure its conductivity to know how much SO_2 is dissolved in solution. In redox titration, gas is bubbled through solution of potassium iodide and liberated iodine is titrated with sodium thiosulphate. In lead candle method SO_2 is passed on lead dioxide to form lead sulphate consequently a change in weight gives idea about SO_2 absorbed on lead dioxide. This method is used to know sulphation rate. However, most reliable method is PRA or p-roseaniline where in the solution of sodium tetrachlormercurate, SO_2 is absorbed to form stable complex, then p-roseaniline is added with formaldehyde. The resulting red coloured complex is measured at 548 nm on spectrophotometer. The working range is 1 to 10 μg/ml, At pH > 1.6 colour is measured at 548 nm and pH < 1.2 is measured at 575 nm.

(b) Monitoring of Sulphurated Hydrogen

The most simple and reliable method for monitoring of H_2S gas is flow colorimetry. Instead of using any kind of chromogenic ligands, it was worth exploring elementary chemistry of second group of qualitative analysis. Amongst metals tested, *viz.* Cu, Cd, As, Sb, Bi, Sn it was found that arsenic gives reproducible results by formation of green-yellow coloured sulphide which conforms to Beer's law. The details of such H_2S analyser, which was indigeneously developed in I.I.T. Mumbai by us is furnished in Table 8.10 and Fig. 8.12. The tape coated with arsenic chloride is slowly moved, K_2CO_3 is impregnated on glassfibre filter to

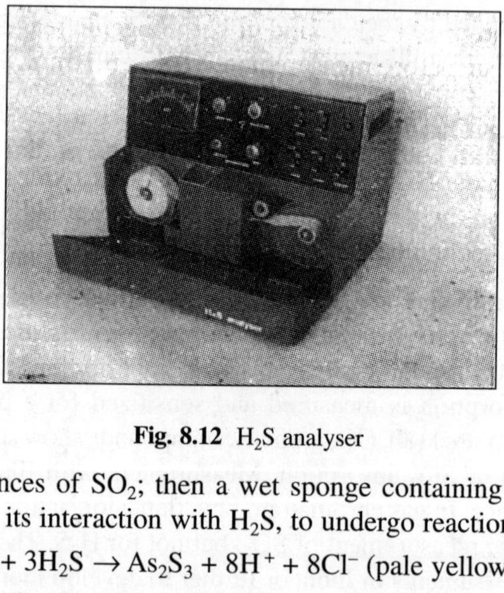

Fig. 8.12 H_2S analyser

eliminate interferences of SO_2; then a wet sponge containing dilute HCl reacts with tape is before its interaction with H_2S, to undergo reaction as follows:

$$2AsCl_3 + HCl + 3H_2S \rightarrow As_2S_3 + 8H^+ + 8Cl^- \text{ (pale yellow colouration).}$$

The lowest detection limit is 5 ppm, with working range is 1 to 800 ppm. The instrument is provided with multiple switch for measurement even in high concentration. The model works both on AC (230 V) and DC (6 V). The instrument can be attached to 10 mV recorder (x–y type). It is worthwhile to consider components as shown in Table 8.11. Excepting pump which is working on a musical car horn all other components are indigenously available. An imported model of this instrument is expensive. This model would cost, much less. The instrument is thus simple.

Table 8.10 H_2S analyser

• Working principle	Flow colorimetry
• Laboratory methods	Acid-base and redox titration methods
• Monitoring methods	Molecular luminescence, colorimetry
• Transducer	Photo tube sensor, involves transmittance measurement
• Threshold limiting value	5 ppm (TLV)
• Limit of analysis	1–800 ppm
• Power supply	230 V AC mains or 6 V DC (car battery)
• Recorder	10 mV recorder possible
• Digital display	Can be adopted with $3\frac{1}{2}$ digit meter

Since H_2S is foul smelling gas therefore even small trace concentration of gas is not tolerated by human being. There are many colorimetric methods of analysis. Most popular method is ethylene blue method. In this method cadmium sulphate, ferric chloride and sodium hydroxide are allowed to react with H_2S in the presence of N N'diethyl p-phenyl diamine to produce blue colour complex which can be measured at 670 nm. The colour is stabilised if extracted with chloroform. The most reliable method for the quantitative analysis of H_2S is spectrophotometry, no matter what kind of chromogenic reagent is used for the development of colour before measurement. The vital components of model are shown in Table 8.11.

Table 8.11 Vital components of H_2S analyser

Pump working on DC/AC
Photo tube
Analogue meter
IC-chips
Gears
Taperecorder motor
Ball bearing and resistances
Dry cells (1.5 × 6) volts
Spools, knob, cover
Miscellaneous components

(c) Monitoring Oxides of Nitrogen

In atmosphere, we have NO and NO_2 while all other oxides of nitrogen are converted to NO_2 by interaction with oxygen. The best method for analysis is chemiluminescence technique. The reaction is as follows:

(*i*) $NO_2 + O_3 \rightarrow 2NO + 2O_2$

(*ii*) $NO + O_3 \rightarrow \overset{*}{N}O_2 + O_2$

(*iii*) $NO_2 + h\nu = \overset{*}{N}O_2$ and

(*iv*) $\overset{*}{N}O_2 \rightarrow NO_2 + h\nu$

The activity is directly proportional to the amount of NO_2 present in the sample. The colorimetric method based on the formation of coloured dye in the presence of sodium nitrite is most reliable. The NO and NO_2 from atmosphere is bubbled through sodium hydroxide to form sodium nitrite. The compound formed namely sodium nitrite is useful for diazotisation reaction. This method was first discovered by Saltzman hence it is called as "Saltzman reaction". A gas is bubbled through solution of sodium hydroxide, followed by interaction with triethanolamine, sulphanilic acid, glacial acetic acid and N-naphthylethylenediamine hydrochloride (NEDA) to develop dizotised orange coloured complex with an absorption maxima at 550 nm. The molar absorptivity is 4×10^4. The other colorimetric methods which involve xylenol orange, phenoldisulphonic acid, sodium arsenite or triethanolamine all compounds acting as chromogenic ligands are also good.

Various methods used for monitoring of oxides of nitrogen, are listed in Table 8.12. Of these the best method is colorimetry which is widely used as the Saltzman reaction.

Table 8.12 Monitoring method of $NO–NO_x$

Methods of monitoring	*Remarks*
• Colorimetric technique	Saltzman method, needs somewhat longer time for colour development.
• Chemiluminescence technique	O_3 used to convert NO_2 to NO
• Ion selective electrodes	Nitrate in aqueous phase is measured
• Electrochemical transducer	Slow response time
• Non-dispersive infrared/	Interference from SO_2, H_2S not good.
• UV spectroscopy	fluorescence shows good specificity and selectivity

In chemiluminscence method NO with ozone gives positive interference. Such ion may overlap the spectral interference in region of emission; fortunately no such molecule exists in the atmosphere. The ions which show quenching of chemiluminescence gives negative error. For instance O_2 and N_2 show quenching, but their concentration in the atmosphere is fixed and is constant. A thermal conversion of $NO_2 \rightarrow NO$ is utilised. Gold, stainless steel, carbon impregnated metals are used for such conversion. In ion selective electrode method nitrite formed is oxidised to nitrate and is measured with ion selective electrode. Electrochemical transducers are slow to work, as their response time is very poor. In NDIR method, SO_2 and H_2S seriously interfere, one has to use resonance fluorescence method in such a situation. For *in situ* monitoring, gas cell correlation technique is favourable.

In an interferometer Raman scattering for detection of NO *in situ* analysis is best. Finally, in Jacob's Hocheiser method, NO–NO_x are collected over sodium hydroxide to form sodium nitrite so formed is used for colorimetric analysis. NO measurement can show large variation if dye is not properly formed. NO, SO_2, invariably exhibit interference. The basis of NO–NO_x meter developed in IIT Mumbai by us was same as described above. The details of such instrument are given in Table 8.13. It detects 0.02 to 600 ppm of NO_2. The weight of instrument being 8 kg. All items except pump are locally available. The cost of manufacturing is reasonable in preference to imported instrument from abroad. The vital components are shown in Table 8.14.

Table 8.13 NO–NO_x meter

• Principles	Flow colorimetry
• Transducer	Photo tube sensor for transmittance
• Range of analysis	0.02–600 ppm
• Power supply	230 V AC or 6V DC accumulator
• Recorder	10 mV recorder possible
• Digital display	is adopted with 3.5 digit meter
• Reading solution	NEDA (1–naphthyl)–ethylenediamine–hydrochloride and anthranilic acid in sodium hydroxide.
• Interferences	None ions interfere
• Weight of meter	8 kg (approx.)
• Recorder print out	10 mV is coupled
• Special feature	High accuracy, less time for analysis, no maintenance, trouble free working, low cost
• Toxic effects of NO–NO_x	Irritation of nose and throat, eyes and skin, dermatitis, lower respiratory track affected, vertigo, vomiting.
• Source of pollution	Atmosphere burning of nitrogenous matter and disel fuel, lightening conductor conversion, autoexhaust emission

Table 8.14 Important components of NO–NO_x meter

Phototube
Analogue meter
IC-chips
Gears
Taperecorder motor
Dry cells (1.5 × 6) V
Spools, knobs, cover
Miscellaneous component
Tungsten lamp
Digital display

8.5 MONITORING OXIDES OF CARBON

The best method for monitoring of CO is NDIR *i.e.,* non-dispersive infrared spectroscopy provided water vapour is absent in the sample. The second best method is indirect interaction of CO on either mercuric or palladium chloride to produce phosgene with shining metallic mercury or palladium, which in turn is measured by reflectance spectroscopy. Silica gel is impregnated on ammonium molybdate in sulphuric acid to react with CO to give blue coloured solution with absorption maxima at 660 nm however H_2S, moisture, and organic matter interference. The analysis of CO_2 is very simple. Carbon dioxide is absorbed in stream of excess of alkali hydroxide and the unreacted solution of alkali hydroxide is titrated with standard solution of strong acid. From the amount of alkali consumed one gets idea about amount of CO_2 in the sampled air.

Table 8.15 Monitoring methods for CO, CO_2

Method	*Remarks*
• Non-dispersive IR	Water vapour interferes, but it is the most reliable method used as reference method useful in analysis of CO from autoexhaust emissions
• NDIR spectrometry	Specific, sensitive, reliable technique
• IR fluorescence spectroscopy	Sensitive, no interference by water vapour
• AAS (Reduction of HgO–Hg)	Need charcoal filter, but H_2O and hydrocarbons interfere
• Electrocatalytic method	Needs selective scrubbing of SO_2, NO_2 but H_2 interfere
• Electrochemical transducer	Ethylene and acetylene interfere seriously, it is battery operated, simple, inexpensive instrument
• FID (after CH_4 formation)	Very sensitive method as compared to NDIR
• Hopacilite based CO monitor	Temperature rise for converting to CO_2 is measured, most reliable technique

The various methods for monitoring CO are given in Table 8.15. All are useful for the analysis of CO. One rarely need instrumental method for monitoring of CO_2, as the conventional classical titration technique is superior to any instrumental method. In NDIR technique, the extent of absorption of CO in infrared energy by a column of sample of gas it a specified which has narrow wave number region (v–1800 cm^{-1}) for measurement.

A pneumatic detector is used in conjunction with interference filters of about 9.1 mm length. Sample needs no preconditioning but dust and moisture must be absent. Gas flow rate need not be controlled. The NDIR technique is specific selective and is satisfactory. The IR fluorescence method is very sensitive, but excess water vapour creates problems. AAS method measures Hg after reduction of HgO to Hg by cold vapour AAS. Hydrocarbons and H_2O vapour however show strong interference. In the electrocatalytic method, one has to use scrubber, while in electrochemical transducer ethylene and acetylene show strong interference. The instrument works on battery, the model is portable and also inexpensive; but shows excessive drift posing a serious problem. Gaschromatography with FID gives best results where CO is hydrogenated to CH_4, nonmethane hydrocarbon is measured by this method.

A novel method for CO monitor is Hopcalite method which is commonly used. The rise in temperature is measured. Such rise is due to heat generated in the exothermic conversion of CO to CO_2 in the presence of Hopcalite catalyst. Oxides of Mn or Cu serve the purpose of such a catalyst. Humidity affects the measurement. It is necessary to maintain catalyst at a temperature of 100°C, while making measurement in Hopcalite technique.

(a) Monitoring of Hydrocarbons

Different methods for monitoring of hydrocarbons, ozone and oxidants are summarised in Table 8.16. Gaseous hydrocarbon may be reactive, *i.e.* ethylene and also non-reactive gas like methane. Gas chromatography is the technique for analysis with flame ionisation or thermal conductivity detectors. Hydrocarbon level is expressed as methane equivalence hydrocarbon. Preconcentration of hydrocarbon gives reliable results. Silica gel column is useful for lighter organics. The reactive hydrocarbon is measured with chemiluminescence technique. Less than 0.1 ppm of ethylene is detected by the chemiluminescence detector at ppb level on silica gel column. The polyaromatic hydrocarbons (PAH) are collected with glass fibre filters. Various instruments including mass spectrometer are used for such analysis. PAH is best extracted in benzene and then analysed by GLC. TLC detects them, but HPLC offers best results. NDIR method is good for hydrocarbons emitted from heavy duty vehicles. The iodometric method involving wet chemical technique is useful for the analysis of oxidant, but SO_2 and NO_2 show interference.

Table 8.16 Monitoring of hydrocarbons and ozone

Method	Remarks
• Gas chromatography	is good for mobile source, light organics with GLC
• FID detectors in gas chromatography (HC)	Coupled in gas chromatography is useful for reactive hydrocarbons
• Chemiluminescence for hydrocarbons	$CH_2 = CH_2$, measured
• Nondispersive IR spectroscopy	Ideal for heavy duty vehicles
• Iodometric method	Wet chemical technique
• UV absorption technique	Change in intensity of beam of light on passage through O_3 is measured.
• Chemiluminescence for CO_2	$CH_2 = CH_2 + O_3$ gives light which is measured
• Thermistor catalyst	When O_3 is passed, heat generated is measured by imbalance in electrical circuit.

Although many methods are described for analysis of hydrocarbons, the best method is gas chromatography, with flame ionisation or thermal conductivity detectors however, preconcentration of sample is necessary. Either methane or acetylene predominates in the sample. As described earlier the polyaromatic hydrocarbons (PAH) are extracted in benzene and then analysed by GLC, HP TLC, or HPLC. The hydrocarbons emitted by heavy duty vehicles are analysed by NDIR technique. The other alternative method for analysis of the hydrocarbons is to use chemiluminscence technique. Formaldehyde generated in photochemical smog is colorimetrically measured with chromotropic acid. Methane if present in large concentration in atmosphere, should be ignored.

8.6 MONITORING OF SUSPENDED PARTICULATE MATTER (SPM)

Various methods for monitoring of SPM are summarised in Table 8.17.

Table 8.17 Monitoring methods for suspended particulate matter

Method	*Remarks*
• Gravimetry	High volume sampler (12–24 hours) filter paper weighed
• β-gauge analyser by dilution	β-rays used to note loss in weight of tape
• Piezoelectric balance	Sensitive method, change in weight is noted
• Thimble sampling	Change in weight of cellulose, borosilic or glass ceramics filter is measured
• Nephelometer	0.1–10 μm diameter is measured by scattering of radiation.
• Lidar method	Measures reflection of light with laser beam
• Acoustical particle	*In situ* analysis (5 μm) by measuring changes in velocity of sound.
• Transmissometer	Measures optical density; low cost, cannot detect mass
• Electrostatic precipitator	Measures particle flow

Table 8.18 Visibility changes and aerosols particulates (%)

S. No.	*Kind of particulate*	*Western location of planet (%)*	*Eastern location of planet (%)*
1.	Soil and dust (SPM)	10–20	10–15
2.	Carbon black	15–25	10–15
3.	Organic particles	15–35	10–15
4.	Nitrates	5–45	10–15
5.	Sulphate	25–65	60–70

The change in visibility due to SPM is shown in Table 8.18.

We often read in newspaper that various flights in airport are delayed (*e.g.* in Palam airport in Delhi) on account of fog which completely reduces the visibility. This is due to water vapour settling on land at low temperature. However, most important cause of differed visibility in towns is on account of aerosols which largely consists of respiratory suspended particular matter (RSM) from air. The extent of dispersion is confined to Eastern or Western side of the earth. Apart from

SPM carbon black (15–25% western) organic particulates (15–35%) the alkali and alkaline salts in form of their nitrates (5–45%) or Sulphate (60–70% in eastern front) causes poor visibility. If in addition to fog and dust sunlight enters in them they cause the photochemical fog. Therefore, environmental scientist have to take strong measures to restore the clear visibility and agglomeration of aerosols.

Table 8.19 Particle size measurement

S. No.	*Method of estimation*	*Actual particle size* (μm)	*S. No.*	*Method of estimation*	*Particle size* (μm)
1.	Cascade impactor	0.2–8	5.	Elutriation	5–100
2.	Centrifuge/sedimentation	0.05–3	6.	Electrical counter	0.6–200
3.	Sieving	44	7.	Sedimentation (simple)	2–50
4.	Microscope	0.3–100			

The size of the dust is also of great importance. Table 8.19 reveals methods for the analysis of particle size from 0.05–200 μm. The smaller is particle size more is the danger of affecting ones lungs with rise in value of respirable, suspended particular matter. Many times microscope is used to ascertain its size. The centrifuge (0.03–3 μm) is used in the process of sedimentation to ascertain particle size of the component. The most popular device is cascade impactor. Electric counter, microscope, sedimentation chamber are various devices to ascertain the particle size. The centrifuge or cascade impactor facilitates measurement from 0.05–8 μm. The electric counter has higher limit of analysis as 200 μm. The process of elutriation facilitates measurement in the range of 5–100 μm. In order to get clear insight of particular matter and dust we shall examine fiber filters.

Table 8.20 Various types of fibre filters for dust collection

S.No.	*Type of fabric*	*Temp of °C operation*	*Acid resistant*	*Base resistant*	*Remarks*
1.	PTFE	260	inert	Inert	Chemical segregation ideal
2.	Acrylic	127	Mineral acid	Good	Used in steel furnace
3.	Glass fibre	260	Fair	Fair	Nonferrous materials
4.	Cotton	82	Poor	V. good	For abrasion dust
5.	Woollen	93	Good	Best	At low temperature is efficient
6.	Nylon	93	Fair	V. good	For abrasive dust
7.	Polypropylene	93	Best	Best	Good at low temperature
8.	Polyester	149	Fair	Good	Chemical, steel furnace

The Table 8.20 shows variety of fiber filters starting from those made of cotton to one like nylon, wool, plastics and glass fibre filters. Many filters operate at elevated temperature (125–250°C) such as PTFE, acrylic or glass fiber filter. It is useful in chemical industry and in steel plants. Woollen, cotton, nylon work at temperature of 90–100°C. Cotton filter is cheap and most suitable for abrasive dust from metal fabricators along with nylon filter. At low temperature polypropylene filters are most suitable so also woollen filters. For handling nonferrous material one must use glass-fibre filter. For simple segregation all these fabric filters are satisfactory however if we have to collect large volume of dust in continuous process then one has to use electrostatic precipitator (Table 8.21). The details of electrostatic precipitator (ESP) is now discussed.

Most of the industrial processes involving steel, paper rocks, minerals and metals one has to use electrostatic precipitator. It works both at room temperature as well as at elevated temperature. Open hearth furnace (Table 8.21) and analogous metallurgical operations involving calcination or roasting. For paper factory and power plants involving boilers ESP and cyclone is best suited. (Table 8.21).

Table 8.21 Electrostatic precipitator (ESP)

S. No.	*Kind of industry*	*Process used for the concentration of pollutant*
1.	Steel industry	Open Hearth; cupola; one roaster; oxygen furnace
2.	Paper factory	Boiler for recovery of kraft, soda and lime
3.	Power plant	Coal, oil, wood needs cyclone
4.	Rock material	Powder of alumina, bauxite, lime and cement concentrated
5.	Mining and metals	Used for roasting and smelting and ore beneficiation
6.	Unmarked place	Municipal incinerator, refinary, metal recovery plants

The mechanism in separation by cyclone is worth examining. When particle moves in circle it is under influence of centrifugal and ceninpital force directing toward centre of centrifuge. The fuel force drives within the centre while centripetal force throws in tangent direction the material outside in the direction by the tangential force. Those weighing light materials are thus removed from heavy particles by cyclone. The higher is the rotational field better is the efficiency for the segregation. This practice is common in power plants.

(a) Monitoring of Suspended Particulate Matter Efficient Methods

Most reliable method is high volume sampler. SPM is collected on filter paper, millipore glass fibre or nucleopore filter using air, such as pumps and residue is weighed. Pump works between 12 and 24 hours. Moisture is removed. The calibrated flow meter measures total volume of air which is sampled; β-absorption analysis is a good method. The air is sampled through filter tape, which passes through radioactive source detector like GM counter. The decrease in count rate is recorded and it is related to level of SPM. In piezoelectric balance, two quartz crystals oscillating at same frequency are used. One crystal is encapsulated, while the other crystal is open, coated with selective chemical, which absorbs SPM. The rise in weight is measured at known temperature. In Thimble sampler, change in weight on deposition of SPM on cellulose filter (150°C), boroglass filter (300°C) or ceramics filter (>300°C) is accurately measured. For very small particles nephelometric technique, is best suited where beam of light is focussed on spot and air is sampled through. Light is scattered, which is measured by photocell. The scattering of light at right angles is utilised for measuring particle density. In

Lidar method, laser beam is used as light source and is used for measurements. The important methods include accoustical particle counter, which involves *in situ* measurement of individual particles above size of 5 μm. It needs sample conditioning. In transmissiometer, optical density of suspended particles is measured, which has a low cost of operation. Only limitation of this technique is, it cannot detect mass of the particles. In electrostatic precipitator, it measures particle flow rate, the system has low potential as mass monitor. To evaluate particle size, electron microscopy, light scattering, impaction, minicyclones, laser doppler velocity meter and changed particle drift spectrometry are used. The efficency of dust collector is given in Table 8.22. It varies with size of the particle but ESP is best technique.

Table 8.22 Efficiency of dust collector according to particle size (%)

Kind of collector	*Size 10 μm*	*Size 5 μm*	*Size 2 μm*	*Size 1 μm*
• Inertial collector	30	16	7.0	3
• Medium cyclone	45	27	14	8
• High capacity cyclone	87	73	46	27
• Spray duster	98	93	75	40
• Spray tower	97	94	87	55
• Wet impinger scrubber	99	82	92	80
• Disintegrator	89	98	95	90
• Venutari scrubber	89.9	99.6	99	97
• Electrostatic precipitator	89.5	99.5	99.5	99.5

Table 8.23 Additional methods for analysis of particulate matter

Name	*Mode of operation*	*Technique*
• High volume	Filtration	Gravimetry
• Paper tapes	Filtration	Transmission density meter
• Durham	Impaction	Counting
Anderson cascade		Microscopic examination
• Midget impinger	Impingement	Gravimetry
• Cyclone	Centrifugal separation	Gravimetry
• Electrostatic and thermal precipitator	Precipitation	Nonquantitative Gravimetry

Table 8.23 summarises some additional methods for the analysis of particulate matter. They are based on the same principle as narrated in the earlier section. The qualitative analysis of sample is followed by separation and quantitative determination. In analysis of the suspended particulate matter, one considers its mass, size and chemical nature. In America, PM_{10} standard is used *i.e.,* mass is measured as μg/m^3. This mass is determined by weighing. The multi stage impactor is used to measure size (μ/m^3) in range from 00.1 to 1.0 μm. First small and latter large size particulates are segregated by passage of electrical field. The light scattering technique in form of nephelometry is best for quantative analysis of fine

particles. The X-ray fluorescence and neutron activation analysis is used to know the chemical composition. The trace metal are present are analysed by atomic absorption spectroscopy. Many of trace metals are invariably detected and also determined in SPM or dust from air. The process of the sedimentation is used to sample the dust or suspended matter before the analysis. The Table 8.24 furnishes an information on kind of fans and hoods used, Ringoven methods for the trace analysis is useful.

Table 8.24 Hood and fans for control of dust

S.No.	*Type of devised*	*Hoods*	*Fans (% efficiency)*	*Remarks on use efficiency*
1.	Cyclone	Slot	Forward curbed blade (75)	Works at temperature
2.	Fibre filter	Flanged slot	Radial blade (70)	Need good planning
3.	Fibrous filters	Plain opening	Radial tripped (78)	Not good at 400° C
4.	(Wet) Electrostatic precipitator	Flanged open	Backward blade (85)	Expensive
5.	Wet washers (low energy)	Booth	Axial (85)	dry product, not useful
6.	Aggregate filters	Canopy	–	Needs good planning

This Table summarizes various kinds of hoods and fans used in the collection of dust. The optimum selection of hood or fans is critical specially when used in conjunction with cyclone or fibre filters. ESP needs flanged hood with backward blades giving 85% efficiency. A canopy is used for aggregate filters. The process involving wet washing is feasible in ESP or canopy device. All fans have radial blades with axial symmetry.

8.7 MONITORING OF AMMONIA

There are several methods for analysis of ammonia where it reacts with mercury chloride and potassium iodide to form brown coloured complex Nessler's reagent which can be measured spectrophotometrically at 450 nm. In the presence of sodium hydroxide when ammonia is bubbled in mercury anode, the reaction of $2\,HgI_4^{2-} + NH_3 + 3OH^- \rightarrow N_2Hg_2IO$ (brown) $+ 7I + 2H_2O$ but aliphatic amines and H_2S interfer in such methods. Other colorimetric methods involve use of indophenol or bromine as the chromogenic ligands but Nessler's reagent is best.

8.8 MONITORING OF OZONE

The best method is chemiluminscene method, by interacting ethylene with O_3, Ethylene ($CH_2 = CH_2$) must be added in requisite concentration to produce ozonide. This ozonide is excited to produce luminescence. Other methods for analysis of O_3 involves volumetric method. O_3 is bubbled through solution of potassium iodide and free liberated iodine is titrated against standard solution of sodium thiosulphate. This titration is carried out both in acidic or alkaline media. Other colour forming reactions are with phenolphthalein. For monitoring of ozone biphenylamine-sulphonate, N-tetraethyldominophenylmethane in the presence of phosphate buffer is used. The potassium iodide solution gives coloured complex with absorption maxima at 350 nm, however SO_2, NO_2, H_2S show strong interference. Most popular method is fluorimetry or the chemiluminescence method which is used with O_3 and rhodamine B probe on silica gel and NO in gas phase. Photochemical reactions measures level of ozone. Photolysis of NO_2 followed by chemiluminescence detection of NO helps to analyse ozone. Ozone is formed by photochemical decomposition of NO_2 by sunlight in the lower atmosphere. Ozone is monitored with wet chemical methods, where in total oxidant is bubbled through neutral buffered KI reagent and liberated iodine is titratred against standard sodium thiosulphate with starch as indicator. In chemiluminescence technique, ozone is reacted with ethylene and absorbance produced is measured. In UV absorption technique, proportional intensity changes of UV beam as it travels through ozone is measured. Finally ozone is passed on two thermistors, one coated with a catalyst. The heat of decomposition of ozone is then measured on thermistor bridge circuit.

8.9 MONITORING OF METAL POLLUTANTS AT TRACE LEVEL

The methods for monitoring metal pollutants or trace elements from the atmosphere involves use of instruments like atomic absorption spectroscopy or ion selective electrodes, fluorescences, plasma spectroscope, neutron activation analysis, thermogravemetry techniques, *e.g.*, Hg is analysed by flameless cold vapour AAS from air, while Cd, Se, Pb are measured by electric discharge; for XRF the great advantage it is the non-destructive method of analysis. Cd, Be and other trace metals are measured by ICP-AES. Spark source mass spectrometer (SSMS) is used to measure elemental composition. The hyphenated TGA coupled with mass spectrometry (TGA-MS) gives analysis of complex molecules. Important elements encountered in the atmosphere are Hg, Be, Pb, Fe, Cd, Se, As, Ni, V, Cr, Mn, Cu, Sb, Zn, Ba, Sn. The typical methods used for their monitoring are Hg (AAS, UV, XRF), Fe (XRF), Be (AAS and spectrophotometry), Pb (NAA, XRF, AES; spectrophotometry) Cd (AAS, AES, spectrophotometry), Se (Spectrophotometry); Ni (AAS; spectrophotometry); Cu (AAS, AES); Sb (spectrophotometry), Zn (AAS,

Table 8.25 Toxic metal analysis by ring-oven technique

Metal ion	*Amount taken µg/litre*	*Amount found by spectrophotometry µg/litre*	*Chromogenic ligand in spectrophotometric analysis* (λ_{max})
• Pb	340.0	360.0	Dithiozone (520 nm) method
	220.0	230.0	with extraction in chloroform
• V	78.0	73.0	N-benzoyl-N-phenyl-
	62.0	68.0	hydroxylamine (525 nm)
• Se	26.0	27.0	3,3′-diaminobenidine
	24.0	28.0	(420 nm) photometry
• Cd	13.5	14.0	2,2′-bipyridyl (526 nm) as
	16.0	19.0	chromogenic ligand in photometry

XRF and AES); Ba (AES) so also Sn (AES). As advancement in research takes place, newer and better method come into the forefront. Tables 8.25 and 8.26 indicate experimental results of the analysis of metal pollutants by ring oven method. from air, *e.g.*, Table 8.25 indicates how a simple ring–oven technique is used for analysis of Pb, Se, V and Cd from air. While Table 8.26 indicates analysis of trace elements from aerosols. It is necessary to take a number of samples and an average value of the result are considered for drawing any conclusion in ring-oven technique. Table 8.26 indicates analysis of particulates in atmosphere. The sampling time varies from 4 to 18 hours. Some more details on analysis of lead from auto-exhaust emission is also given.

Table 8.26 Trace elements in the aerosols

Metal ion	*Vol. of absorption liquid taken ml*	*Amount found, μg/10 ml (Triplicate determination)* (I)	(II)	(III)	*Average μg/10 ml*	*Average μg/litre*
• Pb	2.0	0.20	0.25	0.20	0.21	21.0
	5.0	0.45	0.45	0.50	0.475	47.5
• V	5.0	0.25	0.25	0.25	0.263	26.3
	10.0	0.50	0.45	0.50	0.483	48.3
• Hg	3.0	0.30	0.40	0.25	0.31	31.0
	5.0	0.45	0.55	0.30	0.288	28.8
• Se	2.0	0.10	0.15	0.10	0.113	11.3
	6.0	0.30	0.25	0.30	0.288	28.8
• Cd	5.0	0.45	0.55	0.50	0.50	50.0
	10.0	1.10	0.90	0.90	0.967	96.7

Table 8.27 Analysis of particulates, in the atmosphere

Sampling duration (hr)	*Wt. of paper sample (g)*	*Wt. of filter paper (g)*	*Wt. of particulate (g)*	*Mean flow rate 1 pm*	*μg of Pb/m³ of air*	*μg of V/m³ of air*
• 4	0.787	0.049	0.038	142.5	1378.05	193.00
• 6	0.789	0.750	0.039	135.0	763.96	152.07
• 16	0.771	0.719	0.052	135.0	343.78	11.59
• 18	0.803	0.724	0.079	135.0	3667.00	73.34

For preventing the deposition of black soot, lead tetraethyl [Pb $(C_2H_5)_4$] is added as the ignition control additive to petrol. This lead is released in atmosphere in form of vapour and it is present as elemental lead. As discussed earlier there are series of methods for the analysis of lead. The rapid and reliable method is atomic absorption spectroscopy (AAS) or inductively coupled plasma atomic emission spectroscopy (ICP-AES). One can also analyse it by spectrophotometry by formation of its extractable complex with dithiozone in chloroform. 4(2-pyridylazo) resorcinol (PAR) or 1-2 (pyridylazo) napthol (PAN) as chromogenic ligand to form soluble complex in carbon tetrachloride in ion chromatography is very popular.

For the rapid analysis of metal pollutants at the microgram concentrations there is no better method than the atomic absorption spectroscopy or spectrophotometric analysis with suitable chromogenic ligand.

8.10 AMBIENT AND STACK EMISSION MONITORING

Earlier we have considered laboratory methods for the analysis of pollutants we had also considered in greater details continuous measurement or monitoring of the pollutants. However, the monitoring at source (stack) is different from the overall monitoring. The ambient air monitoring confines to the monitoring of air pollution at any particular place irrespective of where from it emerges. While source or stack monitoring is quite intense it involves the measurement at the very source. In early days dispersion of pollutant in the atmosphere was done through tall chimneys. These chimneys are main source of pollution. It is called as stack (chimney) monitoring at the source. The methods of ambient monitoring are not same as those for stack however there lies a common thread of similarity between lab analysis of ambient and stack monitoring.

(a) Stack Sampling

The sampling or monitoring of stack at source is of atmost importance. The knowledge of stack gives idea about kind of methods used for pollution control. In ancient times the best remedy for abatement of smoke or gases was to fix it in tall stack (chimney) in the permises of factory (Fig. 8.13). The idea of the dispersion of pollutants in the upper atmosphere *i.e.,* toposphere was to mainly to dilute it with copious supply of fresh air to render it harmless. By the time the plume from stack reaches the land it is completely diluted and is rendered harmless. If the dilution is not satisfactory immediate steps should be taken to increase the height

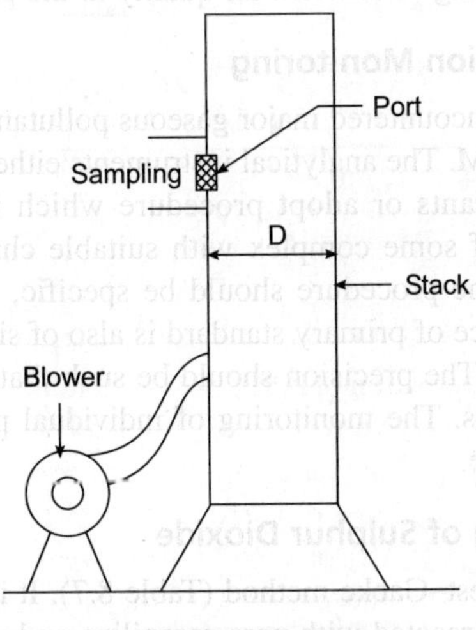

Fig. 8.13 Stack sampler

of stack to release plume in upper atmosphere *i.e.,* in stratosphere. However, this was not sufficient enough, because the release of plume in atmosphere, and its dispersion and subsequent dilution depends upon the metetorological parameters like wind direction, wind velocity, temperature as well as relative humidity present in the atmosphere.

Therefore, in order to control pollution one must have efficient stack sampling process and monitoring methods. The purpose of source or stack sampling is to produce accurate data on sample. The sample must be representative of entire emission emitting from stacks. There should be maximum accuracy of sampling. The collection of sample at base in bottom or at tall end of stack at top should be inexpensive. The information should be useful for devising control measures. The random or grab sampling is most suitable for the ascertaining quickly the quality of emission. A source test is performed. All background material is reviewed. Gas flow measurement is one of the important source test. One uses pitot tube for the purpose. With anemometer gas velocity is measured. The sampling train should not leak. The principle objective of stack sampling is to assess the quantity and quality of pollutant emerging from stack, and evaluate the efficiency of pollution abatement technique resorted to. To undertake monitoring one needs emission standards to minimise the pollution. The process of sampling involves selection of sampling site, gas flow measurement for velocity of gas in stack analysis and recording temperature (Fig. 8.13).

The sample is collected at straight portion of stack, the samples are collected at different points (minimum four points). Simultaneously the gas flow is measured, so also gas velocity with use of manometer and pitot tube is recorded. The sampling is done in isokinetic conditions (*i.e.,* velocity of gas at inlet and outlet is same). Temperature measurement reveals gas properties. The SPM is determined as usual with impinger, vacuum pump, pitot manometers. The sampling of gaseous pollutants involves use of absorber or adsorbent and then measured by methods as described for sampling of ambient air quality in the previous section.

(b) The Stack Emission Monitoring

The most commonly encountered major gaseous pollutants in stack are SO_2, NO-NOx, CO-CO_2 and SPM. The analytical instruments either measures any physical property of the pollutants or adopt procedure which involves wet chemistry involving formation of some complex with suitable chromogenic ligands. The main requirement is the procedure should be specific, reproducible and rapid. The accuracy and choice of primary standard is also of significance, specially for gas phase monitoring. The precision should be such that the measurement agree with mean observations. The monitoring of individual pollutant emerging from stack source is possible.

(c) Stack Monitoring of Sulphur Dioxide

The method used is West–Gaeke method (Table 8.7). It is wet chemical method. The sulphur dioxide is reacted with para rosaniline and methyl sulphuric acid to give red coloured complex, which is determined spectrophotometrically at 575 nm. The other method involves absorption of sulphur dioxide in hydrogen peroxide to form sulphuric acid which is then determined by titration with standard alkali hydroxide. PRA or West–Gaeke method is selective and is specific for sulphur dioxide. Alternatively SO_2 can be measured either by conductimetry or coulometry. However, chemiluminscence technique is most specific, where SO_2 is excited as $SO_2 + h\nu = SO_2^*$, $SO_2^* \rightarrow SO_2$ + fluorescence. The quantum intensity of the fluorescence is proportional to the amount of SO_2 in the sample as system conforms to Beci's law.

(d) Stack Monitoring of Oxide of Nitrogen

Out of the series of oxides of nitrogen, NO_2 is largely encountered in the atmosphere. NO_2 is analyzed by Saltzman method, wherein NO_2 is bubbled in solution of sodium hydroxide to form sodium nitrite. It is then reacted with solution of N-naphthylethylenediamine hydrochloride (NEDA) and MBT to form coloured complex which is measured spectrophotometrically at 550 nm. In the presences of sodium arsenate, SO_2 does not interfere in such analysis but the method of choice is chemiluminscence; where NO_2 is excited to $\overset{*}{NO_2}$ as follows.

$NO_2 + h\nu \rightleftharpoons \overset{*}{NO_2}$, $\overset{*}{NO_2} \rightarrow NO_2$ + fluorescence. If the sample contains NO it is oxidised to NO_2. $NO + O_3 \rightleftharpoons \overset{*}{NO_2} + O_2$. This facilitates direct analysis of NO as pollutant. Most of the gases like SO_2, Cl_2, CH_4, C_2H_2, C_2H_4 do not interfere in the analysis of oxides of nitrogen.

(e) Stack Monitoring of Oxides of Carbon

The analysis of carbon dioxide is directly carried out by titrametric method by bubbling it through the solution of alkali–hydroxide followed by titration with acid. While CO is analyzed by non-dispersive infrared spectroscopy (NDIR). The absorbing species in mixture of stack sample are CO_2 and H_2O, but water vapour interferences in IR measurement, so it is eliminated. A frequency of measurement is at 1800 cm^{-1}. In AAS method CO is passed on mercuric oxide to form the lustrous metallic mercury and CO_2. The mercury is measured by AAS. In Hopcalite method CO is passed on the catalyst of manganese and the rise in temperature is noted and related to concentration of CO in sample. This is the most reliable method of monitoring.

(f) Stack Monitoring of Suspended Particular Matter

It is analyzed by high volume sampler using glass or membrane filter. A large volume of air is filtered through the sample. The toxicity of the maternal is reduced by the process of dilution. For stationary source the control measure should be specific. It depends upon the industry from which such pollutant is emerging. The control of mobile source of pollution has been already considered under auto-exhaust emission. Inspite of very efficient control methods and reproducible monitoring methodology is available, air pollution is not controlled unless the man who has many fold activity in air. He is quite conscience about his responsibility to keep the atmosphere clean. No amount of acts or regulations will solve the problem of the pollution unless and until man has intrinsic will and desire to keep the atmosphere clean and free from pollutants.

8.11 CONTROL OF AUTOEXHAUST EMISSION

Amongst mobile sources, transportion is the major source of air pollution. It is true for automobile emission. In such case crankcase, exhaust emission and evaporative loss by fuel tank and carburretor is easily controlled by using alternative fuel. The exhaust gases are burned and oxidized before emission by use of catalytic converter. The use of unleaded petrol is strongly recommended to prevent mainly hydrocarbon emissions. The control of hydrocarbon reduces level of CO in the exhaust emissions. The gas recirculation and catalytic reduction controls also NO-NO_x emissions. The elimination of these emission prevents formation of photochemical smog and peroxyacelyl nitrite (PAN). In India very little attenuation is paid by state *Pollution Control Boards* to adhere strictly to standards of emission. In America, when people in Los Angles suffered heavily on account of photochemical smog immediately US-EPA formulated clean air act and set clean air standards. Further, subsequently they continued clamping very rigorous standards. The very old cars were not allowed to ply in America whereas in India a model of 10 years old is considered to be reasonably new. In New Delhi and Mumbai car models of more than 15 years old are banned to ply on streets and are slowly phased out from city streets. It is necessary to tighten road emission standards, then sincerely implement PUC *i.e.*, pollution under control and get vehicles checked annually. The use of catalytic converter, or control of air/fuel ratio to ideal number. 1/13 is recommended so as to have clean environment. It is essential to encourage users to shift over to CNG fueled engine instead of petrol or diesel engine for the

Table 8.28 Efficiency of dust collector with particle size variation

S. No.	*Type of dust collector*	*Efficiency in percentage (%)*		
		Size 1 μm	*Size* 5 μm	*Size* 10 μm
1.	Fabric filter (moving type)	99.0	99.5	99.5
2.	Fabric filter (pulse-jet type)	99.6	99.9	99.9
3.	Electrostatic precipitator (ESP)	99.5	99.5	99.5
4.	Venturi scrubber (High energy)	98.5	99.9	99.9
5.	Disintegrator	91	98	99
6.	Wet impinger scrubber	80	97	99
7.	Cyclone (tabular; cellulor with low efficiency)	42	87	97
8.	Spray tower	55	94	87
9.	Cyclone (High efficiency)	27	73	87
10.	Internal collector	3	16	30

automobile as latter are principle polluting agents. Table 8.28 exhibits mode of dust collection. This is because all our public roads are full of dust and SPM and is related auto pollution.

There are variety of dust collectors ranging from simple fibre filters to electrostatic precipitator and cyclones. The best mode is electrostatic precipitator. The overall efficiency for all these devices varies from 3–99.5% for particle size varying from 1 μm to 10 μm. For use of dust collection at high temperature. Venturi scrubber is best. This is interesting process, wherein fountain of very fine droplets are spread in dusty environment to dampen the effect even at elevated temperature. For wet dust impinge is used. The scrubber when large quantity of dust is to be collected then cyclones are used. The spray tower is similar to one used in Venturi scrubber. The best efficiency is shown by fibre filters and electrostatic precipitator.

8.12 CONTROL OF AIR POLLUTION IN STACKS

The control is carried out at the source of the air pollution. Natural uncontrollable sources like volcano cannot be easily controlled. It is best controlled of their own if effective monitoring of pollutants is carried out. The air standards must be rigorously clamped. The control is effectively done by process of changing, of fuel if fissible and locating control equipment at source. Though total removal of pollution is difficult one should prefer least expensive alternatives for such control.

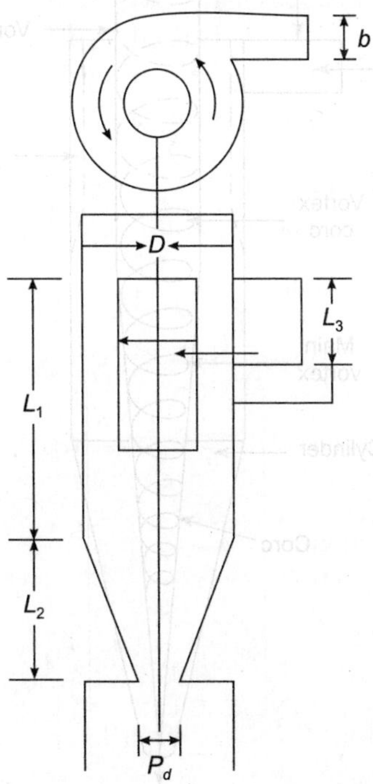

Fig. 8.14 Dust hopper

Old process can be preferably discarded if alternative pollution pre-process is easily available and if it is economical and reliable. The change of fuel considerably reduces emissions. The total removal though difficult of pollutant is the best way of control. The efficient control devices are thus available in the market.

(a) Control of Particulate Matter

It is controlled either by using filters, electrostatic precipitators (ESP), (Fig. 8.14) Venturi scrubber (Fig. 8.18) and inertial methods like sedimentation chamber. For filtration cloth is used.

There are various kinds of devises to eliminate particulates. They include stack sampler (Fig. 8.13). Dust hopper (Fig. 8.14) cyclone separator (Fig. 8.15) Spray tower (Fig. 8.16). Cyclone Scrubber (Fig. 8.17), Venturi scrubber (Fig. 8.18) and electrostatic precipitate (Fig. 8.19) should be also used. Filters are gravitational but thermal precipitators works better based on difference in temperature gradient. The bag house filtration method is very cheap and efficient. However, high voltage electrostatic (ESP) precipitor (Fig. 8.20) is the best one and it is ideal to remove SPM. The technique operates at high temperature but it is the useless for combustible particulate. A 30 kV DC is applied between central wire electrode

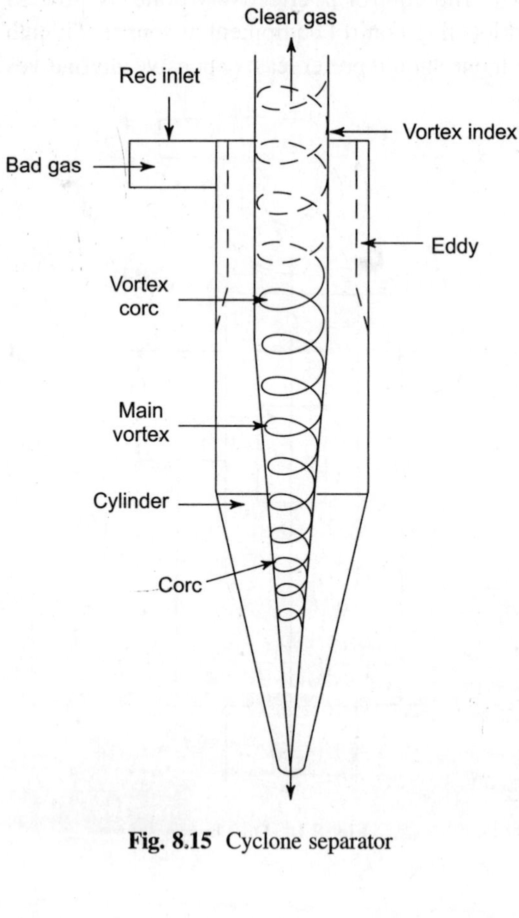

Fig. 8.15 Cyclone separator

and ground surface. On account of static charge, particle are attracted to bottom. However, inertial collection is very cheap. It is effected with use of cyclone (Figs. 8.15 and 8.17) such cyclones are effective for large sized particles (10 mm). The change of radius of curvature, particle size and its diameter, gas flow influences working of the cyclone. Scrubbers are two types dry and wet scrubbers (Fig. 8.14). They permit wet collection. The illustration of latter is Venturi scrubbers (Fig. 8.18). The bag house is cheapest, ESP is moderately costly, cyclones are expensive but Venturi scrubber with fine sprinklers in wet process is most efficient in climinating suspended particulate matter.

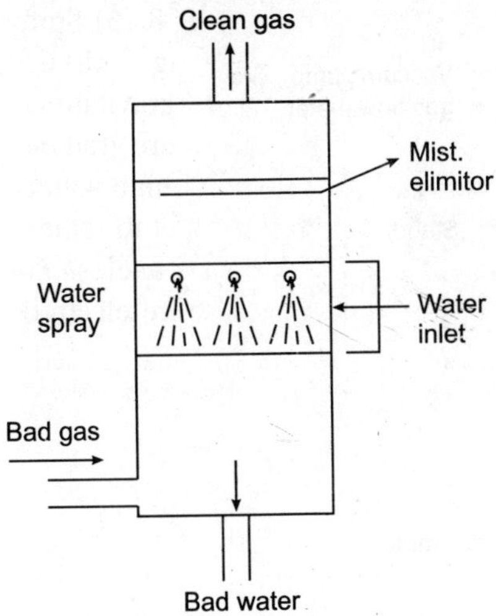

Fig. 8.16 Spray tower

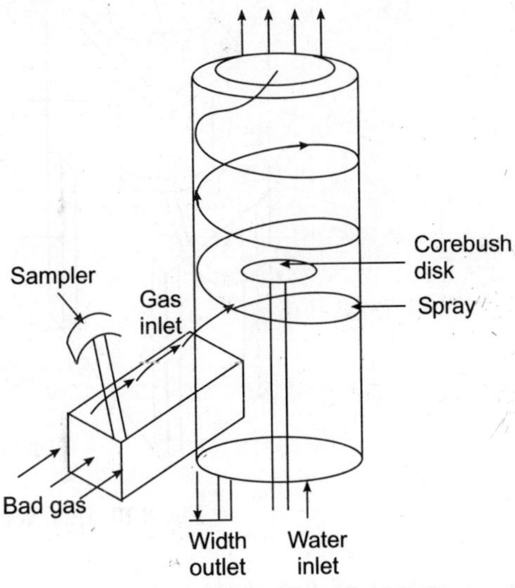

Fig. 8.17 Cyclone scrubber

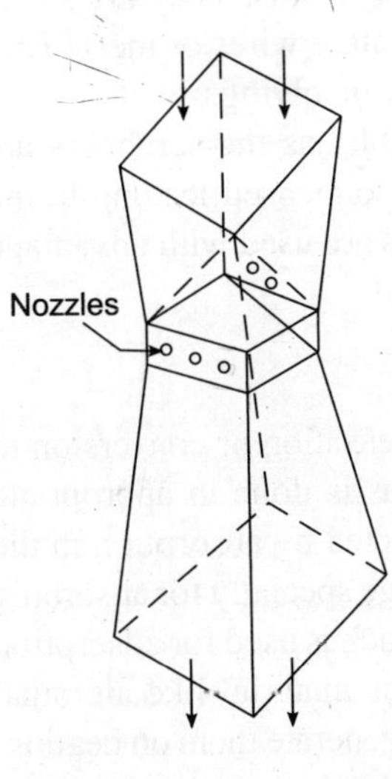

Fig. 8.18 Venturi scrubbers

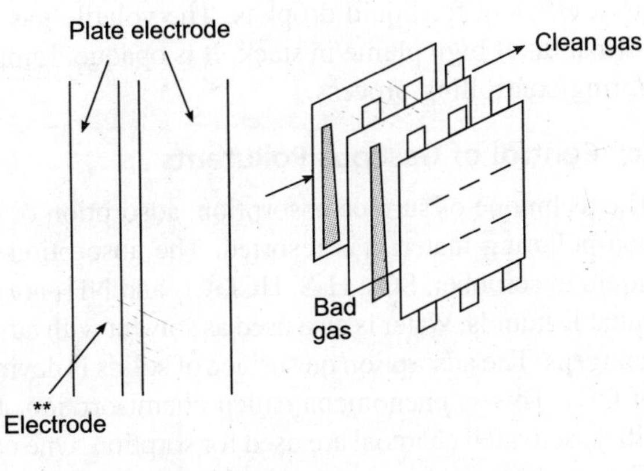

Fig. 8.19 Electrostatic precipitator (ESP)

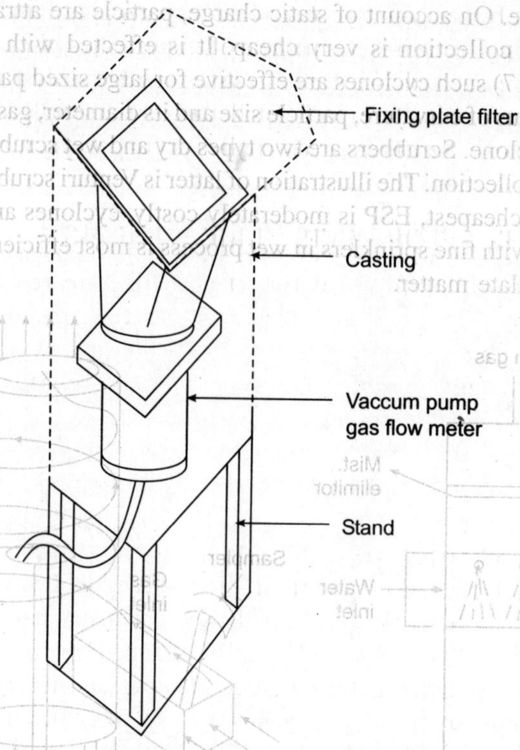

Fig. 8.20 High volume sampler

(b) Control of Aerosols

The liquid droplets mixed with solid particles is called aerosols. They are solid-liquid in nature. For their control one uses filters with knitted wires or mesh. ESP for droplets are used to remove mist. The inertial collector involving use of cyclone which is efficient. The system is inexpensive and reliable; as the scrubbers are most efficient for liquid droplets. The volatile gas gets condensed leading to the formation of high plume in stack. It is opaque. Impingers are used with advantage during controlling process.

(c) Control of Gaseous Pollutants

The technique of surface absorption, adsorption or condensation or conversion to non-polluting material is resorted. The absorption of gas is done in appropriate liquid in scrubber. SO_2, H_2S, HCl, Cl_2 and NH_3 are collected by absorption in the suitable liquids. Water is also used as solvent with advantage specially for absorbing halogens. The adsorption on surface of solids is device which is used for adsorption of CO_2. This is phenomena called chemisorption. Porous material like alumina, silica, activated charcoal are used for sorption. One can regenerate them on heating. The condensation is resorted to if aerosol or gases pollutants are condensable.

This can be done by reducing the temperature by coolant. Finally, the conversion in to non-polluting form is best method of controlling gases pollutants. These transformation are effected by use of catalyst, however catalyst should be changed from time to time. The odour producing pollutants are controlled by use of activated charcoal. The odour reduction is accomplished by passing a gases pollutant on granulated activated coal (GAC).

8.13 FUTURE DEVELOPMENTS IN MONITORING

In India, the research and development activities are restricted to national laboratories and institutions of national importance. Attempts are made to indigenously develop monitoring instruments within country. Such instruments are inexpensive but the co-ordinated approach is lacking. Most of the efforts are directed towards air quality monitoring instruments. Such development leads to standardisation of procedure in data collection, analysis and calibration. A considerable expertise for development is available within the country and really import of know how from abroad is not at all necessary. Personal monitoring instruments are developed within country. Improved aerosol sampling methods, which are size selective, are essential in future years; as fine particles should be measurable with absolute accuracy. Analytical chemistry has moved in the past decade from manual one-by-one sampling procedure to modern automatic techniques with micro-processor but such methods are not extended to routine environmental monitoring. Trace organic analysis must be considered in future. Good gas chromatograph, specially portable, with battery operated models, are required for field work. Instruments based on remote sensing will have to be developed within the country. The work on low cost techniques for detection of gas in indicator tubes will also have to be strengthened in years to come. LIDAR technique will have to be improved with tunable dye laser to monitor upper atmosphere.

We have considered in great details various monitoring methods of the air pollutant. There are selective methods for analysis of the air pollutant either from ambient or stack samples. However, all these efforts will have no value unless we design a efficient methods for control of pollution. Such control methods are inexpensive but are efficient.

8.14 CONCLUSION

Amongst various kinds of pollution, air pollution is very important and needs immediate attendation. To understand it, one needs basic knowledge of meteorology which covers study of winds, their velocity cyclones and anticyclones, wind direction and their measurements. Most useful guideline is wind roses (a plot of velocity against time for wind). It helps to device appropriate control measures, but it does not throw much light on effect of temperature or phenomena of inversion. Several kinds of meteorological instruments are available. It is followed by monitoring and use of suitable instruments. The monitoring methods involve several kinds of principles. The sampling before monitoring is most critical and important. Several methods are available for monitoring of SO_2, H_2S, NO-NO_x, CO, CO_2, HC, SPM, NH_3 and O_3 and trace elements. These methods are applicable for ambient air quality monitoring while the stack monitoring involves measurement of pollution at the source. The sampling of pollutants at bottom and top of stack yields reliable results. The stack emission monitoring concerns pollutants as like SO_2, NO-NO_x, CO, CO_2, SPM with best monitoring control one can do effective control measures. Such control measures include control of autoexhaust emissions, air pollution, particulate matter, aerosols and gaseous pollutants. The proper controlling cannot be effected merely with strict legislation but by creating an awareness of environmental pollution in the society if it becomes alert to mitigate the pollution at the source.

ADDITIONAL READING

1. R.W. Boubel, D.L. Fox, D.B. Turner, A.C. Stern, *Fundamentals of Air Pollution*, 3rd edition, Academic Press (1994).
2. B.S.N. Raju, *Fundamentals of Air Pollution,* Oxford & IBH Publisher, New Delhi (1997).
3. W.L. Faith, A.A. Atkinson, *Air Pollution,* Second Edition, Wiley Interscience Publication (1972).
4. J.O. Ledbetter, *Air Pollution Part A Analysis*, Marcel Decker Inc, New York (1972).
5. J.H. Seinfeld, *Air pollution–Physical and Chemical Fundamentals,* McGraw Hill & Co. (1975).
6. K. Wark and C.F. Warner, *Air Pollution: Its Origin and Control,* A Dun-Donnelley Publisher, New York (1976).
7. A.C. Stern, *Air Pollution*, Vols. I to V, 3rd Ed., Academic Press, New York (1977).
8. J.H. Seinfeld, *Atmospheric Chemistry and Physics of Air Pollution*, Wiley Interscience, New York (1986).
9. R.C. Flagan and J.H. Seinfeld, *Fundamentals of Air Pollution Engineering*, Wiley Inc., New York (1988).
10. K.R. Spurny, *Physical and Chemical Characterisation of Individual Airborne Particles*, Ellis Horwood Co. (1986).
11. R.D. Ross, *Air Pollution and Industry*, Van Nostrand Reinhold Company, New York (1972).
12. H.C. Perkins, *Air Pollution*, McGraw Hill Kogakusha Ltd., Tokyo (1974).
13. W.L. Faith and A.A. Atkinson Jr., *Air Pollution*, Second Ed., Wiley Interscience, New York (1972).
14. W. Strauss, *Air Pollution Control,* Wiley Interscience, New York (1971).
15. V. Brodine, *Air Pollution*, Academic Press Inc., New York, 3rd Ed. (1977).
16. A.K Watson, R.S. Bates and D. Kennedy, *Air Pollution, Automobile and Public Health*, National Academy Press, Washington (1988).
17. G.M. Hidy, *Aerosols: An Industrial and Environmental Science*, Academic Press Inc., Orlando (1984).

18. A.K. Ganguly, Report of the Panel on *Environmental Monitoring Instruments,* Electronics Commission, Government of India, New Delhi (1976).
19. T.E. Harvey, Notes on *Environmental Pollution Monitoring and Control,* Tottenham College of Technology, London (1978).
20. B.L. Deekshatulu, Report on *Environmental Monitoring Instrument,* Department of Environment, New Delhi (1984).
21. P.N. Cheremisinoff, A.C. Morresi, *Air Pollution Sampling and Analysis,* Desk Book Ann Arbor Science Publication (1978).
22. S.M. Khopkar *Environmental Pollution Analysis,* Second Ed. New Age International Publishers (P) Ltd. (2012).

9 Water Pollution

9.1 INTRODUCTION

We have so far considered the analysis of toxic pollutants as well as the analysis of air pollutants. Now in the next two chapters, we propose to consider water pollution and its analysis. First the analysis of potable or drinking water will be considered. It will be followed by discussion on the analysis of water after its treatment, used for domestic and industrial purposes. A fresh water cannot be used directly for drinking purposes due to contamination and pollution. So treatment is essential before it is used for drinking, or for industrial processes. The quality of water depends upon its source or history. The history of water signifies the terrain through which water is flowing, its origin and most important the extent to which it is contaminated on its way by impurities, sediments and industrial waste. The solubilisation and fragmentation of the terrain through which it flows determines its quality. The extent of dissolved solid materials present in water determines its quality. Such quality is also decided by the solubility of the geological deposits, contact of water with sediments, time of interaction and special factors related to environment. To ascertain suitability of water for consumption, it is necessary to undertake examination of quality of water. Such quality is ascertained by examination including physical examination of water, chemical characteristics and biological studies (Table 9.1).

Table 9.1 Water use all over the world

S.No.	*Country*	*Capital city*	*Consumption*			*Average*
			% Drinking	*% Factory*	*% Farming*	*cab/km*
1.	Canada	Ottawa	13	45	42	45.1
2.	England	London	41	45	14	15.3
3.	France	Paris	16	69	15	37.7
4.	Germany	Frankfürt	10	70	20	46.3
5.	Italy	Milan	14	27	59	50.2
6.	Netherland	Amsterdam	5	61	34	7.81
7.	Portugal	Lisbon	15	37	48	7.29
8.	Spain	Basel	12	26	62	30.7
9.	USA	Washington	13	45	42	46.34
10.	Wales	Cardif.	40	45	15	16.0

The Table 9.1 shows consumption of drinking water all over the world. The consumption in Tropical countries is more than countries which are located near north pole. Thus, UK, Wales and Scotland consume largest % of water inspite of having severe winter and cold breeze. While Netherland consumes smallest amount (~5%) of potable water.

The agricultural consumption for farming is the highest in Italy (70%) and Portugal (61%) while nonfarming nation like UK (London) (14%), France and Wales (~15%) need less quantity of water for the cultivation and in farming.

Finally, if we consider overall picture for whole consumption we note that Italy, Germany, Canada and USA (> 50%) consume highest percentage of consumption. It is not only related to the size of land but total population of users in that country (Table 9.1).

9.2 PHYSICAL EXAMINATION OF WATER, CHEMICAL CHARACTERISTICS AND BIOLOGICAL STUDIES

Table 9.2 indicates the characterisation of water from Powai Lake situated near IIT Mumbai, wells and municipal taps in the city of Mumbai, while Table 9.3 describes important characteristics of well water in typical coalfields in Eastern India, where most of the water comes from wells. Both the tables give prevailing status about the quality of water. Thus there is too much of chromium, hardness and dissolved solids in Powai Lake water. Also the MPN count is alarmingly high. It is 2400. Powai water is therefore unfit for drinking. The (Table 9.3) throws much light on the quality of well water in east. Powai water and a typical lake in Bombay contains very high solids, enormous amount of anions, poor BOD high COD and high hardness. We noted in Table 9.1 the extent of consumption of water in various nations in the world.

Table 9.2 Characterisation of water from Powai Lake and few wells

Source	*pH*	*Hardness* $CaCO_3$ *ppm*	*Dissolved oxygen ppm*	NO_2^- *μg/ml*	F^- *μg/ml*	*MPN per 100 ml*
Powai	8.1	74.4	7.0	0.6	2.0	2400
	7.9	71.6	7.2	0.8	1.0	430
	8.3	80.0	8.1	0.6	2.0	430
	8.2	74.7	5.6	1.3	1.0	2400
	8.0	74.8	8.0	0.6	2.3	2400
	8.2	78.2	8.2	0.7	1.6	1100
	8.2	76.8	8.4	0.6	2.4	2400
Potable water	7.0	12.5	12.5	0.1	0.2	100
Well water	7.2	301	1.4	1.2	–	1000
	7.9	95.2	1.4	0.7	–	1000
	7.1	124	1.4	1.1	–	1000
	7.4	251	1.8	0.9	–	1000

Table 9.3 Characteristics of well water from coalfield area in Northeast India at Jorhat

Parameters	*Average values (mg/L)*
pH	7.0
Dissolved solids	672.0
Total hardness	617.0
Nitrate	78.0
Sulphate	47.0
Chloride	62.0
Oil and Grease	0.038
D.O.	6.0
B.O.D.	0.82
C.O.D.	4.5
Iron	0.10 μg/litre
Manganese	0.003 μg/litre
Fluoride	0.23 μg/litre

9.3 PHYSICAL EXAMINATION OF WATER

Major information on the quality of water is obtained by physical examination (Table 9.4). Such examination includes the study of colour, conductivity, temperature, odour, turbidity and hardness.

Table 9.4 Physical characteristics of water

S.No.	*Parameters*	*Quality*
1.	Acidity	Nil
2.	Alkalinity	10–500 mg/L
3.	Colour	50 plate count
4.	Hardness	5–1000 mg/L
5.	pH	6.0–9.0
6.	Specific conductance	30–1000
7.	Temperature	0–30°C
8.	Turbidity	0–1000 JU
9.	Odour	3 TON

(a) Colour

The colour of the water is due to the presence of minute quantities of metallic ions like Cu, Cr and peat humus materials from decaying vegetable matter. Industrial waste also contributes to colour of water. Such colour is classified into two categories, *viz.*, true colour and apparent colour. True colour is the real colour of water. Such colour does not depend upon background when viewed. While apparent colour is colour due to reflection of sky, *e.g.*, blue colour of sea water or reflection of trees as green colour of well water. The classical method for measurement of colour consists of the comparison of colour with water prepared by dissolving known weight of dipotassiun hexachloroplatinate or cobalt chloride. This is called as the platinum-cobalt method for the purpose of comparison. The unit of colour is one produced by 1 mg platinum/litre in the form of chloroplatinate ion. Thus, 1.25 gm of K_2PtCl_6 and 1 gm of $CoCl_2 . 6H_2O$ if dissolved in 100 ml of water and concentrated hydrochloric acid and made upto one litre with distilled water, then resulting stock solution has colour of 500 units. However, this method of analysis involves personal error. The spectrophotometric method is the most reliable method, wherein the absorbance of water is measured between 400 and 700 nm.

The colour may be due to elements like copper, chromium, cobalt, nickel. It is necessary to remove turbidity before colour measurement. This is not advisable as the filtration removes colour. The centrifugation is the best method for removal of turbidity. Cobalt-platinum method is valid only for potable water and not for industrial waste water. It is necessary to specify pH, when colour is measured. The colour is identified in terms of primary colours as red/green/yellow in terms of the dominant wavelength and degree of brightness by luminance. Tristimulus colorimeter with three filters is used to measure the transmittance of sample of water. Transmittance is reciprocal of absorbance.

(b) Conductivity

The equivalent conductance of various ions is listed in Table 9.5. The conductance is the measure of concentration of mineral constituents present in water. It gives a quick method to ascertain quality of water. The conductance is reciprocal of resistance, which is measured between two electrodes kept one cm apart, with area of cross-section as one cm^2. Its value depends upon presence of total concentration of ions. It checks the quality of distilled water. The average value should be less than 2 μ ohms. The self-contained conductivity instruments are available for such measurements. In conductivity cell, it is necessary to evaluate cell constant. The conductivity is measured at a fixed temperature. Table 9.6 gives conductivity as well as other parameters of the potable water from various suburbs of Mumbai, as well as that of supply of water for city from lake sources like Tansa Vaitarna, Bhatsa, Tulsi, Vihar and Powai. They supply water to the city of Mumbai (Fig. 9.1). The results show low conductivity for less polluted water due to absence of ionic impurities, but sea water at *Chowpati* has the highest conductivity due to presence of large proportion of inorganic salts. The water from Bhatshai lake which is less polluted has the minimum value for conductance. This lake is situated quite far off and away from habitat hence is well protected from human interaction.

Table 9.5 Equivalent conductance of various ions

S.No.	*Anion*	*Conductance μmoh/mg/litre*	*S.No.*	*Cation*	*Conductance μmoh/mg/litre*
1.	Cl^-	2.14	6.	H^+	—
2.	SO_4^{2-}	1.54	7.	Ca^{2+}	2.60
3.	CO_3^{2-}	2.82	8.	Mg^{2+}	3.82
4.	HCO_3^{2-}	0.71	9.	Na^+	2.16
5.	NO_3^-	1.15	10.	K^+	2.00

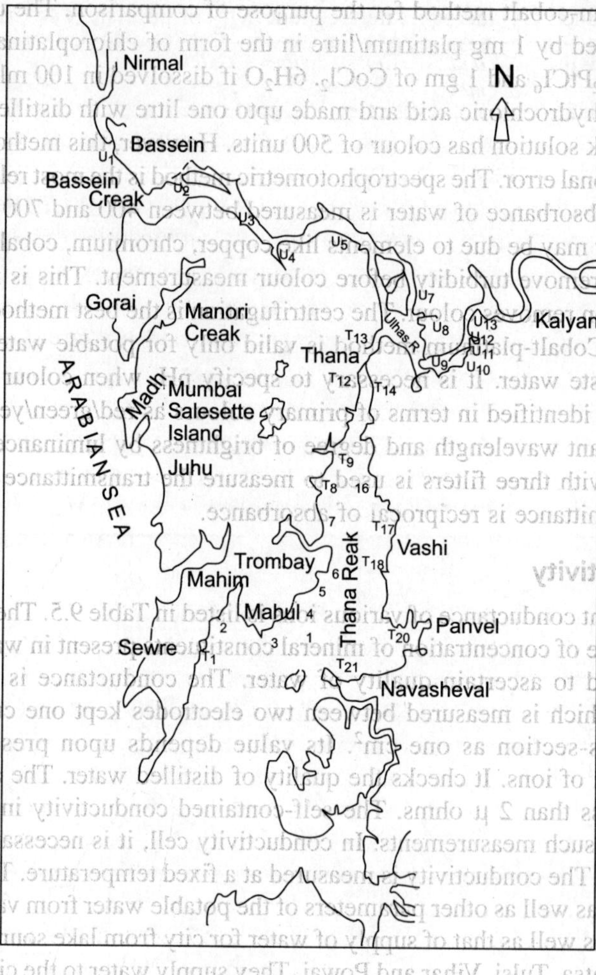

Fig. 9.1 Mumbai island

The conductivity is numerical index of ability of an aqueous solution to carry an electric current. Such ability depends upon the presence of ions in the sample of water as well as on their total concentration, mobility, valancy and temperature. These values are used to assess degree of mineralisation, variation in dissolved mineral levels, or estimate of total dissolved solids. Since conductivity depends upon temp., temperature must be kept fixed. KCl is used as the standard during such measurements. Conductivity and equivalent conductivity is given in Table 9.6.

(c) Temperature

Temperature is measured immediately after collecting the water sample. It should preferably be measured on site itself.

This parameter is useful for calculating various factors such as alkalinity or acidity of water. The elevated temperature has adverse ecological effects on water. The thermometers must be properly calibrated before measurement.

Table 9.6 Conductivity and equivalent conductivity of potassium chloride at 25°C

S.No.	Concentration (M)	Eq cond. μm/cm/eq	Conductivity μm/cm	Calculations
			–	The cell constant (θ)
1.	1.0×10^{-4}	149.86	14.94	
2.	1.0×10^{-3}	146.95	147.0	$\theta = \dfrac{\text{measured resistance}}{\text{specific resistance}}$
3.	1×10^{-2}	141.27	1413	while $K = \dfrac{1}{R} = \dfrac{C}{R}$ is reciprocal of resistance
4.	1×10^{-1}	128.96	12.900	If K = specific or just conductivity
5.	1.0	111.87	111.900	which is measured in terms of 'Siemon' or mohms.

Table 9.7 Characterisation of water from various locations in Mumbai

Location	Place	pH	$[\bar{F}]$ mg/litre	[DO] mg/litre	Hardness $CaCO_3$/ mg/litre	Turbidity NTU	Conductance μmohs/ mg/litre
Lakes:	1 Tansa	7.52	0.219	5.56	0.50	0.60	131.0
	2 Vaiterna	7.72	0.134	6.66	0.45	0.55	126.9
	3 Bhatshai	7.36	0.177	6.80	0.37	0.40	98.27
	4 Vihar	7.77	0.156	5.60	0.68	3.23	190.3
	5 Powai	7.09	0.112	5.95	0.93	0.50	335.8
Sea shore:	6 Juhu	7.39	0.909	4.0	8.3	2.76	5794.2
	7 Chowpati	7.11	0.376	3.70	6.81	2.36	4955.3
	8 Dadar	7.81	0.109	5.45	0.60	1.20	233.3
Towns: (Eastern Mumbai)	9 IIT, Powai	7.24	0.141	5.53	0.93	0.55	163.7
	10 Mulund	7.22	0.139	4.75	0.68	0.60	188.3
	11 Dombivali	7.29	0.136	5.75	0.80	2.50	221.1
Towns: (Western Mumbai)	12 Grant Road	6.81	0.121	5.50	0.70	0.76	122.8
	13 Vile Parle	7.29	0.116	5.45	0.55	1.03	114.6
	14 Goregaon	6.83	0.113	5.20	0.56	0.90	137.0

The depth temperature is required for limnological studies, which may be measured with a reversing thermometer or thermophone or thermistor. The last devise, *viz.*, thermistor is the most reliable amongst measuring instruments. Table 9.7 presents information on hydrological factors of water.

(d) Odour and Taste

The volatile compounds generate odour. The dilution of sample at which odour is just perceptible is a measure for its intensity. The odour is commonly described as medicinal (phenolic) and fishy (algae), earthy (decaying matter) or chemical (chlorine). Odour is one of the quality factor influencing acceptability of potable water.

In spite of advancement of science and technology no instrument has so far been developed for the measurement of odour. Such measurement largely depends upon contact of a stimulating substance with appropriate human recepter cell. Such stimuli are chemical in nature and hence termed as *chemical sense*. The details of odour, its sampling, measurement and control is very well described elsewhere in this book. The odour of water is measured in terms of TON *i.e.*, threshold odour number, indicating the number of times the dilution of water one should carry out with odour free water (in order to get no perceptible odour) *e.g.*, TON = 4.0 indicates if we dilute with clean water in the ratio of 1:4, no odour will persist. Obviously, smaller the value of TON, better is quality of water. Accepted average value of TON = 3. The chemical senses are used to characterise odour and taste. Food, beverage and pharmaceuticals preparations necessarily need odour free water. The odour is measured at 40°C or at room temperature. Free odour free water which is obtained by passing water over activated charcoal. For good results panel of at least 5 and not more than 10 members is needed for smelling. Threshold odour number is TON $= \left(\frac{a+b}{a}\right)$, if a = ml of sample; b = ml of odour free water added to sample. The TON corresponding to various dilution of 20 ml of sample water is 1.0 for (200 + 200); 2(200 + 100); 4(200 + 50), 8(200 + 25); 50(200 + 4), 100(200 + 2), 200(200 + 1) if the order (TON) (sample of odourless water is added). Threshold odour number (TON) is the dilution ratio at which odour is just detectable. Now taste refers to sensation to the tounge to soft palate as flavour needs nose for comparison. The profile threshold test (PTT), flavour is needed for comparison. The flavour threshold test (FTT) flavour rating assessment (FRA) flavour profile analysis (FPA) are terms used in food industry. FRA is used to assess mineral contents. FPA is used to ascertain offensive flavour against background of recorded sensory quality which is as judged if acceptable.

(e) Turbidity

It is a measure of the light absorbing properties of the water sample. It is measured either with nepheloturbidimeter or by conventional Jackson candle turbidimeter. The turbidity is caused by suspended matter. It is an expression of optical quality of water. The standard method for determination of turbidity is based on Jackson candle turbidimeter, but lower turbidity values is measured by nephlometer. In visual or Jackson turbidity measurement, a candle turbidimeter is kept on ground glass. The candle is lighted and held below the cylinder. Water is then continuously poured in turbidimeter and the flame is viewed from top. When flame disappears the reading on the cylinder is noted. The units on cylinder indicates turbidity units of water. Alternatively, it is very easy to measure turbidity of water by nephelometer in terms of NTU units. The instrument permits measurement from 100 NTU, while

Jackson model permits measurement from 25 to 1000 JU limits. So far no direct correlationship has been established between units of Jackson candle turbidimeter and NTU units of nephelometer.

The turbidity is most acceptable for water used for human consumption. The process of coagulation and sedimentation removes turbidity. It is caused by clay, slit, finely divided organic and inorganic contents. Turbidity is also an expression of the optical property of water which causes light to be scattered and absorbed rather than transmitted. The main cause for the variation in turbidity analysis results in the use of the suspension of different types of matter having different available optical properties, refractive indices and varying particle size. As nephelometer are available Jackson candle method nowadays is not used. The hydrazinc sulphate or methylene tetramine are used to prepare standard turbid solution for comparison. The mixture of 1 gm hydrazinc and 10 gm hexamethylene tetramine in 100 ml sample of water gives a turbidity of 400 in NTU units.

Table 9.8 Turbidity of water in NTU

Range	*Value, NTO*	*Range*	*Value, NTO*
0 + 10	0.05	100–400	10
10 – 40	1.0	400–1000	50
40–100	5.0	> 1000	100

(f) Hardness

The total hardness is defined as the sum of calcium and magnesium concentration expressed both as the calcium carbonate hardness in milligram per litre. It is greater than the sum of bicarbonate and carbonate alkinity. This is termed as *carbonate hardness*. The amount of hardness excess of this is called *noncarbonate hardness*. The calculated hardness is obtained from amount of calcium and magnesium present while hardness is experimentally evaluated by titration technique. Many heavy metals inferences in complexometric titrations which are eliminated by use of CDTA as inhibitor. Various indicators like erichrome black T, calmagite, mureoxide are used in EDTA titration for determination of calcium and magnesium. The hardness is expressed as $(CaCO_3)L = \dfrac{a \times b \times 100}{\text{ml sample}}$, where a = ml of titrant, b = mg of $CaCO_3$ equivalent to 1 ml of EDTA titrant.

The hardness should have been classified as the chemical property of water. Hardness of water is caused due to the presence of sulphates and chlorides of calcium and magnesium. Hardness sometimes is attributed to the sulphates or chlorides of iron, manganese and aluminium. This causes what is called the permanent hardness, while temporary hardness is caused due to the presence of bicarbonates of calcium and magnesium and is eliminated by mere boiling of water. In order to ascertain the hardness of water, one has to use soap test. Water will form soft and beautiful lather with soap if water is soft. However, if water is hard then Ca and Mg will combine with stearates from soap to form scum or curd insoluble lather of calcium-stearate or magnesium-sterate. Alkali metal stearates are soluble. The hardness is expressed in terms of $CaCO_3$/litre. Table 9.9 lists hardness of water for practical purposes.

Table 9.9 Classification of hardness

S.No.	*Hardness* *$CaCO_3$ mg/litre*	*Remarks*
1	0–40	Soft
2	40–100	Moderately hard
3	100–300	Hard
4	300–500	Very hard
5	500–1000	Extremely hard

Thus, a water with 25 mg/litre $CaCO_3$ is considered soft water, while water with 500 mg/litre of $CaCO_3$ is termed as very *hard water*. The method for analysis of hardness is titration method, one involving $KMnO_4$ titration, while an another method is involving the use of EDTA for the purpose, latter is more popular. The reactions involved in permanganate titrations are as follows:

$$CaCl_2 + H_2C_2O_4 \rightarrow CaC_2O_4 + 2HCl \text{ (precipitate filtered)}$$

$$CaC_2O_4 + H_2SO_4 \rightarrow CaSO_4 + H_2C_2O_4 \text{ (in solution)}$$

$$2MnO_4^- + 5H_2C_2O_4 + 6H^+ \rightarrow 2Mn^{2+} + 10CO_2\uparrow + 8H_2O.$$

The most common method is EDTA titration with mureoxide as the indicator as it involves reaction as follows:

$$CaCl_2 + 2EDTA \rightarrow Ca(EDTA)_2 + 2NaCl \text{ (with metallochromic indicator)}$$

During titration the pH of solution is fixed at 4.5. If magnesium is present, then the reaction is

$$MgSO_4 + 2EDTA \rightarrow Mg\,(EDTA)_2 + Na_2SO_4$$

The indicator used is Eriochrome black T, where pH is maintained at 10.0. EDTA combines first with Ca from water; then magnesium is precipitated as $Mg(OH)_2$. So titration value gives the amount of calcium only. Solochrome dark-blue is also used instead of mureoxide indicator, with equal efficiency for calcium. When erichrome black-T is used, one gets reading for both Ca and Mg. EBT is grounded with solid NaCl in the ratio of 1:1, and is used during titration. A new indicator called *Patton Reeder indicator* is best for determination of calcium in hard water. It permits simultaneous analysis of both calcium and magnesium in water. It is most popular with chemists.

We have considered physical properties of water, as colour, conductivity and turbidity. However, physical properties alone cannot provide definite information on quality of water. Most of the methods so far discussed are largely physical with few exception like hardness based upon the physiochemical properties. Similarly, acidity/alkalinity or salinity is classified in chemical composition of the water.

Now we would consider purely chemical methods involving characterisation of metals as well as nonmetallic ions. Those of the elements which are rarely encountered at low concentrations are considered separately as trace elements.

9.4 CHEMICAL CHARACTERISATION OF WATER

Most important task is the chemical characterisation of water. Table 9.10 lists important chemical constituents of water, which are analysed to assess its quality. In addition to chemical parameters, this table also lists important physical properties of water, which we have already discussed in the preceding section. The biological factors which are investigated are also listed in the same table. The various components which are present in major concentrations in potable water are calcium, magnesium, sodium, potassium, chloride, sulphate, carbonates, bicarbonates and dissolved solids. The important minor constituents of potable water are aluminium, barium, boron, fluoride, bromide iodide, nitrate, nitrite, phosphates, polyphosphates, iron, manganese and trace elements. We also consider other important properties such as acidity/alkalinity, dissolved oxygen (DO), biochemical oxygen demand (BOD), chemical oxygen demand (COD) and nitrogen contents in from of ammonia, nitrite and nitrates.

Table 9.10 Physical, chemical and biological examination of water

Chemical characteristics		*Physical properties*	*Biological investigations*
Major: Ca^{2+}	Minor: Al^{3+}	Colour	Total coliforma
Mg^{2+}	Ba^{2+}	Conductivity	Faecal coliforma
Na^{+}	B^{3-}	Temperature	Faecal *streptococci*
K^{+}	F^{-}	Odour	Crenothrix
Cl^{-}	NO_3^{-}	Turbidity	Plankton
SO_4^{2-}	NO_2^{-}	Hardness	Algae
CO_3^{2-}	PO_4^{3-}		Nitrosomonas;
HCO_3^{2-}	Fe^{3+}		Protozoa
	Mn^{2+}		Diatmalgae
			E.coli

Table 9.11 Major components of water (mean concen. in bracket)

Component	*Concentration mgs/Litre*	*Component*	*Concentration mg/Litre*
Ca^{2+}	0–250 (150)	Mg^{2+}	0–100 (15)
CO_3^{2-}	0–10 (< 5)	Mn^{2+}	0–0.2 (0.25)
HCO_3^{2-}	0–300 (100)	NO_3^{-}	0–5 (1)
Cl^{-}	0–500 (50)	K^{+}	0–25 (15)
Dissolved solids	0.0–175 (300)	SiO_2^{2-}	0–100 (25)
F^{-}	0.20 (0.5)	SO_4^{2-}	0–500 (100)
Fe^{3+}	0.0.5 (0.25)		

Table 9.12 Limits of the ions in drinking water (mg/litre)

Element	*Public health service—limit*	*World health —limit*
As^{3+}	0.05	0.20
Ba^{2+}	1.0	None
Cd^{2+}	0.01	Nil
Cr^{3+}	0.05	0.05
Cu^{2+}	1.0	1.5
Fe^{3+}	0.03	1.0
Pb^{2+}	0.05	0.10
Mn^{2+}	0.05	0.05
Se^{4+}	0.05	0.05]
Ag^{+}	0.05	None
Zn^{2+}	5.0	15.0

Table 9.11 describes the major components of water and their probable concentration. The values in bracket indicates mean level of the components present in sample of water. The metals constitute an important portion of drinking water. Table 9.12 shows prescribed WHO limit of metals, which is in agreement with that prescribed limits by public health services (PHS) in India. It provide guidelines to control purity of drinking water, by selecting proper water treatment process. The two important aspects of chemical constituents are their significance in determining quality of water and second analysis in the laboratory.

(a) Calcium

It is a major component of natural water. It dissolves from rocks and soils which cause hardness and is deposited in conduit tubes and pipes. The concentrations upto 100 mg/litre of calcium is capable of forming scales in pipes and boilers. Fortunately, it has no adverse physiological manifestation on human system. A person consuming water containing certain amount of calcium is likely to have less chances of heart trouble or cardiac disorder, than a person drinking soft water without any calcium contents. The analysis of calcium is carried by gravimetry, if present in large concentrations. It is weighed as CaO, after its precipitation as the oxalate and ignition to oxide.

$$Ca^{2+} + H_2C_2O_4 \rightarrow CaC_2O_4 + 2H^+;\ CaC_2O_4 \rightarrow CaCO_3 \rightarrow CaO + CO_2 \uparrow$$

However, if the level is small, one can use $KMnO_4$ titration by dissolving the oxalate in sulphuric acid and carrying redox titration which is the best method. In addition to mureoxide, one can also use indicators like calcium purpurate. Fe, Mn if present are masked at pH 10.0 with alkali cyanide. The conversion factor, is 1 ml of 0.01 MEDTA corresponding to 1 mg $CaCO_3$ or 0.4008 mg of $CaCO_3$.

Calcium is analysed by atomic absorption spectroscopy or by inductively coupled plasma atomic emission sepctroscopy. It is determined in air acetylene flame at 317 nm or analysed by ICP-AES at 315 nm.

(b) Magnesium

Magnesium is present in a smaller concentration. It is determined by titration with EDTA with EBT (Eriochrom Black T in NaCl) at pH 10.0. If a large amount is present, gravimetrically it is weighed as $Mg_2P_2O_7$ as:

$$MgCl_2 + (NH_4)_2\,HPO_4 \rightarrow 2MgHPO_4 \xrightarrow{\Delta} Mg_2P_2O_7 + H_2O$$

It can be also determined by spectrophotometrically, with brilliant yellow as the chromogenic ligand.

The amount of magnesium in gravimetric estimation is calculated as:

$$\text{mg Mg/L} = \frac{\text{mg } Mg_2P_2O_7 \times 218.4}{\text{ml of sample}}$$

Reproducible results are obtained by double precipitation, followed by ignition and weighing precipitate as pyrophosphate.

(c) Sodium

It is a major component of potable water. The average level of sodium is >100 mg/litre. If large amount of sodium is present, it will render boiler operations difficult. Sodium has medicinal effect on health, but if present in large concentration in blood it leads to hypertension. The best method for analysis is by flame emission spectroscopy at 590 nm, at this wavelength potassium does not interfere, as it has absorption maxima at 770 nm. One can also use standard addition and internal standard method during flame photometric analysis.

Amongst AAS and ICP-AES, one prefers flame photometry or atomic emission spectroscopy. The spectral interferance if any is eliminated by use of internal standard. As small as 100 μg/L is determined by flame photometric analysis.

(d) Potassium

It is not present in high concentration in water. The ratio of sodium to potassium is 10 : 1 or 20 : 1. The method of analysis is flame photometry at 770 nm. If moderate levels are encountered, one can resort to colorimetry with sodium cobaltinitrate solution. AAS and ICP-AES is also used for the quantitative analysis from sample of water. A direct reading with internal standard method at 766.5 nm gives best results. We detect as small as 0.1/mg/L or 10 μg/ml of potassium in the sample.

(e) Chloride

The concentration of chloride varies from sample to sample. It has no serious or adverse effects on health, but it imparts bad taste to drinking water. With increase in level of chloride in water, corrosiveness increases. The methods for the determination of chloride are Mohr's and Volhard's methods. The important reactions are:

$$NaCl + AgNO_3 \rightarrow AgCl + NaNO_3$$

$$AgNO_3 + NH_4CNS \rightarrow AgCNS + NH_4NO_3 \text{ (Equivalance point)}$$

$3NH_4CNS + Fe^{3+} \rightarrow Fe(CNS)_3 + 3NH_4^+$ (Red colour after end point)

We add excess of $AgNO_3$ to water containing chloride, and titrate excess of unreacted $AgNO_3$ with KCNS or NH_4CNS. After end point, blood red colour appears due to ferricyanate. In Mohr's method, we use K_2CrO_4 as an indicator for direct titration. The reactions at pH 7.0 – 10.0 is as follows:

$NaCl + AgNO_3 \rightarrow AgCl + NaNO_3$ (Till end point)

$2AgNO_3 + K_2CrO_4 \rightarrow Ag(CrO_4)_2 + 2KNO_3$ (At end point)

Both methods are excellent for analysis of dissolved chloride.

Chloride is major anion in potable and industrial water. About 250 mg/L anion imparts bad taste to potable water. But in the presence of calcium and magnesium even 1 g/L chloride does impart bad taste. A high concentration of chlorides affects growth of vegetation. For turbid water containing chloride, potentiometric method is best suited for automated analysis. Ferricynide method is used for all practical purposes. The ionchromatography is an excellent method of analysis. Alternative method includes use of mercurous nitrate for titration to purple colour at pH < 2.0 – 2.5. In potentiometric method lunar caustic solution is used as the titrant till one gets end point. Finally, in the automated ferricynide method, mercury thiocyanate liberates thiocyanate ion by the formation of mercuric chloride. Initially mercurythioncyanate, ferric nitrate are taken and polyoxyethylene aurylether is also used.

(f) Sulphate

It is a major anion present in water. It is formed by biological oxidation of sulphur compounds. It has no adverse effects upon health. If the amount is large, it is gravimetrically estimated as $BaSO_4$. If the amount is moderate, it is determined by the nephelometric method. It is also possible to estimate it photometrically with sodium rhodiazote as chromogenic ligand. Gravimetry is useful if SO_4^{2-} amount is greater than 10 ppm. Titration method involves interaction with $BaCl_2$ with thorin as an indicator. The method is best if SO_4^{2-} is greater than 5 to 150 mg/litre. Formaldehyde is added if interfering ions like SO_3^{2-} are present.

Table 9.13 Fluoride removal process and its efficiency(%)

S.No.	*Process for removal of fluoride*	*% Removal efficiency*	*Remarks*
1.	Use of alumina	85–90	Most efficient
2.	Application of ferric Hydroxide	1.0	Poor process
3.	Coagulation/Sedimental/Filtration	5	Moderate unsatisfactory
4.	Ion exchange separation	1–2	Expensive
5.	Reverse Osmosis-membrane treatment	40–60	Economical, effective

The sulphate is widely distributed in nature. Sodium and magnesium sulphates exert adverse actions. Ion chromatography is the ideal method of analysis. Several ions interfere in the gravimetric estimation of sulphate as the potassium sulphate *e.g.*, heavy metals like chromium and iron give low results in such analysis. Turbidimetric method is suitable for low concentrations. As small as 1 mg/L of sulphate is analysed by nephelometry. In automated methods methythymol blue is used. At high pH barium reacts with methythymol blue to give blue chelate. The useful range is 10 to 300 ms/L of sulphate anions.

(g) Carbonates and Bicarbonates

They render water temporarily hard. They are formed due to dissolution of CO_2 in water at lower pH (bicarbonates) or at higher pH (carbonates). Their level is 40 to 400 mg/litre. They form a scale in pipes and boilers. The temporary hardness is removed by the following process of boiling or lime addition:

$$Ca(HCO_3)_2 \xrightarrow{\Delta} CaCO_3 + H_2O + CO_2 \text{ (By heating)}$$

or $Ca(HCO_3)_2 + Ca(OH)_2 \rightarrow 2CaCO_3 + 2H_2O$ (By addition of lime)

They are estimated by the acid-base titration.

(h) Solids

These are present in the range of 10 to 20 mg/litre. Certain waters contain as much as 1000 mg/litre. The excess level in drinking water causes stomach upset, fever and impart salty taste to water. Total solids are determined by evaporating a known volume of water to dryness and then weighing it.

The solids are present in water as suspended solids as well as the dissolved solids. Their presence affects water quality. They give rise to physiological manifestations. The level should not exceed more than 500 mg/L. Total solids inturn are used to indicate residue left after evaporation of water. It includes suspended solids and fixed solids. The term used to indicate residue of total suspended or dissolved solids after ignition. Weight loss is referred to volatile solid loss. Then the settleable solids is material settling out of suspension within fixed amount of time. Temperature of ignition is critical. One can classify total solids at 100°C; total dissolved solids at 200°C total suspended solids at 100°C then volatile solids at 300°C. Some settleable solids at 103 to 105°C total solids are weighed after ignition. The total dissolved solids is ascertained at 180°C. The sample of water is filtered and the filtrate is evaporated to dryness and weighed to give information on dissolved solids. Now total suspended solids is filtered, ignited, dried at 105°C and then weighed. The fixed and volatile solids are measured by carrying out the ignition at 550°C.

(i) Calcium Carbonate Saturation Test

It is used to ascertain scale forming capacity or scale dissolution tendency of water. The saturated water precipitates $CaCO_3$ while unsaturated water promotes dissolution of calcium carbonate. Two important indices are used to ascertain saturation from precipitation/dissolution data. These are not absolute measures. In precence of phosphate, precipitation is prevented. Positive indices indicate good water while negative indices indicate corrosiveness of water. Tendency to precipitation of $CaCO_3$ or dissolution $CaCO_3$ is experimentally determined. This is called *saturation index* (SI) or *relative saturation index* (RSI) SI = $(pH–pH_1)$ pH is measured pH while pH_1 is pH of water if it is in equilibrium with $CaCO_3$ at the existing Ca^{2+} and HCO_3^- level. Now $pH_1 = (pK_2 - pK_1) + p(Ca) + p(HCO_3) + 5fx$, if K_1 and K_2 are the dissociation constants of HCO_3 acid and solubity product of $CaCO_3$; fx = active coefficient of monovalent species. The saturometers are also available calcium carbonate precipitation capacity (CCPC) or (CCCP) indicates index of saturation or of dissolution of $CaCO_3$. We relate relative saturation to SI index as SI = 10g ₹ if ₹ = ratio of $CaCO_3$ activity products to $CaCO_3$. The solubility product constant. However, this in formation on $CaCO_3$ saturation is of less importance for potable water and is of some significance for industrial water.

9.5 MINOR COMPONENTS OF WATER

We have so far considered the major components of water. The minor components are aluminium, barium, boron, bromide and iodide. Aluminium passes through clays and minerals in water. There level is 1 mg/litre. Fortunately, it has no ill-effects on health. Aluminium is determined spectrophotometrically with aluminon as the chromogenic ligand. Barium is present in concentration range of 1 mg/litre; it has toxic effects upon nerves, heart and blood vessels. It is determined flame photometrically at 554 nm. Boron is another minor element used as micronutrient in the soil. It helps in farming, specially the growth of citrus fruits like oranges and lemons. It has no physiological effects. It is analysed spectrophotometrically with caramine red as the chromogenic ligand. The phosphates and polyphosphates are present in the range 0.01 to 0.5 mg/litre. The aquatic life, flora and fauna, do not survive in water if there is no phosphate in water. The method for its analysis is by $(NH_4)_2\ MoO_4$ method. A canary yellow solution is reduced with $SnCl_2$ to molybdenum blue and then measured spectrophotometrically. As small as 0.002 mg/ml of PO_4^{3-} is analysed. In place of $SnCl_2$, one can also use aminonaptho-sulphonic acid as the reducing agent. The anions of importance among minor constituents are: fluoride, nitrite, nitrate, hence their analysis is considered in some details.

(a) Fluoride

This is most important component of treated potable water. The level of 1 mg/L is conducive for arresting dental decay. It occurs naturally in water as shown in Table 9.11 to the extent of 10 mg/l in water. The methods commonly used for analysis include the spectrophotometric methods with zirconium alizarin complex or use of ion selective electrode in ion analyser. Even ion chromatography furnishes best results. Samples containing fluoride should never be kept in glass container as latter reacts with it. Chloride, phosphate, sulphate may cause inferences in quantitive analysis. The ion selective electrode is simple method of analysis. The cell used is as shown below

$$||AgCl \rightarrow Ag\ Cl - (0.3m): F\ (0.001m)\ LaF_3||.$$

It is used in combination with SCE *i.e.,* saturated calomel electrode). Al^{3+} and Fe^{3+} interfere; for which CDTA is used as sequistering agent Next best method is use of SPADNS which forms coloured complex with zirconium. The fluoride on contacting it bleaches dye and reduce intensity of coloured solution (Fig. 9.2). SPADNS is sodium (2-parasulphopenylazo) 1, 8 dihydroxy 3,6 napthalene sulphonic acid. One should use low strength of dye. The complex is measured around 530 nm. Apart from alizarine, is made of alizarine fluoride blue, lanthanum reagent to give blue complex which is measured at 620 nm. The chromogenic ligand is made by mixing acetate, buffer, alizarine fluorine blue as reagent in lanthanum nitrate. Polyoxythylene lauryl ether is used as surfactant. This is good method for the automated analysis. As small as 0.1 to 2 mg/L of fluoride can be analysed. For very high concentration of fluoride (>10 mg/L) it is always advisable to use ion analyser with ion selective electrode. In SPADNS method temperature during complexation as well as during photometric analysis must be maintained constant in order to get reproducible results.

Table 9.14 Fluoride in drinking water in India

S.No.	*State*	*Name of district*	*Average fluoride level, mg/litre*
1.	Tamil Nadu	Chinglepet	4.5
		Salem	
		Madurai	
		Trichirapalli	
		Coimbatore	
2.	Karnataka	Belgaun	0.8–1.2
3.	Andhra Pradesh	West Godavari	
		Nalangonda	
		Vellore	
		Anantpur	
4.	Gujarat	Mehsana	4.0
		Banaskantha	
		Sabarkantha	
		Panch Mahal	
		Surat	
5.	Punjab	Bhatinda	3.0
		Ferozpur	
		Amritsar	
6.	Haryana	Gurgaon	3.6
		Hissar	
		Karnal	

In Table 9.14 out of 26 states of Republic of India, six states have considerable amount of fluoride in potable water. Although in small concentration it causes dental crevices, acute poisoning of central nervous system; excess of it gets deposited in bones, as it has a great affinity for calcium. Dust containing fluoride if inhaled causes irritation of nasal passage. Gastric troubles, loss of appetite, nausea and vomiting are also observed. In concentrations greater than 74 mg/litre, it is considered toxic. It shows diffuse osteoporosis of bone with calcification of ligaments and restriction of mobility of columns and thorax as confirmed by X-ray therapy. There is a growing controversy regarding role of fluoride in toothpaste and drinking water. In the USA they allow its use freely, while in UK a controversy exists as to whether one should really use fluorodised potable water. In India, in most of cities we do not have fluorides in water supplies; though 0.8 to 1.2 mg/litre is a safe concentration for potable water, it is good for growth of teeth of children. The best method for analysis of fluoride is shown in Fig. 9.2.

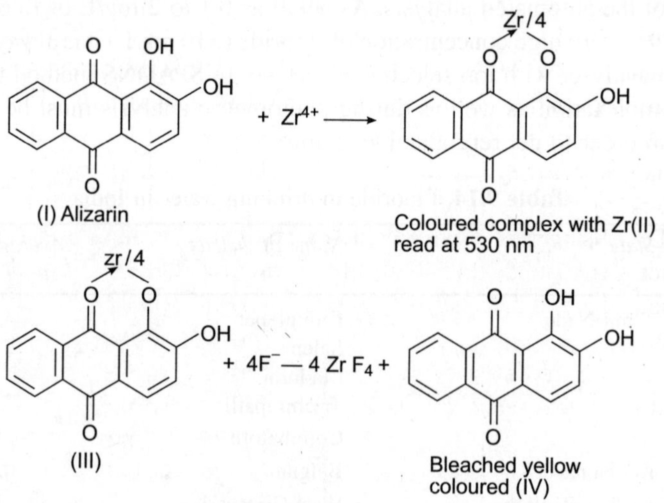

Fig. 9.2 Reaction mechanism of fluoride with Alizarin reds as chromogenic ligand

Alizarine (I) solution is allowed it to react with zirconium (IV) ion to form (II) (Fig. 9.3) complex, which is violet in colour. This complex (III) reacts with excess of fluoride as it bleaches colour to form ZrF_4 or ZrF_6^-. The decrease in intensity of colour indicates concentration of fluoride. In addition to alizarine, erichrome cynine R or SPADNS (*i.e.,* 2-parasulphophenylazo), 1, 8 dihydroxy 3-6 napthalene sulphonate are best reagents, but in such analysis $AlPO_4$ and SO_4^{2-} shows strong interference at 570 nm. However, the best method for analysis is use of ion analyser with specific electrode or use ionchromatography with efficient detectors.

(b) Nitrogen of Ammonical, Nitrite and Nitrate Origin

The nitrogen in water undergoes oxidation to form ammonia, then convert to nitrite and finally nitrate. The nitrogen originates from vegetable materials from land runoff, due to sewage pollution. Infants should not drink water having nitrogen content greater than > 45 mg/litre, as it will cause methaemoglobinemia. The synthesis of protein and aminoacids is affected by nitrogen. Nitrate occurs in trace quantities in surface water. A limit is 10 mg nitrate nitrogen per/litre of drinking water. Nitrate is actual etiologic agent for methoglobinemia. Of this ammonical, nitrogen (NH_3–N) is determined photometrically by the Nessler's reagent.

The presences of nitrogen in from of nitrate, nitrite, ammonia and organic nitrogen is of decreasing importance. Ammonia with organic nitrogen is termed as 'Kjeldal's nitrogen; while total oxidised nitrogen is sum of nitrate and nitrite. The concentration of 10 mg/L is optimum limit of nitrate nitrogen in drinking water. The corrosion inhibitor contain nitrite. Excess of chlorine is removed by treatment with ammonia. Ammonia from water is analysed by Nessler reagent or by phenate colorimetrically method. As small as 20 μg/L of ammonia is analysed by Nessler' reagent which consist of $HgCl_2$ KI in solution of sodium hydroxide. It is measured at 420 to 425 nm in the range of 5 to 60 μg/L of nitrogen. The phenate method consists of use of phenol in sodium hydroxide. The absorbance of complex is measured at 600 to 660 nm or at 630 nm. If range is 0.1 to 5 mg/L of nitrogen. Kjeldal method involving titration with standard acid is best employed if high concentration of ammonia is encountered. A mixture of methyl methylene blue is used as indicator. Ion selective electrode is also used for analysis of ammonia.

Nitrite-nitrogen is best analysed by spectrophotometer with colour developments with NEDA (N-inapthyl ethylene diamine) dihydrochloride at pH 2.0 to 2.5 with absorbance measurement at 540 nm. Thus 1 to 180 mg/L of nitrate is analysed by this method. This was discovered by Saltzman hence it is called as *Saltzman method.* Free chlorine as well as Sb, Fe, Pb, Hg show strong interference. Ion chromatography is the ideal method for analysis of nitrite. The addition of sulphanilaminde gives best resulting in Saltzman technique.

Nitrate-nitrogen is analysed by spectroscopy at 220 nm provided if organic matter is absent. If present absorbance should be measured at 275 nm. Alternatively it is best analysed with brucine and phenol disulphonic acid coulorimetrically. In few instance a chromotropic acid *i.e.,* (4.5 dihydroxyl-2.7 disulphonic acid) is used as chromogenic ligand in spectrophotometric analysis. Nitrate is best analysed with ion selective electrode in the range of 0.1 to 1500 mg/L. The common method involving reduction with cadimum, titanous chloride and hydrazine is used to reduces the ion. It involves reduction of nitrate-nitrite to ammonia when 0.1 to 20 mg/L is limit of analysis NO_2^- is analysed by Saltzman method.

Organic nitrogen is determined by Macro Kjeldal method. $HgSO_4$ in K_2SO_4 is used as catalyst during reaction to convert organic nitrogen to ammonia. Semimicro Kjealdal method is also used for low concentration of nitrogen. The ammonia so generated is determined photometrically by Nesslerisation method.

(c) Iron

The large amount of iron is encountered in water flowing through basaltic rock region, similar to Deccan plateau in India. Murud, a town in district Raigarh of

Maharashtra has high level of iron in potable water. The average level is 1 mg/litre *i.e.,* 1 μg/ml. It causes staining of laundry and ceramics ware. The growth of iron specific bacteria raises the level of iron in water. On account of aeration, iron (II) gets oxidised to iron (III). It is determined spectrophotometry by its complextion with 1–10 phenanthroline or bathophenanthroline. cis or trans pyridyl ion is used for a similar purpose in place of 1–10 phenanthroline as the chromogenic ligand; at pH 3.2 to 3.4. The presence of phosphate or polyphosphate interfere in analysis. Bathophenanthroline is selective for iron in the presence of copper as impurity.

The most favoured method for the determination of iron is I,10-phenanthroline. As low as 10 μg/l of iron is analysed by this method. The results are reproducible in the presence of hydroxylamine hydrochloride (NH_2OH-HCl; 10%). The method is valid for divalent iron. The absorbances are measured at 510 nm. This complex is selectively extracted in isopropyl ether as it is analysed with greater accuracy.

(d) Manganese

Water samples if collected in city of Nagpur or Panjim in Goa have manganese. Average level is 0.05 mg/L. Manganese imparts objectionable and tenacious stain to laundry. The presence of manganese in water gives metallic taste to tea as several complexes of managnese are formed with ingradient of tea. The best method for analysis is the persulphate method. $K_2S_2O_8$ or $KClO_3$ are used to oxidise bivalent to heptavalent manganese. It is then determined spectrophotometrically at 535 nm. Formaldioxime is also used as chromogenic ligand. Organic matter shows strong interferance.

Manganese in boiler feed water breaks down at elevated temperature to form scales. AAS and ICP-AES methods are used for the direct determination. Manganese occurs in water in +4 and +3 state where persulphate photometric method is best for analysis. As small as 210 μg/L manganese is detected by this method. The use of $(NH_4)_2SO_4$ is most common as an oxidising agent. The absorbance of the coloured complex is measured at 525 nm.

(e) Silica

It is the common kind of impurity in drinking water. It is determined gravimetrically if the amount is greater than 20 mg/litre but a small concentration is estimated by spectrophotometric method involving reduction of manganese with 1-amino 2-napthol-4-sulphonic acid. All operations need to be carried out in polyethylene vessels, as glass contains silica. In molybdosilicate technique, colour formed with ammonium molybdate is measured spectrophotometrically at 410 nm. The heteropoly blue method is more sensitive. Average level of silica in water is 1 to 30 mg/L it is removed from water by anion exchangers. In platinum crucible it is determined as SiO_2. With HF it forms H_2SiF_6 which is evaporated and difference in weight is measured to ascertain impurities Molybdosilicate method is photometric method for the analysis of silicon in range of 1 mg/L SiO_2 colour is measurable at 410 nm. The yellow sample is mixed with aminonapthol sulphonic acid to form hetropoly acid blue which is measured photometrically at 810 nm. In flow injection analysis molybdenum blue method is resorted as 5 to 50 mg/L of silica is analysed by this method. Nowadays ICP-AES is also used for such analysis if present at trace levels.

(f) Acidity and Alkalinity of Water

Acidity of water is the quantitive capacity to react with strong base at known pH. This is measure of aggregate property of water. Acid contributes to the corrosiveness, influences reaction rate and biological process. This is done by titration method. The titration gives a measure of the capacity of water to neutralise H^+ and is expressed in terms of equivalent amounts of $CaCO_3$. It is determined by titrating 50 ml of water with 0.02 N NaOH to pH 8.3 or 50 ml of H_2O with 0.02 N H_2SO_4 till a pH value of 4.5. Alkalinity is expressed as phenolphthalein and total alkalinity. During titration, CO_3^{2-} is converted to HCO_3^{2-} at pH 8.3. The end point at pH 8.3 is called *phenolphthalein alkalinity*. However, if same titration is continued further, HCO_3^{2-} reacts with acid to form H_2CO_3. The reaction is complete at pH 4.5. The amount of acid required to react is termed as *total alkalinity*. The alkalinity is expressed in terms of $CaCO_3$. While acidity originates due to dissolution of CO_2 from atmosphere, CO_2 is produced in water due to biological oxidation of organic matter. Mineral acidity is present in many industrial wastes. The salts of trivalent metals (*e.g.*, Fe, Al) hydrolyse to release mineral acidity. The mineral acidity is measured by titration to pH 4.5. When methyl orange is used as an indicator, it is called *methyl orange acidity*. The titration of sample to phenolphthalein end point of pH 8.3 is called *total acidity* or *phenolphthalein acidity*. This is also expressed in terms of $CaCO_3$. As $CaCO_3$ has equivalent weight of 50, N/50 NaOH when used give 1 ml = 1 mg of acidity in $CaCO_3$.

The alkalinity of water is acid neutralising capacity. It is the sum of all the titrable base. It is measure of aggregate property of water and is expressed in terms of specific substances with known chemical composition. Alkalinity gives information to decide mode of treatment of water. The acidity is expressed in terms of $CaCO_3$/ml as shown by following calculations:

$$\text{Acidity} = \frac{(a \times b) - (c \times d) \times 50{,}000}{\text{ml sample}}$$

If a = ml of NaOH, c = ml of H_2SO_4

b = Normality of NaOH d = Normality of sulphuric acid

While alkalinity is expressed as

$$\text{Alkalinity mg CaCO}_3\text{/L} = \frac{a \times b \times 5000}{\text{ml sample}}$$

If a = ml of a standard b = Normality of acid

While total alkalinity is expressed as

$$\text{Total alkalinity} = \frac{(2b - c)\, N \times 50{,}000}{\text{ml sample}}$$

If b = ml of titrant c = Total ml of titrant

N = Normality of acid.

(g) Salinity

It is important for industrial water. It is the measure of mass of dissolved salts in given volume of water. It is obtained by indirect method by measurement of the physical property like conductivity, density, sound speed or refractive index. Amongst physical parameters conductivity has better precision. The salinity dependence on conductivity (R) which is function of temperature to a standard. It is also measured by density method in preference to electrical conductivity method.

(h) Frequency of Analysis

In the chemical characterisation of water certain parameters like dissolved oxygen, BOD residual chlorine, pH, odour and bacteria are determined on the spot and immediately, while some aspects like hardness, Na, K, Ca, Mg, F, Cl, SO_4, colour, turbidity, specific conductance, alkalinity, dissolved solids can be determined at leisure in the laboratory. Nitrogen, ammonia, nitrate-nitrogen, suspended solids or heavy metals need addition of some preservative, before commencing analysis in laboratory. However, we use knowledge of chemical characterisation as demonstrated in Table 9.15, where a typical analysis of well water collected from city of Jorhat adjacent to Civil Hospital is given. This speaks about the quality of health of people in the region. The accepted standard for potable water indicating maximum, minimum and average limit of different constituents for various countries is presented in Table 9.16, knowing such characterisation is of extreme importance in deciding kind of water treatment process to be followed.

Table 9.15 Analysis of water sample from Jorhat (Assam)

Parameter	*Sample A (Surface)*	*Sample B (bottom of well)*	*Standard WHO*	*Remarks*
Colour	70 Hazen	70 Hazen	5 Hazen	Very high
Turbidity	75 JU	85 JU	5JU	Very high
pH	6.5	7.0	7.8–8.5	Slightly acidic
Hardness	105	110	100	Slightly high
Aluminium	0.3	0.2	1	Tolerable
Chromium	0.8	0.1	0.050	High
Iron	2.5	2.0	0.1	Very high
Manganese	0.5	0	0.05	Very high
Chloride	80	85	200	Tolerable
Fluoride	1.5	2.0	0.70	High
Nitrate	25	20	22.6	Slightly high
Dissolved oxygen	0	0	1.5	Worst

Table 9.16 Comparison of standards for drinking water stipulated by different standardising agencies

Parameter		*EEC-Europe*	*EPA-USA*	*Canada*	*France*	*India*	*Remarks u.r.l. India*
Dissolved solid	–	–	–	–	500	–	No standard
Colour	–	5	3–15	15	5	5	High
Turbidity	–	5	1–5	5	5	5	High
pH	–	6.5–8.5	–	6.5–8.3	7–8.5	7.0–8.5	Reasonable
Conductivity	–	400	–	–	2000	–	No standard
Hardness	–	35	–	18	–	100	Very High
Dissolved oxygen	–	5	–	–	1-1.5	–	Tolerable
Sulphate	200–400	5	250	500	250	200	Average OK
Chloride	–	5	250	250	200–600	200	Acceptable
Free chlorine	–	–	0.2–0.3	–	–	–	No standard
Nitrate	45	–	45	10	50–100	–	No standard
Cyanide	0.05	0.05	0.01–0.2	0.01–0.2	0.05	0.05	Acceptable
Fluoride	1.5	0.7–1.5	1.4–2.4	–	1.5	0.70–1.0	Reasonable
Ammonia	–	0.05	–	0.5	0.05	–	Reasonable
Boron	–	–	–	5	–	–	No standard
Phosphorus	–	0.3	–	0.002	–	–	No standard
Calcium	–	100	80–100	200	–	5	Good
Magnesium	–	30	80–100	150	–	30	Good
Silver	–	0.01	0.05	0.05	–	–	No standard
Arsenic	0.05	0.05	0.05	0.01–0.05	0.5	0.05	Good
Barium	–	0.1	1.0	1.0	–	–	No standard
Cadmium	0.01	0.005	0.01	0.01	0.005	0.01	Good
Chromium	0.05	0.05	–	–	–	–	No standard
Copper	–	0.05	0.2–1.0	1.0	0.05	0.05	Good
Iron	–	0.3	0.05–0.3	0.3	0.1	0.1	Acceptable
Mercury	0.001	0.001	0.002	0.05	0.01	0.001	Good
Manganese	–	0.05	0.01–0.05	–	0.05	0.05	Good
Nickel	–	0.05	–	–	–	–	No standard
Lead	0.1	0.05	0.05	0.05	0.05	0.1	Acceptable
Antimony	–	0.01	–	–	–	–	No standard
Selenium	0.01	0.01	0.001	0.01	0.01	0.01	Acceptable
Zinc	1.5–5.0	0.1–0.2	5	2	–	5	Slight High

9.6 IMPORTANT TRACE ELEMENTS IN WATER

Apart from sodium, potassium, calcium, iron, magnesium, manganese other elements are also encountered in the sample of water. The list includes aluminium, antimony, arsenic barium beryllium, bismuth, cadmium, caesium, chromium, copper, gold, iridium, lead, lithium, mercury, molybdenum, nickel, palladium, rhenium, selenium, silver, strontium, thallium, thorium, tin, titanium, vanadium, zinc. However of these elements only eight are commonly observed in drinking water hence only these elements from the point of quantative analysis shall be considered.

(a) Aluminum

Aluminium compounds are used as the coagulating agents to settle suspended impurities. The average levels 50 μg/L. In addition to AAS and ICP–AES it is possible to analyse it spectrophotometrically with eriochrome Cynine R or Solochrome cynine R-200 if aqueous solution is used. The coloured complex is measured spectrophotometrically 535 nm. PO_4^{3-} and F^- interfere hence they must be absent. In flow programming method pyrocatechol is used as the complexing ligand for aluminium.

(b) Arsenic

The presence of arsenic in drinking water in West Bengal specially in Damodar harbour area had created a havoc for the last few decades. In some parts of Bangladesh, there the rivers which contain good amount of arsenic in water. It is slow poison, causes vomiting, amount exceeding 10 mg/L is injurious to the health. It is carcinogenic in nature. AAS with hydride generator is used but, it is analysed by with silver diethyldithiocarbamate as extracting agent and measured at 535 nm spectrophotometrically.

(c) Barium

It stimulates muscles of heart. Our nerves get affected if dose is greater than 500 L/mg. Averge amount of barium in drinking water is 49 μg/L. The best method for analysis is AAS or ICP-AES. If the concentration is very large classical gravimetric or nephelometric analysis involving weighing as insoluble $BaSO_4$ is common.

(d) Cadmium

It causes a disease called *Iitai Iitai*. In Japan large number of people had suffered due to cadmium poisoning. It is a deadly cumulative poison and resides in our body for as much as eight years and it shows problems when body resistances is reduced in old age. Amount > 200 μg/L is toxic apart from AAS and ICP-AES extractive spectrophotometry involving dithizone as the chromogenic agent is used. The dithizone complex is extracted in chloroform and measured photometrically at 518 nm.

(e) Chromium

This is very carcinogenic in hexavalent state. Water is contaminated from tannery waste. Waste contains substantial amount of dichromate used for treating hide and leather. With AAS, and ICP-AES or by photometrically it is analysed with sym-diphenyl carbazide in hexavatent state at 540 nm. The molar absorptivity is 4×10^5 l/g/cm at 540 nm.

(f) Copper

In real sense copper is not toxic but in large dosages it causes problems with health. Copper compounds are used in drinking water to arrest biological growth and catalyse oxidation of manganese. Our health needs 1 mg/day of copper. Apart from AAS and ICP-AES it is determined by extractive photometry with neocuporine (I) and bathocuporine (III) at 457 nm and 484 nm respectively.

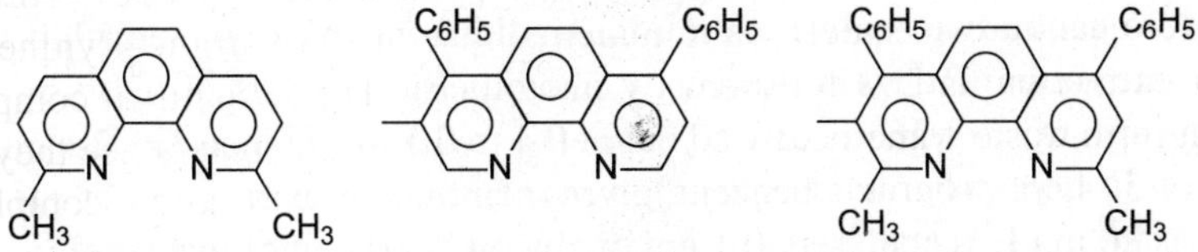

Neocuporine (I) Bathophenantnooline (II) Bathocuporine (III)

Fig. 9.3 Heterocyclic compounds

The copper complex with (I) is extracted in mixture of methanol; chloroform. The pH for complexation is 3.0 to 9.0 for analysis of Cu(I). $NH_2OH.HCl$ is used as reducing agent for reducing Cu(II) to Cu(I). The (Fig. 9.3) reagent (II) *viz.*, bathophenantnooline forms extractable complex with iron in chloroform and is selective in the presence if copper present in sample of water.

(g) Lead

Autoexhaust emission is main source of lead. It is cumulative poison (greater than 5 μg/L) is analysed with atomic absorbance or plasma spectroscopy but it is best analysed by extractive photometry with dithizone in chloroform at 510 nm as at pH 2.0 it forms extractable complex.

(h) Nickel

The best method for analysis of nickel is extractive spectrophotometry with heptoxime or dimethylglyoxime in chloroform. Heptoxime permits analysis in aqueous medium at 445 nm but chloroform is used in the presence of copper and iron. Dimethylglyoxime develops fast colour within few minutes. It is measurable at 445 nm photometrically.

(i) Silver

It causes *argyria i.e.*, permanent blue grey discoloration of the skin and eyes which gives bad appearance. Dose of 0.4 to 1 mg/L is injurious to health specially for kidney, liver, spleen. The compound in small dose is used to disinfect swimming pools. Apart from absorption in emission spectroscopy the extractive photometry with dithizone is best method for analysis of silver. Since silver dithizone complex degrades in sunlight, one must avoid excessive exposure to sunlight to arrest photochemical degradation. The dithizone complex is extracted in carbon tetrachloride and measured at 620 or 460 nm by mixed colour technique.

(j) Zinc

It is essential element for human growth. Amounts greater than 5 mg/L in potable water causes bitter astringent taste and opalescence in alkaline waters.

Galvanisation and rayon industry waste water releases considerable amount of zinc. Apart from atomic absorption and emission spectroscopy extractive photometry with dithizone or modified method or zincon method are standard methods for quantitative analysis. A minimum dithizone in carbon tetrachloride is taken for extraction and its followed by photometric analysis at 620 nm. Zinc extraction from waste water is carried out at 0.4 to 0.5 ml. Zincon *i.e.,* 2-carboxy-2' hydroxy-5' sulphopharmyl benzene gives quantitative extrauction at pH~9.0. As small as 20 mg/L is analysed. 0.1 gm of zincon in 100 ml of methanol in used. Cyclohexane is used as the solvent where it dissociates zinc cyanide complex which in turn is recovered from effluents. The absorbance is measured at 620 nm. but copper strongly interferes.

9.7 BIOLOGICAL INVESTIGATION OF WATER

Apart from direct bacteriological examination, indirect proof for the presence of microorganism and biodegradable organic matter can be ascertained from the knowledge of dissolved oxygen (DO) and biochemical oxygen demand (BOD) of water.

(a) Dissolved Oxygen in Water

All living organisms are dependent upon dissolved oxygen to maintain the metabolic process which produces energy for growth and reproduction. N_2 and O_2 dissolve poorly in water, but their solubility increases with temperature (Henry's law). At saturation, dissolved oxygen is 38 per cent oxygen. The solubility is 14.6 mg/litre at 0°C and it decreases to 7 mg/litre at 35°C at one atmospheric pressure. The rate of dissolution of O_2 in polluted water is much less in comparison to pure water. DO determines whether biological changes are brought out by aerobic or anaerobic organisms. Former uses free oxygen for oxidation to produce innocuous end products. DO is one single test to indicate how aquatic life is supported; as all aerobic processes depend upon DO. The sample of water for DO analysis is collected in outdoor fields. The dissolved oxygen from water is determined by Winkler's method. The important reactions are as follows:

$$MnSO_4 + 2KOH \longrightarrow Mn(OH)_2 + K_2SO_4$$

$$2Mn(OH)_2 + O_2 \longrightarrow 2MnO(OH)_2 \text{ (basic hydroxide)}$$

$$MnO(OH)_2 + 2H_2SO_4 \longrightarrow Mn(SO_4)_2 + 3H_2O$$

$$Mn(SO_4)_2 + 2KI \longrightarrow MnSO_4 + K_2SO_4 + I_2$$

$$2Na_2S_2O_3 + I_2 \longrightarrow 2NaI + Na_2S_4O_6$$

The manganese hydroxide is oxidised to basic manganic hydroxide by dissolved oxygen. This manganic hydroxide in turn is converted to manganic sulphate which in turn reacts with KI to liberate free iodine, which is titrated against standard solution of thiosulphate with starch as indicator. The amount of iodine consumed represents the dissolved oxygen present in water. The oxidising agents in water produce, positive error, while the reducing agents produce negative error. NO_2^-,

Fe^{3+} can oxidise I^- to I_2^0 and show high results; also reducing agents like Fe^{2+}, SO_3^{2-} or S^{2-} show negative results, as they reduce I_2^0 to I^-. The Winklers reaction is given in ionic form as follows:

$$Mn^{2+} + 2OH^- \longrightarrow Mn(OH)_2$$
$$Mn^{2+} + 2OH^- + 1/2\ O_2 \longrightarrow MnO_2 + H_2O$$
$$(\text{or } Mn\ (OH)_2 + 1/2\ O_2 \longrightarrow MnO_2 + H_2O)$$
$$MnO_2 + 2I^- + 4H+ \longrightarrow Mn^{2+} + I_2 + 2H_2O$$
$$2Na_2S_2O_3 + I_2 \longrightarrow 2NaI + Na_2S_4O_6$$

If excess of nitrite is present in water then method needs modifications by Ashlery Winkler's method called *Azide modification*. It involves the addition of azide to destroy nitrite as the reaction proceeds:

$$2NO_2^- + 2I^- + 4H^+ \longrightarrow I_2 + N_2O_2 \uparrow + 2H_2O$$
$$N_2O_2 + 1/2\ O_2 + H_2O \longrightarrow 2NO_2^- + 2H^+ \uparrow$$

Such interference is eliminated by addition of sodiumazide (NaN_3) in modified method

$$NaN_3 + H^+ \longrightarrow HN_3 + Na$$
$$HN_3 + NO_2^+ + H^+ \longrightarrow N_2(g) + N_2O \uparrow + H_2O$$

Thereby, nitrite interference is eliminated. The Rideal-Stewart modification eliminates many interference caused by reducing agents. $KMnO_4$ is used for pretreatment. Excess of $KMnO_4$ is removed with $K_2C_2O_4$ *e.g.*,

$$5NO_2^- + 2MnO_4^- + 6H^+ \longrightarrow 5NO_3^- + 2\ Mn^{2+} + 3H_2O$$
$$5Fe^{2+} + MnO_4^- + 8H^+ \longrightarrow 5Fe+3 + Mn^{2+} + 4H_2O$$

then $5\ (COO)_2^- + 2MnO_4^- + 16H^+ \longrightarrow 10CO_2 + 2Mn^{2+} + 8H_2O$

After this treatment, regular Winkler's reaction is carried out. Apart from Winkler's method, modern trend is to use DO meter or ion analyser with ion specific electrode for dissolved oxygen. Ion-chromatograph is also useful.

Table 9.17 pH and reduction potentials (V) (E_H) of water

S.No.	*Source of water*	*pH and quality*	*E_H (V) reduction potential*
1.	Rain waters	5.0 (Acid)	0.55 V
2.	Stream waters	6.0 (near neutral)	0.40V
3.	Ground waters	9.0 (alk)	– 0.15
4.	Mine waters	4.0 (Acid)	0.60
5.	Ocean-Sea water	9.0 (alk)	– 0.30
6.	Soiled water	3.0 (acid)	– 0.10
7.	Saline (organic) water	9.0 (alk)	– 0.40

The Table 9.17 indicates the reduction potential at specific pH. One observation is as more is dissolved oxygen present in water better would be the quality of water with good purity.

The dissolved oxygen (DO) content substantially changes with pH of sample of water. The DO of weakly acidic water is high (~ 0.55 X in terms of H^+ ion potential) one never consumes water which is distinctly alkaline as is encountered in seawater or estuaries. A notion or the misconcept that the rainwater is pure is not always correct as rain pours down on precipitation on its way downwards it dissolves suspended material from atmosphere and gets contaminated. The alkaline water has always low level of dissolved oxygen as is reflected in it reduction potential (*viz.* –0.15, –0.30 or –0.40) S.Nos. 3, 5, 7 in the Table 9.17.

The analysis of DO is key test in water pollution. The interfering Fe (II) can be eliminated by $KMnO_4$ as shown above in modified method. To get best results sample of water should not be excessively agitated. DO analysis must be carried out immediately. Azide modification is must if the water contains nitrogen in the range of more than 50 mg/L of nitrite. On an average at room temperature water has DO of 6.9 mg/L. It is 12 mg/L at 0°C while at 50°C its less than 4.39 mg/L.

Table 9.18 BOD of typical samples of water

Type of sample	*BOD, mg/litre*	*Remarks*
Pure water	1.0–3.0	Reasonable
River	5.0–20.0	Tolerable
Sewage	50.0–100	Very bad
Industrial waste	100–10,000	Extremely poor

The ferric ion interference is elminated by addition of KF and sodium azide but is ineffective for oxidation of reducing agents *e.g.*, SO_3^2, $S_2O_3^{2-}$ polythionate. The samples high in suspended solids need alum flocculation modification for coagulation. In presence of active sludge in effluent, copper sulphate-sulphuric acid modification is needed. The membrane electrode method is best method for the continuous measurement. Membrane electrodes are used for DO analysis in outdoor fields of polluted water. In such devise diffusion current is measured. Polyethylene or fluorocarbon memberane are commonly used. It represents high temperature coefficient log $\phi = (0.43\ mt + b - 1)$ if t = temperature, m = constant for membrae, b = constant related to thickness of membrane while ϕ represents electrode sensitivity. The accuracy of the method is around $\pm$ 0.05 mg/L DO.

(b) Biochemical Oxygen Demand

BOD is defined as the amount of oxygen required by bacteria while stabilizing decomposable organic matter under aerobic conditions. BOD represents quantity of dissolved oxygen in mg/litre required during oxidation of decomposable or biodegradable organic matter by aerobic biochemical action of bacteria. The decomposable organic matter at a time serves as the food for bacteria and this energy is obtained due to such oxidation. BOD gives an idea about the extent of pollution. It serves as a test to evaluate the purifying capacity of receiving bodies of water. BOD test is a bioassay test devised to measure oxygen consumed by living organisms, while using organic matter present in waste water. The samples are protected from sunlight, from excessive agitation and is kept at a fixed temperature in an incubator. This favours uniform bacterial growth. To complete such growth 20 hours are required. BOD test is a wet oxidation procedure. A 5-day BOD_5 test provides a reliable information on quality of water. Two 300 ml of sterilised bottles are filled with water and dissolved oxygen of first bottle is determined immediately by Winkler's method. The second bottle is incubated under 20°C in the dark for 5 days (sometimes 3 days; or need to keep it for 20 days in order to get a complete picture) and dissolved oxygen is once again measured. The reduction in oxygen content is due to demand exerted by the microbiological population and is a measure of oxidisable organic matter present in sample value of 5-day BOD. The DO varies from 9.2 to 1.0 mg/litre showing 8.2 mg/L as BOD value. Typical pH values of different samples of water are listed in Table 9.17. The reduction potential is indicated in last column while BOD of various kinds of water is given in Table 9.18.

The consolidated study of various hydrological parameters of Ulhas river in Bombay are given in Table 9.19. A typical illustration is for Fig. 9.1, p. 230 for various lakes around city of Mumbai.

Table 9.19 Water quality parameters of Ulhas river at different sampling stations in Mumbai

Station numer	*pH*	*DO mg/litre*	*NO_2^- mg/litre*	*PO_4^{2-} mg/litre*	*SO_3^- mg/litre*
1	7.8	4.8	0.9	0.09	2.8
2	7.8	4.1	0.4	0.09	2.9
3	8.0	4.3	0.7	0.08	2.7
4	7.4	3.7	2.0	0.05	2.1
5	7.5	4.2	2.1	0.08	2.3
6	7.6	3.1	1.8	1.10	2.9
7	7.6	3.6	1.1	0.05	2.5
8	7.4	3.6	0.8	—	2.7
9	7.3	3.2	4.8	0.06	2.1
10	7.3	2.8	2.7	0.06	2.2
11	7.3	1.9	3.7	—	2.8
12	7.4	2.2	3.2	0.04	2.1
13	7.2	2.8	3.1	0.05	2.2

The bacterial population grows logarithmically. The danger of damage to the ecosystem is great due to lowering of oxygen level. If system becomes anoxic anaerobic bacteria will take over leading to formation of CH_4, H_2S, NH_3. Mercury becomes toxic due to its conversion to Hg $(CH_3)_4$ by the bacteria. BOD account for chemical and biological transformation in water. BOD infact is defined as quantity of oxygen used by bacteria in the process of aerobic decomposition of organic matter. Initial loss is due to carbaceous oxygen demand after 8 days. The nitrosomnas exert measurable oxygen demand. Sulphur bacteria also demand oxygen (Fig. 9.4). Average value is 1 mg/L primary and secondary treatment of effluents reduces oxygen demand. The combined sewers demand also increases BOD value. The proximity of dairy or food industry increase BOD of surface water.

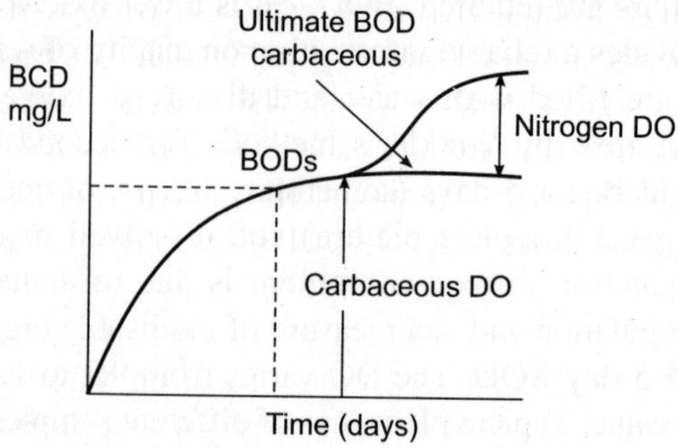

Fig. 9.4 BOD graph

Table 9.20 Technique for biological examination

S. No.	*Bacteria*	*Technique*	*S. No.*	*Bacteria*	*Technique*
1.	Total Coliforma	Membrane filtration also MPN	5.	Iron-crenthroxine	Microscopic examination
2.	Fecal Coliforma	Membrane, MPN	6.	Sulphur bacteria	Microscopic examination
3.	Streptococcus	Membrane MPN	7.	Actynomycetes	Plate count
4.	Heterotropic count	Pour plate method	8.	Klebsiella	Membrane filter

The greatest problem in maintaining quality of water is not only organic/inorganic impurities but also various kinds of microorganisms present in water (Table 9.20). The organisms like Coliforma, streptococus are commonly present. There are also iron and sulphur carrying bacterias which are detected only by microscope.

There are several methods for removed of these bacteria from water. The MPN count or most probable number is the quantitive parameter to categorise the sample of water. The methods of treatment include use of membrane filter, pour plate technique, but microscopic examination gives reliable MPN count for water sample drawn from lakes or river. The water is classified on basis of MPN count (see Table 9.21).

9.8 MICROBIOLOGICAL EXAMINATION OF WATER

The disease producing organism, *i.e.,* or pathogens must be removed from water. Those producing infectious diseases like typhoid or cholera are called viruses. The common indicator organisms are from coliforma group present due to sewage contamination. By special test, their number is determined. Faecal coliforms and faecal *Streptococci* are also isolated. They are determined for their population expressed in terms of MPN, *i.e.,* most probable number. For example, for untreated water, coliforma density should not exceed 5000/ml. Table 9.20 list other kinds of bacteria which are present in water under special circumstances. The MPN or plate count throws good light on the quality of water. It is therefore necessary to undertake a thorough microbiological examination of water to detect presence of coliforma faecal *Streptococcus* actiomyetes, pathogenic bacteria, enteric viruses fungi, protozoa in sample of potable water. The presence of coliforma bacteria gives idea about the quality of water. It is given in the form of MPN count. It is an index of coliform bacteria present. Membrane filter count per 100 ml is also another criteria to judge the quality of water. Faecal *strepococci* are also indicators of level of the pollution of water. The heterotropic plate count gives an idea of total number of viable bacteria in water. It provides information on efficiency of water treatment process. The sample of the water should be representative of whole bulk. WHO has set international standard for drinking water. During analysis the apparatus should be sterilised at 170°C for 60 minutes. This covers mainly sample bottles. The dehydrated media is stored at 30°C with low humidity in air. The cultured media must be used within a week. One must avoid exposure to sunlight. Chlorine from chlorinated water must be removed. Commercially available liquid media is convenient to use. Sodium thiosulphate is used as dechlorinating agent. The examination should be done within 60 minutes of collection of the sample. For fast analysis seven hour fecal coliforma test is carried out. Agar is used as media which can be prepared in laboratory as it contain yeast, polypetone, lactose manitol, common salt, sodium lauryl sulphate and indicator *viz.* phenol red.

Table 9.21 Classification of water on basis of MPN count

S.No.	*Class*	*Fecal Coliforma counts per 100 ml sample of water*
1.	I	MPN < 200 (recommended), > 400 bad. 5 samples tested during a month > 800 worst
2.	II	MPN < never it exceeds > 800 in one day
3.	III	MPN ≥ 200 per month, results from ten samples in a month

The Table 9.21 gives quantitive picture of the quality of water in terms of MPN count. The count for feccal coliforma is reliable and it provides reliable measure in ascertaining the quality of water. The MPN count of < 200 is considered to be acceptable figure. While the MPN count of > 800 is considered to be serious contamination of water. All are calculated on the basis of one litre (1000 ml) of water.

Water is filtered through membrane filter and mixed with media. It is incubated at 41.5°C for 7 hours and then yellow faecal coliforma on colony on microscope counted. Coliphage counts is equally beneficial to give idea of faecal coliforma speciality if water is heavily chlorinated. In specially prepared media, stressed bacteria do not grow, as due to chlorination or presence of heavy metals. The heterotropic (HPC) plate count is very useful. It is also called as *Standard plate count*. It gives idea of live bacteria and change in their number after water treatment. Pour plate method is simple and common, for which incubation is at 35 to 40°C in agar media for 48 hours. Membrane filter is other reliable method. pH should be 7.0. One must use Qubec colony counter for plate counting. This is done by multiple tube procedure. Coliforma are defined as gram-negative nonspore forming rods that ferment lactose with evolution of gas at 35ºC within 48 hours. Membrane filter produce red colony in 24 hours. Now we consider various types of microorganism and their characteristics.

(a) Faecal Streptococcus Count

It consists of number of species which give positive reaction. It grows in human intestine. It gives idea about human contamination of water. Its presence indicates human contamination. Multiple tube technique is also used for counting at pH 7.2 at 25ºC. The membrane filtration technique is used with advantage.

(b) Iron and Sulphur Bacteria

Their presence gives rise to slime in water. Both cause fouling and plugging of wells and distribution system, while sulphur bacteria cause rusty water and tuberculation of pipes. Sulphur bacteria reduce SO_4^{2-} to sulphides in water and promotes corrosion with green or purple in colour.

(c) Actinomycetes

Earth musky odour is objectionable. It is volatile metabolites. It is not fungi but filamentous branching bacteria.

(d) Pathogenic Bacteria

These are enteric microorganisms, which mainly cause water born diseases *e.g.* Salmonellae are common in water. Its contents varies from sample to sample. Swab techniques is used for counting. For detection of Salmonella, immuno-fluoroscene technique is used. They are quantitatively analysed. 'Shigella' occurs in polluted water. *Escherichia coli* is detected in digestive track, causing disease. With *E-coli*, causing diarrhoea, vibrio cholerae is etiological agent of cholera. The occurrance of pathogenic leptospires is rare and variable Legionellaceae occur during outbreak of disease. They are transmitted through air. Yersinia also causes gasterointestine disorders. The Table 9.23 list the water born disease producing living organs.

(e) Enteric Viruses

It is found in sewage and disease of liver *e.g.*, hepatitis. It is excreted by infected person. It multiplys within body of person.

(f) Fungi in Water

It includes yeast and filamentous species or moulds with organised nucleii and rigid walls. It is parasitic soil fungi and is most common. It is indicator of pollution. It is detected in the warmer water to indicate thermal pollution. It is aerobic or the microaerophile. It is estimated by pour plate spread technique. Plate and membrane filter technique are other means of detection of fungi. It is classed as zooaporic fungi, aquatic hyphomycetes.

(g) Pathogenic Protozoa

It causes digestic disorder. Giardia is identified etiologic agent of water borne outbreaks. It causes cholera like diarrhoea. Giardia lamblia is in cyst stage with lifetime of two months at 8°C. Enterhomoeba histolytica is also found in potable water by contamination with sewage from pipes.

(h) Plankton, Periphyton, Macrophyton, Bentric Macrointerverbate

Plankton, periphyton, macrophyton, bentric and macrointerverbate are of less importance for man. Their main use is to know turbidity of water, presence of biological form to oxygen; source of water identification, clogging of pipes, effectiveness of water treatment plants; study of biological pollution, self purification phenomena provides data of any aquatic system.

Table 9.22 Kind of decay

Reaction	*Compounds containing*	*Aerobic decay*	*Anaerobic decay*
(*i*)	C	CO_2	CH_4 CO_2
-	P	H_3PO_4	PH_3
(*ii*)	N	NH_3 NO_3^-	NH_2 and amines
(*iii*)	S	SO_4^{2-} SO_3^{2-}	H_2S

$$(i)\ CH_2O + O_2 \longrightarrow CO_2 \uparrow + H_2O + \text{Energy}$$

$$(ii)\ 5CH_2O + 4NO_2 \longrightarrow 2N_2 + CO_2 \uparrow + 4HCO_3^- + 3H_2O$$

$$(iii)\ 2CH_2O + SO_4^{2-} \longrightarrow H_2S \uparrow + 2HCO_3^-$$

9.9 WATER POLLUTION AND DISEASES

Water-born diseases arise due to untreated water or its contamination with sewage. Pathogenic bacteria are main source of epidemic diseases like cholera, typhoid fever, or dysentery, paratyphoid, fever. Fortunately, 90% of bacterial population dies off within 48 hours. Coliforma bacteria such as *Escherichia Coli* (*i.e.*, *E.coli*) and *Streptococcus* are most common (~50 millions per gm). The bacteria are classified in three groups (*i*) Coces-round cell (*ii*) curved spirilla (*iii*) rod shaped species. They are gram-negative. Non-pathogenic bacteria are used as pollution indicators. On an average effluents have 3-million coliforma per 100 ml water. For testing membrane filters are best where water is drawn through membrane (millpore 0.43/mm filter) using vacuum pump. The bacteria are collected on membrane which in turn is incubated with media. On dilution colonies are counted by microscope. The bacteria are of two types *viz.*, 'heterotrophys'. They use organic matter as source of energy. We have aerobic bacteria and facultative bacteria. The decomposition of organic matter proceed as shown in Table 9.22. These are typical decay reactions as indicated in various chemical equations.

(a) Algae

It has planktonic form, it is autotrophic (generate their own food). Algae bloom is rapid. Cyanophyta is blue-green algae. It is microscopic in nature. It imparts bad taste to the water.

(b) Pathogens

Viral infection is caused by viruses. These are ultramicroscopic. Infective hepatitis is serious enteric disease. Salmonella causes gasteroenteritis or typhoid. Shigellosis causes bacillary dysentery. Leptospirosis originates from accumulated puddle of water due to animal contamination.

(c) Viral Infection

Viruses are intracellular parasites. It cannot reproduce and is ultramicroscopic. Enteric viruses is grouped into four classes as are polyviruses coxsackie A, coxscakie B, and Echoviruses in water. They cause meningitis – a disease of brain. The adenoviruses causes respiratory problem while rotaviruses causes gastro-enteritis. Then hepatitis viruses cause infective hepatitis. Insufficient sunlight, cold weather and absence of oxygen promotes their growth. They are excreted by the infected persons and contaminate water supplies. Their lifetime in water is less man 20 days.

(d) Bacterial Infection

They are large in size hence are filtered. Salmonella cause typhoid fever. The developing countries have no problems of viruses. Shigellosis causes dysentery. Cholera is caused by vibriocholera, vibrio vulnificux. It affects liver or causes impaired immune system.

(e) Protozoa Infection

The amoebic dysentery is caused by them. The species is *'Entamoeba bistulytica'*. The cyst is carrier; it is resistant to chlorination but it is filtrable. Maleria producing protozoa are 'larva' which breed in stagnant water.

(f) Worm Infection

These parasitic worms reside in water. Trematoda and Cestoda are few organisms amongst them. Nematoda is another class of parasites, it is 'roundworm'. Principle of competitive exclusion does not allow some kind species in water as they cannot exist in similar environment.

(g) Water Hyacinthis

It is actually *"Eichhornia crassipes"*. Phosphorus compounds multiples its cultivation in lakes. No soil is needed for their growth. They absorb toxic metals.

They spread malaria and spoil appearance of the lake. The chemicals like TFM (3 trifluoromethyl) 4-nitrophenol (~ 3-9 ppm dose) and lampricide (5, 2 dichlor, 4 nitro salicyal nitride) are used to control larva growth in lakes. It has done well in Tankbund in Hyderabad but not Powai in Bombay.

9.10 WATER BORNE DISEASES

Most of the problems associated with the digestive system are caused by many kind of organisms, pathogens, viruses. It is clearly depicted in Table 9.23. The main source of the water born microorganism originates from human food feccus, excreta and sewage. Table 9.24 shows microorganisms contribute the spread of pollution. It shows both men and animals are responsible for causing pollution. One caused by human beings is shown in Table 9.25.

Table 9.23 Water born diseases

S.No.	*Microorganism*	*Name of disease*	*Incubation period*	*Symptoms*
1.	Hepatitis A	Hepatitis	15–45 days	Fever, Jaundice, anorexia
2.	Rotavirus	Gastroenteritis	1–2 days	Vomiting, diarrhea
3.	Lamblia	Giardsis	7–10 days	Cramps, Flatulence, odours, diarrhea
4.	Entamoeba	Amebiasis Dysentry diarrhea	2–4 wks	mild diarrhea with blood and mucus dysentry, fever and chills
5.	Virus-27	Gastroenteritis	1–7 days	Vomiting, diarrhea, fever
6.	Norwalk	Gastroenteritis	1–7 days	Cramp, headache, fever, vomiting

Table 9.24 Water born microorganism

S.No.	*Name*	*Source*	*Illustration*	*Control process*	*Effect of dis-infection*	*Size Å*
1.	Viruses	Occurring in both Human, Animals presenting in food	Hepatitis Rotaostrorses	Resistant to UV light radiation	Resistant to ozonolysis	0.1–1.0
2.	Bacteria	Food, Human animal excreta	Salmonella, E.coli and Vibro-cholerae (Chlora)	Resistant to process of chlori-nation	Inert form of species	2–3
3.	Protozoa	Human, animal sewage decaying matter	Giardia, Amoeba	Sedimination, filtration slow sand	Resistant to any treatment	1–20

Table 9.23 shows various names of disease caused by various pathogens while Table 9.24 indicates kind of microorganism present in polluted sample of water which are capable of spreading diseases like Hepatitis, Amoebiasis Giardias, gastro intestinal forma. All diseases have varying incubation period the minimum one and maximum (30) days period being shown in S. No. 1 in Table 9.23 in order to show early symptoms of disease. All are leading to water born diseases creating very serious problems with digestive system, involving Liver. However with advancement in the science of medicine almost all diseases are easily cured within 6–8 weeks time with good rest.

The pathogens are one which must be removed from potable water. For instance Table 9.25 list several pathogens which are passed through by human beings. Amoeba, Gastric problems producing pathogens are injurious.

Table 9.25 Pathogens which are passed through by human being in water

S.No.	*Organism*	*Name of disease*	*S.No.*	*Organism*	*Name of disease*
1.	Entamoeba hystolinea	Amoebic dysentry	8.	Giardia instentianal	Giardia
2.	Hepatic A virus	Hepatitis	9.	E-coli forma	Gastroentritis
3.	Salmonella typhoid	Typhoid fever	10.	Vibro para-tiacmolytias	Gastro problem
4.	Balanitidum coli	Balontidiasis	11.	Polio virus	Polymyelits
5.	Versina entero-colitica	Gastric trouble	12.	Campylobacter fens	Gastroentritis
6.	Salomonella species	Gastric problem	13.	Shigella species	Bacillary dysenty
7.	Vibrio Cholorae	Cholera	14.	Yersinia entrocolitica	Gastric trouble

Table 9.26 Effect on water by pollutants

S.No.	*Source*	*Their Effect*	*Remarks*
1.	Heated water	Dissolved oxygen is reduced	Causes thermal pollution
2.	Plant nutrients	Gives offensive odour and bad taste	PO_4^{3-}, NO_3^- must be removed
3.	Organic waste	Rise in value of BOD	Anerobic degradation
4.	Pathogenic organism	Several diseases are caused	Hepatitis caused
5.	Sediments, soil	Oxygen and light exposure is prevented	can carry organisms with several diseases
6.	Radioactive waste	Cancer, hereditary diseases	Increase Vai Food chain
7.	Inorganics waste	Increase salinity, renders it toxic	Removal favourable
8.	Pesticides	Cancer, nerve damage, cause hereditary disease	Nondegradable, spread through food chain

Thus Table 9.26 indicates the effect on water by pollutants of various nature. The plant nutrients, pesticides, pathogenic organism are responsible for all kind of water born diseases affecting seriously human health.

In order to conform to best standards of water. It is imperative we adhere to international standards specially for drinking water. The United States environmental protection agencies (US-EPA) have stipulated and prescribed certain standards which must be strictly followed by both advanced and developing countries. Such EPA standards given in Table 9.27 which can be easily practised by Municipal Corporation.

Table 9.27 EPA Standards

S. No.	*Maximum Permissible limit mg/L*	*Removal by*	*Contaminant*	*Formula*
1.	4.0	Ion exchange; Revers Osmosis; (RO)	Fluoride	F^-
2.	1.0	Ion exchange; (RO)	Nitrite	NO_2^-
3.	10	Ion exchange; (RO)	Nitrate	NO_3^-
4.	0.2	Ion exchange, RO, Chlorination process	Cyanide	CN^-
5.	0.002	0.0005, Alumina, ion exchange	Thallium	Tl^{3+}
6.	0.1	Reverse Osmosis Coagul. ion exch., Lime softening process	Chromium	Cr^{3+}
7.	0.005	Reverse Osmosis coagul, ion exch., Lime softening	Cadmium	Cd^{2+}
8.	10	No. special method	Total Nitrogen	N^0
9.	0.005	Activate carbon; aeration	Benzene	C_6H_6
10.	1.0	Activated carbon; aeration	Tolyene	$(C_6H_5)(CH_3)$
11.	10	Activated carbon; aeration	Xylene	$(C_6H_4)(CH_3)_2$
12.	0.07	Activated carbon; treatment	2-4 D herbicides	–
13.	3×10^{-8}	Activated carbon; treatment	2,3,7,8 TCDD	–
14.	0.002	Aeration in tower	Vinyl Chloride	–
15.	0.005	Aeration, activated carbon	Trichloro ethylene	–
16.	0.010	Chemical treatment process	Bromate	BrO_3^-
17.	–	Special treatment	Bromoform	$CHBr_3$
18.	1.0	Special process	Chloride	$CHCl_3$
19.	0.060	Coagul; activated carbon, Lime Softening process	Halo acctic acid	CH_3COO X
20.	0.080	Coagulation, acti carbon, Lime softening process	Trihalo methane	–
21.	40	Coagulation, filtration, oxid. disinfection, treatment	Coliform	–
22.	–	Speciality designed filtration	Viruses	–
23.	30	Coagul; ion exchange; Lime softening; Reverse Osmosis	Uranium	U^{6+}
24.	5	Ion exch; Lime softening, Reverse Osmosis	Radium 228	Ra^{6+}
25.	1.0	Membrane Filtration	Turbidity	–

The comparison of these EPA standards with those given by WHO, ISI (India), ICMR (Indian Council of Medical Research) show most of them are very close to each other as shown in Table 9.28.

While the Table 9.28 defines separate standards for the presence of inorganic impurities as well as organic compounds present in water.

We have close look at primary and secondary standards. Such standards are listed in Table 9.30 for the inorganic as well organic compounds.

One observation is common. Whether one uses water for drinking or industrial purposes it must conform to universally given standards. The developing countries should not compromise on the standards at the cost of human health. Unfortunately this is not done and therefore we have various kind of diseases in the world many of them are fatal.

In Table 9.24 one can locate all water borne microorganism. Such as Amoeba, Salomenella, E. coli form and vibro chlora. They are one which promote spreading of diseases like dysentry, diarrhea and similar diseases. All these are called water born diseases which are causing very serious health problem. Hepatitis (A, B) is disease of liver which unfortunately is not easily curable. The size of microorganism varies from 0.1–2 Å and disinfection process like chlorination, ozonolysis, ultraviolet radiation kills these microorganisms within 48 hours of life cycle. Protozoa is one which is immune and resist to any kind of treatment. They are passed through the slow sand filtration in order to remove most of the bacteria from water.

Table 9.28 Comparison of water quality standard

S.No.	*Element present*	*WHO standard (μg/L)*	*ICMR standard*	*ISI Standard*	*Average threshold limit mg/ml*
1.	Chromium (cr)	50	–	0.05	–
2.	Zinc (Zn)	–	–	5.0 mg/L	–
3.	Lead (Pb)	10	–	0.10 mg/L	0.10
4.	Arsenic (As)	10	–	0.05 mg/L	0.05
5.	Selenium (Se)	10	–	0.01 mg/L	0.01
6.	Cadmium (Cd)	3.0	–	0.01 mg/L	0.01
7.	Mercury (Hg)	1.0	–	0.001 mg/L	0.001
8.	Manganese (Mn)	–500	0.1	0.1 mg/L	0.5
9.	Iron (III) Fe	300	0.1	0.3 mg/L	1.50
10.	Copper (II) Cu	2000	0.05	0.05	1.5
11.	Magnesium (II) Mg	–	50 mg/L	0.3	100
12.	Calcium (II) Ca	–	75	75	200
13.	Chlorides (Cl)	250	200	250	200
14.	Sulphate (SO_4)	250	200	150	1000
15.	Nitrate (NO_3)	50	20	45	–
16.	Fluoride (*F*)	1.5	1.0	0.5–1.2	15
17.	Cyanide (CN^-)	70	–	0.05	0.002

There are very efficient methods to get rid off pathogens from potable water. Thus Table 9.25 shows the kind of water borne organisms, pathogens or virus causing serious health problems. Apart from problems with Liver, (of Hepatitis,

Jaundice, Cirrhosis) in addition we have fever producing pathogens like salmonella typhoid; Entamoeba hystolinea. In several parts of India the water carries these pathogen on account of lack of hygiene and education. One notices symptoms leading to fatality with pathogen/virsus or typhoid fever, cholera, polio (by Polymyelitis). In fact water purification should get highest priority in Public Health Department by Municipal Corporation.

Apart from pathogen viruses, bacterias present in water. Table 9.26 shows other sources which constituents sediments, radioactive waste, insecticides or pesticides in large does and plant nutrients. In water they produces all kinds of health problem (see last column) of Table 9.26. It is absolutely necessary to give efficient water treatment process by Municipal Corporation before its distribution in the cities or towns.

Table 9.29 Water parameters hydrological parameter

S.No.	*Element present*	*WHO standard*	*ICMR standard*	*ISI standard*	*Average threshold limit mg/ml*
1.	Colour (Hazen unit)	–	5	10	25
2.	Odour	1:3 dil.	No smell	No smell	Zero
3.	Turbidity	5 NTU	5 NTU	10 NTU	25 NTU
4.	Dissolved Solids (TDS)	–	500	500 mg/L	1500
5.	pH	6.5–10	7.0–8.5	6.5–8.5	6.5–9.2
6.	Hardness as $CaCO_3$	70	300	300 mg/L	600
7.	Phenols (Aromatic)	–	0.001	0.001	600
8.	PAH (poly-nuclear aromatic hydrocarbons)	0.40	–	–	–
9.	α-emitters	–	–	10–8 (micro curie)	3 microcurie
10.	β-emitters	–	–	10–7 μc/ml	30 picocurie
11.	Colour	15			

Table 9.30 Primary standards for inorganic and organic compounds

S.No.	*Primary standard for inorganics*	*mg/L*	*S.No.*	*Primary standard for organics*	*mg/L*
1.	Barium	1.0 (Ba)	11.	Benzene	0.05
2.	Chromium	0.05 (Cr)	12.	Vinyl chloride	0.002
3.	Silver	0.05 (Ag)	13.	Carbon tetrachloride	0.005
4.	Arsenic	0.05 (As)	14.	1-2 dichloroethane	0.005
5.	Selenium	0.01 (Se)	15.	Lindane	0.004
6.	Lead	0.05 (Pb)	16.	Endrine	0.0002
7.	Cadmium	0.01 (Cd)	17.	Methoxychlor	0.10
8.	Mercury	0.002 (Hg)	18.	Tri chloroethylene	0.0005
9.	Nitrate-nitrogen	10.0 (NO_3–N)	19.	p-Dichloro benzene	0.075
10.	Fluoride	4.0 (F^-)	20.	Trichloroethane	0.10

The Table 9.27 shows water standards stipulated by environmental protection agencies of United States of America. The table indicates maximum permissible limit of contaminants in water, while Table 9.28 shows comparison of water standards prescribed by Indian standard institute, EPA and ICMR.

Table 9.31 Secondary standard for inorganic and hydrologic parameter

S.No.	*Element/ion*	*Level mg/L*	*S.No.*	*Element/ion*	*Level*
1.	Copper $(Cu)^{2+}$	1.0	8.	Corrosivity	Zero
2.	Iron $(Fe)^{3+}$	0.3	9.	Foaming property	0.5 mg/L
3.	Manganese $(Mn)^{2+}$	0.05	10.	Hardness	0.3 mg/L
4.	Zinc $(Zn)^{2+}$	5.0	11.	pH	6.5–8.5
5.	Chloride (Cl^{-})	250	12.	Colour	15.c.u.
6.	Sulphate (SO_4^{2-})	250	13.	Turbidity	1-5 NTU
7.	Total dissolved solids (TDS)	500	14.	MPN (Coli forma) count	Zero

In India different municipalities and institutes prescribe different standards depending upon the end use of water. We have the Indian Standard Institute (ISI), Indian Council of Medical Research (ICMR) and State Water Pollution Control Boards exist in every State of Republic of India. There are primary inorganic stands (Table 9.30) as well as organic standards. These standards are comparable to the standard prescribed by United States Environmental Protection Agency (US–EPA). A new term was coined in India as MPL *i.e.* maximum permissible limit, indicating mean to avoid stringent measures clamped by US-EPA. However, it is not healthy practice. At the cost of human health the community must not compromise the ideal standards followed all over the world.

We have seen primary standards in Table 9.30 while in Table 9.31, we note secondary standards of the elements as well as the hydrological parameters like colour (Table 9.29). It does not deviate from earlier standard prescribed by others.

9.11 CONCLUSION

The water being important commodity we cannot afford to pollute it. In order to know level of pollution, one must examine the physical, chemical and biological properties. Such physical properties include colour, odour, conductivity, taste, temperature, turbidity and hardness of the sample of water. While chemical characteristics of water includes the study of calcium, magnesium, sodium, potassium, chloride, sulphate carbonate, bicarbonates, dissolved solids and calcium saturation limit. The minor components include fluoride, Nitrogen-ammonical, nitrogen-nitrate, nitrogen-nitrite, iron, silica, manganese, acidity alkalinity and salinity of water. While the important trace elements include aluminum, arsenic, barium chromium, cadmium, copper lead, nickel, silver and zinc. The biological examination have wide scale ramification over several microorganisms. This is specially very much important for the potable water.

The microorganisms include, pathogen, viruses fungi, protozoa, planton and water hysynim. A detailed investigation is very much necessary to identify these organism present in water with the kind of the disease it produces. The origin of source must be located and proper control measures have to be followed at any cost specially for potable drinking water.

The different agencies viz ISI, ICMR, US-EPA and several others state bodies prescribe their own standards for potable water and also for the water used in the industry. This is specially true in ease of potable water. Most of the small municipalities do not adhere to these prescribed standards. Unfortunately very few municipal corporations even in the metropolitan areas like Mumbai, Kolkata, Chennai, Bengluru, Hyderabad, Delhi adhere to strict standard on the quality of water. In fact untreated water promotes all kind of water born diseases. The situation in the villages is far from satisfactory with no standards. The work should begin from the villages, town and then cities. There should not be board at water fountain that it is potable water. That means all water from all kind of sources is infact potable water. But such day is too far in developing countries including India although it is possible in advanced countries like Japan, Europe and parts of Russia to do it.

ADDITIONAL READING

1. D.C. Adriano, *Trace Elements in Terrestrial Environment*, Springer-Verlag, New York (1986).
2. K Grasshoff, *Methods of Sea Water Analysis*, Verlag-Chemie, Weinhem (1975).
3. D.C. Burrell, *Atomic Spectrometric Analysis of Heavy Metal Pollutants in Water*, Ann Arbor Science Publishers, Ann Arbor (1974).
4. U. Forstner and G.T.W. Whittman, *Metal Pollution in the Aquatic Environment*, Springer, Verlag, New York (1979).
5. C.N. Sawyer P.L. McCarty, *Chemistry for the Environmental Engineering*, **3rd Ed.** McGraw Hill and Co. (1978).
6. H.S. Samant, *Methods for Chemical Analysis of Water and Waste Water*, Surveillance Report EPSS-AR-73-12 (1973), Canada.
7. I.L. Marr and M.S. Cresser, *Environmental Chemical Analysis*, International Textbook Co., New York, Blacki and Sons Ltd. (1983).
8. N.F. Voznaya, *Chemistry of Water and Microbiology*, Mir Publishers, Moscow (1981).
9. Mayuri Gandhi and S.M. Khopkar, *Indian Journal of Environmental Protection*, **8**, 12 (1988).
10. R.J. Schinitz-*Water Pollution Biology* Asia Publishers (1996).
11. J.C. Lamb, *Water Quality and Its Control*, John Wiley and Co. (1985).
12. S.A. Abbasi, *Water Quality Sampling and Analysis*, Discovery Publishers (1998).
13. R.E. Bartlott, *Surface Water and Sewage*, Applied Publisher London (1981).
14. American Public Health Association, *Standard Methods for Examination of Water and Waste Water* 20th Ed. (2000).
15. L. Hodges, *Environmental Pollution* **2nd Ed.** Holt Rinhart (1977).
16. D.W. Connet, *Basic Concepts of Environmental Chemistry* Lewis Publication (1992).
17. S.E. Manahas, *Environmental Chemistry* **7th Ed.** Lewes Publication (1999).
18. C. Baird, *Environmental Chemistry* W.H. Freeman and Co. (1995).

19. R Hartung, B.D. Dinmon Ed., *Environmental Mercury Contamination*, Ann Arbor Sci. Pub. (1974).
20. R.M. Harrison, D.P.H. Laxon–Lead *Pollution-Causes and Control* Chapman and Hall (1981).
21. J.G. Nriagu, *Arsenic in Environment Part II Human Health and Ecosystem Effect*—John Wiley (1994).
22. Taskforce, *Health Effects of Drinking Water Treatment Technology*-Lewis Publication (1989).
23. J.N. Moore, *Inorganic Contamination of the Surface Water*, Research and Monitoring Spring Verlag (1990).
24. S.M. Khopkar, *Basic Concept of Analytical Chemistry* **3rd Ed.** New Age International Publishers (P) Ltd. (2005).
25. S.M. Khopkar, *Environmental Pollution Analysis* **2nd Ed.** New Age International Publishers (P) Ltd. (2012).

10 Water Treatment

10.1 INTRODUCTION

The fresh water is very rarely used for drinking purposes, because the water is contaminated with impurities during its transportation to the city reservoir. Even, the water which is used for industrial process also needs a pretreatment. For instance water for textile industry should not contain too much of iron, as it causes staining of fabric. Water for food industry cannot afford to have manganese, as it causes staining of containers and adversely affects the taste and quality of material cooked in that water. The boiler feed water should not contain excess of salts of calcium and magnesium, as they consume more heat due to insulation of containers and pipes by deposition of scales. The methods for analysis of treated water are more or less similar to those for analysis of potable water. However, overall monitoring or analysis of water on regular basis presents a formidable problem. In this chapter, various treatment processes for water, followed by a review of overall monitoring methods for water quality management are considered.

10.2 IMPORTANT STEPS IN WATER TREATMENT

The Table 10.1 shows different ways through which water is consumed:

Table 10.1 Consumption of water for various purposes

S.No.	*Area of use of water*	*Average quantum of water used*	*Duration of consumption*
1.	Domestic consumption	150 liters per person	Day
2.	Nursing home, hospitals	300–500 liters per patient	Day
3.	Office, workhouses	70 liters per worker	Day
4.	Hotel, restaurant	400–600 liters per visitor	Day
5.	Weekwise peak demand	120–140% of yearly consumption	Year
6.	Peak demand summer	140–180% of annual average	Year
7.	Leakage, pilferage, stealing	15–25% of total supply (lakes)	Day
8.	Leakage with good surveillance	1–1.5 liters of supply	Day

The water is such commodity that is required everywhere. The average domestic consumption (Table 10.1) is roughly 150 liters per day per person. The health enterprises consume 300–500 liters of water per person per day but hotel, restaurants consume maximum level of as much as (400–600) liters of water each customer. The summer season shows highest demand (~ 140–200%). The water is lost to extent of 15–20% (specially treated water) in the leakage. Therefore, there is a need for efficient surveillance to protect the water resorb and in water carrying pipelines. These thieves from slums not only do pilferage but also contaminate it with microbiological species. They have gone to the extent of boring hole in supply to city and draw water without any automization or charges.

The treatment procedure vary depending upon its use. However, overall picture of water treatment, irrespective of end use shall be considered. An endeavour is made to comprehend the basic chemistry involved in water treatment process. The important stages involved in treatment include coagulation or flocculation; sedimentation; filtration (slow sand, rapid sand filtration); disinfection (including chlorination and ozonolysis); removal of iron and manganese; softening by lime-soda ash process or deionisation method; scale and corrosion control; taste and odour removal; prophylaxiation treatment *i.e.,* fluoridisation; and specialised treatment for a specific purpose.

Figure 10.1 indicates various steps for water resource management. The main source of water is clouds, rains, melting of ice-caps. It is collected in water-shed areas and it goes to reservoir, from where it is directly let off for distribution in city without processing depending upon its quality and end use. Such process involves preliminary treatment or an advanced treatment. After this treatment, it is taken to storage tank for regular distribution to city and industries.

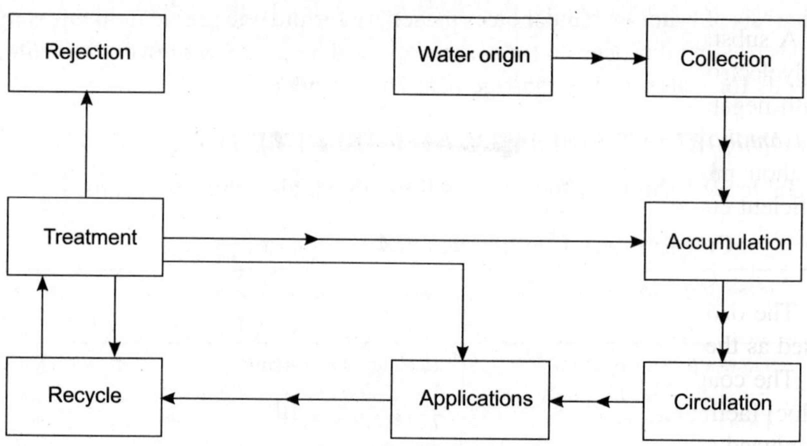

Fig. 10.1 Water management

(a) Coagulation

This is the first step in the water treatment. The principal coagulants used in water treatment consists of aluminium sulphate, ferric chloride, ferrous sulphate (Table 10.2). The important reactions involved in floc formation with alum are as follows:

$$Al_2(SO_4)_3 + 3Ca(HCO_3)_2 \longrightarrow 3CaSO_4 + 2Al(OH)_3 + 6CO_2 \uparrow$$

$$Al_2(SO_4)_3 + 3Ca(OH)_2 \longrightarrow 3CaSO_4 + \underset{\text{Flock}}{2Al(OH)_3}$$

$$Al_2(SO_4)_3 + 3Na_2CO_3 + 3H_2O \longrightarrow \underset{\text{Flock}}{2Al(OH)_3} + 3Na_2SO_4 + 3CO_2 \uparrow$$

$$Al_2(SO_4)_3 + 6NaOH \longrightarrow 2Al(OH)_3 + 3Na_2SO_4$$

This flock of $Al(OH)_3$ absorbs dirt and colour during sedimentation. The reaction with ferric chloride coagulation process is as follows:

$$2FeCl_3 + 3Ca(HCO_3)_2 \longrightarrow 3CaCl_2 + 2Fe(OH)_3 + 6CO_2 \uparrow$$

$$2FeCl_3 + 3Ca(OH)_2 \longrightarrow 3CaCl_2 + 2Fe(OH)_3$$

With $FeSO_4$ and chlorine,

$$Cl_2 + 2FeSO_4 + 3Ca(HCO_3)_2 \longrightarrow 2Fe(OH)_2 + 2CaSO_4 + 6CO_2 \uparrow + CaCl_2$$

$$FeSO_4 + Ca(OH)_2 \longrightarrow Fe(OH)_2 + CaSO_4$$

$$FeSO_4 + Ca(HCO_3)_2 \longrightarrow Fe(OH)_2 + CaSO_4 + 2CO_2 \uparrow$$

$$2Fe(OH)_2 + 1/2O_2 + H_2O \longrightarrow 2Fe(OH)_3$$

The last reaction in the presence of dissolved oxygen is very critical. The effectiveness of a coagulant is determined by the magnitude of *zeta potential.* The zeta potential is defined as the charge on ions surrounding suspended particulate matter. The charge is negative and is expressed in terms of millivolts. The agglomeration of floc particles as a result of polymerisation is critical. The various kinds of coagulants used for water treatment are listed in Table 10.2.

$$2[Fe(H_2O)_5(OH)]^{2+} \longrightarrow [Fe_2(H_2O)_8(OH)_2]^{4+} + 2H_2O$$

A substantial progress has been made in the field of synthetic coagulants or polyelectrolytes. These coagulants are cationic with positive charge and anionic with negative charge. Those with both positive and negative charges are called *polyampholyte* or *nonionic polyelectrolytes*. Their size vary in the range 1 to 100 μ. Without proper coagulation, sedimentation will be useless. The naturally occurring efficient coagulants are copper sulphate, which favour floc formation as:

$$CuSO_4 + Ca(HCO_3)_2 \longrightarrow Cu(OH)_2 + CaSO_4 + 2CO_2$$

$$CuSO_4 + Ca(OH)_2 \longrightarrow Cu(OH)_2 + CaSO_4$$

The ozone is also used to expedite process of coagulation. Activated silica is used as the flocculating agent.

The coagulants are agents which when added to water form bulky precipitate (floc) facilitating subsequent sedimentation and filtration process. The artificially produced coagulants aids are not natural coagulating agents but are one which are artificially produced to promote floc formation. The floc carries positive charge to interact with negative charged colloidal particles. The pH control is important, water with pH ~ 7.0 reacts best with coagulant but not the water with pH < 7.0 or pH > 7.0. Various salts of iron and aluminum are used as the coagulants. The minimum dose is 5 mg/L but a dose of 15–50 mg/L sodium aluminate is useful in solution of pH > 7.0. Iron salts are used in conjunction with lime. Hydrated ferric sulphate is most common. It is not used for treating coloured or turbid and acidic water. Ferric sulphate and chloride are also used. The reactions with ferric chloride or ferric sulphate is as follows:

$$2FeCl_3 + 3Ca(HCO_3)_2 \longrightarrow 2Fe(OH)_3 + 3CaCl_2 + 6CO_2 \uparrow$$
$$Fe_2(SO_4)_3 + 3Ca(HCO_3)_2 \longrightarrow 2Fe(OH)_3 + 3CaSO_4 + 6H_2O$$
$$2FeCl_3 + 3Ca(OH)_2 \longrightarrow 2Fe(OH)_3 + 3CaCl_2$$
$$Fe_2(SO_4)_3 + 3Ca(OH)_2 \longrightarrow \underset{\text{Flock}}{2Fe(OH)_3} + 3CaSO_4$$

The floc is hydroxide specially useful at low pH of water. The coagulants aids promotes flocculation *e.g.*, lime, soda, activated silica and few polyelectrolytes. The synthetic materials are starch based or polysaccharides. Other coagulating aids are nonionic polymers or anionic polyelectrolytes *e.g.*, polyacrylamide or polyacrylic acid. Polystyrene sulphonates are also used. The jar test is carried out to determine the optimum dose of coagulant to be added. It cannot be scaled up. However pH, alkanity floc time can be evaluated.

Table 10.2 Kinds of coagulants used

S. No.	*Formula*	*Sp. gravity (SG)*	*Mol. wt.*	*State/ Form*	*Remarks*	*pH*
1.	$Al_2(SO_4)14H_2O$	1.34	595	Solid	About 8% Al_2O_3 is used	2.7
2.	$Fe_2(SO_4)_3$	1.58	400	Liq.	Only 40% w/w used	–
3.	$FeCl_3$	1.45	102	Liq.	About 45% used for treatment	–
4.	$Al_2(OX)_2Cl_2$	1.20	High	Liq.	10% w/w Al_2O_3 is used	3.5
5.	$Al_2(OX)_2(SO_3)_2(SiO_2)$	1.34	V. High	Liq.	8% w/w alumma used	4.2
6.	$Fe_2(SO_4)_y$ Polymerized form	1.60	High	Liq.	45% w/w is used for treatment	–

The phenomena of coagulation is to clear water by suspended matter. Since ancient times Alum ($Al_2(SO_4)_3$ K_2SO_4, $24H_2O$) is most popular material for such processing. Most of the coagulants are used in liquid form. The efficiency of coagulation not only depends upon the physical nature but also on the chemical characteristics of the coagulant. For instance alum has highest molecular weight while Ferric chloride is lightest coagulant. Their use is confined to the concentration range of 8% (alum) to 45% (ferric alum). They are used at different pH of the water samples however in most of the samples the acidic pH between 2.5–4.0 is preferred. With all advancement in water coagulants alum remains a favourite coagulant and important water purifiers by common man in rural or urban environment (Table 10.2).

(b) Sedimentation

This treatment does not involve any chemical process, nevertheless it is an important aspect of water treatment. This is a physical process of settling of floc. Sedimentation occurs within 15 to 60 minutes after vigorous stirring of water with baffles. This in turn expedites the agglomeration process. The colour of water is removed, as coloured molecules form basic insoluble salts. The settling tanks are of various sizes and shapes. They have horizontal flow or circular flow or stay in static settling tanks. Sludge clarifier ensures proper circulation and controls the turbulence, or excess of stirring during process of settling. The large particles settle early in comparison with small particles. The shallow depth sedimentation is efficient compared to spiral flow basins.

The settling basins situated near sea shores have some trouble as breeze set up a surface current and eddies diffusion process reduces sedimentation process. An ideal tank is one where floc settles rapidly and settled sludge is removed easily. The theory of settlement assumes condition of non-turbulence, in very shallow horizontal flow basins. If the velocity is increased then turbulence interfere in the process of sedimentations. Most of the settling basins work on vertical or horizontal flow principle but in few settlers water flows in upward spiral path. However, pure theory is of less use in designing a settling basin. The average time of retention vary from 1 to 4 hours in absence of coagulating aids. The factors like excess of suspended solids, high colloidal contents, low temperature, constant disturbance by winds, are not conducive for rapid sedimentation. Use of the baffle prevents "streaming" *i.e.,* where incoming water does not mingle with main bulk of water in basin but it quickly passes out of basin stream and breaks the floc. It cannot be easily reformed again. The wrong dosage of polyelectrolyte as coagulating agent have adverse effects on process of coagulation. The knowledge of zeta potential is very essential to decide the dose. For voluminous sludge mechanical scrappers is needed. The lamella separation has 30°C angle through which settled water flows there by separating sediments from rest of the water in short-time.

10.3 FILTRATION

The main role of filters is to retain the particles contained in a liquid on the surface of filter media or in-depth. Surface filtration requires supporting media, while in-depth filtration is performed through a filter bed. The dissolved solids in the presence of chloride, sulphates of magnesium and sodium increase bed penetration by floc. The real filtration takes place in the first 3 to 4 cm in total height of 80 cm of filter bed. The slow sand filters involve filtration of water without previous treatment, while rapid sand filters are used for water which has been previously treated by coagulation or sedimentation. Anthracite coals is used for filtering media along with sand and gravel. The filter bed is cleaned by back washing. In rapid filtration, water passes through bed. Washing of filter bed facilitates the expansion of the filter bed. However, simultaneous air and water washing proceeds without expansion of filter bed.

The filtration follows sedimentation. The efficient sedimentation process reduces load on filtration process. If turbidity is greater than 5 NTU one needs the process of filtration. Rapid gravity sand type filters are most commonly used. It should be efficient to filter water of 10 NTU turbidity. The pressure filters is most common. The mixed media filters is refinement of rapid gravity filters *e.g.,* green leaf filters. Slow sand filter works without coagulant. The water of 30 NTU turbidity is also filtered by slow sand filters, but it cannot remove the colour. In rapid sand filtration sand of size 0.4 to 1.0 mμ is used. The better efficiency is with more depth of water flowing at rate of 3.9 to 7.10 m/hr. The high temperature facilitates filtration. Fineness of grains attributes more surface area for filtration. The filters must be periodically cleaned. The upward flow of water improves efficiency of filtration. A coarse layer of light weight material on top of sand has downward flow, filter promotes rapid filtration *e.g.,* anthracite or pumice used as the top layer. A good filtration model contains 10% high density sand, 30% silica bed and 60% anthracite bed facilitating flow at rate of 24 m/hr. The green leaf filter is rapid gravity filter with control system of different design. The slow sand filters are out moded- though it used to give filtrate of very high quality. Three filter beds consists of gravel and sand which are required for good results. No chemicals are required and bacteria also are removed, but they cover large area and are expensive. As surface of sand filtration takes place after strainers are used before actual filtration to prevent the large size particles. Microstainers are more efficient and effective. Granular material is best as filter media *e.g.,* garnet sand, silica sand, anthracite coal. When filtration media is clogged, the back washing is required. Apart from slow and rapid sand filters, precoat filters are also beneficial, which have septum to support filter medium and pressure and vacuum pump to control the flow. The direct filtration is done in slow sand filters, but flocculation prior to filtration is advisable for turbid water. This avoids step of sedimentation. It also removes colour. A coarse grade of diatomaccous earth is used after coagulation with alum or suitable polyelectrolyte to promote simultaneously coagulation as well as the filtration.

10.4 DISINFECTION

The elimination of taste and smell, the destruction of pathogenic microorganisms is done by process of disinfection with chlorination, ozonolysis or ultraviolet light treatment. However, most favoured method is chlorination. This is because chlorine is a cheap material. The treatment with iodine is only used for swimming pools. The disinfecting gas kills virus bacteria and germs from the water. The source of such disinfectant is chlorine gas or hypochlorates of calcium and sodium, *e.g.,* CaCl(OCl) bleaching powder. The reaction of chlorine with water is as follows:

$$H_2O + Cl_2 \uparrow \rightleftharpoons HCl + HOCl$$

At low pH, hypochlorous acid predominates, while at higher pH greater than 7.5, hypochlorate ion (–OCl) prevails. HOCl penetrates through organism cell walls and oxidises matter within the cell. Relatively OCl^- is not that effective. Fe^{3+}, Mn^{2+}, Ca^{2+}, Mg^{2+}, NO_2^-, CO_3^{-2}, HCO_3^- and NH_3 interfere in such a reaction. The most troublesome interference is due to ammonia. It reacts with chlorine to form mono-, di- or trichloroamines at different pH as:

$$NH_3 + HOCl \longrightarrow NH_2Cl + H_2O \ (pH > 8.0)$$

$$NH_3 + 2HOCl \longrightarrow NHCl_2 + 2H_2O \ (pH \sim 4.3 - 5.0)$$

$$NH_3 + 3HOCl \longrightarrow NCl_3 + 3H_2O \ (pH < 4.3)$$

Though these chloroamines also have germicidal action, they act very slowly. Combined residual chlorination involves chlorination with residual chlorine left behind in water after treatment, since free residual chlorination is one which gives free available chlorine through destruction of ammonia or organic matter. The total chlorine residue remaining after specified contact period is called *combined available residual chlorine*. Residual chlorine acting as HOCl or OCl^- ion is called *free available chlorine*. The chlorine demand is defined as the difference between the amount of chlorine added to water and amount of residual chlorine left behind at the end of specified contact period. The demand varies with time of contact temperature and pH. The germicidal action of iodine is more effective over broader pH range, as elemental iodine I_2° and HIO are active germicidal agents. However, chloroiodides like chloroamines are not formed easily. Ozone is also a good germicidal agent. Ultraviolet radiation at 253.7 nm has good germicidal effect on water.

The contact of disinfecting agent and water during the process of chlorination is most vital. Thus Table 10.3 shows importance of duration in chlorination process.

Table 10.3 Chlorination period (time)

S. No.	Disinfecting agent	Physical state	Contact time in seconds	pH	Temp °C	Concn. (M)
1.	Free chlorine (Cl_2)	Gas	24	6.0	5°	0.1
			360	8.5	20°–30°	0.1
			60	8.5	20°–30°	0.5
2.	Monochloroamine (NH_2Cl)	Liquid	360	4.5	15°	0.1
			3600	4.5	15°	1.0
3.	Dichloroamine ($NHCl_2$)	Liquid	60	9.0	15°	1.0

Of all the process of disinfection of water the chlorination is the one process (Table 10.3) which has become universal all over the world. Although the operation needs critical control of period of contact the break point process is still best. It is sure way to kill microorganisms from potable water. In these plants of operations the contact time is of very important which varies from few seconds to minutes chloroamines are replaced by chlorine gas in many operations (Table 10.3 S.No.1) however with chloroamines time needed for disinfection is very long (*viz.* 3600 seconds monochloroamine). In comparison the dichloroamine is more efficient needing just one minute to attain full equilibrium. On an average pH is between 4.0–8.5. Most of the time operation is carried out at room temperature with use of as little as 0.1–1.0 M concentration of the disinfectant. In initial period the chlorine gas reduces oxidants present in sample and as we increase the dose of chlorination, all microorganisms are killed till a plato is reached in break point chlorination curve. So graph of % Cl_2 added *vs.* residual chlorine becomes parallel to *x*-axis (see Figs. 10.2 and 10.3).

(a) Break Point Chlorination

Chlorine is mainly added as the disinfecting agent; an excess dose is added to kill microorganisms. Chlorine removes foul smell. The demand of chlorine is noted by ascertaining the difference between amount of chlorine applied and amount of chlorine left which remains as residue after some contact period. Such demand is tested in sunlight. The demand depends upon various factors such as time of contact, pH of chlorine, temperature and quantum dose used. The demand suddenly rises if compounds like sulphur mustards, hydrolysis products are present in water. The best method to ascertain concentration of free available chlorine required for killing of microorganism is by plotting graph as given in Fig 10.2. If a plot of pH versus total residual chlorine gives a peak which indicates the dose of chlorine demand for complete killing of microorganisms and pathogenic bacteria.

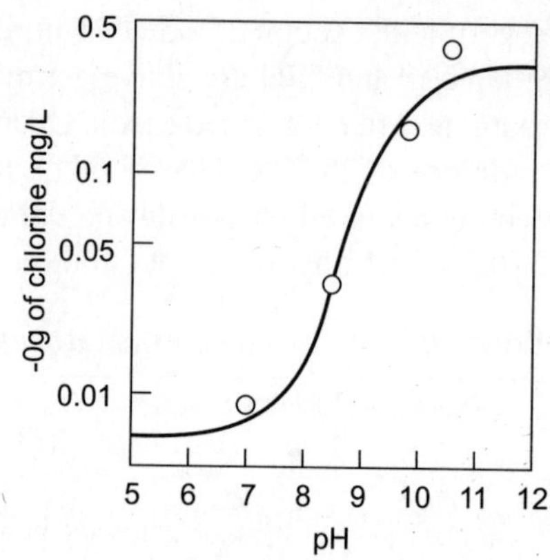

Fig. 10.2 Variation in chlorine with pH

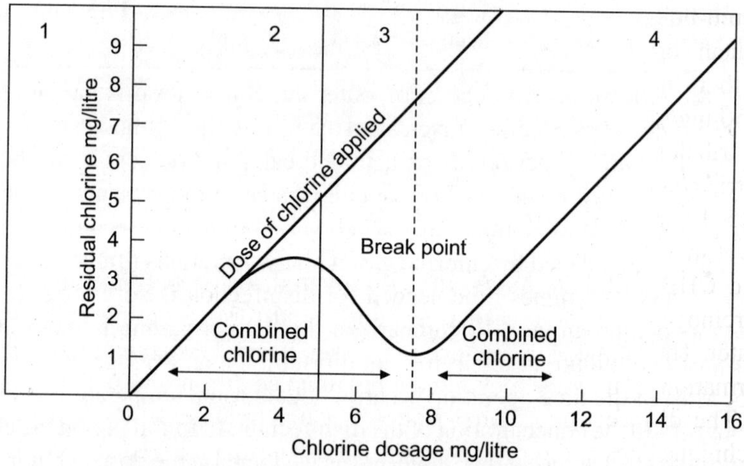

Fig. 10.3 Break point chlorination

A graph indicates residual chlorine curve, showing a typical break point chlorination. A close look at Fig. 10.3 reveals in zone (1) all chlorine is consumed for destruction or interaction of reducing compounds. While zone (2) represents formation of chloroorganics and chloroamines, when quantum of chlorine dose is rising. In zone (3) the level of residual chlorine tapers off, as all chlorine is consumed with no residual chlorine left. On further injection of chlorine in water, zone (4) shows formation of free chlorine with or without combined chlorine. The inter-junction of zone 2 and 3 indicate chlorine demand and it is termed as the break point chlorination point. This is the optimum dose of chlorine, which is a must if the disinfecting action has to be effective. Thus, initially no residual chlorine is noted. The break point chlorination is effective for bactericidal action, removal of taste and odour. Ammonia is sometimes deliberately added to produce combined chlorine residue. Chloramines last longer and have bactericidal effect also. The toxicity of the dosage of chlorine has limit of injection *e.g.*, 1 ppm is the permissible limit, 3.5 ppm imparts odour, 15 ppm gives throat irritation, 30 ppm induces cough, 40 ppm is maximum tolerance by man; 40 to 60 ppm is injurious to the health and 1000 ppm is fatal dose for a person. Apart from ozone, other disinfecting agents which are used with advantage are $KMnO_4$, bromine water, chlorine-bromine mixture, ultraviolet radiation at 200 to 300 nm (cf Aquaguard available in market) the ionising radiation of 25 Ci/g and action of silver in ionic form.

(b) Trihalomethanes

These are the by products generated in water treatment plant during disinfection process by chlorine. The rate of their formation depends upon contact time, chlorine concentration, pH and chlorine dosage. Chloroform is such toxic product which is carcinogenic. The simplest method of analysis is solvent extraction with gas chromatography. The technique of GC-MS is used for such analysis. Chloroform, bromodichloromethane, dibromochloromethane and bromoform are analysed by liquid-liquid extraction coupled with mass spectrometry. Sample is extracted with pentane or hexane, methylcyclohexane or trimethylpentane as the extractant and it is then injected in GC with ECD detector. At low concentration of less than < 50 mg/L only GC is used but for higher level GC-MS is required. A 5–200 mg/L of trihalomethane is analysed. Trihalomethane is toxic hence all operations are carried out in hood. The varying retention time is *e.g.*, $CHCl_3$ (1–4.9 mts), $CHBrCl_2$ (1.5–1.1 mts), $CHBr_2Cl$ (2.6–23.1 mts), $CHBr_3$ (5.5–40 mts). The average dose level in sample of water (mg/L) is: $CHCl_3$ (9.1); $CHBrCl_2$ (1.2); $CHBr_2Cl$ (1.7) and $CHBr_3$ (2.9) minutes. It is discovered that trihallomethanes (THM) are carcinogenic in the presence of humic acid formed during chlorination of the water. The humic acid produces trihalomethanes by reaction with chlorine. Such formation is minimised by removing humic acid from the sample of water.

The disinfection is final stage of water treatment. Most of the filteration technique does not remove bacteria. The ozonisation is also powerful disinfecting agent as it does not affect taste and odour of water. Bleaching powder and sodium hypochlorites are efficient in liquid form (~ 1% useful) while use of 0.5 to 1 mg/L chlorine makes water sterile. When chlorinate water gives nascent oxygen it kills bacteria. The meaning of break point chlorination is the chlorine dose which is added to oxidise any of reducing compound; it is increased to form lasting chloroamine and free chlorine. The rate of killing of bacteria is influenced by low temperature and high pH as action of chloramine is reduced. The addition of ammonia retains chlorine in water. If water is highly contaminated then super chlorination is used. The excess of chlorine from water is removed by sulphur dioxide. The chlorination is done before process of sedimentation or filtration (2–5 mg/L dose), specially when there is slime formation in water. Chlorine in requisite dose only is added to water. Chlorine dioxide is very useful for removal of phenol, iron and manganese from the water (dose 0.5–2.5 mg/L).

(c) Ozonolysis and Ultraviolet Radiation Exposure

The ozonization is common process of disinfection specially in Europe. It provides high quality water. Ozone has to be generated on site before passing through water. It has powerful bactericidal action. It does not impart taste to water. It is expensive process. Ozone is not very persistant and water treated with ozone at source gets reinfected at later stage in the distribution system. The UV radiation is quite cheap. It is extensively used in Russia. The method is suitable for batch method but unsuitable for plant scale. For India chlorine is best and cheapest method. Table 10.4 provides the details of process when water is exposed to UV radiation.

Table 10.4 Exposure to ultraviolet radiation for water purification

S. No.	*UV-quality*	*Efficiency (%)*	*UV-dose (ml/cm)*	*Low pressure*	*Medium pressure*	*High pressure*
1.	UV-wavelength	< 200 nm	–	185–250 mm	250–300 mm	250–300 mm
2.	Output in watts	–	–	60–100 mm	500–2000 mm	2500–3000 mm
3.	Life of UV Lamp (hs)	–	–	8000 mm	4000 mm	400 mm
4.	Temperature of operation	Room temp.	–	At (50° C)	(100° C)	(100°C)
5.	UV-dose used	90.0	5.4	–	–	–
6.	UV-dose complete	99.0	10.8	–	–	–
7.	UV-dose complete	99.9	21.5	–	–	–
8.	UV-dose complete	100.0	21.5	–	–	–

A close examination Table 10.4 gives idea about effect of exposure of water to UV radiation in order to kill the microorganism. The efficiency of operation is optimum (*i.e.* 99.9%). The operation is successful at room temperature and elevated pressure. The UV-dose used is 5–20 ml/cm while pressure varies from 150–3000 mm. The process of treatment is relatively cheap and it is used on mass scale in Soviet Union. The best results are obtained in batch operation and the method fails to show positive results at industrial scale treatment.

10.5 REMOVAL OF IRON AND MANGANESE

From drinking water, Fe and Mn must be removed, as they cause corrosion of pipes, affect appearance of water, impart metallic taste and cause laundering problems. The paper and textile mills do not tolerate their presence in processing water. In underground water, they are present in reduced form for want of oxygen. The metal is present in complexed form. They are converted to stable oxidation state by the following reaction:

$$Fe^{2+} + O_2 + 8OH^- + 2H_2O \longrightarrow 4Fe(OH)_3$$

$$Mn^{2+} + 2ClO_2 + 2H_2O \longrightarrow MnO_2 + 2O_2\uparrow + 2Cl^-\uparrow + 4H^+\uparrow$$

The black film of manganese is difficult to remove from containers. The prescribed limit is 0.3 to 0.05 mg/litre. Such metals are removed after pepitisation or oxidation, which proceeds by aeration or action with Cl_2, $KMnO_4$ or oxides of chlorine.

$$Mn^{2+} + O_3 + H_2O \longrightarrow MnO_2 + O_2\uparrow + 2H^+$$

$$3Mn^{2+} + 2MnO_4 + 2H_2O \longrightarrow 5MnO_2 + 4H^+$$

A dose of 2.5 mg/litre ClO_2; 1.9 mg/litre $KMnO_4$ and 0.87 mg/litre O_3 is adequate. If small quantities of iron and manganese are present, then one has to take resort to ion-exchange method, at the cost of clogging the bed. The process is expensive. Zeolites are cheaper. Zeolites are complex alumino silicates of alkali metals. The reaction with zeolites is as follows:

$$Na_2Z + Fe^{+3} \longrightarrow Fe\text{-}Z + 2Na^+$$

$$Na_2Z + Mn^{3+} \longrightarrow Mn\text{-}Z + 2Na^+$$

if $Z = Na_2O\ Al_2O_3\ SiO_2\ H_2O$

The presence of Cu, Fe and Mn are problem in potable water and needs immediate removal. The brewing of tea and flavours of food are seriously affected by Fe and Mn. The pE α pH diagram gives idea of species of iron present and quantum of dose of oxygen needed to oxidise ferrous to ferric state. Value of pE decrease as pH is raised. Ferrous is oxidised to ferric state and precipitated as $Fe(OH)_3$. It is then removed by sedimentation. Iron at lower concentration is removed by ion-exchange process. The stabilisation of iron by dispersing agents like polyphosphate or silicate is another method of removal. Diatomic filtration process is useful for segregation. In ion-exchange separation the regeneration is economical for resin. With the zeolite the process is satisfactory if manganese is present in ground water. The presence of organic matter with iron is bad as it complexes with it. Tannic acid is used for such removal. The dissolved silica interferes in process of iron removal. Sodium hexametaphosphate *i.e.*, Calgon is used for removal of iron since the manganese has seven oxidation states but divalent manganese is only the objectionable impurity. Cl, ClO_2, $KMnO_4$ are used as oxidising agents.

The best oxidant is $KMnO_4$ at pH 7.2 to 8.3. For lower concentration of manganese ion exchange/zeolite process is used. Calgon is used if manganese is present in greater than 2 mg/L concentration.

10.6 SOFTENING OF WATER OR REMOVAL OF HARDNESS

The softening of water is necessary, for many industrial processes. $Ca(HCO_3)_2$ and $Mg(HCO_3)_2$ render it temporarily hard, while $CaSO_4$, $MgSO_4$, $CaCl_2$ and $MgCl_2$

render it permanently hard. The reliable test to ascertain hardness is soap test; if no lather is formed with soap water, it is considered to be hard. The best process for softening are three, *viz.*, lime-soda-ash process, deionisation or demineralisation and Calgon process. The hardness is also called as the carbonate and non-carbonate hardness. In their presence the scale formation is increased. It is formed in form of metal silicates.

(a) Lime Soda Ash Process

The lime soda ash process is discovered in Aberdeen in Scotland. Henderson later modified the process as cold lime soda ash process with conventional type design which is most common in industry. In hot lime soda ash process all reactions are carried out at elevated temperature, accelerating rate of precipitation with rapid sedimentation.

The important chemical reactions after addition of $Ca(OH)_2$ and Na_2CO_3 occurs at pH 10. The mechanical agitator is used for mixing. The settling occurs within 3 to 4 hours.

$$Ca(HCO_3)_2 + Ca(OH)_2 \longrightarrow 2CaCO_3 + H_2O + CO_2 \uparrow$$
$$Mg(HCO_3)_2 + Ca(OH)_2 \longrightarrow MgCO_3 + 2CaCO_3 + H_2O + CO_2 \uparrow$$
$$CaCl_2 + Na_2CO_3 \longrightarrow CaCO_3 + 2NaCl$$
$$MgCl_2 + Na_2CO_3 \longrightarrow MgCO_3 + 2NaCl$$
$$CaSO_4 + Na_2CO_3 \longrightarrow CaCO_3 + Na_2SO_4$$
$$MgSO_4 + Na_2CO_3 \longrightarrow \underset{\text{Pot}}{MgCO_3} + Na_2SO_4$$

The spiractor is device which is used for fast settling. A conical tank consists of the catalyst *e.g.*, calcite or waste green sand. $CaCO_3$ so formed is deposited on catalyst where the detention period in spiractor is much less *viz.*, 8 to 12 mts only as compared to 3 to 4 hrs in conventional process for settling. The hot lime soda ash process is followed to accelerate the process of precipitation at 100°C, thereby facilitating fast process of the sedimentation. CO_2 for neutralisation of lime is not required. Both the cold and hot process undergo identical chemical reactions.

(b) Deionisation or Demineralisation Process

The cation exchange resin is in $[H^+]$ form, while anion exchange resin is in $[OH^-]$ hydroxyl form. A strongly acidic resin (like vinyl styrene DVB copolymer with sulphonation) is used as cation exchanger, while basic anion exchanger (also vinyl styrene base with labile OH – group) is used for removal of anions. The important reactions on resin (H_2R) are as follows:

$$H_2R + CaCl_2 \longrightarrow CaR + 2HCl$$
$$H_2R + MgCl_2 \longrightarrow Mg\text{-}R + 2HCl$$
$$H_2R + CaSO_4 \longrightarrow CaR + H_2SO_4$$
$$H_2R + MgSO_4 \longrightarrow MgR + H_2SO_4$$

Then water is passed on anion exchanger RNH_3OH in hydroxyl form

$$RNH_3-OH + HCl \longrightarrow RNH_3Cl + H_2O \text{ (Regeneration)}$$
$$RNH_3-OH + H_2SO_4 \longrightarrow RNH_3SO_4 + H_2O \text{ (Regeneration)}$$
$$[RNH_3-OH + H_2O \longrightarrow RNH_3OH + H_2O \text{ (no change)}]$$

The greatest advantage of demineralisation process is possibility of reusing the resin again after regeneration. The regeneration of the resin is as follows:

$$CaR + 2HCl \longrightarrow H_2R + CaCl_2 \text{ (cation exchange, } H^+ \text{ form)}$$
$$Mg\text{-}R + 2HCl \longrightarrow H_2R + MgCl_2$$
$$RNH_3Cl + NH_4OH \longrightarrow NH_4Cl + RNH_3-OH \text{ (anion } -OH^- \text{ form)}$$
$$RNH_3SO_4 + 2NH_4OH \longrightarrow (NH_4)_2SO_4 + RNH_3-OH$$

In place of synthetic ion-exchange one uses naturally occurring sodium zeolite ($Na_2O\ Al_2O_3\ SiO_2$). It is regenerated by NaCl. The principal reactions of exchange on zeolite are:

$$Ca(HCO_3)_2 + NaZ \longrightarrow CaZ + 2NaHCO_3 \text{ (soluble)}$$
$$CaSO_4 + NaZ \longrightarrow CaZ + Na_2SO_4 \text{ (soluble)}$$
$$Mg(NO_3)_2 + Na_2Z \longrightarrow MgZ + NaNO_3 \text{ (soluble)}$$
$$CaZ + 2NaCl \longrightarrow Na_2Z + CaCl_2 \text{ (regeneration of zeolite)}$$
$$MgZ + 2NaCl \longrightarrow Na_2Z + MgCl_2$$

In 1756, J. Thomas and Way discovered zeolite process. The choice of ion-exchange or cold lime soda process is decided by the economic consideration and need of quality was wasted. The demineralised water has low colour turbidity, less hardness, with no sludge disposal problem. Only problem in ion-exchange process is brine disposal. The problem of sludge in lime soda ash process can be handled by dewatering, recalcination or process of coagulation. Some precautions are necessary in the deionisation process. Water is of highest quality. The load of impurities is determined by the total exchange capacity of resin.

During regeneration, chambers containing cation exchange and anion exchange resins is disconnected to facilitate the reconversion of resins to H^+ and OH^- forms, with HCl and NH_4OH as regeneraters, respectively. There is a growing trend to use mixed bed resins, only limitation is during regeneration the anion and cation exchangers will have to be separated before physically carrying out regeneration process.

(c) Calgon Process

This is useful for outdoor treatment for a limited supply of water. The salt sodium hexametaphosphate $Na_6P_6O_{18}$ is added to water for precipitation of insoluble phosphates of calcium and magnesium,

$$MgSO_4 + 2NaH_2PO_4 \longrightarrow Mg(H_2PO_4)_2 + Na_2SO_4$$
$$3CaSO_4 + 3Na_3PO_4 \longrightarrow Ca_3(PO_4)_2 + 3Na_2SO_4$$
$$3Ca(HCO_3)_2 + 2Na_3PO_4 \longrightarrow Ca_3(PO_4)_2 + 6NaHCO_3$$

(d) Reverse Osmosis—a Glimpse

Within treatment procedure the most useful technique is membrane separation. As told earlier variety of membranes are made out of cellulose such as (Table 10.5) polypropylene, polyacryl nitrate, as polyether sulphate are available. Such membranes finds extensive applications in the process of electrodialysis and Reverse Osmosis. In both the methods the ions present in sample of water is allowed to migrate under the influence of potential gradient. Of these two processes Reverse Osmosis is used on industrial scale in South East Asia and United Arab Republic (UAR). In normal circumstance if in two compartments water is kept between screen of membrane liquid flows from high to low concentration. However, in RO the diluted sample tries to migrate from low dilution level to high concentration in the compartment.

Table 10.5 Reverse osmosis process

S.No.	*Kind of membrane*	*Remark*	*Abbreviation*	*Demerits*	*Merits for use*
1.	Cellulose	Not good	CA	Ineffective pH	Chlorine immune
2.	Polypropylene	Good	PP	Hydrophobic	Cheap material
3.	Polyamide	Good	PA	Stable, selective	Small dose of chlorine used
4.	Polyacryl nitrite	Not good	PAN	Resistant to hydrolysis, oxide	Brittle, hydrophobic
5.	Polysulphone	Good	PSU	Stable material	Hydrophobic
6.	Polyether amide	Not good	PEI	In alkali unstable	Thermal resistance is there
7.	Polyether sulphone	V. Good	PES	Hydrophobic	Good stability

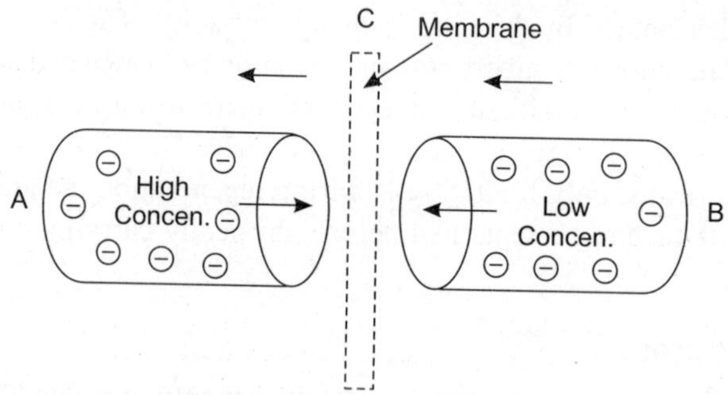

Fig. 10.4 Reverse Osmosis

In the adjoining Fig. 10.4, we see there are two compartments *viz.* (A) Feed and (B) receiving phase while C is the semipermeable membrane (Table 10.5).

On application of pressure or electrical potential liquid from compartment (B) tries to migrate to compartment (A) with higher concentration of ions. The process works on continuing basis and it works well on the industrial scale.

10.7 THE MEMBRANE SEPARATION AND REVERSE OSMOSIS

Based upon the knowledge of the removal of impurities in water samples, reverse osmosis is the most efficient method for the removal of the contamination. In ordinary dialysis or osmosis process the liquid migrates from high concentration to the lower concentration in the compartment. However in Reverse Osmosis the sample solution containing the contaminants migrate from dilute to the highly concentrated solution. Hence the process is called 'Reverse Osmosis' (RO).

Variety of membranes are used to carry out RO process. We have different kinds of membranes (Table 10.5) such as the cellulose, polypropylene, polyamide, polysulphonate, polyether sulphonate etc. of these polypropylene and polyamide is best but they are hydrophobic. Some are inefficient in alkaline (pH 76.0) media as shown in Section 10.7.5. The details of the separation are described in this section on the membrane separation.

It is worthwhile at this stage to consider the overall efficiency of Reversed Osmosis process as the separation unit. It depends upon what is the feed concentration and note the efficiency in removal of ions. The common elements which are separated by RO include calcium, magnesium, sodium or anions, such as chloride, sulphate, silicate with dissolved solids (TDS). The best separation is feasible for calcium and magnesium. The feed concentration varies from 7–700 mg/L while separation efficiency varies from 84–96% at low concentration. While in high range of concentration efficiency varies, (if 25–7000 mg/L is the concentration the corresponding efficiency) is 98.3–100% (optimum level). It will be clear after examining Table 10.6.

Table 10.6 Efficiency of reverse osmosis technique

S. No.	*Constituent*	*Feed concentration (mg/L)*		*Removal efficiency (%)*		*Remarks*
		Low	*High*	*High*	*Low*	
1.	Calcium (II)	52	440	96.5	100	Best
2.	Magnesium (II)	7	38	91.0	100	Best
3.	Sodium (I)	535	2180	85.6	99.2	V. Good
4.	Chloride (Cl^-)	760	2560	84	99.1	V. Good
5.	Sulphate (SO_4^{2-})	810	2615	99.7	100	Best
6.	Silica (SiO_2)	5	25	81.0	100	Best
7.	TDS (dissolved solids)	3370	7190	89	98.3	Good

After membrane separation process, we consider problems of less importance such corrosion—its causes and prevention, the aesthetically important factor as taste and odor while fluoridization is an extremely important criteria in ascertaining the quality of water.

10.8 REMOVAL OF COLOUR

There are several compounds which render a characteristic colour to the sample of water. *e.g.* All kinds of triphenyl basic dyes even in trace concentration give coloration to the water sample. Few kind of organic compounds like Lignine sulphonate imparts coloration to water. No doubt even traces of metal pollutants like chromium, cobalt, copper in any form render colour to the water. There are several methods for the decolorization or removal of colour of water.

Of all the methods studied use of activated carbon or the charcoal gives cent percent results. The beauty of the process is that it has dual role to perform not only removing the colour water but also removal of odor, or smell imparted by organic compounds is also eliminated.

A look at Table 10.7 shows physical properties such as particle size, specific surface area and the pore volume which are of important consideration while using decolorizing agent. Very fine particle size with very large surface area of coal or coke and quite large pore volume gives good results. Even other physical parameters such as bulk density, specific gravity and the iodine number are of equal importance. Larger is bulk density better is outcome of decolorization. The specific gravity has no significant impact on quality of water and charcoal. However the iodine number specially in the presence of organic amines, esters is important. This proves best quality of activated charcoal (through which steam is passed to render it porous) is very useful for the removal of color as well as odor of sample of water.

Table 10.7 Quality of charcoal used for decolorization of water

S.No.	*Property*	*Importance*
1.	Particle size	The small particle size preferred
2.	Specific surface	The large area give better result
3.	Pore volume	Larger volume, better result
4.	Density	Bulk density important
5.	Sp. gravity	No much influence
6.	Iodine Nos	16–28° A. size good results

10.9 CORROSION PREVENTION

The corrosion causes irreversible damage to the metallic surfaces. Corrosion is an electrolytic process in which dissolved oxygen plays vital role. Low pH promotes corrosion. High dissolved CO_2 lowers pH of water. The dissolved oxygen must be reduced, and dissolved carbon dioxide should be totally eliminated from water. Corrosion inhibitors prevents corrosion. Lime reduces level of carbon dioxide to $Ca(HCO_3)_2$. Dezincification is another mode of corrosion mitigation if water has pH less than 8.2. Hot pressed brass readily undergoes dezincification. One should avoid the dissimilar metals in contact with each other. It promotes corrosion by acting as thermocouple. Copper, zinc, aluminium in proximity of each other have adverse effects. Sulphate reducing bacteria also promotes corrosion. The anaerobic bacteria and aeration kills them but iron bacteria are aerobic in nature. They absorb oxygen from the air and promote corrosion of iron. There are several methods for the prevention of corrosion.

The chemical correction and conditioning of water is done in several ways. This also prevents organic growth and fouling of water. The first step is to control pH. The alkaline solutions are not conducive for corrosion of pipes or seams. The other alternative process is to inhibit precipitation, *e.g.*, polyphosphate [$M_4P_2O_7n$ (MPO_3)], prevents scale formation *e.g.*, if M = Na, we have $Na_4P_2O_7$, $NaPO_3$, $Na_2P_4O_7$ and $Na_5P_3O_{10}$ (Polymetaphosphate). It is possible to prevent corrosion by reduction of oxygen content in water. The corrosion inhibitors like Na_2SiO_3, polyphosphates, nitrites and chromates are useful. Organozinc compounds are also beneficial. The layer of $CaCO_3$ inside a pipeline prevents further corrosion. Soft water promotes corrosion, by the process of recarbonation as:

$$Ca^{2} + 2OH^- + CO_2 \longrightarrow CaCO_3 + H_2O$$

$$Ca^{2+} + CO_3^{2-} + CO_2 + H_2O \longrightarrow Ca(HCO_3)_2$$

$$2Na^+ + 2OH^- + CO_2 \longrightarrow Na_2CO_3 + H_2O$$

The sodium hexametaphosphate (Na_3PO_4) is added to prevent deposition of calcium. The concentration range 0.5 to 1 ppm is ideal, as 5 ppm of $CaCO_3$ forms protective coating on interiors of pipe. The corrosion is prevented by chemical treatment of water or electrochemical treatment of metals. Occasionally "Langelier Saturation Index" is used to study of corrosion. It does not indicate how much $CaCO_3$ will be deposited in water to control the corrosion. It is also not a proper measure of the forces tending to develop calcite coatings in water line. However, polyphosphates are best for inhibition of corrosion 1 to 1.5 ppm of $Na_6P_6O_{18}$ prevents precipitation of $CaCO_3$ at pH 10. Lower concentration of hexameta phosphate is useless. 2 ppm of salt prevents $CaCO_3$ precipitation. The continuous treatment with $Na_6P_6O_{18}$ salts is best. Zinc orthophosphate is also used for the prevention of corrosion. At pH 7.5 about 0.5 mg/L prevented corrosion of pipes. Copper shows excellent resistance to corrosion unless environment is oxygenated. At pH less than 6.5 in presence of CO_2 it corrodes. Lead is used less in plumbing as greater than 0.05 mg/L of Pb is prohibited by US-EPA.

10.10 TASTE AND ODOUR REMOVAL

The dissolved organic substances such as phenols, sulphurated hydrogen, chloramines and chlororganics cause odour. Algal decay produces foul smell. The phenols with chlorine form obnoxious products. This is prevented by aeration, coagulation, break-point chlorination and application of certain agents, like activated carbon. The activated carbon is best, as it not only removes odour but also removes colour of water. Granular carbon is not effective. By the process of adsorption impurities are removed, but dyes, detergents inhibit this reaction.

Taste and odour are organoleptic qualities of water. Algae and actinomycetes imparts taste and odour to potable water. Chlorophenols also imparts odour. The threshold odour number (TON) test of water is most reliable. It is dimensionless. The odour intensity index (ODI) is used to assess odour as TON = 2 ODI. The standard method provides the details to determine TON. Taste producing compounds are phenolic. Actinomycetes impart earthy taste. Algae is most important to render taste and odour for the water. Ether extraction followed by NMR reveals the chemical structure of odour generating compounds like nucidone, geosmin, argosmin-C. Many mercaptons give typical odour of sulphur compounds. Phenols from water react with chlorine during chlorination to produce chlorophenols. The drinking water has iodine which imparts medicinal taste. Inorganic compounds impart bitter taste to water. The taste are classified as $CaCl_2$ (bitter), $MgCl_2$ (bitter sweet), $NaHCO_3$ (very sweet), Na_2SO_4 (salty), Na_2CO_3 (bitter) and NaCl (salty). The refrigeration of water improves its taste. The dissolved oxygen of water imparts metallic taste to water also. Cu, Fe, Mn, Zn gives taste and odour. The activated carbon and chemical oxidants like Cl_2, $KMnO_4$, ClO_2 removes taste and odour from water, but chlorination is best agent for the control of taste and odour. ClO_2 is best for such purpose specially if phenollic compounds are present. It operates also at high pH. Dioxide of chlorine does not react with ammonia and is available as HOCl ClO_2 destroys chlorophenols generated by chlorination of water. The process is more effective at low temperature. The significant merit is chlorine oxide treated water is not carcinogenic.

10.11 FLUORIDATION

Figure 10.5 indicates relationship between dental carries and fluoride level in drinking water. The term fluoridation is preferable to fluorination, as the element is used in the form of fluoride. The removal of fluoride is called defluoridation. A small quantity of fluorine (0.4 to 1 mg/litre) in water promotes formation of dental enamel and protects teeth against carries. Too much fluoride leads to destruction of enamel and causes fluorosis—leading to dental disorder, decalcification, mineralisation of tendons, digestive and nervous disorders. The excess of fluoride (1.5 mg/litre) is dangerous to health. Water is fluoridised in Australia, South Africa,

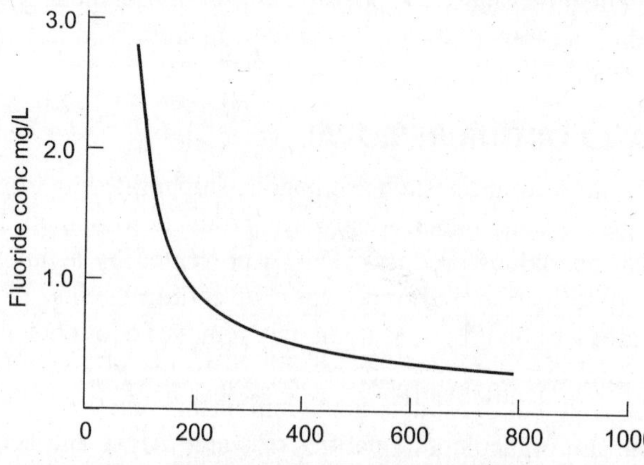

Fig. 10.5 Variation in dental problems and fluoride level

South and North America and Europe. Water is treated with fluorine. Na_2SiF_6, H_2SiF_6, NaF are also used as the common fluoridation agents. About 0.4 to 1 mg/litre of fluoride is added in water. The excess of fluoride is removed by treating water with $Ca_3(PO_4)_2$, $Al_2O_3SiO_2$, or $Ca(OH)_2$, or filtration through activated carbon. Fluorides occur in natural water. Their level is around 1 mg/L which is beneficial for prevention of dental decay, but level more than 3 to 5 mg/L as is found in few districts in Andhra Pradesh, Gujarat and Karnataka is injurious causing mottling of the teeth. Fluoride range more than 1.5 mg/L is removed by $Ca_3PO_4l_2$, or ion exchange resins or activated alumina. It is better to abandon source of water if it contains high level of fluoride. In developed countries (which face severe problem of dental decay) water is fluoridised with sodium fluoride or sodium silico fluoride (Na_2SiF_6) as latter process is economical. However, administration of fluoride is done with atmost care least it would cause health problems.

10.12 TREATMENT OF WATER FOR SPECIFIC PURPOSE

Water for a specific purpose needs a special treatment; *e.g.,* water for swimming pool, boiler feed water, industrial process, hydrometallurgy. Such treatment depends upon the quality of raw water, *e.g.,* for well water no chemical treatment is required; while surface water needs chemical treatment. The desalting plants use flash distillation of sea water, or process of reverse osmosis, wherein the water passes from less saturated to more saturated solution through membranes. Electrodialysis is equally effective. Swimming pool water needs recirculation, prefiltration, disinfection with bromine or ozone for killing of algae, while boiler feed water needs purification with cooling circuits and antifouling measures for prevention of scale and corrosion formation. Industrial process needs treatment according to end use.

Table 10.8 Pesticide concentrations in drinking water

Name of pesticide	*Permissible concen.*	*Name of pesticide*	*Permissible concen.*
Dieldrin	0.407	Lindane (BHC)	0.112
Endrin	0.133	Chlordane	0.169
DDT	0.316	Carbamates	0.380
Heptachlor	0.048	2-4 D	< 10.0
Heptachlor epioxide	0.067	2,4,5 J T	< 10.0
Aldrin	0.85		

The treatment of water for swimming pool is specialised job. Treatment consists of filtration followed by application of high dose of chlorine. Alumina and soda ash are used if necessary as coagulants. pH 7.4 is maintained, algae growth is prevented with $CuSO_4$. Removal of excess of detergent from water is also essential. The level of 0.2 mg/L is permitted but removal is complex job. The spraying of pesticide, fungicide and weed killer get contaminated with potable water

(Table 10.8). Activated carbon is best material to remove impurities. In Malaysia and Bangladesh contains as much as 0.05 mg/L of arsenic from the fungicides. Lead is encountered in drinking water, due to contamination by lead service pipes. Lime should be added to remove excess of lead. Nitrates greater than 45 mg/L is very harmful for growing children. It causes methaemoglobinaemia. Nitrate is best removed by anion exchange resin. One can resort to appropriate technology to keep water clean, but such technology is not always helpful to treat the water.

Table 10.9 Organic compounds produced by chlorination in water

Organics	*At pH 7.0 (acidic)* µg/L	*At pH 11.0 (alkalin)* µg/L
Fulric acid	28	39
Humic acid	29	42
Tannic acid	11	61
Lignine sulphonate	3	9
Aspartic acid	2	85
Phenol	24	31

10.13 ORGANIC COMPOUNDS CHARACTERISATION

The water contains organic compounds like trihalomethanes, few anthropogenic compounds, pesticides, polychlorinated bisphenols, phenolic compounds. The chromatography, NMR and mass spectrometry methods facilitated their characteristics and determination (Table 10.9).

(a) Trihalomethanes

The agricultural land serves as percursors for THM. There is seasonal variations of THM in treated water. Average level is $CHCl_3$ (73.1%), $CHBrCl_2$ (21%), $CHBr_2Cl$ (5%) and $CHBr_3$ (0.8%).

(b) Pesticides

Pesticides imparts taste and odour to the water. Carbon tetrachloride extraction and spectral characterisation the presence of DDT aldrin, o-nitrochloro benzene and phenylether is carried out. Compounds like dieldrin, heptachlor, aldrin, organo-phosphorus or carbamates are detected. Also DDT, DDE, DDD lindane and BHC are also detected in river water (Table 10.8).

(c) Polychlorinated Biphenyls (PCB)

It is detected by GLC technique. It resides in solid phase *e.g.*, sediments (0.1 mg/L). Reverse osmosis is used to concentrate organic compounds in the water.

(d) Halogenated Hydrocarbons

The $CHCl_3$ and CCl_4 are present in level of 10^{-9} gms. Trichlorofluoromethane is freely detected. The chlorination leads to the formation of halogenated hydrocarbons. The model compounds or degradation products of humic and fulvic acids as resorcinol, pyrogallol, catchol, orcinol, pathalic acid. The percursor to trihalomethane by chlorination of potable water is complex mixture. Humic substances and low molecules mass compounds containing acetyl moiety are also encountered. Algae is also percursor gives information of their derivatives. The coagulation removes chloroform percursor from both acids prevention of trihalomethane formation. Water is disinfected by agents other then chlorine. NH_2Cl or $NHCl_2$ is used (1.5 to 1.8 mg/L dose). It kills pathogenic bacteria. ClO_2 and O_3 are also recommended for the disinfection but EPA objected as they affect red blood cells, so chlorine remains the best available alternative.

(e) Phenolic Compounds

Phenol needs special mention as it affects the odour and taste of water. It is obtained from natural sources but its anthropogenic source is most important. Its level is 108 to 128 μg/L. The marine water contains several phenols due to contamination of water with the industrial effluents. Microbially mediated degradation reduces their level in water. The presence of cresol, xylenol and phenols is analysed by the gas chromatographic methods. It has organophillic effect on water. Fish readily is affected by phenolic compounds. As much as 0.02 to 0.07 mg/L dose is fatal for any kind of fish in water.

(f) Halogoenated Phenols

These are formed by chlorination of water. When HOCl is added to substituted chloro or nitrophenols at pH 3.5 to 6.0, several products are formed within 20 to 24 hour of period. The superchlorination of water promotes their formation. Waste water is main source of phenols. Chlorophenols are formed during the chlorination of water. Bromophenols are also formed in the presence of bromide anion during bromination of water for swimming pools. Pentachlorophenol (PCP) occurs in sediments only.

10.14 REMOVAL OF ORGANIC COMPOUNDS FROM WATER

The process involves adsorption. The granular activated carbon is used for removal of taste and odour, organic, trihalomethane, or their precursor. Some efforts are made to use synthetic adsorbent for the removal of organics. During such adsorption pore size of activated coal is of atmost importance. The surface area, particle size, its nature, effect of pH or temperature influences the process of adsorption. Powdered activated carbon and the granulated activated carbon is used for the process of adsorption. The ion-exchange resins are best substituents for activated carbon. The surface area of activated adsorbent is determined by BET method.

Activated charcoal is obtained by carbonisation of peat and wood. Activation process renders particles porous. Adsorption increases the concentration of particular constituent at the surface or at interphase between two phases with several applications.

(a) Removal of Taste and Odour

Odours of biological or industrial origin are best removed by activated coal *e.g.*, chlorophenolic compounds give medicinal smell but it is completely removed by activated carbon by process of adsorption.

(b) Removal of Polynuclear Hydrocarbons

Wide range of organic compounds with various structure and size functionality are adsorbed by gas adsorption chromatography. The adsorbility of all compounds is not uniform. Gas solid chromatography with granulated activated carbon removes polynuclear aromatic hydrocarbons. Nitrosoamines are also removed.

(c) Removal of Chlorination Products

The chlorination products which are formed by chlorination of the water are removed. Level is lowered upto 0.1 mg/L. We need high dose of activated carbon. Of these compounds chloroform is poorly adsorbed on the surface of coal.

(d) Removal of Humic Acid Products

Humic acid and analogus products are poorly adsorbed but ClO_2 and O_3 can eliminate them from water sample.

(e) Removal of Free and Combined Chlorine

Superchlorination kills bacteria and algal growth and ammonia fused produces several chloramines are formed during such chlorination as are:

$$C + HOCl \longrightarrow C^{+}O + H^{+} + Cl^{-} \text{ when } OCl^{-} \text{ is free chlorine species}$$

$$C + 2NHCl_2 + H_2O \longrightarrow C^{+}O + 4H^{+} + 4Cl^{-} + N_2 \uparrow$$

$$C + NH_2Cl + H_2O \longrightarrow C^{+}O + H^{+} + Cl^{-} + NH_3 \uparrow$$

10.15 BIOLOGICAL ACTIVATED CARBON FOR MITIGATION OF GROWTH

It is produced to promote biological oxidation of microorganism in addition to adsorption of organics. It is used extensively in water treatment plants. The reactivation is quite simple. It involves removal of adsorbent and heating at 800°C in inert atmosphere. Apart from this one can use synthetic adsorbent for the removal of organics. It includes polymeric adsorbents, ion-exchange resin and synthetic carbon adsorbent. It is based upon the cross linked polymers with polystyrene, phenol formaldehyde or acrylate structure. It is easily regenerated in comparison to BAC. These are microrecticular resins, which are porous with large surface area. Pore size is controlled during synthesis. They remove chlorinated pesticides, dyes methonol and isopropanol. They exhibit step adsorption isotherm. While synthetic carbaceous adsorbent are prepared to partial pyrolysis of beads of copolymer *e.g.*, the commercial form is Ambersoly XE-340. It is strongly basic and is selective. The synthetic anion exchange resins is used for the removal of organic. For such purpose strongly basic resins are best. Trihalogens are best removed on resins like Dowex 21K or Amberlicte IRA-400. Phenol, p-nitrophenol and 2-4 dichlorophenol are best removed from water by process such as ion-exchange resins, which is regenerated by alkali. However, granulated activated carbon is considered to be best alternative in water treatment plants.

10.16 ANALYSIS OF ORGANIC POLLUTANTS FROM WATER

Most of these compounds are analysed by spectrophotometry. Such compounds are either composed of phenol and its derivatives, hydrocarbons, detergents, pesticides and plant health products or micropollutants. Level of phenol is 0.1 to 0.01 mg/litre. Biodegradability of hydrocarbons is slow. It prevents reoxygenation of water and gives a typical smell to it. Surfactants are bad for health. 4-aminoantipyrine reacts with phenol at pH 10 in the presence of $K_3Fe(CN)_6$ to form colored antipyrene dye. It is extracted into chloroform and is measured at 460 nm. Pentachlorophenol and 2, 3, 4, 6 tetrachlorophenols are extracted in benzene and analysed by gas chromatography. If formaldehyde is present in water, it is reacted with acetylacetone in the presence of ammonium salt to form the yellow compound of diacetyl dehydrolutidine, which is measured colorimetrically is at 420 nm. 1 to 8 ppm of it is easily analysed. Humic acid if present in water is directly analysed spectrophotometrically at 250 nm. Amount of 0.1 to 20 mg/litre is easily analysed. Finally, lignin if present in water is used to reduce tungstophosphoric acid to produce a blue colour, which is measured at 624 nm by spectrophotometer. Alkylbenzene sulphonate is measured after extraction in carbon chloroform extracts.

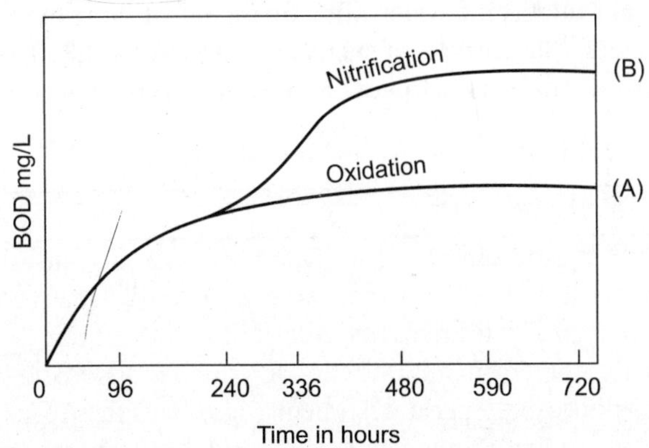

Fig. 10.6 BOD curve with (A) and nitrification (B) at 20°C

Figure 10.6 represents BOD curve (A) for oxidation of organic matter and second curve (B) shows influence of nitrification. These are plotted at 20°C for a period of one month. As time passes BOD demand rises. It indicates change in contents of organic matter during biological oxidation of polluted water under aerobic conditions. The amount of oxygen is used for biochemical oxidation is known we get a parabolic curve. The curve has characteristic behaviour during initial 200–240 hrs. Then BOD curves decreases subsequently after 720 hrs are over.

Table 10.10 Frequency of the analysis of water

S. No.	*Component*	*Limit*	*Frequency*	*Remarks*
1.	Conductivity	1–2 μ mhon/cm	Daily	Throws light on ions present
2.	pH	5.7–7.5	Daily	Quality acidic/alkaline
3.	Ammonia	< 0.1 mg/L	Monthly	Geb evaporated in hot weather
4.	Heterophic count	<1000 cou.	Monthly	Rarely encountered
5.	Total org. carbon	<1.0 mg/L	Annually	Once in year must be done
6.	Trace element single	<.005 mg/L	Annually	Easily analyzed by AAS or ICP-AES
7.	Trace metal (total)	< 0.1 mg/L	Annually	Spectral methods for analysis
8.	Free chlorine	< 0.1 mg/L	Monthly	best OTA method for analysis

It will be clear from Table 10.10 that few parameters such as conductivity; pH undergoes changes with lapse of time therefore the daily analysis is essential. While NH_3 Heterophic count and free chlorine should be preferably absent as they undergo change hence analysed once in month to check quality of water. Total organic carbon, trace elements mostly transition metals are best analysed once in year by AAS or ICP-AES. The elements like mercury Selenium, Tellurium need hydride generator in analysis by AAS technique.

10.17 FREQUENCY OF ANALYSIS

In order to ascertain quality of water after treatment, it is analysed for a fixed number of parameters. The purpose of such analysis is two-folds. The Table 10.11 shows frequency of analysis. However, by and large it is not possible to

Table 10.11 Frequency of analysis of water

S.No.	*Parameters*	*Frequency per day*
1.	Alkalinity	12
2.	Chloride	2
3.	Fluoride	1
4.	Hardness	2
5.	Iron	1
6.	Manganese	1
7.	pH	12
8.	Sodium	1 (3 days)
9.	Sulphate	2 (7 days)
10.	Taste and odour	1
11.	Total solids	2 (7 days)
12.	Trace elements (As Cu Pb Se Zn)	1 per quarter (3 months)
13.	Turbidity	12 (daily)

analyse all the parameters in one single instance. As seen, alkalinity or acidity or pH needs frequent measurement (Table 10.11). The trace metals are analysed once in a quarter year, chloride, hardness fluoride, manganese, taste and odour are analysed daily. Sulphate, iron, total solids are analysed once a week or fortnight. This schedule is valid under normal circumstances; however if there is some emergency due to contamination or pollution of treated water, then it is necessary to undertake more frequent analysis. Thus, an exotic or random analysis is performed during emergency only.

(a) Carbon Dioxide

The total concentration of carbon dioxide changes periodically. It should be determined on the spot near the source. As in transportation it absorbs more of CO_2 from the atmosphere. The titration of water sample with 0.045 NaOH or 0.023 N Na_2CO_3 is carried out with precautions. The reactions encountered during titration are as follows:

$$CO_2 + 2NaOH \longrightarrow Na_2CO_3 + H_2O$$

$$CO_2 + Na_2CO_3 + H_2O \longrightarrow 2NaHCO_3$$

If organic impurities are present, they produce CO_2 by aerobic and anaerobic reactions. Further CO_2 imparts corrosive properties to water as concentration greater than 20 mg/litre is objectionable. However, it has no adverse effect upon health of human beings.

(b) Chlorine

The methods are based on the oxidising property of chlorine gas. Manganese (II) and nitrites have adverse effect on such oxidising property. The qualitative tests consists of starch iodide test with reaction as:

$$Cl_2 + I_2^- \longrightarrow I_2^0 + 2Cl;\ I_2^- + \text{starch} \longrightarrow \text{Blue colour}$$

Orthotoludine method (OTA) is the best method for spectrophotometry. It is shown by the reaction (Fig. 10.7).

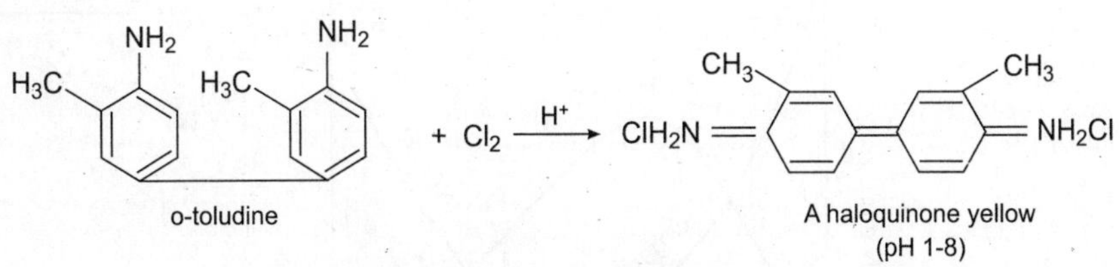

Fig. 10.7 Reaction mechanism of chlorine with o-toludine

Since the nitrites and manganese (II) oxidise o-toludine to haloquinones, it must be removed from water by treatment with sodium arsenite as their presences gives wrong results for free and combined chlorine. The use of amperometric titration, stabilizes neutral orthotoludine or NN' diethyl p-phenylenediamine (DPD) reactions; or NN' dimethyl-aniline techniques (Lecuo crystal) phenyl arsenic oxide (C_6H_5AsO) all are used in amperiometric titratant; at pH 6.5 to 7.5. The slow reaction of *o*-toludine at neutral pH is used when buffered at pH 6.5 to 7.5. A blue colour is spectrophotometrically measured. In DPD method, red colour formed is measured when pH for reaction is 6.2 to 6.5. In leucocrystal method NN' dimethylaniline produces violet colour with chlorine, which is measured spectrophotometrically.

(c) Coagulation Test

It is termed as jar test. The idea is to artificially simulate such conditions in the laboratory and check how much of coagulant is needed for completion of the reaction. It decides its dose at fixed temperature and pH. The flash mixing is done when best appearing floc is formed. The relative merit of coagulant or coagulant aid is ascertained. Zeta potential of floc and colloidal material is evaluated by electrophoresis cell. The difference should be such that more colloidal material is attached to floc. The addition of polyelectrolytes should not increase the alkalinity.

(d) Phosphate and Phosphorus

These compounds are used for corrosion control. Nitrogen and phosphorus are conducive for growth of algae (Fig. 10.8). The critical levels is 0.005 mg/litre or 5 mg/ml. Sewage contains abundant amount of phosphates. Detergents contain polyphosphates (12–13% P). The method for analysis of phosphate and polyphosphate are relatively simple, *e.g.*, by gravimetric method the formation of pyrophosphate (< 50 mg/litre) by precipitation reaction is weighed. The overall reaction is as follows:

$$PO_4^{3-} + 12(NH_4)_2 MoO_4 + 24H^+ \longrightarrow (NH_4)_3 PO_4 + 12MoO_3 + 21NH_4^+ + 12H_2O$$

$$(NH_4)_3 PO_4 + 12MoO_3 + Sn^{2+} \longrightarrow \text{(molybdenum blue)} + Sn^{4+}$$

The colour of molybdenum blue is spectrophotometrically measured. The complex is extracted in benzene, isobutanol and measured colorimetrically providing better accuracy (Fig. 10.9).

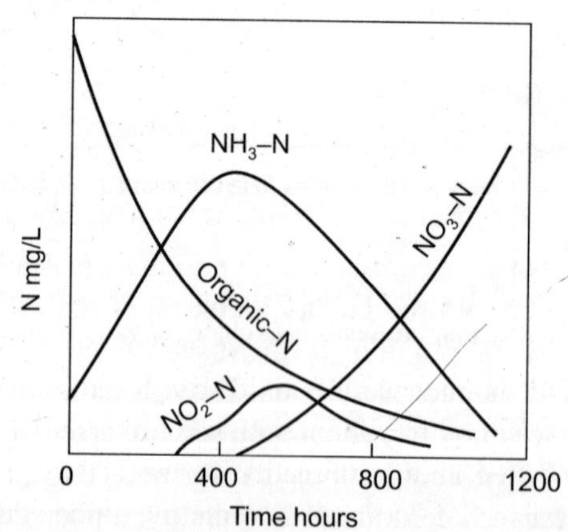

Fig. 10.8 Transformation of N_2 in aerobic conditions

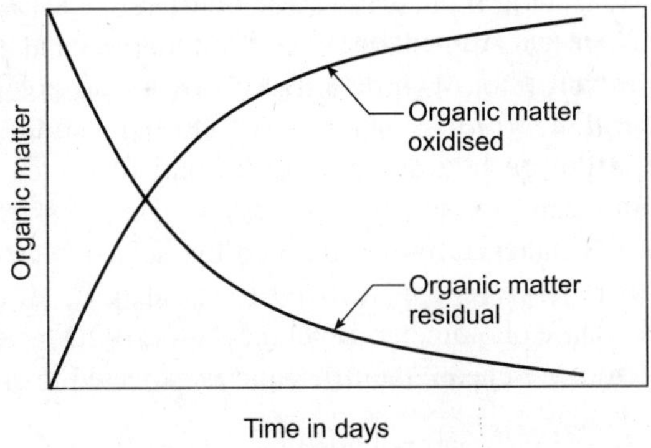

Fig. 10.9 Degradation of organic matter

10.18 WATER QUALITY MONITORING INSTRUMENTS

In 1978, a committee was appointed by Government of India, Dept. of Science and Technology in order to ascertain need of such instruments by various users in India. The findings of such committee are summarised in Table 10.12 through Table 10.13. The (×) indicates the need of the instrument.

Table 10.12 Demand of monitoring devices by typical industries

S. No.	*Industry*	*No. of units*	*Turbidity meter*	*Suspended Solid*	*Tempe-rature*	*BOD*	*COD*	*Trace metals anal.*
1.	Sugar	300	×	×	–	×	–	–
2.	Breweries	100	×	×	–	×	×	–
3.	Soda ash	30	×	×	–	–	–	–
4.	Fertilizers	70	×	–	×	–	–	–
5.	Oil refineries	15	×	×	–	×	×	×
6.	Synthetic fibre	30	×	–	×	×	×	–
7.	Textile mills	950	×	–	–	×	×	–
8.	Paper industry	200	×	–	–	×	–	–
9.	Drugs	300	×	×	–	×	×	–
10.	Pesticides	70	×	×	–	×	×	–
11.	Thermal plants	50	–	×	×	–	–	×

We have considered various parameters, which are measured for potable water or treated water for industrial purposes. However to measure large number of samples with constraint of time, it is imperative to use rapid methods of analysis on a regular basis, to ascertain the quality. Such rapid measurement is possible only with the use of water quality monitoring instruments. Thus, it is worthwhile to examine requirements of such instrument by various industries. Table 10.12 provides demand of such monitoring instruments by industrial enterprises. All important industries are listed, and few parameters are considered for such measurements. The average demand for a year is then roughly calculated. All industries need to measure suspended solids; BOD and COD while trace metals or oil and grease is determined in thermal plants and refinery. The annual requirement for sugar industry is the largest, so also textile industries, specially in cities like Mumbai, Delhi, Kanpur and Ahmedabad. The drug industry has a large demand. Food industries, thermal plant, synthetic fibre factory do not need too many measurements. Table 10.13 gives the need for monitoring instruments by research laboratories, state pollution boards and educational institutes in India. Only important water monitoring instruments are listed. The list shows that there is highest demand for pH meter, turbidimeter, and ion selective electrode analyser and spectrophotometer. There is less demand for AAS, GC, HPLC, as they are quite expensive. The flame photometer, BOD incubator, BOD meter, DO analyser and conductivity meters are cheap, their demand is expected to rise in future.

Table 10.13 Needs for water pollution monitoring instruments (1980)

S.No.	*Instrument*	*R and D Labs.*	*Pollution Boards*	*Educational Institutes*	*Total demand*
1.	pH meter	4500	100	500	5100
2.	Conductivity meter	–	100	500	600
3.	Dissolved oxygen meter	–	100	500	600
4.	Turbidity meter	3000	100	500	3600
5.	BOD incubator	–	100	100	200
6.	COD meter	–	100	100	200
7.	Mercury analyser	30	40	100	170
8.	Atomic absorption spectrometer	–	20	100	120
9.	Gas chromatograph	–	20	100	120
10.	Spectrophotometer	–	20	100	120
11.	Ion selective electrode	1000	20	100	1120
12.	TOC analyser	20	20	100	140
13.	Gas chromatograph Mass spectrometer		5	100	105
14.	High pressure liquid chromatograph	20	5	100	125
15.	Polarograph	–	20	100	120
16.	Ion chromatograph	–	5	100	105
17.	Infrared spectrometer	–	5	100	105
18.	X-ray fluoroscence	–	5	100	105
19.	Flame photometer	200	100	100	400
20.	Thin layer chromatography	–	40	100	140

10.19 TYPE OF WATER QUALITY INSTRUMENTS

The Tables from 10.12 to 10.16 outlines the need for water pollution monitoring instruments in small, medium and the advanced research laboratories. Table 10.14 lists instruments for the measurement of physical parameters such as temperature, pH, conductivity, turbidity, humidity, suspended particulate matter and sunshine recorder. This set is good for a very small laboratory. Table 10.15 gives a set-up for a relatively big laboratory. It measures many parameters. The important

Table 10.14 Water quality monitoring instruments for small laboratory

Parameter	*Instrument*	*Limit of analysis*
Temperature	Thermistor	0–50°C
pH	pH meter	0–14 pH
Conductivity	Conductivity bridge	1 mho to 1 micromho
Dissolved oxygen	DO meter	0–20 ppm
Turbidity	Comparison tubes	1–100 JU
Humidity	Hydrometer	0–100% humidity
Microscopic examination	Microscope	1 × 100 magnification
SPM—measurement	Dust collectors	Large size collection

Table 10.15 Water quality monitoring instrument for medium size laboratory

Instrument	*Parameter*	*Limit of analysis*
Thermistor thermometer	Temperature	0–50°C
pH meter	pH	0–14
Conductivity meter	Conductivity	1 micromho to 1 M mho
Dissolved oxygen meter	Dissolved oxygen	0–20 ppm
Turbidity meter	Turbidity	0–10,000 JU
Ion analyser	Ionic concentration	10^{-1} mg-μg level
BOD analyser/incubator	BOD for 3 days	0.1 mg/litre
Flame photometer	s-block metals	Na, K, Ca filters
Spectrophotometer	Transition metals	325–825 nm
Microscope	Biological investigation	× 500 magnification

Table 10.16 Water quality instrument for advanced analytical laboratory

Instrument	*Parameter*	*Limit*
pH meter	pH	0–14
Conductivity meter	Conductivity	1 mho to 1 micro mho
Dissolved oxygen meter	DO	0–20 ppm
Redox monitor	Redox potential	± 2000 mV
Turbidity meter	Turbidity	0–10,000 JU
Ion selective electrode	Ionic concentration	mg-μg, broad
BOD and COD monitor	BOD/COD	0.1–5 mg/litre
Nephelometer	Turbidance	400–700 nm
Spectrophotometer	Absorbance	200 to z2000 nm
Atomic absorption Spectrophotometer	Metal pollutants at nanogram level	190 to 800 nm
Gas chromotographs	Volatile organics	With FID, ECD, TCD detector
IR spectrophotometer	Organic compounds	With KBr pellet or Nujol technique

chemical parameters are dissolved oxygen, alkali metals, BOD; metal pollutants and plate count (MPN). It gives information on the most vital parameters such as conductivity; DO; turbidity, metal pollutants, and biological plate count. Table 10.16 contains a comprehensive list of water quality instruments for an advanced analytical laboratory. One gets a reliable information not only on physical, but also chemical *viz* inorganic as well as organic pollutants. Table 10.17 lists recommends water quality instruments. The last column lists principles upon which these methods are based. This set-up is ideal for Indian conditions. Figure 10.10 gives a picture of water pollution monitoring kit, which was developed by in the

Table 10.17 Recommended most essential water quality monitoring instruments

Instrument	*Parameter*	*Principle*
Water analysis kit	pH, DO, temperature conductivity	— Temperature 0 to 55°C — Conductivity 1.0 mho tol mohms — Dissolved oxygen 0–20 ppm
Digital pH meter	pH	0–14
Chloride meter	Chloride	Coulometry, technique, (Faraday law)
Chloroscope	Residual chlorine gas	Visual comparison with standard coloured disc
Polarograph	Metals and pesticides	Ilokovic equation, half-wave potential
Spectrophotometer	Organic and metal pollutants	Beer's Lamberts law at 350–700 nm
Turbidity or Nephelometer	Scattering or absorbance of suspended particles	Scattering of radiation

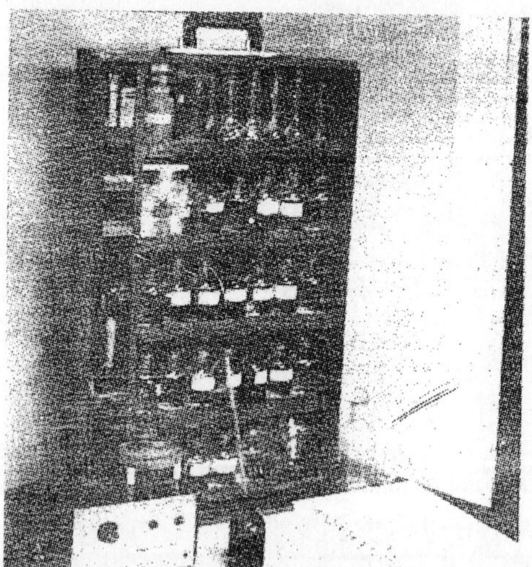

Fig. 10.10 Water pollution monitoring kit developed in IIT.B

Lab of Centre of Environmental Science and Engineering in IIT, Mumbai. This kit measures as many as eighteen-parameters which are important for ascertaining the quality of water. It is a portable kit which weighs six kg. The principle of Ring-oven Technique is used for analysis of metal pollutants.

The method of volumetric analysis is recommended for analysis of acidity, alkalinity, CO_2, NH_3, hardness analysis, while one day rapid test is recommended for plate count and BOD analysis. The extensive field tests were carried out to assess its suitability for field and outdoor work.

10.20 PERSPECTIVE PLANNING FOR FUTURE

Several instruments are used for water pollution monitoring. They are listed in Table 10.18. This table lists fifteen vitally important instruments useful for water quality monitoring. Out of these instruments majority of them are available in India; while few are at developmental stages while limited of these instruments have to be imported. A perspective planning for the future is essential. All efforts should be made to develop these instruments in India on the long run.

Table 10.18 Instruments available in India

S.No.	*Monitoring instrument*
1.	Photoelectric photometer
2.	Spectrophotometer
3.	Flame emission spectrometer
4.	Atomic absorption spectrometer (AAS)≠
5.	Turbidimeter
6.	pH meter
7.	Ion analyser≠
8.	Conductivity bridge
9.	Gas-liquid chromatograph≠
10.	Polarograph
11.	Mass spectrometer*
12.	Nuclear magnetic resonance (NMR)*
13.	X-ray fluorescence (XRF)*
14.	Dissolved oxygen probe (DO)
15.	Biological oxygen demand monitor (BOD)
16.	Electron microscope*

* Imported, ≠ Development stage.

10.21 CONCLUSION

The quality of water after treatment needs examination. The important steps in water treatment include sedimentation which permits settling of flock formed by addition of coagulants. It is followed by filtration which includes slow sand and rapid sand filtration. Injection involving chlorine is most important part in the process of chlorination of water. The concept of break point chlorination is important. Trihalomethane formation is great hindrance in chlorinated water. Ozonolysis and UV radiation are rapid methods of disinfection but are prohibited by US-EPA. The removal of iron, manganese hardness by lime/soda ash or deionisation process is best method. The Calgon process works on small scale. Taste and odour are very offensive for drinking water. Fluoridation is efficient process. Some needs special treatment. Many organic compounds like trihalomethanes, pesticides residues, PCB, halogenated hydrocarbons, phenols contaminate water and their removal is possible with granulated activated charcoal or ion-exchange resins. Excess chlorine is harmful hence it needs removal. The characterisation of organic compounds is most commonly carried out by spectrophotometry or gas chromatography. The frequency of analysis must be raised if water pollution is serious. Rapid analysis includes analysis of CO_2 Cl_2, PO_4^{3-} and the different coagulants. The water pollution monitoring instruments for continuous measurement are very limited. The demand in India for different kinds of laboratories and minimum plan of requirement is chalked out. Much work needs to be done for design and development indigenously water pollution monitoring instruments. The water pollution monitoring kit developed is outcome of such modest efforts in IIT Bombay. Only NITs and Central Universities should undertake this task of fabrication.

ADDITIONAL READING

1. W.J. Weber, *Physio Chemical Process for Water Quality Control*, Wiley Interscience (1972).
2. *Standard Method for Examination of Water and Waste Water, 20th Ed*, American Public Health Association, New York (2000)
3. R.A. Horne, *Chemistry of Environment*, Wiley Interscience (1978).
4. I.M. Kolthoff, P.J. Elving, M.J. Stross, *Treatise in Analytical Chemistry, Vol. 2*, Part III, Wiley Interscience (1971).
5. C.N. Sawyer and P.J. McCarty, *Chemistry for Environmental Engineering, 3rd Ed.*, McGraw Hill and Co. (1977).
6. L.L. Ciaccio, *Water and Water Pollution Handbook*, Marcell Dekker, N.Y. (1972).
7. *Water Treatment Handbook, 5th Ed.*, Degremount Halsted Press of John Wiley and Co. (1979).
8. N.F. Voznaya, *Chemistry of Water and Microbiology*, Mir Publishing House (1981).
9. F.I. Belan, *Water Treatment*, Mir Publishing House, Moscow (1984).
10. I.L. Marr and M.S. Cresser, *Environmental Chemical Analysis*, Chapman and Hall, New York (1983).
11. T. Harvey, *Notes on Environmental Monitoring and Control*, Tottenham College of Technology, London (1978).
12. D.B. Shinde, Mayuri Gandhi and S.M. Khopkar—Ind. J. Env protect **11, 801** (1991).
13. C. Baird, *Environmental Chemistry,* W.H. Freeman and Co. (1995).
14. R.J. Schmitz, *Water Pollution Biology,* Asian Book Co. (1996).
15. G. Sinethrw, *Basic Water Treatment for Applications,* Worldwide—Open University Book, 2nd Ed (1988).

•

16. S.D. Faust and O.M. Aly, *Chemistry of Water Treatment,* Butterworth Annarbor Science Book (1983).
17. J.C. Lamb, *Water Quality and Its Control*, John Wiley (1985).
18. J.W. Moore, *Inorganic Contaminates of Surface Water*. Res and Monitoring Priority, Springer Verlag (1990).
19. S.E. Manhan, *Environmental Chemistry, 7th Edition*, Lewis Publisher (1999).
20. S.M. Khopkar, *Environmental Pollution Analysis*, Second Edition, New Age International Publishers (P) Ltd. (2012).

11

Waste Water

11.1 INTRODUCTION

Water after use is disposed off into the sea, or a stream. Such water which is used for domestic or industrial purposes is considered useless from the point of further use and is therefore it is disposed off. Such disposable and used water is called as *waste water*, indicating thereby that it is waste as far as its consumption is concerned. Out of the total water consumed by human being, more than 50% of it is consumed in industrial activity; and only a very small proportion is used for drinking purposes. The water which is emerging out of industry after processing is termed also as industrial effluent. The water which emerges out after domestic consumption in toilet and washing which is largely in form of sewage is called as *domestic effluent* or *sewage*. It is not proper to term this water as waste water, because it is always possible to recover useful materials from it and reuse it by recycling or treatment for some other purposes. The pollutants associated with industrial effluents are organic matter, inorganic dissolved solids, fertilizing materials; thermal constituents in the form of heat, suspended solids and microorganism and pathogens. Organic pollutants decrease the limit of dissolved oxygen, impart bad odour and colour to the effluent. If contaminated with marine environment, it would have substantial rise in its salinity. If there is a high concentration of phosphate and nitrate which is normally the case with it, it will cause eutrophication. Thermal pollution of waste water causes deoxygenation and causes serious ecological problems. Food processing industry effluent promotes viruses and bacterial growth posing health hazards with high value for BOD.

In order to eliminate problems of liquid waste as well as solid waste, new laws are coming into existence all over the world. UNEP and OECD are working out international code pertaining to hazardous waste, its treatments and disposal. EEC have already defined toxic waste and prescribed norms for its transportation but these norms are poorly implemented. Switzerland and France enacted a practical legislation on waste management. UK is somewhat cautious in enanciating laws however the USA-EPA is accepting best of all existing laws in the world. Their waste legislations are in the dynamic state of transition all round the world, therefore it is felt all over the world to have laws. If it is soon realised in world it would have legislations to regulate the easy transportation of industrial waste to a place where the best treatment is successfully given with confidence so as to maintain clean environment. The treatment of industrial waste waters with new technology processes, approaches and modification are all the order of the day. The knowledge of mass transfer, chemical kinetics and system analysis is valuable in treatment of waste water. The waste water treatment is broadly divided into primary treatment (screening, flotation, neutralisation) and secondary treatment (activated sludge process, lagoons, trickling filters) and the tertiary treatment (precipitation, adsorption, ion-exchange disinfection etc). The main source of waste water is domestic sewage, industrial waste water, agricultural runoff and storm water, urban runoff waste water after treatment is discharged into natural body of water. It depends upon the country *e.g.*, in Saudi Arabia much costly process like reverse osmosis is employed to get fresh water from effluent stream. Waste water if not treated has adverse effect on environment and health. The deoxygenation of streams leads to less value for DO. It being least in early morning. It also leads to decomposition of carbonaceous and nitrogenous organic matter. There is eutrophication—which is natural process of lake aging with algae bloom. The surface, ground and meteorilogical water are three kinds of water supply. Water contamination may be chemical, physical or biological. Heavy metals contaminate waste water, biological contamination leads to water-borne diseases. On account of scarcity of water due to uncertain rainfall the methodology of water harvesting has come forward. Several state government (*e.g.*, Maharashtra) have made it mandatory for builders to water harvesting. It is storage of rain water in new constructions (2002).

11.2 EFFLUENT TREATMENT AND LEGISLATION

Table 11.1 Standards for effluents

Parameter	*Stipulated norms*	*Water (River)*	*Water (Marine)*
pH	6–8	6–8	1–13
BOD	500–100 mg/l	10–20 mg/L	10–200 mg/L
Suspended solids	1000 g/m^3	10–30 g/m^3	150–300 g/m^3
Metals (Hg, Cd)	0.1 μg/m^3	0.1 μg/m^3	0.1 μg/m^3
Metalloid (all)	10–20 g/m^3	5–10 g/m^3	10–20 g/m^3
Ammonia	20–100 g/m^3	10–100 gm/m^3	—

Such legislations varies from country to country. EEC tried to regularise different laws in various places. There are several options for dealing industrial effluents like amend the process, treat effluent at plant or at site to discharge it to fresh or tidal water. The ultimate goal is to conform to legal stipulation of maintaining a quality of the effluents of some parameters relatety to pH, DO, H_2S, metals, nutrients, NH_3, organic mass. Legal requirements stipulate certain standards (Table 11.1) for parameters for effluent discharge.

11.3 CHARACTERISTIC OF WASTE WATER

Waste water contains soluble organics, suspended solids, trace organics and heavy metals, which reduce DO, promote release of gases, cause taste and odour, impart colour or turbidity, promote eutrophication, or accelerate air pollution by generating H_2S. The test such as BOD, COD, TOC and TOD throw some light on the organic contents of waste water. Solid hazardous wastes is ignitable, corrosive, reactive and toxic in nature. The effects of the waste or sewage of human beings are significant. The inorganic constituents promote the growth of microscopic plant life. Wastes are corrosive in nature. The organic matter exhausts the oxygen contents of water or dissolved oxygen. The suspended solids cause odour and decrease level of oxygen floating solids like grease oils. Abstract passage of light through water is measured in terms of Lux and it stops aeration process. Colour also prevents light transmission and reduce photosynthesis. Toxic chemicals kill flora and fauna in water. The bacteria help degradation of organic matter but those which are pathogenic in nature spread disease. The suspended solids lead to sedimentation at bottom or clogging of filter media. Industrial waste also contains toxic heavy metals (Cu, Cd, or Zn) which arrest biological oxidation, while detergents cause foaming, generate acids, corrode pipes and rags clogg pumps.

It is difficult to classify industrial effluents on the basis of its composition, on account of diversity of modern industrial process and practices. It may be possible to classify waste water on the basis of its contents, or rather origin from which it emerges. For instance, effluent from food industry contains too much of organic matter, while effluent from textile industry contains detergents while effluent from plating industry contains cyanide and metal pollutants. Hence classification is based upon the sources and procedures used for specific industrial situation.

(i) Effluent from Chemical Industries

The waste water emerging from chemical industries, such as heavy chemicals and fine chemical factory or explosive factories, fertiliser plants and pesticide factories belongs to this category. The waste water is coloured, waste water has strong offensive odour, is acidic (pH 2.6); power plant waste is highly acidic while waste water from pesticide industry contains abnormally high concentration of organic phosphorus compounds, which are toxic to flora and fauna in water. Phosphatic industry waste contains tallow and slimes, suspended matter with acidic character. All waste have high BOD. The non-degradable matter increases BOD due to presence of soaps, detergents and fatty acids. The waste from material and chemical industry are similar in many ways. Chemical waste includes acids bases, toxic materials with high BOD, low suspended solids. Such waste needs treatment before its final disposal. Acid waste demands neutralisation with lime. The acid waste is sometimes diluted before process of the neutralisation. The sulphuric acid containing waste is hazardous and therefore it needs a special treatment. Corn starch waste is also harmful and needs specific treatment. It contains volatile organics. A process of trickling filters is employed for its treatment. Phosphatic waste is encountered in mines and rocks. The volume is high, it contains also fluoride. The process of lagooning, oxidising and settling and final centrifugation is used. Soap and detergent industries produce less waste. They cause frothing. The contents are not easily biodegradable. The explosive industry (*e.g.*, TNT factory) and those making firearms require special treatment. The TNT waste is coloured with high load of volatile solids, bad odour and acidic in nature. For their treatment coagulation and sedimentation is not effective but process of chlorination though costly is essential. Aeration and biological oxidation is other mode of treatment. Colour is something which has terrible nuisance value. The formaldehyde waste needs special treatment. High rate trickling filters is used for treatment at controlled pH of 4.5 to 8.5. The waste from insecticide industry is very troublesome. It contains harmful chemicals. It is passed through filter bed of activated carbon but is expensive proposition. The waste containing DDT, DCP; 2, 4 D is toxic. The best process is to keep these insecticides, herbicide, or pesticides away from water course and not allow them to contaminate. The Table 11.2 summarises typical characteristics viz. BOD and Suspended Solids (SS) in different effluents emerging from various industries.

Table 11.2 BOD_5 and suspended solids in waste water from processing industry

S. No.	*Kind of industrial process*	BOD_5	*Suspended solids*	*Remarks*
1.	Concrete, plastic product waste	310	10000	High susp. matter
2.	Dairy products	2100	370	High BOD
3.	Fats oils and waxes	1300	1100	High BOD susp. matter
4.	Flat glass, ceramic industry, potteries	310	370	Low BOD
5.	Food preparation	4100	930	V. High BOD
6.	Grain, mill processing plant	3200	4500	V. High BOD susp. matter
7.	Industrial organic material	310	370	Low BOD
8.	Industrial launderers, clothing	870	1100	Low BOD
9.	Leather and tanning industry	1300	1700	High BOD high susp. matter
10.	Meat fish products, marine waste	800	520	Medium BOD
11.	Medicine, pharma products, breweries	4500	4700	Waste V. High susp. matter
12.	Petroleum, combustion products	310	370	Low BOD
13.	Preserved fruits, vegetables	1400	370	High BOD
14.	Primary metal products	310	370	Low BOD
15.	Paints, pigments, varnishes	2500	600	High BOD
16.	Bakery confectionery products	2500	1100	High BOD High susp. matter
17.	Sea food, fish, marine products	1400	600	Low susp. matter

(ii) Waste Water from Food Processing Industry

In India food and beverage factories are limited to cities like Mumbai, Kolkata, Delhi and Chennai. However, in western India we have a network of such industries including. The effluent from such sources have a very high BOD, suspended organic solids, dissolved organic matter. The effluent from a canned food, dairy products, meat poultry preparation, contains high level of proteins, carbohydrates, aminoacids, alkali metals and phosphates. Rice polishing waste contains a high level of nitrogen, with pH 10.8 and BOD of more than 430 mg/litre. Liquid effluents from fish processing industry has a strong odour, while pickel waste is badly coloured. Table 11.4 contains characteristics of distillery waste. It has a high concentration of nitrogen, chloride, sulphates with extremely high value for BOD. While Table 11.3 contains list of components irrespective of whether it is inorganic or organic material and their level.

Table 11.3 Toxic level of waste

S.No.	*Inorganic waste*	*Concn. (mg/l)*	*S.No.*	*Organic waste*	*Concn. (mg/l)*
1.	Ammonia (NH_3)	1500	11.	Isopropanol	100
2.	Arsenic (As)	1.6	12.	Acryl nitrile	5
3.	Boron (B)	2.0	13.	Benzidine	5
4.	Cadmium (Cd)	0.02	14.	Chloroform	10–16
5.	Chromium (Cr^{2+}, Cr^{3+})	5–500	15.	Carbon tetrachloride	10–20
6.	Copper (Cu)	1–10	16.	Methylene chloride	100–500
7.	Iron (Fe)	5	17.	Trichloroethane	1.0
8.	Magnesium (Mg)	1000	18.	Trichlorofluoro ethane	5–20
9.	Sodium (Na)	3500	19.	Alcohol, octyl	200
10.	Zinc (Zn)	5–20	20.	Alcohol, ally	200

Table 11.4 Characteristics of distillery waste

S. No.	*Parameter*	*Spirit (con)*	*Molasses (con)*	*Wine (con)*
1.	Colour	Brown-black	Black	Black
2.	Odour	Offensive	Bad	Pungent
3.	Temperature	89–96°C	80°	75–80°
4.	pH	4.0–4.6	4.1	3.8
5.	BOD	3500–4500 mg/L	34,100	21,000
6.	COD	3500–9300 mg/L	High	High
7.	Total solids	5200–8600 mg/L	43,000 mg/L	10,000 mg/L
8.	Suspended solids	2000–14000 mg/L	40,000 mg/L	8,000 mg/L
9.	Total nitrogen	1000–1500 ppm	–	–
10.	Sodium	120–250 ppm	–	–
11.	Potassium	800–12000 ppm	–	–
12.	Calcium	300–800 ppm	–	–
13.	Iron	30–80 ppm	–	–
14.	Sulphate	1500-4500 ppm	–	–
15.	Chloride	4500-8000 ppm	–	–

The perusal of Table 11.3 indicates that the extent of toxic compounds both inorganic as well as organic. The results shows that ammonia, magnesium and sodium are tolerated at very high level while some materials are tolerated at very low concentration as Cadmium as well as Trichloroethane. In any case when we desire to recycle the waste water (grey water) we have to remove even traces of metals and other organic products.

The food industry encompasses canning, dairies, breweries, distilleries, sugar and some pharmaceutical industries. BOD varies are from 100 to 100,000 ppm. Suspended solids is 120,000 ppm pH = 11.0 or 3.5 and the confectionery waste contains fruits and vegetable matter. It has high moisture contents. BOD varies from 100 to 7000 ppm while suspended solids from 30 to 200 ppm. The treatment consist of screening, precipitation, lagooning and spray irrigation. The biological oxidation is used. The dairy waste contains milk cheese, cream and icecream in untreated form. Such wastes are slightly alkaline and undergo fermentation to become acidic and produce odour. The technique of aeration, trickling filtration, activated sludge treatment is resorted for their treatment as anaerobic digestion is best. Aeration reduces BOD. The brewery involves fermentation process with decomposition of organic substance to ferment. A good example of the fermentation is of grapes. Yeast is by-product of such a waste. The BOD decreases with trickling filters. Electrodialysis, anaerobic digestion is also used for treatment. Meat industry waste needs good treatment. It is coloured with high BOD and suspended solids. The quality is similar to domestic sewage. The screening, sedimentation precipitation trickling filter or activated sludge treatment is followed. The chlorination is also employed. Sugar industry waste is common in North India in Uttar Pradesh and Uttaranchal states. The reuse is resorted for land spraying and lagooning. The coffee production units and soft drink waste needs special treatment. The colloidal material is common. It is alkaline contains suspended solids. Such waste is mixed with domestic sewage for further treatment.

(iii) Effluent from Textiles, Tanneries Industry

Table 11.5 presents characteristics of waste water from textile industries at various stages of processing. The quality of waste water from various textile processing operations is given in terms of pH, BOD and solid contents, while Table 11.6 gives quality of waste water from textile industry. A close examination of Table 11.6 indicates that the average pH value of waste water in all cases exceeds 8. The COD is high for textile industry, the rayon waste contains high level of zinc, *viz.*, 6.20 and finally leather and tanning industries has high level of the chlorides, alkalies and metals like Cr, as $K_2Cr_2O_7$ is used for hide treatment and tanneries waste.

The industrial effluent from textile industry in particular has very high BOD, suspended solid and temperature. It has a bad colour due to dyeing operation and is alkaline processes in nature. The waste water from wool mills contain soap, oils, detergents; while ammonia, copper, salt, acetic acid is detected in silk industry waste. The leather industry waste contains high percentage of proteins, precipitated lime, chromium in the form of dichromate, sodium chloride, ammoniacal nitrogen and suspended solids.

Table 11.5 Quality of Textile waste while processing

S. No.	Stages of processing	Significant observation	BOD lb/1000	% load Solids
1.	Desizing	High BOD, pH, total solids, alkalinity and high temperature	53	35
2.	Bleaching	High BOD, pH, and suspended solids, chlorine	8	3.0
3.	Mercerising	Low BOD and solids, high alkalinity	6	1.0
4.	Dyeing	High BOD, neutral or alkaline pH, unreacted dyes	0.5–32	15.30
5.	Printing	Colouring matter, acidic effluent, suspended matter	12	7.0
6.	Finishing	Waxes, starch products, solids, low pH	50	1–2

Table 11.6 Quality of waste from clothing Textile, Rayon, Leather industries

S. No.	Parameter	Textile	Viscose rayon	Leather
1.	pH	7.0–11.8	8.6–9.4	8.0
2.	BOD	100–900	–	1700
3.	COD	250–1800	50–200	3500
4.	Sulphate (mg/litre)	–	1500–7000	–
5.	Chloride (mg/litre)	–	–	4600

The textile waste is coloured and is alkaline with high BOD and suspended solids. Starch waste constitutes (16%) major share, 53% BOD, 37% suspended solids. The processing constitute, 65% of total volume. Wool industry waste may contain organic solvents, oils and greases. Wool scouring and finishing product effluents with pH 9–10 with 900 ppm BOD 3000 ppm suspended solids. Major BOD contribution is by dyeing process. Rayon is made of regenerated cellulose, *nylon* is cellulose acetate fiber or long chain polymer, *orlon* is trade name containing acrylic units while *dacron* is polyesters fiber from ethylene glycol and terephthalale acid. The volume and strength needs immediate action. The worst among apparel waste is tannery industry waste. It has 8000 ppm suspended solids 1000 ppm proteins 40 ppm chromium and 1000 ppm BOD with pH 11–12. The process of curing, fleshing unhairing, lime splittering, bating and decreasing are the important steps of leather treatment. Primary sedimentation, lagooning chemical precipitation are main process of treatment. The laundry waste is service industry waste. It has high pH 10.3 with BOD of 1800 ppm and total suspended solid 2000 ppm. The COD is 350 ppm. Chemical floccalation and precipitation should be tried however in most of the cases it is mixed with domestic sewage waste water and disposed but it is unhealthy practise and should be discarded.

(iv) Waste Water from Material Industry

These industries consists of paper pulp, steel, electroplating, foundry, smithy, rubber and glass industries. Table 11.7 summarises kinds of pollutants liberated, by such material industries. The paper mill waste has colloidal colouring matter, sulphate nondegradable lignine sulphonates, waxes, dyes and bleaching agents. While steel industry waste is acidic due to high mineral contents, cyanides, and alkalis; the pickel waste contains zinc, chromium, iron, and latex waste contains coagulated rubber, suspended solids and has pH value of 3.2 to 7.9.

Table 11.7 Material waste

S.No.	*Source*	*Pollutants present*
1.	Leather	Sulphides, organic, lime and chromates with colour. Alkaline pH, large BOD/COD, dissolved solids
2.	Textiles and apparel	Alkaline pH, sodium, organic matters, dissolved and suspended solids and colouring matter
3.	Milk and food products	High BOD, colloidal solids, slow rate of biodegradation, offensive odours, dissolved and suspended solids
4.	Slaughter houses	Very high BOD, bad odour, proteins and is toxic have phosphates
5.	Drugs and pharmaceuticals	High or low pH, total solids, toxic organics, metal pollutants
6.	Electroplating bath	Acidity and toxic metals, cyanides
7.	Paper pulp factories	Strong intense colour, sulphide of sodium, alkaline earths, lignite sulphonate, black liquor and quebacha.

Such waste is categorised into three groups: wood fiber, metal and liquid processing. The paper pulp is important class of the material waste in India. All materials are converted in to fiber for further processing. It contains soda, sulphite in black liquor. Its BOD varies from 100 to 700 ppm and suspended solids range from 150 to 1800 ppm. The pH ~ 9.5 with colour. The black liquor mainly contains lignin, sugar, sulphur and calcium. The main process of treatment is sedimentation and floatation followed by chemical precipitation. Activated sludge, lagooning is followed. Photographic waste is common in towns in south India. It is material industries waste, where attempts are made to recover silver. The second category is metal wastes which consists of wash from steel mills, plating industry. It comes from ammonia stills with pH ~ 8.9, cyanide 100 ppm, BOD of 4000 ppm and phenols of 2000 ppm level. Dilution with sewage reduces phenolic contents. Neutralisation with lime is costly proposition. The wash from other plate industry contains copper, zinc, chromium, iron and sulphuric acid. Chemical precipitation is preferred method of treatment. To recover metal by electrolysis is possible. The bath is acidic. The cyanide bearing waste is treated by alkaline chlorination at high pH of bath. Chrome plating waste is process of reduction as well as precipitation. It is last case of liquid material industries waste. The oil glass and rubber industry produces liquid waste. It produces chlorides (25,000 ppm) with sodium (60,000 ppm) and calcium (12,000 ppm). The main treatment consist of elimination of foam formation reduction in leakage, removal of floating oil and separation of the useful products. Rubber waste which is hazardous has high BOD ~ 13,000 ppm. Glass industry waste has low BOD is alkaline, and is coloured red. Coagulation is used for treatment otherwise aeration, chlorination sulphonation, biological treatment is resorted for treatment of this kind of waste.

(v) Effluent from Energy Industry

The effluents emerging from thermal as well as nuclear power plants is considered. It contains silica, sulphate, fluoride and iron, aluminium, manganese, calcium, indium. The nuclear waste contains radioactive waste. Table 11.8 indicates analysis of effluent from power industries. It contains high level of metals.

Table 11.8 Analysis of metal ions from power industries

S. No.	*Metal*	*Level (ppm)*	*S. No.*	*Metal*	*Level (ppm)*
1.	Pb^{2+}	750	8.	Ca^{2+}	84
2.	Cu^{2+}	500	9.	Mg^{2+}	30
3.	Al^{3+}	500	10.	Ni^{2+}	100
4.	V^{5+}	925	11.	Cl^-	85
5.	Fe^{3+}	2000	12.	SO_4^{2-}	400
6.	Zn^{2+}	4000	13.	HCO_3^{2-}	16
7.	Hg^{2+}	625	14.	F^-	0.5

Table 11.9 Analysis of waste water from mines and metallurgical operation

Components	*Mine waste ppm (I)*	*Mine waste ppm (II)*
Flow	2500 g/pmt	900 g/pmt
pH	3.7	6.2
Free acid	124	4.0
Total acid	460	13
SiO_2	14	9.6
Al	17	1.9
Fe	22	0.2
Mn	10	4.6
Ca	95	34
Mg	55	12
SO_4^{2-}	750	170
Cl^-	9	2.4
F^-	0.3	0.5
Dissolved solids	1800	733
Organic matter	4000	70
Fixed mineral matter	5000	660

The power plant needs large amount of water for cooling towers. The power plants generates heat to get steam to run the plant. The release of hot water in stream causes thermal pollution. Waste water contains acidic or caustic solution. Fly ash results at thermal plant and it has major problem of disposal. Cyclones are used for separation of fly ash. Due to high temperature the biological treatment of waste is not possible. Acid mines drainage waste results from mines. The small particle anthracite is collected.

(vi) Effluent from Service Industries

The waste from laundry contains soap and detergents and it is alkaline in nature, while waste from photographic industry is composed of developers hypo, silver bromide spent solutions, fixing inorganic reducing agents. It contains large amount of suspended solids with turbidity of 300 to 400 JU. It contains nondegradable organic matter. The study of physical and chemical properties of waste gives an idea about its source, *e.g.* Table 11.10 gives concentration of metals in Thane

Table 11.10 Quality of the Thane creek

S. No.	*Station at*	*Concentration (mg/litre)*		
		Pb	*Zn*	*Mn*
1.	Sewree	33.0	21.2	6.8
2.	Mahul A	24.1	93.6	12.7
3.	Mahul B	84.0	79.2	3.8
4.	Mahul	24.0	51.2	5.2
5.	Trombay Jetty	18.2	64.8	6.7
6.	Vashi bridge	19.2	110.0	13.8
7.	Thane and Vashi bridge	13.8	110.0	3.0
8.	Thane Town	15.2	86.5	6.8
9.	Vashi A	30.5	70.5	3.6
10.	Vashi B	21.0	106.8	6.8

Table 11.11 IS-2490 specification for waste water

S. No.	*Parameter*	*Surface discharge*	*Effluent (public sewers)*	*Effluent (soil irrigation)*
1.	Suspended solids, mg/L	100	600	200
2.	Dissolved solids, mg/L	2100	2100	2100
3.	Oil and grease, mg/L	10	20	10
4.	Ammonical nitrogen, mg/L	50	50	50
5.	BOD	30	350	100
6.	Temperature, °C	40	45	42
7.	pH	5.5–9	6.5–9	5.5
8.	Chloride	1000	1000	600
9.	Sulphate	1000	1000	1000
10.	Lead	0.1	1	–
11.	Mercury	0.01	0.01	–
12.	Zinc	5	15	–

creek in Mumbai. The Thane creek is a confluence of industrial waste from alkali, rayon, heavy chemical and petrochemical industries. The position of trace elements in the creek is known. It gives an idea about the pollution at various monitoring stations, which are located on both sides of the creek. The samples of effluents are collected all throughout the years on quarterly basis.

Table 11.11 gives tolerance limit of industrial effluent as per the ISI specification No. 2490. It shows interesting features, *viz.*, suspended solids do not exceed 500 mg/litre, while dissolved solids are permited within 2000 mg/litre; ammonical nitrogen 50 mg/litre, pH acidic (5.5); sulphate and chloride contents is less than 1000 mg/litre, metals like Pb, Hg are present in small concentrations, while high level of zinc is encountered.

11.4 TREATMENT PROCESSES FOR WASTE WATER

The primary and the secondary treatment removes objectionable impurities from waste water. The treatment processes are classified as chemical, biological and advanced or tertiary treatment. The selection of treatment process depends upon the quality of waste water, as well as its cost. The chemical treatment consist of operations such as equilization, neutralisation, sedimentation, oil separation, followed by coagulation and precipitation. The biological treatment covers lagooning, activated sludge process, trickling filtration and covering special methods covering absorption, ion-exchange, chemical oxidation and sludge disposal.

(1) Chemical Treatment

It covers several operations. The equalization involves control of quality of waste water. It provides damping of organic matter, control of pH, lowering of flow surge, control of discharge and avoiding toxic material without affecting subsequent biological operation. The mixing is done to get equilization. In neutralisation process, wash water is acidic/alkaline is neutralised before other treatment. Acidic and basic wash is mixed to bring pH to 6.5 to 8.5. Use of lime for acidic wash while mineral acid for basic waste is used. This is followed by sedimentation in order to remove, suspended solids, flocculent settling is used, where settling velocity of particle increases as it settles down the tank. Zone settling is characterised by activated sludge and flocculated chemical suspensions if concentration is greater than 500 mg/L. The clarifiers is used which has rectangular or circular shape to remove sludge. Oil separation is done if effluent is from petrochemical industry. The flotation process is used for the removal of suspended solids and oil grease form effluent. These operations are termed as *preliminary treatment*. While the chemical treatment covers coagulation and precipitation. It is useful for removal of wash in suspended or in colloidal form. It prevents agglomeration. The stability of colloid is due to electrostatic force. Therefore, zeta potential (ρ) is determined as per the following equation:

$$\rho = \frac{4\pi v}{ex} = \frac{4\pi\eta EM}{\epsilon} = \text{Zeta potential}$$

where v = particle velocity, η = viscosity of medium, x = applied potential, EM = mobility. It is lowered by changing concentration, addition of oppositely charged ions or contraction of diffuse part of the double layer. The coagulation results with decrease in zeta potential. Several coagulatants are used for the purpose. Coagulations aids are also available in market. It clarifies the waste. The removal of heavy metals is possible by chemical precipitation as hydroxide by the addition of lime or soda. But before this cyanide, ammonia other complexing agents are removed by alkaline chlorination or catalytic oxidation. Arsenic cadmium, copper, iron, manganese, mercury, nickel selenium and zinc need special treatment. The precipitation removes all these metals. The anions like fluoride is also removed by precipitation with lime to give calcium fluoride. The ion-exchange is best method for removal of all these ions.

Table 11.12 Effluent treatment for metal recovery

Metal	*Con mg/L*	*Method of removal (precipited as)*	*Source for metals*
As	0.05	Sulphide	Glass, ceramic, tannery, dyes
Ba	0.5	Sulphate	Paint pigment, rubber
Cd	0.05	Hydroxide	Alloying, photograph, textile
Cu	0.02	Hydroxide/sulphide	Pickle bath, plating, alloy
Hg	0.01–0.001	Ion-exchange/sulphide	Chloroalkali industry
Ni	0.10	Hydroxide	Steel, foundry, aircraft, printings
Se	0.05	Sulphide	Fly ash, pigment dyes
Zn	0.1	Hydroxide	Rayon, wood pulp.
Pb	0.01–0.04	Sulphate	Storage battery
Mn	0.5–1.0	Hydroxide/oxidation	Dry cell, glass, paints, dyes
Ag	0.01–1.4	Chloride	Photography, ink

The process of aeration is used for transferring oxygen. It is useful for biological treatment for stripping solvents from waste water and also for removing volatile gases like ammonia and sulphurated hydrogen. In such process temperature for mixing and liquid depth is of prime importance. The aeration equipment consist of air diffusion unit, surface aeration equipments.

(2) Biological Treatment

Anaerobic and Aerobic biological treatment is of importance (see Table 11.13 and Table 11.4). Raw waste is converted to bacterial cells. In suspended growth treatment bacteria are flocculated, when oxygen is supplied to liquid. The microorganism use organics for energy and their growth in five day BOD gives idea of organics present in the effluent. The amount of microbial sludge oxidised depends upon the energy. The process of absorption, stripping and biodegradation is used to remove organics. The important process utilised in the biological treatment of waste water consist of lagoons and stabilisation; activated sludge process and trickling filters. Table 11.3 describes aerobic and anaerobic process while Table 11.4 lists various compounds produced.

Table 11.13 Anaerobic and aerobic processes

S. No.	Merits	Difference in two processes		Anaerobic bacterias present
		Anaerobic	Aerobic	
1.	Does degrade compounds like lignin			Desulfovibrio sp.
2.	Degrade Xenobiotic	Slow process	Fast process	Desulfo marculum sp.
3.	Better dewatering of sludge	High sensitivity	Low sensitivity	Metanobacterium formidcum
4.	Generates valuable methane	Start up time slow	It is fast	Methan obacteria proplonicum
5.	Reduction in pathogens			
6.	Facilitates use of biosolids			

A close examination of Table 11.13 pertaining to the anaerobic and aerobic treatment of waste water reveals interesting factors lignin ordinarily considered to be non-degradable is decomposed by slow anaerobic process Xenobiotine are degraded. One has better dewatering of sludge to generate methane (CH_4). It simultaneously kills pathogens. It is useful for biosolids.

Table 11.14 Chemical generated by anaerobic digestion of waste

S. No.	Name of compound produced	Formula	S. No.	Name of compound produced	Formula
1.	Ammonia	NH_3	12.	Acetic acid	CH_3COOH
2.	Caproic acid	$CH_3(CH_2)_4COOH$	13.	Formic acid	$HCOOH$
3.	Carbon dioxide	CO_2	14.	Methane	CH_4
4.	Valeric acid	$CH_3(CH_2)_3COOH$	15.	Indole	$C_8H_{13}N$
5.	Carbon disulphide	CS_2	16.	Methylamine	CH_3NH_2
6.	Pyridine	C_3H_6N	17.	Trimethylamine	$CH_3–NCH_3CH_3$
7.	Carbon monoxide	CO	18.	Dimethyl sulphide	$(CH_3)_2S$
8.	Thyoglycollic acid	$HSCH_2COOH$	19.	Propyl amine	$CH_3CH_2CH_2NH_2$
9.	Hydrogen sulphide	H_2S	20.	Ethyl amine	$CH_3CH_2\ NH_2$
10.	Dimethyl sulphide	$(CH_3)_2S$	21.	Nitrous oxide	N_2O
11.	Nitrogen gas	N			

A look at Table 11.4 shows very interesting observation we get very valuable products by anaerobic digestion process.

The important compounds generated include gases as NH_3, CO_2, H_2S and N_2O, while organic compounds generated are acetic, formic acid, CH_4, $(CH_3)_3NH$. Then quality wise these compounds are comparable with pure products.

(3) Lagoons and Stabilisation

The stabilisation is common method of organic treatment. There are two processes *viz.*, impounding and adsorption lagoons. No overflow is permitted in lagoons. Faculative ponds have anerobic or aerated lagoons. The oxygen generation proceeds by photosynthesis in colourless effluent. A aerated lagoon is a basin of large depth (8′–16′) where oxygenation proceeds by mechanical or diffused aeration units and through induced surface aeration. The dissolved oxygen and suspended solids are uniformly maintained in all process. Oxygen in upper liquid layer or basin is obtained. Temperature influence lagooning process.

(4) Activated Sludge Process

The main aim in this process is to remove soluble as well as insoluble organics from effluent stream and convey it to flocculent microbial suspension which is settlable. Ping flow process uses long narrow aeration basin. In complex mixture activated sludge process consists of mixing of diffused and mechanical aeration. Sludge washing is minimised in extended aeration. The oxidation ditch system needs good channel velocity for mixing. The high purity oxygen is mixed in reactors to function as the respirator. Final clarification is of crucial importance. The best way is to treat industrial waste water with municipal activated sludge leading to generation of large suspended solids. The toxic materials are priority pollutant for removal.

(5) Trickling Filterater

It is packed bed of media covered with slime growth over it on which waste water is passed. As waste passes in rough filter organic matter is removed in form of biological film. 90% BOD is lowered, CO_2 diffuses out of slime. Oxygen transferred from air passing through filter to the film of liquid passing over slime. Temperature affects performance of filtration. Decrease in temperature reduces efficiency of filteration. Plastic pack filters are employed. Finally in anaerobic decomposition involves breakdown of organics to gas as methane and carbon dioxide in absence of oxygen. The elevated temperature gives better results. The anaerobic breakdown of benzene nucleus proceeds via photometabolism or methanogenic fermentation. All of them degrade finally to CO_2 and CH_4. The process is used for food processing effluent at pH 6.6 to 7.6. Lime is used to raise the pH. The inorganic salts in very low concentration help aerobic transformation.

(6) Comparison of Chemical and Biological Treatment

The chemical treatment is feasible at a times. Biological method needs more space and is initially costly but running cost is low. Chemical treatment is fast with low reagent consumption. It needs less space and automatic control is done. Cyanide is best removed by biological treatment but not by chemical treatment. Temperature does not influence the chemical treatment; Erratič pattern is sometimes observed in biological method. The biological treatment is used when effluent is low in organic contents. It facilitates removal of high dosage of ammonia. Activated sludge with lime addition works well. However, most of the time, choice is made on the basis of economic grounds.

(7) Tertiary Treatment of Waste

It is specialised method which involves process such as ion-exchange, reverse osmosis, electrodialysis, chemical oxidation or nutrient removal. The ultimate goal is to get good quality effluent. The suspended solids removal is of importance in order to improve quality of the effluent. Microscreening filtration or coagulation processes is resorted. Activated carbon adsorption involves the concentration of a solute at the surface of a solid due to imbalance in surface forces. The activated carbon is considered to be best adsorbents for van der Waals' adsorption process. The ion-exchange process where ions are held at functional group on the surface of resin by electrostatic forces. The complete demineralisation, process involves either cation, or anion exchange or both the process operating simultaneously. Reverse osmosis is modern process, wherein contaminated effluent is kept in contact with membrane at pressure more than that of solution. Pure water permeates through membrane and leaving behind contaminates in other compartment of unit. In electrodialysis used for desalination as the passage of ions through membrance is increased by application of potential across the membrance. The chemical oxidation process involves chlorination and ozonisation working as the disinfecting agents. The nutrient removal (*e.g.*, P and N compounds) is accomplished by precipitation or use of activated sludge process. Ferric chloride or alum is used for chemical coagulation to effect removal of phosphorus. Nitrogen removal involves nitrification, ammonia stripping or biological or ion-exchange process.

The tertiary treatment produces an effluent of good quality suitable for final disposal. These processes are mainly beneficial for reclaiming water. Tertiary methods are really the polishing methods for the effluent and these methods will have to be resorted to where stringent effluent standards are clamped. This may so happen in near future certainly in developed countries.

11.5 CHARACTERISATION OF WASTE WATER

After considering the treatment of waste water, let us consider characterisation of the waste water. There are several objectives to undertake such process.

The main purpose of analysis is to evaluate method of treatment, with the sole aim is to reuse or disposal ascertain quality of waste water and recovery of valuable products from waste effluents. The purpose of analysis is to assess the material balance for the process to permit evaluation of efficiency of treatment. For this, it will be necessary to analyse various parameters, which would throw light on quality of waste water. The main choice of method for such analysis expect to get reliable information, for accurate and sensitive results. The frequency of analysis is important. The method of sampling and transportation decides the actual choice of particular method of analysis. The measurement is carried out *in situ*, or it is based on automated techniques. The *in situ* analysis involves on the spot field analysis, where we may not always get representative sample. Instrumental methods for *in situ* analysis are limited; however, automated methods furnish valuable information on physical, chemical and biological character of the industrial effluents. The spectrophotometric methods are best for automated analysis. When close control of quality of water is needed, then regular monitoring is essential. Environmental analytical chemist should select his approach for analysis after careful diagnosis of the total problem. Such a diagnosis depends on the objective of analysis, speed and accuracy sought, interferences, environmental conditions of sampling and the cost of measurement of various parameters of industrial effluents.

The analysis of waste water is somewhat complicated; the reason being one does not encounter the kind of impurities and deleterious material which are dumped into stream by different industries. Further, the waste water from different industries, mixed together, before merging into the sea or at disposal point, form very complex mixtures. Such water has a bad colour, offensive odour, turbidity, bad taste; high or too low pH, or high alkalinity and acidity; contain dissolved solids, organic materials, in the form of pesticides; and metal pollutants like As, Ba, Cd, Cr, Cu, Pb, Fe, Mn, Se, Ag, or Zn and anions like F^-, NO_3^-, PO_4^{3-}, SO_4^{2-}, CN^-. These constituents affects aquatic life, promote corrosion, hardness and have a tendency for formation of foam. The intensive measurements are carried out to characterise the quality. The *situ* analysis gives immediate idea about quality of water. Instrumental methods for *in situ* analysis involve temperature measurement, turbidity, pH, dissolved oxygen, and conductivity analysis.

The waste water produced by industry and not the one sewage generates is covered separately in next chapter on sewage. The rapid screening test gives preliminary idea about waste. The test should help us to identify unwanted components in a sample before deciding disposal technique. Such analysis should throw light on the amount of waste, concentration and mobility, and probable chemical reaction and trend in concentration of the effluent.

(i) The Sampling of Effluents

A sample must be randomly drawn and should be a representative of whole lot. The total number of collected grab samples must satisfy the statistical requirements of the sampling programme. The human error is eliminated by the use of manual as well as an automated samples. The determination of gases like O_2, CO_2, Cl_2, CH_4, or H_2S is done by *in situ* analytical methods.

At the same time temperature and pH of effluent must be noted on site. The effluent analysis comprises of three components, *viz.*, the physical methods for characterisation; the analysis of organic pollutants, involving nonspecific and specific analysis, the analysis of metals largely involving instrumental methods and analysis of anions and dissolved gases. The various methods of sampling to obtain a representative sample are considered.

The sampling of waste water is complicated. The waste which appears homogeneous is not dependable. Samples are taken from surface of waste water. A sampling technique includes various factors like the frequency, number, point of collection, method of collection, kind of data sought, time, statistical handling and ultimate aim of the analysis. The samples should be periodically collected. Adequate number of the samples should be collected. 4 to 6 samples provide dependable results. The point for collection of sample should be carefully chosen. The location should be upstream, a stream below pollution site, stream at worst condition but stream midway will be best. Sampling in tidal estuaries is tedious, here sampling on high and low tide time should be resorted to. Sample should be collected at depth of ½ feet to 1½ feet from surface in glass bottles. For biological examination sterile bottles are needed. Long-term analysis should involve physical, chemical and biological analysis of the waste water. For quick analysis temperature BOD, DO gives adequate information of quality of waste. For potable water biological examination is absolutely necessary. Samples must be analysed immediately after collection. Sample should be preferably kept at 4°C temperature. The stream survey in summer gives best results.

11.6 PHYSICAL METHODS FOR CHARACTERISATION OF WASTE WATER

These methods of analysis depends upon the purpose of analysis, nature of constituents present, and the nature of analytical procedure to be adopted. The important physical properties which are generally accounted for waste water are: density and viscosity; temperature; conductivity; turbidity; particulate matter and dissolved solids; oil and grease; colour, radioactivity and odour.

(i) Density and Viscosity Measurement

The determination of density is of utmost importance for characterisation of sea brines, to know dissolved materials. Such determination is carried out at 20°C by

Table 11.15 Hydrological parameters of Ulhas river effluents in Mumbai

S.No.	*pH*	*Temp. °C*	*NO_2-N mg/L*	*PO_4^{3-} mg/L*	*SO_4^{2-} mg/L*	*Alkalinity (phenolphthalein)*	*Total alkanity*
1.	8.0	30.0	0.9	0.09	2.83	6.9	71
2.	7.8	31.5	0.4	0.09	2.94	6.9	70
3.	7.8	32.0	0.7	0.08	1.01	6.8	72
4.	7.6	32.0	2.0	0.05	2.15	7.3	74
5.	7.5	31.8	2.1	0.08	2.29	7.8	79
6.	7.6	32.5	1.8	1.1	2.42	7.9	80
7.	7.7	32.0	1.1	0.05	0.7	6.8	72
8.	8.0	32.0	0.8	0.05	0.9	6.7	73
9.	7.5	31.0	8.4	0.06	2.1	8.0	78
10.	7.6	32.5	7.2	0.06	2.2	7.8	81
11.	7.8	33.0	7.3	0.05	2.9	7.2	72
12.	7.8	33.0	5.8	0.05	2.9	8.1	81

finding weight of exact volume of waste water. The viscosity determination gives direct information on the resistance of liquid to flow, if water contains solid sludge. It is very useful while dealing with oil pollution. Pure water has viscosity of 1.009 CPS at room temperature. Utility of such analysis is demonstrated by determination of some hydrological parameters of Ulhas river presented in Table 11.15 to trace its source in Mumbai.

(ii) Temperature

When there is thermal pollution or, if water is emerging from cooling towers or venturi scrubbers, such measurement is beneficial. It throws light on extent of oxygen present and presence of flora and fauna in waste water. It gives an idea of bio-chemical activity in effluent. It is of great relevance while assessing consequences of thermal pollution on quality of water. For the 10° C rise in temperature the reaction rate nearly doubles. It has relevance in analysis of 5 day BOD of waste water (BOD_5). The details are spelled out in chapter on Thermal Pollution. Ratnagiri power plant has serious problem of thermal pollution of estuaries.

(iii) Electrical Conductance

The measurement of electrical conductivity of effluent provides information on ionic contents of waste water. The quality of surface or ocean water is quickly ascertained from salinity by simple measurement of electrical conductivity. Such measurement should be carried out at a constant temperature. This is also useful in chemical oceanography to ascertain the quality of waste water. The conductivity meter such as Wheatstone bridge, is useful for such determinations.

(iv) Turbidence Measurement

It is a measure of light scattering characteristics of water. The turbidity is ascribed to the presence of colloidal and suspended particulate matter in waste water. Jackson turbidity test is based on measuring the length of light transmitted through the solution, at which flame of standard candle disappears. If effluent is highly turbid, it should be diluted with turbidity free water. If turbidity is greater than 1000 JU, Jackson candle method should be used, but if it is less than 25 NTU, a nephelometer is best for the purpose of analysis.

(v) Volatile and Dissolved Solids

The information is obtained by filtration and weighing similar to gravimetric analysis. The total suspended matter is removed by ultrafiltration, while dissolved matter is weighed after evaporation of known volume of the effluent. This test is good for control of quality in plant operation of water. It has furnished very valuable information on the source of contamination. This test is also called as test of loss on ignition. This test gives how much organic material has volatilised off on ignition. The temperature maintained is 55°C but loss may be also due loss in water of crystallisation. The material is burnt in the presence of 1% ammonium nitrate solution, which itself is volatile hence used in firearms and crackers.

(vi) Oil and Immiscible Liquids

These are removed by liquid-liquid extraction, in petroleum ether when the effluent is emerging from an oil refinery. The information on oil, grease and immiscible liquids throws light on the quality of the effluents. Either benzene, chloroform, carbon tetrachloride or diethylether is used for the purpose of extraction. The infrared spectroscopy is utilised for the gross determination of volatile and non-volatile oily matter in the effluent. The amount of extract on a filter paper gives circular spot. The diameter of spot gives the petroleum extractable material.

(vii) Colour

The colour of the waste water may be its true colour or an apparent colour. Platinate units are used for expressing intensity of such colour. It is also expressed in Hazen units. Majority of the industrial effluents are coloured. A comparison is made in Nessler tube with standard colour solutions made from potassium hexachloro-platinate tinted with small amounts of cobalt chloride. A 1 mg/litre of Pt (from K_2 Pt $Cl)_6$ gives a standard unit of colour. A solution containing 500 mg/litre of Pt has 500 units. The samples with more than 70 units of colour are diluted first and then compared with the standard solutions. It is also possible to measure colour by tristimulus colorimeter which is special devise to ascertain colour.

(viii) Odour Measurements

It is a measure of physiological response to olfactory nerves. Odour is present due to volatile organic matter and biological materials such as algae and actinomycetes. Odour is expressed in terms of TON, *i.e.,* threshold odour number. TON represents the greatest dilution of sample which still persists and has perceptile residual odour. Odour depends upon temperature, hence all measurement should be carried out at fixed temperature, say at 25, 40 or 60°C. When the effluent emerges from food, beverage industry or canning and fish processing plant, then it is imperative to measure intensity of odour.

(ix) Radioactivity

It is measured if the effluent emerges from a nuclear reactor. Waste water from such source is in a state of nuclear instability and emits ionising radiation to attain stability. Such details are spelled in chapter on radioactivity in Chapter 22. A water below Vashi bridge in New Mumbai indicated presence of radioactivity.

(x) Halogenated Organic Compounds

A nonhalogenated organic solvent is taken and extract of waste is made. It is then separated. A hot clean copper piece is heated and dipped in organic extract and once again introduced in flame to note its colour. In the presence of halogenated organic compounds imparts greenish blue flame. Further investigation is carried out by gas chromatography technique.

(xi) Cyanide Test

It is very important to test for cyanide as effluents specially from electroplating industry, as it contains considerable amount of cyanide ion which is deleterious to human health. To effluent containing cyanide, 25% sulphuric acid is added. The colour of the indicating tube becomes red in appearance. This test is bad for cyanide containing complexes. Alternatively a sample solution is mixed with buffer of pH 7.0 then 1–2 drops of chloromine T and few drops of reagent containing barbituric acid, pyridine and hydrochloric acid are added to give red colouration. As small as 0.01 to 1 mg/L of cyanide is characterised by this test.

After consideration of physical characteristics of waste water it is worth to consider nonspecific analysis containing evaluation of DO, BOD, COD and TOD of industrial effluent.

11.7 ANALYSIS OF ORGANIC POLLUTANTS

The presence of organic matter has damaging influence on quality of waste water. To know the exact nature of organic pollutants, it is essential to carry out both nonspecific and specific analysis of the effluent. The nonspecific method involves evaluation of BOD, COD (*i.e.,* chemical oxygen demand), total organic carbon (TOC), while specific analysis involves characterisation and analysis involving UV, visible, IR, NMR, fluoroscence, GC-MS techniques. First nonspecific analysis is considered. It accounts for quantities of oxidisable organic material present in the effluent. BOD is initially employed for measurement of susceptibility of waste to biological oxidation. On the contrary, the measurement of concentration of organic matter oxidisiable by dichromate reflux method is determined by chemical oxygen demand *i.e.,* COD.

The organic contaminants are obtained from the knowledge of oxygen parameters including ThOD, COD, BOD, TOD and the second one carbon parameter inclusive of Th OC and TOC analysis.

(i) Theoretical Oxygen Demand (ThOD)

It is the stoichiometric amount of oxygen needed to oxidise entire amount of organic matter expressed as mg/L. It is theoretical value and is evaluated only when complete chemical analysis of waste water is carried out. In analysis of waste water, no attempt is made to ascertain theoretical oxygen demand (ThOD). Such value is hypothetical and is used in some stochiometric calculations to ascertain organic loadings of waste water.

(ii) BOD of Industrial Effluents

A biochemical oxygen demand test is a bioassay method involving measurement of quantities of oxygen consumed during biological oxidation of organic waste matter under controlled conditions. BOD is defined as the amount of oxygen required by bacteria, while stabilising decomposable organic matter under aerobic conditions. BOD test is used to ascertain pollution strength of waste in terms of oxygen demand, if discharged into natural water sources which is aerobic in nature. It is a bioassay test for which toxic substances in water must be absent to promote bacterial growth. It is a wet oxidation test. The rate of such oxidation depends upon population of number of microorganisms and temperature. Inorganic nitrogen and nitrifying bacteria reduce BOD. The addition of methylene blue or allyl thiourea (ATU) inhibits nitrifying bacteria. The amount of oxygen required is fixed, BOD gives idea of gross concentration of organic matter and oxygen consuming tendency of waste water. BOD is useful for determination of amount of oxygen likely to be consumed by waste upon discharge in receiving water. The main limitations of 5-day BOD test is the need of patience to wait for five long days to get reliable information. The biochemical oxygen demand is used to measure the amount of oxygen needed for oxidation of biodegradable organic matter present in waste water by process of aerobic biochemical action.

Oxygen demand is exerted by carboceous matter used as food for aerobic organism, oxidisable nitrogen obtained from nitrite, ammonia and organic nitrogenous compounds (*e.g.*, nitrosomonas, nitrobacteria) and chemical reducing compounds Fe^{2+} SO_4^{2-}, S^{2-} are oxidised by dissolved oxygen. Water for analysis is diluted before hand. Such dilution ratio should not exceed 100 :1 (bad water) to 4:1 (reasonably good waste) oxygen utilisation in BOD test is very slow, hence 5-day BOD_5 is preferred. An ultimate BOD_{10} is obtained only after 20 days. The ratio of 5-days BOD_5 to 20 days BOD_{20} varies for sewage. It is 0.77. As told toxic materials interfere with BOD analysis by reacting with microorganism in waste water. The presence of algae affects BOD test, as it survives in dark. Even if algae die their cells contribute to increase in TOC and hence high BOD is obtained we have relation of $BOD_5 = 0.77 \times BOD_{20}$ for theoretical evaluation.

(iii) Dissolved Oxygen

Without the knowledge of DO, we cannot evaluate BOD. The Winkler's method is used for the determination of dissolved oxygen. The azide modification is made to remove interferences caused by nitrites. A variation in method of phenylarisine in oxide (PAO) is used as it is stable. DO analysers are readily available in the market. The BOD is analysed by manometric methods. Although DO or BOD are the reliable test to ascertains quality of waste water, it is observed that some organic matter is resistant to biochemical oxidation, the IDDO, *i.e.,* immediate determination of dissolved oxygen demand is devised. This is a 15-minute test to ascertain the rate of oxidation of ferrous to ferric or sulphite to sulphate or sulphide to sulphate state. In order to avoid photosynthetic bacterial degradation, the test is carried out in dark. Toxic matter retard biological activity. Aromatic hydrocarbons are resistant to biological activity as they undergo decomposition, but aliphatic compounds like ester do not undergo degradation. Similarly, macromolecules or biologically inactive and inert matter do not decompose, irrespective of the conditions. In such a case one has to take resort to COD *i.e.,* chemical oxygen demand (COD).

(iv) Chemical Oxygen Demand (COD)

It corresponds to the amount of oxygen required to oxidise entire or total organic matter in sample which is susceptible to permanganate or dichromate oxidation in acidic solution. This is widely used as a means of measuring pollution strength of industrial effluents. It allows measurement of total amount of oxygen required for oxidation to CO_2. It is based on the premise that all organic compounds are oxidised by strong oxidising agents in acidic media. Hence COD values are greater than BOD values. COD is too large, if great amounts of biologically resistant organic matter is present, *e.g.*, lignin. COD cannot differentiate between biologically oxidisable and biologically inert organic matter. The rate of oxidation is not precisely understood in COD analysis. The outstanding feature of COD in comparison to BOD is short-time required for valuation. In three hours all valuable information is obtained. A variety of oxidising agents like ceric sulphate, potassium iodate are used, but potassium dichromate is best for the purpose. Other useful oxidising agents are $KMnO_4$, $K_2S_2O_8$, $HClO_4$, HIO_3 and HNO_3. For $K_2Cr_2O_7$ to oxidise organic matter, the solution is made acidic in 50% sulphuric acid, under anhydrous condition. Reflux condensers are used to prevent loss of volatile organic compounds. Low molecular weight fatty acids are not oxidised, unless a catalyst like silver salt is added. The pyridine and aromatic hydrocarbons are also not easily oxidised. The interference is caused by chloride. It is eliminated by addition of mercury salt, which precipitates chloride as $HgCl_2$, *e.g.*, $Hg^{2+} + 2Cl^- \rightarrow HgCl_2$ ($K_{sp} = 1.7 \times 10^{13}$). Sulphonic acid is added to oxidise nitrites to nitrates. But the chloride interfere as: $6Cl^- + Cr_2O_7^{2-} + 14H^+ \rightarrow 3Cl_2 + 2Cr^{3+} + 7H_2O$, hence mercuric sulphate is added to destroy chloride. Organic nitrogen reduces dichromate, but slow addition of acid gives good results, when volatile matter is present.

The measure of 80% theoretical oxygen need, or 90% of oxygen requirement with silver-catalyst is assessed by COD. A ratio of COD/BOD is used in data interpretation. A 0.125 N $K_2Cr_2O_7$ is used, but 0.25 N $K_2Cr_2O_7$ gives best results. An excess of oxidising agent should be present in COD analysis when excess is added the actual amount be reduced. Ferrous ammonium sulphate is used for back titration,

$$6Fe^{2+} + Cr_2O_7^{2-} + 14H^+ \longrightarrow 6Fe^{3+} + 2Cr^{3+} + 7H_2O$$

Ferrion (ferrous 1–10 phenanthroline sulphate) is used as an indicator; with sharp colour change. The COD test is very useful for analysis of industrial waste. Within short-time results are obtained. COD gives an idea of toxic conditions and the presence of biologically resistant organic compounds present in the waste water. One never gets 100% oxidation of biological maternal in a sample. As sample with ThOD = 100% may have COD of 70 to 85%. The BOD may be 55 to 85% of theoretical oxygen demand is 100 and total oxygen demand is 92. The standard $K_2Cr_2O_7$ is preferred in redox reaction. Such reaction is carried out in the presence of sulphuric acid in reflux condenser for two hours in presence of Ag_2SO_4 as catalyst. The reaction is

$$Cr_2O_7^{2-} + 14H^+ + 6e^- \longrightarrow 2Cr^{3+} + 7H_2O$$

Excess of $K_2Cr_2O_7$ is titrated against standard solution of ferrous ammonium sulphate but chloride interferes. Silver catalyst oxidises straight chain alcohols and acids. The end point in titration is red brown colour with Ferron as an internal indicator. The reaction is

$$Cr_2O_7^{2-} + 14H^+ + 6Fe^{2+} \longrightarrow 2Cr^{3+} + 6Fe^{3+} + 7H_2O$$

One uses permanganate for redox reaction. Waste water is boiled with permanganate then cooled excess of ammonium oxalate is added. Then excess of unconsumed oxalate is titrated against $KMnO_4$ by back titration. The reaction is

$$5C_2O_4^{2-} + 2MnO_4^- + 16H^+ \longrightarrow 10CO_2 + 2Mn^{2+} + 8H_2O$$

A rapid COD test involves digestion for 15 mts. Around 65% of organic matter is easily oxidised. Instrumental COD methods are very fast and give reproducible results. For the purpose precious results. *Aqua rator* is used. The ratio and COD/BOD is very useful in chemical analysis. BOD is always less because organic compounds oxidisable by $K_2Cr_2O_7$ are not biochemically oxidisable. Further, certain inorganic anions like S^{2-}, $S_2O_3^{2-}$, SO_3^{2-}, NO_2^-, Fe^{2+} are oxidised easily by dichromate solution, thus accounting for inorganic COD.

(v) Total Oxygen Demand (TOD)

One gets COD in two hours rather than using 5 day BOD. However, COD cannot oxidise the contaminants like pyridine, benzene and ammonia in waste water. For this total oxygen demand analysers (TOD) rapid are available for analysis in three minutes. No common ions show any interferences. It is different from ThOD.

(vi) Measurement of total Organic Contents (TOC)

These tests are based upon the oxidation of carbon of the organic matter to CO_2 and analysis of CO_2 by absorption in KOH or by infrared analysis (ND-IR).

This fact involves analysis of carbon, hydrogen, nitrogen, sulphur, phosphorus and oxygen contents of the effluent. Such analysis supplements BOD or COD determination for the estimation of pollution potential of industrial waste. Nitrogen is estimated volumetrically by Kjeldahl's method, phosphorus is estimated gravimetrically as yellow ammonium phosphomolybdate, while sulphur is gravimetrically estimated, as sulphate and carbon is determined by Carius method by difference.

One uses knowledge of ThOD and ThOC ratio to find out the extent of organic matter. Wet oxidation method is used for the analysis of TOC. The dichromate is used in the presence of sulphuric acid to oxidise organic product. One also uses KIO_3 or H_3PO_4 as the oxidising agents to oxidise to CO_2 which is passed through alkaline potash and then analysed. The rapid method for analyse of CO_2 is by nondispersive infrared spectroscopy.

Alternatively, the ratio of ThOD/ThOC where the terms represent theoretical oxygen demand and theoretical oxygenated carbon is also used to assess organic contents. For pyridine ratio is zero. While for methae the ratio is 6.5. It is interesting to compare the value of these two terms as shown in the Table 11.16.

Table 11.16 ThOD/ThOC ratio

	Compound	*Ratio*		*Compound*	*Ratio*
Acetone	(CH_3 CO CH_3)	3.5	Pyridin	C_5H_6N	3.33
Ethanol	(C_2H_5OH)	4.0	Methanol	CH_3–OH	4.0
Phenol	(C_6H_5–OH)	3.12	Benzoic acid	C_6H_5–COOH	2.86
Benzene	(C_6H_6)	3.34	Canesugar	$C_{12}H_{22}O_{11}$	2.67

Lower value indicates difficulty in biodegradation of compound *e.g.*, pyridine, benzoic acid or sucrose.

11.8 SPECIFIC ANALYSIS OF ORGANIC POLLUTANTS

We assess the presence of organic pollutant by spectral methods. The problem is complex, as we have to handle a mixture of organic compounds from the effluent. The compounds are present in very small concentration. Biochemical degradation or chemical transformation complicates the analysis. The nature of waste is complex and variable. The sample is present in diluted form. It should be concentrated and separated before spectral characterisation. Such concentration is done by evaporation or distillation. If it is nonvolatile which are concentrated by cryogenic sampling. They are isolated by the process of solvent extraction, selective precipitation, fractional crystallization, selective adsorption or separation involving paper, thin layer or gas chromatography. The organic compounds are identified by detection of the functional groups with chromogenic ligands to give characteristic colour reaction. UV, IR, NMR are used for further confirmation, *e.g.*, thermal pollution is detected by IR measurements. Phenolic compounds are recognised by UV spectroscopy due to bathochromic or blue shift to longer wavelength in spectrophotometric analysis. The phenolic compounds are characterised at nanogram level by mass spectrometry. Carbohydrates are detected and determined by spectropolarimetry and phosphorimetry. GLC and fluorimetry helps us to analyse major compounds like phenols, pesticides and surfactants. Pesticides are found in agricultural waste, while surfactants and detergents are encountered in textile effluents and in domestic effluent. It causes foam formation, Biodegradable surfactants are limited in use. They are less harmful and hence environmentally important. Biodegradation is a measure of susceptibility of organic compound to microbial metabolism, which may proceed either in aerobic or anaerobic environment. This process is determined by type and number of microorganism, structure of organic compound and other environmentally conducive conditions. NMR/ESR is used for confirming the analysis if one has doubt.

When rapid analysis is required one resorts to carbon-chloroform extract. It is same as TOC. The results are related to the weight of organic constituent. It is mixture of organic compounds absorbable on the activated carbon. It is gravimetric adsorption-extraction method. Volume is reduced and organic material is determined by weighing. The method is valid for low organic contents of the waste water. It is interesting to compare these values of different sample.

Table 11.17 Carbon tetrachloride extract values of different water samples

Sample	*Value (mg/L)*	*Sample*	*Value (mg/L)*
Well water	0.1	Surface (summer) water	0.4
Spring water	0.1	Surface (winter) water	0.5
Surface water (average)	0.3	Polluted water	0.9
Potable water	0	Heavy polluted water	1.2

Other organic compounds encountered in water are phenol, surfactants, pesticides, halogented compounds, tannin. Gas chromatography is used for analyses of organochlorine and chlorinated phenoxy acid herbicides in effluent. The phenols are present in various form in water. A chlorophenol or para and meta phenols are analysed colorimetrically with and aminopryine at 460 nm, while compounds like cresol are analysed by aqueous gas-liquid chromatography, specially the chloro- substituted phenols. In colorimetry, oxidising agents, sulphur compounds and oils must be absent as they interfere in analysis.

The sludge digestor gas contains CH_4 and CO_2 generated during anaerobic digestion. Traces of H_2S, O_2 and N_2 are also detectable. They are analysed by volumetric method or gas chromatography. The gas is first absorbed in KOH in Orsat analyser, alkaline pyrogallol for O_2 and heated on CuO to remove H_2 but gas chromatography is best method. Enormous amount of the surfactants are encountered in waste water as alkyl benzone sulphonate. Methylene blue method is used for characterisation of surfactants. Carbon absorption IR technique is also useful. A cationic dye methylene blue reacts with it to form coloured complex which is extracted in chloroform and then absorption is measured spectrophotometrically at 625 nm. Method is quite sensitive. Tannin and lignine sulphonate are encountered if effluent which is from paper and pulp industry and tanneries. They contain aromatic hydroxyl group which react with tungston molybdophosphatic acid to give blue colour. As small as 0.1 mg/L is detected. The absorbance of the coloured complex is recorded between 600 to 700 nm on photometer. Finally, the halogenated methane and ethanes like chloro or bromomethane, vinylchloride chloroform, carbon tetrachloride, 1, 2 dichlorothane/methane and chlorobenzene are encountered in waste water. They are formed due to chlorination of water. They have adverse effect on the health. The organics are extracted in to purge gas (inert), and analysed by programmed temperature gas chromatography.

11.9 ANALYSIS OF METAL POLLUTANTS FROM WASTE WATER

Several industrial effluents from alloy industry, electroplating baths, refineries, fertilizer complex, tanneries, electronic industry consists of a large concentration of metal pollutants. Out of 104 elements so far discovered seventeen are toxic and out of these only five to six are encountered in chemical effluents. Table 11.18 indicates presence of metal pollutant from typical industrial effluents. The metals encountered were mercury, cadmium, chromium and lead. They were analysed by spectral methods as well as by ring-oven technique a semi-quantitative device. The results match with one another. The spectrophotometric methods have maximum applications. Sometimes it is necessary to undertake separation and concentration of these ions before analysis. Ion exchange or solvent extraction is commonly used for their separation. The common methods used for such determination include analytical, molecular and atomic absorption spectroscopy; emission (molecular and atomic) spectroscopy, activation analysis and electro-analytical methods. However, AAS and ICP-AES are most favoured and coming to forefront in such analysis.

Table 11.18 Metal pollutants from industrial effluents

Metal pollutant	*Amount* in mg/*10 ml*	*Average* μg/*ml*	*By ring-oven method* (μg/litre)
Hg (II)	0.10	0.01	10.0
	0.25	0.025	25.0
Cd (III)	0.10	0.01	10.0
	0.30	0.03	23.0
Cr (VI)	0.10	0.01	10.0
	0.10	0.01	10.0
Pb (II)	0.50	0.05	55.0
	0.60	0.06	60.0

The presence of metals in waste water is rarely useful, and is mostly trouble-some. Most of the metals are determined by the instrumental methods of analysis because these methods are rapid and in absence of interference spectrophotometer is best alternatively. Atomic absorption spectroscopy is ideal when inference are there. Sampling is based upon filterable or non-filterable metals as the name implies. Samples of second kind are acidified with mineral acids. The sample for mercury needs special technique of cold vapour AAS. The metal is directly processed for analysis. In both cases acid digestion with hydrochloric acid is beneficial. Nitric acid digestion is also useful, HNO_3, $HClO_4$, combination is resorted for the exhaustive digestion. Volatile samples are analysed by dry ashing. The acid combination is also used for sludge digestion with higher refractory organic compounds. AAS is most popular method because it is rapid, has no problem of interference and is applicable at microgram concentration. Few metals are directly aspirated into flame *e.g.*, Cd, Cr, Co, Cu, Fe, Pb, Mn, Ni and Ag. All are chelated with ammonium pyrolindine dithio carbamate (APPC) then extracted in MIBK and then aspirated. While Al, Be are chelated first with 8-hydroxy-quinoline and then aspirated in to flame of AAS. Metals like As, Se, need hydride generator while Hg needs cold vapour AAS technique. The interference of PO_4^{3-} and silica is eliminated by addition La and calcium respectively. In flame AAS, air acetylene is used. Nitric oxide acetylene flame is used for Al, Ba, Be, Mo, Si, Th, TI, and V. However, electrothermal AAS is best for samples present with less than 1μg/L concentration.

The sample must be very thoroughly homogenised. Table 11.19 shows metal pollutant analysis in the environment.

Table 11.19 Metal pollutants in air, water and food in Himachal and Punjab (μg/ml)

S. No.	Metal pollutants	Himachal-rural (μg/ml)			Punjab (rural)			Punjab (Urban)			Himachal-Urban		
		Air	Water	Food	Air	Water	Food	Air	Water	Food	Air	Water	Food
1.	Zn	0.15	95.0	24.3	0.65	583	31.4	2.7	1457	23.9	0.24	700	30.1
2.	Cu	0.61	14.1	13.1	1.18	9.5	34.5	0.6	12	22.9	0.50	4.3	11.8
3.	Cd	–	3.0	–	–	4.8	–	2.34	5.3	–	0.62	13	–
4.	Pb	0.11	9.0	18.1	0.26	55	4.35	0.56	32	4.6	0.13	26	20.34
5.	Ni	0.01	14.0	1.9	0.17	23	11.0	0.15	2.9	18.0	0.03	10	1.9
6.	Mn	0.02	36.0	48.4	0.52	3.9	77.1	0.93	3.7	–	0.10	5.8	43.5
7.	Cr	5.4	12.0	5.81	0.065	22	13.65	0.09	104	28.6	0.05	264	7.78

(i) Atomic Emission Spectroscopy Technique

This technique comprises of flame emission and inductively coupled plasma ICP-AES atomic emission spectroscopy. Molecular emission spectroscopy covers fluorescence spectroscopy. The flame photometry is used for analysis of alkali and alkaline earth metals. They are commonly present in sea brine. ICP-AES technique is an extension of AES with use of argon plasma torch. The advantage is argon flame ensures complete atomisation. Multi-element analysis favours possibility of rapid determination. In molecular luminescence spectroscopy like fluorescence spectroscopy metals are analysed with Morine (Be) dibenzoylmethane (U), alizarine (Al) 8-hydroxyquinoline (Zn). In Tables 11.20 and 11.21 results are

Table 11.20 AAS determination of elements from Thane creek estuary in New Mumbai

Station number	Concentration in μg/litre					
	Mn	Fe	Cu	Zn	Cd	Pb
1.	3.40	54.00	10.60	82.80	1.50	19.2
2.	6.30	45.00	13.80	73.80	1.40	12.7
3.	2.60	60.30	10.80	38.40	1.10	13.8
4.	12.10	44.00	10.10	69.40	1.30	16.2
5.	17.50	47.00	10.80	45.60	1.60	13.5
6.	6.80	52.00	14.20	69.00	1.70	10.5
7.	3.80	73.60	9.20	70.50	1.20	17.2
8.	2.50	80.40	7.80	80.20	1.40	17.8
9.	3.60	64.20	10.80	70.40	1.30	27.2
10.	6.80	72.40	18.80	106.80	1.00	17.8
11.	2.40	58.80	10.40	108.90	1.10	21.8
12.	13.60	147.20	10.10	52.00	1.50	17.8

Table 11.21 AAS determination of elements from Ulhas river effluent in Mumbai

Station number	*Concentration in μg/litre*					
	Mn	*Fe*	*Cu*	*Zn*	*Cd*	*Pb*
1.	3.6	50.2	11.4	53.5	1.4	19.0
2.	3.9	37.5	13.2	73.5	1.4	16.6
3.	3.5	32.5	7.2	32.0	1.1	14.4
4.	4.4	29.1	14.0	35.0	1.9	15.8
5.	2.7	32.5	12.4	29.5	1.4	13.7
6.	2.6	37.5	6.8	37.2	1.4	14.1
7.	8.0	31.5	8.5	84.0	1.9	42.0
8.	10.2	39.5	12.3	45.6	1.7	55.0
9.	8.2	42.6	16.4	110.0	1.4	15.3
10.	1.8	41.5	8.2	97.5	1.3	11.2
11.	7.8	30.4	5.8	104.2	1.2	12.5
12.	5.4	40.5	6.2	96.4	1.4	11.4

presented for analysis of metal pollutants with AAS from Ulhas river effluent and Thane creek estuary. The important metals like Mn, Fe, Cu, Zn, Cd and Pb were analysed by AAS. Their important source is effluent emerging from adjoining factories, *e.g.*, pesticides (Cu), rayon (Zn), nuclear reactors (Cd), auto-exhaust emission (Pb), chloroalkali industry (Hg), foundry and smithy (Mn). The monitoring is carried from selected stations located on both sides of the river. The metals are concentrated on Chelex-100 resin and eluted with dilute hydrochloric acid and are determined by AAS. The results are interesting. A work on chemical speciation with ion chromatography also revealed interesting information.

(ii) Molecular Absorption or Emission Spectroscopy

Such techniques are no doubt good however the matrix must be pure as any kind of interference is not tolerated in such determination. In an event any of the interferring ion is present it must be masked by sequestering agents or alternatively be removed by selective solvent extraction before resorting to spectrophotometric analysis. Several metals encountered in waste water are analysed by colorimetry *e.g.*, Such metals with name of chromogenic reagent are listed in Table 11.22.

These methods cover molecular spectroscopy and atomic absorption spectroscopy. In former Beer's law, ($A = abc$) is obeyed. A suitable chromogenic ligand is complexed with metal pollutant to form coloured complex. The sensitivity of analysis is enhanced by controlling various factors such as pH, λ max; reagent or metal concentration. However, most popular technique is Atomic Absorption spectroscopy. The principal merit is that, no separation of interfering ions is necessary, multiple samples for multi-element analysis are analysed at nanogram levels. This technique has made dramatic revolution in metal pollutant analysis. Only limitation of AAS is, metals like mercury are to be analysed in vacuum by cold vapour AAS, while elements like Sn, Sb, Se, Te, are analysed with hydride generator. Although flame AAS gives rapid results, graphite furnace provides accurate results due to Zeeman effect.

Table 11.22 Spectrophotometric analysis of metal ions with chromogenic ligands

Cation	*Ligand*	*λ max (nm)*	*Anion*	*Ligand*	*λ max (nm)*
Al	Eriochromcyanine R	535	B	Curcumin	540
Ba	Aluminon	515	Cl^-	o-Toludine	480
Cr	s-diphenylacarbazide				
Cu	Neocuporine or	457	CN^-	Chloramine T	578
	Bathocuporine	484	SCN	Ferric nitrate	480
Fe	1–10 phenanthroline	510			
Pb	Dithizone	465-510	F^-	SPADNS	550–580
Mn	Persulphate	582	I^-	Leuco crystalviolet	450–500
Hg	Dithizone	492	NH_3	Nesslers reagent	450–500
Ni	Heptoxime/DMG	445	NO_2^-	NEDA	543
Se	Aminobenzidine	420	PO_4^{2-}	Molybidophosphatic	540
Ag	Dithizone	620	SiO_2^{-2}	Molybidic silicate	650
V	Gallic acid	415	SO_4^{2-}	Methylthymol blue	426
Zn	Dithozone	535-620	S^-	Methylene blue	600

(λ_{max} = absorption maxima)

(iii) Polarographic Analysis and Electroanalytical Methods

In Polarographic analysis, Ilkovic equation is used, it states that $i_d = 607\ (n\ D^{1/2}\ m^{2/3}\ t^{1/6})\ C$, where i_d = diffusion current, D = ficks diffusion coefficient, m = rate of flow of mercury, t = time in seconds between two successive drops and C = concentration. If we keep D, m, t, n, constant, then we have $i_d \propto C$. It follows a linear relationship with concentration. The distinct advantage of polarography is that the knowledge of half-wave potential for identification of metal pollutant is made. Amongst other electrometric methods, conductance measurement and ion analyser and anodic stripping voltammetry (ASV) provides valuable information. The ISE is used for analysis of anions. It is based on potentiometric technique.

The metals like Cd, Cu, Pb, Ni and Zn are analysed by the polarographic method. But apart from polarography (Table 11.23) many electroanalytical methods are used for analysis of metals or non-metals. They are analysed by potentiometry and amperometry.

Table 11.23 Electro analytical methods

Technique	*Metals analysed from water*
Polarography	Cd, Hg, Pb, Zn, Fe, Ni
Potentiometry	Cl^-, DO, pH, Several anions
Amperometry/ASV	I, Cu, Cd, Zn, Pb, Hg, Fe, Ni
Conductometry	Alkal, alkaline earths, pH, SO_2

(iv) Activation Analysis and Nuclear Methods

These are rarely used due to paucity of neutron source. One needs a reactor with neutron flux of 10^{14} to 10^{12}. The portable Be-Sb neutron source needs periodic recharging. It has a flux of 10^7. The important equation used is $A = \delta f\,(W\phi/M)\,(1-e^{-\mu t})\,(6.2 \times 10^{23})$, where A = activity, (dps) f = flux in barns, s = cross-section of activation, l = decay constant, W = weight of element, ϕ = fractional abundance, t = irradiation time, M = atomic weight. If two elements are compared under identical conditions, then $A_1/A_2 = C_1/C_2$, where C_1 is computed if C_2 is known and the activity of sample (A_1) and analyst (A_2) is measured. The principal advantage of NAA is high sensitivity, rapid analysis and nondestructive testing of sample.

From the sample of waste water the ions like strontium, radium, radioactive iodine caesium, tritium are best analysed by these radioactive methods. The substochiometric extraction is also resorted for quantitative analysis using neutron activation analysis technique.

11.10 ANALYSIS OF NON-METALS AND GASES

The main purpose in such analysis is to analysis of gases like chlorine, different form of nitrogen gas and phosphorus. Such measurement have significance for potable water. The acidity/alkalinity is ascertained by simple titration but several anions are analysed by different process as shown in Table 11.24.

Table 11.24 Analysis of nonmetals and anions

S. No.	*Non-metal present*	*S. No.*	*Anions present*
1.	Boron – Colorimetry (Caramine red)	12.	Bromide-Redox titration
2.	Nitrogen–(Nesslers reagent) NH_3 colour	13.	Chloride-Precipitation titration or Volhard's methods or Mohr's method
3.	Nitrogen (organic) Kjeladal's method		
4.	Oxygen –Winklers'method	14.	Chlorine (residual) Amprimetry (o-toludine arsenite method)
5.	Ozone – Iodometry redox titration	15.	Cyanide – Chloramine T. (colorimetry) or ions elective electrode
6.	Phosphorus—Phosphomolybidic–colorimetry	16.	Thiocyanate – colorimetry ($FeSO_4$)
		17.	Fluoride – ISE/SPADNS/Alizarine
7.	Silica—Molybidosiliae acid–colorimetry	18.	Iodide – Lecuo crystal violet colorimetry
8.	Seleni●m— diaminobenzidine		
9.	Telurium—nephelometry, sol. gel	19.	Nitrite – NEDA colorimetry (dizotisation)
10.	Arsenic—Molybdenum blue (colour)		
11.	Antimony—Rhodamine B (colorimetry)	20.	Sulphate – Nephelometry
		21.	Sulphide – p-aminodimethylaniline (colorimetry)

These anions are concentrated by anion exchange chromatography. The fluoride is analysed by zirconium alizarine complex spectrophotometry method. Sulphides occur in tannery waste, septic tanks, oil refinery and viscose rayon waste. It is detected with lead acetate paper, and is determined by complexation with p-aminodimethylaniline hydrochloride, to produce methylene blue colour, which is measured spectrophotometrically. The sulphites are rated to be in paper and pulp industries waste, while cyanide exist in electroplating effluents. It is determined by interaction with ferroin at a pH of 9.2 to 9.7. The blue coloured complex so formed is extracted in chloroform and determined spectrophotometrically. Chlorimine T is used in colorimetry. Chlorides are determined by Volhard's or Mohr's method, involving precipitation titrations.

Amongst dissolved gases we have to primarily consider dissolved oxygen and chlorine. The dissolved oxygen is determined by Winkler's method, with azide modification in presence of nitrite interferences in iodometric titration. The reaction of interference and elimination of interference is as follows:

$$2NO_2^- + 2I^- + 4H^+ \rightarrow I_2 + N_2O_2 + 2H_2O \text{ (interferences)}$$

$$2N_2O_2 + O_2 + 2H_2O \rightarrow 4NO_2^- + 4H^+$$

$$NaN_3 + H^+ \rightarrow HN_3 + Na^+ \text{ (Elimination of } NO_2^-\text{)}$$

$$N_3H + NO_2^- + H^+ \rightarrow N_2 + N_2O + H_2O$$

This modification is termed as Winkler's Ashlterberg's method. The method for analysis of dissolved chlorine is same as OTA spectrophotometry. The best method for analysis however will be ion analyser fitted with suitable ion selective electrodes or by ion-chromatography technique.

11.11 AUTOMATION IN EFFLUENT ANALYSIS

A typical group for automated analysis comprises of sample turn table, proportionating pump to draw effluent sample, a suitable mixing coil, an efficient separator for segregation of solids and liquids; thermal set-up and online analyser comprising of refractometer, colorimeter, conductometer any suitable device coupled with the recorder. The analytical data so obtained is stored in computer and retrieved when required. Such kind of retrieval system exists for surveillance of rivers and streams in the USA and Canada.

With advent of time analysis of 5 day BOD_5 and suspended solids is not good enough to characterise waste water. Under more stringent regulation multiple sample analysis lead to the online analysis of the effluent. A continuous flow analysis technique is used (See Fig. 11.1).

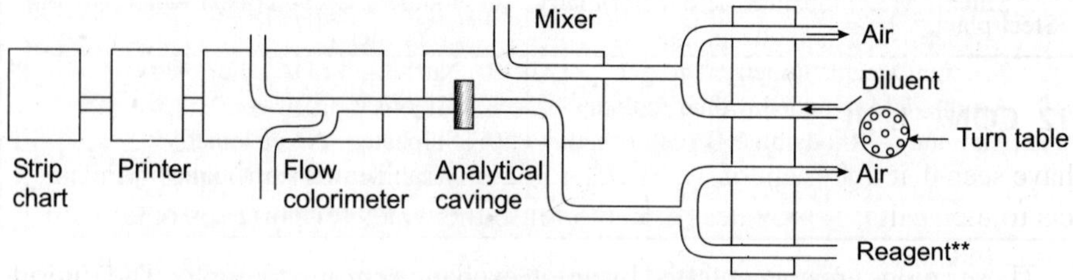

Fig. 11.1 Continuous flow system for effluent analysis

The model involves sampling, mixing, removal of suspended solids, heating, flow inject measurement of intensity of colour. The idea is to reduce the requirement of manpower. AAS, TOC, GLC are also used as cartridge to know the concentration. Autoanalyses has facilitated handling of large number of samples. Just as clinical analysis of blood leads to right treatment, this auto-analysis also leads to better treatment of the effluent.

Now-a-days increasing use of liquid chromatograph for the effluent analysis is used. The separation and determination is specific and selective. An array of details is available for rapid analysis. All nations have their own standards for effluent disposal. The Table 11.25 shows Indian standard tolerance limit of various effluents.

It gives Indian standards for tolerance limits of different effluents.

Table 11.25 Indian standards on tolerance limits of different effluents

Tolerance limits for effluents discharged into surface water	*Serial No.*
1. Part 1: General limits	2490–1974 (Part I)
2. Part II: Distillery industry	2490–1974 (Part II)
3. Part III: Tanning industry	2490–1974 (Part III)
4. Part IV: Strawboard industry	2490–1947 (Part IV)
5. Part V: Electroplating industry	2490–1974 (Part V)
6. Part VI: Dyestuff and dye manufacturing industry	2490–1976 (Part VI)
7. Part VII: Coke ovens	2490–1976 (Part VII)
8. Part VIII: Phosphatic fertilizer industry	2490–1976 (Part VIII)
9. Part IX: Nitrogenous fertilizer industry	2490–1977 (Part IX)
10. Tolerance limits for effluents discharged into marine areas	7968–1976
11. Effluents discharged into sewers	3306–1974
12. Effluents discharged on land irrigation	3307–1977
13. Inland surface waters subject to pollution	2296–1974
14. Sewage effluents discharged into inland surface waters	4764–1973
15. Criteria for controlling pollution of marine coastal areas	7967–1976
16. Distillery effluents	8032–1976
17. Effluents of canesugar industry	4903–1968
18. Effluents of dairy industry	8682–1977
19. Effluents of electroplating	7453–1974
20. Effluents of pulp paper and board	5061–1978 (Part I)
21. Effluents of tanning industry	5183–1977
22. Steel plant effluents	8073–1976

11.12 CONCLUSION

We have seen that treatment of waste water not only facilitates removal of harmful effects to the health. It provides means to reuse the water for purposes other than drinking. In UAR and other middle east countries every effort is made to conserve every drop of the water. Instead of using word waste water which illustrates shear loss we nowadays use word effluent *i.e.,* one which emerges out of industrial unit after processing or use. The quality of waste water emerging from different industries is not same. The effluent from chemical, pharmaceutical and drug, apparel, material industries and the service industry is all together different with varying proportions of impurities and each needs unique mode of treatment. The treatment consist of chemical biological and advanced treatment. It is called as primary, secondary and tertiary treatment to render it safe. In order to decide what kind of treatment is needed its obligatory to first analyse the waste water. A careful sampling is necessary. The physical methods of examination include checking density temperature, conductance, turbidity volatile, immiscible, matter colour, odour, viscocity and radioactivity. The organic contents of effluent is ascertained from the knowledge of DO, BOD and COD.

The above is a nonspecific analysis while in specific analysis, UV IR spectroscopy, fluoroscence, mass spectrometry measurement are used. Although metal pollutants are analysed by spectral methods, there is the growing trend to use atomic absorption spectroscopy and inductively coupled plasma atomic emission spectroscopy. The reason being analysis is not only rapid but they permit multielement analysis and tolerates interference. Polarography is scarsely used so also activation analysis. However, spectrophotometric methods along with ion selective electrodes as well as the ion chromatography are extensively used all over world for analysis of anions. The automated methods are coming to forefront with flow injection analysis or conductivity determination in online analysis.

ADDITIONAL READING

1. G.M Gair, J.C. Gayer and D.A. Okun, *Water and Waste Water Engineering*, Vol. **I** and **II**, John Wiley and Sons (1968).
2. R.A. Horne, "*The Chemistry of Our Environment*', John Wiley and Sons, New York (1978).
3. I.M. Kolthoff, P.J. Elving and M.J. Stross, *Treatise in Analytical Chemistry; Analytical Chemistry in Industry*, Vol. 2, Part III, John Wiley and Sons, New York (1971).
4. C.N. Sawyer and P.J. McCarty, *Chemistry for Environmental Engineering*, 3rd Ed., McGraw-Hill and Co. (1978).
5. K.H. Mancy, *Instrumental Analysis for Water Pollution Control*, Ann Arbor Science Publ., Ann Arbor, Michigan (1971).
6. D. Purves, *Trace Element Contamination of the Environment* Elsevier, Netherlands (1977).
7. H.J.M. Bowen, *Environmental Chemistry of the Elements*, Academic Press, London (1979).
8. K.H. Mancy and W.J. Weber, *Analysis of Industrial Waste Water*, Wiley Inc. (1971).
9. N.L. Nemerow, *Liquid Waste of Industry*, Addison, Wesley, (1971).
10. E. Bosselover, M. Schwartz-*Treatment of Industrial Waste*, 2nd Ed. McGraw-Hill and Co. (1975).
11. S.M. Khopkar, *Indian **J. Env.** Protection*, **7**, 268 (1987).
12. S.K. Sahoo and S.M. Khopkar, *Ind. J. Env. Protection*, **5**, **257** (1985).
13. S.N. Nimbhorkar and S.M. Khopkar, *Indian J. Technology*, **24, 658** (1986).
14. S.K. Sahoo and S.M. Khopkar, *Industrial Engg. Journal*, **15**, **37** (1986).

15. S.K. Sahoo and S.M. Khopkar, *Environmental Management and Planning*, 291 (1988).
16. S.K. Sahoo and S.M. Khopkar, *Ind. **J. Env.** Prot*. **8**, **417** (1988).
17. S.M. Khopkar, *Environmental Management and Planning*, **111** (1988).
18. S. Cherian, Mayuri Gandhi, S.M. Khopkar, *Ind. J. Env. Protection* (1992).
19. N.L. Nemerow, *Theory and Practice of Industrial Waste Treatment* Addison Wesley (1963).
20. G. KaKa budse, *Chemistry and Effluent Treatment* Applied Sci Pub (1979).
21. W.N. Eckenfelder, *Introduction to Waste Pollution Control* McGraw-Hill & Co. (1989).
22. R.S. Ranotho, *Introduction to Waste Water Treatment* Academic (1977).
23. H.H. Benjes, *Handbook of Biological Waste Water Treatment* Garlend TPM press (1980).
24. K.R. Muller, *Chemical Waste Handling Treatment* Springer Verbg (1981).
25. E.A.R. Quario, *Principle of Waste Water Treatment*, Biological process Garlend TPM press (1980).
26. P.N. Cheremisnoff, *Waste Water Treatment,* Pocket Book Publishers (1955).
27. S.M. Khopkar, *Environmental Pollution Analysis,* Second Edition New Age International Publishers (2012).

12 Recycling and Reuse of Waste Water

12.1 INTRODUCTION

Although the source of water in advanced as well as in developing countries is satisfactory, the situation in middle east countries and few places adjacent to deserts like "Sahara" in African nation is somewhat grave. This is because there are no rivers to provide fresh water. They do not have ponds and lakes to get ample supply of water. Such water hungry countries have to import the water for drinking as well as for industrial purposes from developed nation *e.g.* In Kuwait such proposition of import is quite expensive.

Therefore in order to surmount these difficulties several nations in the world have started rethinking as to how best we again use waste water for non drinking purposes like car washing, plantation. Although aesthetically so far no one thought of its use for drinking purposes, users are very much interested in reuse specially for agriculture, cooling towers in industry and numerous other applications in industry.

However, the main drawback in the process of the treatment of waste water for reuse is we have very limited methods for purification. Many effluents needed sophisticated methods of treatment like Reverse Osmosis or biotreatment. In order to facilitate successful treatment of waste water for reuse, one must first know the quality of waste water, its history, its important components and impurities. Further, one needs a thorough knowledge of recovery and reuse of valuable products from the supply of waste water.

It is proposed to consider resources important properties the novel methods of treatment and then derive comprehensive information on recycling as well as its reuse in agricultural fields either by direct or indirect use. Finally some attention must be paid to the regulation for quality of water all over world and need of training programme to control the good quality of recycled water or analysis products from the nature.

The middle east countries use 95% of potable water from desalination of sea water at prohibitive cost. Thus, 70–80% of fresh water consumption leads to the formation of waste water so far middle east countries have not succeeded in developing viable strategy towards efficient utilization of waste water. The problems linked with utilization are complex. Consequently the problem of the treatability therefore attains paramount importance. The suitable legislative measures in form of laws, bylaws, regulations with reference to water quality should solve the problem. However, one must remember that the legislation prepared for other countries specially the developed nations does not always give acceptable results on account of variations in the rate of industrialization and the climate and some variations in the existing degree of enforcement. A continued research and development efforts will lead to the progress in reliable and safe reuse of water. While handling the waste water three important criteria must be taken into the consideration *viz.* how serious is the pollution; whether suitable technology is used to control the pollution and finally what is the probable cost of treatment waste water?

12.2 CHARACTERISTICS OF WASTE WATER

Before undertaking the plan on recycling of waste water it is necessary to discuss three important aspects *viz.* nutrient control; toxicity evaluation recovery of any worthwhile product and application knowledge of modern coordination chemistry to regain the transition metals.

(i) Nutrient Contents and Control

The nutrients are chemical elements or compounds attainable from plants, animals moving in environment. The nitrogen and phosphorous are significant nutrients. The nitrate is common impurity one avoids Entrophication and hypoxia. Former process promotes excessive plant growth which in turn reduces dissolved oxygen from water. Low oxygen contents state is called 'hypoxia'. Nitrogen is bioessential element. It is present in NH_3, NO_3^-, NO_2^- and organic nitrogen. The excessive nitric acid causes methanoglobimia. Phosphorous is key element which supports growth of plants and animals.

The organo phosphorous compounds originate from pesticides and fertilizers or detergent. These are banned in USA. Flow analysis determines nitrogen and phosphorous. Recent trend is to use chromatographic methods and capillary electrophoresis for separation.

(ii) Toxicity Evaluation

Most of the effluents are toxic in nature such testing is not obligatory; though conventional toxicity test which are available are used. This step is of vital importance if we propose to recycle and reuse the sample of waste water. The DO, BOD, COD, TOC does not throw much light on toxicity of waste water. It is tested after pre or post treatment of waste water. The units to express eco-toxicity are: EC_{50} (*i.e.* at 50% toxicity is noted) LOEC (Lowest observable effects), NOEC (Non observable effect concentration) (See Fig. 12.1). Eco-toxicity value is obtained by studying quantitable effects. One uses LC_{50} term in preference to EC_{50} term. LC_{50} is point at which 50% inhibition is noted. The source of toxic compounds in effluent vary. The health units, Hotels dispose of such toxic material in the stream. The pH adjustment and addition of complexing ligand reduces the degree of toxicity.

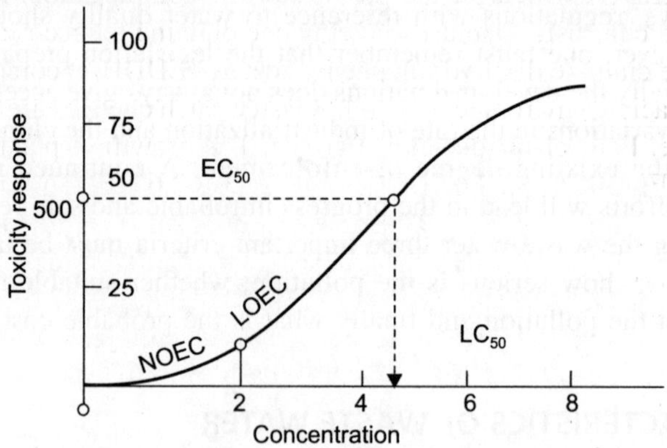

Fig. 12.1 Sigmodal response curve (mg/L)

There are several ways for testing toxicity. The bacterial luminescence nitrification inhibition throw some light on toxicity. The respirometer also detects toxicity. Effluent toxicity requires a scale for the quantitative measurement. Fish, bioassay indicates something on human toxicity. Plant algae bacteria are used for the bioassay. There are many modes to mitigate toxicity *e.g.* by addition of the chemical equilisation basin when pH is controlled. Source must be identified. Let us consider two example *e.g.* recovery of aluminium and iron from waste water.

(iii) Recovery of Aluminium by Liquid Ion Exchangers

For the purpose of coagulation in water treatment, alums are used an extensive scale and the isolation of excess alum becomes a serious problem. The throwing of aluminium-sludge degrades the environment. The excess of aluminium in drinking water causes a disease of alzheimer as well as kidney problem. The sludge is dissolved in any of the three mineral. Hydrochloric, nitric and sulphuric acids 6N *e.g.* di(2 ethylhexyl) phosphoric acid (HDEHP) is used as liquid cation exchanger. The reaction proceed as:

$$Al^{3+} + \underset{\text{(Liquid exchange)}}{H_2R} \rightarrow \underset{\text{Org phase}}{Al-R} + \underset{\text{Soln.}}{2H^+} \text{ (at pH~2.0)},$$

One stage extraction and two stages for stripping are followed. Hexane is used as the diluent (V_w/V_0) in ratio of 1:1. At high concentration the liquid cation exchanger undergoes polymerization. One uses 5N minimum sulphuric acid for stripping *e.g.*

$$\underset{\text{Org phase}}{Al-R} + \underset{\text{Aq phase}}{H_2SO_4} \rightarrow \underset{\text{Org phase}}{2H^+} + \underset{\text{(Aq Ph)}}{Al_2(SO_4)_3}$$

only Ca, Mg, Mn, Zn are co-extracted therefore, optimum conditions of the extraction must be rigorously followed.

(iv) Removal of Iron as Its Chelated Complex with Plants

It is called waste water hydroponics chelated iron. The ligands used are EDTA, E DDHA and HEDTA which for the purpose of the complexation. It controls the disease of iron chlorosis. One uses Fe-ethylene diamine tetracetric acid (EDTA) or Fe-ethylene diamine di-ohydroxyphenyl acetate (EDDHA) complexes. EDTA is effective in acidic environment of soil or water. Such chelates are stable and are toxic in nature. Four plant species are grown. The growth of plant had order of Fe-HEDTA > Fe-EDDHA > Fe EDTA is noted at pH 7.6 HEDTA is most effective for plant growth. The amount of depletion of iron from waste water is expressed in terms of gram dry weight. For first ten days the depletion is maximum. We note auxin-like effect. The complex so formed is unstable at pH ~ 7.6. The variety of plants such as pepo (squash), sativas (cucumber), esculentum (tomato) and Vulgaris (beans) are used. The growth is highest in squash and it is very low in beans.

Table 12.1 Comparative growth of plants on iron chelates (gdw – gram per weight)

S.No.	*Iron chelate (s)*	*c-pepo Squash (gms/wt)*	*c-sativas Cucumber (gms/wt)*	*L-esculenum Tomato (gms/wt)*	*P-vulgaris Beans (gms/wt)*
1.	Fe-HEDTA	147.0	109.0	10.0	6.0
2.	Fe-EDDHA	82.0	55.0	20.0	20.0
3.	Fe-EDTA	36.0	29.0	36.0	30.0
4.	O-phen-Fe chelate	19.7	13.0	69.0	56.0

The changes in dry gram weight (gw) is ascertained (Table 12.1). The squash shows highest depletion while bean show least amount of iron. The higher depletion are noted in first ten days. The system undergoes alkaline hydrolysis, calcium fixation and chelating other elements. The limiting factors are iron availability, its interaction syerigism and sequential activity. These studies help to decide the use of waste water for irrigation of agriculture land.

12.3 TREATMENT OF WASTE WATER FOR REUSE

There are many methods used for the treatment of waste water which we have discussed in the earlier chapters but many methods are slow and time consuming. The rapid methods involve the use of the technique of the reverse osmosis and applications of the biosensors which we shall discuss in details from the view point of mass scale operation and wide applications.

(i) Reverse Osmosis for Desalination of Waste Water

The method provides provision of good quality water at the reasonable cost. We get water not only free from chemical impurities but also free from microorganism as viruses and bacteria *e.g.* the blackish water by process of reverse osmosis (RO) provides almost pure water from the sea water. This has been successfully practiced in middle east countries. Thus, chlorination filtration are the usual primary methods of purification however direct use of water for drinking is strictly prohibited due to ethical reasons. The pressure and the slow sand filters are used for preliminary treatment (sand size 0.75–1.25 mm). We use high pressure pump with operating pressure of 15–25 bar to drive out clean water Polyamide membrane is also used. The reverse osmosis plant is shown in Fig. 12.2. The chemical dosing rate is as follows: Fe (5 mg/L); cationic polyelectrolyte (1 mg/L); sanitizing agent (3 mg/L) dechlorination (2 mg/L).

We see schematic diagram (Fig. 12.2) of typical reverse osmosis plant while Table 12.2 clearly indicates what kind of elimination of impurities occur after Reverse Osmosis treatment. We need primary secondary and tertiary treatment before undertaking reverse osmosis process.

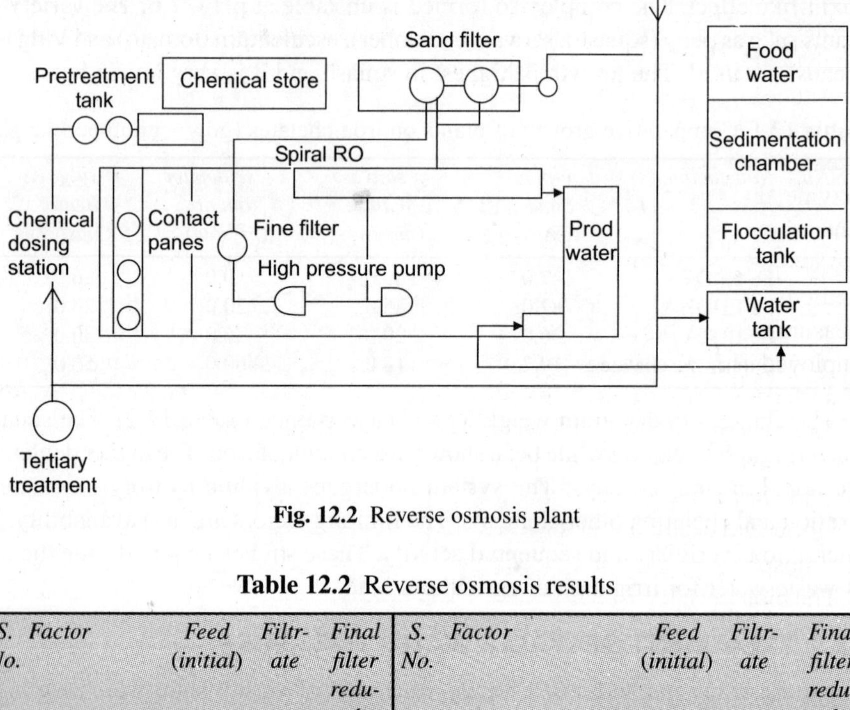

Fig. 12.2 Reverse osmosis plant

Table 12.2 Reverse osmosis results

S. No.	*Factor*	*Feed (initial)*	*Filtr-ate*	*Final filter redu-ced to*	*S. No.*	*Factor*	*Feed (initial)*	*Filtr-ate*	*Final filter redu-ced to*
1.	pH	7.0	7.0	5.7	9.	Ammonia (mg/L)	10	10	6.2
2.	BOD (mg/L)	21.0	21.0	0.1	10.	Magnesium^{2+} (mg/L)	20	20	0
3.	COD (mg/L)	40	20	2.0	11.	Calcium^{2+} (mg/L)	70	70	0
4.	TSS (mg/L)	20	6.1	0.5	12.	Sodium^{1+} (mg/L)	287	275	10.5
5.	TDS (mg/L)	1000	700	300	13.	Chloride^{-} (mg/L)	280	265	12.5
6.	VSS (mg/L) (Volatile)	10	1.5	2.0	14.	Sulphate^{2-} (mg/L)	287	275	12.0
7.	Turbidity (NTO)	20	3.7	0	15.	Alkalinity (mg/L)	135	135	0
8.	PO_4^{3-} (mg/L)	10	10	0.2	16.	Conductivity (μs/cm)	1680	1670	10.0

From Table 12.2 shows feed before treatment and the quality of the water filtrate after treatment shows only total suspended solids (6.1) (S.No. 4). Total dissolved solids (700) (S.No. 5). Volatile suspended solids (1.5) (S.No. 6), turbidity (3.7) (S.No. 7), sodium (275) (S.No. 12), chloride (265) (S.No. 13), sulphate (275) (S.No. 14) and conductivity (1670) (S.No. 16). Shows remarkable reduction in extent of pollution after treatment with concentration while rest of the factors indicate no change after treatment. Filters have to be back washed after every 8 hours. The last column in Table 12.2 shows final quality of emerging effluent after careful application of reverse osmosis. Fecal coliform (0), Salomonellu is zero. Low feed pressure (8.5 bar) gives good results after treatment.

(ii) Biosensors in Biological Monitoring

This kind of the treatment is very useful for treating sewer system, waste water plants for environmental monitoring. A "biosensor" is defined as the devise (analytical) made up of biologically active material directly attached to signal transducer. This belongs to group of biocatalytic materials having bioaffinity and microbe based system. Immunosensors are popular. Such sensors are used only in research and development stage. The biocatalytic materials sensors involve use of enzyme, the bioaffinity sensor have antibodies as nucleic acid. The microorganism sensor involve the process of inhibition of cellular respiration of these. We have two classes *viz.* electrochemical and optical electronic sensors. The well known methods of potentiometry, amperiometry, anodic stripping voltammetry with measurement of the absorbance, fluoroscence or intensity of Luminscence is employed in the first category while latter group of optical electronic model consist of surface plasma, resonance spectroscope, quartz crystal, micro balance with surface accoustic wave. These are used in water monitoring assembly. Online and intensity analysis are main uses. The micro organism based biosensors are routinely used to control BOD of waste water. The field of optical fiber immunosensors is fast growing *e.g.* chlorine-sterase sterase biosensors are used to monitor pesticides in atmosphere.

The biological monitoring is related to the control of pathogens and those which are causing feccal pollution. The changes in the electric properties caused by metabolic activity of microorganisms is used for biological monitoring. More specificity is possible in amperiometric methods. The bioaffinity based biosensors is useful for immunoassay in biological monitoring. The chlorophyll fluoroscence is used to measure presence of algae in waste water. The biological monitoring methods are faster in comparison to classical methods of analyses. Only limitation of this technique is validation of these devices. A good biosensor is influenced by several interferences. However, with careful control of conditions as well as of devices one gets reproducible results. The monitor must be compact and portable and inexpensive.

12.4 RECYCLE AND REUSE OF TREATED WASTE WATER

The irrigation by waste water is common practice all over the world. This is also equally true for India. The process is economical. Food, cash crop in Vadodara

(Baroda) in Gujarat were cultivated on recycled water. Primary worry is about health of persons handling the waste water, although it is treated by clean water.

Table 12.3 Comparison of results with three different sources of water

S.No.	Information	Waste water		Tube well		Rain water	
		MSU	ESU	MSU	ESU	MSU	ESU
1.	Family size	4.9	4.98	4.4	4.54	4.6	4.95
2.	Distance from source (m)	160	90	175	75	–	230
3.	Total band holding	3.5	2.7	3.4	3.1	2.6	2.4
4.	Years since used	8.3	8.6	0.7	0.7	0.1	0.4
5.	Off form cover	1.7	1.4	1.3	1.3	1.6	1.8
6.	Income in rupees	1756	1835	1513	1927	1890	1715

MSU = Municipal Sewage; ESU – Effluent Sewage.

In Table 12.3 MSU is municipal sewage use; ESU is effluent channel waste water is used in unregulated and sub-optimal areas. The waste water processing is viewed from the point of view of disposal problem rather than recycling problem and its reuse. It is used in absence of ground water. A meticulous planning is required to increase the benefits obtained from recycled waste water.

(i) Recycling and Reuse of Distillery Waste Water

Ecofriendly biological treatment of spent waste generates biogas. The spent wash and its chemical characteristics is indicated in Table 12.4.

Table 12.4 Quality of spent wash in sugar industry (mg/L)

S.No.	Property	Value (mg/L)	S.No.	Property	Value (mg/L)
1.	Sulphate (mg/L)	4000–7000	6.	COD	85000–100000
2.	Chloride (mg/L)	5000–6000	7.	Phosphorous (mg/L)	800–1000
3.	Sp. gravity	1.04	8.	Total solids	80000–90000
4.	Potassium (mg/L)	8000–10000	9.	Volatile solids	55000–60000
5.	BOD	35000–40000	10.	Total nitrogen	1200–1500

From Table 12.4 we note that the quality of waste water is poor with very high value for COD, BOD and total solids. We have therefore to adopt "Recycle-Reuse-Reduce" concept. We consider the utilization and not the disposal of waste water. The spent wash when it is used for agricultural farming the treated spent waste is used as liquid manure along with the irrigation of water for the crops. This results in twice the grain yield increase its size. The sunflower growth is very rapid as practiced in South India. It is useful for soil reclamation and bio composting process. Is used as liquid manure in the agricultural management.

(ii) Recycling of Waste Water-Status in India

The situation in semi and part is not very good. 28% or more population stays in urban towns. Around 73000 hectare acre of land is irrigated with waste water. The use and reuse is carried near banks of rivers. Many peninsular rivers have no satisfactory flow. Along the river the water is diverted to canal. The area covered in Andhra Pradesh at town called 'Musi' is 40, 500 hectare acre which is irrigated by waste water. This is significant contribution to control pollution.

(iii) Reuse of Waste Water

Not only for agricultural irrigation but also used in industry and urban cities. The salinity is major problem while handling. Its sodium content is very high. The level of boron, chloride as well as sodium is unusually high. Trace elements accumulate in plants and soil. The reasonable standard for cultivation is the BOD_5 must be less 10 mg/L turbidity should not exceed 2NTU, pH be between 6–9; suspended solids soil < 5 mg/L and the residual chlorine < 1 mg/L while utilising it in industry one must guard against foaming, corrosion (specially copper based) and also less interference by chlorine as it prevents growth of microorganisms. It avoids scale formation, thereby preventing clogging and staining from iron and manganese. One must also control bacteria, Protozoa, viruses, Helminth eggs and antibiotic are resistant gene. The factors influencing reuse is to pursue more valid list of retained water indicators in near future.

12.5 HEALTH GUIDELINES BEFORE REUSE OF WASTE WATER

WHO as well as agencies such as US-EPA have provided certain guidelines to protect health of the person(s) who is handling hazardous waste. The following two tables *viz.* provide for WHO and US-EPA guidelines for safe use of waste water.

Table 12.5 WHO guidelines for reuse of waste water

Type	*Conditions of reuse*	*Persons exposed*	*Intenstinal nematodes per 100*	*Feccal coln. form per 100*	*Treatment recommended*
A.	Irrigation of crops (uncooked) at sport fields, public parks	Farmer worker	< 1	< 1000	It stabilises the pond
B.	Irrigation of cereal, fodder pasture and trees	Farmer	< 1	No standard	Retention in pond for week
C.	Localised irrigation	Peasant	–	–	Pretreatment by irrigation teçhnology

The two tables *viz.* 12.5 (for WHO) and 12.6 (for US-EPA) show that pH of water should be between 6–9. The BOD level should be between 10–30 mg/L, colour should be absent as it is objectionable and if present it should not be more than 2 NTU. All processes need secondary filtration involving high dosage disinfection by chlorine, one needs good filtration media most of the samples cannot tolerate pathogens and the quality of water must be monitored on weekly basis while microorganism must be checked almost daily. The quantum of water which is treated varies from 15–90 m. No nutrient must be present in any kind of water. Most of it is needed for spray irrigation.

Table 12.6 Criteria for reuse of recycled water

S. No.	Kind of reuse	Treatment	Water quality	Water monitoring	Set back (if any)	Remarks
1.	Agricultural reuse (non food crops)	Disinfection	pH 6–9 BOD 30 mg/L	Weekly (8 ds) monitoring	Potable supply	Avoid clogging, low nutrient level preferred
2.	Agricultural reuse (food materials)	Disinfection	pH 6–9.0 BOD ~ 30 200 feccal MPN count coliform	Weekly (8 ds) Measure-ment	80 m to potable water	Spray irrigation needed No nutrient preferred
3.	Agricultural reuse (unpro-cessed food)	Filtration Disinfection	pH 6–9–0 BOD–10 color 2NTU	Weekly (8 ds) few daily	15 m to potable water	Add coagulant before filtration, no pathogens tolerated.
4.	Fixed irrigation field	Disinfection	1 mg/L residual chlorine	Weekly (8 ds)	90 m to portable water	No nutrients, chlorine high dose. Spray irrigation high. Reliable treatment needed.
5.	Land scape, parks	Filtration, disinfection	pH ~ 6–9.0 BOD-10 color 2 NTU, No feccal, coliforms	Daily (1d) monitoring pH/BOD weekly monitoring	15 m to potable water	Low level treatment coagulant added, none pathogens, clear No odor. High chlorine dose.

These pungent requirements by WHO or EPA indicates that the life of worker is not endangered if minimum health precautions are taken.

(i) Health Protection

There is great risk associated with the use of recycled water in form of pathogenic microorganism such as virus, bacteria, helminth and protozoa; but proper control measure should mitigate this problem. The primary and secondary treatment should be perfect. The tertiary process is needed if it is used for unrestricted irrigation. The important process for treatment of waste water includes polishing, chlorination, UV radiation and/or ozonation. The chloride dose varies from 5–20 mg/L while highest dose is 100–450 mg/L. Incompletely nitrified effluent, it causes problem. The UV radiation dose recommended is 25–140 mJ/cm^2 with no by product; but measuring actual dose of UV treatment is cumbersome. The bacteria grow faster if insufficient dose of treatment is there. Ozone contact for 5–10 mts is good.

Ozone reduces color and odor. A suitable irrigation method must be used. It includes flood irrigation, furrow irrigation, sprinkler irrigation and drip irrigation. All process except last one are of low cost. The anaerobic wastage must be avoided in sprinkler irrigation. The level of risk varies for recycled water. Non consumption for crops like cotton do not pose any problem. The raw crop is never used (*e.g.* potatoes egg plant beets) but these are processed by boiling before consumption. Many kinds of pathogens cause varied diseases in human beings if not removed.

This is because virus, bacteria, protozoa, nematodes cause infection. The recycled water is never used for human consumption. The waste water treatment for water recycling includes physical (screening flotation) biological (activated sludge, trickling filters), non conventional natural system (lagooning, perculation, infiltration; soil equifiers) and the better advanced treatment (tertiary filtration, chlorination, UV radiation exposure, ozonation, membrane filtration with use of membrane bio reactors). In order to keep water in good quality better treatment process are employed.

Table 12.7 Choice of disinfection treatment technique

S. No.	*Criteria*	*Chlori-nation*	*UV-radiation*	*Ozono-lysis*	*Membrane filtration*	*Membrane bioreactors*	*Matura-tion*
1.	Plant dimension	All size	Small	Medium	Medium	Small	Small
2.	Pretreatment	All levels	Secondary	Primary treatment	Secondary	Primary	Secondary
3.	Reliability	Good	Good	Good	Very good	Good	Fair
4.	Complexity	Simple	Simple	Complex	Complex	Reasonable	Simple
5.	Safety aspects	Safe	Unsafe	Safe	Unsafe	No inform	Unsafe
6.	Transportation	Normal	Minimal	Less	Less	Less	Normal
7.	Microorganism removal	Poor-good	Good	Good	V. good	V. good	Good
8.	Toxicity	Toxic	Non toxic	Not expected	None	None	None

12.6 RECYCLED WATER-USE IN METROPOLITAN CITIES

In big towns like Mumbai, Kolkata, Chennai, Delhi, Banglore and Hyderabad there is growing urbanisation with several industrial units where professional activities have come up. With this rise there is a spectacular growth of the population which needs water for food, shelter and domestic work.

Further with the vagaries of rain in developed cities drinking water becomes serious problem not only for human being but also of cattle and living entities. Consequently, there is famine in certain parts of states with immediate need of providing clean water at least for drinking. This is possible if such clean water is not used for car washing, agricultural, and plantation in the gardens and recreation purposes.

To mitigate the shortage of clean water big cities like Mumbai are insisting that newly constructed apartments and towers must provide two things *viz.* Rain water harvesting and the other recycling of used water (other than sanitary use) by installation of water purification plant in the building. Such plants primarily consists of two process *viz.* The passing of waste water through slow and filters to remove suspended solids and objectionable impurities while subsequent process involves the passing of previously treated water through bed containing activated charcoal to get rid of colour as well as odour which in turn is imparted by organic matter. Once the water goes through these two processing tanks, it appears clean fit for the reuse in garden, car washing, street cleaning but certainly not for human consumption.

In Mumbai the state government has made it obligatory to have water harvesting and waste water recycling plants for newly constructed buildings. If they fail they are not provided no objection certificate (NOC) for the occupation. Even in old buildings, if there is sufficient space they are encouraged to instal recycling plant and water harvesting unit. The installation of water harvesting plant is easy. All waste water accumulated on the terrace is collected in pit with soft soil on ground, the soil remains wet and saturated with water. This in turn is used during summer for harvesting the soil. This is the most inexpensive process instead of wasting water dumping in sea.

12.7 CONCLUSION

We have considered the possibility of using recycled water mainly from the view point of agricultural applications. We have to follow good agronomic practice and specially must guard against negative impacts of irrigation. One has to strive hard to improve the operation of water reuses. We must consider livelihoods and profitability. One has too many times to change attitude and implications. One has to develop and apply holistic and appropriate health guidelines. One should explore it to apply other management options. An exhaustive research work needs to be carried out in order to understand the intrinsic knowledge and quality of the waste water before recycling.

Whatever amount of measures we take to conserve water, a long term planning is in order. We may do water harvesting or grey water recycling the criminal waste of water by civic society has to be scrupulously avoided. Whatever stock of water we have must be preserved and wastage due to the spillage, sewage contamination must be avoided.

ADDITIONAL READING

1. V. Lazarova, A. Bahri, *Water Reuse of Irrigation, Agriculture, Landscapes and Turf grass*, CRC Press, USA (2005).
2. C.A. Scott, N.I. Iavuqui, L. Rastide Sally, Ed. *Waste Water Use in Irrigated Agriculture, Confronting the Livelihood and Environmental Realities*, CAB International Press (2004).
3. P. Quevauviller, O. Thomas, A. V. Beken Ed. *Wastewate Quality Monitoring and Treatment*, John Wiley and Sons (2006).

4. J. Al-Sulaim, T. Asano, *Wastewater Reclamation and Reuse Ed.*, New Age International Publishers (P) Ltd. (2000) .
5. M. Csuros, C. esuros, *Microbiological Examination of Water and Waste Water*, Lewis Publishers (1999).
6. S.N. Kaul, L. Szpyrkowice, A. Kumar, *Wastewater Treatment and Technologies and Environment*, Daya Publishing House, New Delhi (2004).
7. M.H. Gerardi, *The Microbiology of Anaerobic Digestion*, Wiley Intersciences (2003).
8. S.M. Khopkar, *Environmental Pollution Analysis Second Edition*, New Age International Publisher (P) Ltd. (2012).

13 Sewage

13.1 INTRODUCTION

A sewer is defined as the channel intended for carrying out domestic waste while sewage is the water-borne waste product of mankind. Previously the sewage was just discharged into tidal water without treatment. The dissolved oxygen varies with temperature. *e.g.*, for clean water at 0ºC it is 14.6, at 10ºC is 11.6, at 20ºC is 9.1, at 30ºC is 7.6 mg/L. On release of sewage in to sea, its oxygen contents decreases. For sewage BOD of 10 mg/L was considered bad while 1 mg/L BOD indicate it is reasonably clean water. A sewage should not have more than BOD 20 mg/L. The sewage treatment covers removal of solids and grit; treatment of storm sewage with removal of suspended solids with aerobic biological treatment, thereby effecting improvement of effluent and finally easy mode of treatment and disposal of sludge. The main objective of treatment is to produce a disposable effluent without causing any trouble to the community. There are various types of sewers and different variety of sewage as combined, crude, dilute, domestic one indicating their origin or characteristics. All sewage contains solid which are organic or inorganic. Odour is due to organic solids present in the sewage.

13.2 OBJECTIVE AND METHODS OF TREATMENT

The primary aim of treatment is to protect human health and prevent pollution of potable water. It is definite health hazard as it contains pathogens and disease carrying organisms. It is a liability to community. Recovery of useful material in sewage partly covers the cost of treatment *e.g.*, fertiliser, cooling agent. The methods are classified as process involving screening; sedimentation; chemical and biological treatment. It is also grouped as the primary and secondary treatment. The first involves physical methods of screening, filtration and sedimentation. In secondary treatment involves chemical and biological treatment. Latter treatment gives clean effluent. The removal of solid, grit, oil and grease and partial disinfection is covered in primary or preliminary treatment of the sewage. This is followed by sedimentation, coagulation.

13.3 WHAT IS DOMESTIC EFFLUENT OR SEWAGE?

The sewage is also called as the *domestic effluent*. This domestic effluent is composed of sewage, sullage and waste water from man's activities in environment.

On an average a human being discards 135 to 270 gram of faeces and 1 to 1.3 kg (1–1.5 litre) of urine per day. Its composition is a faeces with about 66 to 80% moisture, 88 to 97% organic matter; 5 to 7% nitrogen; 3 to 54% phosphorus; 1.0 to 2.5% potassium, 44 to 55% carbon and 4.5% potassium; 17% carbon and 6% of calcium. Since it contains pathogenic and disease carrying organism, it is extremely dangerous for health. Sewage has offensive odour and bad colour. In raw form it is harmful to health.

A sewage contains 99.9% water and 0.1% solids; out of this 0.1% solids it contains 30% inorganic matter and 70% organic matter. The inorganic solid contains, grit, metals and salts, while the major portion of organic solid contain proteins, fats and carbohydrates. Sullage consists of chemical detergents, soap, fats, grease used for washing utensils in kitchen, clothes and milk products (Table 13.1). The strength of sewage gives an idea about its quality. Such strength is expressed in terms of 5-day BOD and COD. One has to consider COD, because a lot of nondegradable materials like soaps, detergents, esters and flavours are present in domestic effluent. On an average a sewage with 200 mg/litre BOD or less than 400 mg/litre COD is termed as weak sewage, while sewage with 500 mg/litre of BOD or 1000 mg/litre COD is termed as strong sewage and one with more than 750 mg/litre of BOD or more than 1500 mg/litre of COD is termed as extremely harmful (Table 13.2). The average composition of sewage in India with 5-day BOD is 280 mg/litre, 402 mg/litre of suspended solids, 1000 mg/litre of dissolved solids, 200 mg/litre of chloride and 25 mg/litre of ammonical nitrogen. With rise of temperature, the 5-day BOD value also increases proportionately.

Table 13.1 Composition of sewage

S. No.	*Parameter*	*Values in mg/L*
1.	pH	5.5 to 9.0
2.	Total suspended solids	600
3.	Temperature	< 45°C
4.	BOD (5-day)	500
5.	Oil and grease	100
6.	Phenolic compounds	5.0
7.	Cyanides	2.0
8.	Radioactive materials	10^{-7}
9.	Chromium	2.0
10.	Copper	3.0
11.	Lead	1.0
12.	Nickel	2.0
13.	Zinc	15.0
14.	T.D.S.	2100
15.	Sulphate	1000
16.	Chlorides	600
17.	Boron	2.0
18.	Sodium	60

Table 13.2 Comparison of BOD_5 *vs.* COD_5 of various effluents containing organic chemicals

Domestic effluent contents	*COD mg/litre*	*5-BOD mg/litre*	*BOD in % of COD*
Ethanol	2080	1820	87.4
Acetone	2170	1680	76.5
Acetic acid	1070	860	80.0
Phenol	2380	1100	46.0
Glucose	1010	600	59.3

13.4 TREATMENT OF SEWAGE

The principal objective of treating sewage of domestic origin is two-folds to reduce toxicity and arrest spread of diseases by pathogens and to prevent the pollution of surface and ground water. One of the ideal ways to prevent such pollution of surface waters is to render it beneficial end use after pretreatment, *e.g.*, for protein production, irrigation of soil, growth of algae and fish. The pipes carrying sewage are called *sewers*. When one considers the treatment, one has to know the objective of such a treatment. The main aim is first to remove inorganic solids like grit, dust by the process of sedimentation. It is followed by degradation or disintegration of organic matter into easily assimilable form, with simultaneous liberation of methane and leading to refining the effluent to make it fit for reuse for the agricultural purpose or similar applications only after disinfection. We therefore classify treatment in the following category as: primary treatment (mainly sedimentation), secondary biological treatment (anaerobic and aerobic) and tertiary treatment.

It is worthwhile at this stage to consider quality of sewage and sludge before and after primary treatment as is shown in Table 13.3.

Table 13.3 Composition of sewage before and after primary treatment

S. No.	*Content*	*Percentage*		*Effect*	*Percentage Rise/Fall*
		Before treatment	*After treatment*		
1.	Moisture	93.99	96.40	Rise	2.49
2.	Ashless substance	77.50	81.40	Rise	3.90
3.	Ash	22.50	38.90	Rise	5.49
4.	N_2	3.42	3.10	Fall	0.32
5,	Fats	13.47	9.30	Fall	1.07
6.	Carbohydrate	9.08	7.20	Fall	2.15
7.	Hemicellulose	8.90	7.30	Fall	1.60

It will be noted that although moisture ash and ashless material contents rise by 3%, with 3.90% fats, carbohydrates and cellulose contents they are lowered, 2.2% making it less harmful to human beings. The main objective of any treatment is to remove coarse particles, extract pollutants, absorbs or distill or neutralise all particles if possible, and undertake disinfection by chlorination to so as reduce pathogens and extend biological treatment to promote fermentation and liberation of methane.

13.5 PRIMARY TREATMENT OF SEWAGE

There are several operations involving primary treatment. The operation consist of removal of gross solids. Therefore, it is passed through screens consisting of metal bars with spaces in between. The nature of sewage size of screen and degree of breaking solid matter decides the ultimate quality of the sewage. The next operation is the removal of grit. It is deleterious to health so it is removed to facilitate process of sedimentation. It should be removed in tanks. The next step is removal of oil and grease. It is removed before next treatment step of passing in skimming tanks which accelerates process of settling with use of the coagulants. The important steps in primary treatment are the collection of sewage and its initial treatment. The criteria from the viewpoint of health, reuse, ecological balance, nuisance, cultural and operational aspects, and cost-benefit analysis are considered. Not any system satisfies all the above criteria. The physical process involves screening, removal of grit and organic suspended solids by process of sedimentation and removal of large floating objects. Grit is heavy inorganic fraction of sewage solids, which settles fast in sedimentation tank. Such grit is used for land filling or is disposed off by burial. Sedimentation is the gravitational separation of suspension into its two components as solid and liquid phase. A high degree of clarification is aimed at removal of solids. This reduces load on secondary biological treatment and simplifies treatment in final methods. The density of particle and liquid; velocity of flow temperature, size of particle and gravitational force are of atmost importance in deciding the course of sedimentation process.

13.6 CHEMICAL TREATMENT OF SEWAGE

This process is conducive for the primary sedimentation wherein tanks are employed. A good sedimentation amounts to 50% removal of objectional components from sewage. The Stoke's law shows the factors influencing velocity of particles in liquid state is $V = \frac{2gr^2}{g\eta}(d_2 - d_1)$ if V = rate of fall, r = radius of particle, η = viscocity of liquid, d_2, d_1 is density of solid and liquid resp, g = acceleration by gravity. This law is true for small particles. A shallow tank for sedimentation is preferred. (On sterilisation, biological, flocculation occurs which is not in real sense sedimentation). The artified flocculation favouring sedimentation is enhanced by few aids such as mechanical flocculation, chemical coagulation with hydrated lime or aluminium sulphate or iron salts or use of polyelectrolytes. It leads to formation of insoluble flocculation precipitate which goes down the tank as colloidal matter. The actions are

$$Ca(HCO_3)_2 + Ca(OH)_2 \longrightarrow 2CaCO_3 + 2H_2O \text{ (insoluble carbonate)}$$

$$Al_2(SO_4)_3 + 3Ca(HCO_3)_2 \longrightarrow 3CaSO_4 + 2Al(OH)_3 + 6CO_2\uparrow$$

$$FeSO_4 \cdot 7H_2O + Ca(HCO_3)_2 \longrightarrow Fe(HCO_3)_2 + CaSO_4 + 7H_2O$$

(flocculation of iron bicarbonate).

It leads to reduction of 60% of BOD value of sewage but amount of sludge also increases. The preparation before sedimentation facilitates process of settling. The septic tanks are horizonal flow sedimentation vessels, when settling sludge is digested by anaerobic bacteria. They need little attendation with occasional removal of sludge. The chemical precipitation involves addition of chemical to hasten process of the sedimentation. The process is rapid and it completely removes suspended matter. However, with discovery of biological process its utility is regulated. Colour is also reduced. The putrification in absence of nitrate or DO is higher. Chlorination is very effective and useful. Chemical feed devices are used for uniform dispersion. The use of the activated carbon controls colour, odour, pH, sludge digestion and its quality as it works on principle of process of adsorption. The recirculation favours sedimentation. The chlorination to reduce smell and septric activity, the chlorination is preferably used. It stops corrosion and reduces BOD by 30%. Agitation is also useful. The dose is 10 to 25 mg/L chlorine disinfects the sewage, but gas itself is toxic. Chlorine used is in liquid or gas form. HOCl so generated by reaction with water is in fact useful to kills bacterial cells.

13.7 BIOLOGICAL TREATMENT

As such 0.1% of solids are in sewage, 70% is organic matter consisting of fats, carbohydrates and proteins. They are responsible for generation of bad odour and growth of disease producing microorganisms. These microorganisms contain mainly bacteria, virus, algae and protozoa. Bacteria, algae and protozoa promote biological degradation. The oxidation of organic matter provides food. It tolerates acidic and alkaline conditions and withstands high temperature (< 60°C). The disease carrying bacteria are cholera, dysentery, typhoid fever and diarrhoea. The bacteria useful in aerobic treatment of sewage are rod shaped, facultative and mesophilic. Viruses are peculiar microbes, which do not use organic or inorganic compounds from sewage for their growth. They are reproduced by invading almost all cells, whose reproductive process redirects to manufacture more virus particles. Algae are mostly multicellular photosynthetic organism; carbon dioxide is used by them to reproduce. Their growth is stimulated by phosphates and nitrates from water. It causes what is called as nutrient enrichment or 'Eutrophication' of body of water and extensive algal growth in the form of algal bloom. The protozoa are unicellular proteins ancestral to animal kingdom. They are responsible for putrification of sewage, *e.g.*, in their presence COD it is lowered from 198 to 124 mg/litre, while organic nitrogen is reduced from 14 to 7 mg/litre, while suspended solids decrease by 86 to 26 mg/litre. The intestinal parasites include worms, flukes. They are not necessarily present in every sewage.

(i) Aerobic Activated Sludge Process

This process handles large volumes of sewage with production of better effluents. In earlier days land treatment was used. The biological process promotes coagulation, oxidation, leading to liberation of CO_2 and oxidation of ammonia to nitrite and nitrates. The percolating filters *i.e.,* sprinklers or tricking filters are used. They are useful for biological treatment of sewage at high dosage and loading. A high surface free from dust in filter is the main requirement. The effluent from percolating filter contains 'Humus sludge'. Sludge is removed by the hydrostatic head without disturbing liquid sewage. Filter contains fly insects larvae spiders and other invertebrate animals leading to excessive ponding *i.e.,* production of inferior effluents. Activated sludge process is discovered in 1913 in England. It involves aeration of settled sewage with special bacteria is an active sludge leading to clear effluent. This led to oxidation and nitrification with deposition of brown flocculant sludge. The process is repeated several times to promote purification. A small space is needed it is popular in big cities. A mechanical aeration system is employed. Activated sludge purifies sewage in the presence of DO. Bacterial cells grow divides into segments. The quality of the activated sludge is important. A good variety is golden brown sludge with earthy smell. In dry spell it becomes septic. Sludge activity is measured by rate of oxygen consumption in definite time schedule. Odecometer measures such activity.

Sludge volume index is measure of sludge in terms of volume or density. The

$$\text{sludge volume index (SVI)} = \frac{\text{Settled volume of sluge in 30 mts}}{\text{\% of suspended solids}}$$

It increases during settling process, while

$$\text{Sludge density index (SDI)} = \frac{\text{\% Suspended solids} \times 100}{\text{Settled volume of sludge in 30 mts}}.$$

So $$\text{SVI} = \left(\frac{\text{SDI}}{100}\right)$$

The sludge density is obtained as = $\text{SD} = (\text{SVI} \times 100)$

The sludge age is obtained from $= \dfrac{V \times Sm}{Q \times Sg}$ if V = tank volume, Q = Flow rate of sewage, Sg = solid in sewage, Sm = suspended solids in the mixed liquor. It is average determination time of sludge or floc in activated sludge plant. By nitrification one gets several benefits like getting dense sludge, no bulking, tolerate overload, easy dewatering of sludge, prevention of foaming. The process of nitrification is facilitated by high DO with long aeration time but better nitrification, with working pH 7.5 to 8.0. Only heavy metal cynides prevent nitrification. The oxidation ponds contain the algae to promote putrification, reduction of BOD is cheap. It promotes the growth of mosquitoes. There are several merits of activated sludge process *viz.,* one gets clear non-putrifiable odourless effluent. The controlled nitrification, is an aid to produce fertiliser. Effluent is clear with low BOD and high contents of dissolved oxygen.

The results in Table 13.4 show effect of activated sludge process of treatment. The pretreatment before sludge digestion is used to reduce load on aeration process. It involves sedimentation, chemical treatment, oxidation and adsorption but that

Table 13.4 Comparison of fresh sludge with activated sludge (%)

Constituent	*Fresh sludge*	*Activated*	*Constituent*	*Fresh sludge*	*Activated*
Total Nitrogen	4.5	6.2	CaO	2.7	1.7
P_2O_5	2.25	2.50	MgO	0.6	1.4
K_2O	0.50	0.75	SO_4^-	1.2	2.9
SiO_2	13.80	8.50	Cl^-	0.5	0.5
Fe_2O_3	3.20	7.20	Na_2O	0.8	1.0
Al_2O_3	2.10	3.20	PbO	0.1	0.2

process of aeration is most vital. Preaeration is not essential. The bulking of sludge is a serious problem during treatment. Chlorine gas is injected in sludge to prevent bulking and promote contraction of humus. The settling characteristics of activated sludge is expressed in terms of SVI and SDI. The sludge volume index (SVI) is defined as the volume occupied by one gram of activated sludge after settling the aerated liquid for at least 30 minutes. The sludge density index (SDI) is a factor obtained by dividing percentages of suspended solid (SS) by weight time 100 by sludge volume in the aeration tank settled in 30 minutes times. Both SVI and SDI are useful parameters for control of activated sludge aeration process. It gives prewarning that the sludge is commensing to bulk. It leads to poor effluent. The high percentage of water with no possibility to reduce to small volume called as *sludge bulking*.

The laboratory control of sludge digestion from analysis is done with control of pH. At pH 6.4, cessation of methane occurs while the excess accumulation of organic acid drops the pH value. The efficiency of digestion is measured by reduction in volatile and solids. The quality of sewage is shown in Table 13.5 after treatment.

It is not a general practice in sewage analysis to investigate presence of microorganism in term of M-P-N count. This information is made available from the value of BOD.

The biological treatment depends upon factors like susceptibility of organic substances for biochemical oxidation, concentration of pollutant within optimum level, pH of biological media, absences of surface active substances and presence of micronutrients like nitrogen, phosphorus, potassium, carbon. The sewage treatment involves separation of solid and liquid phases and their further aerobic treatment which gives activated sludge. The processes involves adsorption of pollutants on activated sludge, and mineralisation of pollutants with microorganism. The process is rapid and efficient. In trickling filters the biological filters spreads the microorganisms in sewage uniformly in short intervals. This process is capable of reducing BOD of sewage from 200 to 15 mg/litre. The microorganisms like green algae, biue-green algae, diatoms, protozoa are present in numbers as 226×10^9, 140×10^9, 24×10^9 and 66×10^9 respectively.

The important changes occurring during treatment include decrease in concentration of pollutant and absorption of pollutant on activated sludge, decrease

Table 13.5 Sewage sludge quality after treatment with activated sludge

S. No.	*Chemical test*	*Kind of sludge*	*Remarks*
1.	Moisture, total solid	Raw, treated, humus	Moisture removal facilitates digestion
2.	pH	Digested	Digested condition tested
3.	Alkanity	Digested	The condition of digestion is checked.
4.	Volatile acids	Digested	Initial indication of quality product
5.	CCl_4 extract	Raw, digested treated, humus	Grease, oils, fats, waxes progress of treatment
6.	NPK contents	Raw, digested humus, treated	Valuable as fertiliser
7.	Filter leaf	Treated	Coke yield
8.	Settlability	Mixed liquid	Ease of settling
9.	Sludge volume and density	Mixed liquor	Quality of sludge indicated
10.	MPN count	Mixed, treated	Quality of sludge shown

in amount of organic matter and conversion of ammonical as well as nitrite nitrogen to nitrate nitrogen, *i.e.,* nitrification of sewage and sludge. For trickling filters overload with organic matter, filtration surface become clogged and efficiency gradually decreased. One gram of activated sludge contains 1×10^{12} bacteria with surface area of 1200 square metre in biocenosis of activated sludge. It has a good absorbing power. Protozoa promotes accumulation of nitrogen in order to enhance quality of fertiliser of sludge.

(ii) Anaerobic Treatment of Sewage

It is mainly used to treat sludge. The principal goal is to change the physical structure of the sludge and to decrease the mass of sludge to promote fermentation of gases and soluble salts and to utilise the organic matter as the fertiliser. Methane fermentation is one of the processes where in sludge is separated from sewage and treated. For example, the mineralisation of salts of acetic and butyric acid liberates methane as:

$$2CH_3COOH + H_2O \longrightarrow K_2CO_3 + CO_2 + 2CH_4\uparrow$$

$$(CH_3CH_2CH_2COO)_2\,Ca + 3H_2O \longrightarrow CaCO_3 + 2CO_2 + \uparrow CH_4(g)$$

Such conversion is rapid in the absence of oxygen in anaerobic condition. Other methane producing reactions are as per the following reactions:

$$2C_2H_5OH + CO_2 \longrightarrow CH_4\uparrow + 2CH_3COOH$$

$$2CH_3CH_2CH_2CH_2\text{–}OH + CO_2 \longrightarrow CH_4\uparrow + 2CH_3CH_2CH_2COOH$$

$$4CH_3CHOHCH_3 + CO_2 \longrightarrow CH_4\uparrow + 4CH_3CH_2CH_2COOH + 3H_2O$$

$$CH_3COOH + CO_2 \longrightarrow CH_4\uparrow + 2CO_2$$

Table 13.6 Characteristics of sewage

Sample No.	*pH*	*TDS mg/L*	*DO mg/L*	*Nitrate ppm*	*BOD mg/L*	*Chloride mg/L*	*Alkalinity –*	*Hardness –*	*Heavy metals e.g. Pb (ppm)*	*Remarks*
Solid Sample (Solid)										
A	< 7.0	460	8.6	–	7.6	17	384	–	7.2	Good DO
B	–	620	0.4	3.15	14.4	39	378	–	7.1	V. High TDS
C	–	700	1.75	3.15	24	18.4	402	–	6.7	Good BOD
D	–	750	0.2	5.90	26.4	42.6	624	–	7.2	V. High Chloride
E	–	790	0.1	5.5	39.2	49.2	433	–	7.1	V. High TDS
Liquid Sample (Liquid)										
F	6.7	810	3.4	3.65	–	–	625	387	1.46 (Fe)	Alkalinity
G	6.7	620	4.1	2.8	–	–	646	374	1.0 (Fe)	V. Hardness
H	7.3	710	4.8	9.0	–	–	424	344	0.71 (Fe)	High Fe
I	7.3	720	3.6	59.0	–	–	323	404	1.46 (E)	Too much NO_3^-
J	7.60	550	4.2	25.0	–	–	842	223	2.3 (Fe)	High TDS
K	7.10	1400	1.4	31.5	–	–	433	629	1.75 (Cr)	Hard water
L	7.10	800	5.4	36.50	–	1.6 ppm High CN^-	579	5.278	0.05 (Cu) 0.16 (Cu) 0.17 (Zn)	Present CuZn
M	7.10	1050	4.6	87	–	–	457	415	1.46 (Fe)	High TDS

Thus, in the above transformations, ethanol, butanol, isopropyl, alcohol are converted to CH_4. The formic acid, formaldehyde and methanol also generates methane as:

$$4HCOOH \longrightarrow CH_4 \uparrow + 3CO_2 + 2H_2O$$
$$HCOOH + 3H_2 \longrightarrow CH_4 \uparrow + 2H_2O$$
$$HCHO + 3H_2 \longrightarrow CH_4 \uparrow + H_2O$$
$$CH_3\text{–}OH + H_2 \longrightarrow CH_4 \uparrow + H_2O$$

Water acts as an oxidising agent in methane fermentation reaction. Water acts upon enzymes, itself breaking up to form hydrogen and oxygen. The hydrogen is used by microorganism to reduce CO_2 to CH_4, while oxygen oxidises the decarbonized radical to form acid. Thus, the methane forming bacteria play an important role in circulation of substances and energy turnover in nature. They absorb CO, CO_2 and H_2 to give hydrocarbon, methane and synthesise its own cell substances. Table 13.7 gives composition of liquid sludge during fermentation.

While Table 13.8 gives composition of gas generated. It is worthwhile to study the effects of treatment and products generated, before and after treatment. The characteristics of typical sewage is described in Table 13.6. All eight hydrological parameters are considered in such characterisation.

Table 13.7 Composition of liquid sewage and sludge (mg/L)

S. No.	*Parameter*	*Acid fermentation*	*Alkaline fermentation*
1.	pH	4.9	7.3
2.	Volatile fatty acid	64.2	16.0
3.	Nitrogen of ammonium salt	144	270
4.	Alkalinity	None	30

Table 13.8 Composition of sewer gas let off in air

S. No.	*Gas*	*Acid fermentation*	*Basic fermentation*
1.	H_2S	46%	None
2.	CO_2	45%	26%
3.	CH_4	None	72%
4.	$CH_3\text{–}CH_3$	None	None
5.	H_2	7.5%	None
6.	N_2	None	None

The close examination of Table 13.6 shows that the comparison between quality of liquid and solid sewage. TDS increase in liquid sample, while Do comparatively increase due to exposure to air nitrate level, no special change in BOD, or chloride contents; with substitutional rise in the extent of alkalinity with rise of hardness, with presence of several kinds of transition metals in liquid form is seen *e.g.* Lead contents rises in the presence of iron, chromium, copper and zinc. Thus along with lead the sewage in the liquid state carries Fe (III), Cr (VI), Cu (II), Zn (II) in the range of 1.0–2.3 ppm approximately.

In biological oxidation by bacteria, in such process carbon converts it to CO_2 while organic hydrogen converts to water, organic nitrogen generate nitrate iron. The organic sulphur oxidises to SO_2 while organic phosphorus get converted to orthophosphate.

13.8 TERTIARY TREATMENT OF SEWAGE

It is the final step to improve the quality of an effluent after primary and secondary treatment. It is used to remove additional suspended solids including algae and it shows reduction in fecal coliforma numbers. The suspended solid reduction reduces BOD. Algae are 50% of protein. The solids are removed by flocculation and sedimentation or flotation and microstaining sand filtration and classification on pebble bed. Alum is used to flocculate, while, rapid sand filters are used for staining operation. The removal of fecal bacteria is achieved by disinfection. The fecal coliforma is removed by maturation ponds. They are suitable for treatment of effluent from aerated lagoons. Chlorine is used for disinfection. The difference in comparison with water is a large dose of chlorine, which is required due to presence of a large amount of organic matter (~10 to 25 mg/litre). The contact time of chlorine is also enhanced from half-an-hour to 2 hours. The excess chlorine is removed by treatment with SO_2.

The disposal of sewage into sea and septic tank are quite common. Septic tank is used in rural sewage system. Other methods include sewage dehydration or freezing, thermal treatment, mechanical dehydration by centrifugation and filtration. Sewage sludge is used for fertilisers, fortification of animal feed, as building materials and as biogas.

Table 13.9 Nature of domestic effluent after final treatment

S. No.	*Property*	*Solid effluent (mg/L)*	*Liquid effluent (mg/L)*
1.	pH	6.9 – 7.2	7.2 – 7.9
2.	Total dissolved solids	400 – 600	400 – 600
3.	Suspended solids	70 – 100	50 – 90
4.	BOD	150 – 300	1 – 2
5.	COD	200 – 500	3 – 6
6.	Hardness ($CaCO_3$)	150 – 200	35 – 45
7.	Alkalinity	150 – 200	100 – 150
8.	Chlorides	60 – 80	50 – 60

Table 13.9 gives information of effluent characteristics after final treatment. It clearly shows reduction in pH, SS, BOD, COD and chloride contents. While Table 13.10 indicates efficiency of final treatment in removal of pollutant by various

treatment procedures. The highest efficiency of 80 to 95% is attainable with anaerobic treatment, carbon adsorption process and distillation, while electrodialysis, algae treatment removes a small percentage of the pollutant. Costwise, the reverse osmosis, ion-exchange and carbon adsorption are the most expensive processes, while algae treatment and distillation are the cheapest processes, but have no practical utility.

Table 13.10 Relative efficiency of various processes

S. No.	*Treatment process*	*Elimination of substance*	*Efficiency of process (%)*
1.	Anaerobic treatment	Nitrate-N	80–90
2.	Denitrification	Nitrate-N	80–95
3.	Algae treatment	Ammonia-N	50–90
4.	Ammonia stripping	Nitrogen-Phosphorus	80–95
5.	Ion exchange	Dissolved solids	80–92
6.	Electrodialysis	Organic matter	10–40
7.	Carbon adsorption	Dissolved solids	90–98
8.	Reverse osmosis	Dissolved solids	65–95
9.	Distillation	Surfactants	90–98

The treated sewage has BOD less than 20 mg/L and suspended solids 30 mg/L. The aeration and self purification are final stages of treatment. BOD less than 4 mg/L is ideal for fishing and related activities in summer and value of BOD ~ 10 mg/L is acceptable during winter. Final effluent must be improved by mechanical flocculation, using microstrainer, sand filters, lagoons and land treatment. Such techniques are designated as part of tertiary treatment. The removal of suspended organic solids leads to decrease in BOD. The sewage with humus is subjected to mechanical flocculation. This leads to reduction of suspended solids. The microstrainer is a drum woven stainless steel fabric which is rotated in liquid sludge. It has small orfice. It leads to 28% reduction in suspended solid (SS). Strainer is cleaned with the chlorine once in months. The SS may remain till 40 to 60 mg/L. The suspended matter is removed by sand filters. It reduces as much as the 3.3 mg/L. It removes bacteria if operated at slow speed. Slow sand filters eliminate virus, worm egg and amoebic cysts from the effluent. The upward or immediate sand filters give good results. Gravel clarifiers are also good as little as 6 to 8 mg/L of suspended solid remains after filtration. Sewage if stored in shallow but large lagoons undergoes putrification in presence of oxygen in tropical environment. Large area of land is necessary for treatment but it is best mode if land is freely available. The nitrifying filter is used to improve effluents from activated sludge plants. Nitrate gets converted to ammonia thereby reducing the dissolved oxygen. The filters reduce BOD load. The removal of nutrients such as PO_4^{3-} ; NO_3^- is not necessary so long as water is not used for human consumption. Such nutrients promote the eutrophication (*i.e.*, algal blooms) and promote growth. The process is of ageing and converting land into marshy or dry land. The mode of treatment largely depends upon the size as well as the quality of sewage. No uniform method is adopted for any kind of sewage treatment.

13.9 DISPOSAL OF SEWAGE AND SLUDGE

After treatment sewage is disposed off into sea which is very large body of water. The common method is to dispose it on land. The disposal by dilution is an excellent method provided no sedimentation takes place. The preliminary investigation before disposal is necessary. Life of fish or its use for the recreational facility in water must be examined before disposal. The self purification covers degradation, active decomposition; recovery and get clean water. The value of DO, BOD, TDS gives idea about its quality. The disposal on land is best method such as sewage farming. It has high irrigating and fertilising value. Sewage is then disposed by flooding, surface irrigation, spray irrigation or filtration. The oxidation ponds, stabilisation ponds or lagoons are used. The most important factor is hygiene which must be properly maintained while considering any method of disposal. Sludge may be of three types like the primary sludge, humus sludge and activated sludge. The removal of moisture from sludge before disposal is critical. The liquid sludge is disposed off in sea. Lagoons are used as cold digestion tank. Wet sludge is used for composing land.

(i) Dewatering of Sludge

The chemical treatment given to sewage is the best method for dewatering sludge with coagulating agents. The synthetic organic polymers is also used. Elutriation is the process of washing a sewage sludge before coagulation. The counter current washings is resorted. This is the process of elutriation which reduces 80% of coagulant demand for flocs formation. The freezing is an other method of dewatering. Sludge undergoes fermentation in the process of digestion at raised temperature. It reduces the organic content with generation of CO_2 and CH_4 when pH of 6.8 to 7.8 is maintained. Activated or humus sludge is not easy to digest. 1/3 volume is reduced, when odour disappears, a gas with high calorific value is generated. Pentachlorophenol retards digestion process so also anionic detergents due to high pH, overloading, toxic metals, DO or temperature variation. Sludge drying bed helps dewatering process. Sludge is spread as 9" layer and dried in sunlight. It occupies large area of land. Water contents is 40 to 60% after drying. Filter pressing is old method for dewatering sludge. The pressed cake is used as the manure. Vacuum filtration is expensive proposition. Dorr Oliver have developed such filters on the commercial scale.

(ii) Drying and Disposal of Sludge

Air drying is commonly employed to reduce moisture to 20%. Cyclone separater is used for drying with moisture around 5%. A attritor is used it consists of rotor. The multiple health furnaces is used. The dried sludge is dumped into land in form of layers or it is burned in incinerators of different kinds. However, use as the fertiliser is more productive process. Fertiliser value is due to the presence of nitrogen and phosphorus and potassium (NPK) in it.

13.10 CHARACTERISATION OF SEWAGE

It is complex mixture of minerals and organic matter; floating matter, colloidal dispersion and solution. It also contains living organisms like bacteria, pathogens, and viruses. In few places it may be mixed with industrial effluents 99% is water with 1.0 to 0.1% of solid material which is composed of soaps fats, oils, greases and fecus. The insoluble matter is clay sand, ammonia which is always present in it. The nitrogen, sulphur or phosphorus containing organic matter is harmful to health. The carbohydrate, fats, proteins, detergents constitute organic solid waste. Fresh sewage has dissolved oxygen but not stale sewage. The anaerobic process produces sulphurated hydrogen gas. It is liberated more at pH 5.0 and least as pH 9.6. It gets oxidised to sulphuric acid promoting corrosion. Sulphates cause direct attack on pipeline. The chlorination is resorted to nulify the adverse effect. Sewage processes are biological in nature. The aerobic process depends upon supply of oxygen for the metabolism of bacteria. The nitrification involves the conversion of ammonia to nitrites and nitrates in the presence of oxygen. In anaerobic process no oxygen is present when sewage becomes septic. Looking from substances, sewage oxygen is supplied to undergo reaction. This is similar to process of putrification to generate methane, carbon dioxide. Redox reactions are vital in biological treatment of the sewage. The overall quality of sewage depends upon the method used for treatment.

Table 13.11 Treatment and disposal process

S. No.	*Source of effluent from*	*Method for treatment*	*Method for disposal of effluents*
1.	Gravity	Septic tank, primary treatment	Subsurface disposed
2.	Vacuum	Granular filter	Surface and drip uses.
3.	Pressure	Aerobic-anaerobic treatment	Evaporation, Eva transpiration
4.	Construction	Primary, septic tank	Soil and leach field immersion
5.	Slope gravity	Sand filtration	Wetland dispersion
6.	Mixture	Recycling, flushing	On site containment

The Table 13.11 shows the various additional methods for the treatment and disposal of sewage. There are several methods like septic tank, granular filter, aerobic and anaerobic treatment process sand filtration and recycling or flushing. There are various methods for the disposal of effluent or liquid sewage. It includes disposal on wetland, soil field immersion, evaporation (but very expensive mode) and sub surface disposal. Every method has its own merit as well as limitations. The whole choice is therefore based upon the background from where sewage, sludge is drawn. This in turns depends upon the sampling method of the sewage.

It should be very carefully selected in order get end results which not only reproducible but also reliable.

13.11 ANALYSIS OF SEWAGE

It is the most important aspect of sewage study. Sewage is analysed to know its constituents, which cause problems in its treatment. Effluent is analysed to control its quality. The physical, chemical, biological analysis is done to know its trouble shooting value. The BOD value of sewage rises if it contains large load of organic matter. The suspended solid (SS) analysis also shows the presence of the inorganic matter. Auto-analyser is used but best results are obtained from chromatography (PC, TLC, GLC) and spectrophotometry AAS, polarography and electroanalytical methods. The classical methods are also useful in few instances.

(i) Sampling of Sewage

This is one of the most important operations as the end results of analysis rest on method of sampling. Sewage continuously changes its characteristics, so composite sample is taken through automatic sampler. A representative sample is collected. The samples at surface or deep inside are different. The sampling at point of turbulence where it is mixing sewage it is ideal place for sampling. A grab sample is satisfactory for routine analysis. Sample should be kept in cool place. The physical examination includes measurement of temperature, colour, odour and the turbidity. The chemical analysis includes parameters such as solids (suspend as well as dissolved), BOD, DO, nitrogen, chlorine, alkalinity, fat contents and pH. The biological analysis includes testing of sewage for presence of bacteria and microscopic organism from health point of view (Table 13.12).

Table 13.12 Analysis of sewage and sludge

S. No.	*Chemical test*	*Raw sewage mg/L*	*Treated sewage mg/L*	*Sludge (activated) mg/L*
1.	BOD_5	350	< 20	17.4
2.	Suspended solids (SS)	350	30	22
3.	Nitrogen (ammonical)	35	20	22.8
4.	Nitrogen (organic)	20	4	1.92
5.	Chloride	100	100 (No Change)	30%
6.	Phosphate	12	10	0.2–8.9% (as oxide)
7.	Potassium	12	10	0.1–0.9 (as oxide)
8.	pH	7.0–8.0	6–8	Nil

The main objective of the sewage analysis is to assess the efficiency of various treatments used for sewage, it will be necessary to analyse samples periodically. Depending upon the results of analysis, one steps up the mode of treatment to mitigate the problems of hazards to health. The tests are performed to evaluate the sewage treatment plant. Sewage as such is too complex, and its nature varies from place to place, hour to hour and day-to-day; Therefore determination of exact quantities of all the constituents is not possible. However, it is important to adjudge the chemical characteristics of sewage. Although it is 99% waste water, it carries dissolved and solid matter which is most difficult to analyses. It is not very difficult to analyse organic matter and mineral contents of sewage, but obvinoxious carbonaceous and nitrogenous materials pose a serious health problem. Fresh sewage becomes stale in two hours. The reduction of sludge volume during analysis is also of prime importance. The resulting humus is filtered and all efforts are made to minimise sludge bulking. The efficiency is determined by the gas production and solid reduction process. The complex nature of sewage precludes its complete analysis. Oxygen consumed is easily measured, the concentration of organic matter. It is measured in terms of oxygen consumed for oxidation. This is expressed in terms of oxygen demand. Such oxygen demand is expressed in three ways as DO, BOD and COD.

13.12 ANALYSIS OF OXYGEN IN VARIOUS STATE

In order to characterise quality of sewage it is necessary to analyse DO, BOD and COD. This is because the status of biodegradable and degradable impurities of organic orgin is ascertained from the knowledge of BOD and COD.

(i) Dissolved Oxygen

In saline water oxygen is less soluble. It is necessary to specify temperature when oxygen is analysed. Organic matter reduces the magnitude of dissolved oxygen. The presence of algae increases DO as they consume CO_2 and release simultaneously oxygen in the sewage.

(ii) Biochemical Oxygen Demand

This is the amount of oxygen needed for biological degradation of organic matter under aerobic conditions within known time and temperature. The amount of oxygen consumed is the measure of its content of organic substances. Initially carbonaceous matter is oxidised when the nitrification occurs. It is not always possible to get ultimate oxygen demand value. BOD for 5 days is required but generally BOD for 2 days gives sufficient information to draw definite conclusion.

(iii) Chemical Oxygen Demand

This test involves the chemical digestion of the sample in the presence of dichromate and sulphuric acid. A correlation of COD and BOD is not always possible. However, a ratio of COD/BOD is used. The oxygen consumed test is found out. Sewage is digested with permanganate and oxygen demand is noted for quick information. This test is reliable. The relative stability of polluted water is the amount of oxygen present in terms of total amount necessary for complete stability. For study of raw sewage this test is of no use.

The alternative way of expression of oxygen contents is expressed in terms of ThOD, BOD, COD and ThCOD, so ThOD is the oxygen demand; which is required to oxidise organic fraction of waste completely to CO_2 and H_2O. It is not possible to calculate theoretical oxygen demand. However, it is approximately equal to COD. The COD is obtained as by oxidising waste with boiling dichromate solution. The reaction proceeds to 95% completion. The chief merit of COD determination is rapid three-hour analysis, the only limitation being it does not say anything about the proportion of the waste that is oxidised by bacteria. No light is thrown on the rate of bioxidation while in BOD the amount of oxygen required for oxidation of waste by bacteria is known. It is a true measure of concentration of organic waste which is biodegradable, BOD is carried for 5 days at 20ºC. It is written as BOD_5, while the ultimate 20-day BOD is written as BOD_4. It is seen that ThOD > COD > BOD_4 > BOD_5 >. An interesting relation exists between different stages of untreated domestic sewage. The approximate ratios are as follows:

$$BOD_5/COD = 0.5$$

$$BOD_4/BOD_5 = 1.5$$

The presence of agricultural and industrial wastes may alter these ratios substantially. Table 13.13 shows average breakdown of daily per capita BOD_5 contributions.

BOD is measure of putrescibility of sewage while COD is used all over the world under different names, *e.g.*, permanganate value (4 hour) oxygen consumed; oxygen absorbed; permanganate value; (3 minutes); dichromate value or COD. The ratio of COD/BOD is 2 : 1 for raw sewage it is 5 : 1 on secondary treatment during winter and it is still higher in summer. The difference between two values give an idea about the type of waste. The DO analysis needs modification in the presence of nitrite in sewage. If DO is high, putrefactive odour will be developed. Sodium azide modification for Winkler Alsterberg method involves the following reactions. It avoids positive error.

$$NaN_3 + H_2SO_4 \longrightarrow NaHSO_4 + HN_3$$

$$HNO_2 + HN_3 \longrightarrow N_2 \uparrow + N_2O + H_2O$$

Table 13.13 Daily per capita BOD_5 contributions

S. No.	*Operations*	*Developed countries (gm per person)*	*Developing countries (gm per person)*
1.	Individual washings	9	5
2.	Utensil washing	6	8
3.	Solid waste disposal	31	0
4.	Cloth washing	9	5
5.	Toilet—Faeces	11	11
	Urine	10	10
	Others	2	1
6.	Total average per day per person	78	40

The knowledge of amount of DO is important in activated sludge process for aerobic oxidation but sludge clarification is a problem.

The auto-analyser is used to measure oxygen content of the sewage. The permanganate oxygen technique assess the oxidisable inorganic matter and easily oxidisable organic matter. In spite of limitation BOD of sewage is best single test to ascertain the strength of sewage and of many nitrogenous industrial waste. BOD_5 represents amount of oxygen consumed by one litre of sample, when incubated at 20ºC in 5 days so temperature must be fixed. The BOD_5 of sewage is $3\frac{1}{2}$ times the 4 hour P.V. test (*i.e.*, $KMnO_4$). Here PV stands for permanganate value obtained by taking sample from dilute sulphuric acid, N/80 permanganate to 3 minute and 4 hr at 27ºC. At the end of incubation period excess of alkali iodide is added which reacts with unused permangnate to give iodine which is determined by titration with sodium thiosulphate. For domestic sewage BOD/PV = 4.0 but for the industrial sewage ratio is 2.0 for daily waste it is 8.0 and for farm waste ratio is 2.0.

(iv) Nitrogen

Nitrogen is present as ammoniacal-N or nitrite-N or nitrate-N. The fresh sewage has ammoniacal-N. It has a tendency to degrade to nitrite and to nitrate. The valency change is brought about by living microorganisms. Such change is positive or negative, depending upon whether oxygen is present or absent. The treated sewage has high nitrate ion concentration and is said to be well nitrified. High nitrate and phosphate concentrations in sewage promotes eutrophication, thereby causing algae bloom. The ammonia is determined by Kjeldal's method, while nitrite is estimated by Saltzman method and nitrate by Brucine method. Latter two methods are spectrophotometric methods. In view of easy availability of ion selective electrode for NH_3 and NO_3^-, such analysis is simplified with use of ion analyser.

Nitrogen is present in crude sewage in the organic form and as ammonia. To save time the albuminoid N is measured which represents the fraction of the organic N which is easily decomposed when sample is distilled with alkaline permanganate under standard conditions. This is the index of the nitrogenous organic matter in the sewage. Ammonia is generated during sedimentation. Albuminoid N is measure of the extent of putrification of sewage. It decomposes as follows:

$$2NH_3 + 3O_2 \longrightarrow NHO_2 + 2H_2O; \quad O_2 \longrightarrow 2HNO_3$$

Nitrites and nitrates are normally not found in raw sewage. Nitrate being last product indicates stability of sewage. In wet atmosphere complete conversion is not possible. Activated sludge plant effluents contain more of ammonia. We have five forms of nitrogen *viz.*, free ammonic, albuminoid ammonia organic nitrogen, nitrates and nitrites but last three are most common. Fresh sewage has high organic nitrogen and low in free ammonia but stale sewage has more free ammonia. Nitrite and nitrate are less than one ppm. It is more in treated sewage. Nitrate represents most stable form of nitrogenous matter in the sewage.

(v) Dissolved Chlorides and Chlorine

The sewage contains good amount of chlorides due to large consumption of salt. It will be fine if one has ion selective electrode for chloride measurement with ion analyser. In the absence of such instrument, one resorts to Volhard's or Mohr's volumetric method involving precipitation titrations.

All operations in such a situation are carried out by remote control. Rubber bulb is used for pippething solutions in the pipette. The sample should be kept to 5° C and pH ~ 2.0. The phosphate interferes in Mohr's method which involves precipitation. Chloride level rises due to food and urine excretion. Chlorides are unaffected by biological action. It is used to ascertain strength of sewage. Biological process or sedimentation does not affect them Low level is indication of dilution. It gives idea about degree of dilution. In the disinfection of domestic effluent, chlorine gas is used. A large dose is needed (more than 30 mg/litre) on account of presence of organic matter as well as ammonia in sewage. The excess of chlorine sometimes is eliminated by treatment with sulphur dioxide. Chlorine in solution is present in form of HOCI, Cl^-, and Cl_2 gas, also called *free available chlorine*. It is used to control odour, slime and insects in trickling filters in aerobic treatment and to prevent activated sludge bulking in anaerobic sludge treatment. If one has facility of amperometry, it gives best and rapid results of analysis. Else OTA (*o*-toludine) method is an ideal one, which involves spectrophotometer. Excess chlorine shows that organisms are killed. It is 5 to 50 mg/L in sewage.

(vi) Suspended Solids

In tertiary treatment using rapid sand filter eliminates major portion of suspended solids. Table 13.14 gives the nature of refuse in major cities in India, contributes greatly to suspended solids. A perusal of Table 13.14 will show that Kolkata refuse has a large percentage by weight of dust and ash; while Delhi sewage has considerable amount of vegetable and fruits in the refuse; same is true of Chennai sewage; Nagpur sewage has a large volume of leaves and shell, while Pune follows pattern of Chennai and Delhi. The dissolved as well as suspended solids are likely to be large. They are weighed from known volume of sewage, hence their percentage is calculated.

Table 13.14 Kinds of Refuse in major cities

S. No.	*Nature*	*Kolkota*	*Delhi*	*Chennai*	*Nagpur*	*Pune*	*Remark for highest value*
1.	Fruit, vegetable	16.0	20.3	57	3.8	68	Pune
2.	Leaves, shell	18.0	10.1	8.0	12.9	4.6	Kolkatta
3.	Paper, cardboard	3.2	5.9	4.8	2.0	8.7	Pune
4.	Glass, bones	7.4	0.6	0.5	0.8	0.6	Kolkatta
5.	Metal, tins	0.7	0.6	0.6	0.3	0.7	Pune
6.	Dust, ash	41.6	6.0	–	–	–	Kolkatta
7.	Wt. per person	0.51	0.31	0.56	0.35	0.3	Chennai
8.	Calorific value	6300	6600	6700	5300	7100	Pune

However, the determination of suspended solids is one of the crucial test of sewage. It shows efficiency of settlement tanks, where 50 to 90% solids are removed. The limit is 30 mg/L. The settleable solid indicates the proportion of insoluble solid matter removed by sedimentation. It is an index of sludge forming property of the sewage. The average figure is 5 to 0.3 mg/L. The total solid shows the strength of sewage. The value should be kept as low as possible. In total solid the volatile matter gives idea about the organic contents; which undergoes putrification. SS truly represents extent of treatment needed or how efficient is treatment. The suspended solid is analysed by nephelometric methods. The high dissolved solids indicate sewage is stale or old.

(vii) pH of Sewage

This is determined by portable pH meter. The pH of fresh sewage is more than 7.0 it is highly alkaline, while the pH of the stale or septic sewage is less than 7.5. It is acidic. pH goes down on standing. The degradation of the organic matter is pH dependent. The aerobic biological process is interfered if pH of sewage is either less than 5 or more than 10.0. One can also use indicator to ascertain pH of the sewage. The presence of the industrial waste makes sewage acidic. For biological treatment alkaline media is preferred. pH is mainly useful to control the treatment process. The anaerobic digestion of the organic matter can be controlled by adjustment of pH.

(viii) Total Organic Carbon

By wet oxidation with sulphuric acid and chromic acid a titrametric analysis of CO_2 evolved is measured. The process unfortunately is very time consuming. The fats and greases are recoverable. Their presence creats problem of clogging of filtering media. The analysis of voltile acid is beneficial with the index of progress of anaerobic digestion H_2S, CH_4, CO_2 are important gases in sewage.

(ix) Temperature

Table 13.15 indicates solubility dissolved oxygen in water. The measurement of temperature is of importantance. The temperature of sewage is 11 to 22°C. Initially

Table 13.15 Solubility of oxygen in water at different temperature

Temperature, °C	*Solubility, mg/litre*
15	10.07
20	9.08
22	8.74
24	8.42
26	8.12
28	7.84
30	7.57
32	7.23

the sewage temperature is higher than the atmospheric temperature. The high temperature causes problem of odour.

13.13 BIOLOGICAL ANALYSIS

The organism of various shape and size reside in sewage in form of viruses and pathogens. There are bacteria, which are located by microscope. Such organism may or may not be, harmful. The harmful are pathogenic organisms. The bacteriological and microscopic study gives the idea about their population. Industrial waste mixing with sewage kills these bacteria at pH less than 4.0. The analysis is carried out in study of stream pollution. Algae, fungi are analysed by the microscope. The presence of bacilli, cocci is shown by the microscope. The number *i.e.*, MPN count may be 2×10^6 to 2×10^7 per ml.

(i) Strength of Sewage

The treatment process depends upon the volume and consequently its strength (*i.e.*, treatibility) or the total contents of organic and oxidisable matter. It is measured by the amount of oxygen required to oxidise both organic and inorganic components of a given volume of sewage. Many factors influence the strength of trade effluent mixing. It is measured in terms of strength as

$$\text{Sewage strength} = (\text{ammoniacal N} + \text{organic N}) \times 4.5 + \text{N/8 PV} \times 6.5$$

The permanganate value (PV) indicates also the strength of the sewage.

13.14 CONCLUSION

We see that the methods for the analysis of inorganic constituents are more or less similar as those used for water analysis. For the presence of organic matter much weightage is given to the value of 5-day BOD or 4 hour permanganate value. These two parameters give fairly good idea of organic matter present in sewage thereby, facilitating decision on kind of treatment process. A review of sewage studies is useful. We had considered the objective and methodology of treatment of sewage thereby. There are many methods for treatment of sewage. The samples include primary treatment which composes of physical methods like sedimentation. Then chemical methods are one which largely cover disinfection of sewage by conventional method utilising chlorine. The biological treatment is of two types one in presence of oxygen called as *aerobic activated sludge process* and another is in the absence of oxygen called *anaerobic treatment*. The quality of sewage ascertained in terms of sludge volume index and sludge density index contains information on percentage of suspended solids (SS) and settled volume of sludge in the period of 30 minutes. The anaerobic process leads to generation of gases like CH_4, CO_2. The final or tertiary treatment is equally important to refine the sewage before its disposal. The disposal methods cover land fillings, dilution with large body of water, land filling needs dewatering and preferably drying of sludge. The characterisation is indispensable as it decides the course of treatment. Sewage analysis is vital as it throws light on what kind of treatment is needed or how successful is treatment given to sewage. The determination of DO, BOD and COD gives good idea on quality of sewage. A BOD_5 or 5 day BOD is most common. The ratio of COD/BOD, gives idea of its quality. Nitrogen in form of ammoniacal nitrite is great hindrance in treatment. The analysis of the suspended solids is quick test to know about sewage. The biological analysis never gives correct idea of MPN on population of microorganism present in sewage. The sewage is an important source as agricultural manure, if treated properly.

ADDITIONAL READING

1. L. Metcalf and H.P. Eddy, *Sewerage and Sewage Disposal*, Tata McGraw Hill Book Co. (1972).
2. G.M. Fair, J.C. Gayer and D.A. Okun, *Water and Waste Water Engineering*, Vol. **III**, John Wiley and Sons (1966).
3. P.W. Powers, *How to Dispose off Toxic Substances and Industrial Waste*, Noyes Data Co.
4. D. Mara, *Sewage Treatment in Hot climates*, John Wilety and Sons, ELBS Series (1977).
5. T.H.P. Veal, *The Disposal of Sewage*, Chapman and Hall Ltd., London (1956).
6. K. Imhoff, W.J. Muller and D.K.B. Thistlethwayte, *The Disposal of Sewage and other Waterborne Waste*, Butterworths, London (1971).
7. H.E. Babbit and E.R. Baumann, *Sewage and Waste Treatment*, Asia Publishing House, New Delhi (1958).
8. D. Barnes and F. Wilson, *Chemistry and Unit Operation in Sewage Treatment*, Applied Science Lab., London (1978).
9. S.R. Kshirsagar-*Sewage and Sewage Treatment,* Roorke Pub. House (1965).
10. R.E. Bartlett, *Surface Water and Sewage* Applied Pub. (1981).
11. N. Rajvaidya and D.K. Markandey-*Advances in Environmental Science and Technology,* Vol. **7**, A.P.H. Publishing Co. New Delhi (1998).
12. S.M. Khopkar, *Environmental Pollution Analysis,* Second Edition, New Age International Publishers (P) Ltd. (2012).

14 Land Pollution and Pesticides

14.1 INTRODUCTION

The environmental scientists have paid sufficient attention towards pollution due to the industrial activity. The pollution is largely confined to the urban areas, in cities and towns. Fortunately, it is possible to control such pollution by effectively arresting the faulty industrial growth and related activities. Much worse is pollution of soil and pollution due to pesticide residues. Less attention has been paid towards this problem. As a matter of fact indiscriminate use of fertilisers and excessive use of pesticides has created a great menace. Both of these products find their way into food chain. They have direct impact on human health. The pollution of lithosphere due to fertilisers or pesticides is so widespread in rural areas. In agricultural country like India, it is impossible to control it. It has much wider ramification than other kinds of pollution. A considerable attention has been paid to mitigate soil pollution, to increase yield of crops, and to promote food production.

The crops are destroyed by industrial effluents, but some grow well on them. Apart from consideration of role of nitrogen and phosphorus which promotes eutrophication of effluent, we consider the role of elements like potassium, copper, zinc, iron, manganese, molybdenum and boron as the micronutrient in soil. They promote growth of crops. As such the presence of trace elements from soil, sediments are valuable asset. The pesticides are a gift to man, but also they are a curse if not properly used. Majority of these pesticides are not biodegradable even at elevated temperature. They leave behind a toxic residue in the environment. Such toxicity is determined by LD_{50} value for pesticides. It is essential to study soil pollution—a term which is attaining new dimension in developing countries. An endeavour is made in this chapter to explain what is meant by land pollution and stress the role of NPK micronutrients in soil and their characterisation. The interrelationship between pesticides and agriculture is considered. Attempts shall be made to cover the quantitative analysis of pesticides by conventional as well as by modern methods of chemical analysis.

14.2 ENVIRONMENTAL CHEMISTRY OF SOIL

Agriculture practices affect the quality of the soil. Such practise should be environmentally friendly. The pesticide, insecticides or herbicides are important components of agriculture. Soil consisting of minerals and organic matter is fundamental requirement of agriculture. Weathering of rocks is common phenomena to soil. Soil is mixture of minerals, organic matter and water supporting growth of plant. It has loose texture. It contains 5% organic and 95% inorganic matter. Soil show different layers. Top soil is used for analysis but subsoil is not analysed. Large amount of water is needed for the plant cultivation. Soil contains clay which reacts with water from soil. The soluble manganese and iron are encountered in soil. Both are toxic to plants in high dosages. Inorganic colliods from soil absorb toxic matter. The microorganisms thrive on organic matter from soil. If oxalate is present in soil then calcium dissolves from minerals. Other organic matter in soil is humus, saccharides, nitrogen and phosphorus containing organic compounds. Organic humus contains humic and fulvic acids. The humification is process of formation of the humus. Soil contains H^+, Ca^{2+}, Mg^{2+}, K^+ and Na^+ with low levels of the Fe^{2+}, Mn^{2+} and Al^{3+} in hydrolised form. Common anions present in the soil are HCO^{3-}, CO_3^{2-}, HSO_4^-, SO_4^{2-} and halides. The humus possess very high cation exchange capacity like ion-exchange resins. Soil acts as buffer and maintains its pH. Acid sulphates are generated by interaction of granite in soil. Plants grow if soil has neutral pH of 7.0. In area of low rainfall soil becomes basis of interaction. The exchange of anions by soil is not very well defined. At low pH anions are held by electrostatic attraction, while at high pH, the OH^- ions cleavage to the soil.

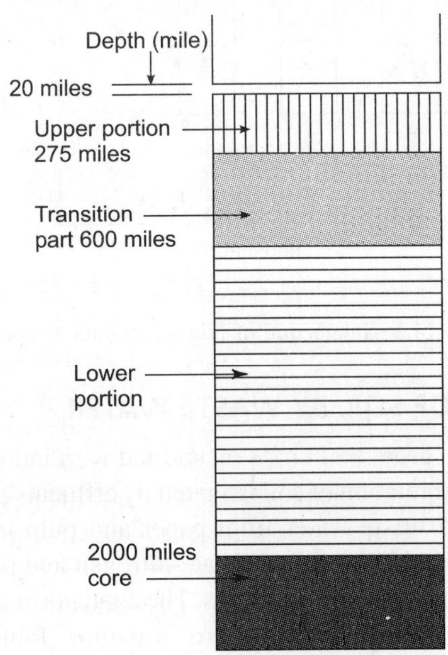

Fig. 14.1 Structure of the earth

The internal structure of the earth is shown in Fig. 14.1. The first 36 km is upper mantle, the next 40 km is transition zone, while the next 3000 km is lower mantle and then we have the core of lithosphere. Figure 14.2 represents lithosphere-biosphere interaction. The atmospheric carbon dioxide reacts with silica, carbon, calcium carbonate to return to lithosphere acting as the great atmospheric sink. These materials return to hydrosphere through water vapour and micronutrients from the soil. Soil contains considerable amount of organic matter. Primary minerals such as silica, limestone and dolomites account for 70% of soil mass. Clay is of significance in soil. The humus is present in soil in colloidal form. Biological activity in soil depends upon the form of water present in it. The microorganisms present in soil are also of great relevance. The important microorganisms present are algae, protozoa and actinomycetes. If these are present then soils becomes productive. These microorganisms play an important role in mineral and fertiliser breakdown in soil formation. A typical fungus produces readily citric acid in soil and then solubilises Si, Al, Fe, and Mg in basalt, as their anionic citrito complexes. Some convert organic nitrogen to inorganic nitrogen. It is worth considering relation of the soil with crop growth with waste water.

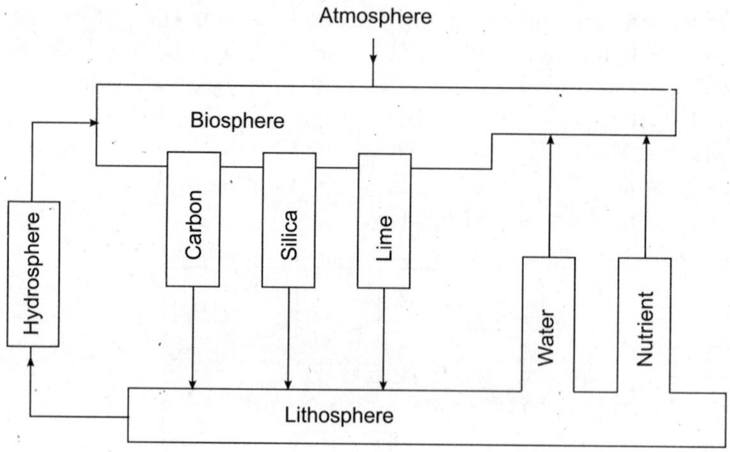

Fig. 14.2 Interaction of lithosphere and biosphere

14.3 IRRIGATION OF SOIL BY WASTE WATER

It is interesting to note growth of crops on soil fed with industrial effluents. Table 14.1 gives typical interpretation of soil irrigated by effluents from different sources such as rain, well and waste water from paper and pulp industries. The soil is alkaline; with considerable amount of nitrate-nitrogen and phosphorus. These are of prime importance for the growth of plants. The contents of exchangeable calcium and magnesium indicate that water is hard in nature. Table 14.2 gives an idea about sustained efforts to grow crops on waste water within a period of six years. The crops grown are paddy, wheat and sugarcane in varying area of soil admeasuring 2 to 25 acre. There is rise in yield of paddy from 2500 to 3500 tonnes; while wheat growth does not rise and sugarcane shows marginal growth in the course of six years. This showed that all crops do not grow well on industrial waste water. Table 14.3 lists certain varieties of trees like nilgiri, babul, rain tree which are grown on ash, as it contains useful micronutrients conducive for their better growth.

Table 14.1 Soil analysis and irrigated by effluents (mg/g)

S.No	*Irrigated by*	*pH*	*Conductivity*	*Organic matter*	*Nitrate-nitrogen*	*Phosphorus*	*Ca/Mg*
1.	Natural rain water	7.5	0.3	0.3	6.3	9.6	24.0
2.	Well water	8.1	0.3	0.9	6.7	12.0	20.8
3.	Waste water from paper mills	8.2	0.5	0.7	7.8	12.0	30.0
4.	Effluent from pulp factory	8.1	0.6	1.2	7.3	20.0	28.8
5.	Irrigated both by paper and pulp effluents	8.5	0.5	1.2	8.1	9.6	22.4

It is observed that effluents replenish important nutrients of soil, and problem of exhaustion of the non renewable resources of lithosphere is made up. The yield of crop in soil better in developed countries than in developing countries; *e.g.* the yield of wheat in the USA per acre is 1440 lbs and rice 2210 lbs, corresponding figures for India are wheat 760 lbs and rice 870 lbs per acre of soil it is good in USA due to modern methods of farming. The per capita food growth has remained

Table 14.2 Sustained effort to grow crops on waste water

Year in succession	*Paddy yield (tonnes)*	*Wheat yield (tonnes)*	*Sugarcane yield (tonnes)*
1.	2300	500	70
2.	780	700	60
3.	2530	1200	65
4.	2600	1100	90
5.	3100	1400	80
6.	3500	450	80

Table 14.3 Trees grown in soil ash containing micronutrients

S.No.	*Botanical name*	*Popular name*
1.	Eucalyptus globulus	nilgiri
2.	Casuarina equisetifolia	saru tree
3.	Pithecellophis dulce	rain tree
4.	Leucaena leuciphalia	subabul tree
5.	Acacia auriculaformis	Australian acasia
6.	Iopmea, lantana, ziziphus	ipoma, tantani, beri

stationary in India. The remedy lies in starting green revolution. This is possible by massive application of fertilisers and use of pesticides. Experiments to use waste water for better growth of plants is not always encouraging. Even if such efforts culminate in partial success, it is not the panacea for stagnating agricultural production.

The Tables 14.4 and 14.5 illustrate how agriculural farming is influenced by use of waste water for growth.

Table 14.4 The waste water in agricultural farming

S.No.	Observations for	Waste water MSU	Waste water ECP	Tube well MSU	Tube water ECP	Rain water MSU	Rain water ECP
1.	Family size	4.9	4.98	4.4	4.54	4.6	4.95
2.	Land holding (net)	3.5	2.7	3.4	3.1	2.6	2.4
3.	Off farm	1.7	1.4	1.3	1.3	1.5	1.8
4.	Total earning (*x*) per annum	1756	1835	1513	1927	1890	1715
5.	Years in use	8.3	38.2	–0	40.1	–0.1	35.7
6.	Distance from Source (meter)	160	90	175	75	–	230

MSU = Municipal Sewage Usage, ECP = Effluent Channel Project.

Thus several attempts are made to use waste water for the agricultural farming. The source of waste water (Table 14.4) is either from municipal sewage or effluent channel. It is used depending on the family size. The time needed for farming varies from 8-years to 40 years. The distance of farm products from source of waste water varied from 75–250 meters. The total earning in terms of rupees varied from ₹ 1513–1835 per annum. The family size of 5 was constant in all experiments. The net land holding varied from 2.5–3.5 acres. The results of the experimentation were not very encouraging for the future planning of application water for agriculture farming.

Table 14.5 Waste water irrigation in different towns in India

S. No.	State	Town	Fish growth	% waste water used	Direct use (ha)	Indirect use (ha)	Vege-tables	Fruits trees	Cotton culti-vation	Rice/ cereals
1.	Gujarat	Ahmedabad	–	0	890	√	√	–	–	√
2.	W. Bengal	Kolkata	√	0	–	12,900	√	–	–	√
3.	Madhya Pradesh	Bhopal	–	52	1214	–	√	–	–	√
4.	Uttar Pradesh	Lucknow	–	0	150	–	√	–	–	√
5.	Tamil Nadu	Chennai	–	0	133	–	–	–	–	–
6.	Kerala	Trivendrum	√	0	–	14,500	–	–	√	√
7.	Andhra Pradesh	Hyderabad	√	24	110	40,000	√	√	√	√

Table 14.5 illustrates how waste water is used for the irrigation in various states of India. From South India in Tamil Nadu, Andhra Pradesh and Kerala, these experiments are carried out while waste coast of India covered only Gujarat and small part of Madhya Pradesh. The Eastern India is represented mainly by West Bengal. The Central India is represented by fertile land of Uttar Pradesh. The water is directly or indirectly used for the cultivation of fruits, cotton, rice, cereals, vegetables and fish farming. The tick (√) mark indicates satisfactory results. Kerala and W. Bengal showed significant fish growth due to proximity of sea. The direct use of waste water shows positive results. In all places vegetable growth is noteworthy. Further rise, cereals grow very well in most of the places. The cotton cultivation is also very good in Kerala and Andhra Pradesh. Therefore the important conclusion is advisable to use waste water for the growth of vegetables as well as food product like rice and cereals. However, it should be done under strict supervision of farmer.

14.4 AGRICULTURAL POLLUTION AND HEALTH

In USA the agricultural product has to be free of genetically modified products. Soil has definite influence on health of man. Soil promoting good growth of plants is due to presence of higher organic matter in soil. The excessive pesticide applications contaminates the quality of soil. A pesticide called 'heptchlor' causes cancer as it is carcianogenic compound. It is noted that the PCB level in soil is high in UK. Pesticides from agricultural use are degraded as chemical, photochemical and bio- degradation materials. The term desertification refers to loss of fertility of soil. While deforestation is serious loss of forests. Water and wind causes soil erosion. The prevention of soil errosion is called *soil conservation*. One such method includes the perennial plant growth as it prevents soil errosion. The soil conservation and protection of water resources are interlinked with one another. The land reforestation conserves both soil and water. In order to know this the analysis of soil is important aspect.

The agricultural activity influences the chemistry of environment in several ways; like disposal of animal plant or food processing waste; the contamination from application of pesticides and fertilisers; depletion of natural soil nutrients and finally salt and mineral accumulation from irrigation. Thus, agricultural waste is more serious than the solid or liquid waste generated due to industrial activity. The waste from food and milk industry poses a serious problem. The excessive growth of fruits like oranges in Vidharbha and apples in Kashmir may pose problem of disposal of solid waste. The food processing industry produces more than 60% of waste from fruit peels. No doubt it is used for animal feed and as manure in soil. Cotton waste is useless as it contains a good amount of pesticide residue, which in the long run is harmful to animal or cattle. The mechanised meat processing industry will produce a liquid waste due to residual blood, flesh and bones which are difficult to dispose.

There is no substantial evidence to prove that fertilisers cause water pollution or contamination however it leads to excess release of nitrogen and phosphorus in soil. Nitrate is the worst enemy of high-yield farming. Nitrate is reduced to nitrite in the digestive system and it causes a disease called *methemoglobinemia*. Phosphate is also a widespread pollutant in agriculture. It travels much slower in the soil as compared to nitrate, but it promotes eutrophication of effluents with algal bloom. Nitrogen and phosphorus pollution illustrate far reaching chemical consequences of man's agricultural activity. The agricultural activity removes these materials from lithosphere and drops them into the sea, which is a permanent sink for chemicals. This agricultural pollution represents a permanent and irreversible depletion of the resources of the lithosphere and steps must be taken to mitigate this menacing problem.

14.5 ROLE OF NITROGEN, PHOSPHORUS AND POTASSIUM IN THE SOIL

Potassium, calcium and magnesium are called *macronutrients* in soil, however the presence of NPK are most essential in soil. The calcium is rarely deficient in soil. In alkaline soil such deficiency is noted. The availability of magnesium depends upon the ratio of Ca/Mg in soil as at high ratio magnesium is present less in soil. Sulphur promotes growth of plant when present in the form of amino acids, thiamin and biotin. NPK plays an important role in determining the quality of soil. 90% of nitrogen in soil is organic nitrogen, generated by biodegradation of plants and animals. The soil fertility is controlled by organic nitrogen. The presence of high nitrogen yields leads to high proteins which are nutritious. Nitrate is beneficial for plant growth. It is provided by legumes—a kind of plants. Ammonium (NH_4^+) is strongly bound to soil and is conducive for growth of rice and paddy, while Phosphorus is present in low concentrations. It is present as PO_4^{3-}, $H_2PO_4^-$ or HPO_4^{2-} but first species is most common. So very little phosphorus is used as fertiliser in the soil. Finally, the role of potassium is important. It activates some enzymes and it balances level of water in plants. The high input of K^+ gives good yield for crops.

14.6 MICRONUTRIENTS IN SOIL

Several transition and main group elements are present in soil (Table 14.6). B, Cu, Fe, Mn, Mo and Zn are considered as essential micronutrients for plants at low concentration. They function as components of enzymes. Mn, Fe, Zn are involved in the process of photo-synthesis while Na, Si, Co are favourable nutrients. Boron is isomorphously substituted for silicon in soil. So also Cu, Cr, Co, As, Se, Ni, Pb and Cd are specific minerals including sulphur. Some plants accumulate high dose of micronutrients. They are called as the *hyperacumulators* (1 mg/g of soil). *e.g.* Ni, Cu get hyperaccumulated in soil. Phytore mediation is process where plants accumulate metals in it. The addition of sequistering agents in soil like oxalate enhance the accumulation of micronutrients in soil *e.g.* uranium with oxalic acid is accumulated as its anionic complex. Mineral contents of the soil gets depleted due to rain, seepage, growth of plants and crops. The soil deficient in mineral contents is unsuitable for further cultivation. Nitrogen, phosphorus and potassium are essential for growth of plants, but they are replenished through organonitrogen and organophosphorus compounds, which are dumped into soil as the sink by plant and vegetable kingdom. However, vitally more important are elements like iron, manganese, zinc, copper, molybdenum, and boron, which are most essential for the healthy upkeep of soil. Each and every plant or crop does not need all of these metals, but they thrive better on at least one of them. The plants have a tendency to extract one or more of these elements. The contents of such an element is termed as '*available element*' contents, while whatever is available in total soil is termed as the '*total amount of a available element*' in the soil. Figure 14.3 depicts the relationship between nutrient availability and pH of the soil. There is good availability in soil of molybdenum, copper, zinc and to a lesser extent iron, manganese, cobalt and aluminium. Calcium, potassium, magnesium, nitrogen, sulphur and phosphorus are otherwise present in substantial concentrations in the soil. The figure is also valid beyond pH 10 in alkaline media. When micronutrients are not available to plants. Tables 14.7 to 14.9 indicate the role of micronutrients in proper growth of soil. A systematic survey was undertaken by Maharashtra government to prepare contour map of nutrients in soils in various districts for growth of sugarcane, paddy, and jawar in fields. The results of various micronutrients in soil are depicted in Tables 14.7 to 14.9 respectively. Table 14.6 shows extent of trace elements in soil all of which all are not micronutrients for soil. The amount present in soil as well as in plants is shown.

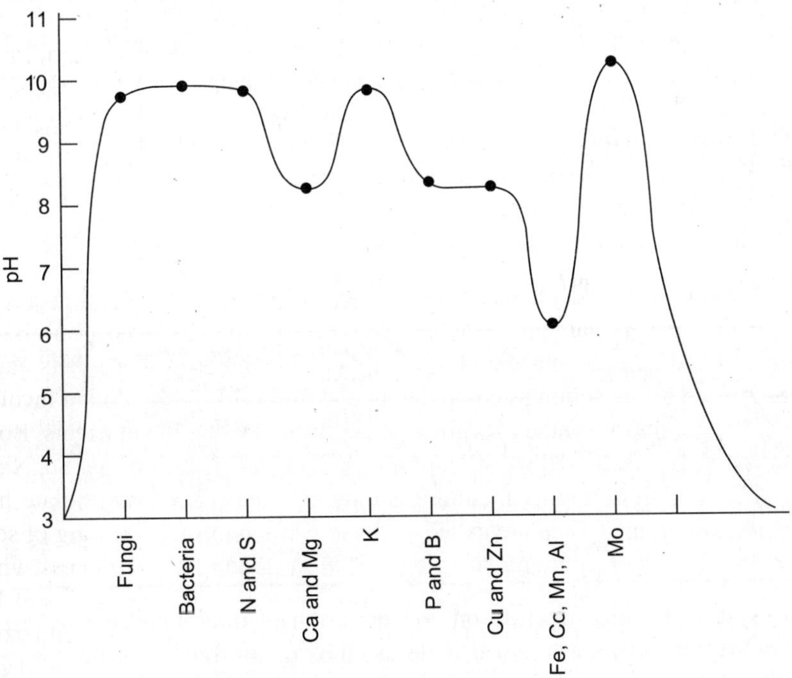

Fig. 14.3 Soil micronutrients as function of pH

Table 14.6 Trace elements in soil and plants

S. No.	Name of element	(symbol)	Amount present in Soil Level (μg/g)	Recom-mended Level (mg/L)	Amount present in plant level (μg/g)	Remarks
1.	Beryllium	Be(II)	1–40	0.10	Nil	Toxic in nature
2.	Boron	B(III)	2–200	1.5	5–30	Useful for growth
3.	Lead	Pb(II)	2–200	–	0.1–10	Low toxicity
4.	Arsenic	As(III)	0.1–40	10	0.1–50	Not essential and toxic
5.	Bismuth	Bi(III)	1–40	–	–	Very Toxic in nature
6.	Selenium	Se(IV)	0.1–2.0	0.02	0.02–2.0	Toxic if > 50 ppm
*7.	Copper	Cu(II)	1–40	0.20	0.05–0.15	Toxic > 20 ppm
*8.	Zinc	Zn(II)	10–300	2.0	0.1–10	Toxic > 200 ppm
9.	Cadmium	Cd(II)	0.01–7.0	0.01	0.2–0.8	Unessential and toxic
10.	Vanadium	V(V)	20–500	0.10	0.1–10	Useful for microorganism
*11.	Manganese	Mn(VI)	100–400	0.20	15–100	Toxicity with iron present
12.	Chromium	Cr(VI)	5–3000	0.10	0.2–1.0	Low toxicity in +3 state
*13.	Molyb-denum	Mo(VI)	0.2–5	0.01	1–100	Required only at trace level (μg)
14.	Cobalt	CO(III)	1–40	0.05	0.05–0.15	required by few plants
15.	Nickel	Ni(II)	10–1000	0.20	1–10	Unessential toxic > 50 ppm

* These are really hard core micronutrients present in soil (B, Cu, Zn, Mn, Mo, Fe)

The Table 14.6 shows various trace elements encountered in soils and plants (μg/g). They consist of Be^{2+}, Pb^{2+}, As^{3+}, Bi^{3+}, Se^{4+}, Cu^{2+}, Zn^{2+}, Cd^{2+}, V^{+5}, Mn^{2+}, Cr^{3+}, Mo^{6+}, Co and in Ni^{2+}. Amongst them vanadium occurs in large proportion in soil (20-500 μg/g) Chromium (~3000 μg/g) and Manganese ~ 400 μg/g) are also present in good level while those found in trace concentrations are selenium (~2.0), Molybdenum (~ 5μg/g) Cadmium (~7.0) Trace level indicator is lower then $< 10^{-6}$ M *i.e.* μg. These are figures for soil but for plants the picture is almost identical. The last column in Table 14.6 indicates the extent of the toxicity of each element and relevant observation on element.

Table 14.7 Micronutrients in soil samples good for sugarcane growth

Iron (%)	Copper μg/gm	Zinc (%)	Manganese μg/gm	Molybdenum μg/gm	Boron (%)
7.95	380	0.90	1810	10.08	0.001
6.02	203	1.10	1187	9.08	0.069
3.51	161	0.51	653	15.10	0.032
6.9	283	0.65	450	4.80	0.071
8.10	150	0.70	750	12.10	0.011
9.20	190	0.90	820	15.10	0.012

The systematic investigation on concentration of micronutrients in selected fields of Western Maharashtra was undertaken by us for four years alongwith few agricultural universities. As many as four stations in Mumbai, Pune and Rahuri were set-up and the analysis of available and total element contents in fields of sugarcane, paddy and *jowar* crop was carried out using atomic absorption spectroscopy. The result in Table 14.7 indicates high levels of copper and manganese, which perhaps is conducive for growth of sugarcane (~ 1810 μg/gm of manganese). Table 14.8 indicates high levels of manganese as well as copper, indicating thereby the copper (310 μg/gm) is the best micronutrient for growth of paddy. Table 14.9 represents micronutrient contents of *jowar* field. The study showed high level of manganese, copper, zinc and iron, which is conductive for growth of *jowar* in the fields investigated.

Table 14.8 Micronutrients in the soil good for paddy

Iron (%)	*Copper* μg/gm	*Zinc* (%)	*Manganese* μg/gm	*Molybdenum* μg/gm	*Boron* (%)
7.99	200	1.00	645	7.01	0.084
9.6	170	2.00	1120	5.0	0.062
9.6	140	0.90	1230	10.0	0.010
9.73	295	1.20	606	4.00	0.007
11.50	290	1.21	1050	18.21	0.095
12.01	310	0.980	950	19.00	0.09

Table 14.9 Micronutrients in the soil good for jowar growth

Iron (%)	*Copper* μg/gm	*Zinc* (%)	*Manganese* μg/gm	*Molybdenum* μg/gm	*Boron* (%)
6.81	160	1.20	1291	15.85	0.090
7.90	170	1.35	1083	16.10	0.091
8.01	150	0.90	1045	12.00	0.061
9.89	198	0.99	833	7.85	0.09
11.01	140	0.69	940	12.01	0.095
11.90	291	0.92	940	8.50	0.025

14.7 QUANTITATIVE ANALYSIS OF MICRONUTRIENTS

Tables 14.10 and 14.11 indicate available trace elements and total trace elements present in soil.

Table 14.10 Available trace element present in soil samples

Soil samples	*Concentration of soil samples in* μg/gm				
No.	*Mn*	*Fe*	*Cu*	*Zn*	*Mo*
Reference	19.80	20.50	4.40	5.40	1.10
1.	32.70	44.60	2.00	6.70	0.08
2.	67.40	42.50	11.00	6.90	0.20
3.	72.00	58.30	10.80	6.30	0.10
4.	102.30	28.50	8.00	6.40	0.20
5.	115.30	19.20	6.00	6.20	0.20
6.	117.60	35.10	11.50	6.80	1.50
7.	120.00	28.20	7.00	6.30	0.10

Table 14.11 Total trace element present in soil samples

Soil samples	*Concentration of soil samples in µg/gm*				
No.	*Mn*	*Fe*	*Cu*	*Zn*	*Mo*
Reference	1260.00	28,40	102.00	70.00	16.00
1	1512.00	20,70	110.00	140.00	5.50
2	1718.00	20,15	110.00	98.00	13.80
3	2074.00	21,75	135.00	81.00	19.20
4	2010.00	19,90	130.00	50.00	7.30
5	2194.00	20,65	195.00	98.00	14.20
6	2521.00	20,70	140.00	92.00	9.20
7	2590.00	20,50	124.00	102.00	11.70

The procedure for sampling of soil is crucial. The surface samples are collected from 10 cm depth. The samples are ground to fine powder (100 mesh), to determine total element content. They are digested in a mixture of nitric perchloric acid. The resulting residue is evaporated to dryness and then extracted with water and made to a known volume before analysis by AAS. For the analysis of available trace elements from soil, the samples are extracted with suitable buffers for various elements as shown in the following Table 14.12.

Table 14.12 Buffers used for analysis

S.No.	*Symbol*	*Element present*	*pH*	*Buffer used*
1.	Fe	Iron	4.8	Ammonium acetate
2.	Zn	Zinc	6.5	Ammonium acetate
3.	Mn	Manganese	7.0	Ammonium acetate
4.	Mo	Molybdenum	3.3	Ammonium oxalate
5.	Cu	Copper	8.5	Ammonium citrate
6.	B	Boron	6.0	Sodium carbonate

All these elements are extracted in appropriate buffers. The organic contents from extract is destroyed by dry ashing with nitric-perchloric acid treatment. The residue is laxivated with water and the available contents of element is analysed by AAS. The difference in the available and total contents gives an idea about the extractability on nutrients by plants.

14.8 CHARACTERISATION OF SOIL

The microscopic examination of the soil is carried out in order to know the quality. However chemical analysis is prefered. It gives information on the composition of soil. Soil is studied from the viewpoint of better plant growth for the human consumption. For chemical analysis soil sample is extracted in acetic acid or ammonium acetate, or hydrochloric acid or EDTA solution. Such analysis shows available nutrient in soil. Potassium chloride is used to extract nitrogen from soil. The particle size distribution of soil is important. This is shown in Table 14.13.

Table 14.13 Classification of soil based on particle size

S.No.	Kind	Particle Size (mm)
1.	Coarse	2000–200
2.	Fine	200–50
3.	Silt	50–2
4.	Clay	2–0

The soil analysis is carried by visual symptoms shown by plants. The sampling and subsampling technique is most essential. The random sampling is preferred. Soil depth is recorded during sampling. Since soil sample is biologically active dry sample is not taken. Overdying of sample destroys micro-organisms. Bulk sample should be divided in subsamples called as increaments. The disolution of soil sample depends upon its contents. It is fused with sodium carbonate in crucible before the analysis.

(i) pH of Soil

It is pH of soil-water which is in equilibrium system. pH gives idea about its metal contents and its exchange capacity. Agricultural soil has pH of 5.0 to 8.0 Zn Mn Fe, Cu are more mobile at this low pH in soil. A high pH induces trace element deficiencies. Microbiological activity is also dependent upon pH. The organic acids or aluminum have buffering action on soil with the formation of hydroxide as ultimate product. The excess of carbon dioxide increases the pH. Acid base indicators identify pH of the soil on the spot in the field.

(ii) Lime Requirement of Soil

Lime is added to soil if its pH is acidic and if pH is too low. Amount of lime is to be added for lowering pH of soil is determined by soil analysis in terms of the exchange capacity, climate, soil particle size. Type of soil decides the dose of lime to be added to soil so as to lower the pH.

(iii) Phosphorus

0.5 M sodium bicarbonate solution at pH 8.5 is used to know the available phosphorus in the soil. The extracted phosphate in solution of bicarbonate is analysed photometrically with ammonium molybdate and potassium antimonyl tartarate to give molybdenum blue in the presence of reducing agent like ascorbic acid. The color is measured spectrophotometrically at 882 nm against reagent blank.

(iv) Nitrogen

The method for the analysis of the available nitrogen is different than for total nitrogen. Nitrogen is converted to ammonia and determined titremetrically by Kjeldahl method (if amount is less than 2%). The total nitrogen throws light on stock of organic nitrogen which is mineralised in typical environment. The nitrogen is determined by the Kjeldahl method. The ammonia so formed is measured by titration or colorimetric analysis with Nessler's reagent.

(v) Exchangable Cation Analysis

The factor of the exchangeable cation shows the abundance and presence of nutrient elements in the soil. Ammonia is used to leach cations from soil. Such leached solution is analysed by atomic absorption spectroscopy. The amount of sodium, potassium, magnesium and calcium is ascertained by AAS method. The ammonium acetate or calcium carbonate is used for the preparation of soil extracts before analysis.

14.9 TRACE ELEMENT IN SOIL ANALYSIS

An examination of Table 14.6 shows what elements are present. AAS is used for their analysis as it avoids time consuming separation technique. The spectral interference is prevented during analysis *e.g.,* Ca^{2+} with PO_4^{3-} forms salt thereby decreasing absorbance during calcium analysis specially if silicate is present. It supreses absorbance of the calcium, magnesium or iron. To prevent such interferences lanthum salt is added as the releasing agent. The interference of incomplete voltilisation is eliminated with hotter flame. Physical interference due to variation in density or surface tension or viscosity of sample is eliminated by matching the sample and standard sample from same solution. The mineral structure of soil is ascertained by X-ray diffraction *e.g.,* clay minerals. The thermal methods are used for mineralogical investigations *e.g.,* TGA or DTA. The trace elements are accumulated by plants. They are called as *hyperaccumulators* (dose more than 1 mg/g). In phyto remediation plants growing on contaminated ground accumulates element and is removed by plant biomass.

The role of fertilisers in soil is also important. The ideal NPK ratio is given as 3/6/4 or 6/12/8 indicating respective % of these elements in soil or fertiliser. The organic manure undergoes biodegradation. Ammonium nitrate is common nitrogen fertiliser, contains 33.5% nitrogen. Urea is best source for nitrogen. The nitrates of sodium, potassium, calcium are also used as source of nitrogen in the fertilisers. For phosphorus, source is tricalcium orthophosphate *i.e.,* fluoroapatite. The phosphate minerals have trace elements like copper, boron, molybdenum, manganese and zinc pyrophosphate. In soil chelates of iron and copper are taken up by the plants. Potassium is obtained from its chloride. Excess intake of potassium by plant is termed as "*Luxung uptake*" by the plant. It is not conducive. It is possible to analyse trace elements from soil or river water or estury which ultimately feeds the soil. Tables 14.14 and 14.15 indicate results of such analysis by AAS outdoor location.

A Van Vee Grab sampler is used to collect samples of sediments. They are dried at 100°C. The dried samples is dissolved in nitric perchloric acid mixture to destroy organic matter. The residue is dissolved in dilute hydrochloric acid and trace elements are analysed. Thus, Tables 14.10 and 14.11 give information on available trace elements and total trace elements in soil. Along with nine samples, a reference sample (from virgin land) is compared in both tables. The result shows high level of manganese in station No. 1. So also iron content is higher than reference source, zinc is high. While Table 14.12 shows high levels of manganese in station No. 3, copper is maximum at station No. 5. This is experimental project to assess metals in soil.

Attempt is made to analyse trace elements from sediments in Thane Creek and Ulhas river estuary around Mumbai. Tables 14.14 and 14.15 present results of such analysis. Manganese and iron contents is high, while cadmium content is very low. The reason for such high concentration of iron, manganese is the location of small-scale industries around Thane belt. Water is alkaline in aquatic marine environment. Hence industrial soil sample suffers from iron and manganese toxicity. The high level of copper (Table 14.14) is due to effluents coming from pesticide industry. Zinc is higher (168.6) (Table 14.15) due to emission of effluents from rayon industry. Lead is large (78.2) in both samples, which is emitted from automobiles on Vashi bridge, where it connects island of Mumbai to mainland of Maharashtra.

Table 14.14 Trace elements form sediments in Thane Creek

	Concentration of μg/gm					
Station number	*Mn*	*Fe*	*Cu*	*Zn*	*Cd*	*Pb*
Reference	658.50	61,17	70.50	102.00	1.20	30.50
1.	783.00	69,56	144.00	273.50	2.00	78.20
2.	722.50	68,36	104.40	209.50	1.70	56.80
3.	922.00	70,36	98.70	159.50	1.80	47.20
4.	1127.00	64,76	90.80	149.00	2.30	53.90
5.	1167.00	72,36	97.20	152.00	2.10	50.70
6.	1467.00	75,46	99.20	168.00	1.80	48.10

Table 14.15 Trace elements in sediments in Ulhas river in Kalyan

	Concentration of μg/gm							
Station number	*Mn*	*Fe*	*Co*	*Ni*	*Cu*	*Zn*	*Cd*	*Pb*
1.	220.0	58,500	38.5	88.0	88.2	43.0	1.4	
2.	198.0	61,200	41.0	87.5	89.5	125.5	1.3	36.4
3.	251.0	63,700	45.7	95.4	91.0	129.0	2.7	36.0
4.	252.0	64,800	43.5	91.7	82.9	130.0	2.7	35.6
5.	208.0	67,900	44.3	96.4	108.0	199.0	3.1	39.2
6.	212.0	68,200	43.8	94.5	97.5	180.0	2.3	33.4

As regards analysis of boron, it is carried out by spectrophotometric technique using caramine red as the chromogenic ligand. The only limitation in such analysis is the need to avoid use of glassware. It is essential to use only polythene, teflon or platinum ware. This is because, glass contains a substantial amount of boron and is bound to give erroneous results during determination of boron. The details of analysis of micronutrients by AAS are given in Table 14.15 and Table 14.16.

Table 14.16 AAS determination of micronutrients in soil

S.No.	*Element*	*AAS wavelength (nm) λ max*	*Detection limit μg/ml*	*Types of flame*	*Recommended spectrophotometric reagents*
1.	B	249.8	2.0	Nitrous-actylene	Caramine Red
2.	Cd	228.8	0.002	Air acetylene	Dithizone
3.	Cu	324.8	0.004	Air acetylene	Cupferron
4.	Fe	248.3	0.03	Air acetylene	1-10 phenanthroline
5.	Mn	279.5	0.003	Air acetylene	Permanganate
6.	Mo	313.3	0.03	Nitrous-acetylene	Thiocyanate
7.	Zn	213.9	0.003	Air acetylene	Dithizone
8.	Pb	283.6	0.02	Air acetylene	Dithizone
9.	Co	240.7	0.02	Air acetylene	Nitrous R salt
10.	Ni	232.2	0.01	Air acetylene	Dimethylglyoxime

Boron is one of the micronutrients amongst nonmetals. It is conducive for the growth of citrus fruits, *e.g.,* oranges, lemon grow in size, if the soil sample is fed with reasonable concentration of boron compounds. The amount of boron is 0.001 to 0.095% in Western Maharashtra. On the contrary, soils in Vidharbha which is the courtyard (orchard) of oranges, shows the good level of boron in the range 0.095 to 0.10% in city of Nagpur.

14.10 ENVIRONMENTAL PESTICIDES

These are the chemicals used to kill pests. Though they are good to protect crop, they are the worst enimies of the environment. Müller was awarded Noble Prize in 1946 for the discovery of DDT. The famous book "silent spring" by R. Carson brought out the hazardous effects of DDT. Pesticides are divided in to three categories as (*i*) Herbicides like carbamates, triazines, (*ii*) insecticides like organo-phosphorus or organochlorine compounds and (*iii*) fungicides like dithio-carbamates. (*iv*) Rodendicide is fourth uncommon class having α-napthol thiourea as its member.

(i) Chlorinated Hydrocarbon Pesticides

DDT is most important member of this class. These pesticides are subdivided in to alkanes, alkenes and aromatic hydrocarbons. DDT is obtained from chloral condensation with monochlorbenzene. The other members are heptachlor, lindane, eldrin, dieldrin, chlorodane, endrin and mirex, (Fig. 14.4). First four belong to cyclodione group. Endosulphone belongs to this class. They have low polarity and dipole moment and are lipophillic. Their environmental degradation is slow, with half-life ranging from 2.0 to 15.5 years in soil. They ultimately degrade to H_2O and CO_2 and other products. All compounds are neurotoxic. The egg shell becomes thin if sprayed with chlorohydrocarbons.

(ii) Organophosphorus Insecticides

These have high mammalian toxicity. Insecticides like parathion, dichloros, dimethate, acetylchloline are of this group (Fig. 14.4). They have better water solubilities. Dichlororos is most soluble (1×10^5 mg/L). They hydrolyse in water. The maximum half-life is 40 days. Therefore bioaccumulation is minimum. They arrest enzyme of ester splitting process. Choline stearase facilities nerve impulse. All of these insecticides by causing interference of muscular function. All of them contain pentavalent phosphorus. Dichloros kills flies. Parathion contains sulphur and it kills bees. Malthione is more toxic with more sulphur and is used to kill insects in backyard and fields.

(iii) Carbamates Insecticides

These are more expensive than organophosphorus compounds *e.g.*, propoxuv (*i.e.*, Baygon) and carbonyl belong to this class. Carbamatic group is hybrid between ester and amide group and is polar. They are relatively soluble in water and possess limited life in the environment, with half-life of 1.5 days to one month. In water they act like organophosphorus insecticide by interference with enzyme mechanism. They are derivatives of carbonic acid. They readily react with water and undergo decomposition. Carbofuran, carbaryl and aldicarb all have the LD_{50} dose ranging from 0.8 to 300 mg/kg. Sevin is trade name for pesticide Pyrethrin is natural pesticide obtained from dried flowers but it is unstable.

(iv) Pyrethrins and Pyrethoriods

These natural insecticide from flowers of chrysanthemum, which contain polar group and hence oily liquids are Lipophillic. They have high boiling point with high molecular weight. They are used in mosquito coil. Pesticide vapourises in air and kills mosquitos, they absorb UV radiation to undergo photochemical reactions. They are neurotoxic. They are absorbed on insect skin. They exhibit 'knock down effect' *i.e.,* temporary paralysis in insects. Allethrin is first synthetic product of this group, with low toxicity.

(v) Phenoxyacetic Acid Herbicides

These are harmone weed killers. They are polar and highly soluble in water; with low toxicity. Dioxins contain toxic compounds (*e.g.,* TCDD *i.e.,* tetrachloro-dibenzo-doxin). 2, 4, 5 T belongs to this category or 2, 4 D is dichloro-phenoxyacetic acid (Fig. 14.4). Both are used to kill weeds in farms 1,4 dioxin is most toxic pesticide. A mixture of 2, 4 D and 2, 4, 5, 7 T is called agent orange. It is used as the defoliant in war. Dioxin is used as preservative and slimicides for wood protection.

14.11 CLASSIFICATION OF PESTICIDES

The pesticides are classified largely into five groups as shown in Table 14.17. The important class is chlorinated hydrocarbons containing aldrine, BHC,DDT, lindane,

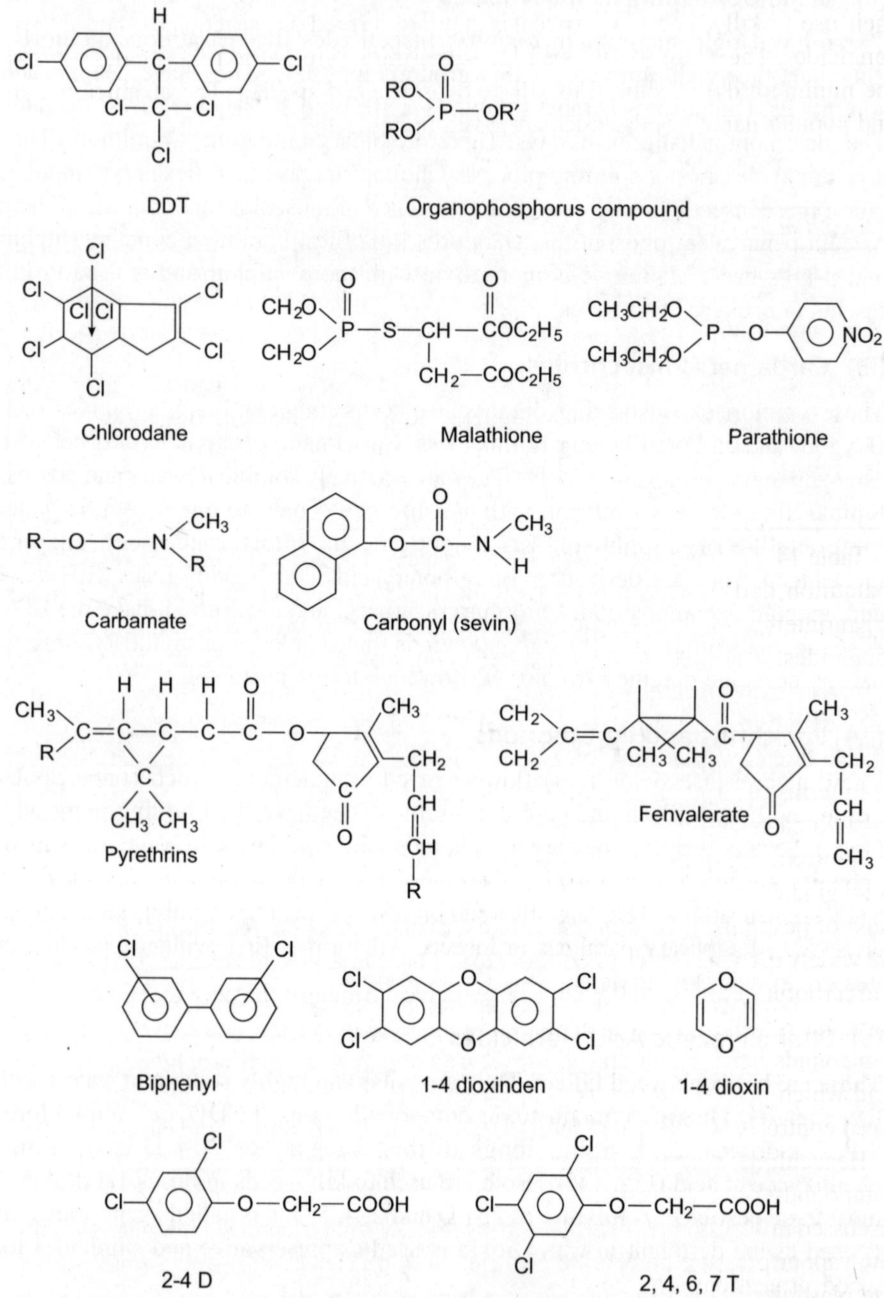

Fig. 14.4 Structres of some pesticides

chlorodane, while organo phosphorus pesticides include malathion, parathion (ethyl and methyl); the third category of the pesticide is carbamate compounds containing zectrion and carbaryl. The inorganic pesticides *i.e.,* fungicides are copper, nickel, lead and arsenic salts, while herbicides are 2, 4 D or 2, 4, 5 T. Depending upon their use to kill insects and rodents, they are termed as insecticides, herbicides, fungicides. The Table 14.18 lists LD_{50} dose (mg/kg) for various pesticides. This is the minimum dose required to kill 50% of affected species. The chemical name and popular name of pesticides are given in Table 14.17.

Table 14.17 Classification of pesticides

S.No.	*Kind*	*Classification*	*Illustrations*
1.	Insecticides	Chlorinated hydrocarbons	Aldrin, chlordane, BHC, DDT, dieldrin, lindane, heptachlor (PCB)
2.	Insecticide	Organophosphorus compounds	Malathion, guthion, parathion (methyl or ethyl), parcoxon chloro pyrifosie durshan
3.	Insectiside	Carbamate compounds	Zectrion, carbaryl (sevin)
4.	Fungicide	Inorganic compounds	$CuSO_4$, $NiCl_2$, PbO_2 As_2O_3
5.	Rodenades	α-napthylthiourea	2, 4, D, 2, 4, 5, T, carbaryl organic mercurials

Table 14.17 shows that aldrin, PCB, carbaryl, DDT, endrin, heptachlor, lindane, malathion and parathion are insecticides, while 2, 4 D, 2, 4, 5 T containing organomercury compounds are herbicides, while inorganic compounds are fungicides. The most toxic amongst them is parathion with LD_{50} of 4 mg/kg. Endrin is toxic with LD_{50} as 5 mg/kg; the least toxic among them is malathion and DDT with LD_{50} ~ 400 mg/kg, 2, 4, 5 T is dangerous with low LD_{50} of 0.03 mg/kg, so also dioxane. Pharsenol is less injurious to human beings.

In terms of structure, parathion is highly toxic while malathion is not; as latter has two carboxy ester linkages which are hydrolyzable by carboxylate enzymes to nontoxic compound. Insects do not detoxify malathion. All of them are biodegradable. Since carbamates are easily degraded and less toxic are favoured class of pesticides. The herbicides like atrazine, simazine, metolchor, and alachor are widely used to control weeds on crop. Thus, carbaryl, carbamic acid, parathicate and carbofuran belong to this class of pesticides. Amongst the bipyridyl compounds paraqual is widely used as herbicide. One containing the heterocyclic nitrogen compounds are a trazin and sensor 2, 4 D and 2, 4, 5 trichlorophenyl oxyacetic acid which belongs to the class of chlorophenoxy herbicides. They are used for weed control. Other less common pesticides are R-mecoprop, and cacodylic acid.

Hexachlorobenze is nondegradable. Similarly, kepone is toxic. Both of these compounds have very simple structures. Polychlorinated biphenyls (PCB) are discussed in details elsewhere. They have high thermal, chemical biological stability low vapour pressure and high dielectric constant. Hence, they are used as coolant and plasticizers. In USA, its manufacturing is prohibited as it is not be destroyed even by incineration.

The anaerobic bacteria degrades them into less harmful cogeners and ultimately to water and carbon dioxide and the inorganic chloride polybrominated biphenyls are fire retardants. In Michigan in USA instead of MgO, PBB was accidentally mixed in animal feed (1973) thereby killing several innocent animals.

The organochloro and organophosphorus pesticides have been widely investigated. Their characteristic is given in Table 14.18.

Table 14.18 Characteristics and LD_{50} of some pesticides

Name	*Solubility in H_2O (ppm)*	*LD_{50} (mg/kg)*
HCB	0.0062	3500
DDT	0.0034	115
Dieldrin	0.20	0.46
Malthion	145	1.375
Parathione	24	3.6
Atrazine	30	1870

The most toxic class of pesticide is 'dioxin' or tetrachlorodibenzodioxin (Table 14.19). Environmental contamination occurs due to dioxin. This leads to cancer. This is starting maternal for herbicides. The effluents from paper industry contains good amount of dioxin in fish.

Table 14.19 Dioxin (TCDD) in food

Food	*Dioxin (ρg/g)*	*Intake in food (ρg/g)*
Fish	500	8.60
Meat	35	6.60
Cheese	16	0.31
Milk	1.8	0.20
Coffee	0.1	0.04
Cream	7.2	0.04
Orange juice	0.2	0.01
Sour cream	10	0.01
Icecream	5.5	0.004

Table 14.20 Congeners of dioxin

Name	*Amt present (ρg/g) in fat*	*Nos of chlorine atoms*	*TEQ chlorine*
2, 3, 7, 8 tetrachloro	11	4	1.0
1, 2, 3, 7, 8 pentachloro	24	5	0.5
1, 2, 3, 6, 7, 8 hexachloro	172	6	0.1
1, 2, 3, 7, 8, 9 hexachloro	22	6	0.1
1, 2, 3, 4, 6, 7, 8 heptachloro	232	7	0.01
Octachlorodioxin	1037	8	0.001

Considerable amount of dioxin are encountered in human fat. There are as many as six congeners of dioxin as shown in Table 14.20.

In Table 14.20 TEQ stands for toxicity equivalent factor given as relative toxicity in comparison to TCDD with value as 1.0.

14.12 DILEMMA OF DDT

The chemical name of compound is 1,1,1 trichloro-2,2 bis (p-chlorophenyl) ethane. It converts to DDE, *i.e.*, 1,1 dichloro 2,2 bis (p-chlorophenyl) ethylene. The average level of DDT in air is 0.015 to 0.149 μg/litre. According to survey conducted in India the per day intake of DDT by human being is 0.178 mg in a restaurant, 0.041 mg in college dinning hall, 0.184 mg in hospital, 0.026 mg/litre in basket fruit, with corresponding figures, for DDE together with DDT in % are for restaurant 37%, college hall 39%, hospital 14% and market 40%. The body fat shows high levels of DDT. Table 14.21 shows levels of chlorinated hydrocarbon pesticides in body fat in different countries of the world.

Table 14.21 Pesticide in body fat (ppm)

S.No.	*Country*	*DDT*	*DDE*	*BHC*	*Dieldrin*	*Endrin*	*Heptachlor*
1.	USA	3.7	6.9	0.40	0.250	0.02	0.10
2.	France	3.1	6.5	1.19	...	...	...
3.	India	18.0	12.0	1.43	0.040	0	0
4.	UK	...	...	0.02	0.210	0.02	0.01

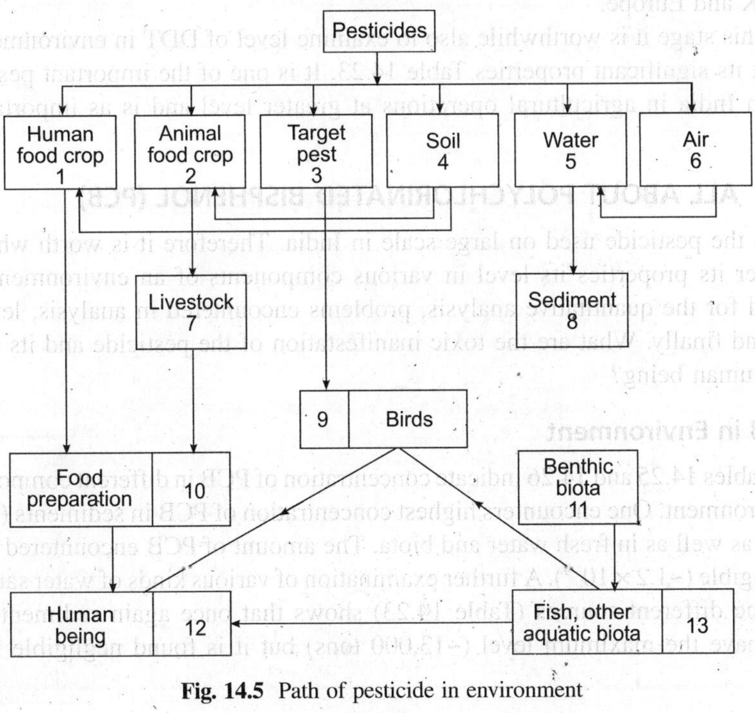

Fig. 14.5 Path of pesticide in environment

The mode of distribution of DDT in aquatic ecosystem is through bottom sediments, suspended solids and water. It goes from water to aquatic plants. Table 14.22 shows quantum of DDT in food such as fish, flesh, water and planktons.

Table 14.22 Level of DDT in eatables

Item	*DDT*	*ppm*
Water	0.00005	5×10^{-9}
Plankton	0.04	4×10^{-2}
Minnows	0.23	2.3×10
Fish	1.33	1.33×10
Animal Feed	3.57	3.57
Duck Flesh	22.80	22.80

It should be noted that in all developed countries the use of DDT is banned however in developing countries like India, Bangladesh, Srilanka and Pakistan. DDT is used extensively in day to day cultivation of crops. An examination of water for DDT contents shows that the fish, animal feed, contains significant amount of DDT as is shown in Table 14.21. It shows duck fish contains highest level of DDT while Plankton has insignificant level of DDT. Virtually Water contains no DDT.

The next Table 14.22 shows level of DDT in eatables. The results show that India has highest level (~18 ppm) of DDT in body fat. This is because a person develops immunity to DDT and is not affected by adverse effects at this level of DDT in fat. In comparison endrin, Heptachlor is absent in fat of Indian farmers. Dieldrin is very high (~0.250 ppm) in person from developed nations like USA and UK and Europe.

At this stage it is worthwhile also to examine level of DDT in environment. A look at its significant properties Table 14.23. It is one of the important pesticide used in India in agricultural operations at greater level and is as important as DDT.

14.13 ALL ABOUT POLYCHLORINATED BISPHENOL (PCB)

This is the pesticide used on large scale in India. Therefore it is worth while to consider its properties its level in various components of an environment, the method for the quantitative analysis, problems encountered in analysis, level in food and finally. What are the toxic manifestation of the pesticide and its effect upon human being?

(i) PCB in Environment

Both Tables 14.25 and 14.26 indicate concentration of PCB in different components of environment. One encounters highest concentration of PCB in sediments (Table 14.24) as well as in fresh water and biota. The amount of PCB encountered in air is negligible (~1.2×10^{-9}). A further examination of various kinds of water samples from the different sources (Table 14.23) shows that once again sediment with water have the maximum level (~13,000 tons) but it is found negligible in air

(~ 500 tons). The microorganism (~4300 ton), marine equatic environment (~2400) contains sizeable amount of PCB.

Table 14.23 Level of DDT in environment

S.No.	Environment	Concent (g/m^3)	S.No.	Environment	Concent (g/m^3)
1.	Air	1.2×10^{-9}	6.	Live stock	9.3×10^{-3}
2.	Water	1.7×10^{-6}	7.	Wild Life	0.48
3.	Sediments (Fresh)	9.3×10^{-2}	8.	Human	0.36
4.	Soil	1.1×10^{-2}	9.	Fresh water-biota	3.0
5.	Vegetation	1.7×10^{-3}			

The examination of Table 14.23 shows that the highest amount of PCB and its analogues is in Fresh water biota as well as Natural soil. It is present in negligible concentration in air as well as in water. The overall concentration varies from 1.2 $\times 10^9$ (g/m^3) to 3.0 gm/m^3.

Table 14.24 Concentration of DDT present in environment (tons)

S.No.	Environment	Estuaries and Creeks	Open sea (Tons)	Remarks and (%) percentage
1.	Atmosphere-air	500	750	0.13–0.21
2.	Aquatic-river	3500	–	0.94–0.98
3.	Marine water	2400	23,000	0.64–61
4.	Sediments	13,0000	110	35–0.03
5.	Land source-soil	2400	–	–
6.	Microorganism	4300	270	39–0.07
7.	Total Loading	14,3000	23,10000	Net load 37,4000

The perusal of Table 14.27 indicates that highest amount of PCB is present in Fish (18.70 mg/kg) while atmosphere contains less than 0.13% of PCB. As compared to open sea it is present in large amounts in estuaries and creek. However aquatic river contains as much as 3500 tons *i.e.* 0.98% in river.

(ii) Characteristic of PCB

There are as many as Ten isomers (Table 14.25) of PCB like deca, nano, octo, hepta, penta PCB. They indicate variable solubility from 2×10^{-2} to 9.3 (gms/m^3) in biphenyl analogue. The boiling points for all the isomers varies from 285–456°C, while melting point varies between the range of 71°–306°C. As expected the higher homolog have high melting and boiling point. The partition coefficient a parameter so useful in Liquid-liquid extraction varies from 4.3–8.3. The higher homologous have high coefficient (Table 14.25).

The Table 14.25 list important physical properties of PCB such as m.p., b.p., solubility, vapor pressure distribution coefficient and level in fish. Deca CB has highest melting point of 306°C while it has also highest boiling point. The distribution coefficient in immiscible organic extractant varies from 4.3 to 8.3 for

Biphenyl to Deca CB. The mono CB has highest vapor pressure (viz 1.1) with highest solubility for biphenyl (Table 14.25).

Table 14.25 Important Characteristics of PCB and its isomers

S. No.	*PCB group (isomers)*	*Vapor pressure*	*Solubility (g/m^3)*	*Amount in Fish*	*Kg partition coeff.*	*b.p°C*	*mp°C (maximum)*
1.	Deca CB	0.0000004	0.00076	0.00000010	8.3	456	306
2.	Naco CB	0.000006	0.00020	0.0000040	7.9	445	206
3.	Octa CB	0.00005	0.00050	0.0000016	7.5	432	162
4.	Hepta CB	0.00010	0.0014	0.000063	7.1	417	149
5.	Hexa CB	0.00058	0.0038	0.000025	6.7	400	150
6.	Penta CB	0.0026	0.099	0.000010	6.3	381	124
7.	Tetra CB	0.012	0.26	0.00040	5.9	360	180
8.	Tri CB	0.054	0.65	6.00015	5.5	337	87
9.	Di CB	0.24	1.6	6300	5.1	312	149
10.	Mono CB	1.1	4.0	2500	4.7	285	78
11.	Biphenyl	4.9	9.3	1000	4.3	256	71

(iii) Problems Encountered in Analysis

PCB is analysed by various methods such as gas chromatography, spectrophotometry and ion selective electrodes but the spectral method is cheap, even for analysis of isolated sample. GC facilities analysis at lowest concentration of PCB. Ion selective electrode shows some errors in analysis. GC needs 300 minutes *i.e.* 40 hrs while spectral methods require only ten minutes for the complete quantitative analysis (Table 14.26).

Table 14.26 Problems encountered in analysis of PCB

S. No.	*Parameter*	*Spectro-photometry*	*Electro-analytical ISE*	*Gas Chromatography*
1.	Cost of analysis overall	Negligible	Low cost	High cost
2.	Cost for one sample analysis	Low	Low	High
3.	Lowest concentration for analyses	0.1 μg	5 μg	1.0 μg
4.	Components measured	organic/ chloride	organic/ chloride	PCBs itself
5.	Any negative results noted?	None	few	Good analyst required
6.	Time needed for total analysis	10 mb	15 mb	5 hours
7.	Nature of analysis	Simple	Simple	Complicated
8.	Manpower requirement for analysis	Not specific requirement	Analyst be reasonably good	Expert analyst is needed

The important methods for quantitive analysis includes spectrophotometry, Electroanalytical methods using ion selective electrode and Gas-liquid chromatography. Spectral method is most rapid (10 mts) while GLC is time consuming needing 5 hours. Costwise GLC is most expensive, one needs a trained manpower for the analysis by gas chromatography. Spectral methods are more sensitive with sensitivity as 0.1 μg/cm/ml (See Table 14.26, item 3).

(iv) Food Contamination with PCB

Since it is very common pesticide it is worth knowing their levels in food product like milk, fish, eggs, cheese (Table 14.27).

Table 14.27 Concentration of PCB in diary product

S. No.	*Food item dairy products*	*ppm PCB*	*PCB present (mg/kg)*	*PCB permitted (mg/kg)*
1.	Fish	2.0	1870	2 mg/kg
2.	Fish by products	3.0	1170	1 mg/kg
3.	Cheese	–	250	–
4.	Milk	1.5	2270	1.5 mg/kg
5.	Eggs	0.3	550	3.0 mg/kg
6.	Potable water	–	Varies	0.1–0.5 ηg/L

The close examination of Table 14.27 gives level of PCB mainly dairy products and fish. Milk contains 2270 mg/kg of PCB being the highest while PCB is absent in drinking water. The permissable level of PCB in potable water is just 0.1 ηg/L. A small amount (250 mg/kg) PCB is present in cheese, but overall concentration varies from sample to sample and it depends upon the source of the sample material.

Table 14.28 Ill effects of PCB on human health with first aid

S. No.	*Site of contact for human being*	*Hazards/adverse effect*	*First aid (instantaneously given)*
1.	Eyes	Irritation of eyes	Use chemical splash and use goggles
2.	Skin	Red and dry skin	Have softly shower to wash.
3.	Inhalation (respiration)	Respiratory track breath infected	Use commercial respirator
4.	Ingestion (breathing)	Cough, short breath, vomit	Have good ventilation to work
5.	Other modes	Affect Liver, carçinogenic cirrhosis of Level, cancer	Wash mouth, avoid excess exposure

The Table 14.28 indicates adverse effects of PCB on human health. Lungs get severely affected by accidental breathing of PCB. The eyes, skin, nose, Liver have very bad effects which are irreversible. Washing with copious stream of water is the best remedy. One should always work in place with free air and well ventilated laboratory.

We summarise following conclusions from series of Tables given. The results in various Tables shows that fish contains objectionable amount of PCB (~2ppm) while cheese, eggs have negligible amount of PCB. Insignificant amount of PCB is encountered in potable water. It exceeds the known permissible level in case of fish and similar products. Milk has large dose of PCB entering body through food chain vai grass consumed by animals and it is given out by animals in the form of milk.

(v) Toxic Effects of PCB

The Table 14.28 shows hazardous and adverse effects of pesticide on human health for which first aid remedies is given as shown in Tables. The eyes skin get readily affected on exposure to PCB. It causes cough breathing upper respiratory (Lungs) problems vomiting and also low respiratory disorders on long term exposure it being carcinogenic has bad effect on Liver. The short exposure is mitigated by capious stream of water. In acute respiratory problem, artificial is respiration is useful. It is better to have good ventilation where PCB is being experimented.

In summary we can state that PCB is common day to day material used in industry extensively in spite of having toxic effects on human being. The main reason perhaps it is economically viability because other pesticides are not that cheap as is PCB.

14.14 DEGRADATION OF PESTICIDES IN WATER

The main problem linked with pesticide application is the presence of pesticide residue. These pesticide residues are formed from the main pesticide. Such residues are injurious to health in comparison with the parent compound, *e.g.*, DDT degrades to DDE. Such degradation is possible by various transformation, such as oxidation (*e.g.*, 2, 4 D undergo hydroxylation), side chain oxidation (DDT converts to OH-form), phorate undergoes sulphur oxide formation, dehydrogenation and dehydro-halogenation, conjugation or metal complex formation like amitrole; hydrolytic cleavage like malathion; exchange reactions like parathion and isomerisation of organophosphorus compounds. Some compounds in this process become more toxic. Such transformation involves no photosynthesis; no chlorophyll synthesis, or absence of oxidephosphyration. The percentage of degradation of pesticide at varying temperatures is large. It will be noted for DDT, if temperature is raised from 600° to 1000°C, degradation is complete, while pesticides like dieldrin shows no degradation; with rise of temperature till 400°C, though it is degraded 0.4% latter. These residue remain in biosphere and lithosphere for more than 30 years, even if use of these pesticides is stopped. A large number of factors are responsible for degradation of pesticide residue in the environment. The rate of degradation depends upon the chemical structure and nature of the pesticide. In spite of degradation they are not totally eliminated from environment and as such degradation is complete or partial. It does not mean end of manifestation of hazards. The agricultural pesticides do not hit target and rarely get degraded to harmless compounds. The pesticide residue in soil is taken up by plants and cause phytotoxicity. They are added to aquatic environment and enter in food web. The important pesticide in common usage with their popular name and chemical

Table 14.29 LD_{50} dose and threshold limiting values of pesticides in India

Pesticides	*TLV* mg/m^3	LD_{50} *dose (mg/kg)*
(A) *Insecticides*	–	–
Aldrin	0.25	54–56
PCB	0.50	250
Carbaryl'	–	340
DDT	1.00	420–800
Endrin	–	5–43
Heptachlor	0.50	90
Lindane	0.50	125–200
Malathion	10.00	480–1500
Parathion	0.10	4–30
Dieldrin	0.25	40
(B) *Herbicides*		–
2,4 D	10.00	666
2, 4, 5 T	–	0.03
Pentachlorophenol	0.50	27–80
Dioxane	–	0.3
(C) *Fungicides*	–	–
$CuSO_4$	–	very high
Pharsenol	–	825

Table 14.30 Transformation of pesticides to other products

S.No.	*Effect of reaction*	*Name of compound produced*
1.	No photosynthesis	Trianzines
2.	No chlorophyll synthesis	Triazoles
3.	No oxide phosphorylane	Carbamates
4.	Harmonic analogue	2, 4 D, 2, 4 5 T
5.	No vit, B synthesis	Chlorihydrocarbon

Table 14.31 Extent of degradation at varying temperatures (%)

S.No.	*Pesticide*	*600°C*	*800°C*	*1000°C*	*Remarks*
1.	Picloram	90.8	95.6	99.2	Partial degradation
2.	Atrazine	87.8	88.8	89.0	Partial degradation
3.	Malathion	95.3	96.3	96.7	Total degradation
4.	Dieldrin	99.0	99.5	99.5	All degradation
5.	DDT	99.2	99.7	100.0	Complete degradation
6.	Parathion	64.0	96.5	97.5	Low degradation
7.	Sevin	88.7	88.8	90.0	Slow degradation
8.	Dapalon	64.3	67.8	97.0	Low degradation
9.	DNBP	99.8	99.8	99.8	Whole degradation
10.	Nemagon	99.6	99.6	99.6	Complete degradation

nomenclature are listed in Table 14.32 while Tables 14.29 to 14.31 show various degradation reactions at different temperature.

The unit of LD50 involves measurement of time for 50% disappearance of the amount applied to start with; *e.g.*, Aldrin—a chlorinated hydrocarbon needs two months for degradation, while carbaryl and phorate needs one month, while parathion, malathion mainly organophosphorus pesticide take 20 days for 50% degradation. All of them need as much as three months to reach harmless residue level of 0.1 ppm, which corresponds to 0.3% of applied dose. There is not a single pesticide which undergoes instantaneous degradation in water. Therefore BOD of effluent does not indicate presence of pesticides residue. Only COD furnishes such information which is most reliable.

Table 14.32 Important pesticides with their chemical names

S.No.	*Popular name*	*Chemical nomenclature*
1.	Aldrin	1, 2, 3, 4, 10, 10 hexachloro—1, 4, 4a, 5, 8, 8a hexahydro 1-4 endo-exo 5-8 dimethanonpthalene
2.	BHC	1, 2, 3, 4, 5, 6 hexachlorocyclohexane
3.	Carbaryl	1–napthyl methyl carbamate
4.	2, 4, D	2,4 dichloro phenoxy acetic acid
5.	DDE	1, 1 dichloro 2, 2 bis (p-chlorophenyl) ethane
6.	DDT	1, 1, 1 trichloro 2, 2 bis (p-chlorophenyl) ethane
7.	Heptachlor	1, 4, 5, 6, 7, 8, 8 heptachloro 3a, 4, 7, 7a tetrahydro 4, 7, methanoindene
8.	Lindane	1, 2, 3, 4, 5, 6 hexachlorocyclohexane
9.	Malathion	S[1, 2 bis (ethoxycarbonyl) ethyl]0, 0 dimethyl phosphorodithioate
10.	Parathion	0, 0 diethyl 0-p nitrophenylphosphorothioate
11.	Phorate	0, 0 diethyl S-(ethylthio) methyl phosphorodiniate
12.	2, 4, 5 T	2, 4, 5 Trichlorophenoxyacetic acid
13.	Endrin	1, 2, 3, 4, 10, 10 hexachloro 6, 7 epoxy-1, 4, 4a, 5, 6, 7, 8, 8a octahydro 1-4 endoendo 5, 6 dimethanophthalene
14.	Dieldrin	1, 2, 3, 4, 10, 10 hexachloro 6, 7 epoxy-1, 4, 4a, 5, 6, 7, 8, 8a octahydro 1, 4 exoendo 5, 6 dimethanophthalene

14.15 EFFECTS OF SOME PESTICIDES ON HEALTH

Such effects have been extensively studied. In absence of pesticides crop production decreases due to the consumption by insects (~ 5 to 15% loss). They control diseases which spread by insects *e.g.*, DDT kills mosquito and stops spread of malaria (malaricuses diseases 750,000 to 1500 persons). Insects on constant use develop immunity and are not killed by the insecticides. Pests on frequent use of pesticides demonstrate resistance to DDT and analogous compounds. The resistance is problem with use of antibiotics. Pesticides also cause harm to species (*e.g.*, bee) which are useful to us. They cause great changes in ecosystem. The consequences on human health are serious. They promote occupational health hazards. Organo-phosphorus pesticide cause instantaneous death (~ 10 to 20 mg) *e.g.* Tik-20. The dose will vary with age, sex, diet, an individual health condition. Food gets contaminated by pesticide. Chlorinated hydrocarbons reside in the body for 30 years fat. Long-term effects are related to carcinogenic, mutagenic and teratogenic properties, DDT, dieldrin, aldrin, heptachlor and mirex promotes cancer *e.g.*, 2, 4, 5 T is confirmed as tertogenic compound to animals. The reproductive system gets affected. Apart from human, wildlife gets affected by indiscriminate use of the pesticides. They get ingested in food (Fig. 14.5) DDT has killed birds. Phenylmercury acetate $[C_6H_5Hg(CH_3COO^-)]$ has killed several birds in Sweden. The chlorinated hydrocarbons interfere with calcium metabolism of birds by inhibiting enzyme carbonic anhydrase. There is decrease in weight and thickness of egg shell layed by birds due to DDT. The laying process is delayed. PCB with high thermal stability and fire resistance property accumulates in fat. Polybrominated biphenols are more toxic than PCB. Fish exhibit acute response to pesticides. Pesticide cause behavioural changes in fish 2, 4 D and 2, 4, 5 T. The herbicides have both positive and negative effects. Crops of grapes are affected by these herbicides. This effect is called '*defoliation*'. The agent reacting is orange coloured mixture of 2.4 D and 2, 4, 5 T.

It is called as *agent orange*; white or blue depending upon their ratio of mixing. By wind, herbicides spread on crops to get disseminated in surrounding areas thereby causing adverse psychological effects on the population. Such chemicals were used in South Vietnam in warfare in 1970 by USA. Dioxin was used in same war. That led to still birth, placental tumours and birth defects (1976). The civilian population was affected for several decades. In America, FDA implement stringent majors to control ill use of pesticides. EPA regulated use of pesticides *e.g.*, production of aldrin and dieldrin is banned in USA. Heptachlor and chlorodane is also prohibited for use in agriculture. An attempt is made in 1910 to control use of the pesticides while full fledged environmental pesticide control act which came into existance in 1974 in USA. In spite of greater awareness of environmental hazards there is no strict legislation on use of pesticide.

14.16 PESTICIDE AGRICULTURE AND POLLUTION

The herbicides and insecticide are the integral part of agriculture production, which in turn is related to soil. The market is large for minor pesticides. 40% of the monetary value of agricultural pesticides stays in its minor use. The contamination of soil occurs due to its interaction with water containing pesticides. Those which are used to control invertebrates are called as the *insecticides* while for control of snails is used mollusc acids while round worms are controlled by nematicides. Vertebrates are killed by rodenticides avicides are used to repel birds. Pesticides control fish population. Herbicides are used to kill plants while fungicides are used to kill fungi, just as bactericides are used to demolish bacteria. Slime is controlled by slimicides, while algae is controlled by algicides. The application of insecticides or herbicides in agriculture is most important as excess had adverse effect on health of man as told earlier. In view of the importance of pesticides in environment we would consider effects of the pesticides like DDT, organophosphorus insecticides, carbamates, herbicides and polychlorinated biphenyls in some details.

The pesticides are the best friend and worst enemy of man on this planet. It not only contaminates lithosphere, and pollutes the atmosphere. Pesticides include herbicides, insecticides, fungicides or rodenticides. These are persistent pollutants obtained during interaction of lithosphere and biosphere. They are cumulative poisons in the body, they accumulate in food chain. They undergo metabolic formation and biodegradation. The pesticides residue is more dangerous than the parent compound. The breakdown in the environment, involving either of the following process, namely oxidation, dehydrogenation, reduction, conjugation like metal complex formation; hydrolytic reaction like cleavage, exchange reaction and isomerisation. The reaction involves interaction with iron porphyrins. The residues are carcinogenic. The metabolic products are dangerous. Some arsenic pesticides have render soil permanently infertile. They may sometimes increase instead of decreasing pest population, due to effect of immunisation. A pesticide like DDT changes fertility of mammals. Pesticides pose an alarming problem for mankind. DDT kills mosquitoes which spread malaria. In spite of this its use in developed countries has gone down due to its harmful effects. However, the production has remained same due to its consumption by developing countries.

Figure 14.6 presents data on production of pesticides in developing countries. Highest production is in 1960 to 1965, with somewhat less production in 1975. Amongst pesticides, highest production is of insecticides, followed by herbicides and finally fungicides. Figure 14.5 shows how pesticide residue enters the environment. A small fraction of pesticides reaches the target pest, some reaches

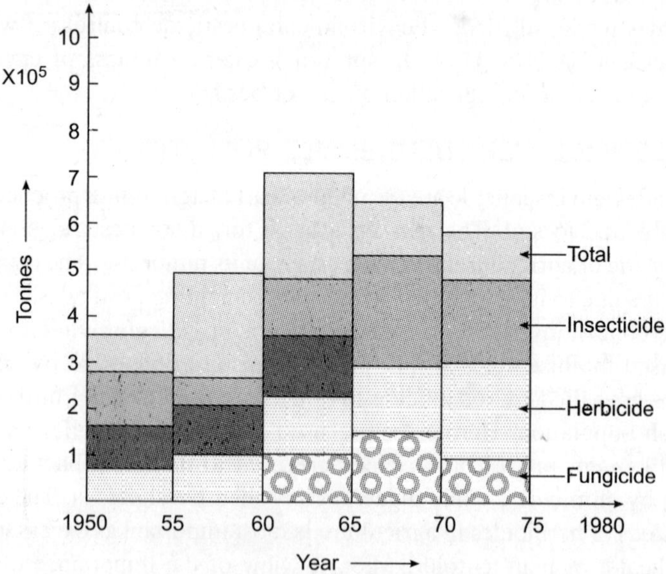

Fig. 14.6 Production of pesticides

Table 14.33 LD_5 of some pesticides

S.No.	Pesticide (mg/kg)	LD_{50} ($\mu g/kg$)	LC_{50} ($\mu g/kg$)	EC_{50} (mg/L)	Solubility
1.	DDT	115	0.4-9	0.37	3.36
2.	Dieldrin	50	0.9-34	250	–
3.	Lindane	125	9-66	460	200
4.	Aldrin	50	5-100	28	130
5.	Malathione	2500	21-3200	1.8	145
6.	Dichlorras	63	0.03 – 3	0.07	10,000

the crop, water, and sediments, some part ends up in the atmosphere. The arsenical herbicide (35%) gets mixed up into air by evaportion. The lithosphere and atmosphere act as sink for these pesticides, as chlorinated hydrocarbons are transported easily in air. DDT, the worst among pesticides is lost to the soil by volatilisation, removal by harvesting of organic compounds, water run-off, and chemical degradation. It is removed from atmosphere by rainfall, settling of aerosols, diffusion and chemical photodegradation.

14.17 ANALYSIS OF PESTICIDES

The pesticides comprises of one of the biggest and important group of compounds. In agriculture, analytical methods are widely used for pesticide analysis involving study of pesticide residue, degradation products and new formulations. Largely chromatographic methods, polarographic technique and spectroscopic methods of analysis are followed for their characterisation. The important chromatographic techniques include thin-layer chromatography, gas-liquid chromatography, and high performance liquid chromatography. While the spectral methods of analysis cover UV visible-IR spectrophotometry, NMR spectrometry and GC-MS technique. Since persistent use of pesticide, the pesticide residue and degradation products accumulate in biota, thus needing accurate analysis. GLC detects nanogram and picogram of pesticides. NMR helps to identify metabolites and degradation products of pesticides. They are extracted by adsorption on column. TLC is a cheap method and is useful for qualitative as well as quantitative analysis of pesticides. For example, carbamates are best analysed by TLC in preference to GLC. In GLC, organochlorine pesticides are detected by electron capture detector. Organophosphorus pesticides are best analysed with flame ionisation detector. The pesticides containing oxidisable or reducible groups are determined by polarography. Pesticide residues are best analysed by IR spectroscopy. NMR technique has low sensitivity, but is useful for elucidation of the structure of a pesticide. Isomers are best analysed by NMR methods. Mass spectrometry is useful (Table 14.34) for identification of new pesticides.

Amongst these organochloro and organophophorus pesticides are encountered in food products. DDT is organochloro pesticide so also aldrin, dieldrin and heptachlor, all have long half-lives. These compounds get accumulated in fatty tissues (1000 μg/g). In 1962, DDT was first recognised as "silent spring" by Ms. Rached Carson.

The important clean up step is to resort to solvent extraction method. Fats dissolved in hexane and are chilled to precipitate, leaving residue in the organic extract in order to shift to DMF extract and then inject it into gas chromatograph for separation and analysis. ECD easily differentiate the various isomers.

The organophosphorus pesticides consist of the members like malathion, parathion, dichlororas. They are very toxic and less stable. They are analysed at the level of 0.0010 μg/g. They are polar and extractable into dichloromethane followed by gas chromatography. The flame ionisation detector (FID) is preferred at 394 to 596 nm. Sulphur and phosphorus are detected in the presence of one another hence dual detector like FID/FPP is used with twin channel chart recorder.

Table 14.34 Mass spectral analysis of pesticides (m/e)

S.No	*Organic compound*	*Peak value (m/e)*	*S.No.*	*Organic compound*	*Peak value (m/e)*
1.	Napthalene ($C_{10}H_5$)	128	11.	Monochlorophenol	128
2.	Phenonthrene ($C_{14}H_{10}$)	178	12.	Trichlorophenol	196
3.	Benzopyrene ($C_{20}H_{12}$)	252	13.	Pentachlorophenol	264
4.	Anthracene ($C_{22}H_{24}$)	276	14.	Dichlorobiphenyl	222
5.	DDT	235	15.	Tetrachlorobiphenyl	290
6.	Aldrin	261	16.	Hexachlorobiphenyl	353
7.	Heptachlor	370	17.	Octachlorobiphenyl	426
8.	Chlorodane	406	18.	BHC	181
9.	Pyrene	202	19.	Dieldrin	378
10.	DDE	246	20.	Endrin	378

14.18 CHARACTERISATION OF PESTICIDES BY SPECIFIC METHODS

The organochlorine pesticides are best detected by TLC, *e.g.*, DDT or DDE with $AgNO_3$–bromophenol blue as spraying reagent in TLC. The presence of 100 to 200 ηg of pesticide is easily detected. The carbamate pesticides like zectron, carbaryl (sevin) and organophosphorus pesticides like phorate, parathion, malathion, are best characterised by TLC technique. Gas chromatography is useful for the analysis of volatile and thermally stable pesticides. The residue analysis of chlorinated pesticide is carried out by GLC. Acetonitrile is used as the solvent. Hexane is used as the solvent for organophosphorus pesticides. From drinking water, chlorinated pesticide is absorbed on a column packed with resin. Amberlite XAD-2 and eluted and analysed by GLC, *e.g.*, lindane, DDT, DDE, aldrin is thus analysed. Polychlorinated biphenyl (PCB) is characterised by GC-MS with glass capillary column. The HPLC is mainly useful for analysis of new formulations. The photometric or fluorometric detectors are used. HPLC is not routinely used for pesticides analysis.

In gas chromatographic separation the solvent used for dissolution of pesticide is important. Hexane is preferred as solvent but in few instances DMF *i.e.*, dimethyl formamide and dichloromethane is also used, for the extraction of polar pollutants. In GC most favoured detector is flame ionisation detector (FID). In most of the cases subsequent to gas chromatographic separation, photometric analysis is preferred for quantitative analysis.

The columns for gas chromatographic separations are also critical. They are run at temperature of more than 200 C. Methyl silicone is used as the stationary phase in the column. The quantitative analysis on the basis of the retention time is not always reliable. The change in the stationary phase from one silicon oil to other as the fixed stationary phase alters sequence of isolation of the organic phosphorus pesticides *e.g.*, diethylglycolsuccinate gives good results in separations of organophosphorus pesticides.

(i) Standards for Pesticide

The standards for pesticide residue is important. The prepared solutions of the mixtures of pesticide is bought from the market. It is diluted according to need *e.g.*, BDH nanogen pesticide standards or supelco standard pesticide are reliable. The gas chromatography permits analysis of important pesticides as aldrin, chlordane, dieldrin, endosulphon, endrin, heptachlore and PCB. These compounds are first extracted with water and then in dichloromethane or hexane. A gas chromatograph with two columns is used, with flame photometric detector while for carbamates Electron capture detector used is for the analysis of 2, 4 dinitrophenyl ether derivative.

(ii) Chlorinated Hydrocarbons

At a times columns are prepared by treating diatomaceous earth as stationary support with dimethyldichloro silane. Many of PCB compounds are carcinogenic. They are less soluble in water. They are analysed by HPLC with fluoroscence and UV detector or analysed with GC with FID detector. One also uses GC-MS technique. Dimethyldichloride is used for the extraction followed by GC analysis. PCB from contaminated drinking water is analysed by GC. The method is equally valid for polynuclear aromatic hydrocarbons such as napthalene, anthracene, pyrene, benzopyrene.

(iii) Analysis of Organochlorine Pesticides

They are bioaccumulating and stable but carcinogenic. GC is used after solvent extraction. GC-MS also gives good results. Pesticides are extracted with ether, hexane or methylene chloride. They are separated by adsorption in column chromatography followed by GC with ECD detector. The level of analysis for lindane is 10 ηg/L while for DDT level is 20 ηg/L.

(iv) Analysis of Phenoxy herbicides

They are weed killers and easily get contaminated with drinking water 2, 4 D or 2 4 5 T belongs to same group. They have adverse effects on the health. The derivatization GC with ECD detector is used. They are extracted with ethyl ether. After hydrolytic precipitation methyl ester is analysed by GC. The limit of analysis is 10 to 50 ηg/L. On the whole 1 to 2 ηg/L is easily analysed by GC.

14.19 POLAROGRAPHIC ANALYSIS

Chlorine containing pesticides are analysed, by polarography *e.g.*, hexachloro-cyclohexane, endrin, aldrin and dieldrin are analysed on DME in LiCl in isopropyl alcohol. The half-wave potential ($E_{1/2}$) of nitrogroup containing pesticides is available in literature. The supporting electrolytes are nitric acid (0.1 M), acetate buffer, sodium hydroxide (0.1 N) and ammonia-ammonium chloride buffer. Half-wave potential varies from – 0.32 V to – 0.72 V for parathion, *e.g.*, – 0.26 V in HNO_3, – 0.62 V in acetate buffer and +0.74 V in ammonia buffer. Voltametric methods is best. The sensitivity of the method is however not very satisfactory. The chief advantage of polarographic analysis is the advantage of identifying a particular pesticide from the knowledge of half-wave potential. It is followed by a quantitative chemical analysis by suitable method.

14.20 SPECTROPHOTOMETRIC ANALYSIS

The UV-visible spectrophotometry is used for formulation analysis. The standardised adsorbents are required for clean up before analysis. The direct reflectance spectrometry is very useful, *e.g.*, analysis of trazine herbicides. IR methods are used for analysis of several isomers of heptachlor or BHC. IR is less sensitive as compared to UV and not suitable for residue analysis; the only advantage is that IR does not need rigorous clean up and offers a choice of peaks. NMR methods are useful for identification and characterisation of pesticide compounds. DDT and DDE are best analysed by NMR. Mass spectrometry, which is the most reliable and definite tool for the analysis of pesticides is useful for the class of carbamates, chlorinated hydrocarbons and metabolites. Chlorophenols is studied by mass spectrometry. The metabolites of 2, 4 D are studied by mass spectrometry. GC-MS gives more reliable information. Lindane 2, 4, 7, 8, T and PCB are best analysed by GC-MS. The development of several ionisation techniques lead to enhancement of sensitivity and reliability in elucidation of the structures of pesticides. The hyphenated GC-MS or GC-HPLC is likely to exhibit spectacular results in future years related to their structure elucidation.

14.21 CONCLUSION

The agricultural pollution and pesticide applications are very closely related. The soil irrigation is partly accomplished by waste water. Micronutrients play an important role in soil chemistry as apart from role of NPK *i.e.*, nitrogen phosphorus and potassium the micronutrients like Cu, Mn, Zn, Mo, Fe, B, also play significant role in promoting growth of the crops. Their characterisation and determinations are valuable as other as component analysis in the soil is. Pesticides are both blessings and curse for human being. It is blessing because enormous amount of foodstuff which is consumed by pests is saved by killing rodants ,pestcides.

While it is considered curse because pesticide like DDT or DDE remain in body fat as long as 30 years and affects health of person. Few of the pesticides do not easily degrade in water even at very high temperature. The quantitative analysis of the pesticide is largely achieved by gas chromatography and in few instances by high performance liquid chromatography. The use of cyclic voltametry and polarography as well as UV-IR spectroscopy is coming into the prominance. The former facilitates identification of the pesticide in suitable supporting electrolyte. In spite of adverse effects of pesticide on health commercial use continues ceaselessly in order to save crops from pests.

ADDITIONAL READING

1. P.R. Hesse, *A Textbook of Soil Chemical Analysis*, John Murray, London (1971).
2. O.A. Black, *Methods of Soil Analysis*, Part 2, American Society of Agronomy, USA (1965).
3. M.S. Cresser, *Solvent Extraction in Flame Spectroscopic Analysis*, Butterworth (1978).
4. I.L. Marr and M.S. Cresser, *Environmental Chemical Analysis*, International Text-book Co., New York (1983).
5. S.K. Sahoo, P.C. Jha, S.M. Khopkar, *Res. Journal of Society of Pollution Free Environment*, **2** 10 (1988).
6. S. Cherian and S.M. Khopkar, *Ind. J. Env. Protection* **11**, 15 (1991).
7. R.A. Horne, *The Chemistry of our Environment*, John Wiley and Sons, New York (1978).
8. M.A.Q. Khan, *Pesticides in Aquatic Environment*, Plenum Press, New York (1977).
9. P.L. McEwen and G.R. Stepenson, *Use and Significance of Pesticides in the Environment*, Wiley, New York (1979).
10. C.A. Edwards, *Environmental Pollution by Pesticides*, Plenum Press, London (1973).
11. K.G. Das, *Pesticide Analysis,* Marcel Dekker, New York (1981).
12. R.F. Krueger and J.N. Seiber, *Treatment and Disposal of Pesticide Waste*, American Chemical Society, Washington (1984).
13. A.P. Dillion, *Pesticides Disposal and Detoxification,* Noyes Data Crop., Park Ridge (1981).
14. R.M. Ladha, V. Sexena, *Pesticide and Environmental Pollution*, Himanshu Publication, Udaipur (1989).
15. S.M. Khopkar, *Environmental Pollution Analysis,* Second Edition, New Age International Publisher (P) Ltd. (2012).

15 Solid Waste

15.1 INTRODUCTION

All materials thrown away of no value are called *solid waste*. Most of solid waste is disposed in India by landfilling and this is most common and important mode of disposal. Solid waste is defined as the material arising from human and animal activities and is being discarded as useless stuff. For instance garbage, refuse, sludge from effluent treatment system or old air pollution control plants is solid waste. The processing involves reuse, recycling or disposal. Old methods of disposal included not only landfilling but also feeding to swine, or incineration but last method causes air pollution. The landfilling contaminates ground water sources in soil. The functional elements are generation, handling and storage, collection and disposal. The volume reduction from bulk is important. Biological transformation produces gas for combustion or provides compost or mannure.

15.2 ADVERSE EFFECTS ON HEALTH

The improper handling of waste leads to spread of diseases. Glass, metal waste, is hazardous. Moist and warm environment favours growth of pathogens. Those of substances retaining water are breeding grounds for insects leading to diseases as gastroenteritis, hepatitis, dysentery and encephalitis. Mosquito and flies promotes typhoid, cholera, which are most prevalent in developing countries. The containers with unused pesticides or herbicides cause problem due to indiscriminate disposal. They lead to explosion if they contain some inflammable materials. The prevention of accumulation of water, controls the breeding of mosquitos which in turn prevents lot of diseases like malaria, filaria and dengu. The organic waste must be stored in dry container to prevent rats infestation. The health of workers at disposal site is affected. Therefore use of dust mask and enclosed the trucks for carrying waste is preferred. The use of protective gloves and eye protectors and safety shoes is always recommended for the safety of workers who handle such waste.

The composting is best process to prevent diseases, as at temperature of 55°C of composting pathogens are killed. The generation of methane from organic waste is hazardous. Good amount of ash results due to incineration. It contains dioxins and metals like Cd, Pb, Hg in form of oxides. The dumping grounds are source of several disease associated, with bad waste.

15.3 SOURCE OF SOLID WASTE

There are many kinds of solid waste like municipal, industrial, agricultural and hazardous and biomedical waste. Municipal waste is made up of garbage, trash, sludge, garden refuse, and construction waste. The food and paper industries produce large amount of trash. Industrial houses generate lot of rubbish due to packing materials. Biomedical waste is recent problem which is covered separately. The industrial waste contains process waste, from refineries or chemical establishments. The agricultural waste originates from farms, fertilisers, insecticide, pesticides in unused form which causes problem. The kind of waste generated before World War II (1945) was changed to fanciful articles by human beings like 40% for paper, 20% for garden waste, 10% for metal, 9% for food, plastics and glass as waste material. The first waste paper is due to progress in packaging technology. For the beverage the throw away containers is slowly increasing. The level of packaging material rose from 37% to 40% within last for 20 years. Printing paper used in newspaper and books increases production of disposable waste. The generation of waste per capita in USA is (1500), UK (800), Japan (900) and Germany (700) lbs/year. The recycling is important method of waste control in USA where per person per day generates 92 kg of waste. The construction activity, street sweeping, landscaping, sewage treatment produces good amount of solid waste. Apart from paper, household waste forms lot of solid waste. It contains glass plastic, leather, rubber, textile. The quality of such waste changes with season. There are also regional variation. Tables 15.1 and 15.2 show quality of waste.

Table 15.1 Consumption of paper for printing (in million tonnes)

Kind	*1990*	*1995*	*2000*
Newspapers	9.11	12.90	16.5
Printed boxes	20.00	26.35	32.0
Books	7.00	7.50	8.0
Journals	2.00	2.20	2.5

Table 15.2 Solid waste with specific weight and particle size

Type	*Sp. weight (lbs/yd^3)*	*Particle size (in inches)*
Paper	135	4–20
Food waste	500	0–8
Plastic	110	0–8
Ash	800	0–4
Metals	250	0–8

In earlier Tables 15.1 and 15.2, we have considered the paper waste as well as specific weight and particle size of typical solid waste. In Table 15.3 relates to proximate and ultimate analysis of solid waste. While Table 15.4 pertains to

Table 15.3 Proximate and ultimate analysis of waste

Proximate analysis		*Ultimate analysis*	
Item	*% of wt*	*Item*	*% of wt dry*
Moisture	25	Moisture	20
Volatile matter	50	Carbon/hydrogen	30/40
Carbon (Fixed)	5	Oxygen/nitrogen	25/0.5
Ash	20	Sulphur/Ash	0.15/20
Total	100%	Total	99.2%

Table 15.4 Reuse of polymeric waste

S.No.	*Name*	*Reuse*	*S.No.*	*Name*	*Reuse*
1.	Polystyrene	Food, foam cup	4.	Polypropylene	Auto industry
2.	High density plastic	Milk container	5.	Low density plastic	Film, grocery bags
3.	Mixed plastic	Fence bench, chair	6.	Polyethylene products	Soft beverage bottles

The polymeric waste Table 15.5 is real headache for big cities.

Table 15.5 Composition of flyash waste

S.No.	*Source*	*Elements percent in flyash waste*
1.	Smelters	Fe Cd Zn
2.	Oiled Power plant	V– Ni Fe
3.	Coaled Power plant	Fe Zn Pb V Mn Cr Cu Ni As Co Sb Cd Hg
4.	Municipal waste inceneration	Zn Fe Hg Pb Sn As Cd Co Cu Mn Ni Sb
5.	Open hearth furnace	Fe Zn Cr Cu Mn Ni Pb

polymers waste and Table 15.5 relates to flyash composition. Flyash is in abundant concentration in and around thermal power plants. There is real problem as to how to get rid of this solid waste. The attempts were made without much success for using it for land filling and manufacture of bricks. The disposal of solid waste in mega cities is serious problem. In cities housing complex do not permit dumping such waste in their neighbourhood. Some dumping grounds are totally saturated (*e.g.* Deonar and Kanjur in Mumbai) where there is no further room to dump this waste. The housing societies have litigation and they have gone to court (*e.g.* Kanjum marg Powai Mumbai) to advice municipal corporation to locate new alternative dumping sites for disposal of solid waste.

There are several inorganic ions which are present in flyash. Iron, is common metal followed by zinc and copper. The oil powered electric generators have metals like vanadium, iron and traces of nickel, however coal power plant (mostly seen in Madhya Pradesh and Bihar) contain all kinds of metals from both transition and main group element. They are series of transition metals such as (Fe V Mn Cr Cu Ni Cd Hg) as well as nontransition or main group metals, such as Pb As, Ca Sb. The Municipal waste contains varying degree of metals depending upon the source of waste so as to examine whether it originates from rural or urban environment. As expected in flyash from open hearth furnace all common metals are detected. It is necessary to a systematic characterise and good disposal method to render environment clean.

Table 15.6 Polymer waste

S.No.	*Name*	*Formula*	*Applications in making of*	*Stability*	*Remarks*
1.	Mixed plastic	–	Fence benches	Partly degradable	Cheap
2.	Polyethylene	PETE	Soft drinks	Nondegradable	Stable
3.	Polyvinyl chloride	PVC	Caps bottles	Nondegradable in any form	Tough
4.	Polypropelene	PP	Battery casting	Nondegradable	Strong
5.	Low density plastic	LDPE	Wrapper, diapers	Can be degraded, on prolonged treatment	Soft
6.	Polystyrene	PS	Foam cup, plates	Never degradable	Ext. stable
7.	High density polyethyle	DFE	Film, grocery bag	Almost impossible to degrade	V. stable

(i) Plastic Waste

One of the unsolved problem of disposal of plastic waste specially in metropolitan cities like Kolkata is severe problem. Plastic is very common and useful material. It is not only used in pharmaceutical or food industries but also day to consumption of groceries, fruits and vegetable. Polymers have unique properties it is possible to make into lowest possible (< 30 microns) thinness. Several attempts were made to discover the substitute for polymer, in day to day life specially to discover a degradable variety. One variety is found with origin in starch. Unfortunately it has failed to replace existing plastic. The greatest problem is their disposal on incineration. This is because it provides obvinaxous gas which is injurious to health. If it is buried in soil it takes several years (in thousands) to degrade in to the soil.

There are several forms of plastic (Table 15.6) such as polyethylene, polyvinyl chloride, polypropelene, polystyrene (most commonly used) high and low density plastic. A good variety (PETE, PVC, HDPE etc.) are used in food industry and grocery shops. Thin plastic cloggs the drain and the location gets flooded during rainy season. The one particular variety used for wrapping food (LDPE) is consumed by animals and its fatal. The variety is used for reuse in form of black variety like garbage bags. Most of the injectibles in hospitals are made up of plastic of vial creating a serious problem bio of waste of disposable. A variety of material is recycled and reused in automobiles industry, furniture fixation in form of black plastic.

Thus the great problem of disposal lies unsolved and it has formed a formidable challenge for research investigators to discover degradable plastic or polymer which should serve as the substitute for present variety of plastic.

15.4 CHARACTERISTICS OF SOLID WASTE

It is worthwhile at this stage to consider physical, chemical and biological properties of solid waste.

(i) Physical Characteristics

It includes specific weight, moisture contents, particle size, field capacity and permeability. The chemical characteristics cover proximate and ultimate analysis, energy analysis and biological characterisation. It contains crude fibre nature biodegradability and smell. The specific weight refers to weight material per unit volume of both compacted and uncompacted waste. Value varies from 300 to 800 lbs/yd^3 (Table 15.6). It varies according to waste *e.g.,* paper (130), plastic (100), food (500), the construction material (800), tin cans (150). Moisture increases the weight. This value decides about compacting capacity and need of volume reduction (Table 15.7). Next is moisture contents, its biodegrability is expressed in wet and dry modes. The value varies from 15 to 40%. It is high for food and garden waste (50 to 80%) and least for rubber waste (1 to 4%) and glass. The particle size is important for processing for recycling and reuse. The field capacity of solid waste is total amount of the moisture against downward pull of gravity. It is useful for landfilling process (Table 15.7).

(ii) Chemical Characteristics

The proximate and ultimate analysis is important. The first property determines the amount of surrogate parameter in place of real chemical contents. The moisture, volatile matter, fixed carbon and ash is analysed. The combustion property is known by proximate analysis *e.g.*, (less water is better for fuel) (Table 15.3). The ultimate analysis is % of each element in solid waste. This gives the idea of chemical composition specially the carbon and nitrogen/contents and moisture contents (Tables 15.3 and 15.8).

Table 15.7 Constituents of solid waste (%)

S.No.	*Name*	*Present %*	*S.No.*	*Name*	*Present %*
1.	Food	10	5.	Metal	110
2.	Paper	40	6.	Cloth	2
3.	Plastic	7	7.	Ash	3
4.	Glass	8	8.	Garden waste, wood	20

A proximate analysis shows moisture (20%), volatile matter (50%), ash (30%) and carbon (7%), while ultimate analysis of typical solid waste has moisture (20%) carbon (30%), oxygen (26%), ash (20%) nitrogen, sulphur, hydrogen (4.5% together). The energy content is measure of heat contents obtained by coulomb (Table 15.11).

(iii) Biological Characteristics

The biodegradability is most important parameter. It is given as BF = (0.83 –

0.028 LC) if BF = biodegradable fraction and LC = ligands contents of voltile solids *e.g.*, BF for food (0.82), paper (0.22), agricultural waste (0.72) is known.

Table 15.8 Moisture contents of solid waste

S.No.	substance	% moisture	S.No.	substance	% moisture
1.	Food	70	8.	Wood	20
2.	Paper	6	9.	Glass	2
3.	Plastic	2	10.	Tin	3
4.	Clothing	10	11.	Metals	2
5.	Rubber	2	12.	Iron	3
6.	Leather	10	13.	Ash	8
7.	Grass	60	14.	Cardboard	5

Table 15.9 Ultimate analysis of solid waste (%)

S.No.	Name	C	H	O	N	S
1.	Paper	45.4	6.1	42.1	0.3	0.12
2.	Plastic	60.0	7.2	22.8	–	–
3.	Cloth	46.2	6.4	41.8	2.2	0.2
4.	Rubber	77.0	10.0	–	–	2.0
5.	Wood	48	6	42	0.3	0.1
6.	Garden	49	6	36	3.0	0.3
7.	Waste food	42	6	28	3.0	0.25
8.	Leather	60	8	12	10.0	0.4

Table 15.10 Gases emitted from landfilling operations

S.No.	Gas	% (vol)	S. No.	Gas	% (vol)
1.	CH_4	60.0	5.	CO_2	50.0
2.	O_2	2.0	6.	N_2	10.0
3.	NH_3	1.0	7.	H_2	0.2
4.	CO	0.2	8.	H_2S	1.0

15.5 TRANSPORTATION OF SOLID WASTE

The storage collection and the transportation of solid waste is of critical considerations. The type of the container is used must be impervious for storage of waste. The garbage container must have cover and are fabricated of plastic or plated metal. It should have wheels for the rolling. A large container is used for housing colonies with as large waste as (0.4–40 yd^3). Solid waste collection is done by municipal office. It costs considerable money. The collection system is fixed or moving container *e.g.*, packer truck, or titled frame hauled container. Solid waste collection from containers is cost effective. The waste collection from large producer is also labour intensive like individual collection. Such collection is directly alone at disposal site. The haul time for disposal site determines the cost. To reduce this transfer stations is located on long distance. The compaction trailers are very useful process for transportation of solid waste. The compacting of waste is best method.

15.6 PROCESSING OF SOLID WASTE

Many companies designate it by different names as physical, chemical or biological processing. The main idea is to recover useful products. If possible, the segregation should be preferably done at the point of generation in dry and wet waste. This is one of the reasons in cities citizens are asked to collect wet and dry waste separately as the former is used for manure and gas production while latter is used for landfilling. Preprocessing is done to produce waste with homogeneous nature with possibility of recovery of materials before shredding. The preprocessing is important. It involves weight testing, storage, pit consideration, retrieval system and refuse conveying. Refuse is weighed before processing to decide its cost. The receiving and storage area act as buffer system prior to processing as processing is slow. Such waste is temporarily stored in pit and crane or live bottom pit, or on tipping floor. In live bottom system bottle moves up. Various types of conveyor belts are in use.

15.7 PHYSICAL TREATMENT OF WASTE

The size distribution and shape characteristics is done before other treatment (Table 15.2). The size varys from 2 to 20". The domestic waste has size of 2 to 6". Hence shredding is accordingly adjusted. The main purpose is to reduce the size for processing. In an hour 300 to 500 tonnes waste is shredded. Different kinds of shear shredders are available. One must guard against fire shredding. It separates oversize particles. The separation by density is also fissible involving liquid flotation which separates materials with lower density than liquid. High density polyethylene container for soft drinks are thus separated. Air classifier involves separators on basis of gravity difference of particles. Magnetic separator are employed for solid waste containing metals. Non-magnetic metals like aluminium is not separated and is thrown away from magnets.

15.8 CHEMICAL TREATMENT OF WASTE

It covers various kinds of the combustion processes. It involves thermal decomposition via thermal oxidation at high temperature of 700°C. With excess of oxygen we have CO_2, H_2O, NO_2 and SO_2 gas. The pyrolsis is an example of thermal combustion/decomposition of waste in absence of oxygen it is called anaerobic burning. Incineration is form of a chemical process involving rapid oxidation of waste. The moisture is evaporated, organic compounds are voltilised and nonvoltile compounds are bounded. Incineration leads to formation of gases, ash and heat liberation (Table 15.10). Like hazardous waste 100% *i.e.*, complete destruction is not mandatory. The high heat value determines type of incinerator used. Fuel with combustion value less than 50% should be preferably burned in earth. The incinerators are of different types as mass burn, refusal derived, fluid bed combustion, multiple chamber incinerator. The combustion in air is necessary to complete combustion. Excess air is provided. It should not cause air pollution. Flyash is main by-product of combustion. Heavy metals in incineration are vaporised and condensed and subsequently cause problem *e.g.*, combustion of plastics product gives hazardous products. Acid gas and dioxone control is important task. At 1000°C, SO_2, NO-NO_x, CO_2, HCl, HF are produced so that they are converted into solid form by precipitation. The acid gases are removed by scrubbers. Dioxin and furans are chlorinated compounds. The temperature of ignition is controlled to prevent formation of furans and dioxins. The scribers control acid emission at 140°C permitting circulation in sprayers. Particulate matter is also washed off. The dry scrubbers neutralise SO_2 and HCI gas. Dry residue is easily disposed. ESP is used to control particulates. Bag house filters are also effective to remove particulate matter. Cyclones are used. Bottom and flyash are disposed. Flyash is rich source of many elements like germanium and tellurium.

15.9 BIOLOGICAL TREATMENT OF SOLID WASTE

The disposal of organic waste is problem. Microorganisms degrade them into useful products. The composting of solid waste is very important. Yard and garden waste is composted. Composting is the biochemical degradation of organic waste leading to the formation of humus. Aerobic composting is promoted by fungi, protozoa. Moisture and temperature is controlled in water as moisture prevents entry of oxygen for aerobic oxidation. The biochemical composting is influenced by moisture plants degrade but not lignine. Backyard composting is a source of reduction of activity. The composting technique is critical. It is either agitating or static. It is done while shaking of waste periodically but static composting is directly done. Window composting needs landspace. In static process aeration is provided by blowing air through perforations. Pyrolysis is act of decomposing organic compounds through application of heat in absence of oxygen. It is kind of distillation process CO, CH_4 are evolved. The operating temperature and pressure needs close control. Life-cycle assessment (LCA) is a system approach for studying pollution sources in a process.

15.10 RECYCLING OF WASTE

The main objective is to explore possibility of reuse and recovery of valuable products. This aspect is considered by manufactures. The toxicity of the waste is due to heavy metal, chlorinated hydrocarbons. There are various ways of use of recycled material *e.g.*, recycled paper is used for newspapers after repulping. Plastics are the bane of environment (9.3% of waste). The recyclable plastics are polystyrene, polypropylene, polyethylene, PVC and polyethylene terephthalate which is mostly used by food industry. New plastic is made from old plastic materials. Al, glass and construction materials is recycled. Yard waste and organics waste is also recycled.

15.11 DISPOSAL OF SOLID WASTE BY LANDFILLING

Landfill is defined as a system designed and constructed to dispose of discarded waste by burial inland to minimise liberation of contaminates in the atmosphere. Landfilling covers hazardous waste, specified waste and municipal solid waste but site selection is important. Thus environmentally unsuitable or unfertile land is preferred. This should not contaminate ground water source. A buffer zone is necessary to isolate it from human habitat. Soil properties have to be studied. It should be permeable, have swelling capacity and capable of support vegetation. The contamination of leaching from waste disposal site must be examined. There are various landfilling techniques such as area method (*i.e.* covering soil) with waste. In trench method solid waste after spreading is compacted in a trenches (10–15' deep). In combination method above two techniques are combined. Cover material is put into landfill at each stage of construction (6"–12" cover). The liquid (*i.e.* leachates) in cover soil of landfill is potential source of pollution. Leachate generation must be minimised. Surface vegetation layer leads to development of parks. Filter layer protects the overlying cover of soil. The drainage layer removes water in filtrating on top soil. The assessment of moisture in landfill is important. Leachates are formed by percolation of water through waste. The hydrological cycle and transportation would control moisture in soil. Surface runoff provides water that drains away from landfill. It is discharged into ponds. It is necessary to estimate leachate generation rate. Landfill operation is complex. Weather also influences landfilling operation. The disposal of asbestos, automobile tyres, furniture is specialised area of operation and action. Good compaction reduces volume, and debris, it discourage rodents, prevent washing of waste in heavy rainfall. For site operation it prevents waste spreading in highwind, cover solid waste to prevent odour.

15.12 CONTROL OF LIBERATED GASES AND LEACHATES

Why leacheats are generated? They are formed as water passes through landfill and end up in ground water source to pollute it. Raining increases leachate formation. Moisture promotes leachate formation, but rain water leakage stops leachate formation. Physical, chemical or biological treatment is used to reduce leachate formation. Aerobic or anerobic treatment is induced in biological treatment like waste water, one uses trickling filters or activated sludge treatment, equilisation and sedimentation is resorted to air and stream stripping is done. In chemical treatment, reverse osmosis, neutralisation, redox reaction is used. Land fill gas generation is another headache, CO_2 and CH_4 are most common gases. Gas recovery is done wherever possible, it is incinerated.

15.13 CONCLUSION

The solid waste is both boon or a curse to society. If not properly handled it is health hazard. There are various domestic and industrial sources of solid waste. One can characterise solid waste by the physical, chemical or biological properties.

Transportation and processing are critical. Such treatment involves physical, chemical or biological processing. The recycling and disposal by landfilling are most common methods which are so far used in developed countries. This includes control of gases and production of leacheats in solid soil.

ADDITIONAL READING

1. K.L. Shah, *Basics of Solid and Hazardous Waste Management Technology,* Prentice Hall, USA (2000).
2. J.T. Pfeffer, *Solid Waste Management Engineering,* Prentice Hall (1992).
3. G.H. Techobanoglous, Thesen and S. Vigil, *Intergraded Solid Waste Management*, McGraw Hill and Co. (1994).
4. W. Robinson, *Solid Waste Handbook*, New York, Wiley Int (1986).
5. L. Hougan, *Chemical Process Principles,* Part I. *Material and Energy Balance,* 2nd Ed. Wiley (1954).
6. C.R. Rhyner, L.J. Schwartz, R.B. Wegnov, M.G. Kohrell, *Waste Management and Resource Recovery,* Lew's Publication (1995).
7. A. Bagchi, *Design Construction and Monitoring of Landfills,* Wiley, New York (1994).
8. S.M. Khopkar, *Environmental Pollution Analysis Second Edition*, New Age International (P) Ltd., Publishers (2012).

16 Hazardous Waste

16.1 INTRODUCTION

The need of getting ISO-9000 certificate for environment is growing in industry. In order to satisfy the requirements of such regulation one needs to control use of the hazardous material and watch their disposal in the environment. Since 1960 awareness for hazardous waste began. Since 1970 regulations came into existance specially in America. Since 1980 actions were initiated for the minimisation of hazardous (HWM) waste material. And in 1990 the ISO 9000 regulation came into existance. The hazardous waste material is defined as the chemicals which are capable of posing risk to health or to an environment. The hazardous waste are dangerous to handle or dispose as it may cause death. The knowledge of chemistry is most essential for the effective management of such waste. Out of 60,000 chemicals generated about 35,000 are listed as hazardous materials. Till 1970 they were disposed off in toxic dumps which leads to enactment of law *i.e.* (RCRA), Resource Conservation and Recovery Act in USA is active. It takes care of future pollution problems. The US-EPA defines "hazardous waste as one which causes or contributes to the increase in the mortality or serious sickness which is irreversible or incapaciting or reversible illness. It poses a substantial potential hazard to human health or environment if improperly treated, stored or transported, disposed of or managed. The characteristics is measured by standardised test or it is detected by generators of solid waste". A waste is considered hazardous if it shows ignitable corrosive reactive toxic properties. Recently act on disposal and transport has been passed in our country also.

16.2 DEFINITION OF HAZARDOUS WASTE

Toxic pollutants and hazardous waste are NOT synonymous. Former are those which threaten and harm to human health or environment to warrant limitations in applications. The latter is defined as one substance which when discharged presents reasonable danger to public health, but not limited to living organism in water. Hazardous waste necessarily contains hazardous material. Toxic material produce injury, mutogensity and carcinogensity. While hazardous material lead to injury due to use of substance in given manner. Toxic refers to intrinsic property while hazardous word encompass the potential for injury to health due to toxic matter. Hazardous material is injurious to human health and environment. It may be toxic, flammable, reactive, corrosive irritating or may be radioactive substances. The extent of consequence be known. The condition under which it shows hazardous nature should be also studied. It need special treatment. Wastes are lethal, nondegradable, cause determental effect. Finally, it is defined as any waste or combination of wastes which due to its quantity or chemical property pose substantial or potential hazard to human health, living organism or to environment. Such wastes are bioconcentrative, inflammable, reactive, toxic, irritating and corrosive. Different countries give different definition but sum and substance is same *viz* they are all injurious to health or to an environment. Next to designate hazardous waste is difficult the listing and criteria are used to classify. The classification depends upon consideration of its properties. Table 16.1 presents the chemical characteristics and applications of hazardous waste.

Table 16.1 Chemical characteristics of hazardous waste

S.No.	*Property*	*Application*	*Remarks*
1.	Colour	Chlorine/sulphur dioxide coloured	Facilitates identification
2.	Odour	More odour more is it hazardity	Easy to recognize from smell
3.	Density	Suppressing fire knowledge	Good to know solid
4.	Firc point temp.	Point at which combustion starts	Identify danger zone
5.	Ignition temp.	Ignition temperature in fuel	Quality of material known
6.	Explosion limit	Limit of explosivity	Noncombustible known
7.	Formula	Identifies chemical family or group	Extent of harmful effect
8.	Molecular weight	Throws information on impurity	Quality of waste is known
9.	Specific gravity	Mostly varies beyond 1.0	Actual value is important
10.	Melting point	Varies in presence of impurities	For solids known
11.	Boiling point	Depends on atmospheric pressure	For volatility known
12.	Flash point	Lowest temperature of ignition in air	Zone of ignition known
13.	Vapour density	More for hazardous waste	Decides flamability
14.	Vapour pressure	High for bad waste	Helps know boiling point
15.	Solubility	Less at high molecular weight	Rarely soluble
16.	Thermal content	Heat generated level	Explosive nature
17.	Physical state	Few in solid state	Limit of hazardity
18.	Threshold toxicity	Toxic effect limit	Most of waste is toxic
19.	Chemical state	Most of it in liquid state	It is in liquid form

The Table 16.1 list several chemical properties of hazardous waste. Apart from physical appearance as colour, odour, solubility the important properties such as fire point, ignition temperature, explosion temperature is most important. The conventional m.p, b.p, molecular weight or specific gravity indicates kind of organic origin. Vapour pressure, vapour density is important apart from explosive nature one must know the toxicity of the hazardous waste. Most of it is present in liquid form with exception of compounds like phenols, napthalene (dye stuff) and polymers.

The remark column in Table 16.1 amplifies its physical or chemical quality and applications.

16.3 CHARACTERISTICS OF HAZARDOUS WASTE

One ennumerates various properties like toxicity, reactivity, infectiousness, flameability, corrosiveness, irritation, bioconcentration, genetic disorder of waste. The characteristic wastes are those which exhibit measurable property.

(i) Flameability

It creates handling problems and also transportation task is rendered difficult. One measures flash point and auto ignition temperature. Flash point is minimum temperature at which liquid ignites. Fire point is temperature at which liquid undergoes combustion. It is higher than flash point. Auto ignition temperature is minimum temperature at which material itself ignite. A liquid with flash point of 60°C is hazardous (see Table 16.1).

(ii) Corrosiveness

It is defined as the ability of substance to dissociate or erode material by chemical change. It is measured in terms of ability of matter to corrode in fixed amount of time. Such waste reacts with other waste and burns. An aqueous material with pH less than 7.0 or pH > 2 or pH more than 12.5 or liquids, which corrod steel. It is called '*corrosive material*'.

(iii) Toxicity

It is the ability of waste to produce injury upon contact with part of body of living organism. It causes severe injury. Phytoxic waste damages plant due to reduction of chlorophyll, retarding growth waste if it contains bioaccumulated food chain or causes irreversible damage. All industries give toxic waste measured in terms of definite parameters. Many metals, insecticides, herbicide are toxic amongst the hazardous waste material.

(iv) Reactivity

It is unstable waste materials which undergoes violent chemical reactions. It reacts without detonating. It reacts readily with water. It forms explosive mixture with water, it generates toxic gases or vapours contain cyanide or sulphide to give toxic gases. The waste may detonate by thermal, mechanical or electrostatic shock. Handling becomes difficult for the oxidising or self reactive materials. One exhibiting autopolymerisation are more hazardous.

(v) Infective Waste

The medical waste belongs to this category. It contains pathogens, bacteria or virus leading to some disease. It poses great hazards to public and one must handle them with care. Sewage waste is not considered as infectious waste. Laboratory, surgical, maternity waste are all biowaste or biomedical waste.

(vi) Irritating Waste

Some waste causes skin problems and hence is directly discharged. It is either acidic or alkaline and is sensitizers. It causes oedema (swelling) and erythema (redness) within 24 hrs of exposure. It has dermal effects causing itching or necrosis due to death of tissue.

(vii) Bioconcentration

These materials are concentrated in a single organism. At low level it causes problem. The bioconcentration factor is defined as the ratio of concentration of the material in organism to the concentration sorrounding environment. For them detoxification, excretion is not possible. Heavy metals are retained by enzyme and proteins of body DDT, PCB are bioconcentrating materials.

(viii) Genetic Activity

The material may be carcinogenic, mutogenic or teratogenic leading to malfunctioning of organs. Much work has been done and also discussed under chapter environmental toxicology of this book.

16.4 SOURCE OF HAZARDOUS WASTE

It originates from industrial or commercial house, agriculture farm. It is small and large quantity generators. Various sources include chemical manufacturers, vehicle maintance, printing, leather, paper, construction, metal fabrication industries. Transportation generates waste so also farmers through pesticides and fertilisers. Millitary activity also produces waste. Apart other agencies like paint pigment, automotive product generate waste. PCB is the confirmed as hazardous waste. Asbestos is also another hazardous waste. It causes asbestosis, lung cancer and mesothelioma (cancer of lining of chest). Pesticides are big problem. Dioxin is most injurious. It is chemically 2, 3, 7, 8 tetrachlorodibenzopdioxin. Methyl isocyanate (Bhopal Tragedy) is hazardous as sevin a pesticide which is prepared from it. Sulphuric acid in large dose and concentration is bad. Lead from oxide cell or in petroleum is injurious for health. Ethyleneglycol, ethers, photoresistant chemicals have adverse reproductive effects. Several air pollutants containing toxic metals are harmful. It is generators responsibility to identify hazardous waste and treat it before disposal. Various generators of the hazardous waste are heavy industry, household, transporters, farmers, military and few biological waste generating laboratories.

16.5 ANALYSIS OF HAZARDOUS WASTE

The sampling and analysis is done for a thorough comprehension of quality of waste. It's impact on environment is well understood. Several properties like water solubility, solid adsorption, moisture, pH, porosity, surface area vaporisation, degradation, chemodynamics and microbial conversion contamination by ground water are studied. It gives idea about the enactment of restrictions on disposal or treatment. The principle objective of analysis is to ascertain extent of hazardity of waste; decide on treatment process; explore possibility of recycle or reuse, know chemical properties, fissibility of land disposal, giving safety information and extent of contaminates. The preservation method, kind of container, type of sampling technique, use of right preservative, as well as analysis of ignibility, corrosivity, reactivity and toxicity is of great importance. This is most crucial in ultra trace analyse.

(i) Sampling

It should be representative sample. The location, frequency, quantum and need should be first examined. Air, liquid and solid are three states. Ground water sampling gives good data. Solid samples are mostly from soil. A line of demarcation is drawn between hazardous and nonhazardous waste. The former contains high level of contaminants. Personal protective equipment must be used while handling. Various kinds of containers are used for storing samples. Glass plastics are best. Some samples need refrigeration. Sampling trace metals is special field. Biological sampling of blood, or serum is carried out as usual tissue or hair is collected on biopsy and autopsy of victim. Sampling process will depend upon physical state of waste, homogeneity, contamination degree, kind of analysis and purpose of study. Special equipment is used for the sampling of liquids. A stastical sampling mode is used if the sample is heterogeneous, large in volume, has unknown contents, and is typical soil.

(ii) Field Analysis

Rapid analysis in field may sacrifice accuracy. We analyse various properties in field itself *e.g.*, organic vapour is analysed by analyser with flame or photoionisation detectors. First works in range of 0 to 10,000 ppm while latter has range of 0 to 2000 ppm. Magnetometry involves detection of iron metal present in sample. Similarly, electrical resistivity is measured. Test kits are used to analyse strip or reagents added to the sample. It detects chlorine, pH, lead chloride, cyanide, PCB and COD of the sample. Portable X-ray set is used in mining industry for metal analysis. Dräger tubes assess the contamination of air. Portable GLC measures volatile organics, O_3, pH, temperature, DO, conductivity. The formaldehyde and lead are analysed by suitable instruments.

(iii) Laboratory Analysis

Such analysis possess high level of accuracy. These are some analytical tests which are used for analysis of nonhazardous material. A number of initial laboratory tests are carried out *e.g.*, pH, conductivity, turbidity, TDS, DO, COD, oil grease TOC, flash point and halogens. Ions like CrO_4^{2-}, PO_4^{2-}, SO_4^{2-}, SO_3^{2-}, F^-, Cl^-, CN are analysed by ion chromatography. The inorganic compounds are analysed by AAS or ICP-AES. The organic compounds are analysed by gas chromatography or HPLC. Halogenated hydrocarbons, aromatic compounds phenol and chlorinated pesticides are analysed by GLC. Nonvolatile and high molecular weight polymers are extracted before GLC analysis. The compounds undergoing pyrolysis or which have low vapour pressure is analysed by high performance liquid chromatography (HPLC).

(iv) Sample Preparations and Analysis

The dissolution is defined as process of dissolving substance in solvent at low temperature with or without chemical reaction. It is done at high pressure and temperature. The decomposition must be complete, with soluble residue. With simple procedure for optimum sample, avoid systemic errors. Wet digestion technique is most suitable specially when using nitric perchloric acid or hydrogen peroxide. A dry ashing process is used. After dissolution preconcentration and separation is useful as the matrix effect is avoided, it raises sensitivity of analysis, promotes caliberation and select right process of analysis. The separation process should be simple and permit use of common reagents, and well-known technique. There are many methods like precipitation, flotation, solvent extraction, chromatography, Ion-exchange, partition, gas, exclusion chromatography and electrolytical methods. The choice of method depends upon quality of sample to be analysed. It is followed by any instrumental method of analysis such as atomic spectroscopy, including absorption and emission spectral methods, electro-analytical methods, nuclear methods, chromatography, mass spectrometry for hazardous metals in environment.

(v) Analytical Methods Instrumentation

Although this discussion aptly fit in for analysis of hazardous metals in the environment it is also valid for organic hazardous materials. Amongst spectral methods atomic absorption spectroscopy as well as atomic emission and fluorescence spectroscopy are most useful for analysis of hazardous waste. Since AAS does not need chemical separation, it is very fast and adoptable at trace level.

(vi) Spectral Methods

In AAS graphite furnace mode is most useful. A Zeeman background correction had improved sensitivity. Hydride methods are adopted for selected metals like As, Se and Sb. AES involving flame emission is most commonly used for s-block metals. However, ICP-AES is considered to be best method so also ICP-MS hypenated method, ICP-AES is multielement method is preferable. A temperature of 5000°C with possibility of analysis of many elements is done by plasma model Only limitation is running cost due to consumption of argon. The ICP-MS permits 100% ionisation of elements. In simple mass spectrometry any element in range of 10 to 12 is analysed. IDMS *i.e.*, isotope dilution mass spectrometry give excellent precision and accuracy. It is useful only if element has two or more isotopes. SIMS secondary ionisation mass spectra is useful for analysis of element on surfaces of biological materials. However, spectrophotometry is most popular due to easy availability of cheap instruments. The molecular absorption spectroscopy in UV visible or IR regions is very useful. Many colorimetric methods need selective separation if chromogenic ligand is not selective for complexation with metal.

(vii) Chromatography

The chromatographic methods are mostly useful for analysis of hazardous organic waste. The components are separated on column by using differential migration front. GC and HPLC are most popular for analysis of organics. Not only metals but organometallic compounds are analysed by GC. With HPLC mobile phase is liquid hence non-volatile compounds are easily analysed. Ion chromatography is best for environmental speciation and analysis of anions.

(viii) Electroanalytical Methods

Unfortunately, electroanalytical methods are not very common in environmental analysis with the exception of polarography. The differential pulse polarography is coming up due to favourable signal/noise ratio. Anodic stripping voltametry is useful at low concentration. Square wave polarography coupled with computer is also very useful. Differential pulse anodic stripping is becoming popular for analysis of As, Cd, Cr, Hg, Pb and Tl present in hazardous waste.

(ix) Nuclear Methods

Amongst nuclear methods, neutron activation analysis and the isotope dilution methods are most versatile. Instrumental neutron activation analysis facilitates analysis of Al, Co, Ni, Pb at level of 10^{-9} *i.e.*, nano gm concentration. The X-ray fluoroscence method is non-destructive method of analysis. As small as 0.1 μg/L of As Cd, Co, Cr, Ni, Pb, Se, Tl and Al is analysed by X-ray fluorescence technique.

(x) Hyphenated Technique

In future, ICP-AES will be more popular than AAS. In AAS one uses graphite furnace. In future ICP-MS hyphenated technique will come up with flow injection analysis. Atomic fluoroscence with laser excitation will analyse 10^{-15} femagram concentration of metals. Computerised potentiometry will have many applications. Use of NAA will continue for radioactive elements. Spectrophotometry in combination with chromatography will provide low detection limit of element in various samples of the hazardous materials.

16.6 TRANSPORTATION OF HAZARDOUS WASTE

Maharashtra was the first state in India to enact legislation to regulate transportation of hazardous waste by enactment of regulation in 1985 to 90. In USA, the Resource Conservation and Recovery Act (RCRA) passed an act (HMTA) hazardous material transportation act in 1975. Many problems originate from bad transportation of waste. Waste haulers cover generators who deliver their own waste; disposers who pick up the waste and contract transporters who provide a service to the generators or disposers. Trucks are common mode of transport. The following table gives the distribution of waste by transports in % according to its type.

Table 16.2 Transportation of waste

S.No.	*Kind of waste*	*Remark*	*%*	*S.No.*	*Kind of waste*	*Remark*	*%*
1.	Acids	High	51	6.	Oils	Medium	55
2.	Pesticides	Low	33	7.	Solvents	Highest	72
3.	Alkalies	Highest	56	8.	Drugs	Lowest	38
4.	Cyanides	Low	35	9.	PCB	Reasonable	45
5.	Chromic acid	Tolerable	38	10.	Herbicides	Lowest	21

Table 16.2 indicates highest transport for oils, acids, alkalies, solvents greater than 50% and is least in Herbicide. Security of disposal sites is also increasing. In Europe most of waste is loaded in ships and it is off loaded in ocean or suitable site. EPA has given instructions regarding packaging, marking, labelling. The material in containers should be inert to hazardous waste, and material should be absorbent or able to consume moisture and liquids and they should be shock absorbers in case of accidents. It is expected to provide correct labels which for such containers with symbol, hazardous class name and UN class number labels which have been assigned colours to indicate kind of the material as shown in Table 16.3.

Table 16.3 International colour code and index of waste

Orange	Explosive, compressed gas (1)
Green	Nonflammable (2)
Red	Flammable (2)
White	Poison (2)
Red	For flammable liquid (3)
White and red strips	Flammable solid (4)
White top bottom red	Combustible (4)
Yellow	Peroxides (5)
White	Harmful poison (6)
White	Infectious substance (6)
Yellow and magenta colour	Radioactive waste (7)
White and black	Corrosive material (8)

(i) Regulations

Transportation of hazardon waste plays significant role in management of waste. It covers important area as preparation for transport, requirements as per legislation and clean up regulations. A generator and transporter has number for identification. A form is filled by transporter. Energy response is essential which stipulate the immediate action to protects human health and environment if released accidentally. Since 1973 greater awareness is created. The regulations are expected to have record labels and comply to transport regulations. Therefore, generation of record, use of labels, maintance of manifest system and assurance of safe transportion is vital. The structure of manifest system is as follows:

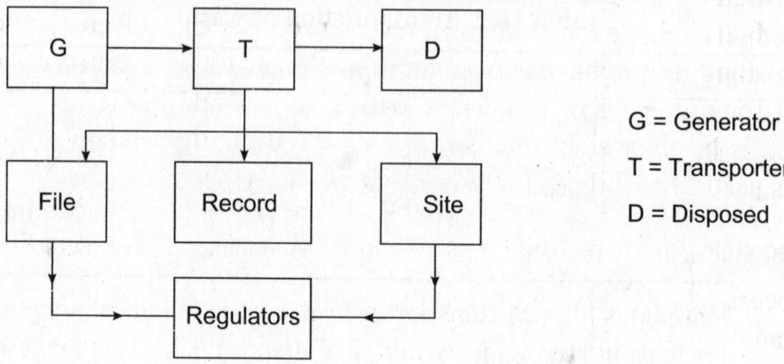

Fig. 16.1 Structure of manifest system

(ii) Precautions during Transportation

The handlers must be trained during loading and unloading of waste. Engine must be stopped with no smoke no alcohol or no drug consumption by driver. The containers should be handled gently with care. There should be proper packaging to prevent leakage. The main considerations are the proper storage. The emergency plan and personnel training is obligatory.

16.7 TREATMENT OF HAZARDOUS WASTE

Waste is detoxified by the physical chemical or biological treatment methods. Effective and economical methods are being developed. US-RCRA *i.e.*, resource conservation and recovery act stipulates minimum treatment before its disposal. The methods for treatment are more or less identical as used for the treatment of waste water. Thermal treatment and pyrolysis is last mode of treatment. Nowadays waste stabilisation and solidification technique is getting popular. By sorption stabilisation and solidification is possible. Free liquid is removed. Soil, flyash, klin dust are used as the sorbent. The lime flyash process involves use of hydrated lime with diatomoceous earth for solidification. This is cheap method. Thermoplastic microencapsulation is also good technique which involves drying and dispersion of waste through heated plastic matter. It is used for disposal of nuclear waste. But it needs mixing equipment. A jacketing system is used to contain toxic waste in drums. This process involves concentration followed by detoxification.

(i) Concentration Method

The main idea is to reduce the volume before detoxification. This is physical form of treatment to remove contamination, dewatering and polishing. The precipitation method is used to decontaminate heavy toxic metals by hydrolysis with lime or sodium hydroxide at pH 10.0. In sedimentation process particles are removed from liquid waste, when heavy materials settles down at the bottom of container by flocculations. It is useful for segeration of solid but not for emulsified oils. It is then followed by filtration. Evaporation is used to concentrate heavy metal salts. Other methods include ion-exchange, reverse osmosis and solvent extraction. For metal finishing ion-exchange concentration is best. Reverse osmosis and dialysis are used for desalting of sea water with semipermeable membrane. Solvent extraction is best for site remediation with fixed facility system. The activated carbon is used as adsorbent for concentrating organic waste.

(ii) Detoxification

This process largely involves oxidation either by chemical or biological means. Biodegradation is done on site, with microorganisms and bacteria (of sewage treatment by activated sludge). The chemical process involves either oxidation or neutralisation. The conversion of Cr (VI) reduces it to Cr (III). Oxidiation involves increase in oxidation number *e.g.* It is oxidised by O_3, Cl_2, H_2O_2. The neutralisation involves acid/base addition. The process is cheap and simple.

16.8 DISPOSAL OF HAZARDOUS WASTE

(i) Incineration

Incineration and landfilling are two important process of disposal. One should not however increase by incineration air pollution like dispersion of particulate in atmosphere. This is alternative disposal method to landfilling. At high temperature oxidation occurs and destroys structure of organic molecules. Capital cost is high for incineration. Incineration involves generation of heat of combustion by chain reaction or combustion of halogenated organic sulphur, nitrogen or phosphorus compounds. Combustion in a sequence of step is chain reaction. Halogenated hydrocarbons have low heats of combustion and process is complex leading to formation of CO_2, Cl_2 gas while sulphur containing compounds liberate SO_2. The nitrogenous organic waste gives NO-NOx. Phosphoratic compounds liberate P_4O_{10}. The organometallic waste leads to formation of ash. When metal gets volatised, rotary klin and liquid injection incinerators are used.

The multiple hearth furnace is used as the incinerator. It is used for the incineration of sludge and hazardous waste containing the metals. Fluidised bed incinerator is used to burn sludge, while catalytic incinerators are used primarily for burning of dilute combustible waste in gas stream. The incineration and detoxification is possible for hazardous waste. Depending upon the kind of the incinerator for organics, acidic, oily halogenated compounds; pesticide, PCB and pathological waste particular type of incinerator is used, but care should be taken to see that there is no air pollution.

(ii) Landfilling Process

The main mode of land disposal technology is landfilling, surface impoundments and injection well. The landfilling is least expensive but should not contaminate soil. For instance PCB, cyanide, halogenated organic compounds and solvents with pH less than 2.0 are used for landfilling. Leachates are collected and analysed. In Europe due to paucity of disposal site, incinerators are favoured. Certain sites accept arduous hazardous waste for disposal. Special sites are needed for disposal of asbestos waste. The common household or trash use municipal landfills, but it is dangerous process. Ocean dumping is discouraged. Deep well injection involves the pumping of liquid waste into underground porous formations as sand but it must not contaminate drinking water. Atmosphere and outerspace disposal is possible but disposal chimney must be very tall and wind direction and velocity should be good. However, in future years, landfilling of waste will be slowly phased out in order to prevent adverse effect on water quality and air quality. It must be considered very carefully. Land should be in low precipitation region. The fixation and encapsulation method involving use of cement, lime thermoplastic material, organic polymer, glass fixation are different modes. In future space disposal may become popular as like space craft they get attracted to sun under gravity and get ignited to ashes in universe.

16.9 CONCLUSION

We have seen what is meant by hazardous waste and how it is different from toxic waste. After defining hazardous waste, we had classified it into group of hazardous material which are separate from solid waste. In the process of characterisation properties such as flammability corrosiveness, toxicity, reactivity, infective value, irritances caused, bioconcentration, genetic activity were considered as important properties to be examined. There are various sources of hazardous waste. The analysis is of paramount importance. It includes sampling and field analysis. The laboratory analysis is best with sophisticated instruments covering classical methods as well as instrumental methods. The latter included spectral methods, chromatographic separation, electroanalytical technique, nuclear methods and some hyphenated techniques. While transporting hazardous waste international colour code is to be followed and regulations obeyed. The treatment of hazardous waste is most critical. It involves methods for concentration, as well as detoxification. The disposal of hazardous waste involves ignition or landfilling but shortage of space creates problem for landfilling. In America, stringent laws have been made by RCRA and enacted but in India such laws are lacking. Further illiteracy amongst workers specially in transportation industry is very much hindrance in enactment of legislation in our country and to adopt scientific mode of disposal is out of consideration.

ADDITIONAL READING

1. K. Shah, *Basics of Solid and Hazardous Waste Management Technology,* Prentice Hall, USA (2000).
2. W.L. Kuhre, *Practical Management of Chemical and Hazardous Waste,* Prentice Hall, USA (1995).

3. G.W. Dawson, B.W. Mercer, *Hazardous Waste Management,* John Wiley and Co. (1986).
4. C.N. Hass, R.J. Vamos, *Hazardous and Industrial Waste Treatment,* Prentice Hall (1995).
5. D. LaGregar, P.L. Bunckingham, J.C. Evans, *Hazardous Waste Management*, McGraw Hill and Co. (1994).
6. M. Stoepples, Ed *Hazardous Metals in Environment,* Elsevier Publishing House (1992).
7. P.N. Chermisihoff Y.C. Wa, *Hazardous Waste Management Handbook Technology Perception* and *Realities*, Prentice Hall (1994).
8. P.L. Nemerow A. Dasgupta, *Industrial and Hazardous Waste Treatment*, Van Nostrand Reinhold and Co. (1991).
9. C.A. Wentz, *Hazardous Waste Management,* McGraw Hill (1989).
10. G.F. Lindgern, *Hazardous Waste,* Printice Hall (1990).
11. R.A. Selg, *Hazardous Waste and Disposal,* McGraw Hill (1994).
12. J.H. Exner Ed., *Detoxification of Hazardous Waste*, Annarbor (1988).
13. S.M. Khopkar, *Environmental Pollution Analysis.* Second Edition, New Age International (P) Ltd., Publishers (2012).

17

Biomedical Waste

17.1 INTRODUCTION

The problem of management of infectious biomedical waste is complex. There are few regulations pertaining to disposal of hospital waste in our country. At many hospitals waste is not at even characterised. The transportation in India is done half hazardly with no concern for health. There are no defined guidelines for its disposal. The question of disinfection is totally neglected and conventional disposal methods are resorted. No priority is given for the minimisation of this waste. No concern is shown for occupational safety and training the manpower. As the medical science is advancing the problem of infectious hospital waste is attaining alarming dimensions. In view of this a detail study of the important aspects of waste are covered in this chapter. The hazardous, medical, solid waste all belong to category of solid waste, but the solid waste is assumed to be harmless in comparison with the hazardous or medical waste. The occupational risk are recognised as there are serious hazards of infections due to medical waste. Let us first try to know the classification and recycling waste and then dispose it off. Hyperdermic syringes and needle itselves are great risk for handlers. Lifetime of infection waste is very long. Natorious anthrax discovered after September 11, 2001 holocast in USA remains alive in soil for several years. The several beaches of sea in America were flooded with medical waste during low ebb. It created panic and lead to enactment of rigorous legislatures. There are several objectives for this waste management. The purpose is to reduce risk and liability, control costs, plan for the future and declare instrumental commitment for protection of human life. The emergency or contingent plans are very important. In 1998 India central government has passed legislation on handling and disposal of medical waste.

17.2 CHARACTERISATION OF BIOMEDICAL WASTE

Infectious waste is one which is capable of producing infectious and contagious diseases; through skin, eyes, wounds, mucuous membrane or by inhalation and ingestion in human body. It is very difficult to exactly identify infectious medical waste from the bulk of solid waste. The microbiological laboratory waste, pathology laboratory waste, blood products, and sharps are considered as infectious waste. The surgical or dialysis unit waste, and discarded contaminated instruments also are medical waste. We classify them into several groups.

(i) Human Blood

It is infectious, as it bears blood borne diseases *e.g.*, HIV, AIDS or hepatitis-B all are serious diseases. The blood soaked bandage is also hazardous. Such material must be steam sterilised before disposal.

(ii) Culture and Stocks Agents

They have infectious microorganisms. The culture must be treated before its disposal. Infectious agent should be characterised.

(iii) Pathological Waste

It coverns body tissue resulting out of surgery. The large body parts must be incinerated or grounded after sterlisation.

(iv) Contaminated Sharps

This cover injection needle, syringes, scapel blades, disposable pipettes, capillaries, slides of microscope and broken pieces of glass, which injure person and causes wound and is contaminated hence should be stored separately. We should presume all sharps are contaminated and handled very carefully.

(v) Contaminated Laboratory Waste

It includes disposable appliances *e.g.*, culture containers, swabs, pipettes, diagnostic tools and protective equipment. All such material must be sterilised and property treated before reuse. It includes contaminated waste from patient care *e.g.*, blood, body fluids, culture and sharps. Diaper, bedpans, cathetors, drainstubes, wet dressings are harmful. The guideline for classification in three groups is first those, which are noninfectious, second those which are centered infectious and third which are sometimes hazardous.

(vi) Discarded Biological Wastes

It includes vaccines. The waste is treated by heat sterilisation and by chemical disinfection.

(vii) Contamined Instruments, Bedding Setts

Unservicable instruments should be handled with precaution. Gloves, masks aprons, labcoats are nowadays disposable and should be immediately discarded.

17.3 TRANSPORTATION OF BIOMEDICAL WASTE

If the handling is not properly done it would lead to contamination of disease to handler. The risk is involved in handling storage and transport. Sharps cause great harm. The pathogens may be unknowingly inhaled. To avoid these harms, waste must be packed, without any leak or spillage, using personal protection devices with minimum handling with no exposure to persons.

(i) Containers

Varying containers for sharps, solids or liquids are employed. The material is puncture resistance, hole proof, impervious, rigid with proper marking. The rigid container is easily stacked before processing. Solid waste is filled in plastic bags, which is impervious and should have right marking. Plastic bag should be 1.5 to 3 mm thick. It should never be overloaded. Liquid waste is preferably stored in glass bottles. For such waste incineration is difficult and it is a new problem of disposal.

(ii) Handling

It should be to minimum extent possible. Mobile carts are used for transportation to treatment site. These carts should be periodically cleaned and should be transported on definite routes. After generation of waste storage should not be for long duration, as immediate treatment must be carried out. It should be securely closed, kept in fixed area, with no easy access and with proper marking. The preliminary treatment involves incineration or steam sterilisation. The containers are directly burried along with waste without emptying them. The big sterilisers for sterilisation are used. The container is compatible with the treatment process. The permeable plastic had to be used only when steam sterilisation is complete.

(iii) Transport to Offsite

The risk of exposure during loading and unloading must be minimised. A double container is preferably used. The spillage should be negligible, the container must withstand transport risk and rough handling till disposal site.

17.4 TREATMENT OF BIOMEDICAL WASTE

The place of treatment, onsite or offsite treatment and different treatment is carefully decided. Onsite treatment means processing in the premises of the hospital. Onsite treatment is good as it gives complete control of waste. Offsite treatment is mostly common as centralised treatment plant. The steam sterilisation incineration *i.e.*, thermal inactivation, chemical treatment or irradiation by radioactive rays are few options for treatment. While choosing the mode, regulatory norms, ease of operation, availability of skilled operators, waste separation or load standardisation is carefully considered. Other aspect include consequence of treatment, volume reduction, exposure to occupational hazards, environmental impact and economic considerations. The waste water after treatment and before disposal should not cause trouble. The process of treatment must be reliable and trust worthy process (Table 17.1).

17.5 DISINFECTION OF MEDICAL WASTE

The most common mode of disinfection is the "sterilisation". High temperature kills pathogen during sterilisation. This is better than dry heat sterilisation. We must always use saturated steam which is water vapour in gas liquid phase boundary

Table 17.1 Camparison of various methods of treatment

S.No.	*Parameter*	*Sterilisation*	*Incineration*	*Chemical processing*
1.	Treatment effect	No change	Ashes	Shredded and ground
2.	Volume change	1/3 reduced	4/5 reduced	4/3 reduced
3.	Hazard	Low	Medium	Medium
4.	Side benefits	None	Energy	Effluent use
5.	Application	All	All	Most of waste
6.	Kind of operator	Trained	Skilled	Trained person work
7.	Standardisation	Necessary	Not required	Sometimes needed
8.	Site on/off	Both	Both	Both
9.	Kind of test	Simple	Complex	Specialised
10.	Separation	Preferable	Not necessary	May need
11.	Release to air	Low risk	High risk	Low risk
12.	Let off to water residue consider	Small risk Landfilling	Small risk Landfill (depends)	Good risk Effluence to sewers
13.	Cost	Low	High	Moderate
14.	Regulation govt.	Applicable	Record purpose	Not applicable

when water is very slowly heated beyond its boiling point. Superheated steam is useless for sterilisation. Steam at 15 to 30 atmosphere pressure is best. Autoclave is preferred for steam generation. The step in operation includes loading, pre-vacuum control, steam charging, steam sterilisation discharge and final disposal. Most important operation is removal of free air from steriliser. The control of time of exposure and temperature attainable is most important. Many problems like interference in waste heating, or dried steam contact occurs, but appropriate waste containment, alternative conditions and other procedures does mitigate these difficulties. One circumvents these problems by increasing depth of number of vacuum cycles, increasing duration of exposure and also temperature. The condition change as per the quality of waste, steam sterilisation destroys spores. Autoclaving and steam sterilisation are not identical. Autoclave for infectious waste are difficult but operator on training, record keeping and risk evaluation are most important stages of disinfection.

(i) Disposal of the Steam Sterilised Waste

The treated and untreated waste looks similar in appearance. Quality assurance and quality control are of great significance so the temperature is regularly checked. For this times and temperature monitors are installed and they are periodically checked. In steam sterilisation the infectious material is exposed to very high pressure and temperature for prolonged duration. Saturated stream is a powerful sterilising agent. Time and temperature is properly controlled to 116°C as time of 30 mts, is needed while for 138°C time needed is 48 seconds. The superheated steam is not good for the purpose of sterilisation. During operation one must take note of loadings, prevacuum (Table 17.2).

Table 17.2 Time for sterlisation on biomedical waste at various temp.

Temperature °C	*Spore killing (wet steam stir) time (hrs)*	*Spore killing (Dry sterlisation) time (mts)*
140	6.3	180
180	3.0	30
240	0.50	30
280	0.75	45

The steam charging and sterilisation facilitates discharge and disposal. Some factors interfere with time, temperature or direct contact of steam. It includes waste heating problem, no contact with steam, improper use with suitable waste containers pose problem. The excessive weight, low heat capacity, and the conductivity interfere with waste heating. Air must be thoroughly removed. Proper load configuration, and carrier and containment must be controlled. Increasing vacuum cycle, exposure time, high temperature improves the technique. The disposal of stream sterlised waste is a specialised job. Since no visible change on surface appears one really does not know whether sterilisation is complete.

17.6 INCINERATION OF INFECTIOUS WASTE

The incineration is the ideal method for medical waste management but the production of large volume of ash and air pollution is serious problem. PCB or dioxin and furan are generated in atmosphere. Ash contains toxic metals, acids, oxides of nitrogen which are generated on ignition. Carbon dioxide enhances global warming. NIMBY (*i.e.,* not in my backyard) protest from neighbouring locality is expected, though it is best for disposal of tissue, and body parts. A controlled air incinerator works with controlled air flow. The municipal incinerator of solid waste disposal is not used for this job. The incineration is chemical process which needs adequate supply of oxygen, it has good volatilisation and atomisation property, it has good turbulence, and temperature and is operative for definite time. The products of incomplete combustion like PCB, dioxine, furan. PAH is generated in absence of sufficient oxygen gas. The destruction of efficiency of incineration is large. It is not improved by long-time of contact or high temperature. One should watch the burns out and burn down process. High density or low

Table 17.3 Air pollution control of biomedical waste

S.No.	*Method*	*Purpose*	*Process*
1.	Venturi scrubber	Homogeneous mixing	Neutralise acid waste and stack gases
2.	Packed column	Acid gases elimination	Large surface area eliminates gases
3.	Lime sprayers	Acid vapours elimination	Neutrilisation of acid vapours
4.	Baghouse	SPM removed	Filters out SPM in air
5.	ESP	SPM eliminated	Charge is separated from neutral particles

surface area far waste creates problem. Old incineration (1970) fail far behind the stipulated standards for efficient combustion. Plastic wastes are difficult to destroy in incinerators as they liberate hydrochloric acid and other obvinoxous gases.

Various methods are used to control emission of suspended particulate matter and acid from incinerator. Such methods are listed in Table 17.3.

The environmental impact assessment stipulates meteorological parameters must be certainly considered and must be given top priority while selecting the location of an incinerator.

17.7 OTHER METHODS OF TREATMENT

Apart from steam sterilisation and incineration other methods involves thermal/ gas sterilisation, chemical treatment, radioactive irradiation or discharge to sanitary sewer. Thermal sterilisation is dry sterilisation method at 120°C spores are killed in 6 hours while at 180°C they are killed in 30 minutes (Table 17.2). Thus, long-time is necessary. Sharp, syringes and needles are best dry sterilised as they melt at high temperature. Gas sterilisers consist of the use of gas like ethyleneoxide or formaldehyde. However ethyleneoxide is toxic and carcinogenic compound hence it must be carefully used. It attacks rubber and plastics. This gas is inflammable. Formaldehyde is used as sterilising agent *in situ* but it is itself hazardous. Chemical disinfection is used for medical liquid waste treatment *e.g.*, idophon alcohols, glutevaldehyde are used for purpose of disinfection specially of medical instruments or surgical appliances. It is used in the range of 25 to 1500 ppm or 0.2 to 2% dosage. Formaldehyde is used as the preservative for all of them contact time, dose is important for better efficiency. The irridation with radioactive devices is very convenient mode of disinfection; but is very expensive. CO_{60} gives γ-radiation which has high penetration power. Maximum precautions is warranted while irradiating waste and handling the source as well as material.

17.8 DISPOSAL OF TREATED MEDICAL WASTE

As a matter of fact we had already considered disposal of hazardous waste in previous chapter. The treated waste is safe for disposal by any conventional method as it poses no risk, but pathological waste or sharp sometimes need additional treatment. Landfill disposal and sanitary sewers are best mode of disposal. Burial in soil is best. This has universal application. Red plastic bags which are disposal only should be used during transportion. Liquid waste is discharged after treatment into the sanitary sewer system. It should never be disposed of as landfill material.

17.9 WASTE MINIMISATION

In order to avoid the trouble of the treatment and disposal, if it is possible in initial stage to minimise the generation of waste, it would reduce health hazards. This is done by reducing the amount of material used, reducing the amount of waste generated, recycling and reuse of waste if possible, reduction in volume of waste and recovery of energy from it. The occupational and environmental risk is substantially decreased on account of disposable items. The quantum of waste has grown since last decade. At source the separation by generator will reduce quantum of medical waste. This is possible by using specially designed containers for infectious waste. Personal is trained to do source separation. The first act is volume and weight reduction, *e.g.,* by incineration volume is reduced by 70 to 80% leaving behind ash. The dry compactness however is very dangerous process if needles and scaps are not properly segregated.

17.10 MEDICAL WASTE OF UNUSUAL TYPE

The antineoplastic drugs, (mitonyan cyclophosphamide, malphalon, uracil mustard) and various kinds of hazardous chemical waste need a special technique for treatment. The chemical waste includes aromatic hydrocarbons, alcohols, ethers, esters, and some mineral acids and corrosive bases. A special treatment as outlined in chapter on hazardous waste management. Management of the radioactive waste is specialised field by itself. Some wastes have multiple hazards *e.g.,* specialised drugs, chemicals, radioactive waste.

17.11 OCCUPATIONAL SAFETY

We must consider health risk, personal risk, prudent practise for control and reduction in risk. One must ground risk through skin, mucous membrane, inhalation and ingestion in digestive track. Injury may cause while handing containers or during transportion. The risk reduction includes immunization of worker, job training, close watch on exposure and fast medical treatment in community as emergency. Planning is done and is kept contingent planning for emergency. One should avoid spills of infectious material, waste or chemicals, one should be extra careful in handling radioactive waste. The long-term solution is to train staff and waste handlers and ordinary haulers the process of completing essential components be expediated. Offside disposal is always bad (Table 17.4).

Table 17.4 Nature of biomedical waste

S.No.	*Type of waste*	*Special features*
1.	Stocks and culture	Discarded vaccine, cultures of diseases
2.	Pathological waste	Tissue, organs body fluids
3.	Blood and analogous products, liquids	Serum, plasma, other blood components, bags
4.	Sharps-used	Hyperdermic needles, syringes, vials, scalpels
5.	Animal waste	Carcasses, body part
6.	Waste specially isolated	Biological waste, excretion, exudates
7.	Sharps-not used	Needles, suture needles, syringes, scalpel blades

17.12 CONCLUSION

In America number of states have regulation enacted by Environmental Protection Agencies. It provides guidelines in medical waste tracking regulations. Such guideline include consideration of norms as purpose of medical waste tracking (its relationship with health); what kind of waste is to be regulated?

The states in USA having stringent regulations are New Jersy, New York, Rhode island, Connecticut. One considers what is tracking of medical waste? What is scope? (Protection for handling), pretransport requirements. (Packaging, storing, labelling, marking), Requirements per generators (50 lb or more/month waste rules) transport requirements (verticle requirements); treatment plans and disposal (Record keeping).

In India, we do not have stringent requirements for disposal of even solid waste. Maharashtra was the first state in the country to enact regulation for transport of hazardous materials' other state governments are now formulating regulations. No clearcut plan for disposal treatment characterisation of the hazardous waste exist. The chemicals used by multinationals as with petroleum, fertilisers, polymers are available. As all the citizens feel there is the need of controlling infectious medical waste specially in metropolitan cities, Mumbai is leading. In any case and we are optimistic as next few decades we will have contingent plans for the regulation of not only solid or hazardous waste but also for biomedical waste. India is one of the few countries which is enormously aware of environmental problems in the world amongst developing countries.

ADDITIONAL READING

1. P.A. Reinhardt, J.G. Gordon, *Infectious and Medical Waste Management,* Lewis Publishers (1991).
2. K.L Shah, *Basics of Solid and Hazardous Waste Management Technology*, Prentice Hall, New Jersey (2000).
3. J.J. Perkins (Ed), *Principles and Methods of Sterilisation in Health Science,* 2nd Ed., Spring Field. Illinois (1983).
4. C.R. Brunnor, *Incineration System: Selection and Design,* Van Nostrand Reinhold and Co. (1984).
5. S.S. Block Ed., *Disinfection, Sterilisation and Preservation,* 3rd Ed., Philadelphia and Febiger (1983).
6. B.A. Goldmon, J.A. Hulme, C. Johnson, *Hazardous Waste Management Reducing the Risk.* Island Press, Wastington (1986).
7. J.H. Exner Ed., *Detoxification of Hazardous Waste,* Ann Arbor (1988).
8. WHO, *Health Hazardous of Human Environment* (1973).
9. C.N. Hoas, R.J. Vamos, *Hazardous and Industrial Waste and Treatment,* Prentice Hall Pub., New York (1995).
10. S.T. Kolaczkowski, B.D. Critendon, *Management of Hazardous and Toxic Waste in Process Industry,* Elesvier Pub. House (1987).
11. S.M. Khopkar, *Environmental Pollution Analysis,* Second Edition. New Age International (P) Ltd., Publishers (2012).

18 Biomonitoring of an Environment

18.1 INTRODUCTION

Of the various methods which were considered in the study of environmental pollution methodology the theme of monitoring is most important. This is because in absence of such data obtained through monitoring it is not possible to adopt measures for the control of pollution. In the process of environmental monitoring, classical methods such as volumetric or gravimetric methods of analysis (*e.g.* dissolved oxygen by the Winkler's method or evaluation of total suspended solid deposits by lead candle method) are used with great success. Subsequently with progress in instrumental methods of analysis these are extensively used such as chromatography and spectral methods of analysis. Only in the limited cases resort is taken to radioanalytical methods and the thermal methods for the quantitative analysis.

However, with advent of time the progress in bioscience and bioengineering promoted to use not only of conventional instrumental methods of analysis but also biomonitoring techniques. These are used with equal ease and have guaranteed success. Such biomonitoring methods include the use of the plants for bio-indication, airborne heavy metals for study of soil contamination. The use of animals for biomonitoring, such analysis involved the use of blood, nails, breast milk and small as well as the large vertebrates and invertebrates, where one has to carefully select cytogenetic parameters for monitoring, as in the aquatic environment microbes are extensively used for monitoring.

In this chapter, we would consider the monitoring of environment with plants, animals, microbes. The basic requirement in such monitoring is need of easily availability of organism, long lifetime, tolerance of organism to the pollutants, easy method of sampling with minimum cost. The most vital parameters is the reproducibility of results specially for air pollution monitoring where here there is greater deviation due to variation of meteorological parameters as due to change in wind direction and wind velocity reproducibility is great problem.

(i) Biomonitoring with Plants

The plants are not only useful for bioindication but also for ascertaining the concentration of the pollutant. Biomonitoring involves use of sensor to ascertain the presence of the pollutant but it also involves measurements leading to the quantitative analysis *e.g.* the transplanted samples of mosses and lichens proved to be most useful in several investigations for biomonitoring with plants.

(ii) Plant as Material of Choice

All plants cannot be used for monitoring. Such plants should first satisfy certain basic requirements *viz.* while responding to the pollutant, one must carefully observe the changes in growth of flowers, morphology and productivity. The plants should grow easily and must not be itself be affected by pest and pathogens. One needs to expose indicator plants to pollutant to note and guard against adverse effect of other biotics such as pathogens, viruses, fungi and bacteria like insect, pest, frost. The best plant will be the one which is sensitive only to one polluting material. One needs standardisation of indicator or of accumulator plants. The criteria to be followed for standardisation includes several factors, such as selection of genetically homogeneous seeds/plants; their uniform growth conditions in the laboratory. Now with similar conditions of soil and water, which is capable of differentiating the climatic changes, act only during vegetation interval, absence of any local contamination, knowledge of the meteorological factors with special reference to air pollution and finally the effect must be specific or representative of effects on other plants.

The methods show changes in distribution pattern, as well as in their growth and morphology with the variation in physiology and biochemistry of the plant. In showing accumulation of the pollutant under examination in the body of plants. The environment should be stress resistant. A biological stress is defined as "any factor having potentially injurious strain, or shift in metabolism". One can study root, leaf, modules and seed output, morpho-anatomical effect and metabolism of the plant.

Before we undertake discussion on biomonitoring by plants. Let us consider how plant materials themselves are analysed in such analysis.

(iii) Plant Analysis

The main operations involved in analysis of plants includes preparation, dissolution of the sample; separation; and finally the determination. The sample plant must be fresh and not old with dead cells. One can collect them and wash, dry and finally grind sample to suitable size (0.2–1 gm). For analysis of silica dry ashing is must while for analysis of sulphur, cyanide and fluoride each time new portion of plant is used. The heating is done in the muffle furnace (525° C) and cooled mass is dissolved in mixture of HCl and HNO_3 *i.e.*, aquariga. Analysis of phosphorus needs separate treatment; however process of wet digestion is more reliable and very easy. The glass beads are added to avoid bumping. The cooled mass is used for subsequent inorganic analysis. One uses flame photometry AAS or polarography for the analysis of metal ions. The analysis of iodine or silicon needs special treatment procedure. One uses autclave while analyzing silicon. The phosphorous is analyzed by colorimetrically as its complex with vanado molybdophosphoric acid at 450 nm. Zinc, lead, cadmium, iron, copper, boron are analysed by AAS while calcium, potassium are analysed by flame emission spectroscopy. There is special method for analysis of "Bryophytes". The 'Lichens' are used for monitoring air pollution. They accumulate metals neutron activation analysis technique is used for the analysis of 'Lichens'.

(iv) Pollutants—Plants Interaction

The effect is studied with special reference to chlorophyll, protein, phenol, carbohydrate analysis. The growth, physiological and biochemical parameters are studied. The leaf area metre is used to measure area on leaf. Some plants show the morphological and anatomical variations. Ascorbic acid (vitamin-C) is always present in plants. 2,6 dichlorophenol indophenol (DCPIP) is converted to coloress sample in biochemical analysis. Chlorophyll contents is measured spectrophotometrically at 645, 663 and 652 nm. The sample is prepared in 80% acetone. One rarely analyses carotenoid contents of the plants. It is done by measuring acetone extract at 480 or 510 nm by spectrophotometer.

The soluble leaf-proteins contents is also easily analysed; colorimetrically with Coomassie brilliant blue. G-250 in the presence of phosphate buffer. The absorbance of the coloured complex is measured at 595 nm with folin–ciocaltean reagent, phenol is estimated as total phenol, it is measured at 650 nm after proper preconditioning. There are special procedures for the analysis of the enzymes with phosphate buffer and ascorbic acid one can measure its contents (*i.e.* enzyme) by colorimetry at 265 nm. For control, boiled enzyme extracts are used. The catalase catalyzes hydrogen peroxide breakdown to water in the presence of the hydrogen donor. The residual peroxide is measured spectrophotometrically. The special 4,1,6 Glucose 6-phosphate dehydrogenase is an important enzyme of oxidative pentose phosphate pathways. The nitrate reductase is responsible to reduce NO_3^- to NO_2^-. It is incubated in potassium nitrate and amount of nitrite formed is measured. One uses the NEDH (*i.e.* 2 naphylene diamine hydrochloride for dizotisation reaction.) The absorbance is measured at 570 nm against a reagent blank by spectrophotometer. The next malate dehydrogenase is estimated colorimetrically in citric acid converting it to oxaloacetate. A change in absorbance at 340 nm is measured. Succinate dehydrogenase in another enzyme. It is reacted with 2,6 DCPIP under controlled conditions and then measured colorimetrically at 600 nm. Apart from, urease, hydrolases we have important enzymes such as Amylase and invertase. The last one promotes breaking of sucrose in plants one can measure the formation of reducing sugars by its action on sucrose. Finally the protease is an endopeptidases and amino and carboxy peptidase.

As regards effect of UV radiations on plants one studies the different stages of reaction undergoing in plants. There is change in growth chlorophyll content, leaf anatomy. By deposition of pollutants the membrane permeability gets adversely affected. The permeability of membrane is analysed by determining concentration of K^+ ions in the leachate.

One also measures metal tolerance and air pollution tolerance index (APTI) easily. The interspecific and interaspecific variation in metal tolerance is measured. The sequential and parallel methods are used but latter mode is most popular. Zinc, cadmium are thus tested and tolerance index (TI) is calculated.

(v) Plants for Monitoring Air Polluting Elements

Some plants are so sensitive that they instantaneously show changes by the action of air pollutants. Some pollutants are deposited on leaves and stem which in turn is directly analysed. The choice of the plant depends upon the showing high occurrences in polluted sites; they have the significant species in pollution location; are characteristics for the species which are having capacity for good accumulation of pollutants. The process of deposition of pollutant is dependent upon plant and soil surface, particle size, wind velocity and overall size of the receptor. The nature of external walls of the epidermal cells, kind of cuticle, structure of hair; kind of epicuticular wàves etc. Rough surface is preferable, wet digestion is followed AAS determination is common route of characterisation. Acids used are nitric, sulphuric and perchloric acids in the different ratios. By knowing the difference between pre and post exposure it throws light on the amount of element deposited. Only limitation is to know time of exposure. ICP-AES and stripping voltammetry is used.

(vi) Plants for Soil Monitoring

The accumulation of soil containing metal is easily analysed by knowing upper critical concentration of elements fungi, lichens, bryophytes and epiphytes plant is used for biomonitoring, Cadmium is detected by Spanish moss. Sulphur dioxide, hydrofluoric acid and heavy metals are analyzed with the help of bryphytes and lichens. One prefers to analyze number of species, degree of cover, frequency of deposition, growth pattern, chlorophyll contents, variation in colour, fertility and reproduction, injury if any and the accumulation. These plants absorb heavy metals specially in the process of air pollution monitoring.

18.2 BIOMONITORING BY ANIMALS

The animals from terrestrial and aquatic environment are used as pollution indicator on account of their longer contact with pollutants. We have sensitive anthropogenic as well as one showing significant reaction in life cycle of animal.

(i) Selection of Animals

The animal must have intense metabolism, long life cycle, good growth (specially for microorganism) possess capacity to attach, good long term contact, ease of sample collection, with very good sensitivity, and with good geometry or size. By and large we have very limited choice from mammals, orthopods, earthworms, wood lice, cricket spiders. The rodents are most useful. Those organisms occupying pore of soil are good. Radionuclides are best characterised by earthworms.

(ii) Bioindication Methods with Animals

One prefers to analyse blood, hair, nails, faeces, breast milk, body component and bones. The blood is intravenously drawn by syringe. Heparin is added as anticoagulant. The small portion (5 ml) is digested in mineral acids, on dry-ashing. AAS is used for quantitative analysis. Hair acts as the minor outlet for trace elements in living being. It is good for metal pollutant analysis. The hair accumulates trace metals very rapidly. Prof Jervis (1966) from waterloo university in Canada found out that the sites of accumulation of eighteen elements in human hair so effective that they are used like finger prints in forensic sciences. The human hair is most reliable species for identifying polluting elements.

The chronic exposure is immediately indicated by nails and hair. The sample after usual dissolution process are analysed by AAS, or ICP-AES. The cleaning hair with 3% water-ethanol is most important step in analysis. Faeces is analysed in similar fashion as hair on nails. Lead, cadmium are usually accumulated in milk. They are digested with strong oxidizing mineral acids such as nitric and prechloric acid and then analysed as usual after dry ashing. The bones accumulates large portions of the pollutants like lead. It accumulates for sufficiently long time. AAS or anodic stripping voltammetry is used for the quantitative analysis metal pollutants.

18.3 BIOINDICATION WITH BIOCHEMICAL TECHNIQUES

Several biochemical methods have been used for qualitative detection of pollutants, or to know biochemical changes in the blood or in the central nervous system. At low concentration insecticides lower the cholinesterase activity. With phosphate buffer, acetyl thiochloline iodine and 5,5′ dithiobis 2-nitrobenzoic acid is used for color development to be followed by spectrophotometric analysis. In blood plasma analysis, blood sugar kectacholamine level is ascertained. The coloured complex formed with the buffer solution of (pH ~ 7.0) with deproteinized serum with o-diansidine. The absorbance is then measured at 450 nm with spectrophotometer. The fluorescence technique analyses adrenaline and noractenaline. The tissue damage in environment is identified with LDH enzymes and transaminase. The latter are located in cytoplasm and mitochondria. Necrosis enhances the presence of enzymes, in blood leading to rise in blood transaminase. Several cytogenetic factors have been summarized for the purpose of monitoring. It includes karyotyping, chromosomal abbreviations, fragment and bridge formation and show sister chromatid exchanges. It is done by visual comparison with standard sample. The damage caused by pollution is discovered by bridges and fragmentation.

18.4 BIOMONITORING WITH MICROBES

The sudden or periodic changes in microorganisms is studied *e.g.*, fish mortality. An early warning of pollution is given by morphological, physiological and genetic characteristics. They are equally effective in fluctuating environment. Ecological indices are also obtained from microorganism on account of small size they are uniformly distributed. Even the extent or level of pollution caused is measured by microorganism *e.g.*, the enumeration of pathogen in the sewage is direct measure of biological pollution. The aquatic system can be monitored by microorganism. The number of coliform group bacterias is used to assess range of pollution by excreta. E-coli is also counted. One needs to count MPN to get authentic information.

18.5 CONCLUSION

The development in biomonitoring is of recent origin. Most of the environmentalists depend upon instrumental methods involving chromatography, spectroscopy and electroanalytical techniques. In proportion to these thermal and radioanalytical methods are rarely used.

Within biosciences, biomonitoring techniques came in to the existence in last two decades. It involved use of plants, animals, microorganism. The monitoring with plants is most popular. In biomonitoring techniques variety of plants are used for the purpose of detection. The morphology and physiology of plant must be noted. Plant themselves should not get affected by an environmental pollutant. The changes in flowering, productivity and morphology decides how specific is plant indicator. Lichen with the exception are analysed by the neutron activation analysis. It is useful for air pollution and soil contents monitoring.

The biomonitoring also involves use of animals or living organism. The earthworm, wood lice, orthopads, spiders; are used for detection and determination. Trace elements in aquatic environment are monitored by living organisms *e.g.* fish mortality is early warning of pollution. One measures the microorganism like Coliforms, E-coli count, to know effect of pollutants on them. The pathogens, viruses is also counted in terms of MPN count.

It will be seen that whatever efficiency is claimed in biomonitoring by plants, microorganism, ultimately final characterisation involves use of physiochemical instruments such as spectrophotometer, fluorimeter or anodic stripping voltammetry. In specific cases even the much neglected neutron activation analysis provides reliable method. By interaction of chemical and biosciences, we expect to witness tremendous growth in biomonitoring technology in future years to come.

ADDITIONAL READING

1. N.C. Aery, *Manual of Environmental Analysis*, Ane Books Ltd., New Delhi, India (2010).
2. APHA, *Standard Method for the Examination of Water and Waste Water*, 18th Edition Washington DC (2000).
3. T.A. Mansfield, Ed. *Effects of Air Pollutants on Plants*, Cambridge University Press UK, p. 87 (1976).
4. L.W. Canter, *Environmental Impact Assessment*, 2nd Ed., McGraw Hill Book Co. (1996).
5. A. Chat, T.M. Roberb, R.E. Jervis, *Scalp Hair as a Monitor of Community Exposure to Lead*, Arch Envir Health **32**, 226 (1977).

6. M.H. Martin, P.J. Coughtrey, *Biological Monitoring of Heavy Metal Pollution, Land and Air*, Applied Sci pub. London (1982).
7. D. Worth, M. Liberman, P. Kaselekas, G. Clarun, *Lead in Drinking Water Environmental Lead*, Academic (1981).
8. M. Csuros, C. Csuros, *Microbiological Examination of Water and Waste Water,* Lewis Publishers (1999).
9. A. Chabt, *et al.*, *Hair Analysis*, Springer Verlag (1998).
10. S.M. Khopkar, *Environmental Pollution Analysis*, Second edition, New International (P) Ltd. Publishers (2012).

19 Environment and Noise

19.1 INTRODUCTION

We have already considered the pollution of atmosphere, and water due to the industrial products. These problems are created by the activities of man in the environment. We have laws and regulations to control all kinds of pollution. In the list of major pollutants we have to add one more type called '*Noise Pollution*', a pollution which is caused by the activity of man in home as well as in industries or in work place. Unfortunately with laws dealing for controlling of air or water pollution, for which the strict legislations to arrest the noise pollution is lacking. The air and water pollution acts are enacted early in sixty's. The comprehensive environmental protection bill (1986) includes noise pollution. As such few states in India like Bihar, Madhya Pradesh or Uttar Pradesh have some legislation covering use of loudspeakers or music in night. However, these are under the perview of police department, who directly do not control the playing of amplified sound like loudspeakers or sound in musical concerts but they restrict the problem to night hours from 10 pm to 6 am. Many festivals are in India. We must consider noise level produced in festivals. The people are not happy unless they celebrate festivals with fan fare with generation of loud noise. It is interesting to examine Table 19.1 listing noise generated by various festivals in India. Such noise is measured in terms of decibel units (dB).

Table 19.1 Festivals and noise in India

Festival	*Level dBA*	*Festival*	*Level dBA*
Diwali	73–114	New year's day	70–80
Dusshera	85–100	Ram Leela	78–85
Ganesh Puja	89–102	Music conference	86–96
Durga Puja	88–95	Wedding Ceremony	92–99
Id festival	93–101	Kumbha Mela	80–90
X-mas	70–90	Durga Puja	80–95

We consider in Table 19.2 the level of noise pollution created during festivals in New Delhi.

Table 19.2 Noise pollution in Delhi in festivals

S. No.	Place of origin	Remarks	1998 level (I)	2002 level (II)	2004 level (III)	Prescribed standards limit
1.	Connaught Place	Exceeding limit	79	65	74	65
2.	India Gate	Excess of stand level	69	34	69	50
3.	AIMS, Ansari Nagar	Twenty times higher	72	35	78	55
4.	Raja Garden	Twenty times excess	76	78	80	55
5.	Income Tax Office	Almost near standard	77	77	77	65
6.	Kamala Nagar	Excess over standard	75	42	78	55
7.	Patel Nagar	Too low in 2002	74	22	73	65
8.	Arjun Nagar	Very high in 1998 and 2004	80	38	81	55
9.	Lajpat Nagar	Too low in 1998 and 2002	50	49	89	55
10.	Mayur Vihar	Very much above standard	79	46	81	55
11.	Friends Campus	Near normal at standard	60	47	90	55
12.	Model Town	Excessive all the years	80	80	88	55

Standard level followed by S.No. 9 and S.No. 11 are lowest.

In Table 19.1, we note that the extent of noise created during various festivals in India while Table 19.2 gives a typical noise of level for various parts of city of New Delhi during years 1998 to 2004. There is substantial rise of noise in 4–6 years in New Delhi and it is far way from prescribed standards of the noise. The Friends Campus (S.No. 11) has highest noise pollution level of 90 dB while India Gate (S.No. 2) is relatively free from harsh noise where existing level is ~ 69 which is much above prescribed standard of 50 dB. The different nagars like Kamala, Patel, Arjun, Lajpat have noise levels ranging from 70–89 dB. This show that they are all noisy dwellings. In all these cases the prescribed standards fixed by Municipal corporation is much lower and is not at all followed.

Table 19.3 Level in metropolitan towns

S.No.	City	Residential area	Commercial area	Industrial area	Average level	Remarks
1.	Alwar	56	80	62	55	Low
2.	Bengluru	67	76	78	67	Satisfactory
3.	Mumbai	70	75	76	66	Unavoidable
4.	Kolkata	79	82	78	79	Acceptable
5.	Hydrabad	65	76	70	70	Little high
6.	Jaipur	75	78	78	77	Reasonable
7.	Jodhpur	68	76	67	71	Slightly high
8.	Kota	54	68	53	63	High level
9.	Chennai	60	78	71	63	Little high

Apart from noise levels in capital of India, namely New Delhi, it is interesting to examine level of noise in metropolitan cities in India (see Table 19.3) which is at alarming levels).

The Table 19.3 gives status of existing noise level in Indian cities. Although metropolitan cities like Mumbai, Bengluru, Hyderabad, Chennai and Kolkata show very high level of noise which is ranging from 65–80 dB on the average. Amongst these metropolitan cities Kolkata has highest level of noise viz 79dB. (S.No. 4)

It will be also interesting to note which town has relatively quiter town in India? Always (Rajasthan) is best place with tolerable level of 55 dB. Then Jaipur, Jodhpur, Kota (S.No. 6, 7, 8) are certainly noisy cities with level of 70–60 dB on average.

We have considered in Table 19.3 level of noise in important cities in India. In all these cities sited industrial noise is highest in comparison to residential or commercial places. The last column in fact gives average of all the noise in various location (Table 19.3) with remarks on the status of average level.

One observation is pertinent here. It is not only in the developing countries like India noise levels are high but also well developed cities all over the world are equally noise as indicated by Table 19.4 on noise levels in world.

Table 19.4 Noise pollution all over the world

S.No.	*City*	*Country*	*Level*	*S.No.*	*City*	*Country*	*Level*
1.	Gräz	Austria	90–120	12.	Frankfurt	Germany	110–170
2.	Amsterdam	Netherland	90–170	13.	London	England	100–160
3.	Athens	Greece	80–120	14.	New Delhi	India	100–160
4.	Bonn	Germany	80–115	15.	New York	America	100–120
5.	Brussels	Belgium	100–150	16.	Paris	France	80-160
6.	Copenhagen	Denmark	120–160	17.	Washington (DC)	America	90–110
7.	Chicago	America	90–95	18.	Stockhome	Sweden	96–100
8.	Paris	France	80–160	19.	Philadelphia	America	98–110
9.	Berlin	Germany	86–110	20.	Hamburg	Germany	80–90
10.	Vienna	Austria	90–120	21.	Toranto	Canada	85–110
11.	Lisbon	Portugal	85–110				

In earlier sections we have considered noise levels in festivals, and also typical noise level in various parts of the city of New Delhi and then we have taken at random some important cities or towns in world. At this stage it is worth while to examine the level of the noise in well known cities in the world (See Table 19.4). In Europe starting from Belgium, Denmark, Franfürt, all have very high levels of noise exceeding 100 dB. While few cities in world like Lisbon, Paris, Hamburg and Toranto have relatively less noise but not ideal level ranging to the lowest level of 80 dB. Copenhagen in Denmark is worst cities with level around 120-160 dB; New Delhi comes next with measured level of 100-160 dB. On an average the noise level spreads from 80–160 dB and certainly it is not conducive for human health for leading comfortable living.

We note that not a single festival is having noise level less than 70 dB. Apart from festivals, our day-to-day activity generates lot of noise. In spite of having made great strides with discovery of robots and computers. Table 19.5 list noise generated by various kinds of domestic home appliances.

Table 19.5 Noise due domestic home appliances

Appliances	*Level dB*	*Appliances*	*Level dB*
Food blender (small)	80	Air conditioner	70
Food mixer	80	Cloth drier	70
Dish washer	75	Shaver	70
Washing machine	70	Table fan	65
Hair dyer	70	Refrigerator	50
Vacuum cleaner	80	Water cooler	75
Can opener	75	Ceiling fan	70
Food disposer	90	Mixer blender (large)	90

From Table 19.5, it will be seen that simple home appliance have sound level not less than 65 dB, the average being 75 to 80 dB. At this stage it is worthwhile to examine not only festivals or home appliances which create noise but also day-to-day activity generating what is called as the occupational noise as shown in Table 19.6.

Table 19.6 Occupational noise levels

Source	*Level dB*	*Source*	*Level dB*
Normal talking	60	Assembly	40
Alarm clock	85	Bedroom	15
Lawn mover	103	Office	70
Pneumatic chipper	135	Truck traffic	100
Jazz music	100	Aeroplanes	125
Rustling of trees	20	Whisper	25
Garden	20	Audibility and tolerance limit	0
Library	30	Threshold pain	140

19.2 WHAT IS NOISE?

Let us consider definition of noise. Sound is a form of energy which requires material medium for propagation. Sound propagates through solids and liquids but not through vacuum. Any kind of vibration is producing sound. In loudspeaker, the diaphragm moves forward and backward to generate sound, wherein on account of compression, gas molecules move back and forth progressively. These oscillating molecules with definite frequency are responsible for creating sound pressure. If the pressure varies regularly and repeatedly, then time between successive high and low pressure points is called as the "*period*". The frequency is the reciprocal of period. Sound is defined as the energy in the frequency range of 0.02 to 20 kHz or 20 to 20,000 Hz. Thus, hertz is the unit of frequency representing cycles per second which has the typical range of hearing of human ears. The lowest frequency which is audible is 20 Hz, while the highest audible frequency is 12,000 Hz. This region is called "*frequency band*". It defines a range of frequencies between the specified or implied limits. The intensity of sound is determined with precision and is related to the quantum of sound energy received per second from the source.

There are practical difficulties in measuring the intensity, but the variation in pressure is easily measured.

The sounds vary in pitch, which is defined as the relative variations of sounds. Pitch is determined by the frequency of sound wave—the rapidity with which it vibrates. A high pitched sound with its fast vibration is more penetrating than one with low pitch sound (Fig. 19.1). The intensity of sound is measured in decibels (dB). This scale is devised to measure the smallest difference in sound which is detectable by the human ears. Its gradations moves up not in simple arithmetic progression, but in geometrical progression based on logarithmic scale, *i.e.,* each increase of one dB represents a large change of intensity of sound.

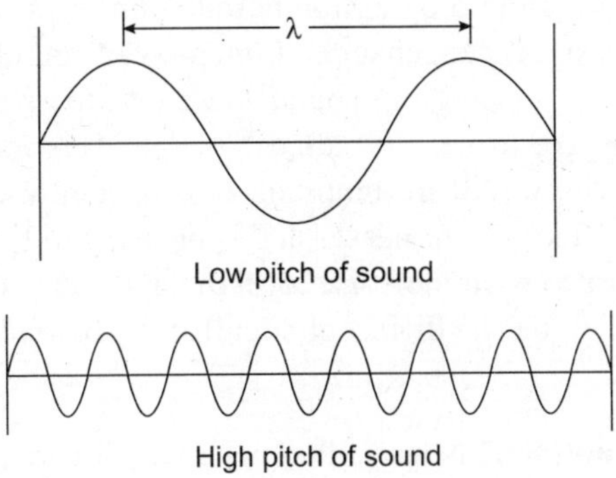

Fig. 19.1 Pitch of sound

19.3 WHAT IS DIFFERENCE BETWEEN SOUND AND NOISE?

The sound requires material medium to propagate. It has been proved experimentally by evacuated bell jar experiments that sound does not travel through vacuum. We observe common phenomenon on rainy days viz., we first see flash of lightening and then we hear loud thunder much latter indicating that the sound travels at much lower speed than light. The sound is a form of energy which is measured in definite units. The unit for measurement of sound is called '*Hertz*'. The environmental sound is in the region of 20 Hz to 20,000 Hz or 20 Hz to 20 kHz. Any kind of sound less than 20 Hz is called as "*Infrasound*". It is not audible. The sound more than 20 kHz or 20,000 Hz which also cannot be heard by us is called as "*Ultrasound*".

When we talk the frequency is around 500 to 2000 Hz while low frequency sound is in region of 20 to 500 Hz. The sound travels through solids and liquids. Any vibrations is capable is producing pressure in form of sound. The change in frequency due to movement of molecules at definite frequency generates sound pressure. If such pressure varies regularly, the time between two successive high and low pressure is called '*period*'. Frequency is reciprocal of period. Sound is defined as energy in frequency range of 0.02 to 20 kHz or 20 to 20,000 Hz lowest audible frequency is 20 Hz while loudest one is 12,000 Hz *i.e.,* 12 kHz. This region is called '*frequency band*'. The intensity of sound is measured in terms of sound energy received per second from source. The so-called intensity level is ten times the logarithm of intensity ratio. It is measured in terms of sound pressure level (SPL) as follows:

Intensity level $= 10 \times \log (P/P_o)$ ...(*i*)

Sound pressure level (SPL) $= 20 \log (P/P_o)$ dBA ...(*ii*)

where P = measured pressure

P_o = is reference pressure (2×10^{-5} Nm^{-2})

The quality of sound is ascertained from what is called as '*pitch*'. It is defined as relative loudness or faintness of sound. A high pitch sound with its rapid vibrations is more penetrating than one at low pitch. On SPL scale therefore gradation moves in multiple progression based upon log scale *i.e.,* each increase of one dB represents significant change of intensity of sound. What we hear from the musical instrument is melodious sound so we love to listen it. On the contrary, whatever we do not like to hear is called "*Noise*". This indicates all unwanted sounds are termed as *noise*. All are annoying and not comfortable while melodious sound has soothing effect on our nerves and is pleasing to listen and one enjoys it in peace. At this stage to examine noise level in day-to-day activities (Table 19.7) as well as level of noise in different localities like residential commercial (Table 19.8).

Table 19.7 Noise pollution in daily life in city

S.No.	*Source*	*Level dB*	*S.No.*	*Source*	*Level dB*
1.	Alarm clock	70–80	18.	Zoological garden	100
2.	City transport	80	19.	Stereophonic sound	117
3.	Heavy truck	90	20.	Pneumatic drill-hammer	120
4.	Motor bike	90	21.	Missile in space	180
5.	Cycle with damper	110	22.	Railway station	70
6.	Aeroplane-jet	100–110	23.	Talk on phone (Landline)	60
7.	Aircraft-small	110–120	24.	Talk on (Mobile) phone	70
8.	Jumbo aeroplane	110–120	25.	Quarell	60–90
9.	Airport	150	26.	Cool conversation	35–40
10.	Train	110	27.	Radio set	40
11.	Tractor	93	28.	Television set	50–60
12.	Cutting saw	82	29.	Soft spoken speech	20
13.	Rockdriller	87	30.	Tree garden	10–15
14.	Compressor	80	31.	Reading library	35
15.	Mixer-grinder	75	32.	Radio stations	20
16.	Cement mixer	75	33.	TV station	30
17.	Printing machines	100	34.	Night road traffic	35

The Table 19.7 gives noise level in due to day Life. The earlier Table 19.6 furnished occupational noise levels ranging from 20 dB for Gardens to 135 to Pneumatic Chipper while Table 19.7 shows noise level for Jet Plane with maximum level of 150 dB on contrary the whisper is just 20 dB. In comparison with bus and bikes the latter produce large noise, under tools compressor is noisy, a person talking on mobile phone generates noise of 70 dB and speaker is mostly unaware of this limit. The library, gardens, music on radio; or station and night traffic are acceptable limits of noise levels.

Table 19.8 Noise pollution in different location

S.No.	*Location*	*Variation during various years*			
		2012 dB	*2011 dB*	*2010 dB*	*2009 dB*
1.	Residential colony	58–74	60–73	62–68	53–83
2.	Commercial plaza	64–83	59–79	58–77	66–106
3.	Road junction	69–80	65–85	64–76	64–96
4.	Silence zone	63–78	55–73	55–73	80–99
5.	Light festival	63–93	62–85	62–85	65–98
6.	Puja or Ganesh festival	63–93	62–85	62–85	60–91

The Table 19.8 illustrates the level of noise pollution in various locations of the city including commercial establishments. The noise level at roadways, silence zones and festivals like Diwali or Ganesh puja festival is displayed (S.No. 6). If we examine result for the year 2012 we note that with the exception of residential premises (S.No. 1) all other locations noise level is in vicinity of 60-90 dB.

Further as we examine levels in different years from 2009 to 2012, one notice that in several places (S.No. 6) it is increasing while at few other locations (S.No. 2, 3, 5 and 6) the level is constant. It is neither decreasing nor increasing. Only at few locations (S.No. 1, 4) the level is substantially going down. Our efforts should be directed towards bringing down the noise to reasonable level of 40-50 dB which is bearable and people can enjoy peaceful life.

19.4 NOISE AND VIBRATIONS

The vibrations play a significant role in generation as well as transmission of noise. The vibrations of transmitter and the radiators lead to the origin of noise. The mechanical vibrations are responsible for the generation of noise. Such vibrations are caused by forces which vary in time. These forces may be rotational, translational, rolling or sliding. They may be associated with either electrical, hydraulic or aerodynamic operations. To reduce the noise one must eliminate these vibrations which are very much at the source. Such vibrating system, has, source, path and a surface. These vibrations is easily eliminated by isolation, adsorption or damping. The sound absorption technique is resorted to eliminate noise from screw machine, punch presses, grinders, riveting or generators in industrial establishment.

The sound barrier is used for damping most of machine type vibrations. The method of damping vibrations is used in machines used for welding, riveting, hopper and conveyor movements. The vibration isolation is resorted to reduce noise. The vibrations are due to grinder, lathes, saws, fans, blowers and printing machines. The vibrations affects comfort of person and cause disorders in the physiological functions of man. The source of oscillations by mechanical energy leads to generate noise. Such vibrations are whole body vibrations or local vibrations. The whole body vibrations are composed of transport vibrations or technical vibrations. These vibrations are transferred to workers hand *e.g.*, rock drill, portable grinder, demolishing hammer. These vibration affects man by ascertaining the root mean velocity and noise level in octave frequency bands. The amplitude of such vibration is measured, at point of contact with human body. Such vibrating forces damage the human tissues. The high frequency vibrations need strong damping. Low-frequency vibrations are transmitted in body or muscles which in turn renders them stiff. Whole body vibrations in rage of 4 to 12 Hz leads to resonance *i.e.*, increase in oscillation amplitude of the human organ or system leading to adverse health effects. Such influences cause malfunctioning of central nervous system. These stresses produces dysfunction of organs and energy loss; or damage of internal organs. Many vibrational diseases are caused leading to pain and numbness of organs. To prevent such adverse effect, the automation or remote control or safe design of tools and use of the personal protective equipment is absolutely essential in industry.

19.5 SOURCES OF NOISE POLLUTION

Let us now examine the source of noise pollution. In Table 19.1, we have identified that various festival in India which are celebrated with noise. While in Table 19.5 we have seen that all home appliances create noise and in Table 19.6 various occupational noises are considered. All these noises are called '*domestic noise*'. In addition we have noise generated by traffic or transport on the road. Therefore, Table 19.4 lists noise levels at principal cities in the world. This noise is primarily due to road traffic. Even the aeroplanes which facilitate our fast rapid transport generates enormous noise as indicated in Table 19.10. It is noteworthy that faster is speed of the aeroplane, louder is the noise it creates in the cities *e.g.*, concord of which use is not permitted in India generates irritating noise.

Table 19.9 Noise produced by vehicles on roads

S.No.	*Type of vehicles*	*Level dB*	*S.No.*	*Type of vehicles*	*Level dB*
1.	Two wheeler on petrol	80	6.	Public transport bus (CNG)	74
2.	Two wheeler on diesel	82	7.	Heavy bus running on diesel (S.T.)	78–85
3.	Three wheeler on diesel	85	8.	Lamberta	75
4.	Light luggage vehicle *e.g.* (Tempo)	89	9.	Tempo run on diesel	80
5.	Heavy luggage vehicle (Truck)	91	10.	Commercial diesel Lorry or Truck	82

The principal source of annoying noise is motor bike or a typical aircraft. Table 19.9 lists level of noise produced by various kinds of vehicles while 19.10 lists noise generated by different types of aircrafts where concord is worst noise producer.

The Table 19.9 indicates various kinds of noise produced by vehicles during travel. These vehicles include two wheeler, three wheeler, high and heavy luggage vans and scooter or lamberta. The diesel and CNG powered vehicles as buses, tempos produce annoying noise. The highest level is 91 dB produced by heavy luggage truck (S.No. 5) while the relatively lowest level is lamberta moped or scooter (S.No. 8) level is 70–75 dB.

An attempts must be made by public authorities to bring down this level by clamping strict legislation. The originator or sources which exceeds prescribe limit should be severely fined and their driving licenses must be confiscated. In many educational institutes like I.I.Ts Mumbai riding a bicycle or the scooter within the campus is strictly prohibited. No matter whether we use petrol, diesel or CNG as fuel the noise level remains at making and constant. A standard value prescribed must be fixed with zero tolerance.

At this stage, it is worthwhile examining the noise generated by aeroplane which is fastest mode of transport and communication. The Table 19.10 summarises noise produced by various kinds of aircrafts like jumbo jet, concord, air bus and small aircrafts.

Table 19.10 Noise level in various types of aircrafts

S.No	*Aircraft type*	*Level dB*
1.	707	114
2.	720	104
3.	727	103
4.	737	102
5.	747	115
6.	DC–8	112–116
7.	DC–9	92–112
8.	DC–10	110–112
9.	Tridentate	130–140
10.	Concord	140–150

It will be observed from Table 19.10 dealing with aeroplane noise that the traffic even in developed countries is headache as it generates noise pollution to the extent of about 150 dBA. Even road traffic noise in cities like London, Paris, Brussels Frankfurt, Amsterdam exceeds 150 dBH. The noise is generated by buses and specially trams in Europe and Australia. Tram is preferred vehicle in Kolkata as it causes no air pollution, but generates noise pollution. In comparison to cities abroad the towns in India are relatively quite. For instance level for noise in Mumbai (90), Delhi (100), Kolkata (90), Bangalore (90), Chennai (90), Hydrabad (90). They are much quiter with noise level less than 100 dB due to less industrialisation as compared to cities in western developing countries. Monorail and Metros will add to noise level in Mumbai.

However, most troublesome source of noise in industry where is all kinds of tools and machines during operation, Table 19.11 list of sources of operational industrial noises while Table 19.12 gives level of average noise pollution in various kinds of industries.

Table 19.11 Level of industrial noise

Type	*Level dB*	*Type*	*Level dB*
Nailing machine	80–85	Pile driver	100–130
Garbage collector	85–115	Rivets	115–120
Concrete mixer	85–110	Blower	100–105
Electric generator	76–115	Chip hammer	118–120
Dozer	87–100	Diesel generator	110–125
Jack hammer	88–120	Ball mill	106–110
Vacuum cleaner	75–80	Power saw	98–110
Rivertor	110–115	Electric cutter	90–110
Scrapper	88–110	Lathe	108–110
Dumper	85–115	Hydrolytic press	98–105
Paver blocks	90–120	Air compressor	85–115
Rock driller	98–125	Pneumatic chipper	100–125

Table 19.12 Average noise level in various kinds of industries

Type of industry	*Noise level dB*	*Type of industry*	*Noise level dB*
Ceramics	95-100	Chemical	94-100
Glass	90-95	Leather	92-98
Food	88-90	Textile	90-110
Confectionary	70-90	Paper and pulp	90-95
Pharmaceutical	90-100	Metallurgical	95-110

From above Tables 19.11 and 19.12, we note that most of the industries generate noise due to complex operations such as nailing, hammering, drilling, riveting, blowing, compressing or chipping with pollution level exceeding > 110 dBA. The least level is in confectionary. Most of the industries are all noise generating sources, which in turn is likely to affect health of man.

The most important source of noise pollution is domestic noise while the one due to generation by industries or transportation is alarming. The most annoying source in the developed countries is industrial noise. One can easily control noise pollution from domestic sources or to some extent even from transportation, but abatement of noise is not at all easy in case of industrial units. For that purpose controlling of such noise we require strict regulations and laws which are implemented by government and municipal corporation.

A review of Table 19.11 shows that in heavy industries include the process involving the pneumatic chipper, chip hammer, and jack hammer are the largest noise producing implements. Similarly, if we take note of various industrial enterprises in Table 19.12 on an average a typical industry produces noise level of 90 to 110 dBA. The foundry produces the largest noise due to various operation in metal cutting. While the food industry produces relatively less noise. All the workers working in such factory or industrial houses are bound to have health hazards due to continuous and uninterrupted exposure to noise. One must take care to avoid this uncalled exposure which otherwise affects hearing sensitivity of worker.

The sensation which is pleasing to the ears, or one which is melodious giving comfort like musical notes is defined as sound. While one which is penetrating and uncomfortable, or one which creates psychological stress is called as *noise*. The source of sound or noise is domestic as well as industrial. Table 19.1 lists domestic sound in decibels. It is interesting to note that threshold of audibility is zero dB. If a pin falls on a hard floor, it gives 10 dB. The sound up to 40 dB is encountered in a garden, a bedroom, in libraries. Whisper (30 dB) is considered to be pleasant is low in level. An average conversation produces 60 dB. Anything between 50 and 90 dB is considered as noise, *e.g.* vacuum cleaner, office, alarm clock, street traffic and pneumatic chipper, while one beyond 90-120 dB is considered to be a health hazard. Such noise is produced by aircraft, pop-music, heavy truck traffic level of noise at road junctions, in Mumbai are presented in Table 19.13 and that at railway stations on central railway in Table 19.14 is quite interesting.

Table 19.13 Noise level at roads in Mumbai

Road junction (New name)	*Noise level (dBA)*
Flora Fountain (Hutama Chowk)	78
Chhatrapati Shivaji Terminus (CST)	81
Byculla Bridge	74
Lalbaugh Junction	76
Parel (Dr. Ambedkar Marg)	79
Dadar (Khodadad circle, Dadar TT)	80
King Circle (Maheswari Udyan)	75
Sion Circle (Laxmibai Chowk)	78

Table 19.14 Noise at suburban central railway stations in south Mumbai

Suburban station	*Noise levels (dBA)*
Masjid	75
Sandhurst Road	76
Byculla	81
Chinchpokli	73
Curry Road	82
Parel	74
Dadar	82
Matunga	76
Sion	78
Kurla	76

Apart from domestic source of noise pollution, industrial activity creates enormous noise. Alarming noise commences from 70 dB and is extended up to 140 dB. It includes noise generated by air compressors, concrete mixers, scrapper, dozer, payer, powersaw, generators, rockdrill and pile foundation operations, riveting process. Such noise is uncomfortable and unwanted by society specially in residential area.

19.6 NOISE AND HEALTH

The noise has several adverse effects on health, much worst than those caused by vibrations. They are cardiovascular problems or pulmonary disorder or skin problems, cerebral disorder, visual handicaps or faulty blood vascular system.

Table 19.15 lists such health problems. It shows extent of damage caused to the health.

Table 19.15 Effect of noise on human health

Health problems	*Symptoms*
Cardiovascular disorder	High blood pressure, slow pulse beats, digestive and gastrointestinal disorder
Pulmonary edema	High pulse rate, high beats, drop in blood pressure; breathing problem.
Dermatitis	Decrease in resistance of skin, cracks, and dryness on the surfaces of skin.
Vision impairment	Dilation of pupil of eye, muscular tension.
Cerebral disorder	Decrease sensation, abnormal conscience state, and brain fatigue, loss of memory.
Blood vascular obstruction	Flow affected, ketosteroid in the urine and plasma cortisol in the blood raised.

It will be interesting to note some of the serious observations in Table 19.15. The common pollutants show deleterious effect on health immediately while the noise pollution shows effect only after prolonged exposure. Therefore noise is called '*silent killer*' amongst several environmental hazards. In the long run of exposure to noise the person will have deafness, high blood pressure and hypertension headache, dry skin, weak eyesight, abnormal conscience state of mind. There is substantial change in the flow of blood with rise in ecenophillia or quality of urine gets affected due to the presence of Ketosteroid.

Table 19.16 Noise exposure with time limit of tolerance

Sound level (dB)	*Exposure (hrs)*	*Sound level (dB)*	*Exposure*
88	12	114	2 mts
90	8	115	1 mts
93	4	118	1/2 mts
96	2	124	1/4 mt
99	1	124	1/8 mt
100	1/2	127	42 seconds
105	1/4	130	2 seconds
108	1/8	133	1.0 seconds
111	1/16	135	0.6 seconds

As told noise causes severe health hazards. Such effects may be physical or mental, which would have long-term consequences on communications, working efficiency, personal comfort and it leads to industrial accidents. The physical health problems may be acute and chronic. The acute effect depends upon frequency of 120 to 150 dB noise which causes permanent damage of ear. If a person is exposed to 90 dB noise for 40 hours in week for 30 years, he is bound to be deaf at the end of his career. A low level noise causes nausea, loss of physical control and physiological changes caused by stress. The important worst effect is loss of hearing. The loss starts at a frequency of 4000 Hz, with more damage done by sudden impulsive noises. The noise causes prolonged loss of sleep also. The mental effect causes lack of concentration and mental disorientation or fatigue. The noise interferes communicability and causes tendency to commit error in judgement. The personal comfort gets affected by destroying peaceful life and enjoyment of leisure. It contracts blood vessel, supplying blood to heart and brain. It causes digestive disorder due to hyperacidity. To mitigate all the health problems it is necessary to measure the noise by instruments in terms of some units. Such discussion is taken in following section of this chapter.

Table 19.18 vivially shows how intensity of sound affects health. Mild sound level till 50 dB is reasonable specially in cities the maximum of 120 dB is unbearable.

Table 19.17 Sound intensity and health

S.No.	*Level*	*Effect*	*S.No.*	*Level*	*Effect*
1.	0	Threshold listening	8.	120	Threshold pain
2.	25	Light speech effect	9.	130	Nontolerable sound
3.	40	Loud talk effect	10.	150	Irreversible damage of skin
4.	80	Irritating voice	11.	190	Damage to ears
5.	90	Injurious to ears	12.	190	Hearing impaired
6.	100	Leads to fast pulse rate	13.	50	Disturbed sleep
7.	110	Ill effect on body skin	14.	70	Causes fatigue, nervousness

The Tables 19.15 as well as 19.17 shows the adverse effects of noise on human health. The Table 19.15 describes the kind of disorders caused such as cardiovascular problems, pulmonary edema, skin or dermatitis problems so also eye, brain and blood circulation problems.

The Table 19.17 list actual value of noise in dB units causing serious health ailments. The threshold limit is zero. The level of 90 dB (S.No. 5) is definitely objectionable. If such level is not controlled the person would become deaf within no time. A level exceeding 100 dB creates serious problem of heart, brain and other vital organs of the body. Some noise above 100 dB causes damage to the skin, ears, blood vascular system. It should be endeavour of city corporators to clamp down all these noises to reasonable level; although zero level may not be always possible to attain. Beyond > 130 dB it is impossible to stand and tolerate noise emission. The best remedy is to bring down to level to 25–40 dB as it is noted in feeble and loud speech in order to enjoy peace and tranquility. As a matter of fact in cities like Mumbai, every attempt is made to create silence zone around hospitals, temples, schools. Even the quite playgrounds are permitted to carry out sports activity with negligible noise but festivals as Ganesh and Durga Puja are banned on open spaces and parks in city of Mumbai. The next Table 19.18 summarises human response to noise of shrill sound level.

Table 19.18 Noise pollution and human response with origin of noise

S.No.	*Human response*	*Sound level*	*S.No.*	*Place of origin of noise/sound*	*Level, dB*
1.	Threshold level	0	12.	Bedroom	25
2.	Faintly audiable	10	13.	Assembly hall	40
3.	Reasonable for normal listener	30	14.	Factory area	30–35
4.	Reasonable, for mildly deaf person	50	15.	Molls, hotel	40–45
5.	Intrusive, not at all good	70	16.	Industrial location	40–60
6.	Not good for listening	80	17.	School, colleges	30–40
7.	Harmful level on health	90	18.	Reading rooms	20–25
8.	Disgusting sound	100	19.	Dispensaries	20–35
9.	Maximum tolerable	105	20.	Normal speech	25
10.	Totally uncomfortable	130	21.	Loud speech	45
11.	Intolerable	140	22.	Acceptable tolerable speech	20–25

The Table 19.18 list the reactions of human being to noise and to ascertain origin of noise from our day-to-day activities. A person with good hearing capacity listens to any audible sound in the level of 30–60 dB. An ideal limit for talking with any persons is 30 dB. One beyond 60–110 dB is definitely harmful to person. The optimum level which is maintained in our place of living or work must be first controlled. Even industrial locations should not exceed limit of 760 dB.

The various limits are prescribed by health authorities in India. Normally speech should not exceed > 25–30 dB. A housing complex having several flats with bedroom, drawing room and kitchen should maintain optimum level less than < 50 for peaceful living. The libraries, dispensaries; molls, should maintain a level of 20–25 dB to get peace. Table 19.19 gives relationship between noise level and

Table 19.19 Permissible limit of noise on health

S. No.	*Duration (hrs)*	*Mints*	*Sound level dB*	*Remarks*	*S. No.*	*Duration (hrs)*	*Mints*	*Sound level dB*	*Remarks*
1.	8	480	90	Uncomfortable	5.	2	120	100	Cannot bear for long time
2.	6	360	92	Intolerable	6.	1	60	105	Very bad
3.	4	240	95	Worst level	7.	1/2	30	110	Nontolerable
4.	3	180	97	Worst level	8.	1/4	15	115	Short time tolerable

time of listening in hours and minutes. The remark column indicates what is healthy sound and bad noise.

It is worthwhile to examine the level of noise at occupational places. The maximum time a person can bear with least comfort is less than 40 dB. Therefore Table 19.19 shows duration of exposure of sound against level tolerable by an individual. The (OSHA) *i.e.* occupational safety and health administration in England fixed limits of tolerance of sound. The investigations were carried out for $\frac{1}{4}$ hrs (*i.e.* 15 minutes) to upto 8 hours (480 mts). Louder is sound less is time of listening *e.g.* A 115 dB level sound is tolerated only for 15 minutes while lower level 90 dB sound is tolerated for as much as 8 hours. Of course, there is personal error for listening power of person.

Although the Flight engineer at ground level at Airport is exposed to level of 100–110 dB. He bears it with only for two hours beyond which a temporary hearing loss is recorded. The level with tolerance time of 4–8 hours (~90 dB) is accepted if it is in form of impulse. A non stop hearing for longer time if sound is continuous will make a person irratic, nervous and perplexed; with all sorts of health problems as described in Table 19.16. As a matter of fact the good town plannars inside on planners trees in row in the area between housing complex and busy street. Not only dust and pollutant but meance of noise is absorbed by bunch of trees to make the dwellings most peaceful and comfortable. Of recent origin is sound barriers which are increasing used between housing complex and express highways. One witnesses this around IIT Bombay or Bandra Kurla complex in Mumbai.

19.7 NOISE LEVEL MEASUREMENT

The chief objective of sound measurement is to finally reduce its level, so as to make it enjoyable as in music; or carry out scientific investigations to reduce its annoying effect, one can ascertain its capability to cause hearing damage and to serve as powerful diagnostic tool to reduce it. Sound travels at the rate of 750 miles per hour or 3 seconds per kilometre or 5 seconds per mile. We measure sound in pascal units, *e.g.* weakest sound is 20 Mpa, *i.e.*, approximately 0 dB (Fig.19.2). Pascal scale is not practical, *e.g.*, 35 dB = 960 Mpa or 70 dB = 70,000 MPa

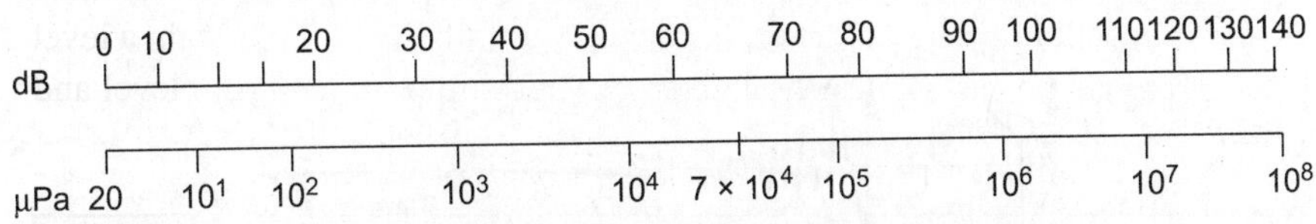

Fig. 19.2 Comparison of decibel and pascal scale

Each time we multiply sound pressure in pa by 10, and then add 20 dB to get the resulting level in dB units. For example, 2000 μpa (2000 micropascal × 10) + 20 = 40 dB. As shown in Fig. 19.2 sound is measured on dB scale. If a sound is of short duration, *i.e.*, less than one second, it is termed as the impulsive sound.

The octave band analyser is used in conjuction with sound level meter to determine the average sound pressure of the standard octave bands. It gives an idea about frequency, contents of noise to decide abatement technique. The magnetic tape recorder is used to record actual noise for storage and laboratory evaluation. If it is run at high speed, it gives a real picture of sound frequency. The pen recorder is fed directly to sound level meter. A continuous record of sound level meter against time is used for storage. The statistical analyser is mechanical or electronic device, which is used in conjunction with a pen recorder. The noise average meter is fed directly on magnetic tape recording to give leg. Leg is equivalent continuous sound pressure level or amounts of energy, with certain limitations, capable of causing the same effect. A noise analyser is fed directly to sound level meter. The company called Brüel and Kajaer in Denmark manufactures excellent sound meters. No attempts have been made to fabricate such devices in India. The sound signal is converted into electrical signal by high quality microphone. The signal is amplified. Such a signal drives the meter to measure sound in dB scale. The microphone has to be Omani model in directional sensitivity, *i.e.*, sensitive in all directions.

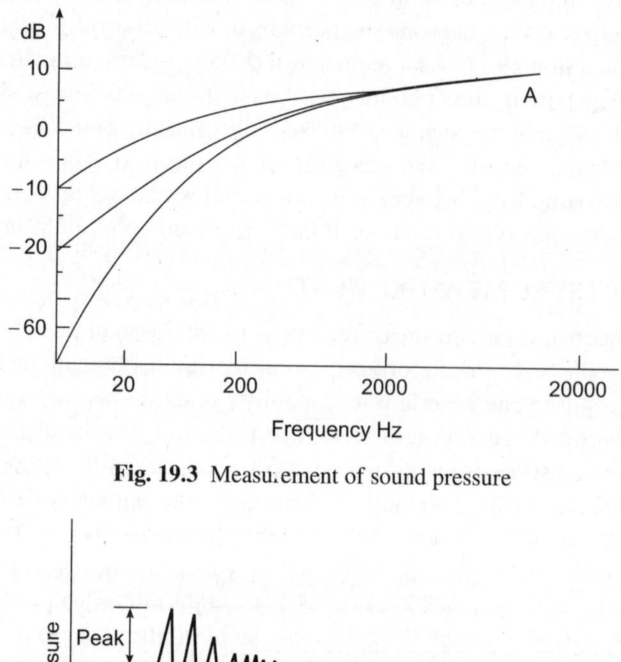

Fig. 19.3 Measurement of sound pressure

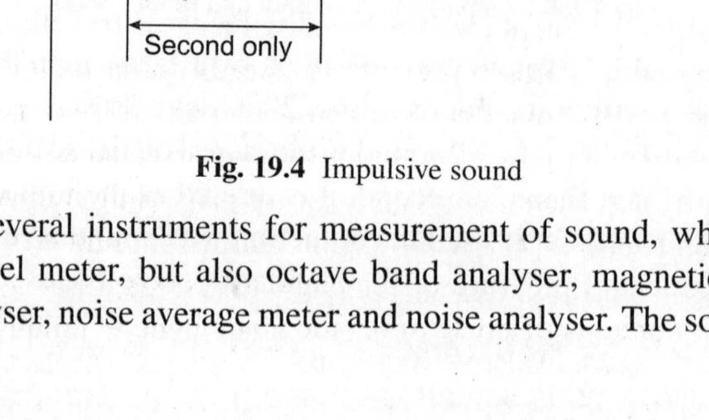

Fig. 19.4 Impulsive sound

There are several instruments for measurement of sound, which include not only sound level meter, but also octave band analyser, magnetic tape recorder, statistical analyser, noise average meter and noise analyser. The sound level meter evaluates sound pressure linearly or on weighted average of scale. The octave analyser determines average sound pressure of standard octave pressure bands. The dynamic property of sound level meter is possibility of measurement of slow, fast or impulsive sound.

A noise less than 50 dB is acceptable but beyond more than 55 to 80 dB is considered as it is noisy, very noisy at 80 to 95 dB and unbearable at 95 dBA. A prescribed limit for cities is 0 to 50 dB for silence zone and 55 dB for residential dwellings, 65 dB for the commercial plaza and 75 dB for industrial establishment. The level of noise corresponding for night duration is less by about 10 units. In SLM, sound meter signal is converted into electric signal on high quality microphone for amplification. Such microphone has sensitivity in all directions, hence it is called "Omni model". The proper use of microphone during measurement of noise is equally important. During measurement of noise, when the wind is blowing around noise meter it gives wrong results, hence a ball of sponge which is made up of porous polyurethane is used over a microphone. Humidity up-to 90% does not affect sound level meter but rain and snow does affect. The model does affect operates in – 10° to 50°C range. A variation in pressure of about ± 10% will not affect measurement. Vibration should be avoided during sound measurements. Foam rubber pads dampen vibrations effectively. The magnetic field influences sound level measurement, hence it should be avoided during measurement.

19.8 NOISE BY TRANSPORTATION

Transportation is the greatest culprit for major source of noise. The variety of noises such as domestic noise, aircraft noise, construction noise, and industrial noise are all leading to discomfort to human beings. Traffic noise makes our lives uncomfortable. To a greater extent domestic noise is easily controlled, by rational use of radio, T.V. Noise in household is minimised by using carpets, drapery and upholstered furniture to absorb sound. The noise of sirens is modulated. The attempts are made to create silent zones around educational institutes, hospitals, in our country but it did not work although it is most successful plan in Britain. Traffic noise is due to cars, motorcycles, trucks and buses. A car gives 60 dB, a bus 80 dB, while a truck creates 85 dB, while motorcycles, scooters, mopeds, lamberta produces noise of the level of 85 to 90 dB. These noises strike on hard surfaces of buildings and are reflected back to the ears. The noise is produced by air turbulence around the bodywork of a moving car; tyres are main source of noise specially on cement roads, specially if a car is travelling at a high speed. In cold countries snow tires make more noise. In India motorcycles are the worst culprits, wherein the noise originates from exhaust and engine. It gives 110 to 120 dB noise. Mufflers are designed in motorbikes to reduce noise. Trees and bushes are planted on highways to reduce noise by dispersing it on leaves and branches. In good town planning, the bedrooms in building are located away from roads to give peace and tranquility to a occupant while spleeping.

19.9 SONIC BOOM

This is the phenomena of sound generated due to an aeroplane on account of difference in velocity of sound and velocity of aeroplane with which it travels in the air.

Aircraft generates too much of noise as shown in Table 19.13. It gives rise to a sonic boom which is caused when a moving body or object crosses the speed of sound.

Aircraft noise is the worst gift to metropolitan cities like Mumbai, Kolkata and Delhi. Fortunately, in India concords are not allowed to fly which would have made our life more miserable. The Jumbo Jets are the main culprits, which cause sonic boom—a loud noise produced when a moving object crosses the speed of sound. An aircraft flying at supersonic speed builds up a shock wave of compressed air, which surrounds the plane and trails behind it (Fig. 19.5). When the trailing edge of the shock wave reaches the ground, it produces sonic boom. The aircraft noise is measured in terms of NNI (*i.e.*, noise number index). It specifies a certain number. An aircraft noise in terms of NNI in busy airport like Chicago is 50, while in our airports like Mumbai with comparatively low aircraft density, it is 35 to 40 NNI. If an aircraft lands at an angle of 60°, it would generate minimum noise. Noise abatement in airports in Narita, Japan is most rigorous. The residents around the Haneda airport in Japan were paid compensation for noise nuisance. The Japanese had therefore shifted their International airport to Narita away from habitat former is about 80 km outside the city limits of Tokyo, while domestic traffic is at Haneda airport, which is located in the heart of the city. The stacking of aircraft is done to minimise noise at airports, this is done in Frankfurt or Los Angles, where large number of planes land. In United States of America the most busy airports is O'hare, in Chicago and Los Angles. In spite of enacting stricter legislation, the life surrounding these airports is noisy. At Heathrow airport in London, the frequency of landing of planes is high. This makes the airport noisy. Fortunately in India, the problem so far is not acute. The Santacruz, and Sahar

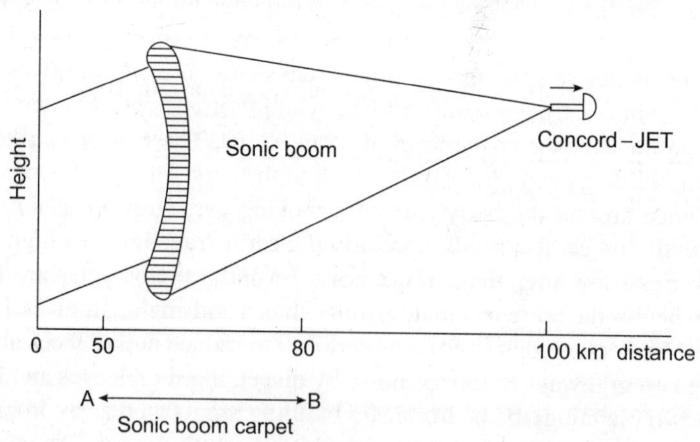

Fig. 19.5 Sonic boom

airports in Mumbai and Palam in Delhi are somewhat busy, while (Dumdum), Kolkata and Meenakumbum at Chennai are relatively less noisy and less populated in comparison to airports in western countries. It is expected that the proposed new Mumbai airport at Panvel will incorporate all new comforts in the airports. New airports at Hydrabad and Bengaluru are reasonably good.

The noise is related to frequency or number of planes which are landing at airport. In India the frequency of landing and take off of planes is low relatively in comparison with such airports in developed countries. In western countries, night operation of aeroplanes after 10.00 pm is banned. They levy heavy taxing charges if plane is to land in restricted hours. In India it is other way round, all foreign aeroplanes start landing or departing specially in Mumbai after 12.00 a.m. in midnight. The most busy domestic airport is Chhatrapati Shivaji Airport at Mumbai, and Indira Gandhi Airport at New Delhi. In comparison with these airports *viz.*, Netaji Subhash Chandra Airport at Kolkata, or Annadurai Airport at Chennai are relatively less busy. The domestic flights at Mumbai and Delhi are too many in relation to other airports. On an average in peak hours for every 30 min one plane takes off or lands at these airports. On an average total at least 48 planes or more depart in a day time.

19.10 IMPULSIVE NOISE

An impulse is very harmful than a continuous noise. A sudden noise of short duration with high intensity but with a low lifetime of less than one second is called as "*impulsive*" noise. Table 19.20 lists impulses caused by an exploding bomb (190 dB), naval gunshooting, firing crackers, pile driving and metal beating. They are capable of producing noise to the extent of 140 dB. An unexpected thud of sound with a short life has high impulse and is harmful. Ultrasonics is a science which deals with sound vibrating at frequencies too high to be heard by human ears (more than 20,000 Hz), however, ultrasound is heard by dogs, horses or dolphins in the sea. The infrasound sound which has intensity less than 20 Hz is not identified by man.

Table 19.20 Impulsive sound very short duration

S.No.	*Source of impulses*	*Level of impact, dBA*
1.	Bomb explosion	190–200
2.	Shooting of gun	160–180
3.	Handgun or torpedos	140–170
4.	Mechanical Pile driving	110–120
5.	Forging of metal in heat	120–140
6.	Crackers	125–150

While the infrasound is too low to be heard with frequency less than 20 Hz. It is easily detected by electronic devices. The sound produces vibration due to natural resonance called as "*Sympathetic Vibration*". They cause acoustic fatigue. The building construction operation produces sound more than 85 to 100 dB due to pile dugging devices.

No attempts are made so far for prescribing the limits of annoying noise. The motorcycle generates noise of 77 to 80 dB while goods truck has 89 to 92 dB, locomotive gives 89 to 92 dB. Even for continuous exposer of human being to noise has limit *e.g.* A noise of 90 dB is tolerated maximum by human being just for 8 hours while 100 dB is heard for 2 hours without damaging ear, one with 150 dB is tolerated only for 10 minutes. So one has to take care of such noises to protect the ears (Tables 19.19 and 19.20).

A definite relation is there between sound level and the tolerance level. It is shown in Tables 19.21 and 19.22.

Table 19.21 Tolerance of noise with time

S. No.	*Sound level dB*	*Time in mts/hours*	*Total mts*	*S. No.*	*Sound level dB*	*Time in mts*	*Time in hours*
1.	90	8 × 60 mts	480	8.	120	1/4 × 60 mts	15
2.	92	6 × 60 mts	360	9.	150	50	~1.0
3.	95	4 × 60 mts	240	10.	140	100	~2.0
4.	97	3 × 60 mts	180	11.	135	300	~5.0
5.	100	2 × 60 mts	120	12.	130	1000	16
6.	105	1 × 60 mts	60	13.	125	3000	50
7.	110	1/4 × 60 mts	30	14.	120	10,000	160

The Table 19.21 gives very interesting parameters for the first reading S.No. 1 to S.No. 8 in table shows how long a person can listen with comforts. The time varies from 15 mt to 8 hours in the noise level of 120–90 dB. While S.No. (9–14) indicates the maximum amount of time for hearing ranges from 50–10,000. Although this is little odd and theoretically true, but because there is another problem of personal factor. Everybody is not sensitive to same level. Further as age advances the hearing capacity is diminishing. A level of 120–150 dB in any case is not tolerable under any circumstances by the sensitive or any persons.

Table 19.22 Noise and health with exposure with time

S.No.	*Noise in dB unit (range)*	*Time of exposure (hrs)*	*Remarks*
1.	80–90	8 hrs	Irritation, hearing loss
2.	90–95	4 hrs	High pulse rate
3.	95–99	2 hrs	Skin affected
4.	99–105	60 mts	Unbearable condition
5.	105–108	110 mts	Change in pulse rate
6.	108–111	10 mts	Skin problem
7.	111–114	< 2 mts	Near threshold pain
8.	114–120	Very few seconds	Threshold pain

Further to the observation of data in Table 19.19, the Table 19.22 shows that the noise level with an exposure and most important observation related to the health which caused hazards. The exposure time is varied from 2 mts to 8 hours *i.e.* 480 mts. The threshold pain limit is in seconds (S.No. 8). One causes several health problems like high pulse rate (90–95 dB) skin ailments (99–110 dB) irritation in ear while listening (80–90 dB) become dumb.

The Tables 19.19 and 19.22 bring us to the conclusion that since threshold limit is only few seconds to minutes, long exposure ranging from 2–8 hours creates irreversible damage to the hearing therefore should be avoided.

19.11 ANECHOIC CHAMBER AND REVERBERATING SOUND

Several heritage sites exhibit such phenomena. Anechoic chamber is so constructed that no sound is reflected but is absorbed. In the reverberating gallaries sound has multiple reflection to produce echo. The classic example is that of the Golghumat in Bijapure in state of Karnataka. It is possible to contain noise danger zone by constructing anechoic chambers or sound absorbing rooms. After measuring sound in field free of reflecting objects, an anechoic chamber is constructed. The roof, sidewalls, ceiling, floor are covered by highly absorbing materials to eliminate reflection. On the contrary as told the sound reflecting chambers are called "reverberation chambers". These are opposite of anechoic chambers. Such reverberating chambers are useful for noise investigations of machines and similar investigations.

An excellent hall holding music concerts has got accoustic or soundproof walls. It is done to give a sterophonic or three dimensional effect to music which is produced on stage. All reflection points are eliminated. Therefore, one then enjoys the sterophonic music generated through two separate channels in the amplifier model. Most of the concert halls in west are fine for orchestra programme, because they are like anechoic chambers to reflect sound.

19.12 NOISE TOPOGRAPHS

In order to ascertain the impact of noise on human health, it is necessary to make a survey of noise levels on site. This is done by noise mapping or noise Topography. The noise is measured at selected sites around noise producing unit. Then those of spots with various noise levels are then marked on the paper. Finally, those of sampling sites or spots which have identical level of sound levels are joined together. This indicates the hazardous zone of noise generating spots (Fig. 19.6). These are similar to isothermal lines in temperature measure.

In Fig. 19.6, the typical site is for generating noise of different intensity *e.g.*, zone A indicates highest intensity of noise in the region of 105 to 100 dB while zone B represents 95 to 87 dB, while zone C shows all spots with less level of 83 to 98 dB and finally outer zones D shows relatively least level of 75 to 70 dB. From this topograph, we note that the area enclosed by zone A is potentially dangerous with highest noise level of 105 to 100 dB while area covered by zone B indicates relatively better zone of 75 to 70 dB. While zone C and zone D are comparatively safe with low sound level.

Noise mapping is specially useful for deciding control measures or total elimination of sound in specific area. The mapping reveals the safe and unsafe zones in the factory or establishment. It is very useful for town planning. The topographs of railway station, airports, cinema houses or commercial plazas, malls should be drawn as these are the main culprits in the generation of noise which in turn affects our health. This is especially most vital in formulating environmental impact (EIA) assessment to assess the effect of noise well in advance on health, it is necessary to undertake a survey of noise levels in different parts of a locality. The sound maps are prepared. The area which are sound prone, like dwellings around industrial establishments, airports, railway stations, cinema houses or commercial plaza are selected for sound mapping in EIA report.

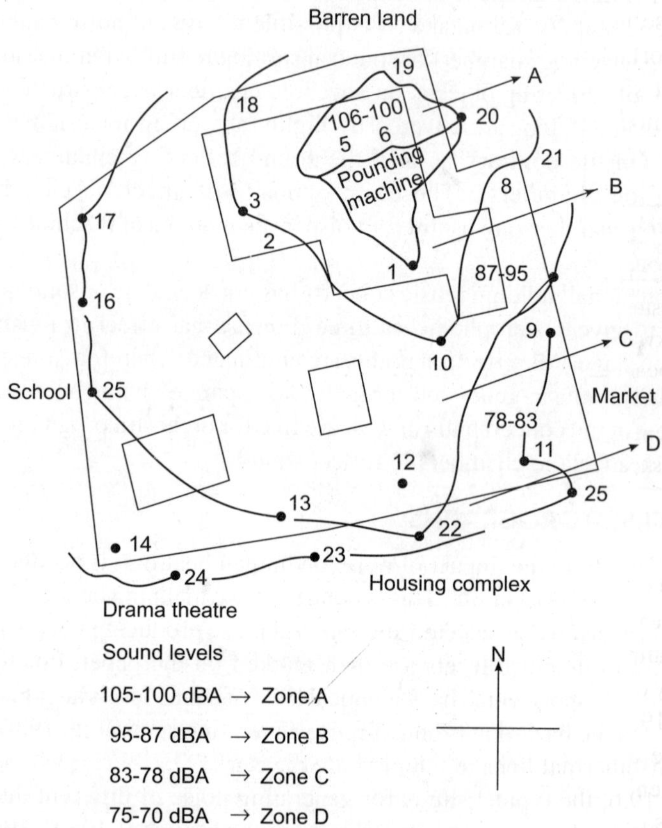

Fig. 19.6 Noise topograph with levels

Noise topograph is obtained by connecting lines drawn between the points of equal sound levels to exhibit sound distribution patterns. A topograph indicates zones of noise danger and is a first step to mitigate or abate sound nuisance. A topograph with 110 dB sound in zone would indicate need of putting ear plugs or ear muffets to prevent damage to hearing sensation.

In summary we have considered several aspects of noise. Difference between sound and noise, as well as correlationship between noise and vibrations, the root cause of the noise, adverse effects of noise on the health, how noise is measured and significance of sonic boom, impulsive sound and anechoic chambers, with great consideration of noise mapping. The effectiveness of noise mapping depends upon what kind of the control measures one is taking to mitigate the sound level. At the same time, it is necessary to consider what kind of material is used to dampen the noise. Such discussions is included in the final section of this chapter under control of noise pollution.

19.13 CONTROL OF NOISE

This is the most important aspects to be carefully studied in order to reduce or minimise uncomfortable noise. The source of noise generating spot is isolated from working area by mapping. To the extent possible various kinds of barriers are kept so as to obstruct and filter the noise. Variety of materials are used to control noise. Such materials are listed in Table 19.23.

Table 19.23 Noise absorbing materials

Material	*Thick (nm)*	*Sound level*	*Material*	*Thick (nm)*	*Sound level*
Asbestos	0.6	26	Plastic board	1.3	12
Brickwork	11.6	40	Compressed wood	5	28
Fireboard	1.2	18	Chipboard	1.8	26
Plywood	0.6	21	Glass fibre wool	50	70
Cement slab	7.6	35	Clinker blocks	7.5	23
Leadsheet	0.5	15	Curtains	0.25	22

It will be observed from Table 19.23 that the best material for absorption of noise is glass wool (70 dB), while brickwork (40 dB) and cement slab (35 dB) or compressed wood (28 dB) are also effective for damping the sound. If the screen is made out of any of theses materials is placed between noise generating source and receptor *i.e.*, person it would considerably reduce the level of noise. A capacity of material to absorb noise is determined in terms of absorption coefficient. (Table 19.24). The absorption coefficient which is defined as the ratio of amount of noise absorbed against amount of incident noise. If all sound is absorbed coefficient is unity. In all other cases, the coefficient is less than unity or expressed in terms of fraction.

Table 19.24 Noise absorption coefficient

Material	*Absorption coefficient*	*Material*	*Absorption coefficient*	*Material*	*Absorption coefficient*	*Remarks*
Glass	0.7	Straw	0.4	Ideal	1.0	Absorption
Wool	0.8	Wood	0.6	Worst	0	No absorption

Thus, this ratio of absorption coefficient represents level of noise absorbed to noise incident if the ratio is zero this indicates noise is totally reflected from the surface and cannot be controlled. On the contrary, if the ratio is unity it indicates 100% absorption of sound. That means all noise incident on the surface is absorbed and nothing is reflected by the surface. In Table 19.24 the value 0.25 as lowest absorption, 0.50 is moderate absorption for straw while, 0.75 is good absorption for glass wool and 1.0 indicates best or total absorption. Therefore, material should be selected in such manner, that the absorption coefficient is in vicinity of unity. The best material is glass wool which is heat sensitive.

The measures which are taken for controlling noise consists of the shielding of source with suitable sound absorbing material. It should be also verified whether sound is continuous or impulsive. If it is continuous, it needs immediate attention for control, but if it is impulsive then its total duration of existance must be noted to decide upon noise abatement measures. The following is case study of noise abatement conducted in typical factory in western subrubs of Mumbai. The Table 19.25 which shows the ambient noise quality standard.

Table 19.25 Ambient noise quality standards

S.No.	*Area*	*Zone*	*Level 6 am–10 pm day time dB*	*Level 10 pm–6 am night time*	*Remarks (specified zone)*
1.	A	Industries	75	70	dB(A) Leq. weighted average
2.	B	Markets	65	55	dB-Leq. frequency of weighing
3.	C	Residence	55	45	The noise level over specified area
4.	D	Silence zone	50	40	Location with school, college, hospitals (~100 meters minimum)

Just as we have ambient air quality standard for gases or the water quality standards for hydrological parameters as presented by federal authorities, we also have noise quality standard for noise (see Table 19.25).

The various locations which are considered span from industries, market, residence and hospital if the latter are under silence zone. The level is measured during day time as well as in night time each for 12 hrs in succession. There is definite reduction of level in night time by 10–20 dB *e.g.* A residential area may have drop from 55–45 dB. The condition is more or less same with on average drop of 10 dB. The only exception is industrial establishment working day and night where we observe drop in level of noise is from 75–70 dB *i.e.* only 5 dB decrease in level. The noise level is worth examining. We take all in weighted average.

19.14 CASE STUDIES

This study was made in workshop of Foundry. At a glance at Fig. 19.6 *i.e.*, topograph, reveals that the central portions of workshop is noisy. This is typical case of metal foundry site which is surrounded by residential buildings on south side, a vegetable market on eastern side. While drama theatre is in south side and school premises is on west. There was barren land on northern side. Foundry is generating impulsive noise of 100 to 150 dB during pounding and forgoing operatings in day and sometimes in night also. In a topograph the zone B is factory shade with relatively less noise while zone C area is outside of working area of factory while zone D represents an area totally outside boundry wall of factory which is accoustically tolerable. With the noise level of 75 to 70 dB while passing three-wheelers or autorikshaws produced more noise of 90 to 95 dB on adjoining road. The control measures adopted is to cover the area shown by zone A by thick asbestos partition and confine here all pounding or forgoing operations. Since noise is due to impulse it is not damaging type. The workers working in the vicinity of pounding machine be provided with ear muffs of sound insulating materials. The final verdict in this case study is that there is no need of closing down the foundry unit provided if the owners take adequate precaution or measures to erect asbestos partition wall around pounding machine, provide earplugs to workers and all forging operations are carried out during day light only.

19.15 CONCLUSION

Our festivals, home appliances and occupational noise is common sources of headache. The noise is measured in decibel units. The source of noise pollution are domestic, industrial and road traffic. All the cities in the world suffer from the noise pollution which range in the vicinity of 80 to 100 dB. The noise generated by industrial establishment is more serious. Various tools and implements produce noise exceeding more than 100 dB. The metallurgical and steel plants also generate uncomfortable noise. In generation of noise, vibration plays a significant role of enhancing the level it needs to be controlled. The noise has serious implication as it produces ill effects like cardiac problem, pulmonary diseases, dermatitis, vision impairment, problems with central nervous system disorder and ill functioning of blood vascular system. Therefore, timely measurement of noise is absolutely essential. Such noise is measured in dB unit by sound level meter (SLM). The other instruments like octave analyser, magnetic tape recorder is used in conjunction with SLM for storing noise. The significance of impulsive sound is very important. It is of very short duration, but is hazardous if its pitch is high. The sonic boom is gift of civilisation generated by fast moving aircrafts in the air. All problems of noise in vicinity of industrial establishment or domestic sources are tackled from the topograph of noise. It involves resorting to proper measurement technique and follow-up of control measures with suitable noise damping materials. The choice of such material is dependent upon its absorption coefficient of the material. One makes several case studies to finally abate noise. Unfortunately there are no strict regulations to prevent noise pollution in India. The social awareness and self-discipline by dwelling community should solve this problem.

ADDITIONAL READING

1. P.F. Cunniff, *Environmental Noise Pollution*, John Willey, New York (1977).
2. C. Jones, S.J. Gadler and P.H. Engstorm, *'Pollution the Noise We Hear'*, J.M. Dent and Sons Ltd., London (1972).

3. W. Burns, *Noise and Man*, J.B. Lippincott (1989).
4. I.L. Faulkner, *Handbook of Industrial Noise Control*, Industrial Press, New York (1976).
5. K.D. Kryter, *Effects of Noise on Man,* 2nd Ed, Academic Press, Orlando (1985).
6. T. Harvey, Editor, Notes on *Environmental Pollution, Monitoring and Control,* Tottenham College of Technology, London (1977).
7. D.F. Anthrop, *Noise Pollution,* D.C. Health and Co., Toronto (1973).
8. R.K. Miller, *Handbook of Industrial Noise Management,* Fairman Press, Atlanta, Georgia (1976).
9. A.A. Walter, *Noise and Prices*, Oxford University Press (1975).
10. R.F. Powell and M.R. Forrest, *Noise in the Military Environment*, Brassey's Defence Publishers, London (1988).
11. S.K. Sahoo and S.M. Khopkar, *Indian Journal of Environmental Protection* **7**, 119, (1987).
12. T.N. Tiwari V.P. Kedesia, *Noise Pollution and its Control,* Pragati Prakashan, New Delhi (1990).
13. C.F. Wilson, *Noise Control*, Harpper and Row and Co. (1989).
14. R.G. White and J.G. Walker, *Noise and Vibrations,* Ellis Horward Pub. (1982).
15. N. Rajvaidya, D.K. Markandey, *Advance in Environmental Science and Technology*, Vol. I to VII, A.P.H. Publisher, New Delhi (1998).
16. S.M. Khopkar, *Environmental Pollution Analysis*, 2nd Edition, New Age International Publishers (P) Ltd. (2012).

20 Odour and Environment

20.1 INTRODUCTION

One of the definite source of indication of pollution is odour. Odour is defined as perception of smell referring to the experience, or one that is smelled by stimulus. Such perception is possible through the receptors (*i.e.*, nose) of olfactory epithelium, in an area of an average one inch within the nasal cavity. A psychologically pure odour is sensed by olfactory receptors. Other odours like chemical smell is termed as impure odour. Such chemical odours have a sense like pain, heat or cold. Such odour originates from chemicals.

The airborne gases, vapours or aerosols have definite odour. It originates from solid, liquid or concentrated gas. Such an origin is called as the odour source. The dispersion of odour in atmosphere is accompanied by dilution. The dispersion is also possible by a process of evaporation, desorption or condensation. Most gases and vapours like P_2, N_2, H_2, CO_2 and most of the noble gases are odorous in nature, while some like CO, have no odour.

Odour just like taste depends upon the contact of stimulating substance with suitable human receptor like nose. The stimuli is chemical sense. Pure water has no odour. But, due to odour, toxic food is be rejected. Odour serves as potential warning of the hazardous environment. Most organic compounds continue to generate odour. Domestic consumers of food, beverage and pharmaceutical industries need odour-free water. Some strong odours are detected even at very low concentration of the substances. Nose qualitatively differentiates between different odours. It gives rough estimate of the quantitative threshold odour concentration. An attempt is to classify different odours with varying smell such as fragrant, sweet, foul etc. Table 20.1 illustrates different kinds of odour with possible source and its response on human beings.

There are variety of odours. This table attempts to classify the odour depending upon the human response. Apart from two common reactions *viz.* pleasant (good) and nauseating (bad). We have in between variety of response like unpleasant, repulsive, pungent, nontolerable, toxic etc.

It is worthwhile at this stage to identify the source, or origin of odour from typical substances emitting characteristic odour. The ethanol and ester like substance which produces fruity smell, while aromatic compounds like phenol aniline produces intense, unpleasant smell. Flowers, fruits give fragrant sweet smell. Muster gives repulsive odour. Coffee, tobacco, smoke give typical characteristic smell. Pesticide give offensive smell not acceptable by human if it is in large doses.

Table 20.1 Classification of odour

S.No.	*Class of odour*	*Examples*	*Response*
1.	Etherial	Fruity ether, perfumes, bees wax	V. good smell
2.	Aromatic	Camphor, citron, almond, spices	Unpleasant
3.	Fragrant	Flowers, vanilla, balsam, scents	V. pleasant
4.	Ambrosiac	Amber, musk	Repulsive smell
5.	Aliceous	Onions, iodine, acetylene	Pungent, irritating
6.	Enpyrenumetic	Coffee, tobacco, smoke, xylol, naphthalene	Nauseating smell
7.	Dairy	Goaty odour; cheese, sweat, chestnuts	Smell causing vomit
8.	Foul	Narcotics, bugs, coriander, flowers	Bad repulsive smell
9.	Nauseous	Carrion, faeces; urine	Bad smell

It is little difficult to classify odour based upon their human response. First a compound may give two kinds of odour. Simultaneously and most important is the personal factor *viz.* Analogous to colour blindness one does not identify typical colour similarly we may have odour blindness where the person cannot differentiate or identify a particular odour. While few persons have such sharp sense of smelling that they identify odour with small variation.

20.2 SOURCE OF ODOUR

If a storage tank is filled with a liquid component from another source, it discharges odour into the atmosphere. A volume of air is saturated with liquid component at prevailing temperature of the liquid. Such odour emanates from a confined source. The odour is confimed when its rate of discharge to the atmosphere is measurable. The characterisation of odour includes knowledge of rate of discharge, temperature, moisture content, location and elevation of the source and finally the description of the state of aggregation of the discharge. A direct human sensory characterisation of a confined odour source is not always possible, due to intolerable human exposure. An example of unconfined source of odour is drainage, sewage, line, ditch discharge. The rate of such discharge is affected by wind direction and wind velocity. Other examples of unconfined source of odour are garbage dump; settling lagoons, chemical storage areas and oxidation pond storing liquid/solid waste.

20.3 SAMPLING OF ODOUR

One directly has sense of odour on inhalation of air but many a times it is necessary to dilute or concentrate this odour. It is necessary to dilute odorant or concentrate it specially before human exposure for its measurement. There are four methods of sampling of odour, like grab sampling, sampling by dilution or sampling by concentration, and sampling by adsorption and absorption on column.

(i) Grab Sampling of Odour

It involves sampling without change in concentration of odorant. The containers for grab sampling are inert and have a large volume-to-surface ratio. The odour may not condense on cooling. Grab sampling is carried out by allowing the air to fill in an evacuated container like stainless steel or glass container, plastic, mylar, teflon or polymeric containers with known volume.

(ii) Sampling with Dilution of Odour

It is necessary to dilute concentrated odour to render it is suitable for human exposure during measurements. The dilution ratio is:

$$\text{Dilution ratio} = \frac{\text{Vol. of sample after dilution}}{\text{Vol. of sample before dilution}} \quad \text{(at constant pressure and temperature)}$$

It is also expressed in terms of pressure rather than volume. However in terms of pressure

$$\text{Dilution ratio} = \frac{\text{Total pressure of sample after dilution}}{\text{Partial pressure of odorant in container}}$$

The container for dilution is a stainless steel vessel and it is odourless and does not contribute any new odour.

(iii) Sampling with Concentration of Odour

A faint odorant will have to be concentrated before characterisation by chemical techniques. In such a case, ratio of concentrations between the odour source and the odorant outdoors is maintained in the range of 10^3 to 10^5. The infrared or gas chromatography is used for characterisation of odour. Most commonly employed methods for concentration involve cooling, use of adsorption on activated coal or cotton pieces.

The odorant air stream is passed through a cold trap, which freezes and holds the odorous substance, but does not retain the major nonodorous components. The liquid air with b.p. – 196°C is used for the purpose of cooling. Oxygen should not be trapped and cooled, as it creates a problem in analysis. Such a pure sample is good, because interactions, among concentrated components are minimised at low temperature.

The odorant air stream is passed through a bed in column of granulated activated carbon, silica gel, or some suitable adsorbent to concentrate odorous substance. The best material for such purpose is activated carbon, as it absorbs organic matter. However, recovery from charcoal is somewhat difficult, however desorption in vacuum is comparatively easy. The solvent extraction process is a less drastic method but it yields poor results.

It is preferable to concentrate and hold an odour sample easily with minimum use of equipment. Thus, mineral odour-free oil or cotton is used for adsorption of odour.

20.4 MEASUREMENT OF ODOUR

An odour is characterised by its intensity, quality, threshold, effective tone or pleasant or unpleasant dimensions. Odour reduction is done by ventilation with exhaust fan or by process of absorption. The measurement is based upon consideration of the parameters like intensity, quality, dilution ratio and acceptability by human being.

(i) Intensity of Odour

It is the intensity of the stimulus produced when a person is exposed to an odorant. It is measured on the intensity scale, where reference points consists of standard odorants for the purpose of comparison. The odour standards does not match the quality of the odour being measured. It is also possible to determine the intensity ratios that is based on certain reference point. This is called as '*ratio scales*'. Some intensities are expressed in simple terms as 'slight', moderate, strong, and extreme odours.

(ii) Quality of Odour

The quality of odour is known by comparison in terms of resemblance to some other odour producing material. Thus, fragrant, putrid, musky, phenolic are common words. No conceptual system is devised which accurately predicts odour quality from the chemical composition of the odorant. The Table 20.2 provides quality of the odour. Such quality is ascertained by comparison with the substances

Table 20.2 Quality of odour of chemicals

S.No.	*Odorant similarity with compounds as*	*Quality*	*S.No.*	*Odorant similarity with compounds as*	*Quality*
1.	Acetaldehyde	Pungent	14.	Dimethy sulphide	Decayed
2.	Ammonia	Pungent	15.	Ethyl ether	V. pleasant
3.	Chlorine gas	Irritating, pungent	16.	Benzyl chloride	Aromatic
4.	Formadehyde	Pungent	17.	Camphor	Aromatic
5.	Sulphur dioxide	Pungent	18.	Trichloroethylene	Aromatic
6.	Propyl mercaptan	Unpleasant	19.	Butyne acid	Rancid
7.	Allyl disulphide	Garlic	20.	Carbon disulphide	Rotten eggs
8.	Allyl mercaptan	Garlic	21.	Ethyl mercaptan	Foul mercaptan smell
9.	Diethylsulphide	Garlic	22.	Hydrogen sulphide	Rotten eggs
10.	Trimethyl amine	Fishy	23.	Phenol	Emphyrematic
11.	Dimethyl amine	Fishy	24.	Pyridine	Bitter
12.	Ethyl mercaptan	Like rotten eggs	25.	Valeric acid	Unpleasant
13.	Methyl mercaptan	Like rotten eggs	26.	Acrolein	Burning

producing odour in simple words as sweet, pungent, garlic, fishy which are commonly known or explains the mechanism of odour perception.

Thus a variety of chemicals generate numerous kinds of odour Table 20.2 summarises odour depending upon its quality. Most of the organic and few inorganic chemicals have some kind of odour *e.g.* Ammonia, acetaldehyde, chlorine, formaldehyde all of them produce pungent smell. The sulphur containing compounds releases garlic smell. The amines mostly produce fishy smell. Benzene, xylene, camphor, ethylene produce aromatic smell. H_2S, CS_2 give smell of the rotten eggs. A burning smell is produced by acrolein. Pyridine gives unbearable intense smell which causes headaches. It is difficult to categorises chemicals on the basis of their smell. As it is difficult task to find out some kind of the correction between chemical constitution and odour. It is possible successfully to predict the colour and based upon the chemical constitution of the compound. The odour is measured in terms of TON value. Table 20.3 summarises measurement of any odour in terms of threshold odour number (TON) after proper dilution of original compound.

Table 20.3 Measurement of odour in terms of threshold odour number

S.No.	*Sample with odour volume (A)*	*Volume of odour free water (B)*	*Total volume after dilution (T)*	*Response human*	*TON (R) (ratio)*
1.	200	0	200	No smell	1.0
2.	100	100	200	Some smell	2.0
3.	70	130	200	Reduced smell	3.0
4.	50	150	200	Further reduction	4.0
5.	35	165	200	Faint smell	6.0
6.	25	175	200	Weak smell	8.0
7.	17	183	200	Dilute smell	12.0
8.	40	160	200	Smell	4.0
9.	20	180	200	Insignificant smell	9.0

The total odour number is defined by following expression wherein 'A' represents ml of odours sample while 'B' represent ml of odour sample of free water added till odour disappears.

$$\text{TON} = \left[\frac{A+B}{A}\right] = R \text{ i.e. (Threshold odour number)}$$

One important criteria is the water used for the dilution is must be totally free from any odour such water is obtained by slowly passing fresh water through finely divided activated column. Although there is spectacular revolution in the development of chemical instrumentation, there is no single instrument so far fabricated which either measure the intensity or the quality of odour emitted out by odorant substance. The nose is most powerful sensing device which gives fairly good idea about the quality of the odour. In order to supplement this observation a scale furnishing quantitative level of odour has been devised called "TON *i.e.* threshold odour number". It depends upon how much dilution is made to allow to vanish/disappear odour of a sample *e.g.* Table 20.4 gives clear idea about TON (*e.g.* S.No. 1) 200 ml of odorous sample with 200 ml of odour free water is added to get rid of odour. We note a 1:1 dilution there for TON = 1.0.

It should be noted that we have to keep total volume constant *viz.* 200 to sample we add odour free water so that it is totally odour free then we note the ratio of dilution (*e.g.* S.No. 2) we add 100 to 100 so ratio is 1.0 so TON = 1.0 (S.No. 1). In next section let us consider experimental aspects of odour measurement.

(iii) Threshold Measurement of Odour

The odour threshold is the bare minimum perceptible concentration of odour, at which an odorous substance is distinguished from odour-free air. It is also called as the detection threshold. This is the limit at which its quality is recognised and is termed as recognisation threshold. The odour threshold level depends upon the nature of the substance as well as on the sensitivity of the judges. The threshold is the concentration at which the odour is detected or recognised by definite population of judges. Threshold data is used to predict conditions under which a given substance will be odorous or odourless. It decides the degree of dilution of ventilation to deodorize or dilute a given odour source. It represents the proportion of odorant that must be eliminated from a space, or it represents the quantity of a substance, that must be eliminated from air to odorize. In fact, this is the volume of air to be odorized by a given quantity of substance. Threshold concentrations are not always reliable prediction of odour intensity. TON is studied quantitatively by other method.

Thus the threshold level (C_t) is measured by quantitative dilution of a given volume (V) of odorant of known concentration (C). Thus, $C = W/V$ and $C_t = W/V_t$, if W = quantity of odorant and V_t is the volume of sample after it is diluted to threshold level, V is volume of odorant and C is threshold concentration. Thus, $C_t = CV/V_t$. The threshold dilution ratio is $V/V_t = C/C_t$. This is similar to reduced Beers' law. It is called as TON or odour perseverance. Table 20.5 tells us how to calculate the possible dilution. Dilution is carried out for perception of odours especially when sample of water is used as diluent. In all these cases, a person testing, odour should never know dilution ratio to avoid predicting the TON of the sample. A 500 ml of sample is diluted in succession with 200, 50, 12 and 2.8 ml of diluent to the sample. Odour of the water is removed by aeration or by passing it for adsorption on activated carbon.

20.5 ODOUR DETERMINATION IN WATER

The following dilutions are used (Table 20.4).

Table 20.4 Threshold odour number corresponding to different dilution

A				*B*			
Quality of smell	*Sample Vol.*	*Pure water with no odour added*	*TON*	*Quality of smell*	*Sample vol with odour*	*Pure H_2O with no odour added*	*TON*
Weak	200	200	1.0	Medium	12.0	188.0	17
Weak	140	60	1.4	Medium	8.8	191.2	24
Weak	100	100	1.0	Medium	5.7	194.3	35
Weak	70	130	2.0	Medium	4.0	196.0	50
Weak	50	150	3.0	Strong	2.8	197.2	70
Medium	35	165	4.0	Strong	2.0	198.0	100
Medium	25	175	5.0	Strong	1.4	198.6	140
Medium	17	183	12.0	Strong	1.0	199.0	200

(i) Experimental Details of Testing TON

The sample bearing strong odour is immediately tested for TON. A person first smells mild odour followed by strong odour during dilution process. TON is in fact a dilution ratio when odour is just perceptible. Smallest TON 1.0, wherein (Table 20.4) 200 ml of sample and 200 ml of odour free water is mixed. It is a geometrical means of the individual threshold. A large panel provides more reliable results. m-cresol or n-butanol is used to test sensitivity of person testing odour. Dechlorinated water must be used for the dilution with no odour. The temperature for measurement of odour be too low or too high during testing (60°C recommended). TON = (A + B)/A when A ml. odorous of sample, B = ml of odour free water. TON is not a precise value specially when single observer is there. Unless all tests conditions are identical one cannot make any comparison. The Fig. 20.1 indicates diagram to procure odour free water. The generator to get odour free water is fabricated indigenously in the laboratory.

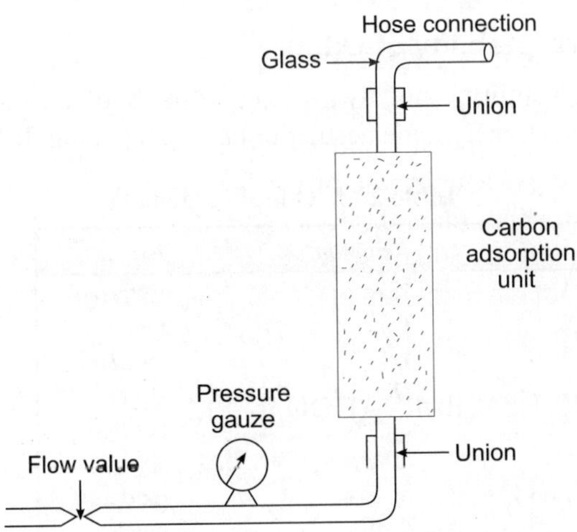

Fig. 20.1 Odour free water generator

(ii) Threshold Cdour Test

TON is determined by diluting sample with odour with odour free water till minimum perceptible odour is accomplished. The sensory capacity of every individual is not identical. It changes even for same person within day or even within few hours. The number of persons selected for odour measurement depends upon the end use of the findings but for better precision large number of persons are essential (5–10 persons). Any high concentration is measured by appropriate dilution. We have already considered different methods for the sampling of odours. They are: sample involving grab sampling, sampling by dilution, or sampling by concentration. The glass or teflon containers are used in all these methods which are odour free. Plastic has smell so that containers are never used. The sample of chlorinated water is dechlorinated before measurement of the odour. The threshold odour number (TON) varies with temperature. The 60°C is standard temperature for the hot threshold odour test. Sometime 40°C temperature is also referred. Use of rubber with smell for testing is also prohibited. Odour free water for dilution is obtained by the process of distillation followed by its passage through column of activated coal. The ratio of flow is 100 ml/mt odour free water generators are easily available in the market or even they are indigenously fabricated. Insensitive persons with lack of concentrations should not be employed for determining TON. Persons with cold cough or allergies be discarded. Non-smoker be preferably selected. An odour free room fitted with glazed titles is used to carry out test. One should not ask persons to smell till he gets fatigued. The coloured glass bottles are used to avoid bias. It is possible in order to differentiate the odour as algae, chlorophenols, mustard. Its better to have TON with greater dilution of sample with odour free diluent yielding a perceptible odour. It is evaluated by an equation as TON = A+B/A if A = ml of sample with odour, B = ml of odour free water or air. Table 20.4 indicates the relationship of TON with various dilutions. Table 20.5 shows acceptibilty of odour.

(iii) Scale of Acceptability of Odour

The scale of acceptability is not always used as per book on standard methods of analysis. It depends largely upon aesthetic sense of a person. It is worth to closely

Table 20.5 Odour judgement

S.No.	*Reaction*	*Extent*
1.	Like	Extreme
2.	Like	much
3.	Like	moderate
4.	No like	slight
5.	dislike	neither
6.	dislike	slight
7.	dislike	moderate
8.	dislike	much
9.	dislike	extreme

examine Table 20.6 dealing with acceptability of odour. A comparison is made real samples with their own odour. Several of the organic compounds have peculiar smell which is used for comparison. It is rated either on a hedonic scale (like, dislike) or on action basis. A typical scale is numbered on like-dislike scale as follows in Table 20.5.

This is called hedonic scales. This scale is not at all foolproof since it involves personal error during measurements therefore is not accepted as standard.

20.6 JUDGEMENT OF ODOUR MEASUREMENT

The following are the criteria for selection of judges during measurement of odour. These judges are called as sensors.

(i) The Criteria of Selection of Person

The judges are able to discriminate among different odours at low or moderate levels of intensity. They should be able to focus their attention on more than one odour quality to characterise a given odour sensation. Their sensory ability is good. The specific items to which one is attentive are speed, interest level, domination, independence and honesty. It is presumed that they do not suffer from cold, cough or any pulmonary problems. They should not be allergic to smell. The person should become familiar with the conduct and execution of sensory testing. If not he should be given proper training to distinguish between various odours for definite period.

(ii) Conditions for Measurement

The space where odour is measured be free of competing distractions. The area should be provided with some means of space odour control, air cleaning is done by local exhaust. The hard surfaced wall panels and mosaic or asphaltic tile flooring are low in background odour. No smoking, drinking, eating, be permitted in the area of measurement. Fair sex be discouraged to use strong perfumes or perfumed cosmetics before such measurement. A gap of at least 30 minutes before measurement is kept and drinking of coffee or hard drinks is strictly avoided.

Table 20.6 Acceptability of odour by comparison

S. No.	*Source*	*Intensity*	*Degree of pleasant or unpleasant*	*S. No.*	*Source*	*Intensity*	*Degree of pleasant or unpleasant*
1.	Amylacetate	2.2	5.0	9.	Ionone	1.8	4.1
2.	Benzaldehyde	2.3	6.5	10.	Methysalicylate	1.5	7.0
3.	Butyric acid (dil)	2.9	2.1	11.	Orange	1.7	5.8
4.	Butylamine (dil)	2.7	2.0	12.	Phenyl alcohol	1.2	5.0
5.	Coffee	1.0	4.4	13.	Safrole	1.6	6.4
6.	Eugenol	2.0	6.5	14.	Terpinol	1.9	4.7
7.	Geraniol	1.7	4.7	15.	Vanilin	1.7	6.3
8.	Indole	1.4	3.7				

The Table 20.6 gives arbitrary scale to recognize odour on the basis of arbitrary response of person to the odour. The intensity is zero while with best value is 4.0 for coffee. A degree of pleasantness or unpleasantness is recovered. Thus, benzaldehyde with smell of bitter almonds has degree of 6.5 while coffee has degree of pleasantness is 4.4. Methysalicylate has 7.0 degree which is highest while butyric acid has degree of 2.1 on this scale.

The scale as shown in Table 20.6 is based on arbitrary response of person to pleasant or bitter smell. Since a personal factor is involved which varies from person to person this scale is not universally accepted. However a scale based on dilution phenomena is most reliable. Therefore, for all the practical purposes TON scale is used for measurement.

20.7 ODOUR-NITROGEN AND SULPHUR CYCLE IN NATURE

An attempt is made to trace the origin of odour. For those of the compounds containing either nitrogen or sulphur they produce odour. There is no hard and fast rule, but organic compounds containing sulphur or nitrogen have intense odours. It is worth to examine the nitrogen cycle (Fig. 20.2) and sulphur (Fig. 20.3) cycle.

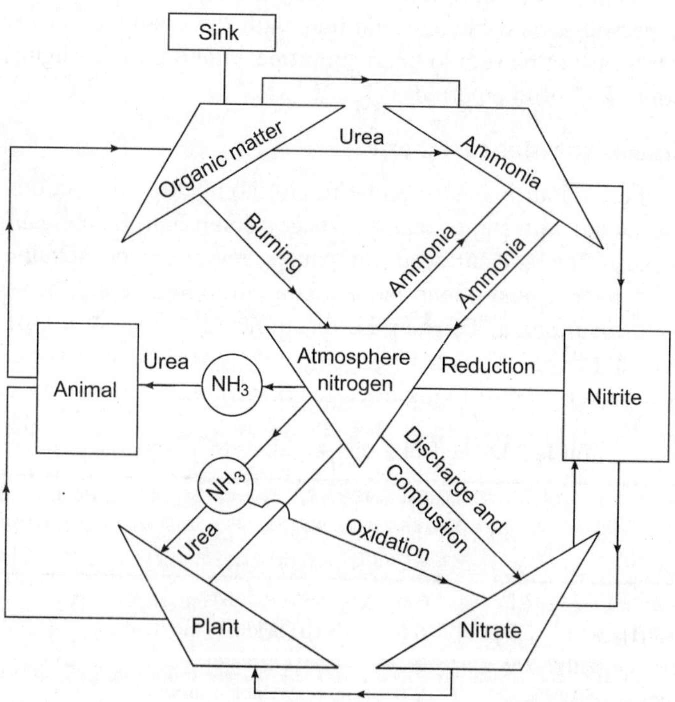

Fig. 20.2 Odour and nitrogen cycle

The nitrogen cycle shows that odour is generated due to oxidation of nitrosomonas or nitrobacteria. The dead organic matter from animal or plant protein gives rise to bad odour. Amongst inorganic compounds containing nitrogen, ammonia, is an well-known example of odours material, which is not hidden as even small traces give strong pungent smell:

As regards sulphur cycle the principal source of odour generation are sulphites, sulphide and animal and plant proteins. Such odour originates from animal feacus and urine. There is no evidence to prove or disprove this argument.

It is interesting to note that in the environmental pollution analysis that in spite of greater advancement in computers, microprocessor and integrated circuit chips, we have failed to produce an instrument to replace olfactory sensory measuring sense. The stimulus is recognised by brain and so far science and technology has failed to devise an artificial brain, though we have mechanical robots to do tedious task.

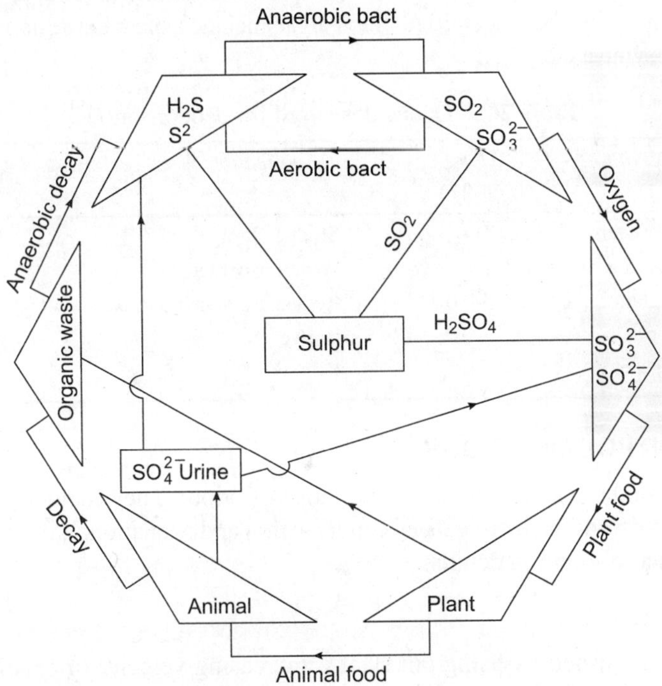

Fig. 20.3 Odour and sulphur cycle

20.8 CHEMICAL CONSTITUTION AND ODOUR

The correlations between odorous substance and sensory measurement is not always possible, though odorants like other substances are amenable to chemical analysis. A chemical analysis is not a final measurement of odour, though it may offer some clue on structural aspects. There is no specific recommended procedure for correlating chemical analysis with sensory measurements of the properties of odorants. The chemical analysis and sensory evaluation should be carried out side-by-side. GC-MS is used with advantage for analysis and one smells the reaction as soon as it [exist] from chromatography chamber. The establishment of correlations between chemical and sensory measurements of complex mixtures is still demanding time consuming mixture of science and art. The closed loop stripping gas chromatograph mass spectrometer is useful for such purpose.

The hyphenated spectrometric analysis (GC/MS) shows that odour producing compounds are *e.g.*, 2 methyisoborneol (MIB) and geosmin. The stripping efficiency affects GS/MS peaks in range of 0.1 to 100 ηg/L lower limit encountered is for compounds like o-dichlorobenzene, geosmin while highest detectable (100 ηg/L), limit is encountered for compounds like trichloroethane, m-xylene, napthalene and diethyl pthalate by GC/MS technique. Other odour producing organic compounds are isobutyl methoxy pyrazine, trichloroanisole, chlorodecane also gives musk smell. The variety of algae produces offensive odour in the sample of water which have been identified. Such algae include synedra, astesionnel, nitella, cestratium, synuva etc.

Table 20.7 Ozone dose used for deodorisation

Application	*O_3 dose (ppm/v)*	*Application*	*O_3 dose (ppm/v)*
Hotel; canteen	1	Sludge storage	10
Sewage plant	1	Wine fermentation	0–50
Phenol plant	3–10	Rendering plants	10
Rubber plant	3–10	Brewery	5–10
Fish process	10	Kitchen, dinning halls	2

20.9 CONTROL OF ODOUR

There are number of methods for the control of odour. They include dispersion, absorption, adsorption, incineration, condensation and ozonation. We would briefly consider each of them in details.

(i) Dispersion

This is accomplished by using tall stacks, increasing velocity of existing gas or dilution with air. The increasing of the buoyancy is also alternative in dispersion of odour.

(ii) Absorption

This method involves scrubbing with $KMnO_4$, NaOH, ClO_2. Spray chambers are not efficient like venturi scrubbers, when odour producing H_2S, mercapturs, SO_2, NH_3 organic compounds due to chemical reaction loose their odour *e.g.* H_2S reacts with $KMnO_4$ to remove 99.5% odour. Ammonia is scrubbed with water or hydrochloric acid when the entire smell disappears.

(iii) Adsorption

Solid surface adsorbs gases. On adsorption the energy of motion is lost. The process is exothermic and energy releasing mode surface area decides quantity of adsorbent to be used. Adsorption increase with concentration. The decrease in temperature, increases adsorption, high pressure favours adsorption. Adsorbent should have large surface area, activated, granular form is easy to regenerate and surface form is cheap *e.g.* Activated charcoal, silicagel, Al_2O_3, Mg_2SiO_3, Fullers earth, clay, bauxite. Coal is best for hydrocarbon.

(iv) Incineration

Complete combustion removes odour and generates CO_2 and water vapour, where time temperature and turbulence are important parameters. Temperature and time are most critical. Some on burning produces more intense odour in absence of incomplete oxidation. Flame, thermal and catalytic operations are modes of operation. Temperature of oxidation is important. Catalysis poisoned therefore Hg, Zn, Pb must be absent. Thermal oxidation is used for spray paint drying process. Gas flame, thermal incineration, is superior as it is cheap, simple and reproducible.

Table 20.8 Comparison of control measure of odour

Process	*Merits*			*Demerits*	
1. Incineration (Thermal)	Simple (50% Effi.)	No maintenance needed	95% Efficiency	High cost	Special equipment needed
2. Oxidation (catalytic)	Low cost (30% Effi.)	No equipment required	Low fuel cost	Replacement necessary	Catalyst poisoning
3. Adsorption	Low cost (35% Effi.)	98% Efficient	No equipment needed	Corrosion problem	Change of adsorbent periodically required
4. Absorption (scrubbing)	Efficient (75% Effi.)	Low cost	Flexible	No change pollution caused	Disposal of scrubble water is problem
5. Dispersion	Simple (30% Effi.)	Simple operation	Low maintenance	Temporary effect	High stack, and cost
6. Condensation	Expensive	Large vol. of water needed	–	Corrosion is problem	Disposal is problem

(v) Condensation

Condensation has limited use. Surface and contact condensers are in use. In first vapors and condensate contact a cool surface, while in latter vapor, condensate and coolants are mixed together. H_2O is coolant.The efficiency is 95%. Latter need more water. No maintenance is required on long term basis.

(vi) Ozonization

This is one of the best method of control of odour though O_3 is unstable but it is powerful oxidizing agent and has germicidal effect. High temperature and moisture accelerates decomposition of ozone to oxygen. $3O_2 \rightleftharpoons 2O_3 \rightleftharpoons 3O_2$.

In place of O_3 one also uses Cl_2, ClO_2, O_2, $KMnO_4$, NaOCl for deodarisation. Other reagents are controversial as disinfectant and cause more odour. It is worthwhile comparing all control system of odour control.

(vii) Comparison of Various Control Measures

We consider some processes. Odour çontrol is one of the formidable task (see Table 20.8). 100% odour removal is essential. Odour threshold value represents minimum concentration (ppm) at which odour quality of odorant is recognised. *e.g.* CCl_4 (100 ppm), Ethyl alcohol (10) but acetic acid (1). It is a serious problem in air pollution. Nose is reliable instrument for its detection. Several unsaturated, halogenated, nitrous or sulphurous compounds generate odour. Odour judgement panel or sensitivity meters detect odour intensity. H_2S, mercaptans, NH_3, CH_3S, SO_2, NO-NOx urea, aldehydes, fluorides, phenols, hydrocarbons, chlorine-compounds produces odour in paper, petroleum, fertiliser, metal casting, pesticide, and food industry. The instrument is used to measure odour threshold. It avoids fatigue of nose and it dilutes 1 : 130 times sample concentration. Most efficient control system is scrubbing (75% efficient). Chemical oxidation is most ineffective (5% efficient). For short term solution, masking or counteractant is best method but it gives only temporary relief.The methods of air oxidation with dried flame gives temperature 1150°C, thermal oxidation gives best results at 450°–750°C and the catalytic oxidation works efficiently at temperature of 250°–400°C range, odour threshold by different substance vary. The perceptible concentration (ppm) for few compounds is worth considering *e.g.* (see Table 20.9).

Table 20.9 Human response to odour (% response)

S.No.	*Source of odour*	*Feeling pleasant response %*	*S.No.*	*Source of odour*	*Feeling pleasant response %*
1.	Acetophenone	56	8.	Diphenylether	44
2.	Camphor	70	9.	Geraniol	81
3.	*n*-caproic acid	9	10.	Heptylaldehyde	7
4.	*o*-bromto compounds	20	11.	Methanol	62
5.	*p*-dichlorobenzene	83	12.	Nitrobenzene	15
6.	Empty bottle (as control)	61	13.	Quinoline	15
7.	Ethylcinnamate	31	14.	Oil of winter green	90

The Table 20.10 is additional table with formula indicating response in percentage. It is based upon approximation. The number of response need not remain same. This is because of the personal error. Every individual has not similar degree of sense of response it may be more for sensitive person and less for nonsensitive person. We have in Table 20.10 source of odour and % feeling presents on the arbitrary scale winter green oil has 90% feeling which is highest while caproic acid as well as heptyl-dehyde has respective % response is 9 or 7 respectively. We can summarise that compounds like (> 50% response) are acetophenone, *p*-dichlorobenzene, Geraniol, Methanol and oil of winter green have very intense odour which cannot be ignored while few compounds (< 10% response) are *n*-caproic acid. Heptylaldehyde has insignificant odour, difficult to smell. But compounds with intermediate response (> 10% but less than 50%) are few namely *o*-bromto compounds, Ethylcinnamate; diphenylether, nitrobenzene, quinoline. There smell is perceptible only with trained person having good sense or response.

Table 20.10 Odour threshold for compounds on basis of 100% response

Compd.	*Threshold*	*Compd.*	*Threshold*	*Compd.*	*Threshold*
CH_3Cl	214	$COCl_2$	1.0	C_6H_5—OH	0.05
CH_3OH	100	$C_6H_5NH_3$	1.0	Pyridine	0.02
CCl_4	100	SO_2	0.5	PH_3	0.02
CH_3NCH_3	100	CH_3COOH	1.0	$C_6H_5NO_2$	0.005
NH_3	46.8	HCHO	1.0	H_2S	0.005
MEK	10	$C_6H_4(CH_3)_2$	0.5	SCl_2	0.001
Acryl nitrile	21.0	MIBK	0.5	Cresol	0.001
C_2H_5OH	10.0	Cl_2	0.3	Butyric acid	0.001
C_6H_5–CH_3	4.7	CS_2	0.2	Ethyl acralate	0.0005
C_6H_6	4.7	$(CH_3)_2CHO$	0.2	Trimethylamine	0.0002

These results show that the members in begining have mild odor but as we go down the series intensity of odour increase with maximum smell for trimethyamine. Table 20.10 list number of compounds with limit of tolerance by human being.

20.10 CONCLUSION

We considered what are probable sources of odour. The various methods for sampling of odour are studied. The measurement of odour is a ticklism task as with all possible precaution exact quantitive analysis is difficult due to relative personal error in measurements. The determination of odour is critical as even with little perceptible odour in potable water it should be rejected. The classical methods of judgements of odour on hedonic scale is justifiably rejected by US-EPA. It is difficulty to correlate odour to either nitrogen or sulphur cycle. However, much needs to be done to ascertain a relationship between chemical constitution and odour. This is formidable task but is easily accomplished with the availability of the precise instruments for chemical analysis.

ADDITIONAL READING

1. P.N. Cheremisihoff. R.A. Young, *Industrial Odour Technology Assessment,* Ann Arbor U.S.A. (1975).
2. W. Sommer, *Odour Pollution of Air,* Leonard Hill (1971).
3. C.P. McCord, and W.N. Whiteridge, *Odours's Physiology and Control*, McGraw Hill, New York (1949).
4. I.D. Morton and A.J. Macleod, *Food Flavours*; Elsevier Scientific Pub. Amsterdam (1982).
5. M. Joseph, *Food Flavourings Composition, Manufacture and Use*, Westport, Conn., AVI, Pub. Co. (1968).
6. E.T. Theimer, *Fragrance Chemistry, the Science of the Sense of Smell,* Academic Press, New York (1982).
7. S.M. Khopkar, *Environmental Pollution Analysis* Second Edition, New Age International (P) Ltd., Publishers (2012).

21

Thermal Pollution

21.1 INTRODUCTION

Thermal pollution is measured to investigate the adverse effects on environment by heated effluents emerging from power plants. It leads to the deterioration of aquatic and terrestrial environment. Major part of water in industry is used for cooling, which consequently leads to decrease in the amount of dissolved oxygen in water. The plants and animals grow better at certain optimum temperature of water. This effect is also called as *"thermal enhancement* or *thermal enrichment*." A large scale change in thermal contents of water changes its ecology for bad effects. The population of fish dwindle if hot water is discharged into stream. The heated water if let off in stream causes pollution which is even worst than discharge of organic waste leading to decrease in assimilative capacity of stream. The electricity plant is the worst source of thermal pollution. Municipal and irrigation resorts causes problem. Sewage increase 10% of heat addition while power plants do increase 73% of heat content of stream. On basis of this information we define thermal pollution as "a process of warming of water leading to adverse effects on living organism or an addition of heat to water to render it unfit for human consumption." The heated effluent causes toxic effect, reduces dissolved oxygen or spread disease. Such pollution reduces population of aquatic organism and impairs the balance of life in aquatic environment. It is considered as the by-product of industrialisation and progress leading to destruction of an environment specially flora and fauna.

21.2 SOURCE OF THERMAL POLLUTION

Most of the thermal and nuclear power plants are based upon cooling towers which in turn causes thermal pollution. In addition industrial effluents and domestic sewage cause also thermal pollution. The nuclear or thermal power plants discharge effluent at > 10° C higher in temperature than a stream. Coal fired power plant is worst culprit. The esturine stream or sea water is used for cooling. The stack looses are about 15%. In terms of heat contents, fossile fuel has 8,500 BTO/kWh while cooling water has 4,000 BTO/kWh and nuclear plants have 10.342 BTO/kWh.

The release of heat by different source is given in Table 21.1.

Table 21.1 Release of heat by various sources

S.No.	*Source*	*BTO × 10⁹ kWh*	*Total (%) release of heat*
1.	Thermal power plant	229	75%
2.	Effluents	19	6%
3.	Sewage	28	9%
4.	Biological activity	12	4%

On the whole the average rise in temperature is 6 to 10°C. Municipal sewage has high temperature. Its DO contents decreases with rise in temperature of a stream, leading to anaerobic condition of water. Hydroelectric power stations have negative effects of thermal loading. There is rise by 20% heat content. Table 21.2 lists some typical power plants releasing definite quantum heat in the environment.

Table 21.2 Discharge of heat by power plants

S. No.	*Type of power plant (capacity 500–15000 MW) (1)*	*Release in aquatic environ. Kcals/Kw per hour (2)*	*Release in atmosphere Kcals/Kw per hour (3)*	*Remarks heat generator (4)*
1.	Ocean power plant	35000	0	V. large heat
2.	Solar energy plant	2500	0	Large heat
3.	Geothermal-hot water stream plant	12000	100	V. large heat
4.	Geothermal-land stream plant	5000	100	Large heat
5.	Turbine plant (800 MW)	11000	200	Large heat
6.	Stream-Gas turbine plant (500 W)	900	150	Reasonable
7.	MHD gas turbine plant	800	120	Reasonable
8.	Nuclear plant (1200 MW)	1700	50	Average
9.	Radioactive plant (1200 MW)	105000	70	V. large heat
10.	Steam extraction and condenser plant	105000	300	Average
11.	Back pressure turbine plant	10000	300	V. large heat
12.	Stream extraction plant	50000	220	Large heat

If we examine Table 21.1, we note that source of release of heat vai different sources which is important. In Table 21.2, one examines the discharge of heat in aquatic and atmospheric environment by different types of power plants. Dozen power plants are in India. The amount of heat released from water is shown in column (3) with observation in last column (4), while heat released in air is shown in another fourth column. We have several kinds of power plants such as ocean, solar, geothermal, turbine, steam gas, MHD gas turbine, nuclear, radioactive, back pressure and steam plant. Each plant is having varying capacity ranging from 500–1200 MW. A close look at this Table 21.2 shows that amount of heat released in Kcals/Kw per hour is highest. Nuclear or radioactive plant, while ocean plant releases 3.5×10^4 Kcals/Kw per hour heat in water. The release of heat in air by back pressure turbine plant as well as in condenser plant produces as much as 300 Kcal/Kw. The maximum amount of heat is generated by back pressure plant in water and MHD gas turbine plants of 500 W in the atmosphere or environment. We would now consider the effect of discharge of heat on environment.

21.3 EFFECTS OF DISCHARGE OF HEAT ON ENVIRONMENT

These effects are classified as the physical, biological and chemical effects. The physical effects involve the change in physical property such as density, viscosity, vapour pressure surface tension, gas solubility and diffusion. Table 21.3 shows changes in physical properties of stream.

Table 21.3 Physical property variation in steam

S.No.	*Temp. °C*	*VP (mm/ng)*	*Viscosity (centi-poise)*	*Density (g/ml)*	*Surface tension (dynes/cm)*	*DO (mg/L)*	*Nitrogen (mg/L) solubility*	*Remarks*
1.	0	4.58	1.79	0.9998	75.6	14.6	23.1	V.P. increases
2.	5	6.54	1.52	0.9999	74.9	12.8	20.4	Viscocity decreases
3.	10	9.21	1.31	0.9997	74.2	11.3	18.1	Density decreases
4.	20	17.53	1.00	0.9982	72.8	9.2	14.9	S.T. decreases
5.	30	31.82	0.79	0.9956	71.2	7.6	12.7	Do reduced
6.	40	55.32	0.65	0.9922	69.6	6.6	10.8	Solution decreases

This Table 21.3 shows that with rise in temperature the viscosity of water decreases, density also decreases O an N_2 contents goes down. Surface tension also decreases only V.P. increases. The rise in vapour pressure increases rate of evaporation leading to effect of cooling with increase in sedimentation. The chemical process of water like filtration, ion-exchange is influenced by rise of temperature. Water with more than 7.5% rise in temperature is unfit for drinking purposes, where the biological effects are significant. At high temperature microorganisms become more active leading to stabilisation of waste. The metabolic activity also rises. The *E. coli* population rises simultaneously with the oxidation process. There is rapid rate of protein denaturation beyond 730°C but rate of oxidation varies with kind of water and type of biological activity. Temperature has bactericidal and viruscidal effect on activity of chlorine in water. The rate of destruction of bacteria decreases with chlorine. Several chemical consquences are encountered. The rate of chemical reaction is doubled with rise of 10°C. The period of chemical reaction is increased. The growth of blue-green algae is enhanced with temperature rise, thereby damaging ecosystem. The bacteria and pathogens also rise in number and rapid temperature produces the thermal shock for fish leading to their death. The rise in temperature is explained by ***"Von't hoff Arhenious law."*** The favourable temperature for fish is 15° C as toxicity rises with temperature. The respiration, digestion, reproductivity is affected by temperature variation. The vulnerability for diseases also increases. With rise in temperature blue algae show algal bloom in water. The thermal effects are not only on marine life, or bacteria but also on man and his environment. It also affects water quality and temperature of streams when enzymatic reaction rises. Water purification occurs at high temperature. It is interesting to note that the favourable temperature for variety of fish to survive such temperature is given in Table 21.4 with acceleration of temperature the extent of death of fish also rises.

Table 21.4 Favourable temperature for fish servival

Type	*Temp. (°C)*	*Acclimatization Temp. (°C)*	*Thermal death at Temp. of (°C)*
Blue gill	32.3	15	30.0
Carp	32.0	20	33.0
Large mouth bass	31.8	30	23.2
Perch	24.2	10	23.2
Pumpkin seed	28.2	26	34.5

The fish undergoes process of acclimatization to survive then. Lethal or thermal death occurs at specified temperature. Beyond this temperature fish cannot acclamatize and does not survive. The population of parasites rises with temperature (36° to 40° range). It thereby rendering water unfit for drinking.

21.4 SIDE EFFECTS OF THERMAL POLLUTION

Apart from loss of living organisms life there are some advantages of thermal pollution. Waste heat from power generation cooling process warms up several houses in winter specially in Europe. The recycling of heat is used for treatment of sewage. Lobsters thrive in warm water. Thermophillic algae survives even at 85° C. The warm water is useful for controlling marine fouling. There is increase in extent of the flocculation. The heat treated waste is more homogeneous than common waste. Cold water is more viscous than warm water. In latter the coarse material quickly settles at the bottom if bed configuration is altered. It is possible to carry out prediction of heat dissipation in river water. It is used for several purpose *e.g.*, heating of buildings or swimming pools, deicing of snow clad streets in cold countries, like USA desalination, aquaculture and agriculture. Deicing process however damages natural ecosystem. The nutrition contents of water for fish is more at high temperature therefore some variety of fish like shellfish thrive. The oysters grow well in warm water due to high nutrients contents.

21.5 CONTROL OF THERMAL POLLUTION

(i) The Cooling Towers, Ponds have their Limitations in Cooling Phenomenons

The artificial lakes or ponds provide a method of cooling. The heated water is discharged into lake 3 to 6 ft. deep and water is withdrawn from beneath the lake (45 ft. deep). The heat is dissipated through evaporation. The cooling towers transfer heat from cooling water to the atmosphere. They are called as the "*evaporative towers*" with natural draft or mechanical draft. In second category out flow is forced by fans. Water is cooled by evaporation by difference of at least 10° C.

Non-evaporative cooling towers are available in cold countries such as UK, where heat exchanger discharge heat. These are termed as "*dry towers*". The cooling ponds are useful for circulating water for central cooling stream stations. Spray system like Venturi scrubbers increases the heat loss per unit area but it also results increase in water loss due to increased evaporation. The rate of loss is 2,500 to 5,000 BTU/h/ft.

The cooling towers in comparison to ponds are expensive. Their cooling range represents water temperature from inlet to outlet. There are several forms of towers as are atmospheric, draft wet cooling, forced draft, induced draft, natural draft, and dry cooling towers.

Several problems are encountered in working of these towers *e.g.*, wet towers are bad but are cheap in cost. Climatic effects on tower are pronounced. Tower has definite effect on regional climatology *e.g.*, there is increase precipitation *i.e.*, raining. There is fog and plummes from wet cooling towers. There is unwanted noise. Foul materials reduces efficiency of tower when the corrosion increases. Water quality is affected. By and large choice of the cooling tower is not simple. System analysis gives proper choice of model. The relative cost of condenser, in cooling tower is not predictable. Chemical waste from cooling tower is also important *e.g.*, scale and flocculant, corrosion, cathodic inhibitors, organic inhibitors and fouling etc.

21.6 PREVENTION OF THERMAL POLLUTION

In order to save aqua world such control is absolutely necessary. Outlet water absorbs heat and releases it in the atmosphere. Apart from cooling towers and cooling ponds, artificial lakes is ideal solution in India. Many limitations exist for cooling tower although they cool it by 10 to 15°C but water is lost (2.5%) by process of evaporation and such water lead to fog formation in atmosphere leading to air pollution. The limitations of cooling ponds is that though they serve as settling tanks and substantially cool water the technique is less desirable and inefficient in terms of airwater contact. It is inapplicable to cold water aquatic environment. The artificial lakes are man-made reservoir of water and offer best alternative to above two processes of cooling. The heated effluent is discharged into lake for purpose of cooling and same. The water is used by recirculation for second portion of cooling. The heat is released in form of evaporation. Overall thermal pollution is prevented through plant silting, channeling of thermal effluents; with cooling ponds, preventing thermal block, also preventing fish migration in hot stream; transporting heat by dispersion, electric power generating system must be improved.

21.7 MEASUREMENT OF THERMAL POLLUTION

This is the most important aspect before undertaking any preventive measures. The (*i*) physical parameters; (*ii*) dissolved oxygen; (*iii*) use Lux meter (*iv*) have the application of electric temperature meter measurements.

(i) Determination of Physical Parameter

This includes factor such as study of temperature distribution, change in magnitude of dissolved oxygen and light attenuation, rate determination by Lux meter. The use of electronic temperature meter involves use of reversing thermometer, resistance thermometer, thermocouples and thermistors. There is a semiconductor diodes, which develops a voltage at the junction. It depends upon current and temperature. The current if kept constant, gives voltage directly proportional to temperature. One electrode acts as reference diode at known temperature, while other diode acts like a sensor. The voltage change is amplified to give correct temperature.

(ii) The DO Meter

DO is an index of presence of organic impurities and thermal pollutants from which one can decide quality of water. In shallow water it is 5 ppm while in tidal water it is 4 ppm. DO meter works like potentiometer or ion selective electrode instrument to read level of dissolved oxygen. It has Rh-cathode and Ag-anode with KCl as the reference solution in gas permeable teflon membrane over cathode when diffused oxygen gets reduced at cathode and permits current to flow. A high impedance operational amplifier configuration with MOSFET imput stage is used if probes are small. The partial pressure of dissolved oxygen is function of temperature. The power consumption is low (viz. 125 MW).

(iii) Lux Meter

It is composed of photosensitive detector connected in equipment to measure photocurrent in terms of 'Lux' in the range of 0 to 5000 Lux. The "light attenuation" rate is evaluated with Lux meter at various depth of water. The maximum depth attainable is mark at which sunlight penetrates. The impurities decrease the high penetration process. Boat is used to go to mid-stream of river to use lower Lux meter. Photosensitive detector measures the photo-current and extent of thermal effluents discharged in stream.

21.8 IMPACT OF HEAT ON LIVING ORGANISMS

The fish is typical indicator of living organism. It is tested for the physical activity, metabolic rate, reproduction, migration, temperature liking and uptake of radio nuclides in heated water. The metabolic rate is measured by determining lactic acid and glucose in blood. In water which is warm fish is adjusted and servive there. The water temperature near power plant is critically monitored. Such reactors are located near seashore. A dye discharged in the condensor effluent gives idea of thermal diffusion and dissipation of heat energy. In high tide, it is 500 to 800 m offshore, while in low tide heated effluents are lead to evaporative cooling in the air. The discharged heat does not migrate beyond 1 to 2 km of outfall. In India in Ranapratap Sagar plant in Rajasthan, dye studies are undertaken on lake 3 km from plant. Rhodamine dye is used and its spreading zone is investigated. Such spreading of course depends upon water movement which in turn is related to wind direction, wind velocity and other meteorological parameters. The rise in level of pollutant is due to low DO, more COD, increase in inlet temperature in relation to outlet temperature.

21.9 THERMAL STREAMS, IMPINGEMENT AND APPLICATIONS

We first consider what is meant by impingement? It is defined as the burden on travelling stream damaging fish and aquatic organism. Such impingement impact is measured by knowing population of killed fish, original population of fish and rate of mortality. In order to know that climatic conditions, temperature and velocity of water, the screen examination and identification is carried out. The high speed results in reduced loss of fishes but loss is bigger for large size fish. Entrainment is the incorporation of small organism into the cooling water flow that passes through 0.9 cm screen. It is serious hazard. The damage is caused by thermal shock, shears, chlorine, toxicity, depletion of oxygen and BOD. Biotic damage is caused by buffeting with heated effluents discharged by thermal power plants. Excess gas kills living organisms. It is called *"gas public disease"*.

There are hot water springs in Vajereswari (Thane Dt) in Maharashtra. Their temperature unlike thermostat remains constant due to mixing of magnetic and meteoric water. These are volcanically active zones. In India 300 thermal springs have been discovered. They have water with pH more than 7.0 few are acidic and sulphurous in nature. Their temperature varies from place to place. The use of natural water and gases is of important consideration. Such water contains sulphates of Na, K, Ca, Mg and bicarbonates of Na and Ca and chlorides of alkali metals. Radon occurs in spring water. They have therapeutic properties to cure rehumatism, gout, skin problem *i.e.*, dermatitis due to water containing radon. Thermal stream gases are Ne, Ar. This produces geothermal energy.

Table 21.5 Prominent hot water streams in India

S.No.	*Location*	*Quality of water*	*Temp. °C*	*pH of water*	*Remark (States)*
1.	Vajerswari	Alkaline	32–39	7.0	Maharashtra
2.	Tatapani	Sulphurous	43–47	8.3–8.5	Odisha
3.	Sitakund	Neutral	56–58	7.1–7.3	Bihar
4.	Rajgir	Acidic	38–45	5.8–7.2	Madhya Pradesh
5.	Hazaribaug	Sulphurous	34–35	7.8–9.1	Jharkhand
6.	Bakreswar	Alkaline	41–68	8.0–9.2	W. Bengal
7.	Manikaran	Acidic	95–97	6.8–7.2	Kulu valley
8.	Tantolol	Alkaline	67–70	8.0–9.0	Uttarakhand
9.	Bhimbandth	Acidic	58–65	4.0–5.0	Bihar
10.	Yellow stone park	Neutral	50–60	7.0–9.0	Wyoming USA

Totally there are 300 thermal springs in India. Major one are listed in Table 21.5. The springs are mostly unfit for survival of the aquatic life. One located in

Kulu (No. 7) has highest temperature of 98° C at an altitude of 6000 ft above hill while one at Vajershwari has lowest temperature of 32°C.

21.10 THERMAL POWER PLANTS

Water control in thermal power plants is very critical. It is essential to control the quality of water otherwise it will promote scale formation and corrosion in condit tubes and in main boiler. To ensure best quality of water; number of samples are taken at fixed interval; and analysed. The technique should be precise, reproductible, simple and rapid. A dependable sample especially of steam which is cooled and analysed is difficult to procure. One examines hardness, salinity, salt and silicon contents, population of trace metals promoting corrosion and gases. One gets the operational quality standards from the comparison. India has abundant supply of coal but 75% of it is of low quality with output of flyash of 45 to 50%. Hence it is necessary to utilise high quality of coal for power generation. Fluidised bed combustion is preferred as here NO-NOx generation is insignificant. Fludised bed combustion based upon integrated gasification combined cycle which is very effective and causes no pollution. Pulverised coal is better containing 30% moisture coal.

The criteria of ideal thermal power plants in India is stipulation environmental impact assessment requirements. It should have electrostatic precipitation, tall stack, air monitoring system and dust separator. Most critical part is proper utilisation of flyash for the purpose of construction of bricks block or preparation of cement useful for construction of roads. We have six major power plants at Andhra Pradesh, Maharashtra, Tamilnadu and Karnataka. Their capacity ranges from 210 MW to 1000 MW. It is ensured by our government that transmission and distribution loss should not be more than 12% (existing 23%). The expertise from Japan and Russia is taken. BHEL had power project utilising exclusively rice straw with 10 MW power station in Punjab. This is monitored by department of nonconventional energy of Government of India. Table 21.6 records various parameters responsible for the working of thermal power plants.

Table 21.6 Thermal power plants working conditions

S.No.	*Conditions of operation*	*320 MW low plant*	*1040 MW high plant*
1.	Water flow (cooling) m^3/s	40	20
2.	Power out put (MW)	780	480
3.	Discharge channel (m^2)	50	30
4.	Air temperature	18.5°C	12.5°C
5.	Relative humidity	60	65
6.	Outfall density	5	5
7.	Wind direction	South East	South East
8.	Wind velocity (m/s)	3	4
9.	Inlet temperature °C	21°C	12.5°C
10.	Outlet temperature °C	27°	20°

The Table 21.6 shows working conditions of typical power plant. The parameters influencing its working largely depends upon water flow, power output, discharge rate air temperature, out fall density the direction and velocity of wind and finally to both inlet as well as outlet temperature. Two plants with low and high power output response as 320 and 1040 MW are considered for examining these conditions. The water flow is moderate while power output varies from 400–700 MW. At 30–50 m^2 the discharge channel operates. Air temperature is virtually same as that of room temperature with humidity of 60–65% with wind velocity of 3–4 m/s. The temperature of working both inside as well as outside varies from 10–27°C.

It should be noted that the meteorology factors are most important. They are wind velocity and wind direction, humidity, air temperature and water flow used for cooling. Thus, the thermal power plants are good so long as we get uninterpreted supply of coal. Unfortunately coal supply is dwindling in India from Bihar and Madhya Pradesh and there is dire need for nuclear power plant (cf. New one in Ratangir Maharashtra and other at Kundokulam in Tamil Nadu) is very necessary in future. So long as we take adequate precautions for safety of people, we should not differ construction of nuclear plants as is done in France which is self-sufficient.

21.11 FLYASH AS THE ENVIRONMENTAL POLLUTANT

It is waste mass from power plant. In India 60 power plants produce 30 million tonnes of flyash. It enhances air water and soil pollution due to presence of suspended particulate matter (SPM). It creates big problem of disposal. ESP gives lot of ash. Koradi (near Nagpur) has created numerous pollution problems. Various agencies like CACRI, Kolkata; CFRI Dhanbad; CBRI Roorkee; all CSIR laboratories and CPRI Pune have made best efforts to fruitfully utilise such flyash and prevent pollution of air and water. They suggested manufacture of bricks and blocks, flyash titles, and recover alumina, germanium from flyash. However, one has to take enormous trouble to utilise them properly. One has to use top surface spoil for brick making, a place for factory, with 100% utilisation of ash, and not letting of slurry flyash in water bodies. It is used for landfilling. Bricks are made from flyash (80%) bottom ash, river sand and quicklime (75%). The technology is still in preliminary stage.

21.12 CONCLUSION

The critical temperature for water use is specified by US-EPA. It stipulates change of only 5°F per hour. Cooling ponds or towers partially mitigate the problem at substantial cost. However, to keep heat away from surface water in order to allow living organisms to thrive such means though expensive are not avoidable. Steam electric plants must not be allowed to belch out heat in nature. According to second law of thermodynamics it is imperative to convert heat into mechanical energy but in reality it is not possible and heat is just wasted. Most of the time heat is then released in waterways by cooling process. With temperature rise viscosity decreases and sedimentation occurs, DO is reduced affecting fish flora and fauna in water. Heat in water increases chemical reaction, it increases growth rate and reduces biomass. A small change may not affect aquatic life in cooling ponds, towers but artificial means are best to be utilised for disposable of heat. It is also sent to air to heat exchangers. Heat is used for warming houses in cold climate in northern hemisphere specially in UK and USA.

ADDITIONAL READING

1. F.L. Parker, P.A. Krenkel, *CRC Physical and Engineering Aspect of Thermal Pollution*, Butterworth London (1970).
2. G.M. Fair, J.C. Gayer, *Water Supply and Waste Water Disposal*, John Wiley (1954).
3. P.A. Krenkel, F.L. Parker (Ed), *Biological Aspects of Thermal Pollution*, Vander Bit University Press Nashville Teen USA (1969).
4. R.M.E. Diamant, *Total Energy,* Oxford Pergaman (1970).
5. S.M. Khopkar, *Environmental Pollution Analysis* Second Edition, New Age International (P) Ltd., Publishers (2012).

22 Radioactive Waste and Environment

22.1 INTRODUCTION

In earlier chapters apart from the conventional air, water, and solid waste we had consideration of noise and thermal pollution. However, with the growing threat of nuclear energy and destructive weapons, the awareness in radiation hazard is growing by leaps and bounds. The first serious effect is that of effect of X-ray on human health. It affects pregnant women with problem of maligancy, ulceration, loss of limbs. Therefore, physicians are advised to use X-ray as the diagnostic tool only in an unavoidable circumstances. However, with the development of nuclear reactors for energy the problem of radiation effects are experienced even by common man. The worst of all is the possible use of such nuclear energy for destructive purposes in form of atom bomb or the hydrogen bomb. This leads to study of radiation hazards, its effect on man. It is important to set radiation standard and prevent over exposure. We discuss effects of radiation, source of radiation, standards for radiation, what are consequences of nuclear energy and nuclear fuel cycle, the effects of nuclear cycle on environment, the monitoring of radiation and what is radioactive waste and how it is disposed off in atmosphere?

22.2 EFFECTS OF IONISING RADIATION ON LIFE

We define radiation as the form of an energy propagated from one to another place. The concerned radiation is "*ionising radiation*". It ionises atoms and molecules *e.g.*, $H_2O \rightleftharpoons H^+ + OH^-$. A free radical results α, β, γ radiation which are ionising. The α-alpha radiation is due to He_2^4. The radiation has positive charge and it interacts strongly with matter. Its charge is twice the charge of an electron. The β-beta radiation is energetic electron (e_{-1}^0). It produces antineutrons. It is strongly charged to interact with matter. The γ (gamma) radiation consists of very energetic photons with short wavelength and have no charge.

In addition H_1^1, H_1^2, H_1^3, n_1^0, have also effects of ionising radiation. These ionising radiation splits molecule leading to direct or indirect effects. The former split DNA while latter split H_2O. The extent of damage done depends upon energy of radiation. The energy lost is expressed as 'LET' *i.e.*, linear energy transfer. 1000 KeV electrons penetrates 5000 μm of tissue with 0.25 LET, while 200,000 protons penetrates 300,000 μm with 0.7 LET but 200,000 of α-particles penetrates

20,000 mm of tissue with 5 LET. This LET increases with decrease in energy. In terms of biology the somatic effects affect directly human body, while genetic effects destroy chromosome or gene in cell. Radiation is expressed as dps *i.e.*, disintegration per seconds. One dps is equal to 1 'becquerel'. Curie is amount of matter giving 3.70×10^{10} dps. 1 gm radium gives 1 curie radiation. While Roentgen is the amount of γ-radiation which produces ionisation of 1 esu of electricity. 'Rad' is quantity of radiation which leads to absorption of 100 ergs/g of absorbing material. 'Rem' is the quantity of radiation which produces the same biological damage as is done by γ-radiation. The exposure of man to 25 to 1000 rads leads to blood changes (~ 50) nausea vomiting fatigue (~ 100 rad) fatality (~ 250) and death. If a person servives he is affected by lukemia. In Japan in the Nagasaki and Hiroshima (1945) atom bomb survivers, mortality was at distance of 1200 meters when children died of exposure. The rate of cancer has substantially increased. Madam Curie and her daughter discovered 'Radium'. Although they were awarded Nobel Prize twice but both have died of cancer. The blood platelets are affected, white blood cells decrease thereby decreasing the mechanism of defence and prevent clotting of blood and passage of oxygen to brain. Intenstine is readily affected. The defects in thyroid glands are discovered after 15 years. Genetic effects are carried to offsprings with birth of handicapped children. Mutations is harmful as it causes change in gene. Threshold level from substance to substance is varying.

The common natural radiation is less harmful than the ionising radiation. The latter readily kills cell. Small dose for long-time creates chronic effects such as epilation (loss of hair), sterility and production of tumor. Enzymes are inactivated. The compounds like nucleic acids, proteins, lipids and carbohydrates are degraded and they cause membrane damage. By controlling time, distance and shielding external radiation is prevented from causing any damage *e.g.*, α-rays are stopped by papersheet while 1 cm perspex sheet stops β-radiation but γ-rays and *x*-rays penetrate through everything except lead sheet which is impervious to these rays.

22.3 SOURCE OF RADIATION

The source is natural or artificial. For instance few isotopes like Ra^{236} (α), U^{238} (α), Th^{232} (α, γ) Rb^{87} (β) and In^{115} give out α, β or γ rays during radioactive disintegration. Cosmic radiation is another source of radiation, which on impact with oxygen and nitrogen from air produces radioactive isotopes like: H^3, C^{14}, S^{35}, P^{33} and Be^7 with short half-life. Only C^{14} has long half-life of 5760 ys and tritium with half-life of as much as 12 years. Chest X-ray gives 200 m rem exposure. However, artificial source largley involves medicine (*e.g.*, radiopharmaceuticals), occupational exposure, radioactive fall out. Atomic energy permits 500 rem/yr dose and 5 m rem/yr for coolant water. Luminous watches, with radium dial give 2 m rem/yr, television tube gives 1m rem/ysr. In the air toposphere and stratosphere get contaminated during nuclear tests. France and China performed such test in open air gives out I^{131} and Ba^{140} in fall out. The other elements are C^{14}, Sr^{89-90} and Cs^{137} with very large half-life in years. Sr and I enters in body through cow milk leading to problems of bones and thyroid gland resp. Nuclear explosion test increases level of radiation in the nature. The soil in Brazil has 2 rem of radioactivity due to presence of uranium and thiorium. The human body contains very small amount of radioactive isotopes *e.g.*, C^{14} and K^{40} totally 22 rem/yrs in body. A person is exposed to cosmic radiation (50m rem) Soil (15) building material (45) air (5), food (25) also voluntary exposure of jet flight (4) watch dials (2), television (5), X-ray (55) so total exposure is 205 m rem/yr.

The exposure to nuclear power plant is restricted to 200 m rem/yr by IAEA. Geneva and to water coolant not more than 5 m rem/yr. The radiologist and dentist perhaps die 2 to 4 years earlier due to exposure to X-ray which is used as digonatic tool. The nuclear waste is principal source of radiation. Cigerrate smoker gets about 40 rem cm/yr dose of radiation from radioactive lead. The Russian Chernobyl nuclear mishap in 1986 caused release of enormous amount of radiation in the atmosphere causing death of several persons in Kiev. In Russia where 2000 persons are affected. Many people died of cerebral haemorrhage, nausea vomiting and problems with bone marrow. The fall out consisted S_r^{90}, Cs^{137} and I^{131} as serious pollutants. I^{131} ($t\,½$ = 8 ds) is most dangerous Pu^{239} used in atom bomb is most dangerous. 4 to 8 kgm is present in bomb. Recent radiation emission in the Fukoka in Japan is very serious one. Therefore we consider in Table 22.1 on property of radioactive elements.

Table 22.1 Radioactive elements

S. No.	*Elements*	*Symbol isotope*	*Mass number (Z)*	*Disintegration*	*Particle emitted*	*Half-life ($t_{1/2}$)*	*Special feature of remarks*
1.	Uranium	U_{92}^{238}	238	α	He_2^4	4.47 bilonys	High half-life
2.	Thorium	Th_{90}^{234}	234	β	e_{-1}^{0}	24.1 ds	Half-life low
3.	Protoactinium	Pa^{234}	234	β	e_{-1}^{0}	1.17 mts	Short half-life
4.	Uranium	U_{92}^{234}	234	α	He_2^4	24,5000 ys	Long half-life
5.	Thorium	Th_{90}^{230}	230	α	He_2^4	8000 ys	Long half-life
6.	Radium	Ra_{88}^{226}	226	α	He_2^4	1600 ys	Long half-life
7.	Radon	Rn_{86}^{222}	222	α	He_2^4	3.82 ds	Half-life in days
8.	Polonium	Po_{84}^{218}	218	α	He_2^4	3.05 mts	Short half-life
9.	Lead	Pb_{82}^{214}	214	α	He_2^4	26.8 mts	Short half-life
10.	Bismuth	Bi_{83}^{214}	214	β	e_{-1}^{0}	19.7 mts	Short half-life
11.	Polonium	Po_{84}^{214}	214	β	e_{-1}^{0}	1.64×10^{-4} sec	Very low half-life
12.	Lead	Pb_{82}^{210}	210	α	He_2^4	22.3 ys	Average half-life
13.	Bismuth	Bi_{83}^{210}	210	β	e_{-1}^{0}	5.01 ds	Half-life in days
14.	Polonium	Po_{84}^{210}	210	β	e_{-1}^{0}	138.4 ds	Half-life in days
15.	Lead	Pb_{82}^{206}	206	α	He_2^4	Stable	Very stable

The Table 22.1 is quite informative. It lists as many as 15 elements which are radioactive. The sixth column indicates the kind of radiation viz α, β, λ decay emitted leading to generation of new elements in the next column No. 7th. The half-life period is very important criteria to ascertain life of radioactive element. This half-life ($t^1/_2$) varies from seconds (S.No. 11 for Polonium) to several years (S.No. 4 Uranium). The last column on remarks in this table gives comments on stability of an isotope based on the information of half-life (column pencitimate *i.e.* 9th column). Many elements are β emitters such as Th^{234}, Bi^{214}, $Po^{21.4}$. Some elements irradiate α-radiation as well *e.g.* Polonium, Bismuth, Lead, Thorium, and Uranium depending upon the condition of transmutation. In addition to U^{238}, Po^{214}, Bi^{210} and $Lead^{206}$ give both α and β radiation-β-emission gives next higher element with rise in atomic number by one unit, while α, emission provides element with mass number less by four units while atomic number is less by two units.

22.4 RADIATION STANDARDS

The consistant use of radio isotopes in medicine and commercial purposes resulted in ill-effects upon health leading to clamping of radiation standards all over the world. International commission for radiological protection (ICRP) devised these standards and led guidelines for safety. The early days standard is 0.1 rem/day in 1940 and 36.5 m rem/yr, in 1960. It is decided that less than 5 rem/day be dose and average dose for the general population be 0.17 rem/year (170 m rem/yr) for whole body exposure. Latter on hue and cry is made to reduce it to 0.017 rem/yr (*i.e.*, 17 m rem/yr) otherwise Leukemia and skin cancer is not prevented. It is discovered that human beings are more sensitive than animals to radiation hence experiments with the animals are useless for generalisation of dose. Youngsters get quickly affected by radiation. US-EPA prescribed maximum dose of 25 m rem/year. A unit of measurement roentgen (R) is established. ICRP reduced the safe dose from 15 rem/yr or 0.2 R/day (1934) to 5 rem/yr (1956). It is called *maximum permissible dose* (MPD). The different parts of body have different standards. For average man tolerable limit 0.5 rem/yr for bone marrow, 3 rem/yr for skin, thyroid, 7.5 rem/yr for hands, feet and 1.5 rem/yr for other organs. The workers have high-dose prescription if working in their environment.

Women should not be exposed for more than 3.0 rem/for 3 month as otherwise their reproductive organs are affected. For life saving operation in case of accident the dose should not exceed 200 rem. Roentgen is used for measuring X-rays or γ-radiation while for other kinds of radiation we use 'rem'. This is equivalent to 1000 millirem = 10,000 00 microrem (μ rem).

22.5 NUCLEAR ENERGY

A first reactor is designed in 1957 (60 MWe) however small reactors (20 MWe) is known within a decade and now it is more than 1065 MWe. In 1942, Lab model of reactor was made in Chicago USA, electricity is produced in 1961, a boiling water reactor is made in 1960 in illinois, in USA gas cooled reactor is made in 1969 in pennsylvania. The nuclear power in 1962 is 40,000 MWe but in 1970 it is actually 150,000 MWe. The fundamental equation in generation of nuclear energy is

$E = mc^2$, where E = energy, m = mass, c = speed of light (3×10^8 m/s). Nuclear energy is produced either by nuclear fission or nuclear fusion, but nuclear fussion power plants are most prevalent with U^{235} as fuel. The boiling water reactor; pressurised reactor; high temperature reactor, liquid metal reactor are build. Heavy water reactor is most common in India. U^{235} is used and heavy deutrium water is circulated to moderate neutrons in fission reaction. These are common in Canada known as CANADU reactors. The breeder reactor uses Th^{234} and U^{238} to make Pu^{239} fissionable for production of nuclear energy through generation of thorium. The breeder reactor is main source of nuclear energy from thorium.

Nuclear Fuel Cycle

Nuclear fuel cycle contains several components. It deals with variety of materials to produce energy. A 1000 MWe reactor contains uranium. Ore is mined and is then milled to produce concentrates (85% uranium) and is then purified to convert it to UF_6. It is then isotopically enriched to increase U^{235} concentration and is then stored in cylinder (0.3%) UF_6 is converted to UO_2 pellets and fabricated into fuel element bundle and sent to nuclear power plant to generate electricity. While spent fuel is removed from reactor and stored in cooling tanks before encasing in lead shielding. Pu^{239} produced is also stored as fuel (Fig. 22.1).

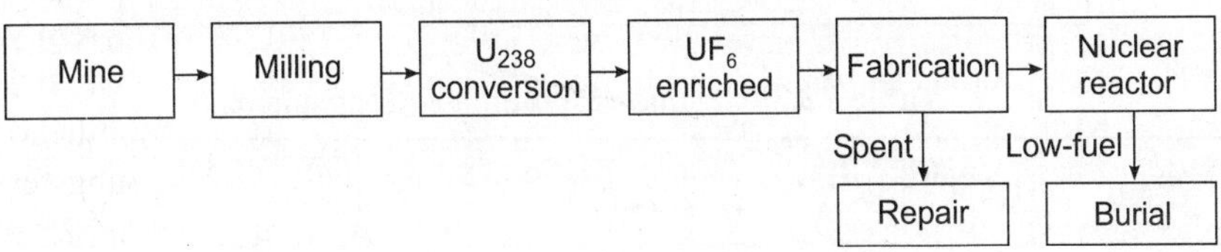

Fig. 22.1 Nuclear fuel cycle

22.6 EFFECT OF NUCLEAR FUEL CYCLE ON ENVIRONMENT

The nuclear power plants are in operation for several years. Such plants have deterimental effects on health of workers. AEC of India as well as US-EPA have extensively investigated health effect in the field of mining, milling, conversion and enrichment plant, fuel fabrication divison, power stations, fuel reprocessing units and waste management plants in operation. In the field of mining some materials are on surface while the others are in underground. The surface materials emit radioactive effluents while the underground mines emit radan gas which is injurious to health. During milling process ore is crushed, reacted with sulphuric acid and converted to yellow cake (U_3O_8). Such operation emits as much as 450 m rem/yr in air and 13 rm rem/yr in drinking water which is injurious to health. During conversion of oxide to hexafluoride as much as 1m rem/yr of activity is detected in 50 miles radius of plant. The enrichment plant generates huge heat during compression needing large volume of coolant however radiation is just 2 m rem/yr which is considered insignificant. The fuel fabrication plant to convert oxides to rod generates 0.1m rem/yr of the radiation. Finally, power plants due to fission produce new radioactive hazardous materials which are serious. They produce thermal pollution. The fission products are Ky, Xe, Cs, Rb, Ba, Sr, I, Br etc. By activation of neutrons Ar^{41}, F^{18}, N^{13} and O^{19} are produced. Radioactive gases leak through cladding and contaminate the coolant. These normal operations does not affect a persons (Table 22.2) but accidents do take place. In spite of atmost precautions accident occurred due to human error. By and large safety records of the nuclear reactors are clean. Fuel reprocessing plant is important part of nuclear fuel cycle with many health effects in usual working (Table 22.3). With the exception of Chernybull and Fukoshima in Japan reactor all others are quite safe.

Table 22.2 Effect of radiation on human health

S.No.	*Dose in rads*	*Effect on health*
1.	25	Detectable effect
2.	50	Changes in blood
3.	100	Nausea, vomiting, fatigue
4.	250	Fatality, but recovery possible
5.	500	Less chances of survival
6.	1000	Certain death

Table 22.3 Cosmic radiation and Toposphere

Isotope	*Half-life (t½)*	*Concen-tration (m)*	*Isotope*	*Half-life (t½)*	*Concen-tration (m)*
H_1^3	12.3 ys	10	S_{16}^{35}	87 ds	0.015
C_6^{14}	57600 ys	4	P_{15}^{33}	23 ds	0.015
Be_3^7	530 ds	1	P_{15}^{33}	14.3 ds	0.02

Table 22.4 Radiation exposure of human beings

S.No.	*Source*	*m rem/yr*	*S.No.*	*Source*	*m rem/yr*
1.	Terrestrial sources	44	5.	X-ray therapy/medicine	72
2.	Cosmic radiation	40	6.	Radioactive fallout	4
3.	^{40}K human tissue	16	7.	Radiopharmaceuticals	1
4.	TV tube	2	8.	Internal sources	2

22.7 MONITORING OF RADIATION

Radioactivity originates in water, waste water by activity of man in the environment *e.g.*, nuclear fuel cycle, nuclear reactor medical use, industrial applications and fallout from atmosphere. Monitoring of radioactive contamination of waste water is done with view of safety of person. The most radioactive elements (Table 22.3) encountered in nature are Sr, Cs, I, U in addition those shown in table. The gross α, β measurements are preferred, but it does not give complete information on presence of isotopes and we have to carry out specific analysis. γ-counting is carried out in rapid with small samples; however during evaporation of such samples activity is lost. Ground water contains radioactive uranium and thorium. While collecting representing sample it must be representive of whole lot. Micro amount is present it readily sticks to glass container and suspended solids.

The radioactive tritium must be analysed in glass. Other isotopes are sampled in plastic or glass. Concentrated HCl or HNO_3 is used to get pH less than 2.0 (exception Cs). It is cooled it for 16 hours. Cr, Cs, K, Rb, Ra, Sr, Sb convert to solid state while Cs and transition metals are held in suspension. Their behaviour in presence of complexing ligands is anamalous. The laboratory must have quality assurance plan to save human beings from radiation.

(i) Radiation and Its Measurement

One cannot sense ionising radiation by any part of body, but several detection devices fulfil these requirement. Such effects cover, ionisation in gases, ionisation in solids; conversion in chemical reaction and neutron excitations, but first mode is most prevalent in nuclear industry. Radiation is measured in differential or integral mode. In first category recording is possible, while second group allows to distinguish between two transformations. Counting measures total disintegrations. The working of ionisation chamber, electroscope, proportional counter, GM counter, neutron detectors are all based on the principal of the ionising radiation. On ionisation of gas, ion pair is formed consisting of positive and negative ions which on application of potential difference between two electrodes promote migration of cation to cathode and anion to anode resulting an electric current proportional to degree of ionisation of gas in a chamber. β-detection needs thin window while pulse detector is used for neutron. Electrons striking anode are called "*Towns end avalanche*". Argon is used as ionising gas; but CH_4 (methane) is also useful substitute. The working of proportional counter involves amplification of electron energy to higher value due to further ionisation since size of pulser current is proportional to the amount of energy deposited by photon. It is called '*proportional counter*'. They have low efficiency for γ-rays but are good for X-rays. The Geiger Müller counter *i.e.*, G.M. counter is most popular, where the voltage is increased so much so that gas amplication rises, with production of large ionisation by single ionising particle resulting in large current. Only resolving time is large (300 m sec). Counting gas is He Ar, Ne at 1000 mm pressure of Hg.

Solid state detectors are those one containing crystalline material which in turn show measurable effects of ionising radiation. It is used in the conductivities, scintilation and thermoluminescence detectors. The radiation dosimetry refers to amount of radiation absorbed by a substance. Most common are chemical dosimeters, film badge dosimeters. They are the radiation detectors. The effect of ionisation of gas, generation of heat in the calarimeter, chemical effects in liquids, thermal current or fluorescence produced by electrons are used in such instruments.

(ii) Radiation Monitoring Instruments

Such device must be portable. It should monitor α, β, γ-rays, as it is easy to operate and give dose in terms of rem/hr unit. The X-ray and γ monitors are devices which indicates also β-radiation. Ion chambers are used at low m rem/hr. Sensitivity is raised with use of G.M. tube. A good response from 0.1 to 3 MeV model is needed. Since neutrons are uncharged ionisation of gases is not fissible but neutrons if they strike proton it causes ionisation of protons which is measured. Thermal neutrons are detected by boron as $B^{10}_{5} + n^{1}_{0} \rightarrow He^{4}_{2} + Li^{7}_{3}$ *i.e.*, ${}^{10}_{5}B$ (n, α) L^{7}_{1} reaction. The emitted α-particles cause ionisation which is measured. With BF_3 in proportional counter is used. The neutron rem meter measures 15 MeV. Thermal neutrons are detected in proportional counter undergoing following reactions as ${}^{3}_{2}He + n^{1}_{0} \rightarrow H^{1}_{1} + H^{3}_{1}$ written as ${}^{3}He$ (*n, p*)${}^{3}H$ *i.e.*, tritum. The proton causes ionisation. There are several kinds of personal monitoring instruments *e.g.*, film badge, fast neutron track plate, criticality locket, electrometer, thermoluminescence device etc. but film badge dosimeter is most common. A photographic film is used to measure extent of blackening of film by densitometer and relate to radiation exposure (range 5 m rem – 5 rem). The use of double film permits measurement upto 1000 rem of radiation. The contamination monitoring depends upon sensitivity of radiation and is done either by direct surface contamination monitoring servilance of air monitoring or biological monitoring. In air monitoring, air is drawn through filter paper (volume known) and it is then counted for activity. While, biological monitoring involves faeces, urine, breath radiation measurements.

(iii) Protection Against Radiation

One has to worry about protection while handling X-rays, radiography, specially use in medicine for Sonography and in research institutions. Operator should not get exposed to X-ray during scanning so also patient must not be exposed for longer duration than necessary which it is used as diagnostic tool. Control should be outside room. In industrial radiography it is used for detection of faults, fatigue or crack in structure. All ionising radiation is handled in closed chamber with warning bell inside it. X-rays are freely used in research for elucidation of chemical structure. Proper shielding is essential for camera and colliminator. X-ray fluoroscence is more hazardous as exposure is 0.6 rem compared to XRD with exposure of 0.1 rem. Radiotherapy is used in treatment of cancer to prevent malignant growth or tumour formation (dose 6 MV). A vial is surgically inserted in body for certain time. In body bone is tested with active Ca^{47} or Sr^{85} (20 m rem), lungs with Xe^{133} and thyroid with I^{131}.

22.8 CHARACTERISATION OF RADIOACTIVE WASTE

The phenomena of radiation existed in outer space much before earth was discovered and as such many radioactive constituents are present in earth, body of human and nature. Becquerel (1896) and Marie Curie (1898) first discovered this radioactivity. Roentgen simultaneously discovered X-rays. As more than 336 persons including Madam Curie died of radioactive exposure causing blood disease. It led to atomic explosion in 1945 and erection of nuclear power station (1950). All the activities led to generation of enormous amount of radioactive waste, creating problems of disposal. Of the total electric generation being 1750×10^9 watts from one nuclear sources is 800×10^9 watts and it is estimated to be 100,000 Mega curie. The radioactive waste is generated. Of this 900 metric tonnes will be actinide waste which includes 12,000 mega curie of α-activity. Pu_{94}^{239} is most active element in waste. The management involves four steps viz. waste treatment; interium storage; transportation and disposal operation. The soil acts as sink, leading to repository degradation. Then there is geosphere, biosphere transport of waste and final consideration of biosphere consequences.

(i) Migration in Lithosphere

It is positive on long storage of the waste, the radioactive waste on storage in repositories or waste storage area is likely to escape in the environment releasing airborn contamination. Also surface contamination gives way to lithosphere through water which percolates to porous rocks. Pit impervious rocks acts as container for long-term storage but their concentration is very dilute. The migration occurres through fissures of soil. The study revealed that displacement of actinide ions from binding sites on rock matrix by quite large concentration of other cations and increasingly easier displacement by more highly charged ions. Radioactivity of actinides held by stony materials leading to the slow rate of migration. A small fraction migrates rapidly than bulk of the species. This shows while considering chemical and geological media, one constructs waste depository which is isolated from environment in spite of major instrusion of water.

(ii) Characteristics of Radioactive Waste

The main source of waste is nuclear fuel cycle. Waste is characterised at low-level, high-level, or actinide contaminated waste. Qualitywise first two are identical in contents but different in concentration of activity. Low-level waste has 1 curie/ft^3 of activity (~30 microcurrents/ft^3). Burying in soil is disposal method for it, but high-level waste originates from reprocessing of spent reactor fuel, present in liquid form. It has 100 to 1000 curie/gallon of activity and it generates heat. Transuranium elements contaminated or actinide waste has more than 710 nanocuries/gm of actinide nuclides.

(iii) Source of Radioactive Waste

It is produced in all parts of nuclear cycle *e.g.*, mining, refining, enrichment place fuel fabrication, reactor and operation and reprocessing. Mining produces mainly dust and radon, so underground mining is preferred. While making yellow cake is (U_3O_8) injurious dust it is produced during refining to give 'mill tailings'. It affects our lungs. U_3O_8 conversion to UF_6 during enrichment produces small active nuclide are washed through in effluents. UF_6 on further processing produces active waste. Laser enrichment is best as no activity is lost in effluents. The rods are made and cladded with zirconium leading to loss of U, Th, Pa in waste water. Maximum waste is produced by reactor operations. Spent fuel contains active elements. The spent fuel is not reprocessed but disposed off. However, U^{238}, U^{235}, Pu is extracted in reprocessing plant from spent reactor fuel (Table 22.5). Washings have 10,000 gallon of activity. Fuel cladding made of zirconium is contaminated and generates solid active waste. In absence of reprocessing, liquid waste is stored in tanks for disposal sometime. But capacity of tank gets full in 5 to 9 yrs demanding closer of reactor. Nuclear reactor is to be shut after 30 to 35 years for decontamination and decommissioning. However, from the point of safety. Dresdent reactor in Chicago was decontaminated at 75% of construction cost in 25 years.

Table 22.5 Radionuclides in spent reactor fuel

Isotope	*Half-life years*	*Emissions*	*Isotope*	*Half-life (yrs)*	*Emissions*
Co^{60}_{27}	5.26	e^{0}_{-1} (He^{4}_{2})	Sm^{151}_{62}	87	e^{0}_{-1}
Sr^{90}_{49}	28.10	e^{0}_{-1}	U^{234}_{92}	2,47,000	He^{4}_{2}
Zr^{93}_{77}	900,000	e^{0}_{-1} (γ)	Pu^{238}_{94}	86	He^{4}_{2}
Ru^{106}_{45}	366	e^{0}_{-1} (γ)	Am^{241}_{95}	438	e^{0}_{-1}
Cs^{135}_{79}	200,000	e^{0}_{-1}	Cm^{244}_{96}	17.6	He^{4}_{2}
Pm^{147}_{61}	2.62	e^{0}_{-1} (γ)	H^{3}_{1}	12.3	e^{0}_{-1}

22.9 STORAGE AND DISPOSAL OF RADIOACTIVE WASTE

Waste constitutes a big hazard and hence is disposed off loosely in environment. It has life of 10,000 years, thus safe disposal is an art and engineering challange. Now we consider different modes of disposal.

(i) Storage of Waste

This is not permanent solution to enclose in container but it is temporary relief and postponement of main problem. US-EPA expects liquid waste to be solidified by calcination, vitrification or synthetic crystalline ceramic form. The calcination is process of evaporation while vitrification is mixing it with borosilicate to form glass. Borosilicate glass conceals several active elements. Crystalline ceramic is alternative involving encapsulation of activity, but it undergoes transmutation and develops cracks. Disposal of spent reactor fuel is critical. Waste cannister do not last longer than 1000 years. Reprocessing will not reduce volume, but it has no special merit from disposal plan.

(ii) Disposal Technologies

Apart from geological isolation, seabead disposal, space disposal and ice disposal are few alternatives. In large concrete air or water cooled valut, spent fuel is stored for 100 years (Table 22.6). Away from reactor, storage is also possible if good transportation is there. Geological isolation involves disposal of radioactive waste deep down within earth's crust. It is good as site of impervious rock is located for disposal. Only ground water should not come in contact with it. The depth should be more than 1500 ft. Sr^{90} and Cs^{137} are lost in soil by disintegration. However, the problem of hydrogeological system, erosion, sesmicity, the tectonic instability, human instrusion must be carefully examined. Super deep holes are 4000 ft. below surface (*i.e.*, 5 to 8 miles deep). Waste due to its heat content melts the rocks.

The disposal media is granite, basalt, shale, tuff. The technical uncertainty of the geological isolation needs serious consideration. The effects upon the host rock caused by repository and burial of thermal hot waste as it is not properly understood. The possible chemical reactions are not known to us. Stability of soil is not reliable. The seismic activity like earthquake is unpredictable. It affects ground water. The response of waste cannister for emplacement in definite geological surrounding and the possibility of cannister retrievability are not thoroughly evaluated, as corrosion may destroy cannisters. Salt disposal has also limitations. The overall behaviour of brine found in cavities need further investigations. The brine attacks cannister made out of glass, alloy, ceramics. Noble metals are attacked. The carbon steel is safe cannisier material for fabrication. The effect of thermal loading on salt needs further investigations. This may cause fracturing and leakage. The exact mechanism responsible to initiate subsidence of rock layers need further study. Plasticity of salt will create problems. It is essential to determine optimum waste form and its effect on repository quality.

Table 22.6 Radionuclides in fuel with long half-life

Years (Range) of activity	*Isotope*	*Half-life (Years) (t½)*	*Emission of particles*	*Effect on human health*	*Radioactivity Curie/meto radiation curie/tonne*
	Cs^{184}_{55}	2½ ys	β, γ	Any part of the body	219
< 10	Sb^{125}_{51}	2.7 hs	β, γ	Kidney	11900
	Co^{80}_{27}	5½ ys	β, γ	Intestine, digestion problem	8610
	H^{3}_{1}	12 ys	β	Entire portion of body ache	3
< 20	Pu^{242}_{91}	13 ys	β, γ	Liver, lymphatic gland	655
	Cm^{244}_{96}	17 ys	He^{4}_{2}, γ	Intestine, kidney	102
	Sr^{96}_{38}	28 ys	β, γ	Bones, marrow	13.2
< 100	Cs^{137}_{55}	30 ys	β, γ	Entire part of body	20.6
	Am^{241}_{95}	458 ys	He^{4}_{2}, γ	Kidney, bones	38.6
	Pu^{240}_{94}	6580 ys	He^{4}_{2}, γ	Bone marrow	485
< 1000	Am^{243}_{95}	7950 ys	He^{4}_{2}, γ	Kidney, bones	170
	U^{234}_{92}	247 ys	He^{4}_{2}, γ	Bones, intestine	1.9
< 100,000	Zr^{93}_{40}	900 ys	β, γ	Intestine	1.9
	Cs^{135}_{55}	2060 ys	β	Entire body	0.2
	I^{129}_{53}	17,000 ys	β, γ	Thyroid gland	0.050

It is interesting to stock of existence of nuclear reactors all over the world. Table 22.7 list different countries with the kind of reactors. It will be noted that all developed countries like UK, USA, Canada, France, Japan, Russia each have more than 30–40 nuclear reactors with large capacity of 35–70,000 MW as on 1990. Although India has five reactors. It is constructing few more in different parts of country.

Table 22.7 Reactors with capacity all over the world

S. No.	*Name of the country*	*Capital*	*Total reactors (1990)*	*Capacity of reactor (MW)*
1.	Argentina	Reojo Galio	2	1020
2.	Bulgaria	–	4	1632
3.	Belgium	Anteweip	6	3474
4.	Brazil	Reo de Janiro	1	626
5.	Canada	Ottawa	16	9521
6.	France	Paris	41	32,993
7.	Finland	–	4	2310
8.	W. Germany DR	Frankfurt	19	16,133
9.	E. Germany FR	Berlin	5	2882
10.	Czechoslovakia	Prague	3	1194
11.	Hungary	Budapesi	2	820
12.	Italy	Millan	3	1194 (1273)
13.	India	Delhi	5	1020
14.	Japan	Tokyo	31	21,751
15.	Korea (South)	Sou	3	1790
16.	Netherland	Amsterdam	2	508
17.	Pakistan	Islamabad	1	125 (600)
18.	Spain	Madrid	7	4690
19.	Switzerland	Zurich	5	2882
20.	Sweden	Copen Hagen	10	7355
21.	South Africa	Pretoria	1	921
22.	United States of America	Washington	85	68,867
23.	USSR (undivided)	Moscow	46	22,997
24.	United Kingdom	London	37	9564
25.	Yugoslavia	–	1	632

The Table 22.7 list countries which posses nuclear reactor with their optimum capacity. It will be seen that America, France, Japan and Russian all super power have 85, 41, 31 and 46 reactors respectively. The less developed Bangladesh has no reactor, Pakistan boast of any one reactors while India posses five reactors. Much depends upon capacity varying from 68000 to 22000 MW. This is official information. One does not know any additional capacity is procured by countries without the knowledge of IAEA in Vienna.

(iii) Space Disposal

Outer space is ideal garbage dumping site, but due to possible hazards on earth it appears to be dubious proposition. Waste if placed in orbital transfer in vertical spacecraft and ejected to Venus, or Moon or Sun. But it needs very high energy to eject it in outer sphere force beyond gravitation of the earth. The worst being ozone layer. It is further depleted and UV radiation enters in the earth's atmosphere. The cost will be prohibitive. If the spacecraft fails to lift and returns with radioactivity will be spread all over upper stratosphere of earth. Transportation of waste to ejection site is also big problem, but NASA is very much interested in this mode of disposal.

(iv) Ice Disposal

The disposal at Greenland or Antartica in north or south pole of the earth in deep ice bed is considered as another alternative. There is geographical isolation. All hot radioactive waste is best cooled by ice. The melt down concepts used to bury cannister at 1 mile distance and allow it to travel downwards by melting in 5 to 10 yrs. Anchored cables are used for retrievability of cannister in a period of 200 to 400 years and it reaches bottom in 30,000 years however ice surge is bad.

(v) Partitioning and Transmutation

This involves separation of radioactive species and transmutation into short lived nuclide by neutron capture or the neutron induced fission. The short lived species will finally disintegrate and disappear. Transmutation should need less energy, remove long-term live isotopes; rate being faster than natural decay and elimination of long lived nuclides. Transmutation is possible through nuclear explosion, charged particle accelerator, fusion reactors, and fission reactor but process will be very prohibitive due to expenses.

(vi) Offshore Disposal of Waste by Drilled Emplacement

This needed a concrete semisubmersible platform. In sea waste is carried to platform and loaded. Then it is transferred from flask to cannister and latter lowered into seabed and guided to previously drilled hole. The malfunctioning like dropped strings of cannister is dangerous. A platform disposes off as much as 400 m^3/yrs of waste. Some restrictions are needed if waste has small diameter. Cost of disposal would be about 0.3 times the cost of generation however cost of disposal is insignificant. The process is reliable for various reactors (Tables 22.6 and 22.8).

22.10 HAZARDS OF RADIOACTIVE WASTE AND MANAGEMENT

One must first consider magnitude and dimensions of hazards in the management of radioactive waste.

(i) Toxicity Consideration

This is known from "ingestion hazard index". This is the volume of water needed for dilution till its suitability as drinking water. Thus, total ingestion hazard index in storage is very-high (Table 22.10) *e.g.*, Sr^{90} or Cs^{137} need 950 trillion cubic meter of water for dilution; as they contain 5700 metric tonnes of spent reactor fuel, needing 2800 trillion cubic water for dilution. No one dilutes waste water to know ingestion hazard index.

(ii) Risk in Storage and Disposal of Waste

The assessment of waste hazardous index is not reliable. Risk analysis is complex and difficult task. One sets upper and lower limits of risk hazards put one cannot evolve full proof system for such assessment. We consider here the repository failure and its consequences. Repository failure may be due to the catastropic tragedies, noncatastropic mild tragedies on human induced error. Such catastropic release waste occurs due to meteorite impact or volcanic or seismic eruption but chances are less for such risk. Ground water intrusion causes non-casterotrophic releases in biosphere, where cumulative effect over period of years is serious. Human induced error occurs anytime. Repository failure is possible in sabotage by terrorist, war or mining operation. The petroleum extraction affects repository or storage. Ground water changes its course and strike cannister which is hazardous.

(iii) Failure of Technology for Management of Waste

Ground water leaching and transport of Tc^{99} leads to failure of management technology, but geological isolation is risk free. Temporary storage possess a great risk. Early repository failure poses also risk but late repository failure poses little or no risk to the human population. From that angle geological disposition is considered safe mode. Physical consequences are added to psychological effect to know the risk. As it stands offshore drilling or geological methods are considered to be most acceptable for disposal.

22.11 CLASSICAL METHODS FOR MANAGEMENT OF WASTE

Whatever is possible in theory it is not possible if it is be implemented in actual practise. In the excitement of the discovery of atombomb and its peaceful and defence uses, everybody totally forgot problem of disposal of high-level waste, leading to catastrophe in world. Then waste is neutralised and dumped in storage tanks. Material of construction of tank is challenged which had 10 to 25 years life only. On the whole carelessness is most predominentely observed. Many states in USA objected for pencil sites in their state. Waste containing 10 nanocurie α-activity is considered as local level waste. Solid low-level waste is buried at assigned site. Soil serves as an effective barrier for radioactivity. To overcome past neglect, national waste terminal storage programme is devised and efforts were made to streamline the process (Tables 22.7 and 22.8).

22.12 SUCCESSFUL PROGRAMME OF DISPOSAL

We consider several aspects as discussed below for disposal.

(i) Dimensions

From nuclear reactor spent reactor fuel is stored in the storage tank. Now they are stored in specified pools at one point. Quantum is very large and is growing day by day several spent fuel assemblies are growing around nuclear reactors although good amount of electricity is also generated.

(ii) Hazards

Pu^{239} causes lung cancer. Small amount of radioactivity escaped in environment causes damage of health. It accumulates in animals, plants and enter human body through food chain (Tables 22.9 to 22.11).

(iii) Successful Disposal Mode

Though several technologies have been developed for safe disposal none of them are full proof. Solidification and emplacement is one method. The disposal in space and specially on sun but is not fissible is ideal.

(iv) Past Practice

No one in past was interested in safe disposal of radioactive waste including federal agencies. So, at several places radioactivity leakage is detected.

(v) Current Programme

Though present practice of disposals is good it is not full proof and much less attention is given on priority basis. Temporary measures are adequate and reliable but permanent long-term solution is yet to be arrived at. A problem is not only technical but has ramification to political and social problems.

(vi) Basic Requirements

The main requirements is fissible programme, which is politically acceptable and socially appreciated. An exhaustive investigations of different parameters lead to technically sound programme for short lived radionuclide. Reliable technology of disposal is available but not for long lived isotopes *e.g.*, transuranic elements. Geological disposal is considered as reliable method, where technical requirement are satisfied on priority basis through R and D output. The repository development proceeds through step by step process. The currently conceived pilot plant project is discarded. The alternative process of disposal is throughly examined. The public support is most essential.

22.13 MANAGEMENT AND HUMAN PROBLEM OF INTRUSION

This arises due to human intrusion into stored or buried waste or an institutional failure *i.e.*, collective human error in planning and execution of disposal technology. The more careless and negligent attention causes human problem of intrusion. Therefore, there should be institutional control on disposal facility; because the surface waste storage is vulnerable by man. The drilling of waste repository causes contamination. As selection of isolated site of disposal does circumvent these problems. Secondly, role implementing institution is equally critical. A wrong site, unfavourable geology and hydrology faulty repository construction, wrong solidification or encapsulation and emplacement programme leads to leakage of radioactivity. Undue haste of implementation is also unfavourbale. Further increasing proliferation of surface storage facility leads to problems related to health of human being unless good methodology is developed for disposal it is futile to expand the generation of energy from nuclear reactors. Extensive involvement of the public in repository sitting and development facilitates control of the institutional failure. A conflict exist all over world between the idea of promotion of nuclear energy and disposal of nuclear waste. This can be avoided if independent waste management organisation is set-up at world level.

22.14 WASTE MANAGEMENT PROGRAMME IN WORLD

It is worthwhile considering programme of disposal in different parts of world. The reactors available in major countries of the world, are shown in Table 22.7. It shows reactors with capacity (MW) existing in Europe.

Table 22.8 Radioactivity in materials of construction

Country	*Material*	*Activity* (bg/kg)	*Country*	*Material* (bg/kg)	*Activity*
America	$CaSiO_3$	2140	Germany	Sandgrave	34
America	U_{308}	4625	Germany	Cement	45
England	Gypsum	29	Germany	Bricks	126
England	Granite	120	Germany	Flyash	341
Finland	Wood	1.1	Sweden	Alumshale	496

Table 22.9 Radioactive series

S.No									
1.	Isotopes	$U^{238}_{92}\rightarrow$	$Th^{234}_{90}\rightarrow$	$Pa^{234}_{91}\rightarrow$	$U^{234}_{92}\rightarrow$	$Th^{230}_{90}\rightarrow$	$Ra^{226}_{88}\rightarrow$	$Rn^{222}_{86}\rightarrow$	$P^{228}_{84}\rightarrow$
		$Pb^{214}_{82}\rightarrow$	$B^{214}_{83}\rightarrow$	$P^{214}_{84}\rightarrow$	$Pb^{210}_{82}\rightarrow$	$Bi^{210}_{83}\rightarrow$	$Po^{210}_{84}\rightarrow$	$Pb^{206}_{82}\rightarrow$	
2.	Half-life ($t_{1/2}$)	4.47 billions 22 ys	24 ds 27 mts 5 ds	1.1 mt 20 mts 138 ds	24500 1.6 × 10^{-4} stable	8000 ys	1600 ys	3.8 ds 1.6 × 10^{-4}	3 mts
3.	Radiation type		He^4_2 He^4_2	e^0_{-1} e^0_{-1}	e^0_{-1} e^0_{-1}	He^4_2 He^4_2	He^4_2 e^0_{-1}	He^4_2 e^0_{-1}	He^4_2 He^4_2

Let us now consider existing programme of radioactive disposal of waste. The Table 22.7 indicates number of nuclear reactors all over the world.

In Europe since land is scarce *e.g.* in Belgium geological disposal of waste is out of consideration while in Canada, fuel is stored in but possibility of geological disposal is bright. France has reprocessing facilities (3200 metric tonnes disposal). Liquid waste is stored; but now they are converting it into solid waste like borrsilicate glass. Geological disposal is being explored, in Germany, it has no facility of its own but it depends upon France. In France attempts are made to have geological disposal facility. In Japan, waste stored in stainless steel tanks, but due to scarcity of land they are exploring possibility of dumping it on isolated island. In Sweden, it is stored in stainless steel tanks. In England, waste is stored in double walled steel tanks and they have plans to convert it to borosilicate glass and then immerse it in geological form. In Russia has small plant for vitrification of waste into glass, but surface storage is most prevalent. Such site had exploded in 1957 killing many persons in area of 800 sq miles in Kyshtym town.

In India, three small reactors are ready and five are under the construction. Plutonium is used to manufacture an atombomb. The expected repository sites is igneous rock formation and the selected sedimentary deposits.

However, brisk activity is on all over the world on fabrication of nuclear power plant in comparison to coal based plant. The former needs very small area (less than 10 acres) compared to thermal power plant which needs more space. The fly-ash problem is absent in nuclear plant. The fossil fuel is getting exhausted hence we have to look for alternative source of the energy like solar energy, wind energy, coal burning but best is nuclear energy. There is one drawback namely accidents occurs if it is not properly controlled and second one must have excellent disposal of activity in the repository and its emplacement in earth or ocean (Tables 22.10 and 22.11).

Table 22.10 Ingestion hazard index of defence waste over years

S. No.	*Isotopes*	*Initial yrs curies*	*10 yrs*	*100 yrs*	*1000 yrs*	*10,000 yrs*	*100,000 yrs*
1.	Sr^{90}_{38}	280 m	73×10^{14}	7.8×10^{13}	16,700	—	—
2.	Cs^{137}_{55}	310 m	1.2×10^{13}	1.3×10^{12}	930	—	—
3.	Pu^{239}_{94}	30.000	6.0×10^{9}	6×10^{9}	5.8×10^{9}	4.5×10^{9}	3.5×10^{8}
4.	I^{129}_{53}	1.05	1.8×10^{9}	1.8×10^{9}	1.8×10^{9}	1.8×10^{9}	1.8×10^{9}
	Total	—	7.4×10^{14}	8.0×10^{13}	8.9×10^{9}	6.8×10^{9}	2.1×10^{9}

Table 22.11 Ingestion hazard index of spent reactor fuel over several years

S. No.	*Isotopes*	*Initial curies*	*10 yrs*	*100 yrs*	*1000 yrs*	*10,000 yrs*	*100,000 yrs*
1.	Sr^{90}_{38}	820	2.1×10^{15}	2.3×10^{14}	5.2×10^{4}	—	—
2.	Cs^{13}_{55}	1100	4.4×10^{13}	2.3×10^{14}	5100	—	—
3.	Tc^{99}_{43}	85,500	2.8×10^{8}	5.5×10^{17}	2.8×10^{8}	2.7×10^{8}	2×10^{8}
4.	Pu^{239}_{94}	1,840,000	3.7×10^{11}	2.8×10^{8}	3.6×10^{11}	2.8×10^{11}	2.2×10^{10}
5.	I^{129}_{53}	250	4.2×10^{9}	3.7×10^{11}	4.2×10^{9}	4.2×10^{9}	4.2×10^{9}
6.	U^{238}_{92}	1700	4.9×10^{7}	4.2×10^{7}	4.2×10^{7}	4.2×10^{7}	4.2×10^{7}
7.	Ra^{226}_{88}	—	—	—	—	1.9×10^{9}	1.9×10^{11}
	Total	2.1×10^{15}	2.4×10^{14}	3.6×10^{11}	2.9×10^{11}	2.2×10^{11}	

So far we have considered ill effects of radioactive waste. At this point it is interesting to examine damage caused by X-rays (Table 22.12). We should carefully note the number of exposure all over the world.

Table 22.12 X-ray in medicine

S.No.	*Country*	*Brain and Head exp. per yr/1000 (Times)*	*Chest exp. per yr/100 (Times)*	*Stomach exp. per yr/100 (Times)*
1.	Sri Lanka	0.3	13	0.11
2.	Japan	59	640	285
3.	Romania	37	850	116
4.	Germany	108.2	334	68
5.	Chile	15	46	17

The technology of X-ray has made greater strides in the field of medicine. It is used for noble cause of diagnosing problems of health *e.g.* lung. It is used by certain nations for diagnosing sex of foetus before delivery in form of Sonography. In India the Sonographic applications are totally prohibited. The X-rays are also used for brain and stomach examination. Table 22.12 shows that in Germany large number of cases are diagonised from head and brain. While Ramania used it extensively for study of lungs and chest (~850). Japan has used it for diagonising diseases of stomach (285). One has to use X-ray very judiciously as pregnant and lactating mothers should not be strictly exposed to excessive exposure to X-ray radiation in order to protect foetus in her body.

Apart from medical sciences, X-rays are used extensively for the elucidation of the structure of chemical compounds. There are few variety of X-ray as X-ray fluoroscences (XRF) and X-ray diffraction (XRD) with single or double crystal models.

With recent tragedy at Fukoshima in estern Japan due to breaking reactors with Tsunami, the scientist are reluctant to go in for new reactor in Japan at Fukoshima. In relation to developing countries, India has to make greater strides in future years for shortage of coal, we will have to replace all the thermal power plants with nuclear reactor with clean technology in near future.

22.15 CONCLUSION

When the conflicts are brewing between two neighbouring countries on global, level best efforts are made to produce nuclear energy not only for power generation but for manufacture of atomic and hydrogen bomb. Although effects of radiation on life are known since long, no serious consideration is given to this problem till nuclear energy is used for generation of electricity. Several source of radiation are available however the main source remains to be nuclear reactor. Although natural radioactivity is emitted from few sources like TV it is not very injurious to health. To evaluate the effects of radiation on man, it is very much necessary to evolve standards of radiation. Number of standards are evolved in terms of curie, rongten, rad however most common unit is millirad (m rem). Nuclear energy is generated all over the world but America and France are on forefront followed by European countries. The Asian countries includes Japan, South Korea and India in commisioning the nuclear reactors. Nuclear fuel cycle needs special attention as its effects on environment are quite serious. This necessitates development of monitoring methods for the measurement of radiation. Most commonly used mode for monitoring are ionisation chambers, but one must protect himself while operating these devices.

Radioactivity waste is of prime consideration for environmental scientist and engineers. Its action on earth, properties, sources, are thoroughly investigated. The disposal of radioactive waste is most critical problem. The liquid waste is dumped in storage tank and kept in isolated place for several years but new technology is growing for disposal. It consists of disposal of activity in soil called geological disposal or bury in seabed container by what is called as off shore drilling operation. The space disposal in universe as well as ice disposal in Greenland and Antarctica are also explored. The problem of transportation and handling of waste is hazardous. The risk on storage as well as failure of technology of disposal needs careful consideration. Classical methods are freshly examined. The successful programmes includes consideration of safety hazards and current practices of protection. Geological disposal involving burying at bottom of seabed or land appears to be common disposal technology. Radioactive waste management programme all over the world shows common practise of disposal taking into consideration human problems of the handling and exposure. The brisk activity is on in different parts of the world to develop reliable disposal technology programme. Only limitation is long $t_{1/2}$ life for spent reactor fuel; ultimate results are not available immediately. In any case future is bright as there is a great awareness of hazards as well as potential of nuclear energy for benefit of mankind.

ADDITIONAL READING

1. APHA, *Standard Methods of Water and Waste Water Analysis,* 20th Edition. American Public Health Association (1999).
2. A.M. Friedman Ed, *Actinides in the Environment,* American Chem. Society Publication (1976).
3. M.R.C. Bury, *The Offshore Disposal of Radioactive Waste* by *Drilled Emplacement,* Graham and Trotman Ltd. Publishers (1985).
4. R.D. Lipschutz, *Radioactive Waste: Politics, Technology and Risk,* Ballingen Pub. Co. of Harper and Row Public (1980).
5. G.R. Chhatwal, M.C. Mehra, M. Satake, *Environmental Radiation and Thermal Pollution and Their Control*, Anmol Publications, New Delhi (1989).
6. S.M. Khopkar, *Environmental Pollution Analysis,* Second Edition, New Age International (P) Ltd., Publishers (2012).

23 Energy and Environment

23.1 INTRODUCTION

The energy problem is not new; but it is recognized since 2500 years. The wood is the main source of energy but solar energy is also used in some form or other. After wood, coal is useful for source of energy. We define energy in simple words as the 'ability to do work'. It is transformed or converted into another form from the other form. It is neither created nor destroyed as per first law of thermodynamics. A stored energy is called as 'potential energy' while the energy in motion is termed as 'kinetic energy'. As per second law of the thermodynamics "Energy goes or is converted from one form to another form which work, as the lower the energy of quality". We use concept of Entropy which is introduced as the measure of the available/nonavailable work to carry out. It is defined by second law of thermodynamic as "the ratio of energy delivered to ratio of energy supplied is critical".

23.2 SOURCE OF ENERGY AND ITS USE

It is produced by oil, natural gas and coal. The last is termed as fossil fuels; which are nonrenewable. The sun, wind are alternative source of energy. They are called as "renewable energy" source. It is measured in 'Joules'. One Joule (exajoule) is equivalent of 10^{18} Joules. In ancient times fossil fuel *i.e.* coal is the main source of energy. The efficiency in its improvement include designing of equipment to give more output while the cogeneration is the number of process used to capture and use waste heat. The target for the development of extra energy efficiency is to construct good building design. In industrial energy uses an appropriate design of automobile is required. The integral urban houses constructed conserve the loss of energy during the days of working.

23.3 THE REGULATIONS PERTAINING TO ENERGY

The sun, wind and biomass are important sources of energy. It is hard to predict demand of energy supply as well as its conversion. It is estimated that by 2030 America would need 120 exajoules (if 1 exajoule = 10^8 energy). This leads to serious consequences in environment leading to its degradation. One depends upon renewable energy source like sunlight, wind and biomass. One works for maximum effectiveness. The system has to be flexible with low technologies. There should be appropriate matching between energy quality and its end use. The 5% user needs clean energy. Although stock of coal in world may last for few centuries, one must think of future source of energy. The supply and demand does not match *e.g.* in west coast of America oil is main source while in eastern coast of America depends upon coal as the source. Around 60–120 exajoules energy is needed by 2030 in America. India being developing nation may then need 80–90 exajoules.

23.4 MANAGEMENT OF ENERGY IN FUTURE

We must have system which is termed as "Integrated energy management". To achieve this we have to procure global sustainable energy as it would provide reliable source. It may not cause harm to global environment. Greater attention must be paid to the source of energy, the available potential for the conservation and efficiency and one must note desired end use of the energy. For better preservation of the environment we badly need sustainable energy, with aggressive energy efficiency, as well as conservation to provide balance between economic health and environment. A balance between source and use of the energy is necessary.

23.5 ALTERNATIVE SOURCE OF ENERGY

Apart from fossil fuel, the most dependable source of energy is solar, hydral, and biomass and coal. These are all alternative to geothermal source of energy. The solar photovoltaic system and hydrogen gas is the dependable source of alternative energy. In this one gets the renewable and nonrenewable energy. The solar and nuclear energy falls into second category of nonrenewable source. The hydal and nuclear source of energy contributes to 3–8% of the total supply of energy.

(i) Geothermal Energy

On basis of geological findings hot geothermal source is defined at temperature > 80°. The hydrothermal source is also a dependable source. The ground water with fixed temperature is another source of geothermal energy. It is used to cool and warm the dwellings in western countries. The environmental impact of geothermal energy should not be neglected. It needs no large scale transportation. It does not cause air pollution, by combustion of the fossil fuel like coal, though it produces a remarkable "thermal pollution". The contribution is only 1% total need. Another renewable alternative sources is solar energy; hydral energy; or from biomass. These are exhaustible with negligible environmental degradation.

(ii) Solar Energy

This is most important component of renewable source of energy. A 13% of energy originate from sun. The passive solar energy system involves the design which absorbs solar radiation and by accepting consequent changes indicates its contents. One uses solar collectors. It consists of flat panels with glass cover plate over black background through which water is circulated in tubes. The photovoltics is the term used for "process which involve conversion of sunlight directly into electricity", with use of solid semiconductors. The water level centre in meteorological laboratory consumes photovoltaic energy. It is also useful to run watches and calculators. One produces 500 kW of power by this process. The conversion efficiency is 20–30% power are expensive. The use of solar ponds is not very common as the temperature is 40–70° C. In pond solar radiation is trapped or collected. The ocean thermal conversion is another source of energy. There is low impact on the environment by any type of solar energy. Only limitation is solar energy is dispersed. The solar power towers have great impact on the land. As much as 20% energy is procured from the solar energy.

(iii) Hydral Energy

Hydrogen gas is strong fuel for the future years. It acts as the source of solar energy. Water power is form of the solar energy. The hydroelectric power provides 15% of total electricity in America. The microhydropower system is used in domestic and household purposes *e.g.* room heating. It produces mechanical or electrical power with use of pump with storage capacity. The tidal power of ocean is obtained from tides of the sea. A 8–15 mt height tide is capable of producing power. This is normally done in great dams. As regards water power and environment, the former source is clean and produces no air or water pollution in the environment.

The wind power like solar power is long known to a man. Wind power is used to generate electricity. The velocity and duration of the wind needs serious and careful consideration. Wind mill produces power as big as one kilowatt however it doesn't solve the energy problem. There are no limitations in wind power generation. The wind mill does interfere with radio or television broadcasting and source away birds from farm. On the whole such power has low environmental impact on generation of energy. It is practised in Maharashtra (West).

(iv) Biomass as the Source of Energy

Biomass is the new name for biomass organic matter. It is burnt. The wood constitutes important source of biomass. Solid waste is used. The net yield calculations of energy are important. Biomass provides greater energy and it is easy way to generate methane or ethane. Its relation with environment is to promote the air pollution when unpleasant odour is produced, then it leads to shortage of wood. The deforestation accelerates the process of soil erosion. It causes water pollution and does promotes carbon dioxide generation by process of burning. The combustion also produces oxides of sulphur as well as oxides nitrogen which are confirmed pollutants in atmosphere.

23.6 NUCLEAR ENERGY

It is the energy of the atomic nucleus. The well known process of radioactive disintegration in the form of fission or fusion is used to generate the power. The fission produces nonrenewable energy. It needs lot of uranium. Therefore, fission reactors are important we define in simple terms as "the nuclear energy is energy obtained from atom by the process of fission or fusion". The process of fission involves the splitting of an atom in to small fragments generating enormous amount of the energy while the nuclear fusion is the process of combining of atomic nucleic leading to the release of energy. These reactions takes place in nuclear reactors. The fission produces nonrenewable energy as it needs uranium as fuel to continue the nuclear reaction in order to generate energy.

(i) Nuclear Fission

Nuclear fission was first carried out in 1942 in USA. The thermal energy produced by coal is equivalent to sixteen tons of combustion of coal and it is produced by as much as one kg. of uranium. Uranium has three isotopes *viz.* U^{238}(99.3%), U^{235} (0.7%) and U^{234} (0.005%). U^{235} is split in the fission reaction by the bombardment of slow neutrons leading to multiple generation of more neutrons as well as fission fragments and generate the heat. The new neutrons in turn bombard U^{235} giving more fission products including neutrons (n_0^1) and heat. The movement of fast moving (n_0^1) neutrons is moderated by heavy water. The reaction occurs in burner reactors. The generated α-particles (*i.e.* He_2^4 nuclei) travel 4–5 cms but it travels much less in human tissue (*e.g.* 0.005–0.008 ml, β-particles are (e_{-1}^0) electrons. The conversion of proton to neutron or vice versa produces new particle called 'neutrino'). The β-particles are stopped from travelling by shield of metal (Pb) sheets. There are (γ)-gama rays with no charge (*cf.* X-rays). The α-rays are harmful to human health. So also γ-rays are equally injurious to the health. U_{92}^{238} ultimately decays to Pb_{82}^{210} or Pb_{82}^{206}. The decay time to produce half the amount of isotope is termed as halflife ($t_{1/2}$). The lowest concentration of fuel is needed to continue the reaction. This is called as "critical" stage. The control rods are capable of absorbing neutrons. They are used in reactor to control and moderate the nuclear reactions. The small nuclear reactors uses heavy water as moderator working under the force of gravity.

(ii) The Breeder Reactors

A nuclear reactor which consumes 40–70% of the nuclear fuel is called as the 'Breeder reactor'. It avoids using U_{92}^{238} or U_{92}^{235} but it uses Th_{90}^{232}. The Breeder reactor is defined as "the reactor which converts fertile nucleus fissionable nuclear". The faster is the rate of fission. The entire process is very expensive and hence prohibitive but such reactors produces less harmful products inclusive of Plutonium (Pu_{94}^{244}). Therefore, one prefers fusion reaction as it involves combination of light elements (*e.g.* H_1^1) to form heavier elements. The fusion generates large energy *e.g.* The deuterium and tritium (H_1^2 or H_1^3) are generated which in turn are injected into nuclear reactor to promote fusion. One needs high temperature, fuel material should have high density producing thereby a 'Plasma' which consists of neutral material and positively charged nuclei and negatively charged electrons (e_{-1}^0).

(iii) Environment and Nuclear Energy

The different kinds of radiation interact with the environment. The radioactive waste material pollutes the environment. U_{92}^{235} promotes generation of radioactive waste. The site selection for disposal is opposed by the neighbouring residents *e.g.* the installing new reactor in Kudnkolam near Chennai and another at Ratnagiri in Maharashtra is in progress but it is severely opposed by environmentalist. The disposal of nuclear waste is a serious problem. The average life span of nuclear reactor is 20–30 years. The process of the fusion is attractive from environmental view point as the land use and the transportation is less problematic. The fusion reaction produces no fission products or radioactive waste. The fusion power is therefore not acceptable. The radioisotopes enter pathways of mineral cycling and food chains. The nuclear 'fallout' is a serious problem as it is encountered in Fukoshima in eastern Japan. It involves deposition of radioactive particles in the environment. This was experienced when nuclear reactors in America, Russia specially in Chernobyl, China, France and England are active *e.g.* Cs_{55}^{187} is dangerous component of fallout. It undergoes what it is termed as biomagnification *i.e.* Ecological food chain concentration. It is consumed in form of meat by human beings. It half-life is $t_{1/2}$ = 15 days.

(iv) Nuclear Accidents

The largest record is that of the accident in nuclear power plant at Chernobyl in Russia. A 3-mile radius of reactor accident is also well known since 1979. It occurred at in town called Harrisburg in Pennsylvania in America but the literature to control this disaster was inadequate. Thus on the whole there is lack of preparedness and willingness to accept nuclear power with minimum of risk. In 1986 many efforts were made to search antitodes without much success for such disaster prevention. The cooling system has miserably failed in Chernobyl in USSR. The reactor temperature rose to 3000° C melting the fuel uranium about 30 persons died and 240 persons were injured. The effect is observed in area of 30 km radius from nuclear reactor. The large population suffered from disease of lukoderma. The thyroid cancer is noticed. The vegetation are damaged near reactor complex. The recent nuclear accident occurred in Fukoshimin Eastern Japan in 2011–12. The after effects are slowly coming out from reactor.

In 1986 the Sweden is the first country in Europe to declare that radiation from radioactive waste is emerging in their land on account of Chernobyl accident in Soviet Union. This happened due to nonfunctioning of cooling towers with water. The temperature rises as much as greater than 3000° C thereby melting fuel element *viz.* $\text{Uranium}_{92}^{237}$ 30 people died and 237 were hospitalized due to this accident. In a radius of 30 km radiation has spread causing damage to plants and animals. One lakh people are exposed and 25,000 persons showed high personal radioactivity. Lukemia and thyroid problems (specially amongst children) is encountered. So far all over the world 34 small or big accidents have occurred therefore in our country *viz.* India the power reactors under construction. In Maharashtra at

Ratnagiri and one at Kudnkolam Chennai in Tamil Nadu is strongly opposed by social organization and environment experts as well as NGO the purpose is in order to protect mankind.

23.7 RADIOACTIVE WASTE AND ITS CONTROL

These are by-products of nuclear reactions in reactors. It is composed of low and high level radioactive waste. The former is less harmful if properly treated before the disposal. The spent fuel (~ 29,000 tons in USA) is serious problem and needs careful handling. So most of it is stored in tank in nuclear sites only. A nuclear waste disposal policy is formulated in the year 1982. An attempt to dispose the western high mountains is being very strongly resented by the neighbourhood population. In an event of the earthquake in the vicinity it does cause serious problem of spreading of radioactivity specially in ground water. As regard future of nuclear energy is concerned it is the big source of energy next to thermal sources in which coal reserves all over the world are slowly diminishing, however from nuclear reactors the hazards are equally dangerous. Coal is better as it do not produce carbon dioxide and monoxide due to incomplete combustion, it does not cause air pollution or prevents the acid rains, if breeder reactor (specialiy in India which consumes. Thorium$^{238}_{90}$ which in turn is so abundant in South India in Kerala in Alwaye town always) is used as it will supplement fuel demand and solve several problems of load shedding. It is claimed by few that the thermal power also causes death of persons and is not safe. However, in Europe and other countries the condition of disposal of the radioactive waste is critically examined before new nuclear plant is installed.

23.8 FOSSIL FUELS AND ENVIRONMENT

Before we conclude we must examine the effect of fossil fuel like coal, oil, gas (natural and synthetic) and specially coal in the environment. Since the consumption of petroleum, compressed natural gas (CNG) or liquid petroleum gas (LPG) is restricted we do not have much serious problem excepting one which is the air pollution, but the real fossil fuel is coal which needs attendation by environmentalist. The process of coal formation is well known. For the moment it is worthwhile to consider coal as sole source of energy.

Table 23.1 Coal from thermal power plant as source of energy

S.No.	*Type of coal*	*Degree of inefficiency*	*Total energy output (Max Joules/kg)*	*Sulphur content (%)*			*Pollutants released*
				High	*Average*	*Low*	
1.	Lignite	Four	16	–	9.3	91.0	SO_2
2.	Anthracite	One	35	43.4	–	97.0	SO_2
3.	Bituminous coal	Two	34	–	27.0	30.0	CO_2
4.	Sub-bituminous coal	Three	23	–	0.4	99.6	SO_2

A critical examination of Table 23.1 for four varieties of coal which are frequently used is Anthracite coal which gives high energy while using low quality coal *i.e.*, bituminous coal has high contents of sulphur which in turn causing air pollution by SO_2. This is because coal is classified as per its level of carbon and sulphur contents. We note anthracite is best fuel while lignite is worst as far as the energy contents considered. Low sulphur content is always preferred. For better efficiency coal containing sulphur is chemically treated with expensive process. The coal reserve in Europe is lowest while it is highest in Asia and specially in Australia. The coal mining causes land reclamation problem. Unreclaimed coal dump causes serious environmental pollution. In such land vegetation also does not grow. It is confirmed from nongrowth of vegetation in Nagasaki and Hiroshima in Japan. The main problem is that of acid rain due to high sulphur content of the coal. The underground coal mining is not safe leading to problem of respiratory (Lung) disorder. The trend is to have low cost transportation devices. The future for thermal source is not so easy to predict due to dwindling supply of coal from in the central India at Jharkhand and Bihar where we are concerned.

23.9 CONCLUSION

It finally shows energy is closely related to the environmental pollution. With rise in energy may lead to more of the pollution. However, conventional energy involving solar energy is best as it causes no problem of environmental degradation. Next to that nuclear energy is best source.

ADDITIONAL READING

1. D.B. Botkin, E.A. Keller, *Environmental Science–Earth as the Living Planet*, Third Edition, John Wiley and Co. (2000).
2. B.L. Cohen, *The Nuclear Energy Option*, Plenum Printing Press, New York (1990).
3. R.L. Murray, *Nuclear Energy– An Introduction to the Concept, System and Applications*, Fourth Edition, Pergamon Press (1993).
4. M. Brown, *Cool Energy, Renewable Solutions to the Environment Problems*, Cambridge MA (1992).
5. T.E. Vankovering, N.J. Sell, *Energy – A Conceptual Approach*, Prentice Hall, Engelwood (1980).
6. D.G. Brookins, *Mineral and Energy Resources*, Merril Publishing Columbus (1990) Ohio, USA.
7. P.I. Liu, *Introduction to Energy and the Environment*, VanNoStrand Reinhold Co. (1993).
8. S.M. Khopkar, *Basic Concepts of Analytical Chemistry*, Third Edition, New Age International (P) Ltd., Publishers (2011).

24 Population and Environment

24.1 INTRODUCTION

Population is directly related to the environment. More is the population then more is also the extent of pollution. This problem has special references to the developing countries like India, Mexico, Nigeria. Even the well developed countries like Europe, USA, UK, China have serious problems of their own with reference to population. A population data has direct relationship with environment. It is new fresh case in point on the millennium development. It has sever impact on millennium like village projects. A good deal of information is available on urban world. It includes public transportation system, growth rate and need of green spaces available in the towns.

In view of these consideration, we consider following important parameters. In population change, *viz.* population size, growing human population and its relation with reproduction. As regards population problems we consider not only quality of life but also we look at fertility rate and concerned governmental regulations. Specially one considers problems of population in developing countries. Finally we must consider population and urban world, where we also consider different urban problems as well as benefits of urbanization. From this viewpoint we take clue for ideal urban planning. Africa has most rapidly growing population adjacent to sub Saharan region. It is expected to react to reach 1.4 billion in year 2030. There is decrease due to growing diseases like AIDS and HIV in society specially in Swaziland. The main cause of growth is lack of education as well as prohibitive cost of patent medicines and antiviral drugs. This has influenced very much the life expectancy in developing countries.

(i) Population Change

In this category one considers two important aspects *viz.* population density and size of population related to reproductive system. One defines population as "a group of individuals of same species that live in the same geographical area at the same time". Population ecology is science dealing with number of particular species present and its change of number in the course of time. A direct relationship is there with population, food and similar resources in the environment. It is of vital importance for scientist working in the field of forestry, agronomy and wild life management to consider these aspects.

(ii) Population Density and Size

The population density is defined as the "number of the individuals of species per unit area or volume at the given time". Such population density varies from season to season or year to year. Mostly the external factors in the environment determines the population density. The size of the population alters due to variation in the rate of birth, death, immigration. The birth rate is expressed as "the number present per 1000 individuals". The rate of birth and death determines the size of population. Immigration (increase in population) and immigration (those leaving population) are two different types of dispersal effects. The intrinsic rate of increase is reflected under 'biotic potential' *e.g.* microorganism grow at faster rates. The exponential growth proceeds with rise in different stages. A population growth occurs if there is constant reproduction at definite interval. The population is growing exponentially when the growth rates remain constant. The environmental resistance arrests the growth of the population. Such resistance arises due to lack of food, water, shelter and rise in diseases. The density dependance factor is most critical. Predation of diseases and competition are few density dependent factors. In mediterranean region mosquito growth is fast in warm tropical climate but entire mosquito population disappears in severe winter. The survival rate is proportional to the new born individuals which are living at given time.

(iii) Human Population and Reproductive Growth

Demography is the science of population and structure and growth. The study of population statistics is termed as 'demographics'. The human population of India is greater than 112 crores in 2006. It is not the birth but cession of death propagates large population. Thus, demography is applied branch of sociology which deals with population. The statistics furnishes population of various countries. Table 24.1 provides world population it being highest in China (1311.4 millions) and it being lowest being for Japan (127.8 millions). The population density which

Table 24.1 World population of different countries

S.No.	*Country*	*Population in crores*	*Population in 2006 (in millions)*	*Density (per mp) (Population/ land area)*	*Consideration of the density*
1.	China	131.0	13,11.4	355	Density good
2.	India	112.0	1121.8	884	Density worst
3.	Bangladesh	14.6	146.6	2637	Reasonable density
4.	Japan	12.7	127.8	876	Lowest
5.	Pakistan	16.5	165.8	539	It is decreasing
6.	Nigeria	13.4	134.5	377	It is fast growing
7.	Indonesia	22.5	225.5	307	Precarious figure
8.	USA	29.9	299.1	80	With growth
9.	Brazil	18.6	186.8	57	Good density
10.	Russia	14.2	142.3	22	Fine density

is most important in environmental action is 355 and 876 millions for respective countries *viz.* Japan and China.

What is most important is not the just number of population figures but also the population density. The worst density is in India (884) with less land and more number of people while in USSR has plenty of land with density is 22 which is quite ideal for living. The growth rate is decreasing. The zero population is possible if birth and death rates are identical China is trying to achieve zero growth in population. By 2050 population would reach a landmark of 9.1 billions (*i.e.* 91000 millions). The developed countries have very slow growth rate (*e.g.* S.N. 8, 4). See America and Japan population and density. It is (29.5 crores for America, 12.7 cores for Japan while the density is respectively 80 and 876).

Table 24.2 The population data

S. No.	*Parameter*	*Well developed country e.g. USA*	*Poorly developed country e.g. Ethiopia*	*Remarks*
1.	Longitivity	78 yrs.	49 yrs.	Less death, more life expectancy
2.	Mortality rate	6.7 per thousand	77 per thousand	Commendable in USA
3.	Fertility rate	2.6	5.4	Good in developed nations
4.	Projected population	± 40%	± 94%	No control on growth
5.	Per capita GNP	$ 41,950	$ 1000	Poor per capita GNP for less developed country

Table 24.2 is self explanatory. Thus much work needs to be done to control the population growth and mortality rate specially in less developed countries. The total fertility rate is 2.7 for Japan-which is a developed country. It has highest living rate of 79 yrs (men) and 86 yrs (women) with low fertility rate, consequently retirement age is much higher in comparison to one in Africa a less developed country place. This is due to long surveying population till ~80 yrs of age. The problem of immigration is attaining serious proportion in United States of America (~35 millions immigrant). They all come from less developed countries like Mexico, India and other Asian countries.

24.2 PROBLEMS OF POPULATION ON ENVIRONMENT

These environmental problems are interwoven with quality of life, fertility rate and its control and to various laws pertaining to the population. The every nation should provide equal opportunity in education for men and women. If population growth is reduced the world will be better to live in with peace.

(i) Quality of Life

One needs comfortable living balanced diet, clean water, good housing and good clothing. We term it in Hindi language as *Roti*, *Kapada* and *Makan*. For this population must be stabilized in order to have the high standard of living. As a rule with environmental growth of the population, there is environmental degradation with the hunger, poverty and health. The population growth should not be in inverse proportion to growth of resources. The food security is of atmost importance. The phenomena of chronic hunger must to disappear a sub-Saharan in Africa and partially in South Asia where we have food insecurity which in turn is caused by famine. The diarrhea, respiratory problems, malaria, measles, dengu kills large population of children in less developed countries. The economic development must solve the world food problems. Fertility rate must be decreased. The overall economic development gets affected by the population growth. The economic development rises with stabilization of population growth in a country.

(ii) Fertility Rate and the Childhood Development

A culture of society influenced the individual by controlling their behaviour. The gender is most important part of culture. The culture is related to fertility and belief. A 250 million child labour is serious problem. This is prevalent in developing countries. Such population group of population kills childhood joy and education. The gender inequality must also disappear; in order to promote development of women folk.

24.3 POPULATION OF THE DEVELOPING COUNTRIES AND ENVIRONMENT

As far as population is concerned China is country with highest population next comes India with large figure of population. Other less developed countries like Nigeria, Mexico are much behind us in population growth. By 2050 India would have (unless properly controlled) worlds highest population. The country like China has taken stern measures to control their population. In India, the highly educated women marries late and consequently she has less children. The education of women have indirect but significant effect on total fertility. Table 24.3 shows relative ratio of family planning with actual birth rate in various countries.

The higher is the population worst is the quality of the environment and life. If it is controlled then Germany is the country. So population control is the most important factor, if we have to zero environmental pollution, China's population is 1.3 billion (*i.e.* 130 crores). Between 1971-1979, China took strict measures for the control of population with late marriage, two children norms and increase in the spacing between two children. Parents with one child derived all concessions. The birth rate has gone down in China. Unfortunately both in China as well as India in population is considered to be great but unfortunately the birth of asset, the daughter is not choosing welcomed. The female foetus killing influences greatly with girls population. There will be serious problem of marriage because of death of girls. India's population is 1.1 billion (110 crores). Since 1976 family planning is being vigorously attempted. The plan of compulsory stabilization has failed.

The population control failure has deteriorated the quality of the environment in our country.

Table 24.3 Family planning and fertility (planning and rate in percentage)

	Pakistan	*Nigeria*	*India*	*Indonesia*	*Brazil*	*Germany*	*Remarks %*
Family planning	45	60	30	35	30	15	Germany best for control
Birth rate	20	10	45	55	70	72	Nigeria worst in planning

The population rise promotes poverty, environmental degradation and causes undeveloped economy. Mexico, Brazil have large population in the comparison with Europe, UK or USA. Specially their urban population is large. The Nigerian and all African countries have largest population (*e.g.* 134.5 millions) with life expectancy of only 44 years. However in Europe population growth is now stabilized. The immigration of people has increased the diversity. A millennium development goal (MDG) is prescribed in summit. It desires to remove disparity, hence the hunger and poverty which have good relation with primary education; it promotes gender equality, reduces child mortality, improves maternal health and controls the spread of deadly disease of AIDs and HIV. The main emphasise the environmental sustainability with good economic development and planning. The developed countries had agreed to provide finance in order to improve the health in the less developed country, but the norm is not regularly followed; though good in principle.

24.4 POPULATION IN URBAN WORLD AND ENVIRONMENT

Chicago is third largest country in USA and 24th largest country in the world with 8.8 million population which in turn is gradually rising. Since 1950 urban areas have witnessed dramatic rise of migration from the rural settings. In fact half the population of world resides in urban areas. Therefore it has great impact on environment. Social and economic development, *e.g.* the substandard housing is big problem in Poland and India. Environment is concerned with natural dwellings and infrastructure and other facilities (*e.g.* Proximity of river or lakes). The number of problems are associated with urban areas what is ideally needed is energy, clean water, clean air, adequate food availability, raw material and good business. In absence of these one encounters waste water, heat, greenhouse gases, air pollution, solid waste problem etc. The proper sewage disposal is greatest problem with rise in the population. The autoexhaust emission contributes to severe problem of air pollution. The warming air exists in cities dust domes and haze of suspended particulate matter is big problem specially in desert of Kutch in Saurashta. The noise pollution is worst in most of the cities in India as well as in abroad noise of human origin. It affects health leading to hypertension or high blood pressure, damaged hearing dilates pupil and muscle contraction.

24.5 ENVIRONMENTAL ADVANTAGE OF URBAN SETTING

The excess concentration of population in cities is not good proposition as it promotes environmental degradation, therefore urban planning is most essential. It makes cities more livable. Chicago in USA without systematic planning has the growth rate of population by 22% with 50% rise in urbanized areas. The public transportation needs encouragement in preference to single cars on road. One has to be very careful while using land. Both economics as well as politics decide land use planning. Finally the transportation is closely related to urban development. The urbanization is accompanied by suburban sprawl. The excessive population causes environmental problems inclusive of the wetland loss, biological habitat, air pollution and water problem. The smart growth is essential in an urban planning and transportation management. One has to carefully consider how cities are made more sustainable. The sustainability should plan the reduction in pollution and reuse and recycling of waste water. It should provide habitat for wildlife and plenty of green space. All the changes aimed at must be people oriented. Roof top growth of plants must be encouraged in high rising buildings.

Table 24.4 Projected population in world (in millions)

S.No.	*Important cities (country)*	*Population as in 1875 (millions)*	*Population in 2005 (in millions)*	*Projected figure in 2015 (millions)*
1.	Tokyo (Japan)	26.5	35.2	35.5
2.	New York (USA)	15.9	18.7	19.9
3.	Mexico	10.7	18.4	21.6
4.	São Paulo (Brazil)	9.6	18.3	20.5
5.	Bombay (India)	13.5	18.2	21.9
6.	Kolkata (India)	7.9	14.3	17.0

Thus, Table 24.4 indicates situation not only in India but also in New York, Mexico, Brazil which show great rise in population. Hence a strict family planning must be resorted all over the world if environment is to kept clean.

24.6 MONITORING AND CONTROL OF POPULATION

A developing nation like India needs serious discussion on abnormal growth of population. A population figure of 112.0 crores is alarming and needs careful consideration in future years to come.

The census of population is carried out in India once in ten years. It is arduous exercise to count population which is floating like those one residing on roads, railway stations and *Dharamshalas*. The figure after the measurement provides easy exit to planned growth in five year plans. As noted in 2015, we must not show any rise in population and should have zero growth in population like China. If necessary for five year planning exact figure of population (floating and stationary) it is most useful to plan various development plans in the country.

As far as control measures are considered there should be strict norms to follow; in birth control. At government level it is propagating use of condom by men or intrauterine device aid. Vasectomy is another surgical device which prevents further growth of population. Like China, India needs to progumalate a legislation to have not more than two children that will indirectly take growth control.

The China has successfully controlled population growth by enacting new laws under communist government. In our country, where there is free and true democracy, the measures for population growth are difficult to vigorously implemented. That will show immediate effect upon the overall growth of population and the quality of environment and life.

24.7 CONCLUSION

We conclude population is curse as well as blessing if it is fruitfully utilized for growth. The population is directly related to the pollution. More is population greater is the environmental pollution. However, if the same population is channelized into some constructive activity it may lead to progress. In last decade or so China has shown, how channelized system leads to positive results. There is no scope for destruction as under strict regimentation things move in right direction. Unfortunately in India there is no focus on population utilization with no positive results due to excessive freedom but things have to change in next few decades if we aim at prosperity of India.

ADDITIONAL READING

1. P.H. Raven, L.R. Berg, D.M. Hassenzohl, *Environment*, 6th Edition, John Wiley and Sons Inc. (2008).
2. Kaplan, Wheeler, Holloway, *Urban Geography*, John Wiley (2004).
3. *World Population Prospects:* The 2004 Revision United Nations Population Division (2004).
4. N.C. Aery, *Manual to Environmental Analysis*, Ane Book Publishers Ltd. (2010).
5. W.P. Cunningham, M.A. Cunningham, *Principles of Environment Science—Enquiry and Applications.* Tata McGraw Hill Publishers (2007).
6. F.M. Duninvant, *Environmental Laboratory Exercises for the Instrumental and Environmental Chemistry*, Wiley Inter Science (2004).
7. P.A. Vesilind, S.N. Morgan, *Introduction to Environmental Engineering*, Thompson Press (2004).
8. S.M. Khopkar, *Environmental Pollution Analysis*, Third Edition, New Age International (P) Ltd., Publishers (2012).

25 Environmental Impact Assessment

25.1 INTRODUCTION

Environmental impact analysis (EIA) concept is in existence since 1980. This is an outcome to reduce suffering of developed nation. It is based on the premise that whatever mistakes developing countries have made, same should not be repeated by developing countries. In order to follow this planning it is necessary to prepare EIA plan to know well in advance before plant or industry is put up, the kind of pollution that the community may face. It gives idea about adverse effects of environment and facilitate to examine whether such effects can altogether be avoided. EIA provides alternative proposal for production or plant control pollution. It provides a clear relationship between short and long-term applications. It helps us to assess whether the damage caused by the environment is irreversible. This is one of the best precautionary measure which is implimented before the commissioning of the plant to mitigate pollution. Several international organisation like UNEP, SCOPE and NEPA insisted on nations to undertake EIA before commencement of new plant. In 1969 NEPA *i.e.*, national environmental policy act was enacted in America. It is stipulated that information like EIA on proposed action, adverse environmental effects, alternative technology, short-term uses of environment, study of irreversible damage is to be studied before any action plan is commenced. It is mandatory requirement in USA. US-EPA is established by NEPA. Thus, EIA is basic tool for undertaking anticipatory environmental policies from early stages of development cycle in developing countries. A useful EIA is built upon the prediction of impacts. Such impact includes physical, chemical, biological and social, economic and cultural problems for evaluation to study impact on environment.

25.2 WHAT IS EIA?

It is a study of the effects of proposed action on the environment. It stipulates considering various alternatives which are available for any project or programme; EIA is largley based on future forecasting. It attempts to weigh environmental effects on common basis with economic cost and benefits in project valuation. It is decision-making tool. In short, it is a study of effect of planned proposal, consider alternative technology, which is based on prediction. It attempts to weigh environmental effects. It is decision-making tool when we consider impacts, we consider several parameters like what is effect of population growth? What are the consequences of urbanisation? What is the impact of expansion of industry? It gives vivid picture of resource utilisation, it focusses on air, water or noise pollution or bad land use and examining ill-effects of environmental pollution on living system and consequently leading to several kinds of health hazards. Sometimes term EIS *i.e.*, environmental impact statement is used synonymous to EIA. However, EIA represents brief examination to ascertain whether or not project needs EIS. For new project EIA is guideline. If it is exempted from guidelines, statement of negative findings is furnished which is short report called *EIS*, which represents a fundamental activity while EIA is a simply introduction to it. EIA generally includes consideration of all technical aspects of environmental investigations. EIS, however summarises the results. Both these terms have, their genesis in NEPA and CEQ (Council of environmental quality) CEQ has formulated few guidelines for projects needing EIA study covers 3/4 of developing nations have carried EIA studies of project. In USA, several books described EIA since 1976. Though developing countries have not verbatically adopted NEPA legislation, as they need modification depending upon socioeconomic and cultural requirements of that particular country.

25.3 EIA UNDER NATIONAL ENVIRONMENTAL POLICY ACT

The EIA is public accountability under NEPA's requirement. The concepts under EIA is very clear. It is fact finding mission and the study of anticipated effects of pollution on society. It is kind of early warning. The EIA law had generated an immediate action throughout federal agencies in first five years. After enactment of law by NEPA through USEPA several questions were raised in USA *e.g.* To whom EIA apply? What actions are needed in EIA? What are uses of EIA? What EIA should include and who should we prepare EIA report?

It is worth considering what type of actions are needed in EIA? It includes making an initial EIA, and identifying type of actions required or not and actions needing statements (EIS). Next one should know what are the contents and uses of EIA? This is an advanced assessment to influence the decision-making, based upon the information on alternatives to proposed plan; the adverse impact which is not to be eliminated has the consequences of depletion of resources, short and long-term implications. EIA forces interospection and evaluation of agencies demanding action, it provides education to internal agencies as it broadens input of or policy formulation. It provides early warning of environmental hazards. It provides balances of socioeconomic factors. EIA provides public accountability. Next question before us is who should prepare EIA? Apart from self study by government agencies main contender of project must carryout EIA themselves. Private proposal by outside agency are permitted by federal agencies in America and in India.

25.4 MYTH ABOUT EIA

Some consider it as bureaucratic stumbling block in path of development specially in developing country like India. Others claim that EIA is clever device by developed countries to sustain escaping poverty in the underdeveloped countries. It is a perceived dichotomy between EIA and developing activity. Initially, environmental laws are also considered as anti developement. It is considered that they are stumbling block and one responsible to slow down development. In fact, it is tool for development and planning in economic analysis. In the decision-making it is reliable, less susceptible to personal bias, it permits comparison in systematic manner. Another myth that exist is EIA is very expensive which actually is not the case. In reality, the cost covers study *e.g.*, actual cost works out to be 0.08 to 1% of total cost of the project. The cost is 0.5 to 1% of overall project and the funding agencies include such expenditure in total cost of the project scoping must to reduce cost. EIA is not a paper tiger. It is neither an exercise in futality nor it is reactive. Some developing countries feel EIA is luxury and is extra financial burden, but prosperous countries believe that development should not lead to environmental degradation. The quality and development of the environment should go hand in hand with the use of EIA.

25.5 EIA IN ACTION

There are various steps in preparing EIA report. It should include preliminary activities, identification of the impact, baseline study, evaluation of impact, elimination of problems, ascertaining alternative processes, documentation, decision-making and final auditing. The preliminary activities include to identify the decision maker, find out coordinator, and decide work allocation, write proposed action and review legislation. List is indicative of first step in EIA and may not be exhaustive. The scoping or identification of impact includes the study of magnitude, extent, significance and sensitivity of impact, in order to know this we need baseline studies. It is record of what existed in the area before plant is installed? The evaluation or quantification of impact is cumbersome and controversial task. The timing of impact prediction depends upon identification of alternative process and should end before decision is taken. The control or mitigation of pollution are important component of EIA. The mitigation measures should be clearly spelled out.

To find out alternative process or technology, one should include positive and negative impacts of environment and it should summarize economic cost and benefits. The documentation is ardous task. We should have two items namely reference and working documents. The reference document will cover detailed record of EIA work while working document will cover immediate action. The comparison with alternative process is not under preview of decision maker. The decision maker is not associated with preparation of EIA report. He accepts one of project alternative, or ask to make further study or altogether rejects the project. EIA should help decision-making process. The post auditing is also important.

This verifies whether predictions made are wrong? This is done after a number of years after starting the project. Thus, one encounters several problems in preparing EIA. There may be various kinds of projects like residential or commercial, industrial; park and recreation, dams and flood control, sewage treatment plan setting new or modification of power plant or construction of new airport or new community dwellings and metro and monorail in cities like Bombay.

25.6 PROBLEMS IN EIA FORMULATION

Several kinds of the problems are encountered while preparing EIA report. It includes too many alternatives available; too many impacts, lack of data or difficulty for expert in quantification, and neglect of cost benefit analysis. Too many alternatives are handled by handling series of choices. The use of planned approach reduces time and cost of alternatives. One should select best type of alternative. Final choice is based upon the indepth study of few alternatives. If there are too many impacts, one resorts to scoping *i.e.*, coarse analysis of possible impact. The lack of data specially in India is greatest hurdle in EIA planning. We therefore carryout synthesis, a process by which data from another location which is analogous to the proposal is utilised. One does synthesise, the missing record by extrapolation. Lack of expertise is problem in the rural areas. The management of EIA is entrusted to coordinator *i.e.*, a local caretaker on behalf of plan or project proposer, who should have general environmental background and good relation with decision maker. Many times the quantification of impact is rather difficult. The Delphi technique is improvement of traditional expert opinion approach to get conscience of opinion. Every member must assess project separately and results are pooled together and then the actions are modified. Many times cost benefit analysis is of secondary consideration. We thus solve problems by already tried approach, scoping, synthesis, management approach, expert opinion taken and numerical methods of comparison are used.

25.7 COST BENEFIT ANALYSIS OF EIA

In developing country like India this aspect is of paramount importance. If such analysis is not applicable numerical method of comparison, or pairwise method of comparison should be resorted with graphical approach. The quantification in costing is difficult task. It is done by examining qualitatively where different advantages and disadvantages are encountered. Technical specification of environmental impacts is not easily available. One should give a monetory value to impact identified *i.e.*, willingness to pay as a measure of damage cost or compensation. One resorts to new technique of assessment, who should know analytical technique which are currently available, their strong and weak points, environmental problems posed by them and need of having such data. Pollution control is not burden on cost if effects savings is made in other cost. Zero pollution attainments is next to impossible hence it should not be that vigorously pursued. The tangible benefits are ignored. The damage is calculated (*e.g.*, air pollution) if range of major pollutants is limited.

25.8 IMPLEMENTATION OF EIA

Let us consider the main institutional arrangements for implementation of EIA. One has to consider policy, machinery, legislation, personnel, information and the involvement of public in general. The national policy should be attainable. Such national policy should be specific and flexible. Finally, the national policy should be responsive to people respecting their culture. Such machinery in India involves ministry of forest and environment assisted by central and state pollution control boards. In India there are comprehensive EIA laws. Such laws include need of EIA; what EIA should have? scope for reviewing EIA and settling disputes if any and legal action of EIA if terms are violated? The minor projects do not require EIA. The EIA defines extent of change, area covered, importance of EIA and special consideration for any sensitivity. Action documents have proposed action plan, result of scoping, baseline study, alternatives possible; anticipated impact, comparison with alternatives and final picture of recommendation. The authorities review the report and work as the arbitrator if required. The decision is taken on balanced environmentally sound principles. Lack of data or information as well as experts is pertinent problem in developing countries. There should be central repository of data on pollution. Involvement of affected public should be taken their comments on EIA. Public participation is necessary to impart it education, explain problems, show methods of problem-solving take feedback, find alternatives if necessary and resolve all conflicts. In public professional relationship the considered opinion of specialist, officials, citizens and public hearings be ignored. One should be constructive and responsible in criticism. The presentation or hearing is vital in EIA process and it provides a strong vehicle for effective implementation of project with good communication. We take up few case studies to clarify the concept.

25.9 CASE STUDIES NO. 1 WATER QUALITY IMPACT ANALYSIS DAM PROJECT

The economic development goes hand in hand with environmental protection. The impact of proposed dam if it has adverse effects, warrants environment impact assessment. The impact should be viewed from physical, chemical and biological point of view.

The construction of new dam changes local atmospheric energy balance leading to increase in local evaporation of water. It reduces atmospheric humidity. The humidity leads to precipitation. Water should not be lost but carefully conserved. Sediment load is affected by dam construction. The natural fertilisers of land are lost. The heavy use of pesticides lead to eutriphication. Fish population is reduced. So also plankton are reduced. Fish harvest drops to low-level.

Thermal stratification occurs in dam, deoxygenation of lakes leads to reduction in population of fish in the water for want of oxygen for breathing.

The slit accumulation in dam leads to erosion in down stream. This erosion threatens the foundation of dam and bridges. Agricultural land is lost due to moving of shore and salt spray from dam.

Their productivity is reduced; with less fish. Water loss is by transpiration wildlife however is not affected by such modifications in dam.

Fish breeding is destroyed. Fish migration is restricted.

Land is lost by establishment. The cultivable land due to dam water is insignificant compared to land lost below dam.

The resettlement of people to new site is expensive and large number of persons are reluctant to move to new site. That is general human tendency to stay where you are.

The stagnant water causes health problems. The diseases like malaria crop up. The other diseases are filariasis and encephalitis and dengue fever.

During construction sand dumping occurs. The aesthetic and archeological value of the vicinity is distorted reducing the flow of the tourist. The power transmission line results in deterioration of aesthetic quality of life. The downstream water quality is affected. The poisoning occurs due to contamination.

The above description thus summarises disadvantages of dam setting. All these problems must be weighed before dam project is cleared and the construction commenses.

25.10 CASE STUDIES NO. 2: SKYSCRAPSER STRUCTURES CONSTRUCTION IN BIG CITIES

The lack of space in big cities necessities construction of tall buildings with vertical expansion. The skyscrapers are considered as the pride of big cities in India. They have few unwanted effects on the environments. They have ecological (water, air, noise and land) and environmental impact (socioeconomic and natural environment). Various ecological impacts are known. Noise is the unwanted sound. It originates from traffic, transportation and the mechanical vibrations. The equipment for the construction of building creates noise. The wind environment is most crucial, the air flow pattern and wind velocity be properly studied. Wind tunnels are created. The air pollution is a major hazard in the building. Wind speed increases with increase in height. Air pollutants are maximum at the inward and less at the windward sides. Wind dilution is restricted. Aquatic environment is an important factor. The pollution is caused by sewage with high-density population. Overuse of ground water creates problem. The concept of conservation of water totally lacks. Light and thermal environment are also of important consideration. If alignment is cast on west, the shadow effect is common, especially for ground floor flats, surrounded by tall buildings. Light reflection in noon is maximum, while at sunset heat emission occurs. Soil environment and refuse disposal is complex problem. Solid waste from dwellings is large and poses problem of disposal. This briefly summarises the environmental impact assessment of tall buildings in the cities and rejects the idea of construction on the plot.

25.11 CASE STUDIES NO. 3: SUPER EXPRESS HIGHWAYS CONSTRUCTION

A distance between Mumbai-Pune is approximately 150 km. In normal circumstances a bus takes four and half hours to cover the distance. However with the opening of super express highway now distance is covered in just two and half hours. The construction of super express highways has caused considerable environmental pollution problems in Lonavala near Pune and its surroundings. EIA studies of such streetway. It considers a national ambient air quality standard which is violated due to emission of CO and NO-NOx from cars. The total highway is around 90 km with six lanes. The project is located in valley of steep slope and lowlying hills. Since air basin is encountered, air quality is affected. The stipulated air quality standards by government are O_3(0.12 ppm), CO (9 ppm). NO-NOx (0.05 ppm), SO_2 (0.03 ppm), SPM (73 $\mu g/m^3$) and HC (0.24 ppm). These figures are for annual average. The rainfall in the ghat is heavy with average of 150 to 400 cms/yr. It good day time wind flows. Wind travels mostly from east to west (occean breeze). High stability occurs along with direction of winds (East-West). The inversion takes place in late evening. Air quality data for five years is required. National air quality ambient (NAQA) is maintained. Automobiles degrade the air quality in the valley. In long-run air monitoring centre should be established on highway. Now let us consider environmental impact. Since then the project is located in a valley of gentle slope from ocean to lowlying hills, then mobile source is main point of air pollution. The maximum traffic is between 6 to 9 a.m. in morning and 16 to 20 hrs in the evening. It causes pollution by vehicles. Impact covers emission by gases on road in the basin of valley which is accumulated. There exists a slow wind directed towards population in high rising building. In next 10 to 15 ys region is expected to experience growth in traffic. Such a growth impact would affect population. Alternatives are buildings exclusive bus way or ramp metering. The project is not very consistent for planned growth but is ultimately executed due to political pressure.

25.12 CASE STUDIES NO. 4: IMPACT OF NUCLEAR POWER PLANT

There are plans to install nuclear plants in Ratnagiri, Maharashtra and Chennai Kudakolom. The nuclear power plant creates havoc if not properly monitored. These are most effective substituent for thermal or hydroelectric power plants. The trouble starts from selection of site for power plant. One must consider various aspects such as the availability of land, the suitability of quality of land, its topography, availability of cooling water facility, public acceptance, resources consumption, communication facility, soil conditions and cost of transmission. The environmental impact study considers water quality, biological consequences, quality of atmosphere and noise, population density and socioeconomic aspects. One should select the alternative site if any of these conditions are not fulfilled. One consider the impact of construction of power plant. One must carefully examine the removal of woodland, impact on flora and fauna; noise and social impact. The additional information on erosion impact, or impact on air quality or influence on resource or aesthetic value is of prime importance. One has to carefully consider impact of station operation and discharges from nuclear power plant.

The discharge of chemical and nuclear waste, loss of heat and effect of cooling water, then sewage disposal along with its consequences of human dwelling, power transmission problems, are all very vital for the consideration. Nuclear waste treatment is most important. The waste consists of fission products, from food matrix, or from primary coolant or release of corrosive products into waste stream. Gases and solid waste is also injurious. The radioactive material has direct access to human being through radiation. The kind of radioactive material, form of material, concentration, influence of dilution by marine environment, consumption by marine biota are considered. The most important aspect is biological effects caused by radiation on human body cells leading to somatic effect or genetic effect are important. Somatic effects are on body while genetic effects are herditatory problems with human gene.

The serious cases of exposure leads to cancer. Factors responsible to affect man include power of radiation, type, energy (meV) close rate, nature of exposure, age of person and his physical health. Most of the effects of radiation are damaging. The exposure is measured in terms of rad (1 rad = 100 ergs/g). Thermal and fast neutrons have large value of rad viz 3 and 10 rads. The human being and non-living organisms also get affected. All materials are dissociated by radiation. Mishaps occur in nuclear power plant due to loss of coolant, transient power, problem with refuelling, rupture of reactor, melting of cladding vapour explosion; isotope migration to coolant, and natural calamities like earthquake, sabotage due to war or accidental leakage. The lack of process of water cobling of the reactors led to the nuclear disaster as in Fukoshima in Japan in 2010–11. Tsunami also contributed to flooding of nuclear establishment. The most significant are socio-economic impact specially for dwellings and population residing in vicinity of reactor. In Canada at Ottawa, the village of Pembrook is vacated around reactor to avoid mishap and all houses are located at distance of 12 to 15 km radius from the reactor. Thermal pollution is significant. There is depletion of dissolved oxygen in water with rise in temperature. Finally, the transmission lines are also effected before and after construction. Impact includes clearing vegetation, rise in surface runoff, during road making. Pest and weed control, generation of electromagnetic noise, but few effects are visible in initial stages. In view of dwindling problem of coal we have to consider alternative source of energy like nuclear plants.

25.13 CONCLUSION

In EIA work ecological and environmental investigation is must, to ensure ecological balance without endangering species in environment. So development project must accompany the reduction of environmental degradation. As a matter of fact it will be now very clear that prevention is better than cure. That proves that it is better to undertake pollution abatement measures well in advamce before plant is commissioned. Any subsequent measure to control on-going pollution will not only prohibitive as far as cost is concerned but also public or outlay and legal actions will entail loss in production, man hours and profit at large.

ADDITIONAL READING

1. Y.J. Ahmad, G.K. Sammy, *Guidelines to Environmental Impact Assessment in Developing Countries*. Hodder and Stoughblon (1985).
2. B.N. Lohani, *Environmental Quality Management*, South Asia Publishers, New Delhi (1984).
3. J.G. Race and D.C. Wooten, *Environmental Impact Analysis Handbook*. McGraw Hill and Co USA (1980).
4. P.E. Black, *Environmental Impact Analysis,* Prager Publisher, CBS Educational Professional Publishers, New York (1981).
5. A.V. Whyte, I. Burton, *Environmental Risk Assessment SCOPE 15,* John Wiley and Sons, New York (1980).
6. J.L. Rodgers Jr, *Environmental Impact Assessment, Growth Management and Comprehensive Plan*, Ballingar Pub. Co., USA (1976).
7. P.A. Fricksen, *Environmental Impact Assessment Principles and Applications,* Academic Press, New York (1979).
8. N. Rajvaidya, D.K. Markandya, *Advances in Environmental Science and Technology* Vol. 4, A.P.H. Publishing Co., New Delhi (1998).
9. G.N. Pandey, *Environmental Science and Technology,* Anmol Publication (P) Ltd., New Delhi (1998)
10. A.K. Sen Ed., *Environmental Management and Planning,* Wiley Eastern (P) Ltd. (1988).

26 Environmental Modelling

26.1 INTRODUCTION

The harnessing of atomic energy and the introduction of many synthetic elements and chemicals has enhanced the environmental hazards. In environmental impact assessment, it is observed that the decision and strategies to control pollution becomes complex. It becomes imperative to predict changes due to natural and man-made destruction of environment. A very promising approach for predictions of changes in environment is possible through modelling. We think of cost and course of action for solutions. These models are useful for the right kind of decision-making. A model represents part of actual world of word with the different scale of operation. Simulation models are of intrisic value. They commences with the behaviour of complex system in varying medium; such that predicated and actual behaviour of the system is almost identical. The simulation modelling of physical, chemical, biological, social system uses several methods from graphical mapping and algebraic relationship to computer technique. Computer models are preferred because they are not only fast to make but stores data and which is retrieved immediately. The computer course goes ahead mechanically with unrealistic predictions as far as the commonsense is concerned. This is its main limitations. The complex simulation models are prepared without computer. Simultation technique is already in use in other fields like aerospace engineering. Meterologist have extensively used simulated modelling. Now in environment the simulated modelling is applied to ecology, soil and population science *i.e.*, demography or to water pollution and interaction of man and environment. It has limitations in biological fields. It is used extensively in developed countries. It is used as the aids to environmental management. It provides better understanding of transportation of pollutant, predict chemical exposure level in future and forecast future condition for management action alternatives.

26.2 PURPOSE OF MODELLING

Models are used for various purposes. They serve as the extension of information system. All possible and available information is available for modelling, with statistical summaries. As means total and tabulation is required. Simulation model is part of background data on system condensing existing knowledge in organised and place format. The another purpose is to use them in environmental management and decision-making. Any decision must have two alternatives, not to do is also a kind of decision. The environmental effects are not well defined. The information helps decision maker. Effects must be accurately defined. The choice must consider future predictions. The institution plays significant role in predictions, but predictions should be objective. Uncertainty must be accounted. The stochastic elements may be included. The simulation is useful for decision maker if model is prepared by him only. Gaming approach is essential. A third purpose of model is to use it as research tool. The resulting consequences of action are deduced in absence of simulation model. The improved understanding of process at the interference *i.e.* link between any two processes will help us to improve the environment. Certain difficult experimental measures are forecasted by simulation models, but experimentation with simulation models is definite way of tackling problem at interface of human and environment. The model serves as research tool for testing hypothesis and to formulate hypothesis of system behaviour. The fourth purpose of modelling is for allocation of research resources. An inter-disciplinary projects is difficult for assessing and allocating funds but model helps the task of disbursement of funds. The very purpose of investigation is to determine uncertainty in system. It constitutes what is termed as 'sensitivity analysis'. The final aim of modelling is education. Certain abnormalities are better explained by model in preference to elaborate explanation. They promote thought provoking on environment. The overall competence of decision maker is refined. A model displays a situation which is likely to answer future questions and suggest means of mitigation of problems.

26.3 PROBLEMS IN MODELLING

Several problem are encountered by decision makers while modelling. There may be problem in model building methodology, which encompases data requirements, temperature and spatial scale, aggregation interface between submodels, validation of model and transferability of the model. Extensive data must be available. Model building and data collection should be simultaneous process and must interact with each another. A preliminary model should be prepared and refined with additional data. A choice of scale is to be made. A model needs different time scales depending upon objective of data collection. In large data, modelling requires aggregate macro simulation of system, or more micro information is needed. Aggregate variable must be defined. In presence of submodel their interfacing is essential. The matching of the model with the real system is difficult. Only relevant data is used for validation. Such of the validation should be within prescribed limits of uncertainty. Simulation model is transferred between people, organisation in different ways. The degree of generalisation be limited. It should not be also too specific. An appropriate environment should be provided for model builder. The builder should withstand pressure of user. There may be problems between modeller and old time scientist. Outdated data or classical concepts have to be shaded out by both. The communication problem between disciplines or between model builder and decision makers may arise. A very close cooperation and communication between expert of differing discipline is essential. The quantitative assessment even for social problems is must. The models and decision makers must think in same direction in tackling problems. The limitations must be recognised by both parties *viz.* modeller and decision maker. The model must be well validated.

26.4 SIMULATION MODELLING AND SYSTEM ANALYSIS

Simulation model helps to decrease the environmental problems either artificial or man-made. The problems of industrialised developed countries are different from those of developing countries. Some problems become common in near future. Such problems are related to food production, forest exploitation, land use, generation of energy and its utilisation, water supply and waste disposal for the both kind of countries. The errors committed by developed nations must not be repeated by developing countries, although for latter outlook may not be always identical. The decision maker should keep away from action group as they are exhypothesis partision in approach and thinking.

The simulation model is based upon mathematical representation of the real life system. It is used when finding solution becomes difficult for control. The computer is mainly used. Model undergoes changes with knowledge of real world system. The changes in system in short period are expressed in terms of state of system initially, with external factors postulated to impinge upon it during the interval. The simulation approach gives flexibility of expression. All functions must be well defined with a system. A determinatistic model is process of logical deduction, well suited for digital computing. Simulation models are predictive tools. Such of the predictions are conditional. The simplistic assumption leads to errors. The decision in environmental management rest on preception of needs, definition of problem, its analysis consideration of alternative strategies, selection of such alternative if required and implementation and monitoring of operations. The advantages of system analysis is the availability of methods and techniques to everyone for further examination. The system analysis basis is conclusion on all scientific methods from various disciplines. It is problem of solving technique.

26.5 ENVIRONMENTAL SIMULATION MODELLING

Let us consider nature of simulation modelling, classification of models, approaches to model building. The article modelling is known since ages. With advent of computer science, job became very simple as a person knowing little mathematics prepares programme the equation of which is good enough to build a model. Simulation is defined as application of computer to trace the causes and effects, relations narrating some complex system and initiate dynamic behaviour of system. The computer keeps track of interactions between different variables. Use of analogue computer is regulated with advancement in the digital computers, latter being fast. Apart from continuous simulators the discrete event simulator and stochastic simulation has to come forward. If images have too many variables influencing decision then discrete event simulation modelling is ideal. If parameters are subjected to change with random fluctuations, then stochastic simulations are fissible. All three types are also used in combinations *e.g.*, in atmospheric pollution all three types are used. Apart from forecasting, simulation models are used to display behaviour modes under variable conditions. They are used for optimisation of conditions. So far economic models are in use. Models vary in scale and end use variation. The classification includes subject (*e.g.*, control, resources) purpose (decision, research, education) and environmental system being studied (*e.g.*, type air, water, size one time). Other aspects are considered as unspecialized events. We consider an approach to model building. A structure is to be defined, section parameters are estimated and finally the task of validation is taken. Non-stationary system model has limitations as it predicts future based on restricted parameters. The physical parameters must be evaluated based upon laboratory experiments. A comprehensive model has many merits, as it enables us to use prior information, permits to incorporate knowledge of behaviour of components, it gives best mode for communication and it summarisation in a systematic form. Of course, there are few demerits *viz.* One gets large amount of data, efforts put are not worthy for procuring such data, many times data does not provide statistical information. The dominant models account for restricted parameter if one knows control theory and system engineering. In large system main model is subdivided in to submodels each differing from other parts of the system.

26.6 AIR POLLUTION CONTROL MODELS

The abatement of pollution is main goal. The model should have wide applications and generalisation, of immediate use, and useful at government level. To make model we must examine following parameters *viz.* (*a*) emission inventory provided. If the data on source of pollution is available, (*b*) regional growth factor: to show growth in emission from present source, (*c*) regional cost data: used to decide cost of control, (*d*) meteorological data: to locate geography of the emission site, (*e*) demographic data to know effect on population, (*f*) growth model for rise in emission expected, (*g*) predicated inventory of growth, (*h*) control technology: to estimate cost of control techniques with all alternatives, (*i*) alternative control includes one of individual control measures, (*j*) meteorological model to predict resultant quality, (*k*) dose response model to estimate cost of damage of human health, (*l*) standard compliances to verify conformation to standards, (*m*) regional economic factor *e.g.*, employment data, input of capital, (*n*) economic impact to test efficiency of control strategies, (*o*) benefit model: to know reduction in human damage and (*p*) decision includes evaluation of each strategy. We examine macro *i.e.*, analytic model and micro or heuristic models. Of these only one is useful for decision-making. Micro model is more useful as pollution at macro level phenomena. In micro model we examine source data management system, concentration of air pollution, source contribution, control cost, and one uses IPP model. The heuristic optimisation procedure is followed. There is a difficulty in procuring data. Such model is used for future forecasting. The micro model gives information on source data management, air pollutant concentration, source contribution, control cost and update programme, emission standards and file regional strategies programme. From model optimisation route is chalked out. All point sources located. Control strategies are finalised. Micro model provides tool for policy planners.

26.7 MODELLING FOR ASSESSMENT OF WATER QUALITY

From reservoir quality management model is prepared in Rasina river at Morava watershed. Increase in capacity of reservoir is the main aim. An additional treatment is another objective of modelling. As it is contained Fe, Mn, organic matter, asbestos which are brought down to standards prescribed limit. Impounding is affecting water quality. Reservoir is designed for city water supply, flood control, sediment deposition and low flow augmentation. One dam is there (33 km distance). Reservoir is 12 km long with surface area of 4 km^2 at maximum water level of 284 m.a.s./volume is 68 × 10^6 cm^3. Inflow to reservoir is 5.25 m^3/s. Temperature and quality is predicated by the model. Stratification time is important due to its complexity. The combined spatial and temporal distribution of quality parameters (*e.g.*, Temperature DO, BOD) are accounted. In absence of sanitary protection, degradation of quality of water took place. One expected to predict treatment process, and new applications. Best quality water is withdrawn when protection measures are effective. The model HEC-5 was best suited. It has flow simulation (HEC-5A) and water quality simulation model (HEC-5Q). Application of model commences with data preparation. Water quality parameters with good record are chosen. There are temperature; DO, ammonia (NH_3-N), electro-conductivity (EC). The 3 years data is used for calibration of model. Next 3 years data is used for the verification process. The calibration is initiated with reproduction of noted temperature. The observed temperature profiles are reproduced with good level of the agreement. Other parameters are adjusted. In verification step, second water quality parameters are mathematically simulated. There is full agreement in simulated and observed values. After caliberation of the model aim is to evaluate impact of new measures or modifications. Simulation runs are carried out for steady state and dynamic conditions.

Simulation shows no impact on temperature. The impact of quality of water on DO (dissolved oxygen) is insignificant, but meteorological factors have insignificant influence on DO. NH_3 has significant effect on quality increasing value of DO from 0.15 to 0.9 mg/L. As regards conductivity it is not affected by any variable. So conclusion is stratification is natural phenomena which occurs regularly. The level of sanitary protection has significant impact on quality of water. With full sanitary protection anaerobic conditions will prevail for ten days. The effect of the meteorological factors is insignificant. The model HEC-5 may be used to assess water quality.

26.8 WATER RESOURCE MANAGEMENT MODEL

In France polluters are fined for creating pollution but unfortunately that failed to deter polluter from creating problems. Cost benefit analysis is best and it allows us to view problem with mathematical programming and sensitivity analysis but global applications are not suitable. Water is limiting factor of growth. In the work programme four phases *viz.* hypothesis of development of basin; forecast model; simulation model and finance model must be considered. In water resource development and utilisation model one considers dynamic model for development and allocation. Then they consider static model for agriculture industry, formulate regional ground water simulation model and use it for applications in the area of water allocation by region, timing of investment in development, they have the integrated operation policy for combined system of water resources simulation model which is multipurpose aquifier model.

26.9 SOLID WASTE GENERATION MODEL

Management of urban solid waste poses a organisational problem. Treatment plants are allocated on basis of modelling. On regional scale collection system must be efficient. Periodic reorganisation is not done in less than three years. Quality and quantity of waste be known. The characterisation is complex task, what we want is in forecasting for definite period of time. The disposal technique must be efficient. The statistical projection are not always reliable. A model is used for a data evaluation. Urban solid waste is in nature is complex species and depends upon the population distribution, institution distribution, service industries and collecting system and living standards of individuals. Hence the job of standardisation is difficult for quality consideration. Fuzzy model solves the problem to some extent. Fuzzy modelling is based on FGA software. The choice of parameter depends upon algorithm calculations to know output, error, least error of the model. Waste analysis is carried out in 13 quarters of town and 3-borderlands, each 15 areas are divided into 6 different sectors and each sector is taken as sample of total 90 samples. The analysis covered organic matter, paper boxes, plastic articles, metals glass. The variable to be considered for input should follow series of conditions. Input variable relate to kg/year of each kind of waste with some relation to population and institution present. As regards output variables it is expressed as % of total waste. Such optimisation methodology is extended in order to obtain, Fuzzy rules system showing relation between the structural parameters of solid waste generation and resulting valuation of solid waste production. A graphic representation for error between real and fuzzy system as well as graph of distribution of output variables or distribution of variable organics between real system and fuzzy genetic model is obtained.

26.10 EXPERIENCE IN MODELLING ABROAD

Some experience in simulation modelling in environmental management in countries abroad is worth considering. The important countries are Australia,

Germany, Japan, Russia, England and America. In Australia, CSIRO and universities have done extensively the modelling but largely for research purposes. In area of agriculture, meteorology such information is used for management guidelines for the country. On account of heavy industrialisation in Germany, there is accumulation of the environmental loading causing damage to ecosphere. German policy makers wants to retain their predominance in industrial growth at the cost of environment. Research institute only are partially involved in simulation and modelling. Japan is forerunner in using models for air and water pollution in future forecasting. However, they are secretative and withhold the vital information. At Nagoya in Japan an interdisciplinary centre is established for simulation and modelling. Russia is highly industrialised country and although vast in size the environmental degradation is visible *e.g.*, greenhouse effect, but they do utilise environmental models for the control of pollution. The British institutes are involved in modelling. They have better rapport with their government agency. Consequently modelling is fruitfully used in the U.K. to control pollution and help future planning. Simulation and modelling is most extensively carried out in academic institutions with eye on decision makers to interact but many of them are highly theoretical with no practical applications. However, simulation is improving with better interaction between modelling on one hand and decision maker on other. As regards India, whole science is in infancy stage with no systematic studies in modelling.

26.11 SCOPE FOR IMPROVEMENT

Modelling is done in broader context but specific goals and priorities must be first identified. An authentic and recent data is used for modelling. Too much old data has no relevance to present day situation. The selection of parameters to be used in modelling should be very carefully decided. The accuracy of model depends upon comparison with real life data. Most important task is to remove first the uncertainty in the model itself so quantitative information is available. This is true specially if model is used for decision-making or for forecasting. A method of compound simulation is resorted to achieve this goal. The sensitive analysis is important. It is mean process of assessing the changes in model behaviour which results from changes in model output variables. Validation is used to describe the process of testing. It is open to subjective judgement and improvements. It involves testing under different intervals for observation. One has to devise strategies for the improvement of human interactions. The interface between various discipline, scientists must be first improved. Submodels are developed by the individuals from different groups. The interphase between models and decision maker must be improved. Priorities for improvement in developed and developing countries are different. One should render modelling methodology compatible with incremental decision-making. There should be clearing house for data and models. There should be training of the modelling project manager in multidisciplinary approaches. One should utilise semi-quantitative and purely qualitative models.

However, priorities for developing countries like India are altogether different. Models for developed countries should be accepted by them with great caution. In conclusion the international recommendation in modelling are as follows:

(*i*) **Education and training:** Modelling courses must be included in undergraduate teaching programme. Training courses should be organised with regional workshops.

(*ii*) **Modelling standards and principles:** Existing model are selected, when data should be always collected with advice of modeller. Client must interact with modeller and decision maker.

(*iii*) **Modelling information and documentation:** A manual on modelling should be at hand for case studies to be included in such manual. Model inventory should be well prepared.

(*iv*) **Research and international cooperation:** Research must be encouraged in modelling. The interfacing of models be done with care for models of different discipline. The above recommendations are made by SCOPE group *i.e.*, scientific committee on problems of the environment in 1978. When the members met in Stockholm in Sweden. A critical study of referees Nos. 5 and 7 gives clear picture of modelling.

26.12 CONCLUSION

Environmental modelling is an important field from the point of view of future forecasting. The modeller and the decision makers must work in consonance. Lot of good measures are taken to preserve environment. Modelling technique is used very extensively in meteorology and aerospace engineering. The purpose of the modelling is not to repeat same mistakes which are already committed in environmental planning in developed nation. One forecasts future problems and suggests measure to solve those problems. There are several problems in modelling specially when decision maker and modeller work in the opposite direction. Old data is also useless for modelling. The simulation and modelling and system analysis is very useful. Environmental simulation modelling works wonders. If worked with computers one extrapolate certain future parameters. Such simulation modelling is used for air pollution control and for assessing the quality of water. It is also used for water resource management and for solid waste generation and management. The developing countries have learnt from developed countries. specially UK and USA have done extensive work in this field in research institutes and decision-making organisation. However, more study is needed for improvement of such modelling. One learns from the mistakes of the developed countries. In long-run the periodical training programme in the field of environmental modelling is useful. The future is very bright only we must have will and desire do work hard to attain excellence in this specialised field.

ADDITIONAL READING

1. F.N. Frenkiel and D.W. Goodall, Ed., *Simulation Modelling of Environmental Problems*, John Willey and Sons (1978).

2. J.L. Schnoor, *Environmental Modelling Fate and Transport of Pollutants in Water Air Soil*, John Wiley and Sons (1996).
3. R.A. Deininger, Ed. *Models for Environmental Pollution Control*, Ann Arbar Science Publishers (1974).
4. D. Daetz and R.H. Pantell, Ed. *Environmental Modelling Analysis and Management*, Powden Hutchinso and Ross in (1974).
5. K. San Jose, C.A. Brebbia, Ed. *Measurement and Modelling in Environmental Pollution*, Computational Mechanics Pub. (1997).
6. T.R. Lakashmanan, P. Nijkamp, Ed. *Economic Environmental Energy Interactions Modelling and Policy Analysis*, Martinus Nijhof Publishing (1980).
7. E.S. Barton, E.H. Pation, W. Senjour, *Models for Environmental Pollution Control*, p. 219, Annorbar Science Publishers (1973).
8. R.R. Barthwal – *Environmental Impact Assessment*, New Age International (P) Ltd., Publishers (2002).

Appendices

Appendix-A

Values of 't' for various levels of probability

Degrees of freedom	*Factor for confidence interval*			
	80%	*90%*	*95%*	*99%*
1	3.08	6.31	12.7	63.7
2	1.89	2.92	9.92	31.6
3	1.64	2.35	5.84	12.9
4	1.53	2.13	4.60	8.6
5	1.48	2.02	4.03	6.86
6	1.44	1.94	3.71	5.96
7	1.42	1.90	3.50	5.40
8	1.40	1.86	3.36	5.0
9	1.38	1.83	3.25	4.78
10	1.37	1.81	3.17	4.59
11	1.36	1.80	3.11	4.44
12	1.36	1.78	3.06	4.32
13	1.35	1.77	3.01	4.22
14	1.34	1.76	2.98	4.14
∞	1.29	1.96	2.58	3.29

Ref.: 1. F.J. Holler, *Principles of Instrumental Analysis,* Harcourt Brace, p. 144 (1992).
2. D.A. Skoog, D.M. West – *Analytical Chemistry*, Holt, Reinhart, Winston, p. 71 (1979).

Appendix-A-1

Values of 'Q' for rejection of quotient at various confidence limits

Number of observations	*90%*	*95%*	*99%*
3	0.941	0.98	0.994
4	0.765	0.85	0.936
5	0.642	0.73	0.821
6	0.560	0.64	0.740
7	0.507	0.59	0.680
8	0.478	0.54	0.634
9	0.437	0.51	0.598
10	0.412	0.48	0.568

Ref.: 1. D.A. Skoog, D.M. West, F.J. Holler, 6th edn., *Fundamental of Analytical Chemistry* - Harcourt Brace, p. 46 (1992).
2. J.S. Fritz, G.H. Schenk—*Quantitative Analytical Chemistry*, 4th edn., p. 38, Allyn & Bacon, p. 38 (1979).

Appendix-B

Chi square distribution

Degree of freedom	*Probability (P)*						
	0.99	*0.95*	*0.90*	*0.50*	*0.10*	*0.01*	*0.005*
1	0.00016	0.0039	0.0158	0.455	2.71	2.71	7.78
2	0.01	0.1026	0.211	1.39	4.61	9.21	10.6
3	0.071	0.352	0.584	2.37	6.25	11.3	12.8
4	0.207	0.711	1.064	3.36	7.78	13.3	14.9
5	0.412	1.15	1.61	4.35	9.24	15.1	16.7
6	0.676	1.64	2.20	5.35	10.6	16.8	18.5
7	0.99	2.17	2.83	6.35	12.0	18.5	20.3
8	1.34	2.73	3.49	7.34	13.4	20.1	22.0
9	1.73	3.33	4.17	8.34	14.7	21.7	23.6
10	2.56	3.94	4.87	9.34	16.0	23.2	25.2
20	7.43	7.26	8.55	14.3	22.3	30.6	32.8
30	13.79	18.49	20.60	29.3	40.3	50.9	53.7

Ref.: H.A. Lattinen, W.E. Harris—*Chemical Analysis*, p. 546, Second Edition, McGraw Hill & Co. (1976).

Appendix-C

Confidence levels for different values of Z

Confidence level (%)	Z
50	± 0.67
68	± 1.0
80	± 1.29
90	± 1.64
95	± 1.96
96	± 2.0
99	± 2.55
99.9	± 3.29

Confidence limit for mean = $x \pm z\sigma$, if σ = standard deviation

Confidence limit for mean (μ) = $x \pm z\sigma/VN$ (N = nos. of measurements)

Ref.: 1. D.A. Skoog, F.J. Holler, T.A. Niemon, *Principles of Instrumental Analysis*, 5th Ed., p. 71, Harcourt, Brace (1998).

2. D.A. Skoog, D.M. West – *Analytical Chemistry*, 3rd Ed., p. 68, Holt, Reinhart, Winston (1979).

Index

B

F

G

J

K

L

M

O

P

U

V

W

X

Z